ENCYCLOPEDIA OF THE RENAISSANCE

Tintoretto. *St. George and the Dragon.* Oil on canvas; 1560–1580?; 158 x 100 cm (62.25 x 39.5 in.).
[See the entry on Tintoretto in this volume and Raphael's interpretation of this theme in the color
plates and in the entry on Raphael in volume 5.] NATIONAL GALLERY, LONDON/ERICH LESSING/ART RESOURCE

ENCYCLOPEDIA OF THE

ENAISSANCE

Paul F. Grendler

Editor in Chief

PUBLISHED IN ASSOCIATION WITH
THE RENAISSANCE SOCIETY OF AMERICA

VOLUME 6

Shakespeare – Zwingli

Systematic Outline
Directory of Contributors
Index

CHARLES SCRIBNER'S SONS

An Imprint of The Gale Group

NEW YORK

Charles Scribner's Sons
1633 Broadway
New York, New York 10019

1 3 5 7 9 11 13 15 17 19   20 18 16 14 12 10 8 6 4 2

PRINTED IN THE UNITED STATES OF AMERICA

Library of Congress Cataloging-in-Publication Data
Encyclopedia of the Renaissance / Paul F. Grendler, editor in chief.
      p. cm.
    Includes bibliographical references and index.
    ISBN 0-684-80514-6 (set) — ISBN 0-684-80508-1 (v. 1) — ISBN 0-684-80509-X (v. 2)
— ISBN 0-684-80510-3 (v. 3) — ISBN 0-684-80511-1 (v. 4) — ISBN 0-684-80512-X (v.
5) — ISBN 0-684-80513-8 (v. 6)
    1. Renaissance—Encyclopedias.   I. Grendler, Paul F.   II. Renaissance Society of
America.
CB361.E52   1999
940.2'3'03—dc21   99-048290

The paper used in this publication meets the requirements of ANSI/NISO Z39.48-1992
(Permanence of Paper).

The typeface used in this book is ITC Garamond, a version of a typeface attributed to the
French publisher and type founder Claude Garamond (c. 1480–1561).

CONTENTS OF OTHER VOLUMES

COMMON ABBREVIATIONS
USED IN THIS WORK

A.D.	*Anno Domini,* in the year of the Lord
A.H.	*Anno Hegirae,* in the year of the Hegira
b.	born
B.C.	before Christ
B.C.E.	before the common era (= B.C.)
c.	*circa,* about, approximately
C.E.	common era (= A.D.)
cf.	*confer,* compare
chap.	chapter
d.	died
D.	Dom, Portuguese honorific
diss.	dissertation
ed.	editor (pl., eds.), edition
e.g.	*exempli gratia,* for example
et al.	*et alii,* and others
etc.	*et cetera,* and so forth
f.	and following (pl., ff.)
fl.	*floruit,* flourished
HRE	Holy Roman Empire, Holy Roman Emperor
ibid.	*ibidem,* in the same place (as the one immediately preceding)
i.e.	*id est,* that is
MS.	manuscript (pl. MSS.)
n.	note
n.d.	no date
no.	number (pl., nos.)
n.p.	no place
n.s.	new series
N.S.	new style, according to the Gregorian calendar
O.F.M.	*Ordo Fratrum Minorum,* Order of Friars Minor; Franciscan
O.P.	*Ordo Predicatorum,* Order of Preachers; Dominican
O.S.	old style, according to the Julian calendar
p.	page (pl., pp.)
pt.	part
rev.	revised
S.	*san, sanctus, santo,* male saint
ser.	series

S.J.	*Societas Jesu,* Society of Jesus; Jesuit
SS.	*sancti, sanctae,* saints; *sanctissima, santissima,* most holy
Sta.	*sancta, santa,* female saint
supp.	supplement
vol.	volume
?	uncertain, possibly, perhaps

ENCYCLOPEDIA OF THE RENAISSANCE

(CONTINUED)

SHAKESPEARE, WILLIAM (1564–1616), English playwright, poet, and actor-shareholder in a theatrical company. William Shakespeare was born in Stratford-upon-Avon, a market town in Warwickshire of about fifteen hundred inhabitants. The christening register of Holy Trinity Church records the baptism on 26 April 1564 of "Gulielmus filius Johannes Shakspere" (William son of John Shakespeare). The exact date of birth, presumably one or two days prior to the christening, is traditionally assigned to 23 April, since that day also honors St. George, slayer of the infamous dragon and patron saint of England.

William's father, John, was evidently the son of Richard Shakespeare, a farmer in the village of Snitterfield, four miles north of Stratford. Richard died in about 1561, possessed of a respectable estate. William's mother, Mary Arden, was the daughter of Richard's prosperous landlord, Robert Arden of Wilmcote, another nearby village. John thus advanced his fortunes by a good marriage. Some time before 1552, John and Mary moved to Stratford, where John rose to considerable local importance. One of the several houses he purchased was the dwelling on Henley Street traditionally identified as William Shakespeare's birthplace. Out of the relatively few existing timbers, the house has been reconstructed and serves as a tourist center. The house is comfortably large, since it served as a place of business for John Shakespeare as well as a domicile. He cured animal skins from which to manufacture gloves and other leather goods, and sold them from the shop in his house. He also dealt in wool, grain, malt, and other farm produce. In an English town like Stratford-upon-Avon such a successful merchant was sure to hold civic offices. John Shakespeare served at various times as ale taster (inspector of bread and malt), burgess (member of the town's governing body, acting also as petty constable), affeerer (one who was responsible for assessing amercements, or fines), city chamberlain or treasurer, alderman, and high bailiff—Stratford's chief municipal office and hence the equivalent of mayor. He seems, however, to have experienced a reversal of fortune around 1577–1578 and afterward; the records indicate that he was often absent from council meetings and was in financial difficulties serious enough to require the mortgaging of his wife's valuable property. He was assessed heavy fines, and, although he managed to keep his seat on the corporation council until 1586–1587, he eventually ceased to be an alderman. Scholars have speculated that John was in trouble because he clung to the old Catholic faith in a time of vigorous religious persecution, but the evidence is inconclusive.

Schooling. Undoubtedly, John Shakespeare sent his eldest son to the King's New School in Stratford. The records of that school have perished with time, but tradition reports that Shakespeare attended a "free school," and one of the town's leading citizens would hardly have passed up the opportunity. There, after having learned to read and write at home or in a "petty" (that is, elementary) school, William would have begun at the age of seven or so a rigorous daily routine of Latin study from 6:00 or 7:00 A.M. until 5:00 P.M., with brief intervals for food and recreation. Strict discipline was maintained, often by means of corporal punishment. In this school, Wil-

The Globe Theater. Detail of a long panorama of London by Claes van Visscher, published in Amsterdam in 1616. The hexagonal shape of the theater is probably inaccurate. © THE BRITISH MUSEUM, LONDON

liam would have read, among other Latin authors, Ovid, Virgil, and (in bowdlerized versions) Plautus and Terence.

These authors plainly leave their traces in Shakespeare's early writings. Plautus is an important model for *The Comedy of Errors,* for example, and Ovid is vitally present in *A Midsummer Night's Dream* and elsewhere. Seneca lies behind Shakespeare's early tragedy, *Titus Andronicus.* Although Shakespeare could read the Latin originals, his plays and poems give evidence also that he consulted English translations. Ovid's *Metamorphoses* had been translated by William Golding in 1567 and was widely available. In 1623 Ben Jonson (1572–1637) condescended to Shakespeare's "small Latin and less Greek," but this was said from the point of view of a proud, not to say arrogant, neoclassicist, and does not deny that Shakespeare could read Latin. The extent of familiarity with Latin that we see in Shakespeare's early plays and poems is precisely what we might expect of the education he received. Hints in the plays give us amusing glimpses of what a boy in

that age might have thought of his schooling: the pedantic schoolmaster Holofernes in *Love's Labor's Lost* with his absurd Latinate neologisms; the sketch in *As You Like It* of "the whining schoolboy, with his satchel / And shining morning face, creeping like snail / Unwillingly to school" (2.7.144–146); the rote recitations of young William Page in *The Merry Wives of Windsor* (4.1) under the watchful eye of his Welsh schoolmaster Sir Hugh Evans, who warns that if William forgets his *qui, quae, quod*s he must be "breeches" (that is, spanked), and so on. These passages betray neither a special animus toward nor enthusiasm for school days, and are entirely of a piece with what we know of Shakespeare's schooling.

Marriage. Shakespeare never attended a university. Instead, he married, at eighteen, a woman eight years older than himself and had a child with her some six months after their hastily arranged marriage in late November 1582. Shakespeare and Anne Hathaway were evidently obliged, by Anne's pregnancy, to seek a special license allowing them to marry after only one reading of the "banns," or official announcements in church of a forthcoming nuptials. Banns were usually read thrice, on succeeding Sundays, to enable any interested party to raise any potential objections. Owing, it would seem, to the pregnancy, and to the awkward fact that banns could not be read during the Advent season, the family and friends of the bride-to-be were required to sign a bond accepting any financial liabilities up to 40 pounds that might accrue to the bishop for permitting the marriage to go forward. The marriage may not have been a happy one, as we shall see, but it did at any rate legitimate the birth of a daughter, Susanna, baptized on 26 May 1583, in Stratford. The only two other children of this union, the twins Hamnet and Judith, were baptized on 2 February 1585. Shakespeare was thus twenty-one when his last children came into the world.

Possibly, Shakespeare's early and precipitous marriage cut off any plans he may have entertained for a university education. His father's financial difficulties could not have helped. Whatever the case—and we have no evidence that he wanted to attend one of the universities—Shakespeare seems to have been thrown on his own resources with a need to support a family. Records are sparse for the years of his late teens and early twenties. An uncertain tradition written down about a century later speculates that he became a schoolmaster for a time. Another hypothesis is that he served out an apprenticeship in Stratford in his father's trade. These are plausible choices for a person of Shakespeare's background and training, but have little else to recommend them in the way of reliability. All we do know is that by 1592 he had gravitated to London, evidently without his family, and had quickly gained some reputation or even notoriety as a playwright and actor.

Shakespeare in London: First Notice. In 1592, Robert Greene, a prolific dramatist and writer of the 1580s and 1590s, singled out Shakespeare for a remarkable attack. By way of warning his fellow dramatists Christopher Marlowe (1564–1593), Thomas Nash (1567–1601), and George Peele (1556–1596) to beware of the ingratitude of a fickle public, Greene lashed out at a certain "upstart crow, beautified with our feathers, that with his 'tiger's heart wrapped in a player's hide' supposes he is as well able to bombast out a blank verse as the best of you. And being an absolute *Johannes Factotum,* is in his own conceit the only Shake-scene in a country" (*Greene's Groatsworth of Wit Bought with a Million of Repentance,* 1592). The diatribe hints darkly

that the "upstart crow" is gaining public favor by plagiarizing from the reigning dramatists of the time—beautifying himself with their feathers. The pun on "Shake-scene" can only be directed at Shakespeare, all the more so since the quip about "tiger's heart wrapped in a player's hide" is an acerbic misquotation of Shakespeare's "O tiger's heart wrapped in a woman's hide" from *3 Henry VI* (1.4.137). The barb has the ring of an envious older dramatist viewing with dismay the appearance on the theatrical scene of a bright new star. The episode confirms that Shakespeare is indeed on the scene by 1592, and that he has become an instant success. Indeed, we know from other testimonials that *1 Henry VI* had been a great hit, perhaps as early as 1589, with its heroic portrayal of Lord Talbot as nemesis of the French. *Richard III* (c. 1592–1594; dates throughout refer to approximate year or years of performance rather than publication) brought instant fame to Shakespeare's leading man, Richard Burbage, in the part of Richard. Shakespeare had arrived.

The unseemly fracas over the charge of plagiarism not only establishes Shakespeare's presence on the London theatrical scene in 1592, but it also gives us our first character sketch of the man. Greene's churlishness led to an apology, not by Greene himself, who died shortly afterward (of an excess of pickled herring and Rhenish wine, according to a contemporary account), but by Henry Chettle, another dramatist and professional scribbler who had shepherded *Greene's Groatsworth of Wit* through the press, and who, not coincidentally, is suspected today of having authored the original attack himself. Whatever the circumstances of that authorship, Chettle saw fit to issue a thoroughgoing disclaimer in his *Kind Heart's Dream,* also published in 1592. Insisting that he has had no part in the business, Chettle goes on to wish that so fine a person as Shakespeare had not been singled out thus for criticism. Referring evidently to Shakespeare, Chettle declares that "myself have seen his demeanor no less civil than he excellent in the quality he professes. Besides, divers of worship have reported his uprightness of dealing, which argues his honesty, and his facetious grace in writing, that approves his art." Chettle thus describes Shakespeare as "civil" in his demeanor and excellent in the calling he practices—the "quality" or professional accomplishment of playwright and actor. Shakespeare is judged upright by "divers of worship," that is, by persons of social dignity and probity. A special talent is his "facetious grace in writing," that is, the great facility and swiftness with which he composed his works, noted in later years (disapprovingly) by Ben Jonson. All this, in Chettle's view, argues Shakespeare's honesty in dealings and his "art"—his superior skill as a dramatist.

One of Shakespeare's earliest literary efforts was the writing of two nondramatic poems, *Venus and Adonis* and *The Rape of Lucrece.* They were published in 1593 and 1594, with dedications to the young earl of Southampton, and the second of these dedications is sufficiently warm to encourage belief that Southampton became a kind of patron for Shakespeare. Quite possibly the young Shakespeare wanted to be a nondramatic poet, like Edmund Spenser (1553–1599). Writing poetry had a cachet that playwriting did not. Shakespeare never saw his plays into print; many were published, but not with his having seen them through the press. He evidently cared enough about his early poems to tend personally to their publication. Still, he was by this time a practicing playwright as well, and must have known that he had talent in that line.

The Authorship Question.

Could the man heretofore described have written the great plays and poems that are attributed to him? Ever since the nineteenth century, a number of dedicated readers of Shakespeare have doubted the identification, chiefly because the life record is of a commoner lacking university training. Shakespeare has left us virtually none of his manuscripts or correspondence; we have, in his handwriting, only a few wavering and variously spelled signatures on legal documents (including his last will and testament) that cast doubt in the minds of some as to whether Shakespeare was even literate. Could a country boy from Stratford, educated if at all only through what we would call high school, have produced such brilliant studies of the lives of kings and aristocrats?

Many candidates have been put forward as the author of Shakespeare's plays—so many, indeed, as to materially weaken the case for any particular individual. Sir Francis Bacon (1561–1626) was the first such candidate in the anti-Stratfordian cause—so called because the movement generally acknowledges that Shakespeare of Stratford did exist as an actor but denies that he was the real author. Others include the earl of Southampton, Anthony Bacon, the earl of Rutland, the earl of Devonshire, Christopher Marlowe, and, most recently, Edward de Vere (1560–1604), seventeenth earl of Oxford. This last person has been a favorite candidate because he did in fact write verse, served for decades as a courtier under Queen Elizabeth, and was involved in various imbroglios that sound at times like plots from some

of Shakespeare's plays. Oxford knew intimately Lord Burghley, who was his father-in-law, and whom many critics and scholars have seen as a model of sorts for *Hamlet*'s Polonius—a careworn, cautious, overly sententious, and pompous statesman.

A major problem with Oxford's candidacy is that the earl died in 1604, before the dates that most scholars assign to *King Lear, Macbeth, Antony and Cleopatra, Timon of Athens, Coriolanus, Cymbeline, The Winter's Tale, The Tempest,* and *Henry VIII,* to name only the chief plays of Shakespeare's later career. But why in any case would the earl of Oxford (or Bacon, or Southampton) wish to see these great plays ascribed to an ordinary actor? The answer from the anti-Stratfordian side is that playwriting was an inglorious trade, a little like script writing today for the film industry or television—remunerative in some cases but well beneath the dignity of England's ruling class. Aristocrats and gentry of the time did indeed profess to scorn commercial publication of the verses that they turned out as gentlemanly exercises. According to the hypothesis, then, Oxford retained Shakespeare as his "front man" in order to avoid the opprobrium of commercial endeavor in a theater world that bordered on the bohemian. A number of people would have had to be in on the secret understanding, or at least colossally fooled by it: Shakespeare himself, of course, and some of his fellow actors, along with Oxford and persons close to him, and then others like Ben Jonson, who knew Shakespeare all his adult life. The very size and breadth of the imagined conspiracy of silence militates against its plausibility. So does the bizarre argument that the earl wished to conceal his playwright's identity during his lifetime and afterward, but then supposedly longed for posterity to uncover the real truth some centuries later. (One anti-Stratfordian reads the Ghost's words in *Hamlet*— "Remember me"—as a covert cry of anguish from the long-dead earl of Oxford, seeking the belated recognition that has been so unjustly denied him but that he nonetheless is supposed to have avoided during his lifetime.)

We need to consider whether university training and life at court would have been necessary to enable Shakespeare to write the plays and poems he wrote. English university training in the sixteenth century was directed in good part at preparing young men for the ministry. Some professional writers of the Renaissance did go to one or the other of the universities—Christopher Marlowe, Edmund Spenser, and Ben Jonson, among them. Others like Thomas Dekker (1572–1632), George Chapman

The Swan Theater. Facsimile of sketch by Johannes de Witt, 1596. BY PERMISSION OF THE FOLGER SHAKESPEARE LIBRARY, WASHINGTON, D.C.

(1559–1634), Anthony Munday (1560?–1633), and William Shakespeare seemingly did not. They all were significant writers. The years of the late sixteenth and early seventeenth centuries were years of a remarkable flourishing of English drama, not by Shakespeare alone. He shared with these other dramatists a crucial characteristic that Oxford (or Bacon, or Southampton) did not: they were professional writers. They had the strongest of motives for succeeding as writers: the desire to say something and the need for financial success. Shakespeare needed to satisfy his customers, as his father had done. Only a snobbery about class, together with a misconception of the nature of university training in the Renaissance and a deep mistrust of authority, can explain the long-lived appeal of anti-Stratfordian sentiment.

London and Its Theaters. These matters of authorship are important because they help determine what sort of man Shakespeare was, and why he wrote. The professional theater served him well, and he served it well. Shakespeare arrived in London

at an auspicious time for English theater. Native drama had long flourished in England, chiefly in biblical and allegorical renditions of divine history from the moment of God's creation of the world down to the day of general doom. Neoclassical forms of drama, reaching back to Plautus, Terence, and Seneca, had recently introduced into that native tradition its roster of character types, including (in comedy) the young lover and his clever servant, the romantic young heroine, the parasite, the braggart soldier, the miserly old man, the careworn father, and still others; and in tragedy the ghost of the murdered person, the revenger, the villain, the loyal friend, and so on. The mix of native and classical traditions gave to English theater a new vitality and versatility; and with it came a new sense of the potential for the English language to serve as a vehicle for literary greatness. The drama was often put to polemical uses in an age of religious wars between Catholic and Protestant, so that drama quickly found its place at the center of national debate.

London, by far the dominant city of England, became the center of this new and burgeoning drama. James Burbage, a former joiner or furniture-maker turned actor, had built a theater in 1576 to the northeast of the city, called the Theatre perhaps because there were no others. (There had been plenty of dramatic activity in inn yards, churches, great houses, and other suitable venues, but no permanent theatrical building.) Burbage and his colleagues located outside the city to be free of the city authorities, who tended to be suspicious of theatrical activity as subversive, ungodly, and unhealthy. Richard Burbage, James's son, became Shakespeare's lifelong friend and leading actor, starring in *Richard III, Hamlet,* and *Othello,* among other plays. Some of Shakespeare's early plays, like *The Comedy of Errors, The Two Gentlemen of Verona, The Taming of the Shrew,* and the *Henry VI* plays, may have been staged at the Theatre, though of this we cannot be sure. In fact, we do not really know what acting company or companies he may have joined until 1594, when his name appears in a roster of the Lord Chamberlain's men, acting chiefly at the Theatre in Shoreditch.

The Theatre appears to have been octagonal or otherwise polygonal in design, with a capacity of perhaps three thousand spectators. Some sat in the wooden galleries; the less well-to-do, including apprentices from the more prosperous guilds, stood in the "yard" in front of a large rectangular stage, perhaps forty-three by twenty-seven feet (thirteen by eight meters). This platform stood five feet (one and a half meters) or so above the floor of the yard. Backstage was a "tiring house" where the actors attired themselves and made their exits and their entrances through two or three doors. A gallery above the doors, in the tiring house facade, may have accommodated well-to-do spectators at times but could also be used for acting scenes "above." The main stage had at least one trapdoor in it, and probably supported two pillars that held up a roof partly covering the stage and providing, especially in later years, a "heavens" from which descents and ascents were possible by means of machinery. We know this much partly by way of analogy with the Swan, a theater for which a sketch has survived from about 1596, along with various contemporary descriptions and legal documents providing building specifications. The Theatre was dismantled in 1599 by Shakespeare's acting company, owing to a dispute with the landlord, and was then reassembled on the south side of the river Thames as the famous Globe theater—re-created in the late twentieth century on a location near its original site. We do not know all we would like to know about the Theatre or the Globe, especially the number and location of the stage doors, but we can gather a sense of what the space was like. Other theaters in the vicinity—the Swan, the Rose, the Fortune, and others—varied in their design and capacity: the Rose was smaller, the Fortune rectangular rather than octagonal. The Globe itself may have incorporated variations from the design of its predecessor, the Theatre, in important details, when the relocation occurred.

Shakespeare's Early Success. In an Elizabethan theater such as we have just examined, Shakespeare began his professional life. *The Comedy of Errors* (c. 1589–1594), an early work, is in some ways Shakespeare's most avowedly neoclassical play in that its whole action takes place in an imagined twenty-four-hour period in one city, Ephesus. The stage doors may have served to represent fixed domiciles throughout the action, facing onto a single street: the house of Antipholus of Ephesus is such a house, with the Priory located nearby at another door. Most of the action is understood to take place in front of Antipholus's house or inside it. The arrangement approximates the staging of Plautus and his imitators in the Renaissance, although in Italy especially the street scene in perspective would also utilize painted scenery to achieve its visual effects. The character types are Plautine as well: the clever twin servants named Dromio of Ephesus and of Syracuse, the maidservant, the zany conjuring school-

master. Shakespeare's play is in fact an astute reworking of Plautus's *Menaechmi* (The twins).

In a similar vein *The Taming of the Shrew* (c. 1590–1593) uses as its secondary plot the story of the wooing of Bianca by her lover secretly disguised as a servant, in competition with a rich and unwelcome rival; this plot is taken straight out of George Gascoigne's *Supposes* (1566), itself a sprightly translation of Ludovico Ariosto's neoclassical *I Suppositi* (1509), which in turn looks back to Terence's *Eunuchus* and Plautus's *Captivi* (c. 200–150 B.C.). Neoclassical character types abound: the aged wealthy wooer, the anxious father, the clever servant (Tranio), the romantic hero and heroine. At the same time, *The Taming of the Shrew* features as its main plot the story of a vehemently male wife-tamer and the woman he tames, taken from a very English ballad.

The Two Gentlemen of Verona (c. 1590–1594) is a romantic comedy of lovers who cope with parental opposition to their union, separation, rivalry, misunderstandings, hairsbreadth escapes, and sudden conversions to virtuous behavior—hardly the stuff of the neoclassical repertory. *Love's Labor's Lost* (c. 1588–1597), too, is a romantic confection of wooing and misunderstanding between the sexes that has little to do with neoclassical conventions. Early in his career, Shakespeare demonstrated remarkable eclecticism as he searched for the comic form that he perfected in his comedies of the later 1590s.

As a writer of history plays, Shakespeare was an important innovator. The English history play as a genre owes everything to his genius. A few earlier experiments, such as the anonymous *Famous Victories of Henry V* (1583–1588), had exploited English history (especially the career of Henry V) for its patriotic themes, but Shakespeare did more than any other writer to give the English history play its form. In the *Henry VI* plays and in *Richard III,* he dramatized (with Raphael Holinshed's 1577 *Chronicles* as his chief source) the prolonged agony of civil war in fifteenth-century England that eventually led to the defeat of Richard III at Bosworth Field in 1485 and the accession to the English throne of Henry VII, grandfather of Queen Elizabeth I. Shakespeare ends the saga triumphantly, in the victory of Henry VII, with a seeming demonstration of a caring providence at work in establishing the Tudor regime, but the story itself is chiefly one of failed leadership, political strife, and savage butchery. To the chaos of civil war Shakespeare gave an artistic shape. The theater building provided a worthy space for such an endeavor, lending its structure to a representation of

Performance of a Shakespeare Play. Contemporary sketch of a performance of *Titus Andronicus* from Longleat Portland Papers I, fol. 159v. REPRODUCED BY PERMISSION OF THE MARQUESS OF BATH, LONGLEAT HOUSE, WARMINSTER, WILTSHIRE/VISUAL CONNECTION LIBRARY

siege warfare, with actors costumed as soldiers attacking the facade of the theater as though attempting to enter a fortress. Here was a truly English theatrical genre, owing nothing to classical precedent; instead, the Shakespearean English history play was indebted to chronicle history and to the great cycle plays of the medieval religious drama.

Major Comedies. With *A Midsummer Night's Dream* (c. 1595), Shakespeare gave to his audiences a perfect example of his distinctive comedy. In a fashion that is definitely not neoclassical, it blends several plots: the story of Theseus's wedding to Hippolyta, the mock-epic quarrels of Theseus and Titania as king and queen of the fairies, the tribulations of four lovers (two male, two female) who seek out the forest as a place of refuge from a sternly forbidding parent and the sharp Athenian law, and finally the bumptious artisans of Athens who aspire to mount a production of "Pyramus and Thisbe" before Duke Theseus on his wedding night. The multiplicity is thoroughly nonclassical; so too is the mix of hu-

man figures and otherworldly spirits that Ben Jonson so deplored.

Midsummer illustrates the genre of romantic comedy in its refreshingly candid approach to the experience of falling in love. First of all, the young men, Demetrius and Lysander, are so much like each other that we are invited to laugh at Hermia's father, Egeus, for insisting that she marry his favorite, Demetrius. As Lysander insists, "I am, my lord, as well derived as he, / As well possessed [that is, with money]" (1.1.99–100). Egeus's choice seems arbitrary, but so, for that matter, does Hermia's. The two women, Hermia and Helena, are just as interchangeable, too; one is taller than the other, but that matters little. Falling in love in this play is sudden, irrational, and comical, enabling Puck to have his fun by interchanging all the love relationships with the magical love juice. Falling in love is a bit like taking some psychoactive drug. The men are typically male in their mercurial inconstancy, falling in love with one woman and then the other, trying to kill each other in their rivalry as rutting males. The women are constant, beleaguered, tearful. The whole experience of falling in love is hard on both sexes. Helena recalls longingly to Hermia the days when they were like sisters, "Both warbling of one song," like "Two lovely berries molded on one stem" (3.2.203–213).

The transition from same-sex childhood confidentiality to heterosexual attachment is portrayed in *Midsummer* as a hazardous journey. The women try to scratch out each other's eyes, doubt their own attractiveness, and think how convenient it would be to die. Yet somehow this nightmare in the forest all comes to a good end and Shakespeare persuades us that true love is eternal. The four lovers wake up as though from a dream, knowing now that they form two couples that are made for each other. Queen Titania is reconciled with Oberon, and the court marriage of Theseus and Hippolyta will go forward. All is well in spite of Puck's amused observation: "Lord, what fools these mortals be!" (3.2.115).

The Merchant of Venice (c. 1596–1597) shows us another distinctive feature of Shakespearean comedy: its fascination with narrowly averted disaster. Shylock's challenge to the Christian community of Venice is meant to be fatal in its consequences, and the life of Antonio (the merchant of Venice) is saved only by the last-minute intervention of Portia disguised as a legal expert. The interplay between this tragicomic plot, complicated by the partly sympathetic portrayal of Shylock as a persecuted Jew, and the more jovially comic wooing of Portia by Bassanio (including the delicious contretemps of the rings at the play's end) is a remarkable signature of mature Shakespearean comedy.

No less definitively Shakespearean is the device of the juvenile male actor playing a young woman who then disguises "herself" as a man. The device, used earlier in *The Two Gentlemen of Verona,* serves Shakespeare to brilliant effect in *As You Like It* (1598–1600) and *Twelfth Night* (1600–1602). Especially in these two plays, the protective coverage of a male disguise enables Rosalind and Viola to befriend the young gentlemen with whom they fall in love. They offer wise counsel on matters of the heart to Orlando and Orsino, so that in each denouement the resolution of sexual identity from that of a presumed male to that of a woman provides the basis for a marriage that neatly combines love and friendship. It is as though Shakespeare is devising strategies for sexual maturation that put the least possible strain on the participants, especially the male. Once again, the transition to heterosexuality is seen as hazardous. Orlando and Orsino both arrive at it by becoming emotionally involved first with what they

take to be young males. Once a deep friendship and trust is established, then sexual difference can be brought into the equation. Moreover, Shakespeare has made things easy for the men in these plays by enabling them to fall in love with young women who are patient, constant, and loyal. Rosalind and Viola offer no threat to the fragile male ego: they are supportive, emotionally generous, and not overly importunate. They are what men sometimes dream of in womankind, and it is that kind of idealization of women that helps give Shakespearean romantic comedy its lift and optimism.

Much Ado about Nothing (1598–1599) arrives at a similarly deep understanding between Beatrice and Benedick, with adroit use throughout of the motif of disguise, albeit with no use of male disguise for the women. The play strikes us as a kind of rewriting of *The Taming of the Shrew,* in which the saga of male supremacy is softened into a quest for mutual respect and affection. Benedick and Beatrice do their best to ruin their chances for happiness by playing mean tricks of deception on each other, even to the extent of persuading themselves that perhaps the other person really is scornful; but these attractive lovers are saved from their own fearfulness toward involvement in love by the amused plotting of their friends. Elsewhere, *Much Ado* flirts with disaster, in the vein of *The Merchant of Venice:* the plot of the slandered heroine (named Hero) comes close indeed to requiring her death as the price for the male jealousy and misunderstanding of Claudio. The interconnectedness of these two plots, one hilarious and one tragicomic, is one of the hallmarks of Shakespearean romantic comedy at its best.

Major History Plays. Shakespeare's history plays of the later 1590s achieve a mastery of form in much the way that his comedies do. He takes up once again a subject requiring a four-play cycle, this time the story of Prince Hal as the once and future Henry V. *Richard II* (c. 1595–1596) commences the story with Henry Bolingbroke, who becomes Henry IV when he seizes the throne from Richard in 1399. The two *Henry IV* plays (1596–1598) chronicle Henry's struggles with political and military rivals and his unhappiness over the waywardness of his crown prince, who nonetheless emerges as England's greatest hope. *Henry V* (1599) completes the saga of Hal's triumph over his political enemies and especially over the French at the battle of Agincourt (1415). The special brilliance of these plays lies in the portrayal of Hal, as he seeks out the company of the disreputable and unregenerate Falstaff and eventually comes to terms with the awesome authority of the father whom he must finally succeed as king. At the level of personal history, these plays offer a deeply moving portrait of a young man seeking to know his father. Indeed, the best known of these history plays, *1 Henry IV,* is as much about father-son relationships as it is about English history—a focus that no doubt helps explain its continued popularity in a world today that is distant from the struggles surrounding the throne in late-medieval England.

Prince Hal's relationship to Falstaff is a wonderful puzzle to us. Is he merely using Falstaff in a condescending way, amusing himself in the tavern and constructing for himself an identity as a young man of flair while he waits for the throne to come to him, or is he deeply attached to Falstaff and unable to give up a relationship that is costing him his father's affection and respect? We see indications of both sorts, and probably both are true. King Henry IV is a forbidding model: stern, unbending, incapable of personal friendships. Prince Hal, in a classic move of the Prodigal Son, takes the opposite course, of irresponsibility. Yet Hal also learns something precious from Falstaff about vitality, warmth, and spontaneity. These are values that will stand him in good stead when he does at last become his father's heir and ascends the English throne. Hal's rivalry with Hotspur, meantime, has sharpened Hal's sense of his own identity and destiny; both young men are named Henry or Hal, both are intensely ambitious, neither can tolerate a rival. Only one can succeed at last. Perhaps Hal succeeds in defeating Hotspur because Hal does learn to become his father's son without falling into the forbidden territory of open rebellion. Hal is, at last, legitimate; Hotspur, for all his incandescent charisma, is not.

Broadly, we can say that the 1590s were, for Shakespeare, a time of writing comedies about romantic love and history plays about the maturing of a young man as he confronts issues of authority, career, and ambition. The two genres are kept quite separate in ways, despite the brilliance of Falstaff as a comic figure: Prince Hal comes to love and marriage only at the very end of his journey, when he marries the daughter of his defeated French enemy. These parallel themes of love and ambition are well suited to a young dramatist; Shakespeare was twenty-six when the decade began. *Twelfth Night* and *Henry V* represent the culmination of his achievement in comedy and history. He also wrote *The Merry Wives of Windsor* (1597–1601) and *King John* (c. 1594–1596) in these veins.

Shakespeare did little with tragedy as a genre during the decade, although history plays like *Richard III, King John,* and *Richard II* do deal with tragic themes. To be sure, Shakespeare experimented with tragedy in *Titus Andronicus* (c. 1593–1594), a mélange of Senecan elements filled with violence and revenge. *Romeo and Juliet* (1594–1596) is a tragedy, and deservedly one of Shakespeare's best-loved plays, but its emphasis on comic wooing in the first half of the play aligns it with the romantic comedies of the period more than with the tragedies that followed. Not until 1599 or so did Shakespeare begin to take a serious look at a genre then well suited to his own more mature years as a writer.

Problem Plays and Sonnets. Between 1601 and 1605, Shakespeare experimented with genre, and produced a group of plays often called the "problem" plays: *Measure for Measure* (1603–1604), *All's Well That Ends Well* (c. 1601–1605), and *Troilus and Cressida* (c. 1601–1602). *Measure for Measure* is a comedy ending in marriage, but the marriages are manifestly bizarre and imperfect because the conditions of human carnality are so exacerbated in this dark tale of vice and corruption in Vienna. Angelo nearly succeeds in getting away with seduction and cover-up through murder; Isabella, about to become a nun, consents to a plot of trading sexual bedfellows; the Duke is a mysteriously manipulative presence. Angelo especially is an amazing character to appear in a comedy: driven by an urge he never knew he possessed to attempted rape and murder, Angelo comes to loathe his own nature and is released from this torment only by a highly unlikely ending that offers him a second chance and a marriage with one of the women he has wronged. Shakespeare is pushing "comedy" into very strange territory. Plainly, he is experimenting with genre.

All's Well That Ends Well is no less puzzling, with its young protagonist, Bertram, so eager to avoid marriage that he runs away until he is hoodwinked with a bed trick. An unattractive protagonist, he is rescued (like Angelo) from his worst self by a forgiving woman and by the contrivances of a "comic" plot that offers undeserved forgiveness. *Troilus and Cressida* is the darkest of the three, and the most nearly tragic, for Cressida does in fact prove unfaithful to Troilus, albeit under circumstances that are eminently understandable, and the great Hector dies an inglorious death at the hands of the shamelessly brutal Achilles. The great heroes of the greatest war in antiquity prove to be fallible indeed. Shakespeare is at work on something devastatingly new.

The *Sonnets* (c. 1593–1603) prove another turning point, for they too give (along with some of the most idealized and noble expressions of love in all literature) a complex portrayal of love and friendship that is fraught with complex eroticism, tortured jealousy, and self-abasement. The central relationship of the *Sonnets* is that of the poet and the young friend to whom he writes. The poet urges his friend to marry, but he also broods over ungratefulness and forgetfulness on the part of the young man. Physical absence is a torture to the poet. So is his own aging and fear of diminishing powers as a writer. The poet is openly jealous of other writers whom the young man patronizes. Clearly this is a deeply emotional love relationship. The poet insists in one sonnet (20) that it is not homosexually physical; since Nature has "pricked" out the young man "for woman's pleasure," the poet must be content to enjoy the young man's less physical love. Even so, the relationship is a tortured one, and raises all sorts of unanswerable questions as to whether the *Sonnets* portray directly an experience in Shakespeare's own life.

The *Sonnets* also portray, toward the end of the sequence, the poet-speaker's compulsive heterosexual attraction to a woman, but the sonnet sequence is no less unhappy in its exploration of love between men and women. The Dark Lady does indeed betray men, and can claim few of the redeeming justifications of Cressida. Unfaithful women had been notably rare in Shakespeare's comedies and histories of the 1590s (though Joan of Arc and Margaret of Anjou of the *Henry VI* plays, both French, do offer exceptions); most suspicions of female infidelity, as in *Much Ado about Nothing,* are the nightmares of a diseased male imagination. Now, however, around 1599–1601, Shakespeare opens new and frightening prospects.

Major Tragedies. *Hamlet* (c. 1599–1601) is darkly misogynistic in Hamlet's obsession with his mother's overhasty marriage to Claudius; a perception of womanly inconstancy destroys Hamlet's own relationship with Ophelia. The circumstances of the play also test Hamlet's friendships. Rosencrantz and Guildenstern suddenly reappear as former friends, prompting Hamlet rightly to suspect that they are spying on him for the king. Horatio, contrastingly, is disinterestedly loyal. Such a true friendship is precious in a world of counterfeiting and secret murder. Hamlet's circumstances prompt him to question everything about human happiness and about himself: "What a piece of work is a man! . . . The beauty of the world, the paragon of animals! And yet, to me,

what is this quintessence of dust?" (2.2.304–309). In Horatio's company he skeptically examines everything, mistrusting, loathing, hating, and yet needing to fulfill his father's dread command to revenge a murder. Ultimately, Hamlet comes partly to terms with his misogyny by bringing his mother to her senses; he is finally reconciled with her, as they both die as a consequence of an immensely elaborate plot. Hamlet's ultimate view is that even the conspiracies and strange turns of events are somehow part of a larger divine plan: "There is special providence in the fall of a sparrow" (5.2.230–231). Yet the blood-filled stage at the play's end leaves stark testimony of the harsh struggle that Hamlet leaves behind. Justice is in some ways served, but at a huge cost of decency and all that deserves to be called civilization.

The hero of *Othello* (c. 1603–1604) is tempted into believing that his wife Desdemona is a whore, much as Claudio in *Much Ado about Nothing* comes to suspect Hero. The difference is that Othello executes Desdemona at Iago's jealous instigation and must then face the reality of a deed for which repentance comes too late. Othello is a tragic hero in an Aristotelian sense: a good man driven by a flaw into fatally disastrous action. The puzzle in this case is how Othello, a mighty warrior and loving husband of Desdemona, could come to loathe her so quickly and on such illusory grounds. The answer must reside in part in Iago, whose villainy is clever enough to fool others in the play and even, in part, his long-suffering wife Emilia. Yet in *Othello* the protagonist must assume the major blame, as a tragic hero should: he chose to marry Desdemona, and he chooses to believe Iago's lies about her. There is something emotionally insecure about him, despite his majestic calm under stress in the play's opening scenes. Is it because he is a black man, and older than Desdemona, and is thus too ready to believe that a younger white woman cannot love him long? These are the racist insinuations in which the play deals, and in the last analysis all Iago has to do is to persuade Othello to believe in his own heart that a black-white marriage is inherently not "natural." Once Othello has accepted that proposition, the rest of his tragedy follows as a consequence.

The protagonist of *King Lear* (c. 1605–1606), driven into madness by the monstrous ingratitude of two of his daughters, reveals a disturbed mind filled with horrid images of the corrupted female sexual anatomy; and indeed Goneril and Regan are everything their father's imagination supposes, for they are in a competition to enjoy sexually the bastard

Edmund, whose very bastardy seems to proclaim the sexual energy with which he was conceived. Lear's tragedy is self-inflicted, to a significant extent, by his banishing of Cordelia, and arises from an insecure sense of being unloved similar to that of Othello. Yet Lear's sufferings far exceed his deservings, and the monstrous behavior of his two elder daughters propels him toward an examination of injustice in the universe that is all the more compelling and distressing because it is uttered by a man who is temporarily deranged. The subplot pursues a parallel course: the earl of Gloucester, ill-advisedly banishing his loyal son Edgar and delivering himself into the clutches of his villainous bastard son Edmund, discovers in his misery an apocalyptic view of human unhappiness and the utopian need for a radical redistribution of the goods of this world, so that the prosperous will no longer be insolent in their wealth and the poor no longer needy. The vision is beautiful but utterly unattainable in an imperfect world. Only through cruel blindness can humans be taught to see the "real" truths of the need for human kindness; only through madness can they see a glimpse of true wisdom.

The protagonist of *Macbeth* (c. 1606–1607) succumbs to the promptings of his own ambition, materially aided by the importunity of his wife and the insinuations of the three Weird Sisters. A terrible crime against kingship, hospitality, and all that civilization stands for is committed by a man who is unable to resist the taunts of his wife that he show himself to be "a man." The inversions of sexual relationship that afflict husband and wife cast Macbeth as "too full o' the milk of human kindness" and his wife as one who demands of infernal spirits, "unsex me here" (1.5.17, 42). Character is fate: Macbeth commits his terrible crime against a fatherly king, despite all his humane promptings to the contrary, because his fate cannot be avoided; it is part of him, so thoroughly so that the Weird Sisters know from the start that they can goad him into killing. As with Iago in *Othello,* the motive of these dark spirits is to get Macbeth to damn himself.

Shakespeare's tragic vision in these great plays focuses on the dark human emotions that must have seemed painfully difficult to a writer who was himself in his late thirties and forties: sexual jealousy, marital strife, aging, anxieties about being forgotten by ungrateful children, the ravages of time.

Greek and Roman Tragedies. Concurrently, as he wrote these great tragedies at the incredible rate of one or so a year, Shakespeare pur-

William Shakespeare. Portrait by John Taylor (d. 1651). BY COURTESY OF THE NATIONAL PORTRAIT GALLERY, LONDON

sued a more sardonic vision of the human predicament by exploring Greek and Roman history. We have already glanced at *Troilus and Cressida,* based loosely on the greatest war of classical antiquity. In a sense *Titus Andronicus* is also a Roman play, although it is not "historical" in the sense of modeling its plot on history or legend. *Julius Caesar* (1599), on the other hand, deals directly with one of the most famous events of the ancient world: the assassination of Caesar in 44 B.C. Here, Shakespeare could anatomize political strife in a world divested of the providential and monarchistic imperatives that were so central to *Henry V* (also 1599). In the world of ancient Rome, Shakespeare could explore politics in a more morally neutral, ambiguous, and ironic framework. In *Julius Caesar* he takes a look at well-meaning but ambitious and self-blinded men, caught in a fearful struggle over republicanism versus strong-man single rule. The upshot is assassination and civil war in which the civil liberties for which Brutus and the other republicans have fought are not achieved but are instead destroyed.

Coriolanus (c. 1608) goes back hundreds of years before Caeser to the founding of the Roman republic

(509 B.C.) in order to arrive at a similarly dispiriting conclusion. History is not providential; its movements are undular, uncertain, dependent on the greatness or the weakness of particular men at any given moment. Coriolanus himself is a mass of contradictions, a superb soldier, arrogant, antiplebeian, emotionally too close to his mother. *Timon of Athens* (c. 1605–1608) is a deeply ironic portrayal of a generous man who discovers how forgetful his friends can be when he is no longer in a position to be generous.

Antony and Cleopatra (1606–1607), arguably the greatest of Shakespeare's classical plays, chronicles the decline and fall of a great-hearted warrior and lover, whose love for Cleopatra is at once a stirring male accomplishment and a shameful betrayal of Roman honor and duty. Antony falls before the relentless might of Octavius Caesar, who is both the greatest politician-emperor of his day and an obsessed puritan who finds sexuality abhorrent and is unwilling to deal honorably even with his own sister. *Sic transit gloria mundi* (Thus passes the glory of this world), one is tempted to say, but at least Antony and Cleopatra achieve a kind of immortality through the visionary poetry of Shakespeare. Cleopatra, by choosing suicide rather than enslavement to the bloodless Caesar, declares that great emperor to be, in her terms, an "ass unpolicied."

Late Romances.　In his last productive years, Shakespeare returned to comedy, but to comedy with a difference—so much so that it is often described as tragicomedy or romance. *Pericles* (1606–1608), perhaps only partly written by Shakespeare and to an extent an unfinished play, sets the tone by its saga of travel, separation, and eventual reunion. The coming together after years of sorrow of father and daughter (Pericles and Marina) is especially moving, and seems expressive of a playwright who was himself approaching retirement and the marriage of his two daughters. (Shakespeare's one son, Hamnet, had died in 1596 at the age of eleven; Susanna married John Hall in 1607, and Judith married Thomas Quiney in 1616.) *Cymbeline* (c. 1608–1610) takes up the story of a daughter who is alienated from her father by her imprudent marriage and is eventually reconciled to him.

The Winter's Tale (c. 1609–1611), even more revealingly, is about a King Leontes who wrongly suspects his Queen Hermione of infidelity, and accuses her so harshly that she appears to die. He destroys the life of their young son, and orders the infant girl born of the supposed adultery to be left on a foreign shore to the mercy of wild beasts. In the play's second half, sixteen years later, not only is the young Perdita (accompanied by her wooer Prince Florizel) reunited with a tearfully penitent Leontes, but Hermione is restored to life in a seeming miracle, having been sequestered all the intervening years by a loyal lady-in-waiting. The resemblance of such a narrative (taken from a novel by Robert Greene) to Shakespeare's own impending retirement to Stratford, and (speculatively) to his hopes for a successful rapprochement with his wife, Anne, is suggestive if quite unprovable. Shakespeare had presumably stayed with his family during vacations in his two decades of working in London, but he seems never to have settled his family there with him.

If we entertain the supposition of some kind of biographical relevance in these late plays, *The Tempest* (c. 1611) ends the story on a cautionary and dispiriting note, for Prospero's wife (mentioned once) is nowhere to be found. Instead, the play focuses on the strong bond between an aging father and his coming-of-age daughter, and provides Prospero with opportunity to do right what King Lear and other fathers before him (such as Brabantio in *Othello*) have failed to do: give his daughter to an eminently suitable young man whom she herself has chosen, and to embrace retirement in their happy company. *The Tempest* sounds like a farewell to Shakespeare's art, but it is also much more: especially today we see that it ponders New World motifs and colonialism in ways that seem remarkably prescient. Prospero's enslavement of Caliban makes us very uncomfortable, and opens up all sorts of ways in which, in the spirit of the French writer Michel de Montaigne (1533–1592), *The Tempest* sets up a radical critique of the most cherished institutions of western Europe. In the last analysis, though, the play's most telling perspective is on the nature of theatrical art. Prospero's setting free of Ariel bespeaks the artist's need to free himself from an awesome burden of artistic creation that is both glorious and perilously close to playing god with the lives of others.

Shakespeare seems to have come out of his retirement or semiretirement to write *Henry VIII* in 1613, and to collaborate with John Fletcher, his successor as chief dramatist for the King's Men, in writing *The Two Noble Kinsmen* in that same year, but Shakespeare stopped work at about this time at the age of about forty-nine. He died at fifty-three, evidently having been in poor health.

Accomplishments and Reputation.
Among his astonishing accomplishments, perhaps

Shakespeare's greatest achievement is his astute portrayal of so many emotional states that are essential to human life: falling in love, experiencing sexual rivalry and jealous fears of desertion or betrayal, knowing the need for friendship and loyalty, struggling with the opposite pulls of the need for autonomy and dependence, going through midlife crisis, raging at ingratitude and growing old, lapsing into tediousness and garrulity, anxiously watching children turn to new attachments, longing for and fearing retirement, sensing the approach of death. No writer has done these things better.

Shakespeare's magic with language is also incalculably great. Not by mere chance, or weight of tradition, is he the most quoted author in the English language. He addresses the weighty issues of human existence in words that enchant us. We sometimes do not realize we are quoting or paraphrasing him when we say, for example, "it was Greek to me" (*Julius Caesar,* 1.2.287) or "What's in a name?" (*Romeo and Juliet,* 2.2.43) or "the apparel oft proclaims the man" (*Hamlet,* 1.3.72), or even "The first thing we do, let's kill all the lawyers" (*2 Henry VI,* 4.2.83). Shakespeare is everywhere among us. As George Bernard Shaw put it (in *Misalliance,* 1910), Shakespeare has a word for everything.

As a result, Shakespeare's influence is incalculable. John Milton, John Keats, William Wordsworth, Herman Melville, Leo Tolstoy, Shaw, T. S. Eliot, William Faulkner—all have responded to his towering presence, sometimes resenting his dominance, always experiencing him deeply. But we cannot do without him. As Matthew Arnold puts it, in a sonnet addressed to Shakespeare:

> Others abide our question. Thou art free.
> We ask and ask: Thou smilest and art still,
> Out-topping knowledge.

BIBLIOGRAPHY

Modern Editions

The Complete Works of Shakespeare. 4th ed., updated. Edited by David Bevington. New York, 1997.

The Norton Shakespeare. Edited by Stephen Greenblatt, Walter Cohen, Jean E. Howard, and Katharine Eisaman Maus. New York, 1997. Based on the Oxford edition.

The Riverside Shakespeare. 2 vols. 2d ed. Edited by G. Blakemore Evans. Boston, 1997.

Bibliographical Guides and Reference Works

Blake, Norman F. *Shakespeare's Language: An Introduction.* London and New York, 1983.

Champion, Larry. *The Essential Shakespeare.* Boston, 1986.

Dent, Robert W. *Shakespeare's Proverbial Language: An Index.* Berkeley, Calif., 1981.

McDonald, Russ. *The Bedford Companion to Shakespeare: An Introduction with Documents.* Boston, 1996.

Spevack, Marvin. *The Harvard Concordance to Shakespeare.* Cambridge, Mass., 1973.

Wells, Stanley, ed. *Shakespeare: A Bibliographical Guide.* Oxford, 1990.

Secondary Works

Adelman, Janet. *Suffocating Mothers: Fantasies of Maternal Origin in Shakespeare's Plays.* New York, 1992.

Barber, C. L. *Shakespeare's Festive Comedy: A Study of Dramatic Form and Its Relation to Social Custom.* Princeton, N.J., 1959.

Boose, Lynda E. "The Father and the Bride in Shakespeare." *PMLA* 97 (1982): 325–347.

Chambers, Edmund K. *William Shakespeare: A Study of Facts and Problems.* 2 vols. Oxford, 1930.

Cook, Ann Jennalie. *The Privileged Playgoers of Shakespeare's London: 1576–1642.* Princeton, N.J., 1981.

Dessen, Alan C. *Recovering Shakespeare's Theatrical Vocabulary.* Cambridge, U.K., 1995.

Dollimore, Jonathan. *Radical Tragedy: Religion, Ideology, and Power in the Drama of Shakespeare and His Contemporaries.* 2d ed. Durham, N.C., 1993.

Dusinberre, Juliet. *Shakespeare and the Nature of Women.* 2d ed. Basingstoke, U.K., 1996.

Engle, Lars. *Shakespearean Pragmatism: Market of His Time.* Chicago, 1993.

Frye, Northrop. *Fools of Time: Studies in Shakespearean Tragedy.* Toronto, 1967.

Goldman, Michael. *Shakespeare and the Energies of Drama.* Princeton, N.J., 1972.

Howard, Jean E., and Marion F. O'Connor, eds. *Shakespeare Reproduced: The Text in History and Ideology.* New York, 1987.

Kahn, Coppélia. *Man's Estate: Masculine Identity in Shakespeare.* Berkeley, Calif., 1981.

Kirsch, Arthur. *Shakespeare and the Experience of Love.* Cambridge, U.K., 1981.

Lenz, Carolyn Ruth Swift, Gayle Greene, and Carol Thomas Neely, eds. *The Woman's Part: Feminist Criticism of Shakespeare.* Urbana, Ill., 1980.

Loomba, Ania. *Gender, Race, Renaissance Drama.* Manchester, U.K., 1989.

Marcus, Leah. *Puzzling Shakespeare: Local Reading and Its Discontents.* Berkeley, Calif., 1988.

Matus, Irvin Leigh. *Shakespeare, in Fact.* New York, 1994.

Novy, Marianne. *Love's Argument: Gender Relations in Shakespeare.* Chapel Hill, N.C., 1984.

Orgel, Stephen. *Impersonations: The Performance of Gender in Shakespeare's England.* Cambridge, U.K., 1996.

Rackin, Phyllis. *Stages of History: Shakespeare's English Chronicles.* Ithaca, N.Y., 1990.

Schoenbaum, S. *William Shakespeare: A Compact Documentary Life.* Oxford, and New York, 1977.

Schoenbaum, S. *William Shakespeare: A Documentary Life.* Oxford and New York, 1975.

Schoenbaum, S. *William Shakespeare: Records and Images.* Oxford and New York, 1981.

Skura, Meredith. *Shakespeare the Actor and the Purposes of Playing.* Chicago, 1993.

Thomas, Vivian. *The Moral Universe of Shakespeare's Problem Plays.* New York, 1991.

Traub, Valerie. *Desire and Anxiety: Circulations of Sexuality in Shakespearean Drama.* London, 1992.

Watson, Robert. *Shakespeare and the Hazards of Ambition.* Cambridge, Mass., 1984.

Wells, Stanley. *Shakespeare: A Life in Drama.* New York and London, 1995.

Wheeler, Richard P. *Shakespeare's Development and the Problem Comedies: Turn and Counter-Turn.* Berkeley, Calif., 1981.

Zimmerman, Susan, ed. *Erotic Politics: Desire on the Renaissance Stage.* New York, 1992.

DAVID BEVINGTON

SHIPS AND SHIPBUILDING. The most important difference among European vessels during the Renaissance was their method of propulsion, which generally meant the distinction between oars and sails. Though a variety of vessels relied on oars, the galley was probably the most famous. The largest galleys could be from five to seven times longer than their maximum breadth (beam), with hundreds of oarsmen on both sides of the hull. Galleys used oars during combat, beaching, entering and leaving ports, and whenever short bursts of speed were essential. For more extended cruising, they used sails. The characteristics of the galley helped to define warfare in the Mediterranean until the late sixteenth century. Galleys also carried passengers and trade goods, especially luxury items of high cost and low volume. Bulky items could be carried more economically in sailing vessels, which were commonly two to three times longer in the keel than the beam, and able to carry more cargo, though subject to the vagaries of winds and currents.

Traditional northern and southern sailing vessels had distinctive characteristics in the Middle Ages, with the northern tradition prevailing from the Atlantic coast of Spain (and perhaps Portugal) northward, and the southern tradition prevailing in the Mediterranean. During the fourteenth and fifteenth centuries the traditions merged, eventually producing the ancestors of virtually all later oceangoing ships. Southern shipbuilders, known for the triangular lateen sails they had borrowed from the Muslims, adopted the essential features of the northern cog in the early fourteenth century: a sternpost rudder and a single square sail. Cogs from both traditions had a straight keel and a straight sternpost, but the stempost of northern ships was straight, whereas that on southern ones might be curved. As time went on, shipbuilders added a second and then a third mast and experimented with combinations of sails. Regarding hull construction, the traditional southern method began with a skeleton of ribs and then added edge-to-edge planking for the hull. The northern method first shaped the hull with overlapping planking, and then added internal bracing. Over time, the southern method gradually prevailed for larger ships because it required less wood and was more efficient overall.

The result of the merger between northern and southern maritime traditions was a ship with three masts, the foremast and mainmast carrying square sails, and the mizzenmast at the stern carrying a lateen sail. The largest of these full-rigged ships, which often featured high castles fore, aft, or both, were called by variants of the name carrack. Smaller versions seem to have been called by the generic *nao, nef,* or *nau* (ship), but "carrack" or "*nao*" might be used interchangeably to describe the same ship. With its combination of square and lateen sails, and a sternpost rudder, the ship of the late fifteenth century was balanced and maneuverable in a variety of conditions. The ships that Columbus used on his first voyage across the Atlantic were typical Iberian vessels of the time. Scholars disagree about the measurements of those three ships, but a plausible set of figures for the *nao Santa María* is 19 feet at its widest point, 58 feet in length (38 of that in the keel), and 10 feet in depth, with about 108 tons carrying capacity and a crew of 40. The larger of the two caravels (*Pinta*) probably measured about 18 feet at its widest point, 55 feet in length, and 8 feet in depth, with 75 tons burden and a crew of 30. The smaller caravel (*Niña*) measured some 16 feet at its widest point, 50 feet in length, and 7 feet in depth, with about 55 tons burden and a crew of 20. Carracks of the time were far larger.

Responding to the global exploration and burgeoning trade of the sixteenth century, European shipbuilders adapted the full-rigged ship to a variety of conditions, a prime consideration being the characteristics of the ports that a ship might frequent, and the purposes for which it was destined. Large vessels with the same basic design might be used for trade, warfare, whaling, fishing, transport, or a combination of functions, and a single vessel might serve all of those purposes at one time or another in its career. Smaller vessels might be used to carry out exploration, dispatch, coastal trade, piracy, fishing, or other functions that required the relative speed and agility of a smaller ship. In short, Renaissance ships were adaptable in size, configurations, and function, and it is impossible to provide a fixed definition for the famous ship types of the period because they continued to evolve, and their evolution varied from

An English Warship. Etching of Henry VIII's warship *Henry Grace à Dieu,* 1546.
<small>PEPYS LIBRARY, MAGDALENE COLLEGE, CAMBRIDGE/EDUARD LEIGH</small>

place to place. By the late sixteenth century, every seafaring people in Europe had developed a set of sailing ships to serve their purposes, comparable to the ships used by their neighbors, but rarely identical.

For example, galleons used by Europeans in the late sixteenth and early seventeenth centuries varied in size and configuration from country to country but displayed certain features in common. Those features included a beak below the bowsprit and a crescent profile, with a low forecastle and a half-deck, quarter-deck, and often a poop deck aft of the mainmast. The galleon generally had two full decks above the waterline upon which to mount artillery, and three or four masts plus the bowsprit. It usually carried two courses of square sails on the foremast and mainmast and lateen sails on the mizzen (and bonaventure mizzen, if the ship had a fourth mast). The hull was heavily built and braced to withstand heavy seas and the hazards of battle. Galleons generally ranged from about three hundred to about one thousand tons burden. With ratios of keel-to-beam between 2.4 to 1 and nearly 3 to 1, the narrower versions sacrificed carrying capacity for increased speed. Oceangoing ships were arguably the most sophisticated creations of their time, combining advanced techniques of forestry, metallurgy, carpentry, rope making, and dozens of ancillary crafts, not to mention the complicated arrangements required to

finance, provision, and crew them. They were the essential tools of European exploration, trade, and empire during the Renaissance.

See also **Exploration**; **Naval Warfare**.

BIBLIOGRAPHY

Gardiner, Robert, ed. *Cogs, Caravels, and Galleons: The Sailing Ship, 1000–1650*. London and Annapolis, Md., 1994.

Mott, Lawrence V. *The Development of the Rudder: A Technological Tale.* College Station, Tex., 1997.

Parry, J. H. *The Discovery of the Sea.* Berkeley and Los Angeles, 1974.

CARLA RAHN PHILLIPS

SICILY. Renaissance Italy knew the kingdom of Sicily (also called Trinacria) as a former pro-papal, pro-French territory lost to the king of Aragon in the revolt of 1282, the so-called Sicilian Vespers, against Charles of Anjou. Separated from the mainland kingdom of Naples, except for the temporary reunification under Alfonso V, called the Magnanimous (ruled 1442–1458), the island kingdom remained a part of the Iberian—not the Italian—political world for more than four hundred years. Thus, Machiavelli has only one reference to Sicily in *Il principe* (*The Prince;* 1513), the ancient story of Agathocles, king of Syracuse (chapter 8), and only thirteen references—all classical—to Sicily or Sicilians in *Discorsi* (*The Discourses;* composed c. 1515–1517). Shakespeare's *Much Ado about Nothing* (1600), with an ancient plot revived in the Renaissance, is set in Messina, where the prince of Aragon holds court, and Sicily again provides scenes at court in *The Winter's Tale* (c. 1610–1611). Sicily remained a classical allusion or a literary itinerary, and its few well-known Renaissance humanists and artists sought fame afar—Antonio Beccadelli (Panormita) (1394–1471) in Bologna and northern Italy before attaching himself to Alfonso and the Aragonese court; Marineo Siculo (1444?–1536) in Spain, where he set up a humanist school; and Antonello da Messina (c. 1430–1479) in Naples and northern Italy, where he mastered oil painting and portraiture.

Monarchical power in Sicily—usually absentee—was often nominal, contested between Aragonese and Angevin claimants, caught up in Mediterranean imperial ambitions, and subject to divisive factions among powerful local barons. Aragonese and Spanish rule after the 1282 revolt can be divided into four periods: 1282–1296, rule by the kings of Aragon until Sicily was exchanged for Sardinia and Corsica; 1296–1409, lordship under a cadet branch of the Aragonese royal house, whose breaking of a marriage-alliance treaty to return the island to the Angevins in 1337 led to renewed hostilities and exhaustive civil war between local noble Latin and Catalan factions, themselves divided, which ended in anarchy; 1412–1516, after a short interregnum, return to the kings of Aragon under a viceroy, with Sicily serving as a staging ground for Alfonso's conquest of Naples but retained by Aragon on the division of his empire at his death; and 1516–1713, rule by Spanish Habsburgs, administered by a viceroy, first under the jurisdiction of the Council of Aragon but after 1558 made part of King Philip II's newly created Council of Italy. In general, contested rule over Sicily (and Naples) was a remnant of the medieval antagonism between the imperial-Aragonese and the Guelf-Angevin factions that passed through marriage and inheritance to the Habsburg and Valois claimants in their sixteenth-century wars.

Sicily's 25,434 square kilometers were divided into three *valli* (main administrative and fiscal units from the early fifteenth century), which comprised subregions distinct by the late thirteenth century for their topography, settlements, and demographics: the Val di Mazara (western Sicily from Termini Imerese and Agrigento to Palermo, Marsala, and Mazara), the Val di Noto (south of Castrogiovanni and Etna from Catania and Syracuse to Licata), and the Val Demone (the northern coast and its mountain hinterlands from Messina to Cefalù). Structural re-

alignment after the fourteenth-century socioeconomic crisis shifted the traditional agricultural dominance of western Sicily and Palermo in grain and wine production to a more dynamic regional economy around Messina, with its increasingly commercialized, specialized economy of wine, sugar, oil, and especially silk. The foundation of the Universities of Catania (1445) and Messina (1590s) give evidence to the island's more dynamic eastern urban centers.

Resistance of the feudal nobility to Aragonese fiscal policies and the developing urban society reflected the continuing importance of local feudal power. Growing impoverishment and the rise of brigandage on the island were symptoms of an aristocracy that tied its privileges to support of the monarchy. Parliament became an ossified institution that existed only to grant payments to the crown. With its growing power, the monarchy exercised special jurisdiction over the church without papal input and introduced the Spanish Inquisition (1487), which likewise was not subject to Rome.

The historiography of Sicily—along with that of the southern Italian mainland—has been dominated since Italian unification in the nineteenth century by the idea of backwardness, as part of the *problema del Mezzogiorno* (the Southern question), with emphasis on the deleterious effects of political development, social institutions, and economic dualism. Contemporary scholars, however, no longer investigate how late medieval and Renaissance Sicily lost its influence and splendor from the time of the Holy Roman emperor Frederick II (ruled Sicily as Frederick I 1198–1250)—Jakob Burckhardt's first modern ruler because of his centralizing practices in southern Italy and Sicily and heir to a complex melding of Greek, Roman, Byzantine, Arabic, and Norman traditions. Instead, scholars attempt to debunk the myth of insular peculiarity and to integrate Sicily into a wider European context, which finds the island's place in the Mediterranean policies of the Catalan and later Spanish Habsburg imperium.

See also **Naples**.

BIBLIOGRAPHY

Aymard, Maurice. "From Feudalism to Capitalism in Italy: The Case That Doesn't Fit." *Review* 6, no. 2 (1982): 131–208. Translation of "La transizione dal feudalesimo al capitalismo." *Storia d'Italia: Annali* 1 (1978).

Bresc, Henri. *Un monde méditerranéen: Economie et société en Sicile, 1300–1450.* 2 vols. Rome, 1986.

D'Alessandro, Vincenzo, and Giuseppe Giarrizzo. *La Sicilia dal Vespro all'unità d'Italia.* Turin, Italy, 1989.

Epstein, Stephan R. *An Island for Itself: Economic Development and Social Change in Late Medieval Sicily.* Cambridge, U.K., 1992.

Koenigsberger, H. G. *The Practice of Empire.* Ithaca, N.Y., 1969. Emended edition of *The Government of Sicily under Philip II of Spain* (1951).

Mack Smith, Denis. *A History of Sicily: Medieval Sicily, 800–1713.* New York, 1968.

JOHN A. MARINO

SICKNESS AND DISEASE. With the word "sickness" people subjectively describe their inability to perform accustomed roles, duties, and desires. Sickness is thus more a human problem than a medical one, and so the humanists had much to say about it. For example, Desiderius Erasmus suffered most of his adult life from pains, aches, and fevers, most notably from kidney and bladder stones, whose passage he likened to severe birthing pangs. Believing some part of his suffering was due to an intolerance for fish, he obtained dispensation to eat meat on fast days. Believing also that only fine Burgundian wines would speed his recovery, he prevailed upon friends to acquire such medicine. Erasmus, like many educated men of the Renaissance, thus frequently relied upon his own understanding of bodily ills and cures, even when he consulted with (and, more rarely, trusted) prestigious physicians. Similarly, Michel de Montaigne spent many of his later years traveling from spa to spa, seeking relief from "stones." Both Erasmus and Montaigne are fairly typical of Renaissance elite: aging victims of chronic diseases, collaborators with their physicians in their treatment, living decades past the average life expectancy of around forty years. The biographies of prominent Renaissance artists, humanists, historians, and even physicians replicate this experience with nonplague and noninfectious afflictions. Many survived to a reasonably advanced age of sixty to seventy years.

While an anecdotal sampling naturally privileges the biographies of those who lived long enough to confront some of the inevitable afflictions of aging, the self-presentation of such pain, suffering, disease, and frailty was not a necessary outcome. Traditional learned medicine offered practical guides for the maintenance or restoration of health, but the willingness to detail, even glory in, one's own sufferings certainly was atypical before the Renaissance. The sufferings of Job, Christ, and the martyrs previously emphasized the transcendence of physical pain and the power that incorruptible, saintly relics had to heal when earthly medicine failed. New to the Renaisssance period is the "real-time" suffering of mere mortals, especially depicted as an ennobling saga of presumed fascination to the ordinary, nonmedical reader. Giovanni Boccaccio's *Decameron* (c. 1350), in Fourth Day, Tenth Story, is the first secular text to mention the use of an opiate to dull the pain of surgery. The innovative Renaissance surgeon Ambroise Paré was the first to proclaim that a patient's pain was in itself a reason to question accepted therapies. He included a chillingly detached description of his fall from a horse: "The broken bones came out through the flesh, stocking and boot, from which I felt as much pain as a man can endure." Paré then described how his poorly set fracture had to be broken and set again, an excruciating procedure most can scarcely imagine enduring without anesthesia. Nonetheless Paré, born in 1510, lived until 1590.

Disease and Social Class. One is often tempted to view life in the Renaissance era as a treacherous venture, navigating the perennial stenches, stinks, sores, and other sufferings associated with urban poverty, occasionally caught in the ship-wrecking storms of periodic plague and pestilence. But the reality for most prominent individuals was far less precarious, although chronic infectious diseases do punctuate the life stories of prominent families and individuals. Great killers familiar in nineteenth-century contexts also stalked the rich and famous of the Renaissance: the poxes, fluxes, scurvies, scrofulas, cancers, consumptions, fevers, rheumatisms, and gouts. Some, such as many members of the Medici family, struggled against the multisystem ravages of tuberculosis, others with the new disease of syphilis (Benvenuto Cellini, most likely, and certainly Ulrich von Hutten, Cyrano de Bergerac, many of the Borgia, and Henry II of France). Malaria was certainly part of the mix of intermittent fevers increasingly troubling sixteenth-century Italians, particularly as rice cultivation expanded. A favorite subject for retrospective diagnosis, Henry VIII of England suffered nonhealing ulcers and fistulas on his legs. From his early forties on, these excruciatingly painful, loathsome sores worsened significantly because Henry was increasingly unable to move around on his own and thus gained girth like Rabelais's Pantagruel. Speculation on the underlying cause has pointed to syphilis, tuberculosis, infection of the bone from a previous fracture, or deepening infection of the skin and muscle from the way his sores were treated. Those who had to endure surgery—for hernia, stones, fractures, toothache, and occasionally even complications of childbirth—often suffered unpleasant chronic ulcers and fistulas, requiring sustained surgical management, but nevertheless lived into their fifties and sixties.

The vast majority living in the time of the Renaissance weathered periodic storms of hunger, infection, squalor, and need. Their cries of misery, their frightening mummy-like faces, their "formless thinness"—in the words of a chronicler cited by Piero Camporesi—were barely perceptible to the wealthiest classes of the early Renaissance. In the century after the Black Death the poor had something of a reprieve, with stable, low food prices compared to wages. By the sixteenth and seventeenth centuries, however, the homeless and hungry became too numerous and too insistent to ignore. Prices outstripped wages at a slow and steadily relentless pace. To some extent, politically and economically secure individuals could avoid the frightening, periodic scourges, both because surveillance to identify cases of feared diseases had become commonplace in Renaissance Italy before the sixteenth century and because the habit of summer retreat to secluded country estates appealed to European elites of this era. Having fewer insults or injuries for their physicians to attend, the prosperous, well-fed, and well-clothed could manage chronic illness adequately. The rich required imported wines, long sojourns at the baths, medicines of marvelous complexity and expense, carefully planned and moderated diets prepared to the physicians' specifications, tuned to the nuances of temperament, age, gender, or the stars. The poor, almost as though they had no human humors to fall out of balance, no need for the moral and literary lessons of the *ars moriendi* (art of dying), were scorned for eating refuse, foraging among inedible plants, and supplementing their blackened bread and gruel with grubs, worms, and insects. The poor were thus seen as an indistinguishable swarm of humanity, distinctive and individual only when seen as dangerous vagrants or criminals. Their bodies were interchangeable and thus as generically serviceable in the novel Renaissance study of human anatomy as they were to the salvation of charitable Christian givers.

Very little of elite medicine (e.g., the potions, drafts, clysters, powders, baths, poultices, and prescriptions for health maintenance) made sense among the famished masses. Some diseases came to belong to the poor, as Girolamo Fracastoro, for example, found that plague did. In his famous work *De contagione et contagiosis morbis* (On contagion and contagious diseases; 1546), Fracastoro reflected on the disastrous years of the late 1520s, when all the four horsemen of the apocalypse seemed to

sweep through Renaissance Italy. One troubling appearance—which he called lenticular or punticular fever because the rash looked like lentils or small pinpricks—put the nobility at greater risk. Fracastoro explained: it was "more prone to attack those who are rather delicate and less robust. . . . The populace, on the other hand, are more robust and of drier temperament, because they exert themselves strenuously, and their diet is more frugal" (*On Contagion,* p. 111). The famous English "sweating sickness" was likewise a disease of the prosperous.

New Diseases. During the Renaissance physicians and laymen began to see many "new" diseases, ailments not well described by the ancients and thus requiring some discussion of the origins of the novelty. Most of these, such as the injuries that guns created, were at first hopefully assimilated into older ways of understanding. By the sixteenth century appropriating the very idea of new diseases could buoy the career of a Renaissance physician or surgeon. Among the new or newly recognized afflictions were the "great pox" (or syphilis, the "French disease"). "Great" distinguished it from the "small pox," which was first described by the Arabs but became a serious epidemic affliction only in the later sixteenth century. The sweating sickness appeared only from the 1480s to the 1550s, primarily in England. Tarantism, a bit like the medieval dancing mania, was seen only in the Puglia region of southern Italy. Miners' diseases, typical in the Alpine areas but also in the silver mines of the New World, were the first occupational diseases well described (by Paracelsus). Epidemic typhus fever, as detailed by Fracastoro, appeared suddenly in the early sixteenth-century wars. Scurvy and yellow fever were first described in relation to overseas conquest and colonization.

Not only diseases were novel. Many organic substances unknown before the discovery of the Western Hemisphere were suddenly available to therapeutic experimentation, and their sudden existence seemed to evoke and support the idea that diseases could be caused by something other than the putrefaction or imbalance of the humors. Both the discovery of medicinal plant substances unknown before European contact with the Western Hemisphere and astrologers' increasing focus on minerals introduced new remedies to late medieval therapeutics. Iconoclasts such as Paracelsus seized the possibilities in new remedies to question the adequacy of Galenic medicine and Artistotelian natural philosophy. Indeed the contagion theory, while evolving as justification for urban antiplague policy, encouraged the supposition that drug substances could be specific. The phenomenon of new diseases prompted an elegantly Renaissance discussion. Could a disease be seen as "new" because the usage of the words to describe diseases (such as rabies) had changed over time? Could diseases be new because they were seen only rarely and intermittently (Thucydides on the plague of Athens formed one locus classicus for such discussion)? Could a disease be new because it was truly a new creation (thus a problem that challenged theology)?

Disease and Population. Recording practices in the Renaissance make it difficult to gain numerical perspective on the differing experience of disease and sickness by socioeconomic class. But we do know that a quarter of all infants born never reached their second birthday—whether born to the rich or to the poor—and that fevers of various kinds and duration were the dominant causes of death in all years. During epidemic years, even in the sixteenth century mortality rates over 10 percent were typical in urban crises. Deaths attributed to plague alone in the great plague years (1520s, 1570s, 1590s, 1630), reached the 15 to 40 percent levels witnessed in the Black Death of 1348–1350. Wealthy individuals probably escaped this general slaughter largely because public health practices increasingly distanced the privileged from the poor in dangerous epidemic times.

Overall the population of Europe began to grow after 1460, fueled by rural to urban migration throughout western Europe. Strong contrasts between urban and rural mortality characterized the slow, but irrevocable, emergence of a Western fertility pattern (later marriage, lower birth rates). Yet for both rural and urban laborers, dependent upon day wages, illness plunged both the victims and their families into a more abject and dependent poverty, in which survival depended upon networks of support as well as philanthropic assistance. Any plague, famine, illness, or accident; a sudden expansion in the number of children or older relatives a family had to support; the loss of a mother in childbirth or a father to urban violence; an economic downturn, soaring prices, or currency devaluation; a war nearby—virtually any change in fortune could plunge modest households into vagrancy. Hospitals and other traditional charitable organizations rarely met these kinds of challenges to families, and so the later Renaissance period was characterized by the widening chasm between the rich and the poor. The

lens of sickness and disease is simply one way this history-shaping contrast became visible.

See also **Demography; Medicine; Plague.**

BIBLIOGRAPHY

Primary Works

Brabant, Hyacinthe. *Médecins, malades, et maladies de la Renaissance.* Brussels, 1966.

Fracastoro, Girolamo. *On Contagion and Contagious Diseases.* Translated and edited by W. C. Wright. New York, 1930. Translation of *De contagione et contagiosis morbis* (1546).

Paré, Ambroise. *The Case Reports and Autopsy Records of Ambroise Paré.* Edited by Wallace B. Hamby. Translated by J. P. Ma Ignaigne. Springfield, Ill., 1960.

Secondary Works

Brockliss, Laurence, and Colin Jones. *The Medical World of Early Modern France.* Oxford, 1997.

Camporesi, Piero. *Bread of Dreams: Food and Fantasy in Early Modern Europe.* Translated by David Gentilcore. Chicago, 1989.

Cohen, Esther. "Toward a History of European Physical Sensibility: Pain in the Later Middle Ages." *Science in Context* 8 (1955): 47–74.

Jütte, Robert. *Poverty and Deviance in Early Modern Europe.* Cambridge, U.K., 1994.

Poynter, F. N. L. "Patients and Their Ills in Vicary's Time." *Annals of the Royal College of Surgeons of England* 56 (1975): 141–152.

Pullan, Brian. "Plague and Perceptions of the Poor in Early Modern Italy." In Terence *Epidemics and Ideas: Essays on the Historical Perception of Pestilence.* Edited by Terence Ranger and Paul Slack. Cambridge, U.K., 1992. Pages 101–123.

ANN CARMICHAEL

SIDNEY, MARY (countess of Pembroke; 1561–1621), English writer, patron of belles lettres. Mary Sidney was the daughter of Sir Henry Sidney and Lady Mary Dudley Sidney, and wife of Henry Herbert, second earl of Pembroke. Her earliest known work is an elegy written for her brother Philip, who had died in 1586. Mentioned in her 1594 letter to Sir Edward Wotton, the elegy is probably "The Doleful Lay of Clorinda," printed with Edmund Spenser's "Astrophel" (1595). During the 1590s she encouraged works that praised her brother's memory, including Spenser's "Astrophel" and "The Ruines of Time," Thomas Moffet's *Nobilis,* and Abraham Fraunce's Ivychurch poems.

Pembroke was a transitional figure in the shift from a manuscript to a print literary culture. She supervised the printing of the 1593 and 1598 editions of Philip Sidney's *Arcadia,* which did much to legitimize print. Despite cultural injunctions to female silence, she printed two translations under her own name, with no apology for her gender or pretense that they had been printed against her will: *A Discourse of Life and Death, Written in French by Phi-*

Mary Sidney. Engraving by Simon van de Passe, 1618.
BY COURTESY OF THE NATIONAL PORTRAIT GALLERY, LONDON

served in a transcript of papers collected by John Harington for Lucy, countess of Bedford; she may well have translated Petrarch's entire *Trionfi,* for other works mentioned by contemporaries have been lost, probably to fire. Two original poems are also extant in only one manuscript, "To the Angell Spirit of the most excellent, Sir Philip Sidney" and "Even now that Care," a dedicatory poem to Queen Elizabeth that mingles praise with admonition. Both poems employ a traditional modesty topos to veil her self-assertion as a writer, although neither mentions her gender. Far more influential were the Sidneian *Psalmes.* Inspired primarily by the French Huguenot Psalter of Clémont Marot and Théodore de Bèze, Philip Sidney composed metrical paraphrases of Psalms 1–43; Pembroke completed the Psalms, using a dazzling array of verse forms and rhetorical devices. She evidently began with the Geneva Bible (1560) and Miles Coverdale's Psalter in the Book of Common Prayer and then consulted virtually every Psalm translation and commentary available to her in English, French, and Latin, choosing renditions closest to the Hebrew. Her poems, praised by contemporary writers such as John Donne and Aemilia Lanyer, influenced the development of the seventeenth-century religious lyric. She also served as a model for English women writers, particularly her niece Mary Sidney Wroth.

BIBLIOGRAPHY

Primary Work

The Collected Works of Mary Sidney Herbert, Countess of Pembroke. Edited by Margaret P. Hannay, Noel J. Kinnamon, and Michael G. Brennan. 2 vols. Oxford, 1998.

Secondary Works

Beilin, Elaine V. *Redeeming Eve: Women Writers of the English Renaissance.* Princeton, N.J., 1987.

Hannay, Margaret P. *Philip's Phoenix: Mary Sidney, Countess of Pembroke.* New York and Oxford, 1990.

Schleiner, Louise. *Tudor and Stuart Women Writers.* Bloomington, Ind., 1994.

MARGARET P. HANNAY

lippe Mornay. *Antonius: A Tragedie Written also in French by Robert Garnier, Both done in English by the Countess of Pembroke* (1592). *Antonius* was innovative in its form, primarily blank verse, and in its content, Roman history used to comment on contemporary events; Shakespeare quotes from it in *Antony and Cleopatra,* and it inspired other closet dramas (plays designed to be read rather than performed), including Samuel Daniel's *Cleopatra* and Elizabeth Cary's *Mariam.* She also permitted the printing of "A Dialogue betweene two shepheards, *Thenot* and *Piers,* in praise of *Astrea*" in Francis Davison's *A Poetical Rhapsody* (1602).

Nevertheless, Pembroke reserved her most important literary works for manuscript circulation. Her translation of Petrarch's *Trionfo della morte* (Triumph of death) in terza rima was haphazardly pre-

SIDNEY, PHILIP (1554–1586), English poet. Although there are a large number of documents by and about Philip Sidney, many aspects of his life are open to interpretation. In the latter half of the twentieth century, his life, works, and attitudes have been used by partisans of various camps to describe him: as an icon of patriotism, as an icon of rebellion or of coerced collaboration, as an idealist, or as a serious person whom you can love or hate, depending on your bias. Few, however, have found him likable, gentle, or funny; few have found him a little tricky, as did most of his contemporaries before his death fighting Spanish soldiers in the Netherlands made him a hero. At the time of his death, Sidney was the most important writer in Tudor literature since Thomas More. He exercised a huge influence on the flowering of English Renaissance letters, arts, and music in the 1590s and thereafter.

Origins. Sidney's life and works are filled with happy ironies. The first occurred at his birth and christening. He was born the first child to Henry Sidney and Mary Dudley on 30 November 1564 in the sprawling mansion of Penshurst in Kent, so warmly described both by Sidney in the second chapter of his novel, *The Countess of Pembroke's Arcadia* (1590), as Kalender's great house, and by Ben Jonson in his bread-and-butter poem addressed to Sidney's younger brother Robert, earl of Leicester, "To Penshurst." Philip was named after his godfather, King Philip II of Spain, the husband of Queen Mary I of England, who happened to be visiting Penshurst. Thus Sidney, ironically, was named after the leading Roman Catholic monarch of Europe, who during Sidney's mature years was constantly preparing to invade England with his Armada. Robert Naunton (1563–1635) recalled that Queen Elizabeth recognized the irony by referring to Sidney as her Philip as opposed to the enemy king and tyrannical overseer—in her propaganda—of the evil continental empire and of the Americas. Philip II remembered the baptism well enough to note on a troop report of Sidney's death "he was my godson."

Although they suffered from relative poverty throughout their lives, Sidney's parents and their forebears moved not only among the aristocracy but among royalty. Young Edward VI had granted Sidney's grandfather William the oft-renovated thirteenth-century castle Penshurst. Sidney's mother, Mary Dudley, was the younger sister of Robert Dudley, earl of Leicester, the queen's putative lover, and she was a perpetual lady-in-waiting to the queen and even caught smallpox while attending the queen's illness. The disease had a far more devastating effect on Mary Dudley's face than on the queen's (although in public and when sitting for portraits, the queen hid her pockmarks with a cosmetic foundation of white powder). Ben Jonson reported that Sidney himself had "pimples," possibly a reference to an even milder case of smallpox that affected Sidney). In his typically odd, autobiographical manner, Sidney memorializes the event of his mother's disfigurement in book 1 of *The New Arcadia* when his

heroine, Parthenia, has her face smeared with poison but is then miraculously cured by love. But the argument that Sidney resented the queen for limiting his family's advancement holds no water. The queen was a fiscal conservative and almost never rewarded her followers with money and advancement unless she had to. Sidney well knew the policy and even approved of it at times because it kept taxation of the old aristocracy in check.

Several of Sidney's forebears, ironically, lost their heads for high treason around the time of his birth, as he himself recounts in *The Defence of the Earl of Leicester* (1584), a witty and vituperative manuscript apology for the tribulations of his oft-slandered uncle Robert Dudley. Both his grandfather, John Dudley, the duke of Northumberland, and his uncle Guildford Dudley were executed, in part for their roles in placing Lady Jane Grey on the throne in London for nine days in 1553, to the exclusion of both Mary and Elizabeth. His aunt, Lady Jane herself, sixteen years of age and a student of the humanities, was beheaded for treason on Tower Hill the year he was born, as was her father Henry Grey, duke of Suffolk. These dire events had little effect on Sidney's life and reputation, unless they prompted him to adopt the ironic role in Elizabeth's court of self-deprecating rebel.

Education and Travel. At nine, Sidney entered Shrewsbury School and four years later Christ Church, Oxford. He received a superb education in Latin and Greek literature and in the Bible from able people of very different theological persuasions. Sidney's teachers were all apparently impressed with his learning and his likely agreement with their theological positions.

At age twenty-two, he went on a full three-year grand tour of the European continent under the worried eyes of some of the most powerful figures in England, including Elizabeth, who licensed him to leave the court for only two years. Elizabeth gave him two official charges: first, to condole the Holy Roman Emperor's court for the death of Maximilian II and to congratulate them on the succession of his troubled son Rudolf II; and second, to stand in as godfather to the new daughter of William of Orange. A guest of his future father-in-law, Francis Walsingham, the ambassador to Paris, Sidney witnessed the Saint Bartholomew's Day Massacre of about ten thousand Huguenot Protestants on and after 24 August 1572. The massacre spread from Paris to the provinces following the forced marriage of Sidney's newfound friend and patron, Henry of Navarre, to

Philip Sidney. Anonymous portrait. BY COURTESY OF THE NATIONAL PORTRAIT GALLERY, LONDON

Margaret of Valois, sister of Charles IX. Sidney's works are rife with scenes of and references to collective violence, although sometimes allegorized as the passions ganging up on reason or sense: occasionally comic, they are always ominous. In the massacre, he lost a newfound friend, the rhetorician Petrus Ramus, who may be the gently satirized model for Sidney's schoolmaster Rombus in *The Lady of May* (written 1578).

During his extended visit to the Continent, Sidney gained great skill in several languages. His insatiable curiosity led to excursions into the Roman Catholic reaches of Italy; to interviews with the painters Tintoretto and Veronese, for whom he sat, in Venice; and, accompanied by Edward Wotton, to discussions with John Pietro Pugliano, the esquire of the stables of the emperor Maximilian II, in Prague. In Warsaw some saw him as a candidate for king of Poland-Lithuania when the throne was left empty by Henry of Valois, who in June 1574 had succeeded to the crown of France as Henry III; the Polish throne was eventually occupied by the brilliant Transylvan-

ian prince Stephen Báthory. Sidney also formed a friendship with William of Orange, who may have wanted to marry him to his sister, a marriage Queen Elizabeth would object to on principle, as she would his candidature for the Polish throne.

Some of the details of Sidney's travels remain unclear because much of what we know comes from veiled autobiographical references in his own works: witness the comic opening to his *Defense of Poetry* (written 1580–1582), or the rather formal Latin correspondence Sidney maintained with the avuncular and rather possessive Hubert Languet, a Protestant convert and political thinker more than twice his age. Sidney's letters to Languet from Italy are clearly self-censored, and at the time they led, ironically, to the rumor that Sidney had turned Roman Catholic, a rumor that was immediately and strenuously denied by Languet. Sidney became acquainted with many of the artistic, scientific, and philosophical minds of the era, and some of their works were dedicated to him.

Life at Court. Anxiety in the court about his travels suggests that Sidney was part of Elizabeth's inner circle of writers, artists, scientists, propagandists, and men of action, a circle that she intentionally kept at home at court for her greater glory and for the country's safety. The queen was never in greater danger than when her impulsive gallants were off in the Americas, Portugal, Spain, or Ireland battling the enemy. Without much official or monetary advancement, Sidney played a large part in the queen's Accession Day entertainments for the public, and in 1578 he even wrote *The Lady of May,* a quasi-masque performed with the queen in the central role.

Apparently, along with the earl of Essex, Francis Drake, Walter Ralegh, and few others, Sidney had something of a royal license to be impetuous: it occasioned both the queen's reproof and her laughter. His letters confirm Fulke Greville's account in *The Life of the Renowned Sir Philip Sidney* (1652) that he gave the lie to Edward de Vere, earl of Oxford, in a fight over the use of a tennis court near Whitehall in 1579: having been called a puppy, he swore his parents were not dogs. He also gave the lie to the anonymous author of the slanderous *Leicester's Commonwealth* (possibly the Jesuit Robert Parsons) in *The Defence of the Earl of Leicester;* however, neither challenge came to a duel. His elegant public letter to the queen, "Touching Her Marriage with Monsieur," designed to dissuade her from marrying the duc d'Alençon in 1579, may have led Elizabeth to compel him to live in the country, away from court. But he naturally spent a good deal of time at the estate in Wilton that belonged to his brother-in-law, William Herbert, earl of Pembroke, and to his beloved sister Mary, countess of Pembroke, and his own letters indicate he was missed at court. Sidney was knighted in 1583, but this was the result of necessity, not the queen's largesse, because his friend, Prince Casimir of Poland, had asked him to stand in for him in his installation into the Order of the Garter, and only a knight could do so.

In September 1584 he signed on with Drake to explore the New World—in fact to frustrate Spanish interests there, a desire he had cultivated from his early days—with his friend Richard Hakluyt. At the moment the queen discovered his plan to sail with Drake, she appointed Sidney governor of Flushing in the Netherlands. He still held this post two years later, when he died from injuries sustained during an attack on well-defended Spanish supply lines. Clearly prejudiced in his idol's favor, Sidney's lifelong friend and fellow poet Fulke Greville (1554–1628) tells the story that, although thirsty from loss of blood on the battlefield, Sidney lent his water to a dying common soldier with the words, "Thy necessity is yet greater than mine." (This phrase Walter Ralegh repeated when he offered his hat to a bald fellow on his dramatic way to the scaffold to be beheaded by James I's authorities over thirty years later.) Sidney's funeral parade and burial in London at St. Paul's put a huge strain on his father-in-law Walsingham's finances. It seems to have served to deflect interest from the trial and beheading of Mary, queen of Scots, eight days before.

Works. C. S. Lewis, in his *English Literature in the Sixteenth Century, Excluding Drama* (1954), names Sidney, Spenser, and Shakespeare the first "golden" authors of the Tudor era and the culmination of the Renaissance in England. Of the three, Sidney was the oldest of the group, the most aristocratic, and the most comic. He provided Shakespeare with the tragic subplot for *King Lear*—that of the blinded Gloucester and his unknown son Edgar; and much of Portia's most moving speech on grace and mercy in *The Merchant of Venice* comes from the end of *The New Arcadia*. But as a consistently ironic viewer of human nature, Sidney has more in common with novelists and autobiographical essayists like Cervantes and Montaigne than he does with Shakespeare, the creator of the glittering falls of heroes and heroines, or with Spenser, the urgent moral iconographer (though Calidore in book 6 of *The Faerie Queene* is a version of Sidney's difficulties as a Knight of Courtesy).

Sidney is a writer's writer, and whatever his reputation among critics of various eras, writers have encoded tributes to him, whether it is Jonathan Swift renaming his mysterious beloved correspondent Stella ("star" in Latin, from Sidney's sonnet sequence, *Astrophil and Stella,* 1591, meaning "star-lover" and "star"); or Samuel Richardson borrowing the name of one of Sidney's heroines in the *Arcadia,* Pamela (from the Greek "pan honey" or "all sweetness"), for the title figure of the first great English epistolary novel, *Pamela* (1740); or Charles Dickens borrowing the names of Philip, Phip or Pip (Queen Elizabeth's nickname for him) and of Stella, as Pip and Estella, for his most profound and dark autobiographic novel, *Great Expectations* (1860–1861; the mildly sarcastic phrase is one of Sidney's sly self-referential coins in his sonnet sequence); or Stanley Kowalski shouting "Stella" up the staircase in Tennessee Williams's *Streetcar Named Desire* (1947).

Sidney is best known for three major works written in part at Wilton from 1578 to 1584. The first is the great critical statement of the Renaissance, *The Defence of Poetry.* Originally published in 1595 in separate editions, as *The Defence of Poesie . . . for William Ponsonby* and *An Apologie for Poetry . . . for Henry Oldey,* it is a dazzling, often self-deprecating, autobiographical essay, that, like Erasmus's *Praise of Folly* (1509), contains a sermon at its center. Extolling the importance of the Renaissance romance form, Sidney's theory is affective insofar as he proposes that the best art causes reader identification and thus moral improvement. Artists have the priestly and exoteric task of making "many Cyruses" of their readers rather than providing one real historical Cyrus—the reference here is to Xenophon's romantic *Cyropedia.* His central image in the work, borrowed from Lucretius and Juvenal, is that of poetry, meaning imaginative literature, as something with curative powers that excel those of history or philosophy. As Samuel Johnson put it in a tribute to Sidney, the reader takes the pill of philosophy's truths because poetry "gilds" them with its sweet coating, that is, with its delightful "feigning" of sex-and-violence-conflicted heroes and heroines with whose stories we feelingly identify. For poetry creates its own golden world that is not an imitation of nature's iron one; and the poet can wing his way across the zodiac of his own wit inventing things that can never be, but should be or might be. It is an essay, in short, that argues for the integrity and separateness of what we now think of romantically as the imagination, but which Sidney thought of Platonically as the mind exploring the Ideas. In the process, Sidney reviews the course of English poetry and challenges his peers to emulate in the vernacular the achievements of the Greek and Roman poets.

Sidney's great-house romance, interspersed with poems and songs, is his *Arcadia,* which has come down to us in three versions (a complete manuscript of the first version was discovered only at the beginning of the nineteenth century). It is the first English novel and contains, as Virginia Woolf recognized, "all the seeds of English fiction" in that it predicts the great novels to follow. It does so both technically in its use of letters; stories within stories; oblique first-person narrative; and *libre indirect,* or limited third-person narrative, focusing from one point of view; and also thematically in its use of what became commonplaces of English novelistic narrative: from near-drowning at sea and near rape to the famous party, crowd, court of law, and royal court scenes, all colored by remarkable displays of female sensibility.

Readers after the early nineteenth century have often had difficulty with *Arcadia* either because they had been told the characters are ideal when they are actually struggling better-than-average figures (as Aristotle had prescribed, or at least noticed, in his analysis of tragedy, *The Poetics*); or because they had to confront a prose-poetry that Sidney adopted in order to convey his subtle moral, psychological, and philosophical messages, and that demanded the same kind of care one gives to lyric poetry. If we take the time to read it aloud as it was for a coterie at Wilton that included his sister Mary, the poet Samuel Daniel, his wife, Frances Walsingham, and his purported beloved, Penelope Rich, we will enjoy a great experimental fictive mind at work.

In his sonnet sequence *Astrophil and Stella* Sidney tells the story of a brilliant self-deluding young man with great expectations frustrated in his pursuit of an adulterous affair with a charming unhappily married young wife, Stella. The model for the wife was purportedly the younger sister of Essex, Penelope (Devereux) Rich, whose father, we know from a letter from his deathbed, wanted her to marry Sidney. As in *Arcadia,* Sidney teases the reader with veiled autobiography, including a long-begged-for kiss. But beyond the big tease, we have a marvelous psychological study of the vanity of human wishes and the joys of poetic ambition, all capped with a visit to the torturous world of love melancholy. It is sustained throughout by a self-mocking engagement with platonic idealizing and with the persistence of desire.

Sidney's other achievements include a comic mini-drama, the masque *The Lady of May* (1578); *Certain Sonnets* (1581–1582), which contains, among some interesting experiments in quantitative verse, some contemplative poems that caught both Fulke Greville's and Shakespeare's eyes; a translation of the Psalms of David (which influenced a future family member, George Herbert), completed after his death by his sister Mary, sections proving the immortality of the soul in his friend Philippe du Plessis Mornay's treatise *The Truth of the Christian Religion;* and a version of the first two books of Aristotle's *Rhetoric* (now lost).

BIBLIOGRAPHY

Primary Works

Sidney, Philip. *An Apology for Poetry.* Edited by Geoffrey Shepherd. New York, 1973. Essential notes.

Sidney, Philip. *Astrophil and Stella.* Edited by Max Putzel. Garden City, N.Y., 1967. Essential readings.

Sidney, Philip. *The Countess of Pembroke's Arcadia.* Edited by Maurice Evans. London, 1977. Modernized text.

Sidney, Philip. *The Countess of Pembroke's Arcadia (The New Arcadia).* Edited by Victor Skretkowicz. Oxford, 1987. Standard edition.

Sidney, Philip. *The Countess of Pembroke's Arcadia (The Old Arcadia).* Edited by Jean Robertson. Oxford, 1973. Remarkable apparatus.

Sidney, Philip. *Miscellaneous Prose.* Edited by Katherine Duncan-Jones and Jan Van Dorsten. Oxford, 1973. Contains *Defence of Poetry, Defence of Leicester,* and *Lady of May.*

Sidney, Philip. *The Poems.* Edited by William A. Ringler Jr. Oxford, 1962. Essential apparatus.

Sidney, Philip. *Selected Prose and Poetry.* Edited by Robert Kimbrough. 2d ed. Madison, Wis., 1983. Strong selection and notes.

Secondary Works

Allen, M. J. B., Dominic Baker-Smith, and Arthur F. Kinney, eds. *Sir Philip Sidney's Achievements.* New York, 1990. Contains various essential essays.

Buxton, John. *Sir Philip Sidney and the English Renaissance.* London, 1954. Provides discussion of patronage.

Connell, Dorothy. *Sir Philip Sidney: The Maker's Mind.* Oxford, 1977. Discusses structures of Sidney's works.

Craft, William. *Labyrinth of Desire: Invention and Culture in the Work of Sir Philip Sidney.* Newark, Del., 1994. Discusses relation to Montaigne and experimentation.

Davis, Walter. *A Map of Arcadia.* In *Sidney's Arcadia.* New Haven, Conn., 1965. Reference to mythological interest.

Doherty, Mary Jane. *The Mistress-Knowledge: Sir Philip Sidney's Defence of Poesie and Literary Architectonics in the English Renaissance.* Nashville, Tenn., 1991. Discusses Sidney's vast intellectual background and his use of the image of Cyrus.

Duncan-Jones, Katherine. *Sir Philip Sidney Courtier Poet.* London, 1991. Rebel theory biography.

Greenfield, Thelma N. *The Eye of Judgment: Reading the "New Arcadia."* Lewisburg, Pa., 1982. Strong reading of female interest.

Hager, Alan. *Dazzling Images: The Masks of Sir Philip Sidney.* Newark, Del., 1990. Discusses Sidney's self-irony, impersonation, and self-portraiture.

Hamilton, A. C. *Sir Philip Sidney: A Study of His Life and Works.* Cambridge, U.K., 1977. Standard recapitulation.

Kalstone, David. *Sidney's Poetry: Contexts and Interpretations.* Cambridge, Mass., 1965. Deals with poetic complexity and pastoral motifs.

Kay, Dennis, ed. *Sir Philip Sidney: An Anthology of Modern Criticism.* Oxford, 1987. Essential articles.

Kimbrough, Robert. *Sir Philip Sidney.* New York, 1971. Careful recapitulation.

Kinney, Arthur F., editor. *Essential Articles for the Study of Sir Philip Sidney.* Hamden, Conn., 1986. Historic essay collection.

Kinney, Arthur F. "Sir Philip Sidney." In *Major Tudor Authors: A Bio-Bibliographical Critical Sourcebook.* Edited by Alan Hager. Westport, Conn., 1997. Pages 418–428.

Klein, Lisa M. *The Exemplary Sidney and the Elizabethan Sonneteer.* Newark, Del., 1998. Recapitulation of influence, Daniel.

Lanham, Richard. *The Old Arcadia.* In *Sidney's Arcadia.* New Haven, Conn., 1965. An early evaluation of the rhetorical complexity of this work.

Lindheim, Nancy. *The Structures of Sidney's "Arcadia."* Toronto, 1982. Presents the idealistic arguments and the notion that Sidney yokes opposites in his work.

McCoy, Richard C. *Sir Philip Sidney: Rebellion in Arcadia.* New Brunswick, N.J., 1979. Presents the new historicist theory of Sidney as rebel.

Myrick, Kenneth. *Sir Philip Sidney as a Literary Craftsman.* 2d ed. Lincoln, Nebr., 1965. Discusses prose narration. Originally published in 1935.

Osborn, James M. *Young Philip Sidney, 1572–1577.* New Haven, Conn., 1972. Solid observation of early years. Includes documents.

Raitiere, Martin N. *Faire Bitts: Sir Philip Sidney and Renaissance Political Theory.* Pittsburgh, Pa., 1984. Discusses Sidney's theory of rebellion and consent.

Robinson, Forrest G. *The Shape of Things Known: Sidney's "Apology" in Its Philosophical Tradition.* Cambridge, Mass., 1972. Presents the Platonic background.

Rudenstine, Neil L. *Sidney's Poetic Development.* Cambridge, Mass., 1967. A rhetorical study of the poetry.

Stillman, Robert E. *Sidney's Poetic Justice: "The Old Arcadia," Its Eclogues, and Renaissance Pastoral Traditions.* Lewisburg, Pa., 1986. Addresses the question of pastoral remedies and justice.

Stump, Donald V., Jerome S. Dees, and C. Stuart Hunter. *Sir Philip Sidney: An Annotated Bibliography of Texts and Criticism (1554–1984).* New York, 1994. An invaluable tool.

Van Dorsten, Jan, Dominic Baker-Smith, and Arthur F. Kinney, eds. *Sir Philip Sidney: 1586 and the Creation of a Legend.* Leiden, Netherlands, 1986. Discusses the distortion of Sidney's character following his death.

Wallace, Malcolm William. *The Life of Sir Philip Sidney.* Cambridge, U.K., 1915. The standard biography. Includes documents.

Weiner, Andrew. *Sir Philip Sidney and the Poetics of Protestantism.* Minneapolis, 1978. Discusses Lutheran and Calvinist backgrounds.

ALAN HAGER

SIENA. [This entry includes two subentries, one on the history of the city and territory of Siena in the Renaissance and the other on artists active in Siena.]

Siena in the Renaissance

Siena was an independent republic in Tuscany. An important commercial center in the Middle Ages and site of a university, it gradually declined in the Renaissance until it lost its political independence to the Holy Roman Empire in the middle of the sixteenth century.

The city's wealth came from commerce, banking, and wool manufacturing. Siena may have had a population of 65,000 just before the Black Death of 1348, which would have made it one of the five or six largest Italian cities. The plague lowered its population to about 15,000, from which recovery was slow. A census of 1558–1562 revealed a population of about 25,000 in the city and another 109,000 in the territory of the Sienese republic.

Government and Society.   From the Middle Ages onward Siena had a complex governmental structure typical of Tuscan republics in north-central Italy. It had a central administration, a chief judicial and police officer (podestà), and a council that oversaw trade and merchant activities, including all guilds except the powerful wool guild. Other officers represented the lower orders of the social hierarchy. The so-called government of the nine, dominated by international merchants, excluded aristocratic families from the highest offices and ruled relatively well from 1285 to 1355.

Sharp divisions between different groups characterized Sienese politics in the later fourteenth and the fifteenth centuries. The chief divisions were between noble families claiming ancient lineage, nobles from the countryside, and wealthy merchants. A series of less stable political regimes followed the government of the nine. These oscillated between more democratic regimes favoring tradesmen and shopkeepers and those serving the interests of the nobles.

The economy stagnated in the later fourteenth century. In 1371 the wool workers rioted in an effort to secure higher wages. A series of political reversals, including the loss of Arezzo, a commune on the Arno, to Florence in 1384, also hurt Siena. Because of the political and economic difficulties, aristocratic groups consolidated their supremacy over the city by the second half of the fifteenth century.

In 1487 Pandolfo Petrucci (1451–1512), a prominent Sienese nobleman, succeeded in establishing personal rule over the city, which his heirs maintained until 1523. Petrucci's major political accomplishment was to block the attempt of Cesare Borgia to incorporate Siena into his short-lived state in cen-

Bullfight in Siena. *Bullfight in the Piazza del Campo* by Vincenzo Rustici. The Palazzo Publico (city hall) is at the right.
MONTE DEI PASCHI, SIENA, ITALY/SCALA/ART RESOURCE

tral Italy. Petrucci also won support from the Sienese through an agrarian act of 1501, which transferred ownership of a considerable amount of land outside the city walls to citizens of Siena. Thus, Siena expanded its economic control over rural areas, changing what was previously a federation between city and countryside. The ruling class of Siena was becoming a landed elite.

But the wars of the sixteenth century involving France, Spain, and the more powerful Italian states left Siena vulnerable. Florence had sought control over Siena for centuries. Even though Siena defeated papal and Florentine troops at the battle of Camollia in 1526, the city increasingly came under Spanish influence. Charles V forced Siena to accept his protection and a Spanish garrison in 1530. In 1552 the Sienese threw out the Spanish garrison and welcomed Florentine refugees who opposed Cosimo I de' Medici, the ruler of Florence. Spain responded with a three-year siege that starved the Sienese into surrender in 1555. On 3 July 1557 King Philip II of Spain transferred the city to Cosimo as a fief in return

for a substantial payment. This ended Sienese independence forever. Even though the Florentine government confirmed Siena's civic autonomy in 1560 and 1565, the city and its territory were part of the Tuscan state of the Medici. A new political order divided the Sienese political and social structure into those permitted to hold office and those excluded. Like much of Italy, late-Renaissance Siena froze into a rigid political and social stratification for the next two centuries.

Culture and Art. Siena's most important cultural activity was to host a major Italian university. Founded about 1240, the University of Siena emphasized law (which was studied by about two-thirds of the students) and had a number of important professors on its faculty over the centuries. The Sozzini family produced a dynasty of distinguished jurists in the fifteenth and sixteenth centuries who taught at Siena and other Italian universities. The University of Siena attracted numerous non-Italian students, especially Germans, who came to study law, throughout the Renaissance.

Two of the three most famous Sienese of the Renaissance were saints: St. Catherine of Siena (Caterina Benincasa; 1347–1380), who worked to persuade the papacy to return from Avignon to Rome; and St. Bernardino (Albizzeschi) of Siena (1380–1444), the most popular preacher of the fifteenth century. Certainly not a saint, the humanist Enea Silvio Piccolomini (1405–1464) came from a small town in the Sienese republic. After he became Pope Pius II (1458–1464), he renamed his birthplace Pienza and had the architect Bernardo Rossellino (1409–1464) erect a complex of buildings (1459–1463). Pinturicchio (Bernardino di Betto di Biago; c. 1454–1513) created a cycle of paintings called the Libreria Piccolomini (Piccolomini library) in the cathedral between 1495 and 1509 to celebrate Pius II's life.

The general architectural landscape of Siena, which is on a hill, has changed little since the Middle Ages. Lined with medieval buildings, its streets wind up and down three ridges. The communal palace (begun 1288) with its slender and elegant tower (1338–1348) dominates the central square and can be seen for miles beyond. The campo (literally "field") in front of the palace is the setting for Sienese urban life. Every July and August, it is the scene of the famous Corsa del Palio, a competition between teams of horses and riders from different sections of the city. The city's cathedral (begun in the tenth century) has inlaid marble and other artistic treasures.

See also **Siena**, *subentry on* **Art in Siena** *and biographies of figures mentioned in this entry.*

BIBLIOGRAPHY

Primary Works

Malavolti, Orlando. *Historia de' fatti e guerre d'Sanesi*. Venice, 1599. Reprint, Bologna, Italy, 1982.

Tizio, Sigismondo. *Historiae Senenses* (Histories of Siena). Rome, 1992– .

Repetti, Emanuele. *Dizionario geografico fisico storico della Toscana* (A geographical, physical, historical dictionary of Tuscany). 6 vols. Florence, 1833–1846.

Secondary Works

Ascheri, Mario. *Il Rinascimento a Siena, 1355–1559*. Siena, Italy, 1993.

Ascheri, Mario. *Siena nel Rinascimento: Istituzioni e sistema politico*. Siena, Italy, 1985.

Barzanti, Roberto, Giuliano Catoni, and Mario De Gregorio, eds. *Storia di Siena*. Vol. 1, *Dalle origini alla fine della Repubblica*. Siena, Italy, 1995.

Pepper, Simon, and Nicholas Adams. *Firearms and Fortifications: Military Architecture and Siege Warfare in Sixteenth-Century Siena*. Chicago, 1986.

PAOLO RENZI

Art in Siena

The republic of Siena's contributions to Renaissance art start with its much-praised fourteenth-century masters, Duccio di Buoninsegna, the Lorenzetti brothers, and Simone Martini. They transformed the late-Byzantine tradition of painting, with its flattened, static forms set against gold backgrounds, by introducing a splendor of vivid color, figures enlivened with greater emotional power, and new representations of landscape and interior spaces. Less appreciated today are the accomplishments of Sienese masters in the fifteenth century, some of whom are known only by modern nicknames, such as the Maestro dell'Osservanza. Also less well-known than they deserve to be are the eccentric personalities Domenico Beccafumi and Sodoma (Giovanni Antonio Bazzi), who dominated Sienese painting during the first half of the sixteenth century.

Fourteenth-Century Painting. Siena's native school of painting starts with Duccio di Buoninsegna (1255?–1318). His most magnificent work for the City of the Virgin, as Siena is known, is the *Maestà* (Madonna in majesty; see the color plates in this volume) made for the high altar of the cathedral in 1308–1311. It presents the Madonna and Child enthroned, surrounded by a heavenly court of gorgeously robed angels and saints, including the four patron saints of Siena kneeling in the foreground. The Byzantine formula in the pose of the Virgin and Child is softened with elegant touches that Duccio learned from the French Gothic style, such as the undulant lines of drapery hems trimmed in gold.

The back of this monumental image of the Madonna as queen of heaven bears many small scenes showing the Passion of Christ. Duccio's exploration of spatial effects and his ability to animate individualized figures come through strongly in the scene of *Christ's Entry into Jerusalem*. Patches of jewellike color on the garments of the crowd welcoming Christ lead along the curving roadway that turns up sharply to pass under a three-dimensional arch of the gateway, opening onto the high-towered city beyond. Only a few paces separate Christ from the eager crowd, and the blank orchard wall that measures out that distance heightens the anticipation of his arrival.

Simone Martini (c. 1283–1344), a pupil of Duccio's, also painted a Marian altarpiece for Siena cathedral. His sumptuous *Annunciation* (1333) betrays French Gothic influence in its pinnacled and gabled frame and in the swooping curves of the lean bodies of the two figures. This is the first large-scale altarpiece to celebrate the angel Gabriel's annunciation to the Virgin, the moment of the incarnation of Christ. Martini envisions the angel arriving wearing a plaid mantle that curves in an arabesque behind him. Across the marbled floor, the aristocratic Virgin leans away from her celestial visitor. An ornate vase of lilies, symbolic of the Virgin's purity, separates the pair, while just above it the dove of the Holy Spirit bursts out of a heavenly glory. Such creations set the stage for the elegant International Gothic style to come.

Just a few years later, in 1338–1339, Ambrogio Lorenzetti (c. 1290–1348) created his famous series of frescoes, *Good and Bad Government,* in the Palazzo Pubblico for the room of the Nine, the governing officials of Siena. These allegories, complete with inscriptions, set forth a philosophical framework for just rulership based on the inspiration of divine wisdom, the distribution of justice, and the concord of all citizens—all male—united together for the good of the commune. Women find their role not among the citizens who stand below the great allegorical figures but as the allegories themselves, reclining Peace and upright Fortitude and her sisters all crowned and seated on a great dais flanking the male figure representing Siena itself.

To accompany these complex symbolic works, Lorenzetti created vast fresco vistas of *Effects of Good Government in the Country* and *Effects of Good Government in the City.* The former is the first panoramic landscape painted since antiquity. A high view of the rolling Tuscan hills includes an early attempt at aerial perspective. Farmworkers toil in the fecund fields or trudge with their goods uphill to the city markets, while a well-off party of hawkers rides out of the city, down into the fields. Ambrogio Lorenzetti's city view constructs open squares flanked by blocky buildings, many with open archways that reveal the flourishing commerce inside.

Pietro Lorenzetti (c. 1280–c. 1348), like his brother, explored the construction of illusionistic space in a painted interior. His *Birth of the Virgin* (1342) effectively evokes the illusion of a boxy room, Anna's bedroom where the birth has just occurred. The room is capped by a vaulted ceiling, visible through the ornate frame as if it were the outer wall of the vaulting. Such experiments anticipated the consistent perspectival illusion so sought after by fifteenth-century Renaissance artists.

Fifteenth-Century Painting. Fifteenth-century Sienese painters built on many of the strengths of these fourteenth-century masters. Ste-

fano di Giovanni (c. 1400–1450), known as Sassetta, extended the Lorenzettis' exploration of atmospheric landscapes and well-articulated illusions of interior spaces. Such effects figure prominently in the now dispersed predella panels for Sassetta's altarpiece for the Guild of the Wool Merchants (1423–1426), made to celebrate the feast of Corpus Christi. Dramatically foreshortened figures and audacious touches of naturalism in the darkening night sky enliven Sassetta's affecting scene of the *Burning of a Heretic.*

Giovanni di Paolo (1403?–1483) maintains the same delicate figure type favored by Sassetta in his ingenious narratives of saints' lives. In his cycle of scenes from the life of St. Catherine of Siena, he invented some of the very first visualizations of this local saint's life. His panel *St. Catherine Receiving the Stigmata* presents the fragile form of the saint caught up in ecstasy, her hands raised to accept the marks of Christ's wounds, invisible to all but herself. [See the biography of Catherine of Siena in volume 1.]

Completing this trio of charming fifteenth-century painters is the anonymous Maestro dell'Osservanza (active second quarter of the fifteenth century). Many fine details of ornament link him to Sassetta, and his feeling for lovely color fits him firmly within a late-Gothic aesthetic. The St. Anthony Abbot series attributed to him offers starkly beautiful landscapes populated by mysterious creatures—a pink-garbed temptress, tormenting demons, a helpful centaur. In *St. Anthony Tempted by the Devil in the Guise of a Woman* the poetic treatment of striated colors in the overarching sky caps the charged encounter of holy man and demon.

Sixteenth-Century Painting. Rather than continue to build on the strengths of Siena's fourteenth-century artistic heritage, two early-sixteenth-century artists of stature working in Siena took the city's painting tradition into distinctly new directions. Both Sodoma (1477–1549) and Domenico Beccafumi (1484–1551) worked outside the city, then brought back knowledge of the latest developments in Rome. Sodoma, whom the art historian Giorgio Vasari denounced for his immoderate style of living, nevertheless won praise from him for his beautiful *St. Sebastian.* Like that work, Sodoma's *Christ at the Column* (1511–1515), although a fragment, poignantly depicts a noble, suffering figure, presented with Leonardesque subtlety in the soft modeling of the flesh.

The giant of sixteenth-century Sienese painting, Beccafumi, is sometimes given the label of mannerist because of his experiments with extreme distortions

Art in Siena. *Mystic Marriage of St. Catherine of Siena* by Giovanni di Paolo. Tempera and gold on wood; 28.9 × 28.9 cm. (11.375 × 11.375 in.). THE METROPOLITAN MUSEUM OF ART, BEQUEST OF LORE HEINEMANN IN MEMORY OF HER HUSBAND, DR. RUDOLF J. HEINEMANN, 1996 (1997.117.2)

of bodily forms. He painted monumental incandescent altarpieces for the churches of the city, principal among them the *Fall of the Rebel Angels* in two versions (c. 1524 and c. 1528). His long-limbed figures, often straining in violent contortions, carry a strong emotional charge. Vibrant color animates even his fresco work, such as his ceiling full of moral examples in the Hall of the Consistory in the Palazzo Pubblico. Beccafumi's subjects taken from ancient history present ferocious models of justice.

Sculpture.   Siena contributed one great sculptor to the ranks of Renaissance masters: Jacopo della Quercia (c. 1374–1438) is perhaps best known for his influential marble reliefs of the *Temptation and Fall* for the doorway of San Petronio in Bologna, or for his failed entry in the Florentine competition for the sculpture of the Baptistery doors. Unfortunately,

much of the work he did in Siena is in a bad state of repair. For the Fonte Gaia in the Campo of the Palazzo Pubblico (1414–1419) he sculpted marble allegories and narrative reliefs that still exhibit a robust plasticity even though reduced to fragments. The *Expulsion from the Garden* relief displays portions of well-muscled, stocky bodies striding out of an illusionistic gateway done in low relief. It is no wonder that Michelangelo Buonarroti, the most accomplished sculptor of the Italian Renaissance, could learn from Jacopo's powerful vision of the human body more than a century later.

Biccherne.   During the Renaissance, Siena's Palazzo Pubblico, the seat of civic life, received some of its painters' finest artistic efforts. Another measure of the strong interweaving of art and government in Siena is seen in a distinctive type of painting made

29

in the city for centuries. This is the *tavolette* (small panel paintings, also known as *biccherne*), which started out as small decorated wooden covers for the financial books of the treasury offices, the Gabella and Biccherna. These modest paintings, fashioned by masters such as Duccio and Beccafumi, give a pictorial history of Siena's current events from the thirteenth to the seventeenth century.

BIBLIOGRAPHY

Borsook, Eve. *The Mural Painters of Tuscany.* London, 1960. Rev. ed., Oxford, 1980. Good illustrations of the Lorenzettis' and Simone Martini's works.

Carli, Enzo. "Sodoma." In *Dictionary of Art.* Edited by Jane Turner. New York, 1996. Vol. 29, pages 1–4. Useful short summary of life and works.

Christiansen, Keith, Laurence B. Kanter, and Carl Brandon Strehlke. *Painting in Renaissance Siena, 1420–1500.* New York, 1988. Exhibition catalog with excellent essays on art and culture in fifteenth-century Siena and many color illustrations.

Domenico Beccafumi e il suo tempo. Milan, 1990. Exhibition catalog in Italian with fine color illustrations of works by Beccafumi and Sodoma.

Martindale, Andrew. *Simone Martini.* Oxford, 1988. Includes twentieth-century debates over the artist's works. Well illustrated.

Os, H. W. van. *Sienese Altarpieces, 1215–1460: Form, Content, Function.* 2 vols. Groningen, Netherlands, 1984–1990. Discusses meaning of religious works in context.

Stubblebine, James H. *Duccio di Buoninsegna and His School.* 2 vols. Princeton, N.J., 1979. Monograph on Duccio.

SUSAN E. WEGNER

SIGNORELLI, LUCA (d'Egidio di maestro Ventura de' Signorelli; c. 1450–1523), Italian painter and draftsman. Born in Cortona, a Tuscan town controlled by Florence and close to the border with Umbria, Luca Signorelli was active in this provincial center throughout his career, and, at the summit of his fame, in Rome and Florence as well. His present renown is linked largely to the recently restored frescoes depicting the end of the world and the Last Judgment in the New Chapel (known by its sobriquet, Chapel of San Brizio) in the cathedral in Orvieto (1499–1504). Thus the densely knotted clusters of nudes pictured here are the subject most commonly allied with Signorelli, and the intensely violent manner in which the nudes are rendered is the style with which he is associated. Current interest in the frescoes resonates with Giorgio Vasari's assertion in *Le vite de' più eccellenti architetti, pittori, et sculteri italiani* (1550 and 1568; trans. *Lives of the Artists*) that Michelangelo was influenced by the Orvieto murals in his *Last Judgment* (Rome, Sistine Chapel; 1536–1541), the supreme manifestation, it may be added, of Signorelli's contemporary impact.

Following Vasari, once again, Signorelli appears to have studied with Piero della Francesca (active 1439–1478, d. 1492) beginning in about 1460. The geometrical simplification, grandeur, and unrelieved sobriety that characterize Signorelli's art seem, indeed, to relate to Piero. But the often aggressive physicality of Signorelli's art, so different from the serene and reflective approach of Piero, and the brilliant draftsmanship and facility in anatomical representation evident in his work, reflect a Florentine current best discerned in the work of Andrea del Verrocchio (1435–1488) and Antonio del Pollaiuolo (c. 1432–1498). Signorelli appears to have been in Florence for several years beginning in 1475, so evidence of such influence should not be unexpected.

The lineaments of Signorelli's career become more secure only with two grand fresco cycles, the first in the sacristy of San Giovanni in the Santa Casa at Loreto (1474–1484) and the second in the Sistine Chapel (c. 1481–1483). The latter, one of the great monuments of the early Renaissance, involved the decoration of the newly built chapel of Pope Sixtus IV (reigned 1471–1484) with scenes of the lives of Moses and Jesus. The full extent of Signorelli's role in this collaborative project that included Perugino and Sandro Botticelli, among others, remains unsettled, although the *Testament of Moses* (1488) is agreed to be his. In this mural, vividly interacting groups of figures, some of whom are likenesses of notables of the day, spread across the broad surface of the work and move into the background, a formula Signorelli would employ in later narrative representations. The beautiful male nude youth representative of paganism, and found at the center of the composition, is an especially telling presentiment of later achievement.

Perhaps partly through a new eminence that resulted from this papal monument, Signorelli's standing in Florence, during these years that immediately preceded Lorenzo de' Medici's death in 1492, reached its apex. The *Court of Pan* (Berlin, Kaiser-Friedrich Museum; destroyed 1945) stands with Botticelli's mythological paintings of this same period as expressive of the defining endeavor of the Florentine intellectual and artistic culture to reconcile paganism and Christianity.

Probably illustrative of a comparable body of ideals, although expressed now in a more conventional religious idiom, is the so-called Medici Tondo (Florence, Uffizi), another work of this Florentine period. Representative of a lifetime engagement with the popular theme of Virgin and Child, Signorelli's characteristic inventiveness in the area of subject matter

Luca Signorelli. *Acts of Antichrist.* Fresco in the Cathedral, Orvieto, Italy; c. 1499. Signorelli included a portrait of himself at the far left, standing next to Fra Angelico, who had decorated parts of the cathedral in the 1440s. Antichrist, a figure mentioned in the New Testament who opposes Christian truth, preaches from a pedestal at right center. ANDERSON/ ALINARI/ART RESOURCE

is suggested by the inclusion of male nudes in the background.

During this time, Signorelli was also developing into one of the great draftsmen of the day. An early master in the use of chalk, he realized to the fullest the potential of the medium for the making of loose, rapid, and sketchy impressions.

The commission awarded Signorelli in 1499 to complete Fra Angelico's abandoned work of 1447 in the New Chapel (Orvieto Cathedral) led to the creation of the most comprehensive (and original) consideration of the Christian "last things" (death, judgment, heaven and hell) in Italian art. In six towering wall murals that recount the universal cataclysm at the end of time, together with vaults embellished with a sprawling image of the heavenly conclave and

a basement region devoted chiefly to an unprecedented ensemble of pagan literary portraits and scenes, Signorelli depicts a world torn asunder and the coming of a merciful God, one nevertheless capable of inflicting horrific punishments.

The subject of these works, expressive of a religious extremism out of place in a culture that generally spurned apocalyptic demonstrations, prepares one for the last decades of Signorelli's career. This was a period of growing isolation for the artist in Cortona, a time in which he came to be surpassed by more progressive contemporaries, such as Raphael, who favored a graceful, restrained, and idealizing style. To be sure, some important contracts were awarded the artist during these years, notably for work in the Vatican apartments of Pope Julius II

(c. 1508) and for decoration of the Petrucci palace in Siena (1509). But, seemingly, Signorelli's contemporary consequence came to an end after Orvieto.

BIBLIOGRAPHY

Kury, Gloria. *The Early Work of Luca Signorelli, 1465–1490.* New York, 1978.

Mancini, Girolamo. *Vita di Luca Signorelli.* Florence, 1903.

Riess, Jonathan. *The Renaissance Antichrist: Luca Signorelli's Orvieto Frescoes.* Princeton, N.J., 1995.

Vischer, Robert. *Luca Signorelli und die italienische Renaissance.* Leipzig, Germany, 1879.

JONATHAN B. RIESS

SIGONIO, CARLO   (c. 1522–1584), Italian humanist of the late Renaissance, historian of antiquity and the Middle Ages. Sigonio taught classical studies known as "humanity," first in his hometown, Modena, then at the university-level Scuola di San Marco of Venice (1552–1560), the University of Padua (1560–1563), and the University of Bologna (1563–1584). He wrote and lectured in Latin exclusively.

Literary theory based on Aristotle's *Rhetoric,* and on the concept of mimesis in his *Poetics,* reached a high point in sixteenth-century Italy. Sigonio was esteemed as a lecturer on both books, by the youthful Torquato Tasso among others, and in 1562 Sigonio had published an analysis of the mimesis used by writers of dialogue, a major literary genre in the ancient world that had regained importance in the Renaissance. In 1583 Sigonio was involved in the publication of a philosophical work, the *Consolatio,* known to have been composed in antiquity by Cicero and purportedly rediscovered. This was in fact a forgery, but Sigonio stubbornly defended its authenticity and most people came to assume that he was the author.

Carlo Sigonio's importance lies in his contribution to historical studies. In the 1550s he edited and published commentaries on Roman inscriptions and Livy's history of the Roman republic, emphasizing the most basic elements of historical study: chronology and prosopography (the identification of individuals and the compilation of the record of their public careers). In the 1560s he published a series of fundamental monographs on the institutions and social history of ancient Rome. In these works Sigonio demonstrated that the archaic aristocracy, the patriciate, had been forced over time to share the state with the plebeians, and that the noble senators of Rome were of mixed patrician and plebeian descent.

In the 1570s Sigonio turned to the study of late antiquity and medieval Italy, following Flavio Biondo over a century earlier. In addition to the range of sources that the printing revolution had made available, he consulted the civic archives of northern Italian cities as a source for their history as medieval communes—a turning point in historical research. The resulting works, *De occidentali imperio* (On the history of the western empire; Bologna, 1578), and *De regno Italiae* (On the history of the kingdom of Italy; Venice, 1574, and Bologna, 1580), provided the first modern general narrative of the period from the third to the twelfth centuries. Particularly at intervals in *De regno Italiae,* Sigonio pauses to survey and interpret the course of Italian history.

In the 1580s Sigonio produced several books on ancient Hebrew society and the history of the church. Four of his works were scrutinized at this time by ecclesiastical censors in Rome, trying to protect the history, true and legendary, of the Western Church, and the papacy against Protestant attacks. The censors stringently criticized Sigonio for failing to adopt the same defensive stance, and although the books in question were never banned, they were not reprinted in Italy until the eighteenth century, whereas there were many editions from the Wechel press in Frankfurt.

BIBLIOGRAPHY

Primary Works

Sigonio, Carlo. *Del Dialogo.* Edited by Franco Pignatti. Rome, 1993. Critical edition of the Latin text of Sigonio's *De dialogo* (1562) with Italian translation and an introduction covering the main points of the sixteenth-century debate on literary theory in Italy.

Sigonio, Carlo. *Opera Omnia.* Edited by Filippo Argelati. Milan, 1732–1737. 6 vols. The most widely available edition of Sigonio's works; but where possible, readers should consult the original sixteenth-century editions.

Secondary Work

McCuaig, William. *Carlo Sigonio: The Changing World of the Late Renaissance.* Princeton, N.J., 1989.

WILLIAM MCCUAIG

SIXTUS IV   (Francesco della Rovere; 1414–1484), pope (1471–1484). Francesco della Rovere was born in Pecorile, near Savona; his father, Leonardo della Rovere, was a small merchant and involved in cloth manufacture. Dedicated to the Franciscan order by his family as a child, he was educated in Franciscan convents and studied at the Faculty of Theology of the University of Padua before embarking in 1434–1435 on a career as a teacher of theology in the universities of Pavia, Padua, Bologna, Florence, Perugia, and Siena. He was minister general of the Friars

Minor (Franciscans) from 1464 to 1469 and was made a cardinal in 1467; he was elected pope on 9 August 1471, taking the name Sixtus IV.

One of the few theologians among the Renaissance popes, Sixtus continued to take an interest in theology and to wear a Franciscan habit under his papal robes. His pontificate, however, marked a significant step in the development of two major abuses of the Renaissance papacy, nepotism and the venality of office. Sixtus made six of his relatives cardinals—including Giuliano della Rovere, the future pope Julius II—and sought prestigious marriages and estates for several lay relatives as well. Most influential over Sixtus were Cardinal Pietro Riario (d. 1474) and his brother Girolamo Riario, who was married to Caterina Sforza, the illegitimate daughter of Galeazzo Maria, duke of Milan, and made lord of Imola (1473) and then Forlì (1480). Girolamo Riario's ambitions involved the pope in the Pazzi War (1478–1480) against Florence (after Riario had backed an unsuccessful attempt to assassinate Lorenzo de' Medici) and the War of Ferrara (1482–1484). While the Riario lost their states to Cesare Borgia and did not recover them, the marriage arranged for Giuliano della Rovere's brother, Giovanni, to Giovanna, daughter of Federico da Montefeltro, duke of Urbino, resulted in their son Francesco becoming the first della Rovere duke of Urbino in 1508. Partly to finance the promotion of his family's interests, Sixtus extended the practice of selling offices in the Curia and creating large numbers of new offices simply in order to sell them, practices that made fundamental reform of the papal administration in the future exceedingly difficult.

Sixtus's desire to project an image of grandeur and temporal power was another cause of expense but brought lasting cultural benefits. One was the Vatican library, reorganized by the pope in 1475 (although he neglected the University of Rome, diverting its revenues to his building projects). Another was the Sistine Chapel in the Vatican, designed as an imposing setting for papal ceremonies and decorated (1481–1483) with frescoes by Sandro Botticelli, Pinturicchio, Domenico Ghirlandaio, and Perugino (Pietro Vannucci), among others. Many Roman churches and monasteries, most notably Santa Maria del Popolo and Santa Maria della Pace, and the Hospital of Santo Spirito, which he had decorated with a large fresco cycle depicting his own life, were restored or rebuilt on his orders. These works, his ordering the cleansing and improvement of the streets in Rome, his construction of the Ponte Sisto across the Tiber, and his encouragement of investment in

building and restoring palaces in Rome by a bull of 1474 allowing clergy who died there to bequeath real property to their relatives (formerly it would have gone to the pope) earned him the epithet of *restaurator Urbis* (restorer of Rome).

[For images of Sixtus IV see the painting by Melozzo da Forli of Sixtus inaugurating the Vatican Library in the color plates in volume 4 and the painting by a follower of Melozzo in the entry "Libraries" in volume 3.]

BIBLIOGRAPHY

Ettlinger, Leopold D. *The Sistine Chapel before Michelangelo: Religious Imagery and Papal Primacy.* Oxford, 1965.

Lee, Egmont. *Sixtus IV and Men of Letters.* Rome, 1978. The first chapter is a biography of Sixtus.

Miglio, Massimo, et al., eds. *Un pontificato ed una citta: Sisto IV (1471–1484).* Vatican City, 1986.

CHRISTINE SHAW

SIXTUS V (Felice Peretti; 1520–1590), pope (1585–1590). Felice Peretti was born on 13 December 1520 at Grottammare, in the March of Ancona. The son of a farmer, he was educated by the Conventual Franciscans of Montalto; at age twelve he joined the order and at thirteen took his vows (1534). Ordained a priest at Siena in 1547, he received his doctorate in theology at Fermo in 1548. Renowned for preaching, he gave Lenten sermons in Rome, Perugia, and Naples in the 1550s. Pope Paul IV made him an inquisitor; twice sent to Venice, he was twice recalled because of his severity. After his second recall he was made consultor of the Roman Inquisition by Michele Ghislieri (the future pope Pius V), then appointed procurator general, and, in 1566, made vicar-general of the Conventual Franciscans. In the same year Pius V made him bishop of Sant' Agata dei Goti. In 1570 Pius V elevated him to the cardinalate and appointed him to the see of Fermo (1572–1577) and to the Congregation of the Index. At odds with Ugo Boncompagni (Pope Gregory XIII, 1572–1585), Peretti withdrew to his villa on the Esquiline to prepare an edition of St. Ambrose's writings.

Elected pope in 1585, he took the name Sixtus in honor of the previous Franciscan pope, Sixtus IV (reigned 1471–1484). In five years Sixtus's ambitious and energetic personality achieved impressive results, though he was often sharply criticized for the severity of his measures. He extirpated bandits in the Papal States, whom he executed publicly, and punished their protectors. Sixtus's economic measures included encouraging farming and wool and silk production, sharply reducing expenses, raising new

Pope Sixtus V. The engraving surrounds the pope with images of the accomplishments of his pontificate, including construction projects that remade the face of Renaissance Rome. © THE BRITISH MUSEUM, LONDON

taxes, generating income by increasing the number and cost of salable offices, and using revenue from public investments (*monti*). Moneys he thus took in provided him with ample means to refurbish Rome with many enormous buildings and artistic works. Sixtus completed the dome of St. Peter's Basilica, enlarged papal palaces at the Vatican and Lateran, enlarged the Vatican library and the Quirinal, and built open public squares and wide and straight paved streets connecting the principal churches of Rome. At four of the major churches he placed obelisks crowned with crosses, the most notable one in front of Saint Peter's. He also provided the city with abundant water fountains (called *Acqua Felice,* or "felicitous water," in a pun on the pope's baptismal name, Felice) by rebuilding the ancient Roman aqueduct of Severus Alexander. Sixtus accomplished these feats and managed to leave the papal treasury with more than four million *scudi,* more than any monarch in Christendom. Sixtus's ambition and his vision to make Rome a manifestly Christian city resulted in the destruction and disparagement of some ancient sites revered for their architecture, such as the Septizonium (a third-century ornamental facade on the southeast side of the Palatine Hill) and the Baths of Diocletian; Sixtus intended to convert the Colosseum into a facility for cloth production, but this plan was never carried out. For many of these projects he relied on the architect Domenico Fontana.

Sixtus was exceedingly generous to the religious of Rome whose charitable works proclaimed Rome's holiness; and he gave generously to the university, increased its staff and their salaries, and continued with the building begun by his predecessor, Gregory XIII. Sixtus did not continue the support of scholarly pursuits as widely as did Gregory XIII, except insofar as they fostered piety and theological learning. When the leading humanist professor Marc-Antoine Muret died in 1585, Sixtus replaced him with Pompeo Ugonio, a scholar of early Christian Rome. Sixtus set up the Vatican press under Domenico Basa principally for the publication of religious works. He gave a sizable annual income to Cesare Baronio for work that supported early Christian history from a Roman Catholic perspective. Sixtus authorized the publication of a new version of the Vulgate (the traditional Latin text of the Bible), which was later recalled because of numerous errors.

The Franciscan order became the primary beneficiary of his patronage, which focused on preaching, religious education, and multiplying churches and religious foundations. In general, preferment went to those engaging in works of a religious na-

ture. Sixtus supported the work of the Jesuits but was critical of their constitutions. In 1585 he required all prelates to visit and report regularly on the status of their dioceses. He officially reorganized the Roman Curia into fifteen distinct congregations assigned particular tasks, thereby giving himself more direct control over internal and foreign affairs.

In foreign policy Sixtus vainly kept alive the vision of a crusade against the Turks to regain the Holy Land; he promised support for the Spanish armada against England but reneged after its defeat. He was successful in promoting Catholicism in Poland but made little headway in France after excommunicating Henry of Navarre (later Henry IV) in 1585. Sixtus strongly resented and resisted Spanish domination in Italy and throughout much of Europe, which exacerbated his already strained relations with Philip II and arguably prolonged the religious wars in France. Sixtus V was an energetic pope who promoted the religious causes of the Catholic Reformation and did a considerable amount of building and urban planning for Rome.

BIBLIOGRAPHY

Ostrow, Steven F. *Art and Spirituality in Counter-Reformation Rome: The Sistine and Pauline Chapels in S. Maria Maggiore.* Cambridge, U.K., 1996.

Pastor, Ludwig von. *The History of the Popes, from the Close of the Middle Ages.* Vols. 21 and 22. St. Louis, Mo., 1923.

Schiffmann, René. *Roma felix: Aspekte der städtebaulichen Gestaltung Roms unter Papst Sixtus V.* Bern, Switzerland, 1985.

Sette, Maria Piera, and Simona Benedetti. *Architetture per la città: L'arte à Roma al tempo di Sisto V.* Rome, 1992.

FREDERICK J. MCGINNESS

SKARGA, PIOTR (Piotr Powęski; 1536–1612), Polish theologian, preacher, prose writer. Piotr Skarga was the son of an impoverished nobleman and lawyer. After his studies at the University of Cracow (1552–1555), he was a rector of the town school in Warsaw until 1560. From 1560 to 1566 Skarga worked in Vienna as a tutor to Jan Tęczyński, a son of the castellan of Cracow. He took orders in 1564 in Lvov, where he later became a cathedral canon and preacher.

A turning point in Skarga's life occurred in Rome where he joined the Society of Jesus in 1569. From 1571 he worked as a lecturer in Jesuit colleges in Poland (Pułtusk, Jarosław, Poznań, Lvov, and Wilno) and as an organizer of such schools in Połock, Riga, and Dorpat. He also was a rector of the Jesuit academy (established in 1579) in Wilno. From 1584 he stayed in Cracow, where he founded several charity organizations and served as a preacher in ordinary for King Sigismund III from 1588–1612, exerting some influence on the political decisions taken by the king.

Skarga's works concerned mainly the defense of the Catholic church against heretical critique, the issue of union between the Roman and Greek churches, the internal matters of Poland (the limits of the political power of the nobility, the freedom of religious beliefs, and the limits of the king's power), and education (including subjects such as modern examples of sainthood and the model of piety and education established by the Council of Trent).

Skarga was a master of homiletic prose. This genre of Renaissance rhetoric (called *postilla* from the Latin incipit of a sermon, *post illa verba*) held great appeal for Polish readers. Its persuasive function was strengthened by the authority of the speaker, and Skarga's prophetic language was impressive. His major homiletic works are *Kazania na niedzielę i święta całego roku* (Sermons for Sundays and the annual cycle of feast days; 1595), which in 1597 were edited together with a political treatise in the form of eight sermons called *Kazania sejmowe* (Seym sermons). In his work Skarga strongly criticized the defects of the Polish state system, which he presented as "disease," such as weak patriotism, lawlessness, the oppression of peasants, religious pluralism, and the deterioration of morality.

Skarga also wrote numerous theological works, including *O jedności kościoła Bożego* (On the unity of God's church; 1577), as well as *Żołnierskie nabożeństwo* (Soldier's piety; 1618), in which he describes an ideal Pole—a Christian knight. Skarga is best known, however, for his hagiographic work, *Żywoty świętych* (Lives of saints; 1579), which is compiled from many sources. *Żywoty świętych* (published eight times in Skarga's life and about twenty by the end of the nineteenth century) is significant for its lively and colorful narration, superb literary language, and suggestive argumentation. Skarga included both biblical and early Christian legends as well as contemporary accounts of the persecutions of Catholics taking place in the countries under the sway of the Reformation, along with moral comments concerning those stories.

BIBLIOGRAPHY

Korolko, Mirosław. *O prozie* Kazań sejmowych *Piotra Skargi.* Warsaw, 1971.

Kot, Stanisław. Introduction to *Kazania sejmowe,* by Piotr Skarga. Cracow, 1925.

Tazbir, Janusz. *Piotr Skarga: Szermierz kontrreformacji.* Warsaw, 1978.

Williams, George Huntston. "Peter Skarga." In *Shapers of Religious Traditions in Germany, Switzerland, and Poland, 1560–1600.* Edited by Jill Raitt. New Haven, Conn., and London, 1981. Pages 175–194.

Windakiewicz, Stanisław. *Piotr Skarga.* Cracow, 1925.

ANDRZEJ BOROWSKI

SKELTON, JOHN.   *See* **Poetry, English,** *subentry on* **Tudor Poetry before Spenser.**

SKEPTICISM.   Skepticism is a philosophical attitude that questions the reliability or even the possibility of acquiring knowledge about the world.

Ancient Skepticism.   Two Greek philosophical traditions served as the sources of Renaissance skepticism. Academic skepticism developed within Plato's Academy; Pyrrhonian skepticism was formulated by Pyrrho of Elis (c. 360–c. 275 B.C.) and was further developed in Alexandria during the first century B.C.

The Platonic philosophers Arcesilaus (c. 315–241 B.C.) and Carneades (c. 213–129 B.C.) argued that nothing can be known. Their primary targets were what they perceived as the dogmatic claims of the Stoics and the Epicureans. Arguing against the possibility of attaining certain knowledge about the real nature of things, the Academic skeptics developed a series of arguments to show that the senses are unreliable sources of knowledge about anything beyond our immediate sensations, that reasoning cannot be trusted, and, therefore, that there is no way of knowing which of our statements is true and which false. *Academica* and *On the Nature of the Gods* by Cicero (106–43 B.C.) were major sources for the knowledge and transmission of Academic skepticism.

Pyrrhonian skepticism received its fullest development in the writings of Sextus Empiricus (c. 200 A.D.). He criticized the Academic skeptics for holding the negative dogmatic view that we can know nothing. Instead, he believed that the limitations of our knowledge should lead us to suspend all belief. In *The Outlines of Pyrrhonism* and *Against the Mathematicians,* Sextus Empiricus laid out the Pyrrhonian arguments, known as tropes, in a systematic attack on dogmatic claims to knowledge. Each of these modes or tropes was designed to demonstrate that evidence from the senses is an unreliable source of knowledge about the real natures of things because it leads to contradictory conclusions about the observed object.

Sextus Empiricus applied these skeptical arguments to all areas of knowledge, including physics, medicine, logic, and mathematics, all of which, he argued, were based on unjustified, dogmatic claims. He believed that the skeptical suspension of judgment produces a state of tranquillity or *ataraxia,* a goal he shared with the Epicureans. He did not doubt our knowledge of the way things appear and regarded such knowledge as adequate for life in the world.

Skepticism in the Middle Ages. Among the few church fathers who considered the skeptical arguments, two different approaches to skepticism emerged. Lactantius (c. 240–320), moved toward fideism, the view that faith is the only reliable source of knowledge. He utilized Academic skepticism to undermine the claims of the philosophers and thereby prepare the way for genuine knowledge, which, he claimed, comes only from God. Saint Augustine (354–430), who attempted to combine Christian theology with Neoplatonic philosophy, struggled with the problems posed by Academic skepticism as presented by Cicero. Rather than viewing skepticism as propaedeutic to faith, Augustine came to see it as an obstacle that must be overcome. In his early work, *Against the Academics,* he concluded that revelation is the only way to defeat the skeptical arguments. Skepticism was not widely discussed during the Middle Ages, although Augustine's approach to Academic skepticism did receive some attention.

In the late Middle Ages, the German philosopher, theologian, and churchman Nicholas of Cusa (1401–1464) adopted the Platonic view that the Good exists in an entirely different realm from the things known by the senses. In *De docta ignorantia* (On learned ignorance; 1440) he argued that knowledge of the Good cannot be attained by any series of inferences that begins with observation and experience. Thus empirical knowledge is completely other than absolute truth. This kind of skepticism impelled him to adopt a negative theology, according to which all that we can know about God is that he is not like any of the things that we experience.

Sources of Renaissance Skepticism. Serious consideration of skepticism revived during the Renaissance with the recovery of the writings of the ancient skeptics. Coupled with the intellectual crisis of the Reformation, this revival led to a general skeptical crisis in European thought. Both Academic skepticism and Pyrrhonian skepticism were revived in the sixteenth century. The humanists' interest in the writings of Cicero produced a greater awareness of the ideas developed in the *Academica.* In the middle of the century, several works were published

that dealt with the arguments of the Academic skeptics in detail, including the writings of Omer Talon (1510–1562), who published a commentary on the *Academica;* Giulio Castellani (1528–1586), who rejected the skepticism of the *Academica* in his defense of Aristotle; and Joannes Rosa (1532–1571), who wrote the most lengthy and detailed commentary on Cicero's work to date.

While the works of Sextus Empiricus were practically unknown during the Middle Ages, Greek manuscripts of his work became known in Italy during the fifteenth century and were gradually disseminated through Europe. The *Outlines of Pyrrhonism* was published in 1562, and all his works were translated into Latin and published in 1569. From that time on, his works were frequently published, and skeptical ideas were in general circulation.

Renaissance Skepticism. Interest in skepticism was sparked by the Reformation debates. Luther's challenge to the authority of the Catholic Church concerning matters of the interpretation of scripture presented philosophers and theologians with the problem of determining a rule of faith. Rejecting the traditional claims of the church, Protestant thinkers argued that the only authority in questions of religion is the word of God as revealed in scripture. To avoid the danger of religious anarchy that they feared would result from the fragmentation of the church, Catholic thinkers fell back on the traditional authority of the church. This debate led to the broader questions of determining a proper criterion for judging among rival claims to authority. Thinkers on both sides of confessional lines appealed to skeptical arguments to discredit the positions of their opponents. Coupled with the recovery of the writings of the ancient skeptical philosophers, this Reformation debate precipitated a general skeptical crisis during which the foundations of most fields of knowledge were questioned.

The Dutch humanist and theologian Desiderius Erasmus (c. 1466–1536) advocated a life of piety and reform of the church. In *Encomium moriae* (1509; trans. *The Praise of Folly*) he adopted a skeptical approach, although he did not give a systematic account of philosophical skepticism. He believed that the Scholastic philosophers, in their quest for certainty, had missed the point—the adoption of a truly Christian attitude. According to Erasmus, it is better to be a Christian fool living a truly Christian life than a theologian tangled in intellectual snares.

The French humanist Michel de Montaigne (1533–1592) popularized Pyrrhonian ideas. In response to his reading of the works of Sextus Empiricus, Montaigne adopted Pyrrhonian skepticism as his own personal philosophy, a view he expressed in the essay "Apology for Raymond Sebond," which he wrote in 1575–1576. Montaigne argued that by challenging the competency of human knowledge, Pyrrhonism supplied a solution to the Reformation quest for a rule of faith. Since the skeptic could defend no belief, he had to rely on faith alone, a position known as fideism. Montaigne found this approach preferable to the endless wrangling of philosophers and theologians and superior to the dogmatism that had occasioned the French Wars of Religion.

Pierre Charron (1541–1603), a French philosopher, theologian, and legal scholar, systematized Montaigne's Pyrrhonism in *De la sagesse* (On wisdom), published in French in 1601. Using skeptical arguments to undermine the capacities of the human senses and human reason, Charron maintained that we must live according to nature. This natural state can only be improved by accepting divine grace and revelation, which is available once skepticism has purged us of any pretense of having rational support for our knowledge. Charron deployed his fideism to defend Catholicism and to attack Calvinism.

Francisco Sanches (1550–1623), a Portuguese physician and philosopher, wrote *Quad nihil scitur* (That nothing is known; 1576) as a philosophical critique of Scholastic philosophy and method. He used skeptical arguments to prove that he did not even know if he knew nothing. He argued that the method of Aristotelian science cannot produce knowledge of anything. Science as the perfect knowledge of things is unattainable. Instead, we must settle for imperfect knowledge based on sense experience and judgment.

The influence of the revival of skepticism in the Renaissance was profound. Many philosophers in the seventeenth century defended their ideas by starting with a skeptical critique of other philosophies and then seeking epistemological foundations for their own views. This approach can be found in the writings of Francis Bacon (1561–1626), René Descartes (1596–1650), and Pierre Gassendi (1592–1655), who were among the most influential philosophers of the day.

See also **Philosophy**; *and biographies of Pierre Charron, Nicholas of Cusa, Michel de Montaigne, and Francisco Sanches.*

BIBLIOGRAPHY

Primary Works

Cicero, Marcus Tullius. *De natura deorum and Academica.* Translated by H. Rackham. Cambridge, Mass., 1979.

Montaigne, Michel de. *The Complete Essays of Montaigne.* Translated by Donald Frame. Stanford, Calif., 1957. Contains Montaigne's Pyrrhonian skepticism, especially in book 2, essay 12, "Apology for Raymond Sebond."

Sanches, Francisco (Franciscus Sanchez). *Quod nihil scitur* (That nothing is known). Translated by Douglas F. S. Thomson. Cambridge, U.K., 1988. Original Latin text followed by English translation. Lengthy and detailed introduction by Elaine Limbrick.

Sextus Empiricus. *Sextus Empiricus.* Translated by R. G. Bury. 4 vols. Cambridge, Mass., 1933–1949. Original text in Greek with English translation on facing page.

Secondary Works

Burnyeat, Myles, ed. *The Skeptical Tradition.* Berkeley, Calif., 1983. Articles on skepticism from Greek times through Kant.

Cassirer, Ernst. *The Individual and the Cosmos in Renaissance Philosophy.* Translated by Mario Domandi. New York, 1963. Translation of *Individuum und kosmos in der Philosophie der Renaissance* (1927). Contains two chapters on Nicholas of Cusa.

Copenhaver, Brian P., and Charles B. Schmitt. *Renaissance Philosophy.* Oxford, 1992. General survey, including discussion of many important thinkers.

Popkin, Richard H. *The History of Scepticism from Erasmus to Spinoza.* Rev. ed. Berkeley, Calif., 1979. Classic work on the history of skepticism. Focuses on the history of Pyrrhonism.

Schmitt, Charles B. *Cicero Scepticus: A Study of the Influence of the Academica in the Renaissance.* The Hague, Netherlands, 1972. On the influence of Cicero and Academic skepticism in the Renaissance.

Schmitt, Charles B., et al., eds. *The Cambridge History of Renaissance Philosophy.* Cambridge, U.K., 1988. Indispensible reference work.

MARGARET J. OSLER

SLAVERY. During the thousand years from the end of the Roman Empire to the beginning of European expansion in the Atlantic, slavery was a reality in the Christian world, and it was reinforced by contact with the highly developed slavery of the Muslims. The persistent and growing influence of Roman law, which contained a sophisticated set of regulations for slavery, helped shape the legal systems of the European west and provided a ready-made set of rules to be put into force easily when slavery again became economically significant. Slavery's resurgence in the sixteenth century was due to the creation of the New World plantation system, which initially produced sugar, and an expanding market economy to absorb the production of the plantations. Sugar growing and refining required intensive labor, and, in the absence of the necessary numbers of Amerindian or European workers, the Spaniards and the Portuguese turned to sub-Saharan African slaves, acquired by Portuguese traders who tapped preexisting trading networks along the West African coast and transported their human cargoes across the Atlantic. The persistence of slavery throughout the Middle Ages thus helped shape the colonial societies in North and South America, and, in very real ways, influenced the evolution of modern society throughout the Western Hemisphere.

Types of Slavery. In western Europe during the Renaissance, slavery was most fully practiced in the Italian and Iberian peninsulas. Even there, however, slavery was never crucial for social and economic development, and it did not exist on any great scale. Nevertheless, varieties of slavery were present. Even though all slaves suffered the same or similar legal, emotional, and ideological disabilities, there were gradations in their material circumstances. Within the two distinct types of slavery, agricultural or rural, on the one hand, and domestic or urban, on the other, wide variations are apparent because the categories often overlapped. Some rural slaves worked in manufacturing on country estates. There were gradations among domestic slaves as well. Much of the employment of domestic slaves was unproductive labor, for slaves were usually assigned to noneconomic tasks, as servants, guards, and sexual partners. In the preindustrial world, much, if not most, of the ordinary manufacturing of goods for common consumption was artisan production, taking place in workshops within the homes of the artisans. In these workshops a few domestic slaves could aid their artisan owners, and collectively their activity made a significant impact on production. Small-scale slavery, in which a few slaves were added to the urban or rural households as domestics and additional workers, was characteristic of both Renaissance Europe and the Islamic world. Gang slavery, which we associate with classical Rome and with New World slavery, was not present at all in Europe, where small-scale slavery was the norm.

Slaves in Renaissance Europe came from two sources: birth to slave mothers or capture in warfare or raids. When slaves entered western European households, they lived under the tutelage of their masters, who legally had the power of life and death over them. Masters could sell, transfer, and move their slaves at will and could use them as sexual partners. Despite their lack of legal standing, many slaves took advantage of laws that permitted them to attain freedom in several ways. Captives were often ransomed or exchanged. Other slaves, once assimilated, could become free through self-purchase or by their master's gift during his lifetime or following his death. Freedmen and freedwomen suffered legal disabilities, but children born to them were fully free.

Italy. In the Italian and Iberian states, slavery received a new impetus as a result of the Black Death, which in 1347–1349 killed a quarter to a third of the European population. One tragic result was a growth in slavery. As a consequence of the high death rate, the workers who might otherwise have become household servants found good jobs in the countryside or the cities. Death struck poor and rich alike, but the elite who survived had even greater sums of money available, because fortunes were supplemented through inheritance. Slavery grew largely because additional workers and domestics became financially possible. The unrestricted importation of slaves from outside Italy was permitted by the government of Florence beginning in 1363, with the sole caveat that they be of non-Christian origin. Perhaps as a result of the large influx of slaves over the preceding two decades, Venice prohibited slave auctions in 1366, most likely to reduce sales. Venetians were still permitted to import slaves, however, although sales had to be by private contract.

Genoa continued to receive enslaved Tatars, Russians, and Circassians during this period, but with diminished access to the Black Sea their numbers declined in the second half of the fifteenth century. The Genoese rectified the situation by looking back to the western Mediterranean. From North Africa, Spain, and Portugal, Muslim slaves were purchased in increasing numbers. In order to distinguish among Islam's varying ethnic groups, the Genoese categorized their slaves by skin color—white, black, *indaco* (indigo), *lauro* (mulatto), and *olivegno* (olive). Relatively few black slaves reached Genoa or other northern Italian cities, although they were fairly common in southern Italy and Sicily.

Responding to political changes in the greater Mediterranean region that limited recruiting grounds for non-Christian slaves, the Venetians turned to indentured servants to meet the demand for domestic servants. Known as "souls" (*anime*) by the Venetians, these indentured servants were predominately young, purchased from their parents in Dalmatia, Albania, Istria, and Corfu by Venetian shipmasters. Distinguished legally from ordinary slaves, and bound only for a defined period of service, servants could buy back their freedom, if they had the money. Although Venetian law prohibited their exchange or sale to another master, the Venetian government had to ensure that they were not taken elsewhere in Italy, where they were in danger of being sold into perpetual slavery.

Slavery could be found throughout Renaissance Italy. Documentary evidence such as account books and notarial records indicate the presence of numerous slaves of various ethnic origins in the Italian peninsula. The portrait painters of the Renaissance were fascinated by slavery. Nevertheless, despite the well-documented presence of slavery, it was not significant in a statistical sense. The Venetian census of 1563 listed only 7 to 8 percent of the population as servants, a figure that included free as well as slave.

Spain and Portugal. The situation was similar in Spain and Portugal. The Iberian states were part of the European world, where slavery gradually declined as serfdom and free labor grew. Yet, unlike the rest of western Europe, the Iberian kingdoms were frontier states, sharing borders with non-Christian states whose inhabitants would be raided or enslaved with complete legality. This meant that slavery persisted there longer and more vigorously than elsewhere in Christian Europe.

The Portuguese and Spanish activities in Africa meant that a large-scale trade in African slaves developed. Many of the African slaves went to the Atlantic islands, and many more went to the Americas as the pace of development increased there in the sixteenth century. Other black slaves ended up in Europe, causing changes in the ethnic composition of the servile population of several European regions. Blacks had been present in Europe in small numbers since the Roman period, and from the ninth century, if not before, Muslims brought African slaves across the Sahara for sale in the ports of the Mediterranean. Aside from Italy and the Iberian countries, however, blacks remained rarities in Europe until much later.

The Portuguese were the main slave traders of Europe in the late fifteenth and early sixteenth centuries. By the 1480s the Portuguese crown had established a Casa dos Escravos (slave house) in Lisbon to administer the trade. By the mid-sixteenth century, black slaves and freedmen made up some 2.5 to 3 percent of the total Portuguese population, with geographical variation: up to 10 percent in southern Portugal and Lisbon, and much lower elsewhere.

Only a minority of the Africans in the Portuguese slave trade actually arrived or remained in Portugal. Portuguese traders supplied slaves to the new Portuguese plantations in São Tomé, the Cape Verdes, and Madeira. They also sold slaves to African rulers and merchants at São Jorge da Mina. The Portuguese sold other slaves to Castilians in the Canaries or on the mainland. Of those who were taken to Portugal, significant numbers were later delivered elsewhere in Europe, particularly to Spain but also to Italy.

Outside Portugal, Seville probably held Europe's highest number of slaves in the Renaissance. Slavery had been a feature of the life of Seville since Roman times. By the thirteenth century, while still under Muslim control, the city had large numbers of slaves. Between the time of the Christian reconquest of the city in 1248 and the mid-fifteenth century, most of the slaves in Seville were Muslims, captured in the constant warfare between Christians and Muslims.

African slaves became more common in the fourteenth century as Spanish and Italian merchants purchased them in North African ports. By the middle of the fifteenth century, black slaves arrived in Seville by sea or overland from Portugal. Once in Seville, most of the newly arrived slaves were sold to private buyers. Seville had no regular slave market, unlike Lisbon, where slaves were sold at the Casa dos Escravos. Slave dealers in Seville took their human merchandise through the streets and arranged sales on the spot, making private arrangements with prospective purchasers. The buyers, at least in the period from 1484 to 1489, were predominately from the artisan class. Age, sex, and physical condition determined the prices slaves would bring. Children brought the lowest prices because, before they could be put to work profitably, they needed lengthy care and training, and were subject to disease and death.

Most slaves in Seville were used as domestic servants. Well-off families usually had at least two slaves. Wealthier families owned greater numbers, much as their contemporaries in Italy did. Slaves were also used in smaller numbers in income producing ventures, such as the soap factory of Seville and the municipal granary. Masters employed slaves as porters and longshoremen, retail sellers in the streets and plazas, assistants for shopkeepers and merchants. Some of the slaves acted as agents for their merchant-owners, and in some cases slaves ventured on business trips to the Spanish settlements in the Americas. Slaves were excluded from membership in the crafts guilds, although some did work as helpers for guild masters.

The presence of black and Muslim slaves in Seville was striking, and several contemporaries said there were as many slaves as free citizens. Such comments were exaggerations. Slaves in Seville were hardly as numerous as free citizens. A census in 1565 listed 6,327 slaves in a total population of 85,538, or

Slavery. Page from *Livro de horas de D. Manuel,* fifteenth century. At top, an African slave waits on table. MUSEO NATIONALE DE ARTE ANTIGA, LISBON

some 7.4 percent of the total population, a lower percentage than Lisbon. The slaves enumerated in the 1565 count were not reported according to their ethnic origin, but after the mid-sixteenth century, blacks probably outnumbered slaves from all other ethnic groups. From the fifteenth century, Seville had a large community of freed blacks.

Mediterranean Europe had other cities in which slavery flourished in the period, even if they were not as racially mixed as Seville. One of those cities was Valencia, an important center for slavery in the fifteenth and sixteenth centuries. Slaves were not as numerous in Valencia as they were in Seville, but they were more varied in their ethnic origins. Most Valencian slaves were Muslim in origin, either from Spain itself or from North Africa. Non-Muslim slaves came from many other places, brought to Valencia by the slave traders. Within the western Mediterranean, the Balearic Islands also served as a nexus of the Christian slave trade and as a place where slaves were used.

Nonetheless, slavery remained exceptional throughout most of Renaissance Europe. The great development of slavery in the sixteenth century was in the Americas, where sugar plantations and other enterprises created a demand for labor that for various reasons could not be filled by American or European laborers. Africa housed the greatest number of potential slaves, and in the sixteenth century the Atlantic slave trade began, with Africans offering other Africans for sale to Europeans, who transported them across the Atlantic to their fates in the American colonial areas.

BIBLIOGRAPHY

Cortés Alonso, Vicenta. *La esclavitud en Valencia durante el reinado de los Reyes Católicos (1479–1516)*. Valencia, Spain, 1964.

Cortés López, José Luis. *Los orígenes de la esclavitud negra en España*. Madrid and Salamanca, Spain, 1986.

Franco Silva, Alfonso. *La esclavitud en Sevilla y su tierra a fines de la edad media*. Seville, 1979.

Heers, Jacques. *Esclaves et domestiques au Moyen Âge dans le monde méditerranéen*. Paris, 1981.

Lobo Cabrera, Manuel. *La esclavitud en las Canarias orientales en el siglo XVI: Negros, Moros, y Moriscos*. Santa Cruz de Tenerife, Canary Islands, 1982.

Phillips, William D., Jr. *Historia de la esclavitud en España*. Madrid, 1990.

Phillips, William D., Jr. *Slavery from Roman Times to the Early Transatlantic Trade*. Minneapolis, Minn., 1985.

Saunders, A. C. de C. M. *A Social History of Black Slaves and Freedmen in Portugal, 1441–1555*. Cambridge, U.K., 1982.

Verlinden, Charles. *L'esclavage dans l'Europe médiévale*. 2 vols. Bruges, Belgium, 1955–1977.

WILLIAM D. PHILLIPS JR.

SLEIDANUS, JOHANNES (Johann Phillipson von Schleiden; 1506–1556), humanist scholar and historian. Born in Schleiden in the northern Eifel in present-day Germany, Johann Phillipson was educated in humanist traditions by the Brethren of the Common Life in Liège, and from 1524 at the Trilingual College in Louvain, where he latinized his name after his birthplace.

Although describing himself as *homo germanus,* his education and scholarly career were thoroughly international. In 1533 he migrated to Paris and then Orléans to study law, the normal qualification for a civil administrator. In 1537 he became Latin secretary to Cardinal Jean du Bellay, bishop of Paris, who, with his brothers Guillaume and Martin (the former of whom was planning an extended history of France on the model of Livy), provided an ideal environment to nurture Sleidanus's interest in French historical studies.

From 1530 he had established close contact with Protestant moderates Martin Bucer and Philipp Melanchthon, a network later extended to include John Calvin. In 1540–1541, having witnessed the failure of the Hagenau and Regensburg conferences between Catholics and Protestants, he settled in Strasbourg, where his friends included the city council leader Jakob Sturm. There he became the first contemporary historian of Protestantism.

Nourished by his reading of Caesar and Polybius, Sleidanus preferred plain historical writing devoid of Italian oratory, and particularly admired the French tradition. Having published in 1537 a Latin translation of Froissart, in 1545–1548 he completed a parallel translation of Philippe de Commynes in two volumes, dedicated respectively to Edward VI and the protector Somerset. A Latin version of Claude de Seyssel's *La monarchie de France* was also published in 1548.

Appointed historiographer to the Schmalkaldic League and inspired by a desire to emulate Commynes in providing a realistic history of his own time, Sleidanus devoted his energies to publication of his *Commentariorum de statu religionis et reipublicae, Carolo Quinto caesare* (Commentaries on religion and the state in the reign of the emperor Charles V; 1555), the first general history of the Reformation period. A second edition (1557) was translated into German, French, Italian, and English. As he wrote, he also undertook diplomatic missions, including one to Henry VIII of England on behalf of the Lutheran princes, to promote reconciliation with France and avert war between the emperor and the

Schmalkaldic League, and another to represent Strasbourg at the Council of Trent. He saw no conflict between commitment to the Reformation and citizenship in an empire under a Catholic emperor, acknowledging in his *Apologia* the latter's constitutional authority and right to obedience "in all things which are not against God." A measure of the fundamental success of his scholarly aims is that the *Commentaries* were initially deemed unsatisfactory by both sides of the religious divide: Catholics found them heretical, while Protestants objected to their moderation and their recognition of Protestant weaknesses.

Concurrently with the *Commentaries* Sleidanus had also written *De quatuor summis imperiis* (Of the four greatest empires; 1561) based on the empires described in Daniel 7–12—Assyria, Persia, Greece, and Rome—and appealing to German patriotism by identifying the Holy Roman Empire as the authentic inheritor of world dominion. Shorter in scope than the *Commentaries,* this work nevertheless appeared in nearly seventy editions and was used extensively for two centuries as a historical textbook.

In the preface of the *Commentaries,* and in an apologia addressed to critics shortly before his death, Sleidanus articulated scholarly ideals that seem to anticipate the nineteenth-century historian Leopold von Ranke. His commitment to write history *"prout quaeque res acta fuit"* (just as each thing happened) is almost exactly equivalent to Ranke's famous phrase *als es eigentlich gewesen.* By contrast with the roughly contemporary Protestant *Magdeburg Centuries* and the calumnies of the Catholic controversialist Johannes Cochlaeus, Sleidanus's history is a model of moderation and balance, despite promoting a view of the Reformation as a miraculous work of God. Rejecting mere legend and unsubstantiated charges, he highlighted the close relationship of religion and civil government and, unlike Erasmus, regarded tumult and disorder as inevitable accompaniments of religious change.

From a modern perspective Sleidanus's limitations as a historian are those of the Renaissance scholarly traditions in which he was raised: a too exclusive preoccupation with the actions of princes and political leaders as instruments of historical change, and a corresponding tendency to ignore the deeper significance of ideas and the complex interaction of religion with social life.

See also **Historiography, Renaissance,** *subentry on* **German Historiography.**

BIBLIOGRAPHY

Primary Works

Sleidanus, Johannes. *Briefwechsel.* Translated by Hermann Baumgarten. Strasbourg, France, 1881.

Sleidanus, Johannes. *The General History of the Reformation of the Church.* Translated by E. Bohun. London, 1689.

Sleidanus, Johannes. *Ioanni Sleidani de statu religionis et reipublicae Carolo Quinto Caesare commentarii.* Frankfurt, Germany, 1785.

Secondary Works

Baumgarten, Hermann. "Sleidan, Johann." *Allgemeine deutsche Biographie.* Vol. 34. Pages 454–461.

Dickens, A. G. "Johannes Sleidan and Reformation History." In *Reformation, Conformity, and Dissent.* Edited by R. Buick Knox. London, 1977. Pages 17–43. Reprinted in Dickens's *Reformation Studies.* London, 1982. Pages 537–563.

Kelley, Donald R. "Johann Sleidan and the Origins of History as a Profession," *Journal of Modern History* 52 (1980): 573–598.

JOHN TONKIN

SOCIAL STATUS. Status was the fundamental basis of social categorization and stratification in European society. It defined a person's rank and place in the social hierarchy. Although there was no absolute consensus over how to assign status, it was generally associated with a hierarchy of groups rather than any one individual. From the Middle Ages these groups fell into three estates, described in terms of functions: the clergy prayed, knights fought, and commoners worked. This scheme, however, was never that simple, for within the estates there were innumerable ranks with no fixed place in time or geographical space. Moreover, by the eleventh and twelfth centuries, urbanization produced a multilevel middle class to add to the social ladder.

The Three Estates. At least until the late fifteenth century the clergy, broken into secular and regular divisions, comprised the First Estate. Entry at all levels required education, training, and ordination, but career opportunities, and consequently status, were determined by social station. The Second Estate was reserved for the nobility, a contender for superiority with the self-proclaimed clerical First Estate. The nobility formed a broad spectrum, from emperor and king to duke, count, and multiple ranks of knight. The Third Estate began with rustic laborers but eventually grew to include commoners from both town and country. It had a very broad range, from lawyers, academics, physicians, jurists, councillors, merchants, and magistrates at the upper levels to bailiffs, soldiers, artisans, and peasants toward the bottom. Status in this hierarchy of groups was determined by a complex constellation of criteria, which included but was not limited to gender, power, birth and lineage, patronage and prestige, legal and customary privileges, honorary titles, education, civic offices, government service, profession or occupation, sources of wealth, degree of purchasing power, and residency in town or country.

The Clergy. The clergy was regarded as the First Estate because its members' involvement in spirituality and prayer was considered a vital contribution to the welfare of society. At the top of the secular clergy were high prelates, most of whom came from the ranks of the nobility, some from wealthy commoner families, and a handful from lower social origins: pope, cardinals, patriarchs, and bishops. Urban priests, cathedral canons, and poor parish priests followed, occupying a considerably lower place on the social scale. Beyond social origins, there was a wide gulf between high prelates and parish priests in terms of wealth and level of education. The former enjoyed income from landed estates, loans, benefices, clerical taxation, and the wealth of their natal families. Moreover, they constituted the learned elite of late medieval society, until Renaissance education bred a new class of scholars from the secular world. The regular clergy, which included the orders of monks and nuns, were also led by the scions of noble houses. Though clerics received religious training and ordination, the orders of regular clergy were class-specific, with the wealthiest social groups filling the most prestigious and established institutions.

The Nobility. The nobility was defined originally by birth and lineage. However, by the sixteenth century, particularly in France and Spain, the rank was infused with new social energies from those who bought land and offices or achieved distinction in military service. Honor and deference to nobles hinged on the prestige of their genealogy, the degree of judicial and political power attached to their land holdings, and their source and level of wealth. There were stark contrasts, from lords of large, landed estates with authority over many peasants to poor noble families in decline. The rich and powerful exercised authority over neighboring villages and peasantry, with the right to seigneurial dues, jurisdictions, and immunities from direct taxation. Nobles, as well as clergy, were often subject to different forms of law than the Third Estate. Variations on the nobility depended on geographical area. The English peerage was for the most part a small, hereditary elite that privileged the rank of baron or higher

over gentry. It was the most socially homogeneous of the European nobilities. The nobles of France, Spain, and the Netherlands largely associated themselves with the courts, while those of the Italian peninsula were a hybrid group entrenched in the land, yet with important political and cultural ties to the cities. Some of the self-perpetuating civic elites of northern Italy also claimed noble status through municipal office as well as family antiquity, accumulated wealth, and a long history of political participation. For half a millennium, for example, Venice vaunted a closed, constitutional elite, deriving from commercial origins, that was praised by royalty and nobility throughout Europe for its stability.

Noble status also hinged on sources of wealth. For the most part, nobles were expected to live on their landed wealth; commerce and craft manufacture were degrading, a concept that carried over from Roman times. The hybrid groups of elites in the northern Italian cities were an exception, though by the sixteenth century, they too were emulating the lifestyles of people of independent means. The acquisition of wealth was a means of ascent into the nobility. Businessmen converted their fortunes and capital investments into land holdings, which were more prestigious than money; bought titles; and adopted noble behavior. People also acquired noble status through outstanding public service to the ruler or states, or by marriage into the nobility.

Noble birth enabled sons and daughters whose parents did not arrange for them to marry to find powerful and lucrative positions in the church, giving them elevated status. Bishops, abbots, and abbesses controlled vast landed properties, received substantive donations, and made profitable investments. Moreover, they held jurisdiction over many subjects and enjoyed important connections with powerful noble families.

Way of life and behavior were important signs of elite status. Landed magnates kept supporting retinues that helped them exercise coercive force. They remained devoted to arms, both in profession and at leisure. Codes of chivalry served as guidelines for protocol and behavior. Manners also identified status. Elites cultivated their speech, the comportment of their bodies, and their facial expressions. They strove to have good manners according to the conventions of the time, and to repress the emotions. Dining rituals, fashion, tournaments and processions, and humanist colloquia were all forms of sociability that represented status. Architectural styles, too, mirrored social station; lavish, costly dwellings distinguished noble proprietors from the rest of the social hierarchy. Mountainous areas were ideal for castles, while the plains were graced with expansive palaces. In these magnificent dwellings nobles held elaborate banquets, staged hunts, and patronized the arts on a grand scale, all activities that preserved and enhanced their status.

Lesser nobles and gentry followed the high nobility in the social order. They defy precise definition in time or geographical space because they derived from composite origins and drew their status from a variety of activities. Some achieved it through military service, others through administrative offices or successful commerce, others through some combination of the two and astute marriage alliances. Lesser nobles and gentry were both oriented toward acquiring land, as that promised the greatest prestige. Both used the marriage market as a means of social ascent to the nobility, creating in time their own coats of arms as symbols of high status.

The Third Estate. Citizenship in a European city or town conferred yet another category of status, often with special privileges that distinguished the citizen from the rest of the urban inhabitants. However, this category had limited resonance as few parts of Europe were intensely urbanized. Citizenship assumed particular importance in northern Italy, parts of Germany, Catalonia, and the Low Countries, taking on characteristics specific to these locales. In these areas citizenship became a fundamental requisite for holding municipal office, the path toward judicial and fiscal benefits as well as prestige. Citizens often enjoyed privileges comparable to those granted by monarchs to their outstanding financial and administrative employees.

Citizen elites were composite groups. On the Italian peninsula they derived from the local nobility and town patricians and tended to marry within their social class. What distinguished these elites was their municipal authority and long record of political participation. Prior to the sixteenth century, too, connections with international trade, manufacture, and landed possessions in town and country contributed to their status. From the sixteenth century on, commerce and industry were abandoned for investments in lands and loans and/or careers in law.

Lawyers and judges, because of their education and functions in society, held critical powers that placed them at the pinnacle of town hierarchies. They stood above the lesser nobility, who were generally privy to the jurisdictional powers advocates enjoyed. In some Italian cities notaries also achieved exalted status because of their wealth and demand,

The Three Estates. Clergy (*top*), nobility (*middle*), and everyone else (*bottom*), from a Breton manuscript of the mid-fifteenth century. The clergy is under the leadership of the pope, who is shown above King Charles VII and the dauphin. The subordination of the king of France to a foreign power appealed to Brittany at a time when it was able to maintain its independence of France. BIBLIOTHÈQUE NATIONALE DE FRANCE, PARIS, MS. 2695, FOL. 6v

as well as their entrenched place in civic offices. The shift in economic activities by the late sixteenth century tended to make some of these citizen elites a sort of rural nobility. Intermarriage with nobles was another means of social ascent for this group as well. Urban patricians with generational power tended to claim a kind of noble status in northern Italy, while the distinction between city elites and nobility in northern Europe remained much clearer.

The middle class that developed as a result of urbanization after the year 1000 was the most fluid of all the orders of society. Level of education, profession or occupation, and wealth were the primary criteria of definition. Lawyers, government officials, physicians, and intellectuals were at the apogee of the order. They were followed by merchants, masters, journeymen, apprentices, urban laborers, and domestic servants. Wealthy professionals, merchants, and manufacturers formed powerful and prestigious corporations and confraternities; they exerted political influence, performed charitable deeds, and staged flamboyant pageants, all symbols of their status. Guild members followed the professionals in rank, and in some cities they exercised considerable social and political influence. In Florence, for example, the fourteen major and seven minor guilds were divided both politically and socially but nonetheless shared business activities, economic values, and moral values. Guild membership separated masters, journeymen, and apprentices from those in the *popolo minuto,* or laboring class. The latter were unorganized, disenfranchised, and at times on the edge of poverty. Status was associated with meaningful participation in the guilds and confraternities; it required both affluence and social prominence. In contrast, the laboring *popolo minuto* held no legal rights. They were legally prohibited from meeting and organizing, a privilege held exclusively by their guild-master employers. Yet even within the *popolo minuto* there were gradations of status attached to degrees of working skills. Tasks that required more brawn than skill earned little or no regard. Low wages, prohibitions against organizing, and vulnerability to market fluctuations, pestilence, and war kept the laboring classes down in Florence as well as other European towns.

The vast majority of the European population lived outside the towns. Rural society was also layered into hierarchical groups that were distinguished from urban social spheres. The first included high prelates with vast landed estates and prominent lay families who spent part of their time in the city. The second, landlords and cultivators, leased their properties from the first group, making their living from speculative activities. In western Europe the third group included independent peasants and small landowners who paid rents and relied on their own efforts for support. They were followed by the highly mobile, landless agricultural laborers, who depended on landlords for animals, seeds, and fertilizers. The position of these last two groups was always precarious because of high rents, taxes, usury, crop failure, war, and epidemics. While islands of serfdom still prevailed in some parts of the West, for the most part peasants achieved free status with the possibility of some mobility and the right to lease or own land. In contrast, rustics in the East fell increasingly into serfdom from the fourteenth century onward. Peasants were reduced to servile workers deprived of any rights to the land in east Germany, Silesia, Bohemia, Poland, Russia, Hungary, and Romania. Their movement was severely restricted, while their labor dues and services multiplied.

A wide range of social and economic structures, tied to occupation, purchasing power, size and type of land tenure, ownership of farm animals, and free or unfree status influenced the place of the European peasantry in the social hierarchy. Apart from the large landowners and wealthy investors, the status of country dwellers, particularly agricultural laborers, was regarded as inferior to that of townsmen. Urban dwellers often mistrusted peasants, and law codes in various cities described them as natural-born inferiors, malicious, insolent, and stupid. Still, the countryside in western Europe was a constant source of labor and recruitment for depopulated cities, making it possible for rustics to improve their material and social conditions and thus raise their status. In contrast, peasants east of the Elbe were bound in service to landowners whose economic activities centered on commercial farming.

Outsiders. Muslims, Jews, gypsies, and slaves remained outside these societal orders, experiencing legal restrictions, economic hardship, and segregation. Women, too, stood in a group apart. A woman's status mirrored first that of her natal family and later, if she married, that of her husband. In society her status depended to an important degree on her maintaining her sexual honor by remaining modest and chaste. Sex and reproduction outside of marriage were prohibited; violation of this strict social code degraded a woman's status and brought shame to her family.

It is difficult to discuss the status of women in terms of social mobility, for the domestic sphere to which they were largely relegated cannot be assessed according to male categories of analysis. Their perspective, together with recent studies, strongly suggests that women maintained vertical bonds of friendship and solidarity with other women. How women perceived and applied distinctions of status is a subject that requires further investigation.

Gender roles, too, assumed various weights associated with status, with activities and qualities—explicit and symbolic—perceived as "feminine" or "masculine." The association of domestic duties with femininity and public roles with the masculine is one example. Others could be drawn from the relationship between gender and politics, science, theology, humanities, arts, professions, and skilled labor in conformity with the social and cultural constructs of society.

See also **Confraternities**; **Guilds**; **Honor**; **Professions**.

BIBLIOGRAPHY

Becker, Marvin. *Civility and Society in Western Europe, 1300–1600*. Bloomington, Ind., 1988.

Cohn, Samuel K. *The Laboring Classes in Florence*. New York, 1980.

Ferraro, Joanne M. *Family and Public Life in Brescia. The Foundations of Power in the Venetian State*. Cambridge, U.K., 1993.

Goody, Jack. *The Development of Marriage and the Family in Europe*. Cambridge, U.K., 1983.

Hale, John Rigby. *Renaissance Europe: Individual and Society*. Berkeley and Los Angeles, 1971.

Hanawalt, Barbara, ed. *Women and Work in Preindustrial Europe*. Bloomington, Ind., 1986.

Kamen, Henry. *European Society, 1500–1700*. London, 1984.

Le Roy Ladurie, Emmanuel. *The French Peasantry, 1450–1660*. Translated by Alan Sheridan. Berkeley, Calif., 1987.

Martines, Lauro. *Lawyers and Statecraft in Renaissance Florence*. Princeton, N.J., 1968.

Martines, Lauro. *Power and Imagination: City-States in Renaissance Italy*. New York, 1979.

Schalk, Ellery. *From Valor to Pedigree: Ideas of Nobility in France in the Sixteenth and Seventeenth Centuries*. Princeton, N.J., 1986.

Wiesner-Hanks, Merry. *Women and Gender in Early Modern Europe*. Cambridge, U.K., and New York, 1993.

Zagorin, Perez. *Rebels and Rulers, 1500–1600*. Vol. 1: *Society, States, and Early Modern Revolution: Agrarian and Urban Rebellions*. Cambridge, U. K., and New York, 1982.

JOANNE M. FERRARO

SOCIETY OF JESUS. *See* **Religious Orders,** *subentry on* **The Jesuits.**

SODOMA, GIOVANNI ANTONIO BAZZI, IL. *See* **Siena,** *subentry on* **Art in Siena.**

SOLDIERS AND MILITARY LIFE. *See* **Warfare.**

SONNET. *See* **Poetry,** *subentries on* **The Sonnet.**

SOTO, DOMINGO DE (1494/95–1560), Dominican philosopher and theologian, important for his work in logic, mechanics, and political theory and for his influence at the Council of Trent. Born in Segovia, Spain, Soto received his early education there and, in 1516, the baccalaureate from the University of Alcalá. He then went to Paris, where he earned the master of arts at the College of Santa Barbara,

studying under Juan de Celaya (c. 1490–1558). He also studied theology at Paris, where he was influenced by John Major (1469–1550) and Francisco de Vitoria (c. 1483–1546). In 1519 he returned to Alcalá, where he completed the licentiate in theology by 1524, working under Pedro Ciruelo (1470–1554). In that year Soto entered the Dominican order at the priory of San Pablo in Burgos, and shortly thereafter he was assigned to the priory of San Esteban at Salamanca. There he taught first in the priory until 1532 and then, with Vitoria, at the university, where he continued to teach until his death. Soto was in Trent from 1545 to 1550, replacing Vitoria as theologian to the emperor, Charles V, whom he also served as confessor from 1548 to 1550.

Soto's early interest was in nominalist logic, and this led to the first edition of his *Summulae* (Small summary; Burgos, 1529). This part of logic he considered to be formal logic, a science that served the needs of nominalists and realists alike. A second, simplified edition was published at Salamanca in 1539 (with eight more editions, to 1582). In the 1540s, concern developed at the university over time being wasted on nominalist puerilities, and Soto was commissioned by the faculty to write textbooks more open to realism. His first project was to treat the remainder of logic, that is, the predicables, the categories, and demonstration. This was published as *In dialecticam Aristotelis* (On Aristotle's dialectic; Salamanca, 1543, with twelve more editions to 1598). In 1544 he began revising his teaching notes on Aristotle's *Physics* from Paris and Alcalá, where he had imported the mathematics of the Parisian "terminists" into this classical text. The first six books he published in two volumes, one a commentary, the other disputed questions, at Salamanca in 1545, just before going to the Council of Trent. Upon his return in 1550 he finished the remaining two books and published the completed work, again in two volumes, at Salamanca in 1551 (with seven more editions of both volumes to 1613). In his questions on the seventh book Soto adumbrates Galileo's law of falling bodies, holding that their motion is "uniformly varying" with respect to time, that is, uniformly accelerated. Other places where terminist influences are apparent are in Soto's treatments of motion, time, and the infinite, where he adumbrates a quantitative physics well before its flowering in the seventeenth century.

All of his logical and philosophical works were written while Soto was teaching theology at Salamanca. At Trent he identified with the Spaniards and was at odds with the Italians, some of whom he saw as favorable to Lutheran teachings, others as opposed to ecclesiastical reform. Still, he was the principal Dominican at the council and played an important part in writing the decree on justification. While at the council he wrote his *De natura et gratia* (On nature and grace; Venice, 1547, followed by eleven more editions to 1589). This was nonpolemical exposition of problems relating to nature, grace, original sin, baptism, and justification—matters treated in the council's fifth and sixth sessions. Toward the end of the council, Soto's dual position as theologian and confessor to Charles V caused him difficulties, and the emperor, at his request, released him from confessorial duties in 1550.

Despite Soto's collaboration with Vitoria at Salamanca for twenty years, his writings on political theory are generally overshadowed by those of the older Dominican. Yet Soto's primary motive for writing his most important work in that field, *De iure et iustitia* (On right and justice), was the unjust treatment of the Indians by the conquistadores. This was published in ten books at Salamanca in 1553, followed by twenty-four editions to 1608. Right (*ius*), for Soto, is the object of the virtue of justice (*iustitia*), and it applies to humans as individuals, as social beings, and as members of the state. Political authority arises not from God but from the community as a whole by translation to the legal sovereign. This teaching was used by later writers to refute the theory of the divine right of kings.

BIBLIOGRAPHY

Beltrán de Heredia, Vicente. *Domingo de Soto: Estudio biográfico documentado.* Salamanca, Spain, 1960.

Bowe, Gabriel. *The Origin of Political Authority: An Essay in Catholic Political Philosophy.* Dublin, Ireland, 1955.

Hamilton, Bernice. *Political Thought in Sixteenth-Century Spain: A Study of the Political Ideas of Vitoria, De Soto, Suárez, and Molina.* Oxford, 1963.

Wallace, William A. "Domingo de Soto's 'Laws' of Motion: Text and Context." In *Texts and Contexts in Ancient and Medieval Science.* Edited by Edith Sylla and Michael McVaugh. Leiden, Netherlands, 1997. Pages 271–304.

Wallace, William A. "The Enigma of Domingo de Soto: *Uniformiter difformis* and Falling Bodies in Late Medieval Physics." *Isis* 59 (1968): 384–401.

WILLIAM A. WALLACE

SPACE AND PERSPECTIVE.

Renaissance painting is associated historically with the affirmation of three-dimensional space as a principal component of the comprehensive realistic treatment of subject matter, in contrast to the highly reduced and conceptualized art of the Middle Ages. The interest in representing realistic space arose in the early fifteenth century in northern Europe, primarily in Flanders and at the principal courts of France, and in Italy, particularly in Florence. Initially, Italian pictorial space was primarily analytical, based on geometric principles: the rules of linear perspective. The pictorial space prevailing in the north, as in the paintings of Jan van Eyck, was synthetic. It combined substantial awareness of linear perspective with the basic rules of atmospheric vision: the appearance of objects according to the agency of light and shade, and the loss of clarity of shape and local color of objects as distance increases. During the fifteenth century, Italian masters, especially Leonardo da Vinci, also became increasingly aware of atmospheric perspective.

Briefly, the evolution of Renaissance perspective can be divided into three parts. First was the age of the precursors—those painters first aware of pictorial depth in their works. These are the great Italian painters of the proto-Renaissance, especially Giotto, active in the late thirteenth and fourteenth centuries. In their paintings tangible pictorial depth does not extend beyond the foreground, and basic rules of linear perspective are not systematically applied. Second was the age of thorough investigation of linear and atmospheric perspective in painting, and of optics grounded in real experience. This period corresponds roughly to the fifteenth century. During this period both linear and atmospheric perspective were thoroughly applied in painting. Third was the age drawing on the lessons of the fifteenth century, beginning roughly with the Italian high Renaissance and climaxing in the baroque, when knowledge of linear and atmospheric perspective evolved into the creation of vast images of the heavens applied on vaults and ceilings of buildings, and otherwise assumed complex, exaggerated, and personal forms.

It should be remembered that certain conceptual conventions such as hieratic scale, traditionally used to identify divinity, continued to appear in the paintings of principal Renaissance masters renowned for their perspectival knowledge (see, for example, the huge Virgin in Masaccio's Pisa Altarpiece of 1426; Piero della Francesca's large Virgin in his Brera Altarpiece, dated before 1473; or Jan van Eyck's small panel of the *Madonna in the Church* in Berlin, of c. 1430).

The Birth of Linear Perspective.

According to Antonio Manetti's biography (c. 1480s), the Florentine artist-architect Filippo Brunelleschi (1377–1446) made the first systematic use of linear perspective in an attempt to imitate an actual urban

Perspective in Sculpure. *The Head of John the Baptist Presented to Herod* from the doors of the Baptistery, Siena, by Donatello. Note the receding perspective through the arches in the background. The panel illustrates the passage in Matthew 14:1–12 and Mark 6:14–29. ART RESOURCE

scene in two experimental panel paintings, dating close to 1413 (they no longer exist). One depicted the Piazza della Signoria in Florence as one enters from the northwest corner. The view of the Piazza della Signoria was cut off at the tops of the buildings, so that, if the panel were seen from Brunelleschi's fixed vantage point, the actual sky would complete the image and bring it to life.

The other panel painting represented the Baptistery. In this work, the process of obtaining the facsimile effect was more complicated. The viewer, facing the Baptistery, stood at the center of the Florence Cathedral facade. He held the back of the panel tight against his face, and looked through a hole (the size of a lentil, located toward the center of the painting) in the direction of the Baptistery and toward a mirror held in his extended hand. Instead of the Baptistery he saw the mirror reflection of the painting. The portion of the painting devoted to the sky above the buildings consisted of burnished silver in which the actual sky was reflected.

It took some years for the lessons of Brunelleschi's experiments—especially the basic rules of linear perspective, which made them possible—to enter the life stream of Florentine art. The rules of perspective were presented in convenient form for artists' use by Leon Battista Alberti (1404–1472) in his *De pictura,* and his *Della pittura,* the Italian version, in 1435–1436. In essence, linear perspective, comprising basic geometric principles, is used to project settings, including objects and/or figures occupying various locations in space, onto a two-dimensional surface (the picture plane). Assuming a fixed vantage point, it is based on the principle that all orthogonals (lines perpendicular to the picture plane) will meet at a point (the centric or vanishing point) located along the central ray or line: the orthogonal extending from the pupil of the viewer's eye. In pictorial practice, linear perspective prefers objects and settings formed by straight lines; this usually means architecture. The presence of squares in positions of perspectival recession enables the viewer, by simple geometric means, to determine precisely his distance from the picture plane. Accordingly, the very geometry of linear perspective introduces the beholder into the painter's spatial structure, and, if a fixed measure is introduced, the distances between painted objects and/or figures can be precisely determined.

Masaccio (1401–1428) was the first painter who thoroughly applied the principles of linear perspective in his commissioned paintings. He did so in two fundamentally different ways. The one system, exemplified in his *Holy Trinity* mural (in S. Maria Novella, Florence, dating before 1428; see the color plates in volume 4), is ordered from below, in accordance with the actual viewpoint of an observer standing before the mural. The other system is found in his *Tribute Money* (in the Brancacci Chapel, in S. Maria del Carmine, Florence, dating before 1428; see the color plates in volume 4), where the individual scenes are applied in superposed registers. There the viewpoint, determined by his perspectival scheme, is directly in front of the mural. Since the mural is located high above the viewer's head, the painter's viewpoint does not correspond to that of the actual beholder. Because in mural cycles superposed register arrangements were then generally preferred, in much of near-contemporary Italian mural painting

the second perspectival order prevailed (see, for example, Piero della Francesca's murals of the *Story of the Holy Cross* in S. Francesco, Arezzo, dating after 1454; or Ghirlandaio's mural cycles in the square apse of S. Maria Novella, Florence, dating 1485–1490). Even when in the high Renaissance individual scenes occupied whole walls, as in the case of Leonardo's *Last Supper* in Milan [see the color plates in volume 3] or Raphael's *School of Athens* in the Vatican [see the color plates in volume 5], the vantage point chosen by the painter remained fixed high above the actual position of the beholder. The preferred location of the vanishing point at the very center of the image often coincided, as in Masaccio's *Tribute Money* or Leonardo's *Last Supper,* with the head of Christ: an open invitation for connecting rational space to Christian faith.

Although linear perspective concerns pictorial depth, following Alberti's analogy of the painted image with a view through a window, painters also investigated means by which the image could extend forward in the beholder's direction. This meant to some extent the dissolution of the picture plane. Such a device is found in Masaccio's tax collector in the *Tribute Money* who receives money from Saint Peter as he walks literally into the picture from the space of the beholder. Piero della Francesca (c. 1420–1492) uses architecture to obtain the same effect in his Brera *Madonna* [see the color plates in this volume]. He introduces the ends of the slanted cornices belonging to the side walls of the missing nave. Their presence locates the beholder in the latter, while the Madonna and the flanking saints appear in the church's crossing.

Perspectival Problems. As the Renaissance progressed, artists turned to the analysis of specific perspectival problems, including the foreshortened and angle view of objects and figures, as can be seen in Mantegna's compacted *Dead Christ* of the later 1460s in the Brera Gallery, Milan, and in Leonardo's studies copied in the Codex Huygens (The Pierpont Morgan Library Codex M.A. 1139).

The classicizing architecture of the high Renaissance and beyond produced large vaults and domes, which were often covered with vast paintings. Their curved surfaces, and the view from below, served as a challenge to effective perspectival projection. The subject matter of these murals conveniently drew on the obvious equation of the vault or dome with the natural and/or divine heavens. This movement culminated eventually in the grand ceiling murals of the baroque and rococo periods, including Andrea

Piero della Francesca. *The Flagellation of Christ.* Piero considered perspective in his *De prospectiva pigendi.* Painted for the duke of Urbino, 1460. The painting illustrates the passage in Matthew 27:27–31, Mark 15:16–20, and John 19:1–3. Pontius Pilate, in the dress of a Byzantine emperor (see the portrait medallion of John VIII Palaeologus at the entry on Pisanello), observes the flagellation. The painting may also depict the dream in which St. Jerome was whipped for his devotion to pagan rhetoric. PALAZZO DUCALE, URBINO, ITALY/SUPERSTOCK

Pozzo's *Ascension of St. Ignatius to Heaven* in S. Ignazio, Rome, of 1691–1694.

Toward the beginning of this trend belongs Mantegna's painted domical vault of the Room of the Newlyweds in the Ducal Palace in Mantua, from the years 1464–1475. Although the main part of the domical vault is decorated with imitation recessed ceiling panels, an oculus, or circular window, is represented at the very top. Beyond, against the sky, foreshortened women and children lean over or hold precariously onto a balustrade as they look down at the beholder. Melozzo da Forlì was also a master of perspectival painting. His vast mural of Christ's Ascension in SS. Apostoli, in Rome (1481–1483), of which only a few fragments remain, filled the entire vault of the apse with figures suspended in heaven, and with a foreshortened Christ, firmly standing on a cloud, looking down at mankind.

The most significant painted vault of the high Renaissance is Michelangelo's huge Sistine Chapel ceiling (1508–1511; see the color plates in volume 4). The perspective structure of the painted vault is highly complicated. Michelangelo introduced an arbitrary classicizing rectilinear architectural grid that conforms in spatial location to the curve of the actual vault, and serves as a frame for the nine principal scenes from Genesis, which extend along the vault's major axis. Only those scenes depicting the beginning of God's creation of the universe offer views of open skies including active foreshortened figures filling much of the available space.

It was Correggio who first transformed entire domical spaces into divine heavens. He did so in his *Vision of St. John the Evangelist* in S. Giovanni Evangelista, Parma (1520–1524), and in the *Assumption of the Virgin* in Parma Cathedral (1526–1530). Here the circular array of clouds and figures, roughly congruent with the shape of the dome, creates a spatial funnel that leads the beholder's eye directly toward heaven. By the end of the century virtuoso pictorial perspectival display on ceilings of subject matter seen from below is widely found, especially in Venice, as can be seen in Veronese's *Triumph of Venice* in the Great Council Hall of the Doge's Palace (c. 1585).

Mirrors have special and diverse connections with Renaissance perspective. It has been proposed that when Brunelleschi experimented with proportionate perspectival construction he was aware of the great medieval mathematician Leonardo Fibonacci (c. 1170–after 1240) and his use of mirrors, or basins of water, for surveying purposes, since this also involved calculations based on proportionate right triangles. As the understanding of pictorial space progressed, artists occasionally chose to challenge themselves with particular problems of optical distortion. In Jan van Eyck's *Arnolfini Wedding* in the National Gallery, London (1434; see the color plates in volume 2), the reflected image in the centrally located convex mirror, duly distorted, offers two men entering the depicted room roughly where the beholder would be standing. Another remarkable example of perspectival (anamorphic) distortion appears in Hans Holbein the Younger's painting of the *French Ambassadors,* also in the National Gallery, London (1533), in which the skull in the lower foreground is at first glance hardly recognizable. From in front of the painting the skull is compressed in height and laterally distended. It assumes its proper shape only if viewed at a sharp angle at some distance from the right side roughly level with the viewer's eyes.

BIBLIOGRAPHY

Primary Works

Alberti, Leon Battista. *On Painting.* Translated by Cecil Grayson with an introduction by Martin Kemp. London and New York, 1991. Translation of *De pictura* (1435).

Dürer, Albrecht. *The Painter's Manual.* Translated by Walter L. Strauss. New York, 1977.

Manetti, Antonio. *The Life of Brunelleschi.* Edited by H. Saalman. Translated by C. Enggass. University Park, Pa., and London, 1970. Translation of *Vita di Brunelleschi* (c. 1480s).

Piero della Francesca. *De prospectiva pingendi.* Edited by Giusta Nicco-Fasola. Florence, 1984.

Secondary Works

Baltrušaitis, Jurgis. *Anamorphic Art.* Translated by Walter J. Strachan. New York, 1977. Translation of *Anamorphoses ou magie artificielle des effets merveilleux* (1969).

Damisch, Hubert. *The Origin of Perspective.* Translated by J. Goodman. Cambridge, Mass., and London, 1994. Translation of *L'origine de la perspective* (1987).

Edgerton, Samuel Y. *The Heritage of Giotto's Geometry: Art and Science on the Eve of the Scientific Revolution.* Ithaca, N.Y., and London, 1991.

Edgerton, Samuel Y. *The Renaissance Rediscovery of Linear Perspective.* New York, 1975.

Kemp, M. "Science, Non-science, and Nonsense: Brunelleschi's Perspective." *Art History* 1(1978): 134–161.

Kemp, M. *The Science of Art: Optical Themes in Western Art from Brunelleschi to Seurat.* New Haven, Conn., and London, 1990.

Panofsky, Erwin. *Perspective as Symbolic Form.* Translated by Ch. S. Wood. New York, 1991. Translation of "Die Perspektive als 'symbolische Form.'"

Panofsky, Erwin. *The Codex Huygens and Leonardo da Vinci's Art Theory: The Pierpont Morgan Library Codex M.A. 1139.* London, 1940.

Sandström, Sven. *Levels of Unreality.* Uppsala, Sweden, 1963.

White, John. *The Birth and Rebirth of Pictorial Space.* London, 1957.

JOSEPH POLZER

SPAIN. [This entry includes two subentries, one on the history of the Spanish kingdoms, the other on art in Spain and Portugal.]

The Spanish Kingdoms

In the fifteenth century, four separate Christian kingdoms and one Muslim kingdom shared the Iberian Peninsula: Aragon, Navarre, Castile, and Portugal represented the Christians, and Granada the Muslims. The words "Spain" and "España" are both derived from the Latin word "Hispania," which the Romans used to designate the peninsula that the Greeks had called "Iberia." The word "Spain" was commonly used in Europe in the fifteenth century to designate either Castile or the entire peninsula except Portugal. There was no "kingdom of Spain" in the fifteenth century and would not be until the eighteenth.

Christians, Muslims, and Jews. In addition to its Catholic majority, Spain in the fifteenth century also had a large number of Jewish subjects and the only sizable Muslim minority in western Europe. After the Muslims conquered most of the peninsula in the early eighth century, they built a brilliant civilization in Spain and made it an integral part of the wider Islamic world. In the beginning, the Muslims failed to take all the peninsula, leaving enclaves of Christian strength in the mountainous north. These enclaves became the basis for the Christian kingdoms. The period known as the Reconquest lasted from the early eighth to the late fifteenth century, during which open hostility and warfare alternated with periods of what the Spanish call *convivencia,* or living together, in neither peace nor war.

During the course of the Middle Ages, Christian power extended slowly and inexorably southward. At the same time, the Christians learned much and benefited economically from the more advanced Islamic civilization across their southern frontiers. Attitudes gradually hardened, and by the fifteenth century, there was a growing sense of implacable hostility between the two civilizations that shared Iberia, and it became increasingly clear that relations among the several religions were worsening. At the end of the fifteenth century, Ferdinand of Aragon and Isabella of Castile followed the path laid out by English and French monarchs two centuries before, and in 1492 they ordered the Jews to convert to Christianity or leave Spain. About half left, going mainly to North African cities and to Portugal. The rest converted. The Muslims were given a similar choice in 1500. With the exception of Muslims in the kingdom of Valencia, who were given several decades of respite, all had to embrace Christianity or leave Spain. Most chose to convert and remain. By the early sixteenth century, there were two significant minority groups in the Spanish kingdoms: the conversos, Christians of Jewish origin, and the Moriscos, Christians of Muslim origin. Many so-called Old Christians resented and feared these New Christians, seeing them as a threat to religious unity. Both groups were considered notoriously bad Christians, and the religious inquisition in operation from 1478 had as its primary aim enforcement of the conversos' Christian orthodoxy.

The Unification of the Kingdoms.

Even after the marrage in 1469 of Ferdinand of Aragon and Isabella of Castile and their subsequent accession to the respective thrones, the Spanish kingdoms of Iberia remained divided among several smaller political entities, each one the product of geography, topography, environment, and history. The crown of Aragon in the east contained three separate units: Aragon, Catalonia, and Valencia. The kings of Aragon also ruled a Mediterranean empire, which included the Balearic Islands, Sicily, Sardinia, and the Kingdom of Naples in southern Italy. Northwest of Aragon lay the small kingdom of Navarre. Dominating the center of the peninsula from north to south was the kingdom of Castile, an accumulation of territories acquired during the long Reconquest of the peninsula from the Muslims during the medieval centuries. Castile included the northern coastal areas of Galicia,

Santiago, Patron of Spain. *Saint James Fighting the Arabs* by Juan de Flandes (c. 1475–1519). Oil on canvas; c. 1500. MUSEO LÁZARO GALDIANO, MADRID/ORONOZ

Asturias, Cantabria, and the Basque regions of Vizcaya, Guipúzcoa, and Álava; León and Castile (Old Castile) to the north of the central mountains, and La Mancha and Extremadura (New Castile) to the south; and the kingdoms of Andalusia and Murcia in the extreme south and southeast. The kingdom of Portugal lay to the west of Castile, formed in its own Reconquest of territory from the Muslims. The kingdom of Granada in south-central Iberia was the last Muslim possession in Europe in the fifteenth century. Ferdinand and Isabella took over Granada in 1492, and it became part of the kingdom of Castile.

There was nothing inevitable about the creation of modern Spain through the amalgamation of Aragon and Castile. There could as easily have been a merger of Castile and Portugal as between Castile and Aragon. After Isabella died in 1504, Ferdinand married Germaine de Foix, heiress of Navarre. The eventual consequence of Ferdinand's second marriage was the absorption of the part of Navarre south of the Pyrenees into Castile. By the time Ferdinand died in 1516, the peninsular area his grandson Charles inherited corresponded closely to a modern map of Spain, its territories divided and accentuated by the rugged topography that makes Spain the second most mountainous country in Europe.

Government. Spain shared many characteristics with other European countries, not the least of which were a monarchical and bureaucratic form of government, the rule of law, and a well-organized Catholic Church. In the fifteenth century, Spanish monarchs were working to extend the sway of royal law, like their fellow monarchs elsewhere in western Europe. Two legal developments proceeded on parallel courses in Castile and Aragon. One was the gradual adoption of Roman law as the primary law of the kingdom, and the second was the gradual imposition of royal law throughout the kingdom, a process still incomplete in the sixteenth century. In the mid-thirteenth century, Alfonso X of Castile produced a new code for his kingdom, known as the *Siete Partidas,* which relied heavily on Roman law. Implemented only after Alfonso X's death in 1284, and then incompletely, the *Siete Partidas* still had a significant influence on subsequent legislation in Spain, both for the home country and for the American colonies. This is apparent in the Laws of Toro (1505) and the New Laws for the Indies (1542). As the legal authority of the monarchy strengthened, so did the bureaucratic apparatus of councils and royal officials. Despite the strength and authority of the monarchs, local traditions still limited what they could do. Certain regions retained *fueros* (law codes) from the Middle Ages that provided guarantees against arbitrary royal actions, and the Cortes (parliament) allowed local spokesmen, usually members of the urban elite and minor nobles, to express local concerns and to participate in the legislative process.

The first rulers of the unified kingdoms, Queen Isabella of Castile (ruled 1474–1504) and Ferdinand, king of Aragon (ruled 1479–1516) and regent of Castile (1506–1516), worked to build an anti-French alliance through royal marriages with the Habsburgs and the English and Portuguese royal houses. At home, Ferdinand ended revolts and consolidated royal power in the crown of Aragon and gained control of the Kingdom of Naples in 1504. Meanwhile, Isabella secured her claim to the Castilian throne, worked out agreements with the Castilian nobles, and completed the Spanish Reconquest in 1492. In the same year, Spanish Jews were given the choice

of converting to Christianity or leaving the kingdom, and Columbus secured royal backing for a westward voyage to Asia and found the Americas in the process. Thus began Spain's transatlantic empire.

Charles I (ruled 1516–1556), as mentioned previously, inherited from his four grandparents the largest empire in Europe. While he was still a child, it was clear that Charles would be the most powerful ruler in Europe, through his inheritance of the combined legacies of the Trastámaras of Castile and Aragon and the Habsburgs of central and northwest Europe. Charles also held the title Emperor Charles V of the Holy Roman Empire (ruled 1519–1556). With power based in several key cities, he ruled an empire that included a large portion of central Europe, the Low Countries (the Netherlands, Belgium, and Luxembourg of today), and the Spanish kingdoms with their possessions in the Mediterranean and on both sides of the Atlantic. His Spanish subjects in the Americas extended the empire with the conquests of Mexico, Peru, and Chile. In Europe, Charles divided his time between Spain and central Europe. Spanish annoyance, based on the assumption that he was a foreigner intent on milking Spain for his imperial ventures in Europe, led to a revolt of the comuneros in Castile in 1520 and 1521 and contributed to the revolt of the Germanías in Valencia during the same years. Both failed, and Charles thereafter had domestic peace in Spain. Elsewhere, Spanish forces took control of Oran and Tunis in North Africa and extended Spanish influence in Italy. Charles considered himself to be the protector of traditional Christianity and expended considerable effort and wealth in trying to defeat the Turks in the Mediterranean and combat Protestantism in Germany.

In 1556 Charles took the extraordinary step of abdicating. He retired to the Extremaduran monastery of Yuste after dividing his empire. His younger brother Ferdinand received the Holy Roman Empire and central European possessions. His son Philip got the rest: Spain and the Canaries, the Netherlands, the Italian possessions, and Spain's American empire.

The reign of Philip II (1556–1598) was a curious mixture of successes and failures. The general domestic peace of Philip's long reign was broken by two important revolts, one in the Alpujarra mountains of Granada from 1566 to 1571 and the other in Aragon in 1591 and 1592. The Moriscos of the Alpujarras were pacified by Don John of Austria only at great expense and cost of life. Afterward, the survivors were enslaved and resettled in towns and villages throughout New Castile. In 1591 long-simmering tensions in the kingdom of Aragon found

an outlet in the monarchy's clumsy handling of the Antonio Pérez affair, and an army of 12,000 was required to put down the rebellion. The remainder of the 1590s were scarred by plague, famine, and royal bankruptcy (1596).

Abroad, Philip oversaw the great Christian victory over the Turks at Lepanto in 1571, but that triumph only temporarily halted the Ottoman machine. After a brief campaign, Philip assumed the throne of Portugal in 1580, but the union of crowns lasted just sixty years. With the addition of Portugal's possessions in Africa, South America, and Asia to Spain's extensive American holdings, Philip II presided over the first truly global empire. In northern Europe he was less successful. In the Netherlands, anti-Catholic and anti-Spanish sentiment led to the Dutch revolt, which began in 1566 and resulted in Philip's loss of the northern provinces. After years of provocation, Philip sought to negate the aid of Elizabeth I of England to the Dutch rebels with the Great Armada of 1588, whose mission was part of a larger plan to invade England with Habsburg forces from the southern Netherlands. The armada's failure is often seen as a metaphor for the beginning of Spain's decline, even though its losses in ships were rapidly replaced, and several other armadas were sent north in the 1590s.

In the reign of Philip III (ruled 1598–1621), Spain signed truces with England, France, and the northern Netherlands. Spain gradually adjusted to the rank of a secondary power, although the Spanish fleet was usually able to protect the annual fleets to and from the Americas and could still project Spain's power in Europe. At home, popular opinion as well as clerical and governmental suspicion held the Moriscos to be insincere converts. That combined with their failed social integration helped to influence the decision for their expulsion beginning in 1609.

The Catholic Church. Throughout the period, the Catholic Church in Spain had a great deal of power, as we have observed. The members of the church formed a category all their own, legally constituting a unified group with collective rights and privileges, but actually mirroring all of society, with internal divisions and a well-defined hierarchy of wealth and status. Members of the secular clergy, those who ministered to the spiritual concerns of the laity, ranged from rich and worldly archbishops, to bishops in smaller cities, canons of cathedrals and churches, and priests in local parishes.

The regular clergy (monks and nuns) usually lived in communes apart from secular society, governed by *regula* (rules) established by the founders of their particular monastic orders. They took vows to serve God through spiritual or charitable works. In Spain the most important of such monastic orders included the long-established Benedictines and Cistercians and the order of St. Jerome, founded in the late fourteenth century. The Jeronimites had their headquarters at Guadalupe in the hills west of Madrid, in the heart of the area that produced many early venturers to America. Consequently, the Jeronimites and the Virgin of Guadalupe had a great influence in the Spanish colonies in the Americas. The late medieval orders of mendicant friars, the Franciscans and the Dominicans, flourished in the Spanish kingdoms as well. The founder of the Dominicans was an early-thirteenth-century Castilian nobleman, canonized as St. Dominic. In the sixteenth century, Ignatius of Loyola founded the Society of Jesus (the Jesuits), which through educational work at home and its missionary activities in Asia and elsewhere became one of the most influential orders. In Castile, St. Teresa of Ávila and St. John of the Cross worked to reform the Carmelites and founded in 1562 the reformed Discalced Carmelites. It is estimated that in 1591 there were about 91,000 members of the clergy (just over 1 percent of the total population), 40,600 of them members of the secular clergy and the rest almost equally divided between male and female members of the regular clergy.

There had always been close relations between crown and church. One of the most visible results of the close relationship was the foundation of the modern Inquisition in 1478 at the request of Ferdinand and Isabella. The governing council of the Inquisition formed part of the royal administration and all members of the tribunals were royal appointees. In the fifteenth and sixteenth centuries, tribunals were set up throughout the kingdoms, from Palermo, Sicily, to Lima, Peru. In addition to punishing those practicing Judaism, Islam, or Protestantism, the tribunals passed on the religious ancestry of applicants to various prestigious positions in the realm, censored works that had been placed on the Index of Prohibited Books, and searched for contraband merchandise passing between the kingdoms.

Queen Isabella also supported the internal reform of the church and its clergy in a program led by Jiménez de Cisneros that helped to end or ameliorate conditions of clerical ignorance and immorality, about which many had complained. In their conquest of Granada, Ferdinand and Isabella secured the right to present candidates for the office of bishop for that kingdom, which gave them powerful control over the direction of church policy. This was later extended to the new possessions in the Americas, and Charles I secured its extension to all his Spanish realms. The right of presentation included many lesser benefices in the realms, guaranteeing the crown infinite opportunities to influence appointments and win allies. From the church, the crown also reaped important sources of revenue through levies on vacant benefices, the sale of indulgences known as *cruzadas,* and contributions from the clergy known as the *tercio* and *subsidio.*

The Spanish crown made a lasting contribution to church affairs through its support for the Council of Trent (1545–1563). Charles V and then Philip II commanded leading archbishops and theologians such as Pedro Guerrero, Diego Hurtado de Mendoza, Melchior Cano, Juan Bernal Díaz de Luco, Bartolomé de Carranza, and Domingo de Soto to attend the sessions. In all, a total of 286 Spanish prelates and theologians participated. There, the Spanish delegates were influential in passing decrees on important points of dogma as well as practical reforms of church administration. On 12 July 1564 Philip II led European monarchs in mandating the adoption of the council's decrees throughout his kingdoms. The interest of the monarchs in ecclesiastical affairs continued throughout the Renaissance period.

Society. Militant Christianity was a medieval legacy that continued in the Renaissance period. The Reconquest shaped the Christian attitudes that there was wealth to be gained from the armed conquest of alien peoples, and that the security of Christian society and indeed its survival depended upon unity and a militant defense of the faith. Nonetheless, we must not draw the erroneous conclusion that the typical Spaniard of the fifteenth century was an armed professional warrior or minor nobleman, whose only interests were war, booty, and the oppression of non-Christians. The Reconquest shaped some of the attitudes of the Spanish population, but the social and occupational structure of the population was much like that in the rest of Europe.

A lack of demographic records before the sixteenth century in Spain, as in most areas of premodern Europe and the world, means that we know little about Spanish population in the formative medieval centuries. We have only estimates made from incomplete censuses, tax assessments, and other official documents. A safe guess for the total number of Spaniards in the late fifteenth century would be something on the order of 5.3 million. By 1591 the numbers reached approximately 8 million. About 81.3 percent of the population and 76 percent of the land of Spain came under the jurisdiction of Castile, with the rest in Aragon and Navarre.

Rural society. Spanish society, like that of most of the pre-industrial world, was overwhelmingly rural and dependent for its food supply on the labor of a large majority of its population. Four out of every five Spaniards worked on the land to produce the vegetable and animal products that society needed to feed itself. Serfdom, which bound people to the land and forced them to make payments to an overlord, was never widespread in Castile and was abolished by the end of the fifteenth century. In Catalonia, serfs joined in the civil wars from 1462 to 1472, rebelled again in 1484 and 1485, and finally won permanent relief in 1486 through the Sentence of Guadalupe that ended the worst abuses of serfdom. In Valencia and Aragon, a large proportion of the rural work force consisted of Muslim serfs who in the sixteenth century were nominally converted to Christianity. Their expulsion, starting in 1609, led to economic disaster for landowners, particularly in Valencia.

Nowhere was the rural population of Spain equal in wealth or status. The majority owned neither land nor animals and usually made a living by working for others, with no security in bad times. Some were *jornaleros,* who worked and were paid on a day-to-day basis. Others could arrange labor contracts for a season or a year. Those who owned a plow team, whether owning land or not, were generally known as *labradores* and were a cut above the majority, who owned no land or livestock. The wealthiest *labradores* owned or leased large farms and employed others to work for them. They often lived very comfortable lives and could aspire to higher social status, even the lower nobility. The land available for leasing was often owned by nobles or clerics, who rented it on terms ranging from a year or two to virtual perpetuity. Such wealthy landowners can also be counted among those who earned their livelihood from the land, despite their social and economic distance from those who actually worked it. The percentage of *jornaleros, labradores,* and rentiers in the population varied enormously from region to region; generally, more independent farmers were found in the north, while virtually all of the Andalusian peasantry was landless. Over the course of the sixteenth century, the agricultural population underwent progressive impoverishment, due to rapid demographic growth, inflation, scarcity of resources, ever-increasing taxes, and well-intentioned but ultimately harmful government regulation of commodity prices.

Spain's agricultural population mostly lived in nucleated settlements, ranging from hamlets of one hundred inhabitants to towns of five thousand, and traveled back and forth to work their land and tend their flocks and herds. This type of settlement pattern originated in part because people need to cluster around the sources of fresh water in the dry plains of Castile, and in part for protection and mutual aid during the centuries of warfare with the Muslims. For their residential status, people identified themselves proudly as *vecinos* (citizens) of the legal corporations of their hamlet, village, or town. Citizenship gave them a wide range of privileges and made them eligible for allotments of communal goods held for the use of all the *vecinos:* arable and grazing land, forest products, and water rights. Clearly their lives were very different from the lives of *vecinos* of large towns and cities, many of whom had lost their rural ties.

The Nobility. At the upper end of the social spectrum, urban and rural, was the nobility, whose ancestors had been given land and status in earlier centuries, usually for military service to the monarchy. This was not a closed caste in Spain, however; movement in and out of its ranks was common in the fifteenth century and thereafter. The standard threefold division of the nobility included as the lowest and most numerous category the *hidalgos*— loosely meaning "children of some distinction"— whose only advantages were a certain amount of local prestige and exemption from ordinary taxation. Above them were *señores* (lords) with *señoríos* (small territorial possessions). At the top of the scale were the *títulos* or titled nobles, often called the *grandes*. The counts, marquises, and dukes who made up this exclusive group were defined by their wealth and power, both of which increased in the fifteenth and sixteenth centuries, as did the number of titles.

The holdings of the *grandes* were scattered, and the greatest among them owned or controlled towns and lands in several provinces. While each titled noble typically had a favored stronghold and various other fortresses, he did not usually reside on his estates. Instead, the Castilian nobility as a whole tended to be urban, with its spheres of action in the major towns and cities of the realm; the greatest nobles followed the royal court. In the towns and cities, nobles moved to dominate municipal governments and judicial positions by gaining supporters among lesser noble families through intermarriage and patronage. At the royal court they sought to establish hereditary control over important royal offices, such as the admiralty of Castile. They also exercised great influence on foreign commerce and over the administration of the Mesta, the crown-sponsored association of flockowners.

By inserting themselves into the highest levels of local and royal government, the Spanish nobility secured and enhanced its economic position, as well as its social status. By the mid-fifteenth century, fewer than two-dozen families had amassed great amounts of lands, titles, wealth, and political positions. Even though the number of important noble families grew in the sixteenth century, their total numbers were still quite small. The wealth of the high nobility rested on a common economic base: the land and its bounty. Whether they raised wheat, wine grapes, or olives, or derived their wealth from wool, meat, and hides from livestock, their primary aim was to secure the greatest possible return from their agricultural and pastoral pursuits. Nobles who lived along the coasts pursued analogous profits from the fishing industry, or from the export trade, either by controlling ports or by direct ownership of shipping. Nobles routinely engaged in business without losing either social status or their titles.

Another important source of wealth for the nobility came from political rewards, both for loyal service (particularly in time of war) and for promises of loyalty (particularly in time of political strife). This was just one way in which their political and economic positions were closely linked. The monarchs had at their disposal a vast array of material rewards to grant as *mercedes* (mercies or gifts). Royal offices, both in the central government and in the provinces and cities, were lucrative gifts, providing salaries and the potential for graft. Titles, most of them with more honorific than real value, were also bestowed as favors from the monarch. Grants of income based on royal taxes and customs revenues, outright monetary gifts and grants of vassals, towns and villages, and the rights to found *mayorazgos,* or entailed estates, were also bestowed on the nobility in return for their service and loyalty. Although very few of the high Spanish nobility migrated to America, they served as powerful role models for those who emigrated in search of increased wealth and status. Their military values, the way they dressed and spent their money, and their willingness to serve the crown in anticipation of substantial rewards, all inspired Spanish conquerors in the Americas.

Other groups. Spaniards of all ages and both sexes who were neither noble, nor members of the religious establishment, nor workers on the land surely did not exceed 5 percent of the total. Urban dwellers almost exclusively, they ranged from wealthy merchants and town councilors to domestic workers, concentrated in a few large urban areas, especially Seville and Valencia. All these groups tend to be studied less thoroughly than the more familiar nobility and clergy.

The Economy. Spain, as well as Europe generally, was experiencing a rise in economic activity from the late fifteenth century on, especially in long-distance trade within Europe and across the Atlantic to the American empire. This helped to explain urban growth in many parts of the peninsula. The most striking growth took place in Seville, which served as the gateway to the rapidly expanding American empire. Madrid, too, grew spectacularly in the later sixteenth century, after Philip II designated it as the capital in 1561. Its growth caused an eclipse of neighboring cities such as Ávila and Toledo. Other traditional centers declined in the same period. Burgos suffered from the decline of wool exports northward as a consequence of the Dutch revolt in the 1570s. In Mediterranean Spain, Barcelona, a vital medieval metropolis, was in decline from the later Middle Ages, its place gradually taken over by Valencia.

In most fair-size towns, artisans supplied the basic needs for food, clothing and shelter, and services. The products of other workers were sold throughout the peninsula and exported abroad. For example, shipbuilders of the Cantabrian coast, western Andalusia, Barcelona, and Valencia produced vessels for European and transatlantic voyages. Many towns manufactured wool cloth for local use, and high-quality cloth from the looms of Segovia, Cuenca, Zaragoza, and Barcelona found a much wider market, although Spain was never a major exporter of textiles. Iron deposits in the north gave rise to important mining and smelting operations.

Nevertheless, the largest component of the Spanish economy remained the agrarian sector, with its production of food and animal products. On the semiarid plains of Castile, dry farming of cereals and livestock grazing (sheep, and to a lesser extent, pigs, goats, and cattle) predominated. In areas where Moriscos lived (Granada, Valencia, and Aragon), irrigation was employed to produce rice, vegetables, and fruits. In Granada mulberry trees were cultivated for the silk industry. During the sixteenth century Spain's forest reserves were drastically depleted, resulting in deforestation and soil erosion in many areas. Most farm production was consumed in Spain,

Spanish Monarchs

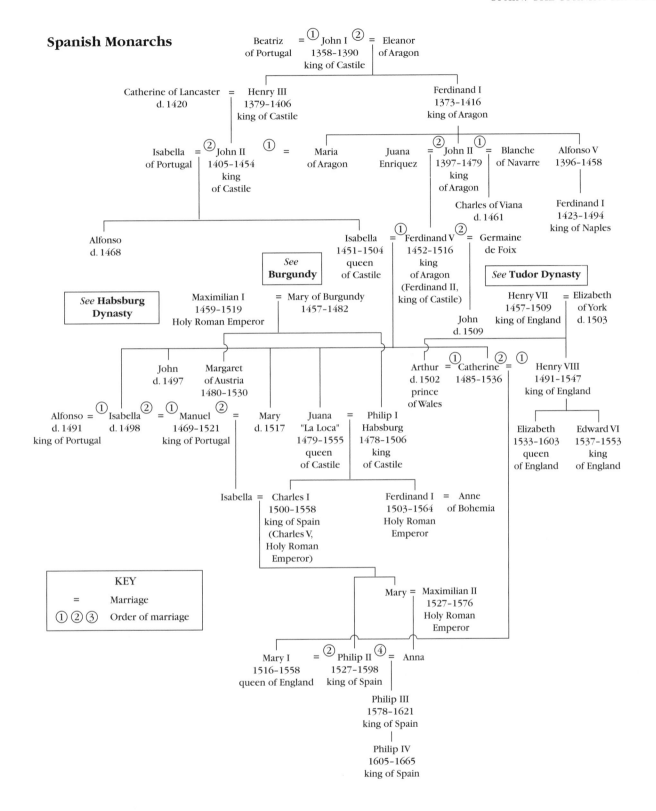

KEY

=   Marriage

① ② ③   Order of marriage

but a considerable amount was exported. For a long period, the merchant tradition in Spain has not received due attention. Given the militaristic legacy of the Reconquest, some historians have even assumed that being a merchant was incompatible with being a Spaniard, or at least with being a Castilian. That hoary misconception ignores the strongly developed merchant tradition in Spain as a whole, and in some regions in particular.

Trade. The Mediterranean empire of the crown of Aragon began in the thirteenth century when the kings of Aragon took over the Balearic Islands and Sicily. In the fifteenth century their descendants added Sardinia and Naples. Merchants from Barcelona, Majorca, and Valencia maintained a strong presence throughout Mediterranean and Atlantic Europe. They operated in a variety of trading networks, from the coast of southern France to northern Italy, from the islands of Corsica and Sardinia to Sicily, and into the Islamic Mediterranean with enclaves in Alexandria and Damascus. They maintained a number of North African enclaves as well, in Tunis, Bougie, and Tlemcen, as well as other places. The North African connection provided access to tropical products and the gold of west Africa. Merchants from Barcelona and other cities in the crown of Aragon traded in northwestern Europe, with establishments in Bruges and later in Antwerp. They were also present in considerable numbers in Seville and Lisbon.

On the Castilian side, foreign trade developed along with religious pilgrimages, particularly along the Way of St. James, which brought large numbers of Europeans across northern Spain to the shrine of St. James at Santiago de Compostela. By the fifteenth century, commercial relations were highly developed, with merchant fairs integrating the interior and exterior trade of Castile. Medina del Campo hosted the most important fair, which met for a total of one hundred days during two periods between May and October. Spanish merchants traveled to Medina from Seville, Burgos, Valencia, and Barcelona, joined by Flemings, Florentines, Genoese, Irish, and Portuguese. Medina was the kingdom's financial center in the second half of the fifteenth century and through most of the sixteenth century. The networks of trade developed by Aragon and Castile in the late Middle Ages encouraged Spanish interest in exploration and developed the commercial organization and business techniques that were incorporated in Spain's overseas empire.

The foreign trade of Castile in the fifteenth and sixteenth centuries suggests the complexity of Europe's commercial networks. The Atlantic coastline defined one major circuit for Castilian merchants, a circuit that stretched from the Cantabrian ports to the Atlantic coast of France and to Flanders, the British Isles, and the North Sea. The ability of the Castilian merchants to supply wool and other goods to the French, Flemish, and English markets depended upon the development of maritime transport. Shipbuilders and mariners on Spain's northern coast had a well-deserved reputation for competence, honed over the centuries. Like the merchants of Burgos, the mariners, shipbuilders, and owners had formed associations for their mutual benefit. In return for royal favor and rental payments, shipowners furnished vessels to the king for warfare and official missions. In general, the mariners of the northern ports served as transporters rather than merchants, contracting for the carrying trade with Castilian and foreign merchants.

The port of Bilbao in the Basque province of Vizcaya became a major center of shipbuilding and of the export trade in iron and wool. Bilbao's hinterland provided timber and naval stores for the shipbuilding industry, and water and fuel for iron smelting. Iron mines in the coastal mountains from Santander to Vizcaya provided ore for the iron and steel industry. Around one-third of Vizcayan iron was exported, usually in the form of bars, but occasionally as pure ore. Another third remained in the peninsula, used especially for the metal fittings in ship construction. The remainder was converted into hardware for export, including nails, anchors, artillery, armor, and weaponry. The region had difficulty producing grain in the hilly damp environment, but this provided a further incentive for trade. With the profits from trade, wheat could be purchased in Old Castile or from the ports of western France.

The trade in manufactured goods, iron ore, and various agricultural products was overshadowed by the export of raw wool. By the fifteenth century, Castile was one of western Europe's chief suppliers of high-quality wool. It attained that position in a process stretching back to the eleventh century, when vast migratory flocks were developed to take advantage of the lands newly conquered from the Muslims. An expanding European market for cloth in the late Middle Ages provided a vigorous demand for raw materials for the textile industry, especially in Italy and Flanders. Castile was in an excellent position to supply foreign demand, as well as its own domestic need for raw wool. With ample pasture and careful breeding techniques, the Castilian merino sheep became the new standard for quality. In the markets of

Flanders, both for consumption there and for transshipment to central Europe, by the sixteenth century, wool from Spain virtually replaced English wool, and Castile at times even sent wool to England. Because of this phenomenal growth, wool production and trade became the single most important element in the Castilian economy before the establishment of the American colonies and even afterwards rivaled the products of the colonies.

The commerce with Flanders clearly exceeded that of all other routes pursued by Castilians in the Atlantic. The primary exports from Castile to Flanders included iron, wine, and fruit, in addition to wool. The primary imports to Castile were various types of Flemish cloth and artworks, primarily paintings. Flanders was more than a manufacturing region, however. The major currents of European commerce met there as well: the Baltic trade of the Hanseatic League; the Italian, French, and English trades; and the Iberian trade from the south.

Due to piracy and war, insecurity on the Castile-Flanders run was constant, and the Castilians created a convoy system in 1436, the precursor of the *flota* of the Spanish Indies. Despite the hazards, enough ships got through to Flanders to enhance the position of the Castilian community in Bruges and to allow the Castilian Cortes of 1453 to describe the transit taxes on exported and imported goods (the *diezmos de la mar*) as the largest single source of royal income in Castile. War, piracy, and trade were intimately linked in the commercial networks of Europe in the fifteenth and sixteenth centuries. In fact, there was no clear distinction between them. Throughout the late Middle Ages and well into the Renaissance, there was no Castilian navy as such. Naval campaigns depended on impressed merchant ships. In those circumstances, merchant mariners learned to confront armed attacks even as they practiced the more peaceful skills of commerce.

Despite intermittent hostilities, England was the focus of much trade from the northern coast of Castile. In the winter months, Castilian and English ships brought citrus fruits, figs, dates, raisins, honey, almonds, and vinegar to Bristol, mostly from the Cantabrian coast, but occasionally from Seville or other ports. In summer, the northbound freight would consist of iron and manufactured goods, from nails and combs to anchors and crossbows, plus olive oil and wine, soap and leather, alum for the cloth industry, salt for fisheries, and some raw wool and yarn. The return cargoes were woolen cloth and a variety of other items useful to Castile: herring and hake, grain and beans, lead and tin. The English even imported some Spanish wool and yarn.

The other great area of Castilian trade was the Mediterranean, where merchants in Castile were active from the mid-fourteenth century onward. Seville and Cádiz on the southern Atlantic coast of Spain, and Cartagena on the southeastern Mediterranean coast, were the most important ports involved in Castile's trade in the Mediterranean, with Seville predominating until the fifteenth century. Thereafter, even though it remained the financial capital, the increasing size of ships and the silting of the Guadalquivir River allowed Cádiz and Sanlúcar de Barrameda at the mouth of the river to seize the advantage. Such was the importance of the latter ports, that virtually every Christian ship on its way through the Strait of Gibraltar stopped at one or the other. There was also a brisk exchange between Seville and Lisbon, where the Portuguese supplied apples, fish, and slaves from sub-Saharan Africa. The products of southern Castile—salt, wheat, barley, beans, peas, tuna, olive oil, wool, silk, and wine—generally sailed for Italy. The return cargoes were Italian manufactured goods along with spices and other oriental products that the Italians obtained in the eastern Mediterranean.

For the most part, Genoese and other Italians resident in Spain traded the products of the south in the markets of northern Europe. Local Spanish merchants participated in the trade, but they did not have the international connections of the Italians or of their compatriots in Burgos and elsewhere in northern Castile. Shortly after its reconquest in 1248, Seville had a Genoese quarter, and rich Genoese merchants intermarried with the local nobility. By the fifteenth century, Genoese merchants were firmly entrenched in Seville, where they prospered as bankers and monopolized certain goods, among them mercury and cinnabar from the mines of Almadén; they shared domination of the wine trade from Jerez de la Frontera with the Florentines. Other foreigners in Castile's Mediterranean trade included Italians from Pisa, Milan, and Venice; Englishmen; Portuguese; some Frenchmen; and other Spaniards—Catalans and above all Cantabrians. Burgalese merchant families also maintained a strong presence in Seville, where they helped to organize the Castilian wool trade, among other ventures. Spanish merchants and Italians resident in Spain helped finance the voyages of Christopher Columbus, and they expanded their operations in Spain's American empire.

Religious Military Orders

Related both to the nobility and to the clergy were several important Spanish religious-military orders, originally founded in the twelfth century to aid in the Reconquest and modeled on the Templars and the Hospitallers. Castile boasted the orders of Calatrava, Alcántara, and Santiago, and the crown of Aragon had the order of Montesa. In recognition of their crucial contributions to the success of the Reconquest, the military orders had received huge land grants from successive rulers of Castile in Extremadura, La Mancha, and on the frontier with Granada in Andalusia. These grants included rich pasturelands eminently suited for winter grazing; as a result, the masters of the orders were intimately involved with the Mesta and transhumant stock raising. The grand masters of the orders had jurisdiction over about one million people and enjoyed the privilege of bestowing nobility on some fifteen hundred individuals, the knights of the orders. They were roughly equivalent to the *señores* or middle ranks of the nobility. Along with the title of knight, or *caballero,* often went jurisdiction over tracts of land belonging to the order. The lands so granted were called *encomiendas* (from the verb *encomender*), because they were commended to the care and protection of the knight, or *encomendero.* The military orders provided respected and influential positions for minor noble families and for the younger sons of great families. Their wealth and power made the orders potential threats to the crown, however. From the fourteenth century onward, monarchs began to assert control over them, a process completed in the reign of Ferdinand and Isabella, when Ferdinand became the head of all three orders. The pattern of granting *encomiendas* to hold newly conquered land was well established during the Reconquest, and it was also used during the Castilian conquest of the Canary Islands.

European Links. We have already mentioned the connections between medieval Iberia and the Islamic world, which had helped to create Spain's religious militancy. Spain also maintained close relations with the rest of Christian Europe in the Renaissance. Its ties to Rome were similar to those that linked the papacy with all parts of western Europe. Spanish cardinals resided in Rome, and Spanish clerics played a large role in the life of the Roman Catholic church, particularly after the Valencian, Rodrigo Borja (Borgia), became Pope Alexander VI in 1492. The Dominicans were always in-terested in education, and their colleges at the University of Paris and elsewhere attracted many Spanish students to study abroad. In 1365 Cardinal Gil de Albornoz, archbishop of Toledo, founded the College of St. Clement at Bologna. Popularly known as the Spanish College, it provided lodging and support for Spanish students of theology and law. Throughout the Renaissance, reciprocal movement brought foreign students to Spanish universities. The University of Salamanca was the most prestigious in the peninsula, receiving royal support and attaining an international reputation quite early. A substantial proportion of young men of good family in sixteenth-century Spain attended university, and in the Americas, universities were established on European models in the sixteenth century.

Artistic works and artists came to Spain from other parts of Europe. One particularly important segment linked the Netherlands with Castile and other parts of Spain. Flemish artists moved to Spain, and Flemish paintings, tapestries, and wooden sculptures were sold to noble, clerical, and royal patrons. Hardly a major church in Spain lacks an example of art from late medieval and Renaissance Flanders. Italian artists gained patronage at the Habsburg courts, as did intellectuals from most parts of Europe. Charles I imported many Germans, ranging from cannon founders to organ makers. At the same time, Spain's power, prestige, and commercial importance in the sixteenth century meant that for a time Spanish became a common second language in elite circles in France, Italy, and the Low Countries.

In governmental structure, economic structure, legal forms, religious organization, intellectual orientation, and political relations, Spain fit firmly within the European context, and was heir to centuries of development, not only in Europe, but also in the Islamic world. Spain's late medieval economic development, combined with the political consolidation brought about by Ferdinand and Isabella, allowed Spain to act as the foundation for the empires of Charles I and Philip II, as Spain became the world's first superpower. Maintaining an empire was costly, as all emperors have known; by the seventeenth century, Spain was able to keep its American empire but in Europe had to adjust to the role of a second-rank power.

See also **Armada, Spanish; Madrid; Peasantry; Seville;** *and biographies of Charles V, Ferdinand of Aragon, Isabella of Castile, John of Austria, Antonio Pérez, Philip II, and Philip III.*

BIBLIOGRAPHY

Bilinkoff, Jodi. *The Avila of Saint Teresa: Religious Reform in a Sixteenth-Century City.* Ithaca, N.Y., 1989.

Braudel, Fernand. *The Mediterranean and the Mediterranean World in the Age of Philip II.* Translated by Sian Reynolds. 2 vols. London, 1972–1973.

Caraman, Philip. *Ignatius Loyola: A Biography of the Founder of the Jesuits.* San Francisco, 1990.

Chaunu, Pierre, and Huguette Chaunu. *Séville et l'Atlantique (1504–1650).* 11 vols. in 8. Paris, 1955–.

Contreras, Jaime, and Gustav Henningsen. "Forty-Four Thousand Cases of the Spanish Inquisition (1540–1700): Analysis of a Historical Data Bank." In *The Inquisition in Early Modern Europe: Studies on Sources and Methods.* Edited by Gustav Henningsen and John Tedeschi. De Kalb, Ill., 1986. Pages 100–129.

Edwards, John. *The Monarchies of Ferdinand and Isabella.* London, 1996.

Elliott, John Huxtable. *Imperial Spain, 1469–1716.* New York, 1963.

Flynn, Maureen. *Sacred Charity: Confraternities and Social Welfare in Spain, 1400–1700.* Ithaca, N.Y., 1989.

Griffin, Clive. *The Crombergers of Seville: The History of a Printing and Merchant Dynasty.* Oxford, 1988.

Hamilton, Earl J. *American Treasure and the Price Revolution in Spain, 1501–1650.* Cambridge, Mass., 1934.

Kagan, Richard L. *Lawsuits and Litigants in Castile, 1500–1700.* Chapel Hill, N.C., 1981.

Kagan, Richard L. *Lucrecia's Dreams: Politics and Prophecy in Sixteenth-Century Spain.* Berkeley, Calif., 1990.

Kagan, Richard L. *Students and Society in Early Modern Spain.* Baltimore, 1974.

Kamen, Henry. *Philip of Spain.* New Haven, Conn., 1997.

Kamen, Henry. *The Spanish Inquisition: An Historical Revision.* London, 1997.

Liss, Peggy K. *Isabel the Queen: Life and Times.* New York, 1992.

Lunenfeld, Marvin. *Keepers of the City: The Corregidores of Isabella I of Castile, 1474–1504.* Cambridge, U.K., and New York, 1987.

Lynch, John. *The Hispanic World in Crisis and Change, 1598–1700.* Rev. ed. of *Spain under the Habsburgs.* Vol. 2. 1969. Oxford, 1992.

Lynch, John. *Spain, 1516–1598: From National State to World Empire.* Rev. ed. of *Spain under the Habsburgs.* Vol. 1. 1964. Oxford, 1992.

MacKay, Angus. *Money, Prices, and Politics in Fifteenth-Century Castile.* London, 1981.

Martin, Colin, and Geoffrey Parker. *The Spanish Armada.* London and New York, 1988.

Meissner, William W. *Ignatius of Loyola: The Psychology of a Saint.* New Haven, Conn., 1992.

Meyerson, Mark D. *The Muslims of Valencia in the Age of Fernando and Isabel: Between Coexistence and Crusade.* Berkeley, Calif., 1991.

Monter, William E. *Frontiers of Heresy: The Spanish Inquisition from the Basque Lands to Sicily.* Cambridge, U.K., and New York, 1990.

Nader, Helen. *Liberty in Absolutist Spain: The Habsburg Sale of Towns, 1516–1700.* Baltimore, 1990.

Nader, Helen. *The Mendoza Family in the Spanish Renaissance, 1350 to 1550.* New Brunswick, N.J., 1979.

Nalle, Sara T. *God in La Mancha: Religious Reform and the People of Cuenca, 1500–1650.* Baltimore, 1992.

Parker, Geoffrey. *The Grand Strategy of Philip II.* New Haven, Conn., 1998.

Perez, Joseph. *La revolution des "Communidades" de Castille (1520–1521).* Bordeaux, France, 1970.

Perry, Mary Elizabeth. *Crime and Society in Early Modern Seville.* Hanover, N.H., 1980.

Perry, Mary Elizabeth. *Gender and Disorder in Early Modern Seville.* Princeton, N.J., 1990.

Phillips, Carla Rahn. *Ciudad Real, 1500–1750: Growth, Crisis, and Readjustment in the Spanish Economy.* Cambridge, Mass., 1979.

Phillips, Carla Rahn, and William D. Phillips Jr. *Spain's Golden Fleece: Wool Production and the Wool Trade from the Middle Ages to the Nineteenth Century.* Baltimore, 1997.

Phillips, William D., Jr. *Enrique IV and the Crisis of Fifteenth-Century Castile, 1425–1480.* Cambridge, Mass., 1978.

Phillips, William D., Jr., and Carla Rahn Phillips. *The Worlds of Christopher Columbus.* Cambridge, U.K., 1992.

Pike, Ruth. *Aristocrats and Traders: Sevillian Society in the Sixteenth Century.* Ithaca, N.Y., 1972.

Rodríguez Salgado, María José. *The Changing Face of Empire: Charles V, Philip II, and Habsburg Authority, 1551–1559.* Cambridge, U.K., and New York, 1998.

Vassberg, David E. *Land and Society in Golden-Age Castile.* Cambridge, U.K., and New York, 1984.

Vassberg, David E. *The Village and the Outside World in Golden Age Castile: Mobility and Migration in Everyday Life.* Cambridge, U.K., and New York, 1996.

WILLIAM D. PHILLIPS JR.

Art in Spain and Portugal

The Renaissance art of Spain and Portugal, inspired as elsewhere in Europe by Italian precedents, at the same time responded to the Iberian Peninsula's distinctive political, cultural, and physical conditions. This response differed from region to region, for although an imperial power and a large country, Spain was riven by profound differences in language, history, and artistic tradition. The continued independence of Portugal is only the most extreme example of this pervasive Iberian regionalism, for Castilian, Aragonese, Catalan, Basque, Andalusian, and Navarrese art show similar independence of style. Still, certain general trends emerged in peninsular art during the course of the fifteenth and sixteenth centuries.

General Trends. Shaped by the Moorish combination of stark planar surfaces and riotously elaborate ornamentation, fifteenth-century architecture in Spain and Portugal was at once more severe and more embellished than its Italian equivalent. This Moorish-inspired style, known as *mudejar,* was named for the medieval Muslim artisans who remained in Spain as it became Christianized. The gorgeous Alhambra palace in Granada (c. 1358) is perhaps the most famous example of *mudejar* architecture. At the same time, Spain's Christian rulers looked increasingly to Gothic style as a way of giving the arts in the realm a more European flavor, but theirs was always a Gothic with a distinctively *mudejar* flair, as flat expanses of wall and the intricate carving of ornament exploited the clear, bright quality of sunlight in an arid climate.

In part because of this Moorish-Gothic legacy, Iberian sculpture maintained a particularly close alliance with architecture, especially in elaborate tombs and the decorated altars known as retablos, discussed below. For its intricacy, this Iberian renaissance amalgamation of architecture and sculpture for building facades, cloisters, and retablos was known as *plateresco* (silversmith-like) style; its derivation from *mudejar* tradition is evident. In the Middle Ages, Spanish and Portuguese sculptors favored large, lifelike devotional images of Christ and the saints, sometimes dressed in real clothing; this tradition continued through the Renaissance period with some striking results.

Painting, especially once Spanish rule had been established over Burgundy in the fifteenth century, drew its chief inspiration from Northern, rather than Italian, sources. Oils were favored over tempera, linear grace over spatial clarity. Like contemporary Northern painting, it was also more apt to emphasize the violence and cruelty of biblical scenes or daily life than did contemporary Italian art. There were good reasons for this development in Iberia, for in 1492 Ferdinand and Isabella of Spain expelled the country's flourishing population of Jews, followed by the expulsion of Muslims from Granada in 1502. In 1497, Manuel of Portugal, eager to marry his son to a daughter of Spain's Most Catholic Majesties, drove the Jews from his country, many of them refugees from Spain. These expulsions and their attendant forced conversions caused permanent disruption to Iberian culture and clearly colored not only the graphic violence of the region's Renaissance paintings—lamentations over the dead Christ, autos-da-fé and bloody martyrdoms—but also, and notably, the psychologically penetrating painting of the seventeenth-century "Golden Age."

In the early to mid-sixteenth century, with the advent of international artistic entrepreneurs such as Raphael and Titian, the general circulation of critical literature on the arts both in Latin and various Romance vernaculars, and the return to Iberia of native artists with Italian experience, attention shifted to Italian style as the guiding force for the peninsula's aesthetic sensibilities. The development of a cosmopolitan, classical style received its greatest stimulus in Spain from the Habsburg monarchs Charles V (ruled 1519–1556) and Philip II (ruled 1556–1598), whose own national identities were fluid, whose political domains stretched from Austria to the New World, and whose sensitivity to art and its communicative power was acute. Charles was Holy Roman Emperor as well as lord over much of Italy; Philip added Portugal to his Spanish, Italian, Netherlandish, and American domains in 1580. Philip's Escorial united all the arts in an architectural complex where government and religion shared pride of place. His collection of paintings at the Alcázar in Madrid, now housed in the Museo del Prado, was one of the very finest in the world, with works by Northern masters (Rogier van der Weyden, Hieronymus Bosch) and Titian among his own favorites.

Portugal, meanwhile, at least until its annexation by Philip II in 1580, maintained a distinct artistic culture, stimulated above all by the long-lived, aggressive military figure King Manuel I (ruled 1495–1521) and his successor John III (ruled 1521–1557), both of whom looked emphatically to Italy for political support and cultural inspiration. Ironically, however, the "Manueline" style that typifies the arts during their reigns now seems more conspicuous for the retention of Gothic elements also recognized in contemporary plateresque design. The age of the Renaissance was also, of course, the age of Spanish and Portuguese exploration in Africa, India, East Asia, and the Americas, all places that produced their own distinctive syntheses of Renaissance and indigenous artistic style, ranging in size from the massive cathedrals of Mexico to the popular Afro-Portuguese carved elephant tusks known as oliphants.

Origins of Renaissance Style. Spain's first involvement with distinctively Renaissance culture dated from 1442, when King Alfonso of Aragon conquered the Kingdom of Naples and moved his royal court from Valencia to Italy. The painters, architects, sculptors, and illuminators sponsored by the Aragonese king and his descendants (1442–1504) reflected both Naples's tradition of involvement with the classical past and a strong link with Florence, the city that produced most of the kingdom's financiers. This classical, Tuscan-flavored taste in turn exerted its own influence on Aragon, a region positioned relatively near the east coast of Spain and thus in closer contact with Italy than much of the rest of the country. If Alfonso's court painter in Valencia had been the Flemish-inspired painter Luis Dalmau (c. 1405–1460), later Aragonese tastes ran to Italians like Paolo da San Leocadio (1447–c. 1520), who brought Emilian style to Valencia in 1473.

The first arguably Renaissance buildings appeared on the Iberian Peninsula in the late fifteenth century. The Colegio de Santa Cruz in Castilian Valladolid (1487–1491), features an austere facade whose elaborately articulated portal combines rusticated masonry, a semicircular arch, and, to each side, two orders of superimposed pilasters over Gothic tracery. The rusticated facade and arched portal of the Medinaceli Palace in Cogolludo (1492–1495) are clearly modeled on mid-fifteenth-century Florentine palazzi like the Medici, Strozzi, and Rucellai, but still more closely resemble buildings from the Aragonese-dominated Kingdom of Naples, like the Palazzo dell'Annunziata, Sulmona (early fifteenth century) or the rusticated Palazzo Penna in Naples itself (1404). It is typical of *plateresco* style for identifiably Renaissance arched portals to coexist with windows framed in Gothic tracery, or the arabesque attic parapet of the Palacio de Cogolludo. Courtyards and cloisters, meanwhile, may recall the proportions of Brunelleschi's Ospedale degli Innocenti though they use low-slung Catalan arches.

The plateresco facade of the University of Salamanca (1494) combines the intricate tracery, stemmata, pointed arches, and spires of Gothic architecture with classical motifs: the Serlian arch, *imagines clipeatae* (portraits enclosed within circular frames), and a fanciful type of Corinthian capital. The same eclectic combination is repeated in the same city on the facade of the Convent of San Esteban (Juan de Alava, c. 1524) and in another university building, the Escuelas Menores (1533).

Working under impetus from King Manuel I (ruled 1495–1521), the Portuguese architect Diogo Boytac (d. before 1528) ushered in the Renaissance style that would become known as "Manuelino" in projects like the Convento de Jesus in Setúbal south of Lisbon (1494–1498), the cloister and "Unfinished Chapels" (1509–1519) of the Gothic monastery of Batalha (begun 1388), and the Jerónimos Monastery in Belém, also near Lisbon (1502–1516). His most important successor was João de Castilho (c. 1475–1561), who took over Boytac's position as chief architect at Batalha (1517–1522) and worked for more than twenty years on the Convento de Jesus at Tomar (1521–1540s).

The Gothic tracery, spires, and elaborate carved decoration of Boytac's Manuelino style coexist with a clarity of compositional line and regularity of proportion that are undeniably Renaissance. Castilho's later work at Batalha reflects his familiarity with Italian architectural literature, particularly Cesare Cesariano's 1521 Italian vernacular translation of Vitruvius, which exerted notable influence in Iberia.

Portuguese Art. Altarpiece for the convent of São Vicente, Lisbon, by Nuno Gonçalves (fl. 1450–1472). MUSEO NACIONAL DE ARTE ANTIGUA, LISBON

Another distinctive aspect of Portuguese Renaissance architecture deserves mention: the ornamental majolica tiles known as azulejos, used to decorate facades as well as floors and fountains. Two spectacular sixteenth-century tiled buildings still survive; the Quinta de Bacalhoa at Azeitão (1565), and the church of São Roque, by Francisco de Matos (1584) at Coimbra.

The Iberian Renaissance made particular use of the alliance between architecture and sculpture, both in the ornamentation of architectural elements such as columns, doorjambs and window frames, and especially in that most distinctively peninsular feature of church architecture, the retablo or ornamental high altar, a huge construction that often included assemblages of paintings, sculpture, and architecture depicting up to sixty sacred scenes. Architects and sculptors often worked in conjunction, as did the Portuguese brothers João and Diogo de Castilho and the French sculptor Nicolas Chanterène, who executed a series of projects in Coimbra in the first quarter of the sixteenth century. A master like the Castilian sculptor Gil de Siloé (active in Spain 1486–1499) created tombs and retablos that were arguably works of architecture in their own right. A similar style of architectural sculpture, the vivid style known as Isabelline, is exemplified by the facade of the Colegio de San Gregorio in Valladolid or San Juan de los Reyes in Toledo, combining Italian-inspired grotesques with Gothic-style clusters of colonnettes and flat ogive arches, tectonic structure with sculptural ornament.

Medieval Iberian retablos, high altars that could extend all the way from floor to ceiling, had already become extraordinarily elaborate architectonic constructions, covered with intricate carving and loaded with paintings and statues. As peninsular tastes shifted from Gothic exuberance to the more linear orderliness of Renaissance classicism, individual elements of retablos, and then entire schemes of composition, began to follow a new set of guidelines. The most beautiful examples, both in Spain and Portugal, were perhaps those *plateresco* altars created at precisely the moment of transition from Gothic to classical: works like the high altar of the Cathedral at Toledo (1498), the Carthusian Monastery of Miraflores in Burgos (1496–1499), and the Sé Velha (Old Cathedral) in Coimbra (1498–1503). Yet with few exceptions, even the most classically restrained of retablos continued to provide a riot of decoration—thus the high altar of San Lorenzo in Juan de Herrera's severely proper design for the Escorial ranges brilliantly colorful paintings (by Italian artists) and gilded statues among the stately superimposed orders of its colored marble columns for an effect that is visually lively as well as conspicuously rich, and provides a marked contrast with the stark harmonies of the rest of Herrera's complex. Indeed, the ubiquity of the retablo as a place to display images of Christ, Mary, and the saints tempted painters like El Greco to try their hand at sculpture in the company of trained stonecarvers and metalsmiths.

Individual Artists.   For most of the Renaissance, Iberian painting was dominated by foreign masters—Flemings and Burgundians in the fifteenth century, Italians in the sixteenth. Bridging these two distinct traditions, the Northern and the Italian, we find figures like the Spaniard Pedro Berruguete (c. 1450–c. 1504) who worked in Italy from about 1475 to 1482 for Federico da Montefeltro, duke of Urbino.

Federico was himself a collector and connoisseur of Northern oils, but he also sponsored artists of the Italian avant-garde like Piero della Francesca. In the Montefeltro court Berruguete learned to create his own distinctive and successful union of Italian spatial clarity with Burgundian precision. Pedro Berruguete's return to his native land (by 1483) and his subsequent work in Ávila and Toledo marked an important point in the transformation of Spanish Renaissance taste from a distinctive eclecticism to a truly cosmopolitan synthesis.

In sculpture the same transformation was effected a few years later by the returning expatriates Bartolomé Ordoñez (d. 1520) and Diego de Siloé (c. 1495–1563), who first collaborated in Naples (then ruled by a Spanish viceroy) on the elaborate Caracciolo di Vico Chapel for the Augustinian church of San Giovanni a Carbonara (1516) and then brought their innovative style back to Spain, where Ordoñez executed the spectacular tombs of the Capilla Real, the Royal Chapel in the Cathedral of Granada (1517–1520). His monuments for Ferdinand and Isabella, Philip the Fair (1478–1506; Philip I of Spain) and Juana the Mad (1479–1555; Joan I of Spain) reflect the influence of Michelangelo in their dramatic freestanding figures. Diego de Siloé and Juan de Juni (c. 1507–1577) continued this same Italianate mode well into the century. Alonso Berruguete (1488–1561), son of Pedro, worked both as a painter and a sculptor in the *maniera* of the sixteenth-century Italian avant-garde, a legacy of his long visit to Italy from about 1504 to 1518, where he made the acquaintance of Michelangelo and Giorgio Vasari and absorbed the principles of their style.

The invention of printing ensured that Renaissance writing on art circulated as quickly as actual artistic creations; in Spain the works of Leon Battista Alberti and printed editions of Vitruvius would prove particularly influential. The Portuguese artist Francisco de Hollanda (c. 1517–1584), who had befriended Michelangelo on a journey to Rome between 1538 and 1542, recalled their conversations in his influential *Quatro dialogos da pitura antiga,* composed in Lisbon in 1548–1549. De Hollanda's sketchbook of Roman antiquities, with its brilliantly colored drawings of the vaults of Nero's Domus Aurea provide a valuable archaeological record and represent virtually all that is known of de Hollanda's artistic output.

Charles V and Philip II.   The most systematic efforts at fostering Renaissance art in Iberia were made by a father and son who were the two most powerful sovereigns to have control of Spain during the sixteenth century. The brilliant Habsburg strategist Charles V (ruled 1516–1555; Holy Roman Emperor 1519) established a residence at the Alhambra in Granada, keeping the *mudejar* building and adding a structure designed by the Italian-trained Pedro Machuca (c. 1495–1550). Conceived after 1526, begun in 1533, still unfinished in 1550, the building's ultimate inspiration was the architecture of ancient Rome. Its distinctive circular courtyard may have been based on a passage from Pliny the Younger or on Vitruvius; the combination of Tuscan pilasters and rusticated details evoked the powerful structures and triumphant Christian symbolism of Bramante's work in early-sixteenth-century papal Rome.

When Charles abdicated and retired to the monastery of Yuste in the last year of his life (1556), he split his own vast domains between his relatives, granting the lands and title of Holy Roman Emperor to his brother and Spain to his son Philip, who reigned (1556–1598) as Philip II.

An avid collector of paintings, Philip II was particularly enamored of Titian, some of whose most voluptuous nudes covered the walls of the royal study in the Alcázar at Madrid, the remodeled Moorish castle that served the king as his chief residence. His library also acted as a repository for writings on art and for sketchbooks, notably the early sixteenth-century Italian sketchbook now known as the *Codex Escurialensis*. A fire destroyed the Alcázar in 1734, making a full assessment of Philip's patronage impossible. However, the enormous monastic complex he erected beginning in the early 1560s at El Escorial, a village some 43 kilometers north of Madrid, survives, its splendor nearly intact. The architectural commission of El Escorial was largely accomplished by the Spaniard Juan de Herrera (1530–1597), who executed the massive monastery, church, and palace complex in a stark sweep of golden limestone, picked out with Doric details and roofed in gray slate. Despite its warm color, the Escorial makes a forbidding statement of Philip's power and the power of the Catholic church he worked so hard to support against the challenges of the Protestant Reformation. The same sense of stern, austere power characterizes the dynastic monuments to Philip and his father, Charles, executed for the Capilla Mayor of the Escorial by the Italian sculptor Pompeo Leoni (1591–1598). Huge kneeling marble figures of Charles and his family, larger than life, face the tomb of Philip II, who kneels accompanied by his three wives (all of whom died young, of natural causes), and his son Don Carlos.

To paint the Escorial's far-flung interiors, Philip invited a team of Italians versed in the latest style to enchant the tastemakers in Florence and Rome—a style its practitioners called the *maniera*. The painters included Luca Cambiaso (1527–1585), Pellegrino Tibaldi, and Federico Zuccari (c. 1540–1609); and their Spanish collaborator, Juan Fernandez de Navarrete (1526–1579), was also called "El Mudo"—the mute. The Italians' lively, acrobatic style and lush colors contrast remarkably with the stiffly formal portraiture produced at the same time by the Flemish-trained court painter Alonso Sánchez Coello (c. 1531–1588).

El Greco. The stimulus provided by Philip's taste, his spectacular personal collections, and the tastes of his court ensured that painting in Spain would never be the same. Nonetheless, one of the most influential Spanish painters of all time was not one of Philip's favorites. Doménikos Theotokópoulos (1541–1614) was a Greek from Crete who trained as an icon painter in the marvelous, entirely distinctive, Western-influenced Cretan style (the island had been a Venetian colony since 1206). In 1568 the ambitious painter moved to Venice, where the impact of artists like Titian and especially Tintoretto caused first a convulsion and then a revolution in his painterly style. By 1570 "the Greek" had transformed himself from a Late Byzantine master working in miniature in tempera to a virtuoso worker of oil on canvas.

After journeying to Rome in 1570 to study the ancients and moderns (and apparently hoping to make a career), he then moved on to Toledo in 1577, where, as "El Greco," he settled for good. A single painting executed for the Escorial, an altarpiece showing *The Martyrdom of St. Maurice and the Theban Legion* (1580–1582), failed to win Philip's enthusiasm; designed to form part of the Escorial's great retable, it was relegated instead to the monastery. However, thwarted in his aspirations at court, El Greco quickly found patrons among the leading citizens of Toledo; perhaps his most famous painting, the monumental *Burial of the Count of Orgaz*, executed for the Toledan church of Santo Tomé in 1586–1588, included portraits of many of them [see the color plates in volume 1].

BIBLIOGRAPHY

Bedini, Silvio. *The Pope's Elephant.* London, 1997. On Manuel I.
Brown, Jonathan. *The Golden Age of Painting in Spain.* New Haven, Conn., 1990.
Elliott, John Huxtable. *Imperial Spain, 1469–1716.* London, 1963.
Moffitt, John F. *The Arts in Spain.* London and New York, 1999.

Rosenthal, Earl. *The Palace of Charles V in Granada.* Princeton, N.J., 1985.

Tomlinson, Janis. *Painting in Spain: El Greco to Goya, 1561–1828.* London, 1997.

INGRID D. ROWLAND

SPANISH LITERATURE AND LANGUAGE.

The definition of the Renaissance as a movement and a period in Spanish cultural history raises several questions. If the Renaissance is viewed primarily as the international development of Neo-Latin humanism, Spanish contributions do not compare with those of Italian humanists, which were of primary importance. However, Antonio de Nebrija (1442–1522), who had studied in Italy and was the first major Spanish humanist, established the study of classical Latin in Spain with his *Introductiones latinae* (Introductions to Latin; Salamanca, 1481), a textbook based on ancient texts and grammarians; Queen Isabella of Castile (1451–1504) encouraged him to translate this work into Spanish so as to make it more widely accessible. By the beginning of the sixteenth century there were several groups of humanists writing Neo-Latin poetry in Spain. Hispano-Latin humanism was institutionalized in 1506 with the establishment of the new University of Alcalá, near Madrid; its founder, Cardinal Francisco Jiménez de Cisneros (1436–1517), organized a team of specialists in Latin, Greek, Hebrew, and Aramaic to publish the *Biblia polyglotta complutense* (Complutensian Polyglot Bible), Spain's major contribution in the scholarly editing of ancient texts.

But it is possible to see the Spanish Renaissance as primarily the establishment in the vernacular, rather than in Latin, of Italian and Erasmian humanism at the end of the fifteenth and during the first half of the sixteenth century. Despite the Spanish Inquisition (founded in the 1470s), inner spiritual reform, especially among converts from Judaism and their descendants, reinforced innovative tendencies at times akin to those of the Renaissance elsewhere. From about 1550, and especially after the Council of Trent (1545–1563), vernacular humanism in Spain was submitted to many ideological restrictions, but it continued to have profound repercussions as late as the baroque literature of the seventeenth century. Traditionally, the so-called golden age of Spanish literature has been divided into two periods: the sixteenth-century Renaissance, during the reigns of Charles I (king of Spain 1516–1556; as Charles V, Holy Roman Emperor 1517–1556) and Philip II (ruled 1556–1598); and the baroque period that had begun by 1613, when Luis de Góngora (1561–1627)

began to circulate his major innovative poems at court. By then the classical Renaissance period of Spanish literature had ended in an explosion of baroque exuberance.

The Castilian (or Spanish) Language and Culture.

Over a period of five centuries, as soldiers from Castile slowly liberated the peninsula from Islamic rule and resettled Mozarabic-speaking territory with landowners and peasants from the north, the Latin-derived dialects of most other Iberian regions, such as Leonese, Aragonese, and Mozarabic, were gradually absorbed by the Castilian dialect; only Catalan in the east and Portuguese in the west survived as independent literary languages. (Basque is not a Latin-derived or literary written language.) Castilian first became standardized as the Spanish language during the reign of Alfonso X (the Wise; ruled 1252–1284). As king of Castile and León, he supervised prose translations from Arabic and Latin into Spanish, and Spanish, not Latin, was the language of his chancery. Although the Aragonese occupied Sicily and Naples, Italy's Renaissance culture had little influence on the language of Spain until the fifteenth century, when borrowings from Italian and classical Latin became increasingly numerous in central Spain, replacing many (but by no means all) Arabic loan-words. Latin classics began to be translated into Spanish, and a highly Latinate poetic style was developed in Spanish by the pre-Renaissance writer Juan de Mena (1411–1456). The first non-Italian sonnets, a substantial collection, were written in Spanish by the Marquis of Santillana (1398–1458) around 1450, but they were not widely circulated. It is convenient to use the year 1492 to mark Spain's cultural coming of age: in that year the last Moorish kingdom, Granada, was taken; Spanish ships commanded by Columbus reached the New World; all unconverted Jews were expelled, as they had been previously from some areas in northern Europe; and Nebrija published the first grammar of a modern European language, declaring Castilian Spanish to be the language of empire.

During the sixteenth century the phonetic and phonological traits of modern Spanish became established, with the following sounds being lost or modified in the spoken language: the aspirated *h-*, from Latin *f-*, was lost in all but a few exceptional cases; the distinction between *b* and *v* disappeared; and three pairs of voiceless and voiced sibilants (written as *ss/s*, *ç/z*, *x/j*, and pronounced like *ss* in the English word "moss" or *s* in "rose"; "ts" or "dz"; and "sh" or "zh", or *z* in "azure") lost their voiced elements, with readjustments in their points of articulation, becoming respectively *sh* of "cash" (written *s*), *th* of English "thin" (written *z*), and *kh* (written *j*). Then, in the south of Spain and the Spanish colonies in America, a further distinction was lost: the sounds written as *z* and *s* merged into a single sibilant similar to the English *s*.

Renaissance developments in vocabulary and syntax cannot be separated from the development of new written or literary styles. In the 1530s the Erasmian religious reformer Juan de Valdés (1490?–1541) wrote in Naples *Diálogo de la lengua* (Dialogue on language), a brilliant and elegant discussion of matters of Spanish style in the form of a dialogue with a group of Italian friends; unfortunately, this work was not generally available until its publication in 1737. The classical vocabulary of Renaissance Spanish was ably defined, etymologically analyzed, and codified in a dictionary entitled *Tesoro de la lengua castellana o española* (Treasury of the Castilian or Spanish language; 1611) by Sebastián de Covarrubias y Orozco (1539–1613). Noteworthy grammars and dictionaries for Amerindian languages were written by Spanish missionaries, especially in Mexico; they give evidence of considerable linguistic sophistication in Spain and the Spanish colonies.

Spanish Renaissance Poetry.
Medieval popular songs had been composed in short lines, customarily of about eight syllables. Courtly love poetry, first written in Spanish in the fifteenth century, had similar metrics. Juan de Mena's learned poetry was written in longer lines with a dactylic rhythm, and the Marquis de Santillana, in his sonnets, came close to the standard Italian meter; but his pieces were little read and were not imitated. New Renaissance genres of Spanish poetry with a fully Italianate meter, style, and ideology were at last introduced as a result of the wedding in Granada in 1526 of the emperor Charles V (Carlos I of Spain) and the Portuguese infanta Isabel, which was attended by an international roster of guests. Discussions among Italian and Spanish humanists at this wedding led two courtier soldiers, Juan Boscán (c. 1490–1542) and Garcilaso de la Vega (1501–1536), to experiment with writing, first, Petrarchan sonnets and *canzoni,* and eventually Horatian epistles, satires, an ode, funereal and Ovidian elegies, mythological poetry, and pastoral eclogues in more or less dramatic form. Their surviving poems were published posthumously in 1543 in a single volume. The publication of this volume, with a prologue by Boscán that is a manifesto for the new Italianate and Latinate po-

Spanish Literature. Title page of the works of Juan Boscán and some by Garcilaso de la Vega printed at Barcelona in 1543. The page carries the arms of the emperor Charles V with his impressa (badge): two pillars (representing the Pillars of Hercules) and the motto "Plus ultra." GENERAL RESEARCH DIVISION, THE NEW YORK PUBLIC LIBRARY, ASTOR, LENOX AND TILDEN FOUNDATIONS

etry, marks the Renaissance revolution in Spanish poetry. It was frequently reprinted and imitated and its styles became dominant during the second half of the sixteenth century.

The basic Italianate metrical form used in Spanish, known as the hendecasyllabic (eleven-syllable) line, is similar in length, stress pattern, and rhythm to English iambic pentameter; while it may occasionally end on the tenth syllable, which is always stressed, it is almost always an eleven-syllable line ending with a feminine rhyme. The Spanish sonnet uses the hendecasyllabic line and follows the standard Italian pattern of rhymes and syntactic divisions: an octet or pair of quatrains (rhyming *abbaabba*) and a sestet or pair of tercets (with two or three differing sets of rhyme words, but never ending with a couplet, as in the Shakespearean sonnet form). In the *canzone* stanza, the hendecasyllabic line is accompanied by a varying number of heptasyllabic (seven-syllable) lines. Other hendecasyllabic stanzas that became established in Spanish were the *ottava rima* (rhyming *abababcc*), used primarily for long narratives; and the *terza rima* (interlocking tercets rhyming *aba, bcb, cdc,* and so on), used for epistles, satires, and elegies. Blank verse was used by Boscán for a long narrative poem based on the classical story of Hero and Leander and by Garcilaso for his informal Horatian epistle, but it was seldom used thereafter.

Garcilaso left only a relatively small body of poetry, but it was aesthetically captivating and was soon recognized as the highest standard for later sixteenth-century poetry in Spain. Most of it was written in Naples under the influence of local humanists and vernacular poets, especially Jacopo Sannazaro (c. 1458–1530) and Bernardo Tasso (1493–1569), but Garcilaso's memorable sonnets and *canzoni* do not form a coherent love story in the Petrarchan manner. In fact, his sonnets include an epitaph, classical epigrams, and mythological vignettes having little or nothing to do with love. His only ode, written in a five-line *canzone* stanza form known as the *lira* (which was invented by Bernardo Tasso and imitates Horace's short stanzas), bears the Latin title *Ode ad florem Gnidi* (Ode to the flower of Knidos) and is a mosaic of Horatian echoes. In it he begs a Neapolitan lady to have mercy on his friend who is dying of love for her; she is warned that if she does not she may undergo an Ovidian metamorphosis into stone. Three of his poems are in epistolary form: a funeral elegy addressed to the famous third duke of Alva (1507–1582), in which the poet offers him consolation for the premature death of his brother; a romantic elegy addressed to Boscán deploring the military campaign in Africa that has separated him from a lady love in Naples, provoking his jealous suspicions; and a typically colloquial Horatian epistle on the theme of friendship, also addressed to his friend Boscán.

Garcilaso's three eclogues are all pastoral poems about love. The first is the most purely Virgilian: two shepherds lament the loss of their loves, one because of his lady's infidelity and the other because of his beloved's death. The second eclogue is a long drama in varied meters with no narrative frame, in which the madness of courtly love is contrasted with the sanity of matrimony. In the third eclogue— which tells of four nymphs who come out of the Tagus River near Toledo to embroider on their tapestries ancient and modern mythological stories of violently lost lovers—the influence of Sannazaro is particularly obvious. Between 1570 and 1580 this brief corpus was edited and annotated as a classic by two scholars working competitively, one at the University of Salamanca in the north and the other in Seville in the south. Garcilaso's poetry was thus definitively canonized as Spain's Renaissance model.

At the University of Salamanca, Luis de León (1527–1591), an Augustinian friar and university professor, became the leader of a group of humanistic translators and poets. He was the descendant of converts from Judaism and a specialist in the Hebrew Bible, facts that contributed to prolonged imprisonment and a trial by the Inquisition; he was, however, eventually acquitted. The brief corpus of his own poetry consists almost entirely of Horatian odes, modeled on Garcilaso's single ode and written in the five-line *lira* stanza. Fray Luis's odes are Horatian, Platonic, and Christian in theme with no traces of courtly or Petrarchan love. In some he describes his idyllic life in the country, far from courtly politics and maritime commerce; in his imagination he rises through the musical spheres to a world of transcendental peace. He even touches quite obviously upon the injustices he has suffered at the hands of his enemies in the Inquisition. These poems, written between 1570 and 1580, were not published until 1631; but meanwhile they circulated widely in manuscript and established the author as second only to Garcilaso as the leading classical poet of the Spanish Renaissance.

A competing figure in Seville was Fernando de Herrera (c. 1534–1597), who edited one of the two scholarly editions of Garcilaso published in 1580; its lengthy and often pedantic annotations not only comment on classical sources, rhetorical figures, and parallels in other Spanish poetry but also contain a number of substantial essays drawing on Italian literary theory. He wrote, and published in 1582, an original Petrarchan *canzoniere* of his own, a carefully planned sequence of sonnets, *canzoni* (two of which are Pindaric odes on military victory and defeat), and elegies. A much more extensive collection of his poetry was published posthumously. He also invented a rationalized orthographic system (which no one adopted).

In addition to lyric poetry, more than fifty long epic poems in Spanish were published in the sixteenth century; the primary model for style and narrative organization was Virgil's *Aeneid* and its Italian imitations, in which *ottava rima* was almost invariably the stanza used. The masterpiece of this genre in Spain was *La Araucana* by Alonso de Ercilla y Zúñiga (1533–1594), published in three parts (1569, 1578, 1589). It tells the story of the conquest of Chile—in which the poet himself had participated (as a soldier)—in classical epic style, portraying the Araucana Indians who fought the Spanish as heroic noble savages. Some of the best Spanish epic poems were religious in subject matter, though none of these approaches the grandeur of Milton's *Paradise Lost* (1667, 1674).

Drama. The only Renaissance drama written in Spanish that is of substantial literary quality is Fernando de Rojas's *Celestina* (1499), which, not having been written for the stage, lends itself to being read as a prose novel in dialogue form (see below). Despite humanistic experiments, the theater as such was only beginning to develop toward the end of the sixteenth century; it now seems a mere prologue to the great popular, polymetric verse theater of Spain, established in the seventeenth century under the leadership of the poet Lope de Vega (1562–1635).

Prose. By the end of the fifteenth century Spanish literary prose style had developed a high level of Ciceronian elegance; one example is the sentimental, or courtly love, novel *La cárcel de amor* (Love's prison; 1492) by Diego de San Pedro (c. 1437–c. 1498). A completely different category, that of the popular spoken language, is brilliantly manipulated by Fernando de Rojas (c. 1465–1541) in the dialogues among masters and servants in his humanistic story in dramatic form *La comedia de Calixto y Melibea,* more popularly known as *La Celestina.* This work obviously draws on classical Roman comedy, but ends in the grimmest tragedy: the old bawd Celestina is murdered, the young lover Calixto accidentally falls to his death, and the seduced girl hurls herself from a tower in the presence of her father. No other work in Spanish classical literature resounds with the deeply pessimistic overtones of this dramatic, but unstageable, masterpiece.

The historians of Spain's conquests in the New World drew on a variety of traditions, from medieval chronicles to Italian, Roman, and Greek historians. More like a typical Renaissance writer is Antonio de Guevara (1480/81–1545), the author of a broad range of prose works, some of which were widely read in other European languages. His *Reloj de príncipes, o Libro aureo del emperador Marco Aurelio* (Dial of princes; or, Golden book of the emperor Marcus Aurelius; 1529) is composed of fictional letters by the Roman emperor, mixed with fables and other lore. His *Menosprecio de corte y alabanza de aldea* (The court despised and the village praised; 1539) is a compilation of Horatian commonplaces on city versus country life, composed in harmoniously balanced antithetic phraseology. Guevara's most creative work is his collection of *Epístolas familiares* (Familiar epistles; 1539–1542), a vast miscellany of epistolary fiction loaded with antiquarian erudition (both authentic and invented) intermixed with courtly and moral advice, sermons, short novels, and other prose forms.

A more modern, scientific attitude is reflected in the *Examen de ingenios* (Psychological investigations; 1575) by Juan Huarte de San Juan (c. 1530–c. 1588/90), a physician who drew on a wide range of established sources, from the Bible to Galen to Aquinas. Besides highly original treatises on physiology, the humors, and psychology, he has much that is new to say about human mental faculties and the education of children. Although some passages were censored in Spain, the *Examen* remained popular there and was translated and widely read throughout Europe.

Spiritual Writings. Two factors were especially important in the renewal of inner religious life in Spain: the "new Christians"—the many well-educated converts from Judaism and their descendants—tended to be more fervent in their devotion to Christ than were the old Christians; while often unjustly persecuted as Judaizers by the Spanish Inquisition (which was established to police the sincerity of their conversions), they promoted the reform of a stagnant Spanish church. This reforming impulse was reinforced by a second factor, the translation and publication in Spain of Erasmus's works. (Indeed, the best general overview of Spanish spiritual life in the sixteenth century is the French scholar Marcel Bataillon's 1937 study of the influence of Erasmus in Spain.) The influence of Luther and Calvin, on the other hand, encouraged only insignificant underground movements in Spain, and the isolated local heretical movements were quickly stamped out by the Inquisition.

The most significant and successful reformer and writer of spiritual literature was Teresa of Ávila (1515–1582), whose grandfather had been disciplined by the Inquisition as a lapsed convert. She set about reforming the Carmelite order to which she belonged, attacking the mechanical observance of external forms and promoting the renewal of inner religious life. Her autobiographical *Libro de la vida* (Book of her life; 1611), written between 1562 and 1565, follows the tradition of St. Augustine's *Confessions* and recounts her own spiritual journey from asceticism to the achievement of mystical union with God. Her *Camino de perfección* (Way of perfection;

1583), written between 1565 and 1570, leads up to her most systematic treatise on the varieties of religious experience, *Castillo interior* (Interior castle; 1588), written in 1577. Lacking the formal literary discipline that came from knowing Latin, Teresa wrote in a highly personal way that has been characterized by modern critics as an apparently submissive, yet insistently effective, feminine rhetoric. She won the support of Philip II and other aristocratic patrons for the founding of reformed Carmelite convents and was canonized in 1622.

Theologically more sophisticated, and a supreme mystical poet, was Juan de Yepes (1542–1591), later known as San Juan de la Cruz (St. John of the Cross) and canonized in 1726. He devoted himself wholeheartedly to Teresa's Carmelite reform movement. Using the *lira* stanza of Luis de León's odes, his rewriting of the Song of Solomon merges erotic imagery with the most intense religious experience as he attempts to express the ineffable; he later rationalized theologically some of his very few poems in detailed and subtle prose commentaries.

Quite different in character is the poet Luis de León's major prose work, *De los nombres de Cristo* (The names of Christ). Begun in 1573 while he was in prison, published first in two parts (1583) and later completed in three (1585–1587), this is not a mystical work, but one designed to teach the Bible at an elevated level in a country where the Bible was accessible only in Latin to just a minority of potential readers. Written in the form of a Renaissance dialogue and using as headings the various names by which Christ was mentioned in the Bible, it brought to the devout Spanish reader a scholarly and analytical summary of evangelical aspects of the Old and New Testaments.

In Spain, as in the rest of Europe, the sermon, like the theater, was a major oral bridge between the high culture of those who read and wrote Latin and the vernacular and the popular culture of the illiterate majority. At Latin mass on Sundays, and especially during the seasons of Advent and Lent, the Spanish public listened to lengthy orations on moral, theological, and political themes, drawn from many different sources: the Bible, Greek and Latin church fathers, humanistic texts, traditional tales or *exempla*, medieval bestiaries, and emblem books. Rhetorical handbooks on the art of teaching were available in Latin and in Spanish; the style of preaching varied among the different religious orders. A few of the many oral sermons delivered were made available, in manuscript or in print, for study by the literate. The most famous Spanish preacher of the period was the Trinitarian friar Hortensio Félix Paravicino (1580–1633).

Narrative Fiction. With hindsight, sixteenth-century Spanish fiction appears as a series of meandering steps toward the works of Miguel de Cervantes (1547–1616). Romances of chivalry called *libros de caballerías* (books about knights) were immensely popular, combining imaginary tales of knightly prowess with scenes of courtly love; in the first and most famous one—the so-called Montalvo version of *Amadís de Gaula* (1508)—such love leads to marriage. This prototypical romance was followed by many others published in the first half of the century; their titles are based on the fantastic names of heroes such as Esplandián, Florisando, Palmerín, and Primaleón. Some of these knights were models of Christian virtue (in addition to killing pagans), but preachers denounced the love scenes, which seemed to appeal primarily to a feminine readership. By the end of the century the vogue for chivalric romances was declining rapidly.

A more typical Renaissance genre of fiction, the pastoral romance, began with a "book about shepherds" entitled *Diana* (1559), written in Spanish by the Portuguese-born Jorge de Montemayor (c. 1520–1561); its closest antecedent is the relatively static Italian *Arcadia* by Sannazaro. Into his groups of shepherds and shepherdesses (or nymphs) who wander through an idyllic landscape, Montemayor introduces discussions of complex Platonic love theory, and love stories that progress toward resolution. The vogue for *Diana* and pastoral romances overlapped with that of the chivalric romance, but the pastoral appealed to a more sophisticated literary readership interested in Renaissance theories of love. Important sequels or imitations of Montemayor include *La Diana enamorada* (1564) by Gaspar Gil Polo (d. 1585) and *La Galatea* (1585) by Cervantes. In these pastoral novels, women's points of view are emphatically expressed by the female characters in dialogues interspersed with songs or lyrical poems expressing the characters' happy and unhappy loves.

Worthy of brief mention here is the Moorish novel, in which the relations among Christian and Islamic knights and ladies were presented in highly idealized form. This genre culminated in what has been called a historical novel published in two parts (1595 and 1619): *Las guerras civiles de Granada* (The civil wars of Granada) by Ginés Pérez de Hita (c. 1544–c. 1619). (This work eventually became the principal source of Washington Irving's *The Alhambra;* 1832).

However, in Spain the more realistic tradition of the novel, as opposed to the romance, has its roots in a brief bit of narrative fiction by an unknown author entitled *La vida de Lazarillo de Tormes* (The life of Lazarillo de Tormes; 1554), which is usually called a picaresque novel. It purports to be the autobiography of a *pícaro,* or rascal, the child of a miller and his wife. His poor mother, soon widowed, gives him to a crafty blind man to be his guide; Lazarillo eventually leaves the blind man, who has abused him, and lives for a while with a parish priest whose stinginess makes him suffer from hunger, a major motif of the novel. Escaping from the priest, the boy goes to Toledo, where a pseudo-aristocratic squire promises to feed him well; but the boy is soon begging in the streets to feed his starving master. Finally, after serving other masters, Lazarillo (now more appropriately called Lázaro) decides to fend for himself and becomes a town crier, monopolizing a few petty commercial operations, including the sale of wine; his new superior is a wealthy archpriest whose mistress he is induced to marry. This narrative is written in the form of a letter addressed to some great man to explain how Lázaro has come to occupy the shameful position of priest's cuckold in exchange for the financial security of being the official town crier. The narrator's control of point of view is amazingly sophisticated; the anonymous author was obviously a humanist, perhaps Erasmian, who used traditional folktales to satirize some of the social problems of early modern Spain.

But the picaresque novel could not be viewed as a special literary genre until the publication (between 1599 and 1602) of the lengthy *Guzmán de Alfarache* by Mateo Alemán (1547–1614). In this work the picaresque narrator tells his story from the vantage point of one who has undergone a moral and religious conversion: after each episode he gives the reader the benefit of the lessons in virtue that he has learned. The publication of the Alemán novel seems to have led to the reprinting of *Lazarillo* and to have stimulated Cervantes's novelistic imagination while he was writing the first part of *Don Quixote.*

Cervantes and the Modern Novel. Miguel de Cervantes as a young man had learned some Latin literature from the Erasmian humanist Juan López de Hoyos at the municipal grammar school of Madrid, where he published his first poetry, strongly influenced by the Renaissance style of Garcilaso de la Vega. His later sojourn in Italy added substantially to

Spanish Author. Engraving of Alonso de Ercilla y Zuñiga (1533–1594) by Juan Moxeno Fejada.

his literary education in Italian poetry, especially that of Ludovico Ariosto. After being ransomed from prison in North Africa in 1580, he attempted in vain to live as a writer in Madrid; his plays were not staged, and his only publication was his pastoral novel *La Galatea* (1585), displaying a wide range of love poetry, in different genres, as well as a growing skill in the art of narration.

Between 1587 and 1600 Cervantes had a difficult life as a government employee in southern Spain but wrote two masterful burlesque sonnets making fun of his country's military pretensions. About 1600 he began the second and mature stage of his career as a writer. Part 1 of *Don Quixote,* published in 1605, met with immediate success and was translated into

English by Thomas Shelton (1612). Encouraged by his national and international success, Cervantes began writing very productively; he published his *Novelas ejemplares* (Exemplary novellas) in 1613, his burlesque *Viaje del Parnaso* (Voyage to Parnassus) in 1614, and both *Ocho comedias y ocho entremeses* (Eight plays and eight interludes) and part 2 of *Don Quixote* in 1615. He died in 1616; his last novel, *Persiles y Sigismunda,* was published posthumously in 1617.

Don Quixote has been widely acclaimed as the world's first modern novel; it has been more acutely read and appreciated abroad than in Spain, where its status as the major national classic, the model of prose style, was finally canonized in the nineteenth century. It tells the story of its title character, an old and impoverished member of the minor nobility, a man who has sold land to buy books and has gone mad from reading the endless romances of chivalry; in his madness, he decides to arm himself and set out as a modern knight to right the wrongs of the world, recruiting as his squire a local peasant called Sancho Panza. Don Quixote is highly literate and his models are always literary, ranging from Amadís to the heroes of ballads; Sancho, who is illiterate but shrewdly intelligent, is a gold mine of popular culture and thus provides an ever-changing counterpoint to his master. The endless exchanges between the two, and their violent encounters with contempory reality, provide an inexhaustible source of humor, both slapstick and subtle.

A new level of complexity is reached in part 2, in which the protagonists meet new characters who have read about them in part 1, just as we have—without being in it. The parody of earlier literature and having readers both inside the book and (ourselves) outside of it make part 2 of *Don Quixote* primarily a book about books, anticipating twentieth-century metafiction. During the nineteenth-century romantic period, some European readers came to see the ridiculous protagonist as an admirable hero, and this reading has come to be a dominant trend in modern Cervantes criticism, both in Spain and abroad.

Second in international importance only to *Don Quixote,* Cervantes's *Novelas ejemplares* is an innovative collection of deliberately varied experimental fiction. Although often reflecting the plots and characters of Italian novellas as well as traditional romance motifs, some of these short novels draw also on Spain's native picaresque tradition and range from vulgar realism to fantasies presented from various points of view. Cervantes's full-length plays are less original than his brief interludes, which are farces using stock comic characters.

Among modern critics, the romantic reading of *Don Quixote* was taken to its ultimate conclusions by the Spanish writer Miguel de Unamuno in his *Vida de don Quijote y Sancho* (The life of Don Quixote and Sancho; 1905). The Spanish philosopher José Ortega y Gasset in his *Meditaciones del Quijote* (Meditations on Quixote; 1914) used *Don Quixote* as a point of departure to make some recent phenomenological concepts accessible to a cultured readership. Cervantes was first studied as the typical Renaissance intellectual by Américo Castro in his landmark study *El pensamiento de Cervantes* (Cervantes's thought; 1925), which characterized Cervantes and his *Don Quixote* as the most advanced intellectual, literary, and linguistic product of the Renaissance in Spain.

See also **Chivalry,** *subentry on* **Romance of Chivalry; Complutensian Polyglot Bible; Conversos; Inquisition,** *subentry on* **Spanish Inquisition; Italian Language and Literature; Novella; Pastoral,** *subentry on* **Pastoral on the Continent; Picaresque Novel; Poetics,** *subentry* **Survey; Spirituality, Female;** *and biographies of figures mentioned in this entry.*

BIBLIOGRAPHY

Primary Works

Cervantes Saavedra, Miguel de. *The Ingenious Gentleman Don Quixote de la Mancha.* Translated by Samuel Putnam. New York, 1958.

Rivers, Elias L., ed. and trans. *Renaissance and Baroque Poetry of Spain with English Prose Translations.* Prospect Heights, Ill., 1988.

Rojas, Fernando de. *La Celestina: The Spanish Bawd.* Translated by J. M. Cohen. New York, 1964, 1966. Translation of *La comedia de Calixto y Melibea* (1499).

Teresa of Ávila. *The Life of St. Teresa of Avila, by Herself.* Translated by J. M. Cohen. Harmondsworth, U.K., 1957. Translation of *Libro de la vida* (1562–1565).

Two Spanish Picaresque Novels. Translated by M. Alpert. Harmondsworth, U.K., 1969.

Secondary Works

Bataillon, Marcel. *Erasme et l'Espagne.* Edited by Charles Amiel. New ed. 3 vols. Geneva, 1991.

Beardsley, Theodore S., Jr. *Hispano-Classical Translations Printed between 1482 and 1699.* Pittsburgh, Pa. 1970.

Close, Anthony J. *Miguel de Cervantes, Don Quixote.* Cambridge, U.K., 1990.

Gilman, Stephen. *The Art of "La Celestina."* Westport, Conn., 1976.

Lapesa, Rafael. *Historia de la lengua española.* Madrid, 1988. The best general history of the Spanish language.

López Estrada, Francisco. *Siglos de Oro: Renacimiento.* Barcelona, 1980. The best general source of information about the literature of the Renaissance in Spain.

Orejudo, Antonio. *Las "Epístolas familiares" de Antonio de Gue-vara en el contexto epistolar del Renacimiento.* Madison, Wis., 1994.

Read, Malcolm K. *Juan de Huarte de San Juan.* Boston, 1981.

Redondo, Augustin, ed. *L'humanisme dans les lettres espagnoles.* Paris, 1979.

Weber, Alison. *Teresa of Avila and the Rhetoric of Femininity.* Princeton, N.J., 1990.

ELIAS L. RIVERS

SPEGHT, RACHEL (b. c. 1597), Jacobean polemicist. Rachel Speght was the daughter of a Calvinist minister who was rector for two London churches. We lack information on her mother, although the daughter claimed her as a great influence. Speght's best-known work is *A Mouzell for Melastomus* (A muzzle for black mouth), published in 1617 in opposition to Joseph Swetnam's *The Araignment of Lewd, Idle, Froward and Unconstant Women* (1615). She also wrote *Certaine Quaeres to the Bayter of Women* (1617), and *Mortalities Memorandum, with a Dreame Prefixed* (1621), which was inspired by the death of her mother.

In her writings Speght demonstrates knowledge of Latin and the rudiments of a classical education, including familiarity with Plutarch and Cicero. Her social standing is not totally clear, but her godmother Mary Moundford was married to a London physician who attended Arabella Stuart and other court figures. While still under her father's governance Speght wrote her response to Swetnam's *Araignment*. Swetnam's provocative work seemed intended to seek response from women or their supporters and to perpetuate a debate over their nature and proper status.

Speght's *Mouzell* is a Jacobean contribution to the long-term *querelle des femmes,* a seemingly endless series of tracts and longer works in Latin and modern languages disputing women's capabilities and their proper place in society and learning. Speght sought to tie her interests with the wives of leading officials and commercial and financial leaders in London by asking for their protection in her efforts at repudiating Swetnam's slander of their sex. One response criticized Speght for lacking the experience of an older, married woman, while the author of *The Worming of a Mad Dogge* (1617) praised her as "the first Champion of our sexe that would encounter with the barbarous bloudhound."

The *Mouzell* incorporated both a personal attack on Swetnam and a demolition of his arguments concerning women's unreliable and disreputable qualities. His tract, she claimed, caused "greater harme unto your owne soule, then unto women." She attacked Swetnam's biblical justifications for women's unworthiness by claiming that Eve and Adam were equally responsible for the Fall since each had free will. The apostle Paul, she argues, does not claim that men were without sin because of the woman's first temptation; in telling them to avoid the touch of women, he is referring to the perilous and unstable period of the early Christian church at Corinth and discouraging marriage in such circumstances.

After undercutting Swetnam's claims of women's failings, Speght put forth her understanding of women's excellence. Women were created by God along with Adam and are encompassed in the Creator's claim of excellence for his handiwork. While Adam was made from the earth, woman comes from a higher substance, being drawn from a human body. She was also made of an excellent "fashion, and proportion" and resembled Adam, not God's inferior creatures. Women were intended to "glorifie God, and to be a collateral companion for man." Such views resemble those of Heinrich Cornelius Agrippa (1486–1535) and later Christian feminists such as Mary Astell (1668–1731), who based their claims of women's equality and respect on God's having created them with all the capacities and spiritual potential of their male counterparts. To achieve such ends, marriage must be a union of jointly respected individuals working to further God's greater glory. This led her to decry men who would use their position as head of the family to think "themselves Lords and Rulers" and expect all their orders to be followed, forgetting the couple's dual duty to serve God.

We have little information about Rachel Speght in her later life, but her writings place her in the forefront of seventeenth-century women who wrote openly in defense of their sex.

See also **Querelle des Femmes.**

BIBLIOGRAPHY

Primary Work

Speght, Rachel. *The Polemics and Poems of Rachel Speght.* Edited by Barbara Kiefer Lewalski. Oxford, 1996.

Secondary Work

Woodbridge, Linda. *Women and the English Renaissance: Literature and the Nature of Womankind, 1540 to 1620.* Urbana, Ill., 1984. See pages 74–113.

HILDA SMITH

SPENSER, EDMUND (1552/53–1599), Elizabethan poet and colonial administrator. Born in London, Spenser attended the Merchant Taylors' School and may have been the son of a clothworker—perhaps a poor one, for in 1569 he was one of six boys given a gown and a shilling to represent the school at the funeral of Robert Nowell, a wealthy lawyer. Since records of his baptism and school enrollment do not survive, most of the little we know about Spenser's background is gleaned from his poetry: his mother's name was Elizabeth, London was his "most kyndly Nurse," and he claimed relation to the ancient house of Despencer as well as to the more recently ennobled family of Sir John Spencer in Althorp. He was not born a gentleman (a crucial distinction in early modern European society), but he did die as one, having elevated his status through university study and then acquiring property through government service in colonial Ireland.

Education and Career. The Merchant Taylors' School, founded under the headmastership of Richard Mulcaster in 1561, was part of the broad Protestant and humanist educational reforms of the sixteenth century. Mulcaster was an influential proponent of the humanist ideal that joins scholarship and rhetorical training to public service. He would emerge in later years as a progressive voice in educational theory, arguing for an open system of public schooling; a number of boys from the Merchant Taylors' School did rise from obscure backgrounds to positions of distinction. In 1569 Mulcaster may have helped arrange Spenser's first, anonymous publication—a selection of verses by Petrarch, Joachim du Bellay, and Jan van der Noot, translated for the English edition of an anti-Catholic volume that had appeared the year before in French and Dutch. He may also have helped arrange payments of twenty-two shillings Spenser received during 1569–1571 from the estate of Robert Nowell.

In 1569 Spenser entered Pembroke Hall at Cambridge as a sizar, performing servant's duties for room and board. Among these would have been service at meals; contemporary references to the adult poet as "the Muses dispenser" combine a witty recollection of this humble status with a pun on his claims to noble lineage (dispenser = butler), playing both off against his literary ambitions. At Pembroke he met Gabriel Harvey, a talented scholar some years his senior whose background and ambitions resembled his own. Their friendship would eventually include strategies of mutual self-promotion, as evidenced by Harvey's role, or roles, in *The Shepheardes Calender*, where he appears both as the addressee of a commendatory letter and as "Hobbinol," Colin's "especiall good freend" and sometime suitor.

Five Spenser-Harvey letters, published in 1580, extend this effort to advertise the authors' abilities and connections.

Spenser received his B.A. from Cambridge in 1573 and his M.A. in 1576. His whereabouts from 1574 to 1577 are not known, but sometime in 1578 he was appointed personal secretary to Dr. John Young, newly consecrated bishop of Rochester, who had been master of Pembroke Hall during Spenser's residence there. *The Shepheardes Calender*, published the following year, may have been written while Spenser was in Young's service; references to the position are encoded in one of the eclogues, and the collection as a whole is marked by allusions to ecclesiastical politics. The *Calender* and the *Letters* have much in common as highly self-conscious advertisements for a pair of young scholars newly gentrified by their education and seeking employment in court circles. When the letters appeared Spenser had already left Young's residence in Kent for the household of the earl of Leicester in London. There, they intimate, he enjoyed the patronage of the earl and "some use of familiarity" with Edward Dyer and Sir Philip Sidney, who shared his literary interests and apparently formed the nucleus of a short-lived coterie nicknamed the "Areopagus."

Late in 1579 Spenser is believed to have married Machabyas Chylde, who would bear him two children, Sylvanus and Katherine. Within a year he had been appointed private secretary to Arthur, Lord Grey of Wilton, the new lord deputy of Ireland. There is some difference of opinion as to whether this was an unqualified honor, since Ireland lay far from the center of Elizabethan cultural and political life. There are hints in Spenser's writing, too, that he may have alienated powerful members of Elizabeth's government by advocating Leicester's cause with too much zeal. As a colonial possession, however, Ireland offered opportunities for the acquisition of land, office, status, and military honor that proved tempting to Elizabethans of varying rank, and Spenser seems to have made the most of these. Based initially in Dublin and later in Cork, he obtained a series of administrative clerkships (by common practice, the duties of such posts were performed by deputies while the nominal officeholder kept the difference in pay). He likely accompanied Lord Grey on military expeditions into Leinster and Munster, where he witnessed the massacre of foreign troops and the remorseless use of starvation as a tactic to subdue domestic rebellion. He also engaged in a series of property transactions during the 1580s culminating in the acquisition of a lease on Kilcolman Castle and the surrounding 3,028 acres in County Cork. This land was part of an ill-fated and probably unrealistic government plan to settle half a million acres in Munster, confiscated from the rebellious earl of Desmond, with English tenants. Spenser took over Kilcolman sometime between 1586 and 1590; when the Munster plantation collapsed during Tyrone's Rebellion in 1598, his estate was sacked and burned.

Grey had been recalled in 1582, but Spenser lived and worked in Ireland for the rest of his adult life. Most of *The Faerie Queene,* the epic poem for which he is chiefly remembered, was written there. He visited London in 1589 to oversee the publication of its first installment (books 1–3), portions of which he read aloud to the queen, and he returned a number of times during the 1590s. Yet Spenser clearly regarded Ireland as his home, and his poetry, for all the symbolic centrality it affords the queen and her court, came increasingly to assert the author's independent status as a celebrated poet and landed gentleman. When Spenser commemorated his 1589 visit to the court of Elizabeth in a pastoral called *Colin Clouts Come Home Againe,* the title was deliberately tricky: the poet's homecoming turns out to be the return not to his birthplace but to his estate in Ireland.

The first installment of *The Faerie Queene* won its author a royal stipend of £50 per annum, and its publication in 1590 secured his literary fame. After the long silence of the 1580s, this triumph served as a second, more emphatic debut: seven volumes followed, including the six-book *Faerie Queene* in 1596. In 1594 Spenser married Elizabeth Boyle; the marriage produced one son, Peregrine, for whom Spenser purchased a castle and lands in 1597. He had just been named sheriff-designate for Cork in 1598 when the popular uprising that destroyed his estate forced him to take refuge with his family and other settlers in the town. In December he returned to London for the final time, carrying dispatches from the governor of Munster to the Privy Council and a petition from the colonists to the queen. These were delivered on Christmas Eve; Spenser died in Westminster on 13 January 1599. The circumstances of his sudden death have been a subject of speculation, including a dubious account attributed to Ben Jonson some twenty years later according to which Spenser "died for lake of bread in King Street" (quoted in Cummings, p. 136.) In the end, though, his death, perhaps simply the result of stress and exhaustion, remains as enigmatic as his birth.

Spenser's funeral was held in Westminster Abbey, his body accompanied to the church by poets who, according to a contemporary report, cast "their dole-

Edmund Spenser. Portrait engraving, 1598.

ful Verses, and pens too into his grave" (quoted in Cummings, p. 316.) The earl of Essex bore the cost. Queen Elizabeth ordered a memorial, but none was erected. The title page to the folio edition of his collected works, published in 1611, calls him "England's Arch-Poet"; a monument set up in 1619 by a descendent of the Althorp Spencers hailed him as "the Prince of Poets in his tyme," and gave the wrong dates for his birth and death.

Relation to Contemporaries. The extent of Spenser's brief, early familiarity with the circle around Sir Philip Sidney is not known; the transparently self-promoting account in *Letters* may imply more than was strictly true. Spenser dedicated *The Shepheardes Calender* to Sidney, who mentions it with approval in *A Defence of Poetry* while taking exception to the rustic diction. Sidney died in 1586; in 1595 Spenser published a belated and somewhat ambivalent elegy commemorating him as "Astrophel" (the name Sidney used in his sonnet sequence).

Spenser met Sir Walter Ralegh in Ireland, where they probably crossed paths while serving in Lord Grey's retinue together from 1579 to 1581. Later they were both undertakers in the Munster plantation;

Spenser's Kilcolman lay about thirty miles (48 kilometers) from Ralegh's estate at Lismore. When Ralegh visited Ireland in 1589 to inspect his holdings, he also visited Spenser. From this time forward, the two developed a close relationship. They were friends and neighbors, but not equals: Ralegh was the queen's favorite, and his estate in Ireland (for example) was about fourteen times the size of Kilcolman. They were fellow poets who recognized each other's talent, yet Ralegh never sought, as Spenser did, to make poetry his chief vocation and service to the state. They were patron and client as well: when Spenser carried the first three books of *The Faerie Queene* to London, it was Ralegh who presented him to the queen. He also contributed a pair of commendatory sonnets published with the poem in 1590.

Spenser's fictional account of these events in *Colin Clout's Come Home Againe* was dedicated to Ralegh, who figures in the poem as "The Shepheard of the Ocean," Colin's sponsor and guide on a journey to the court of Cynthia. An explanatory "Letter of the Authors" appended to *The Faerie Queene* in 1590 was also addressed to Ralegh, who appears in book 3 both in fictional guise as Arthur's squire Timias, languishing from a love wound inflicted by the virgin huntress Belphoebe, and in literary guise as the "gracious servant" whose "sweet verse, with Nectar sprinkled . . . pictured / His Cynthia." Ralegh's patronage cannot have been worth much after 1592, when he fell out favor for marrying one of the queen's maids of honor. But Spenser remained loyal, as he had after Lord Grey's disgrace a decade earlier: in the 1596 *Faerie Queene* he celebrates Grey as the knight of Justice, victimized by wicked detractors, while a new episode involving Timias pleads on Ralegh's behalf for reconciliation with the queen.

In the opening and closing passages of the second three books, added in 1596, Spenser also attacks William Cecil, Lord Burghley, Elizabeth's lord treasurer and the most powerful figure in her administration. He had already satirized Burghley in *Mother Hubberds Tale,* a beast-fable written as early as 1579 and published in 1591. The volume it appeared in was suppressed and became an immediate collector's item; Spenser returned to Ireland, in the words of one contemporary, "in hazard to loose his . . . annuall reward" (Peterson, "Spurting froth," p. 14). The stipend was paid, but the offending poem was left out of Spenser's collected works until 1612, after the death of Burghley's son Robert. Such attacks did not help the poet's quest for a place at court, but they do reflect his ambivalence about the prospect. In more than one poem he lacerates the royal court for hypocrisy, vanity, and greed; a passage in *Mother Hubberds Tale,* for example, that laments "what hell it is, in suing long to bide" rings with personal conviction.

Spenser's Works. Spenser is one of four "major" poets on whose works the canon of English literature is founded (the others are Geoffrey Chaucer, William Shakespeare, and John Milton). Recognized during his own lifetime as the preeminent poet of the age, he wrote memorable and distinctive verse in every genre from the lyric to the epic, including a pair of marriage poems that remain unrivaled to this day. Much of his poetry was experimental in style, not only because he created new verse and stanza forms for so many of his works but also because, a bit like James Joyce in the twentieth century, he cast his most ambitious achievements in a highly artificial language developed specifically for them. At the same time, and without a major precedent in the native tradition, he virtually created the idea of the literary vocation in English; consolidated first by Jonson and then by Milton, his example was central to the culture's emerging notion of the "laureate" career (Helgerson, *Self-Crowned Laureates*). More recently, interest in the cultural history of European colonialism has led to an emphasis on Spenser's role as a colonial administrator and English landholder in Ireland, on his authorship of a political treatise advocating harsh military measures to subdue resistance there, and on the increasing prominence with which Ireland (especially the landscape around Kilcolman) figures in Spenser's later poetry.

The Shepheardes Calender. From its first appearance *The Shepheardes Calender* (1579) presented itself as at once canonical and inaugural. Through a conspicuous, highly sophisticated play of allusion and imitation, its twelve eclogues gather into themselves the long and diverse tradition of European pastoral. Each eclogue is headed by a woodcut engraving and brief synopsis of the "argument"; each ends with a motto, followed by a set of scholarly notes that point out allusions, gloss archaisms and dialect terms, deflect attention from some of the riskier topical satire, and interpret the mottoes, slipping now and then into solemn parody of the scholarly style they affect. The whole ensemble is prefaced by a commendatory epistle and prose argument and framed by verses in which the unnamed poet salutes his work. The effect is to make Spenser's debut poem look like an edited classic, a pretension the commendatory epistle confirms when it invokes the Virgilian *cursus*—a paradigm in which the self-consciously "major" poet launches his career with pastoral before moving on to epic.

Yet even as it lays audacious claim to canonical status, the *Calender* trumpets the humility of "this our new poete" and makes a great show of hiding his identity. The poem cultivates an elaborate air of mystery, matching its multiplication of textual layers with a proliferation of names. The volume is authored by "Immerito," dedicated to Sidney, commended to Harvey, and edited by an unidentified, perhaps fictitious commentator known only as "E. K." The central character is "Colin Clout," a love-sick shepherd-poet glossed as "the author selfe" whose story runs through the collection from beginning to end. He is surrounded by a cast of shepherds and lasses, some corresponding to real persons, who sing, argue, mourn, warn, trade stories, celebrate, and complain. The result is an imposing, suggestive, persistently enigmatic text that continually both prompts and teases its readers.

The Faerie Queene. Published eleven years after the *Calender*, Spenser's *Faerie Queene* (1590) opens by recalling the pastoral disguise in which its author first appeared. In phrasing imitated from Virgil, the poem's first lines allude to the promise implicit in that beginning, turning from pastoral to an epic poem about the building of the English nation. But *The Faerie Queene* is a strange sort of epic. Unlike Shakespeare's history plays, for example, it deals only obliquely with the military and political struggle to found the Tudor dynasty. The narrative is set rather in Faeryland than in England, and King Arthur, the nominal hero, appears not in his celebrated prime as the founder of the Round Table, but in a youthful phase of wandering invented by the poet. Even in this guise Prince Arthur appears only episodically in the poem, passing through each of its local narratives long enough to defeat an allegorical enemy but then wandering off again in an apparently futile quest to find Gloriana, queen of Faerie, who has appeared to him in a dream. This quest for Gloriana, introduced as the overarching narrative into which all the others will be gathered, turns out in fact to be marginal.

But the story of Arthur's quest for Gloriana was never meant to unify the poem on a realistic narrative level in the manner of classical epic. For one thing, Spenser's immediate predecessors—Italian Renaissance poets like Ludovico Ariosto and Torquato Tasso—had already stretched the boundaries of epic by incorporating the wandering, crisscrossing story lines of romance. For another, the practice of allegorical reading and writing had taught literate audiences and authors alike that the substance of great literature lay not in its narrative surface but in the meanings that surface veiled. Spenser takes the multiplying of narratives farther than any of his predecessors had and then unifies his labyrinth of stories on a conceptual rather than a narrative level, through an extensive thematic and symbolic structure. It is to this structure of allegorical meaning, far more than to the actual story lines of the poem, that Arthur's quest for Gloriana proves central.

Each book of *The Faerie Queene* follows the adventures of an errant knight or knights who enact its titular virtue and do battle with fantastic figures that represent corresponding vices. In practice the patrons of holiness, temperance, chastity, friendship, justice, and courtesy not only illustrate but explore and often challenge their assigned virtues. Because the poem continually tests the reader's moral and ethical assumptions, its didacticism is unusually dynamic and open-ended. The second installment, published in 1596, strikes most readers as more defensive and, at times, more strained than the early books. The concluding "Legend of Courtesy," however, is widely admired for the striking generic innovation in which it returns to the poet's pastoral beginnings, reintroducing Colin Clout as he pipes in magnificent solitude to a vision of dancing maidens.

Because Faeryland is a world that admits both the marvelous and the incongruous—magicians, twins that fornicate incestuously in utero, armies without bodily substance, and monsters that vomit books—and because everything in it stands for something else, the poem can assimilate almost any element of European culture and history. In this way it gathers into itself ethics, metaphysics, theology, popular pageantry, classical myth, medieval romance, chronicle histories, political theory, folklore, proverbs, and the entire literary tradition, recombining their styles, themes, and images. The result is rich and elusive rather than simply chaotic because Spenser writes with a sure feel for the contrasting perspectives implicit in these heterogeneous materials; his gift lies partly in the way he manages to play forms and traditions against one another without subordinating them to a single, decisive context.

Shorter Poems. The 1590 *Faerie Queene* was followed by a rich variety of shorter poems. In 1591 *Complaints* appeared with a preface from the printer, who claims to have gathered and issued its nine "sundrie small poemes of the worlds vanitie" on his own. Since this was the volume suppressed for its satire on Burghley, the disclaimer was from Spenser's point of view prudent, though unlikely to be true. A rather uninspired elegy called *Daphnaida* also appeared in 1591.

In 1595 Spenser published *Amoretti and Epithalamion,* combining a Petrarchan sonnet sequence that records his courtship of Elizabeth Boyle with an extraordinary and numerologically intricate marriage poem celebrating their union. In the same year he also brought out a volume combining *Colin Clout's Come Home Againe* with a collection of elegies for Sir Philip Sidney that included his own contribution, *Astrophel.*

The following year, in addition to the six-book edition of *The Faerie Queene,* Spenser published *Fowre Hymnes,* pairing two poems in praise of love and beauty (purportedly written in the "greener times" of the poet's youth) with two more in praise of heavenly love and heavenly beauty purportedly written to "reform" the first and rich in Neoplatonic resonances. Also appearing in 1596 was *Prothalamion,* a "spousall verse" celebrating an aristocratic double marriage, perhaps commissioned in response to *Epithalamion.*

Spenser's "Two Cantos of Mutabilitie," a wonderfully evocative mythopoeic and philosophical allegory unpublished until after his death, was appended to *The Faerie Queene* in 1609 by the printer, who observed that "both for forme and matter" it appeared to be "parcell of some following booke" of that poem. Set on a hilltop near Kilcolman, "Mutabilitie" combines an Ovidian river-marriage story with a high medieval debate in which Dame Nature convenes her court to hear the titaness Mutability challenge Jove's sovereignty over the sublunary world.

In 1633 the English antiquarian Sir James Ware published Spenser's prose dialogue *A View of the Present State of Ireland.* The *View* develops a complex cultural and political analysis of Ireland under English rule, but remains notorious for the harshness of the policies advocated by "Eudoxus," usually taken to be a figure for the author. Little is known about its composition or circulation except that it was presumably written before being entered in the Stationers Register in 1598. None of the surviving manuscripts, however, bears a dedication or other sign of intent to publish, and we do not know why, at whose behest, or for what audience the dialogue may have been composed.

Spenser's Influence. For subsequent generations of English poets, Spenser represents an ex-

alted view of the poet's calling, a synthesis of Virgilian historicism with biblical prophecy that asserts the "laureate" poet as spokesman for his culture's abiding values. Ben Jonson, John Milton, Alexander Pope, and the romantics are among the successors whose model of poetic vocation derived significantly from Spenser. His portraits of feminine experience, particularly in the middle books of *The Faerie Queene,* were crucial for Milton's conception of Eve and of the Lady in *Comus.* Partly through Milton, they exercised significant influence on Samuel Richardson and other eighteenth-century novelists.

In the nineteenth century Spenser's influence as a stylist and formal innovator would earn him the title of "poet's poet"; his most famous contribution to poetic form, the nine-line stanza of *The Faerie Queene,* was put to memorable uses by Francis Thompson, Percy Bysshe Shelley, Lord Byron, John Keats, and Alfred, Lord Tennyson. Spenser's distinctive and highly experimental poetic diction, by contrast, did not survive beyond the first generation of imitators in the seventeenth century. Individual works stood for at least fifty years as preeminent models in English of the pastoral eclogue, the marriage poem, and the epic; well into the eighteenth century *The Faerie Queene* was the touchstone for any serious consideration of allegory; and for more than two centuries Spenser's most characteristic invention—Faeryland itself—was virtually synonymous in English letters with the idea of poetic imagination.

BIBLIOGRAPHY

Primary Works

Spenser, Edmund. *The Faerie Queene.* Edited by A. C. Hamilton. New York, 1977.

Spenser, Edmund. *The Faerie Queene.* Edited by Thomas P. Roche and C. Patrick O'Donnell Jr. Harmondsworth, U.K., 1978.

Spenser, Edmund. *The Works of Edmund Spenser: A Variorum Edition.* Edited by Edwin A. Greenlaw et al. 11 vols. Baltimore, 1932–1957. The standard scholarly edition, authoritative though now somewhat dated.

Spenser, Edmund. *The Yale Edition of the Shorter Poems of Edmund Spenser.* Edited by William A. Oram et al. New Haven, Conn., 1989.

Secondary Works

Anderson, Judith H. et al., eds. *Spenser's Life and the Subject of Biography.* Amherst, Mass., 1996. Essays on aspects of the biography and on the uses of biography as an approach to reading the works.

Berger, Harry. *Revisionary Play: Studies in the Spenserian Dynamics.* Berkeley, Calif., 1988. Seminal interpretations of Spenser's poetry published over three decades.

Cummings, Robert M., ed. *Spenser: The Critical Heritage.* London, 1971. Responses to the works from 1579 through the end of the seventeenth century.

Hamilton, A. C., et al. *The Spenser Encyclopedia.* Toronto, 1990. Comprehensive and authoritative reference on life, works, and influence.

Helgerson, Richard. *Self-Crowned Laureates: Spenser, Jonson, Milton, and the Literary System.* Berkeley, Calif., 1983. Critical study of the "laureate" career in English Renaissance poetry.

Miller, David Lee. "The Otherness of Spenser's Language." In *Worldmaking Spenser: Explorations in the Early Modern Age.* Edited by Patrick Cheney and Lauren Silberman. Lexington, Ky., 1999. Pages 244–248.

Miller, David Lee. *The Poem's Two Bodies: The Poetics of the 1590* Faerie Queene. Princeton, N.J., 1988. Critical study of the poem's allegory as derived from and informed by the fiction of the monarch's "body politic."

Montrose, Louis Adrian. "Spenser's Domestic Domain: Poetry, Property, and the Early Modern Subject." In *Subject and Object in Renaissance Culture.* Edited by Margreta de Grazia et al. Pages 83–130. Cambridge, U.K., 1996. Major reassessment of Spenser's poetic career, focusing especially on the shorter poems of the 1590s.

Norbrook, David. *Poetry and Politics in the English Renaissance.* London, 1984. Salutary emphasis on the complexity of literature's engagement with the politics of the reformation; wide-ranging and well-informed.

Nohrnberg, James. *The Analogy of* The Faerie Queene. Princeton, N.J., 1976. Learned and subtle commentary that enriches detailed interpretation of the text with nearly encyclopedic range of reference to literary, biblical, and philosophical sources.

Oram, William Allan. *Edmund Spenser.* New York, 1997. Informative and insightful critical introduction to the works.

Peterson, Richard S. "Spurting froth upon courtiers." *Times Literary Supplement,* 16 May 1997. Reviews the scandal surrounding publication of *Mother Hubberds Tale* in 1591 in light of newly discovered evidence.

Waller, Gary. *Edmund Spenser: A Literary Life.* New York, 1994. Not a full-fledged biography, but a useful introductory overview of Spenser's life and works.

DAVID LEE MILLER

SPIES. *See* **Espionage.**

SPILIMBERGO, IRENE DI (1538–1559), Italian intellectual and artist. Irene di Spilimbergo was born in Spilimbergo, a castle town northwest of Udine, to Adriano di Spilimbergo and Giulia da Ponte. Her father (d. 1541) was a member of the noble clan that ruled the region, and almost certainly a philo-Protestant. Her mother was the daughter of an affluent Venetian, Zuan Paolo da Ponte. After spending their childhood in the Friuli, Irene and her elder sister Emilia moved to Venice as wards of their maternal grandparents. Zuan Paolo da Ponte supervised their education, which included instruction in Italian literature and music as well as training in the "womanly art" of needlework.

According to her biographer, Dionigi Atanagi, Irene made extraordinary progress in her studies. The learned men with whom she eagerly discussed literary and philosophical topics were much impressed by her intelligence. When she was about eighteen, her keen interest in "undertakings of honor and glory, in departing from the common path followed by other girls" found a new outlet: painting. Taking lessons from Titian, she mastered all the requisite techniques and produced several competent paintings (none now locatable and securely attributed to her).

Just three years later, in 1559, Irene contracted a high fever. After a three-week illness, she died at age twenty-one. The Venetian patrician Giorgio Gradenigo commissioned Atanagi to gather an anthology of verses in her memory. This volume is prefaced by a biography in which Atanagi presents Irene as an exemplary figure who fulfilled humanistic criteria for womanly excellence and surpassed them in her artistic endeavors.

BIBLIOGRAPHY

Schutte, Anne Jacobson. "Commemorators of Irene di Spilimbergo." *Renaissance Quarterly* 45 (1992): 524–536.

Schutte, Anne Jacobson. "Irene di Spilimbergo: The Image of a Creative Woman in Late Renaissance Italy." *Renaissance Quarterly* 44 (1991): 42–61.

ANNE JACOBSON SCHUTTE

SPIRITUALI. "Spirituali" is the name given by contemporaries in 1542 to a group of Italian reform-minded Catholics who despite their diversity were united by their Christocentric piety, deeply personal religion based on the reading and study of the scriptures (especially the Pauline epistles), adherence to the doctrine of justification by faith, and an irenic attitude toward Protestants. In the early twentieth century the French historian Pierre Imbart de la Tour used the term "evangelism" to describe similar attitudes among French Catholics, and the influential Italian historian Delio Cantimori applied it to the religious views of conspicuous figures in sixteenth-century Italy. Other scholars have described Evangelism as a movement among educated upper-class men and women of deep Christian faith who aspired to personal salvation and hoped for reform of the church. Cantimori traced the history of this movement by positing its flowering during the decades from 1510 to 1540, followed by its decline after the reorganization of the Roman Inquisition in 1542. After that date most of its leading members either died or fled Italy. Those who remained had no choice but Nicodemism, which Cantimori defined as outward conformity with the practices and rituals of the Catholic Church combined with private interior faith.

More recent scholarship has changed this image. Evangelism is no longer seen as a movement confined to the social elite because it has become evident that concern with reform of the church was widespread among all classes. The *spirituali* were only one of many social groups that turned to the "pure word of God" as guide to salvation, and they defy neat categorization. They included cardinals, high prelates, noble women, artists, scholars, writers, and poets. The most important spokesman for the ideals of the *spirituali* during the later 1530s was the Venetian Cardinal Gasparo Contarini. As a member of several commissions charged by Pope Paul III with drafting reform proposals, Contarini made a name for himself as a staunch spokesman for church reform. The pope appointed him legate to the last significant meeting of German Protestant and Catholic theologians, the colloquy of Regensburg in 1541. Contarini's efforts produced a short-lived agreement on justification that was rejected by both the pope and Martin Luther. After Contarini's death in 1542, his friend Cardinal Reginald Pole succeeded him as the leading figure among the dwindling number of *spirituali*.

Both Contarini and Pole were at the center of a considerable network of friends whose attitude toward religion was similar. Outstanding among them were cardinals Gregorio Cortese and Ercole Gonzaga (regent of Mantua), bishops Gianmatteo Giberti of Verona and Pier Paolo Vergerio of Capodistria, the poets Marcantonio Flaminio and Vittoria Colonna, her friend Michelangelo, the great preacher and vicar-general of the Capuchin friars, Bernardino Ochino, the Lateran canon Pietro Martire Vermigli, and the Spaniard Juan de Valdés, influential writer and teacher of spirituality. The most famous work associated with the *spirituali* is *Il beneficio di Cristo* (The benefit of Christ's death for Christians; Venice, 1543). It sold thousands of copies before being systematically ferreted out and burned by the Inquisition. Its author was a Benedictine monk from Mantua, Benedetto Fontanini, while Flaminio added revisions and literary polish to the text. The *Beneficio* stressed justification by faith alone as efficacious to salvation and included passages from John Calvin's *Institutes of the Christian Religion*. Whether the theology of the little book is Catholic or Protestant has been the subject of ongoing debates among specialists.

The *spirituali* received a serious blow when some of their best-known figures, including Ochino and Vermigli, fled Italy for Protestant lands in the summer of 1542. Subsequently the Inquisition tried a number of *spirituali* on suspicion of heresy. Most famous among them was Cardinal Giovanni Morone, arrested in 1557 on the order of Pope Paul IV, a former inquisitor; he was later restored to his former position by Pope Pius IV.

The *spirituali* never coalesced into an actual movement. Rather, they serve as witnesses to the religious ferment in early and mid-sixteenth-century Italy and to the complexity of Italian responses to the crisis of the Reformation. Their theological opinions and their dream of reconciling Protestants and Catholics became moot after the canons and decrees of the Council of Trent defined Catholic doctrine.

BIBLIOGRAPHY

Cantimori, Delio. *Prospettive di storia ereticale italiana del Cinquecento.* Bari, Italy, 1960.

Fragnito, Gigliola. "Gli 'spirituali' e la fuga di Bernardino Ochino." *Rivista storica italiana* 84 (1972): 777–813.

Schutte, Anne Jacobson. "Periodization of Sixteenth-Century Italian Religious History: The Post-Cantimori Paradigm Shift." *Journal of Modern History* 61 (1989): 269–284.

ELISABETH G. GLEASON

SPIRITUALITY, FEMALE.

In the two and a half centuries before 1450, new women's devotional movements and a distinctive women's spirituality arose in northern France, the Low Countries, the Rhineland, and Italy. During these centuries women continued to enter traditional communities of nuns, following the Benedictine or Augustinian rules. But some women, commonly called beguines, preferred a less restricted mode of communal living open to members of diverse social origins and free of the enclosure typical of monastic life. Without formal vows and with only a promise of chastity, the beguines commonly supported themselves by their own labor, while undertaking charitable activities such as the teaching of children and the care of the sick and the dead. Freer than nuns to develop their own forms of piety, they contributed most actively to a spirituality rooted in a larger religious movement scholars now describe as an "evangelical awakening," inspiring imitation of Christ in his life, teaching, and suffering.

In addition to other activities, members of both innovative and traditional female communities composed works of Christian spirituality. Some were written in Latin; others were the earliest such writings in vernacular languages: Dutch, German, and French. Modern knowledge about these women comes largely from their own works, often based on visionary experiences, as well as from hagiogra-

Female Spirituality. St. Bridget (Brigitta) of Sweden (c. 1303–1373) inspired by Heaven; the body of Christ appears in the host held by the priest saying mass at the left. From a manuscript of *Revelationes* by Bridget, late fourteenth century. THE PIERPONT MORGAN LIBRARY, NEW YORK/ART RESOURCE, NY

phies, or saints' lives, written about them, chiefly by men. Among the better-known women of this earlier period are Hildegard of Bingen, Beatrice of Nazareth, St. Gertrude the Great, Mechthild of Helfta, Margaret of Oingt, Hadewijch of Brabant, Mechthild of Magdeburg, and Margaret Porete.

In the early fourteenth century the beguine movement was increasingly threatened by official opposition reflected in papal legislation of 1298, imposing strict enclosure on all religious women. Soon growing suspicion of beguines and their presumed association with heresy erupted in the censures and condemnation of the Council of Vienne (1311–1312). Although beguine communities in the Low Countries managed to survive and flourish, they were almost completely suppressed in the Rhineland and other German regions, where they were often succeeded by convents of Dominican nuns.

Nine of these communities left records of their communal spirituality in a unique genre, the so-called sister books (or convent chronicles). Combining the hagiographic with the highly personal, these narratives offer images of saintly women with whom contemporaries could identify. Filled with visions and miracles, the sister books also reveal an environment that fostered profound mystical experiences and spiritual friendships.

Diverse Models of Spirituality, 1350–1400. As the beguine ideal was fragmented in new fourteenth-century movements, the sister books and their makers represented the contemplative aspects of this ideal, while the somewhat later Sisters of the Common Life reflected its active and charitable contributions. These could hardly have been more gravely needed than during the disorders and disasters that beset much of Western society during this century, above all the Black Death but also long wars and a papal schism in the church that lasted nearly forty years.

The Sisters of the Common Life, women followers of Master Geert Grote of Deventer, Netherlands, and his Devotio Moderna in the late fourteenth and fifteenth centuries, were always more numerous than the brothers, as were their houses. Supervised by a rector, or mistress elected by the sisters, like beguines they lived by the work of their hands, chiefly in textiles and sewing, brewing, and book copying, including some of the earliest Dutch translations of the Bible. "Work," one of the sisters wrote, "is a kind of medicinal plaster for the wound of our sins." By the early fifteenth century, the influence of these sisters, who were especially active in the Netherlands and Germany, had extended to the cities of northern Italy.

A century earlier, the Italians had bypassed ecclesiastical legislation regarding beguines by forming various kinds of women's communities. Far more diverse than those of their male contemporaries, these communities added to older beguine-like groups increasing numbers of tertiaries (members of the lay branches, or third orders) of the powerful mendicant orders, especially the Franciscan and Dominican; these tertiaries became exclusively female in the later fourteenth century. Demonstrating what was to many women the irresistible appeal of the unenclosed life, women, especially of the urban middle and lower classes, chose—as tertiaries, lay converts, and penitents—active lives performing desperately needed works of mercy.

A continuing feature of the religious experience of Italian women, diversity is equally striking in the expanding and influential cult of women saints. Not only were they more numerous than ever before, but many of them were lay women, including the two most eminent saintly figures of the fourteenth century, Bridget of Sweden (c. 1303–1373) and Catherine of Siena (1347–1380). Yet, different as they were, one an aristocratic widow and mother of eight children, the other the twenty-fourth child of a Sienese wool dyer, these women shared a single overarching purpose: the reform of the church at its highest levels, beginning with the return of the papacy to Rome after its long sojourn in Avignon.

Although Bridget died before their hopes were realized and Catherine lived to see the beginning of the schism that the pope's return would cause, both achieved other, more effective goals. Before moving to Rome in about 1350, Bridget had founded a new and soon successful monastic double order, dominated on the medieval model by women and guided by men. With male assistance, she had produced an account of her visionary experience, *Revelations.* During the prodigious brief life recorded in Catherine's visionary works and her vast correspondence, this Dominican tertiary achieved a popularity, an influence, and an enduring fame unmatched among the holy women of her century.

Reformers and "Living Saints," c. 1400–1600. With hopes repeatedly disappointed for an end to the Great Schism, religious women directed their reforming efforts more immediately to their own communities. An outstanding example is the Franciscan nun St. Colette (1381–1447) of Corbie in northern France, who was first a recluse, then a beguine, later a Benedictine nun, and finally a member of the Clarists, or Poor Clares. Entrusted by papal authority with the direction of all communities that she might found or reform, she established seventeen new convents in France and Flanders and extended her reforming efforts to more than three hundred Franciscan houses of both sexes. If the extremes of hagiography are reflected in the miracles illustrated in her contemporary "life," so is the adventurous career of this prophet, visionary, and incessant traveler.

Franciscan reformers were also active in Italy during the early fifteenth century, among them Angelina of Montegiove (1377–1435) in the reform of the tertiaries and especially Catherine of Bologna (1413–1463) in the reform of Clarist nuns in northern Italy. Like Colette and Angelina, Catherine began her religious life, after early years at the Este court in Ferrara, in a community of lay women, Corpus Domini, which became after dramatic changes a Clarist abbey. There, as novice mistress and later as abbess of a new Corpus Domini in Bologna, she was an agent of reform, enforcing the strictest version of the rule of St. Clare. A direct witness to her spiritual life, to her doubts, visions, and inner struggles during her formative years in Ferrara, is her semiautobiographical *Le sette armi spirituali* (Seven spiritual weapons), the most revealing record of its kind by an Italian woman of this century.

Evident in the lives and choices of Catherine and her contemporaries, the competing attractions of both forms of women's religious life are equally striking in the experience of their successors, the "living saints"—holy women so designated by their contemporaries in late fifteenth- and early sixteenth-century Italy. Remarkably numerous and popular as both models and "social operators" were the visionary and charismatic holy women, most of them Dominican tertiaries, devout followers of Catherine of Siena, whose prophetic gifts were highly prized at princely courts during this critical time. Similar in their unenclosed lives, though less popular and more reformist in spirit, were the Spanish *beatas,* by this time objects of inquisitorial suspicion after a period of tolerated diversity.

Among religious women in the sixteenth century, none achieved more lasting distinction and influence than two quite different reformers, the Italian Franciscan tertiary Angela Merici (1470 or 1474–1540) and the Spanish Carmelite nun Teresa of Ávila (1515–1582). Often included among the living saints but significantly different from them in her essential goals, Angela Merici envisioned in her Company of Saint Ursula a novel apostolate of women that would encompass the education of young girls and other charitable activities in a flexible society of women living and working in the world. Despite the subversion of her original plan by the decrees of strict enclosure at the Council of Trent (1545–1563), her company survived in the Ursuline communities, congregation, and the famous teaching order of the succeeding centuries.

A tireless reformer of her own Carmelite nuns, Teresa of Ávila, engagingly witty and charming, was an embattled and subtle defender of the validity of her mental prayer and her visionary experiences. Despite the exigencies of the Spanish Inquisition and the Council of Trent, she has held her place among the most profound and certainly the most prolific and enduringly influential of women mystical theologians. She and Angela Merici epitomize the successes and defeats, the challenges and dangers experienced by religious women during this period.

See also **Religious Orders,** *subentry on* **Orders and Congregations of Women;** *and biographies of figures mentioned in this entry.*

BIBLIOGRAPHY

Primary Works
English translations of many works by individuals and groups are published by the Paulist Press of New York in the series The Classics of Western Spirituality. Among individual authors are Angela of Foligno, Bridget of Sweden, Catherine of Siena, Catherine of Genoa, and Teresa of Ávila. See also John Van Engen, ed., *Devotio Moderna: Basic Writings* (New York, 1988).

Secondary Works
Ahlgren, Gillian T. W. *Teresa of Ávila and the Politics of Sanctity.* Ithaca, N.Y., 1996.
Bornstein, Daniel, and Roberto Rusconi, eds. *Women and Religion in Medieval and Renaissance Italy.* Chicago, 1996.
McLaughlin, Mary Martin. "Creating and Recreating Communities of Women: The Case of Corpus Domini, Ferrara, 1406–1452." In *Sisters and Workers in the Middle Ages.* Edited by Judith M. Bennett, et al. Chicago, 1989. Pages 261–288.
Weber, Alison. *Teresa of Ávila and the Rhetoric of Femininity.* Princeton, N.J., 1990.
Wood, Jeryldene. *Women, Art, and Spirituality: The Poor Clares of Early Modern Italy.* Cambridge, U.K., 1996.
Zarri, Gabriella. "Living Saints: A Typology of Female Sanctity in the Early Sixteenth Century." In *Women and Religion in Medieval and Renaissance Italy.* Edited by Daniel Bornstein and Roberto Rusconi. Chicago, 1996. Pages 219–303.

MARY MARTIN MCLAUGHLIN

SPONDE, JEAN DE (1557–1595), French baroque poet. Born in Mauléon, Jean de Sponde was the son of the Calvinist secretary of Jeanne d'Albret, queen of Navarre. Sponde studied in Basel, receiving his degree in 1580. He converted to Catholicism shortly before his death in Bordeaux.

Sponde, an exemplar of the literary baroque, or mannerist, style, unites faith and poetry in his literary productions. Sponde's work shares many of the stylistic qualities characteristic of other Calvinist writers, but it usually remains personal and spiritual rather than political or *engagé,* a dimension that many Calvinist writers—such as Théodore-Agrippa d'Aubigné, Théodore de Bèze, or Philippe Du Plessis-Mornay—do attain.

Sponde's extensive body of love poetry includes sonnets, songs, elegies, and encomiastic pieces. *Les amours* (1597, published posthumously), an accomplished grouping of twenty-six sonnets, three songs, and an elegy, innovates in its refusal to resemble the ubiquitous Ronsardian model; its language is abstract, often ordered by paired contrasts. Such antithetical structuring continues in his religious poetry, the medium for Sponde's inquiry into the dialectical relationship between man and God, heaven and earth. The *Essay de quelques poèmes chrétiens* (An attempt at some Christian poems; 1588), a powerful immolation of the insignificant self and the deceitful world, uses a violent rhetoric to testify that the only meaning of life lies with God, and that the earthly experience is mere *vanitas* and instability. His *Stances de la Cène* (Stanzas on the Last Supper; part of the *Essay*) demonstrate a Calvinist understanding of the Eucharist, but *Sonnets de la mort* (Sonnets on death; also part of the *Essay*) cease to display a Calvinist conception or idiom; they focus, instead, on the universal theme of *vanitas mundi*. Sponde's poetic style can be described as highly metaphorical, relying on an extensive and evocative employment of images without, however, resorting to the macabre or remaining at the level of realism. Sponde's religious sensibility produces a poetry of inconstancy because of his agonized perception of the wrenching away of the terrestrial from the celestial: nothing can be trusted, especially our reason, in such troubled times. Sponde succeeds in sculpting art from agony.

BIBLIOGRAPHY

Primary Work
Sponde, Jean de. *Oeuvres littéraires*. Geneva, 1978.

Secondary Works
Cave, Terence. *Devotional Poetry in France c. 1570–1613*. London, 1969.
Rousset, Jean. *L'intérieur et l'extérieur*. Paris, 1968.
Rousset, Jean. *La littérature de l'âge baroque en France*. Paris, 1954.

CATHERINE RANDALL

SPORTS. The medieval world abounded in sport, from chivalric tournaments to church-sponsored ball games, but the Renaissance infused such activities with new meaning according to changing ideas of individuality, the ancient world, gender, education, the court, the military, and the body. For humanists such as Leon Battista Alberti, the pursuit of sports accorded with the harmonious fusion of mind and body; by following an educational program of controlled and gentlemanly activities, the new scholar-athlete would ensure for himself the correct proportion of mental and physical development necessary for becoming *l'uomo universale* (universal man). Such a man was to be discriminating in his choice of sport: swimming, running, hunting, wrestling, and horseback riding were acceptable, since they abided by the ancient Greek ideal. "The sharp exertion of ball-play" was also selectively permitted and generally treated with historical significance by encyclopedists such as Polydore Vergil. The embrace of sporting activity was not shared by all, however; while Erasmus advocated proper manners and honesty for boys engaged in sport, he also stated, "We are not concerned with developing athletes, but scholars and men competent to affairs, for whom we desire adequate constitution indeed, but not the physique of a Milo" (from *De pueris instituendis*).

On the playing field and among nobler classes, jousting tournaments continued in popularity, despite pleas from men such as Petrarch, who in book 1 of *De remediis utriusque Fortunae* urged men away from such base pursuits. The English king Henry VIII was an avid proponent and participant in such games, which could carry a heavily diplomatic aspect, as his wrestling match with the French king Francis I at the Field of Cloth of Gold pageant in 1520 demonstrates. An equally ardent though altogether more unfortunate jouster was King Henry II of France, who received a fatal blow during a jousting contest in 1559 that left France open to the religious wars that ensued. At court, sports served as a social lubricant, and it was the duty of the perfect courtier, according to Baldassare Castiglione in book 1 of *Il cortegiano* (*The Book of the Courtier*), to gain proficiency not only in the joust but also in other popular and military-derived sports such as archery, swordplay, fencing, and horse racing, along with running, hurdle jumping, swimming, and throwing. The court lady, according to Castiglione, was to stand by and cheer on the athletic displays of her man, who could also engage, out of noblesse oblige, with peasants, though "he should be certain of winning, or else not take part at all, for it is too sad and shocking, and quite undignified, when a gentleman is seen to be beaten by a peasant, especially in a wrestling match."

One of the most popular sports of the Renaissance among the upper classes was tennis, which originated in the cloisters of medieval France and spread outward to other western European countries. Monarchs again set the fashion, with Henry VIII—the owner of seven rackets—joining the emperor

A Tennis Match. The enclosed court in the foreground is part of a greater pleasure-garden complex. Painting, sixteenth century. MARYLEBONE CRICKET CLUB

Charles V in 1523 for a doubles match against the princes of Orange and Brandenburg. Regional variation, however, tended to complicate the game, resulting in a monk named Antonio Scaino de Salo writing a treatise on tennis in 1555 in which he established norms of etiquette and a rational scoring system and mentioned the game's newfound popularity among merchants, students, and artisans. Meanwhile, King James VI of Scotland popularized the ancient sport of golf, which had originated in Scotland and was played not only by the king but also by his mother, Mary Stuart. Golf's short-lived popularity among the English, however, had perhaps more to do with seeking favor from the king than with genuine love for the sport.

While sports among the elite transcended national barriers, sports among the lower classes remained firmly bound to region. In popular culture, games such as *la soule,* born in the twelfth-century villages of France, involved teams of men divided according to parish or marital status (the marrieds versus the unmarrieds, for example), whose aim was to drive a ball forward and past a goalpost with the foot, the hand, or sticks of various kinds. The church had long sponsored events such as *la soule,* though some clerics had from the beginning called for its prohibition, even threatening excommunication for those who engaged in a game that bred such "ill feeling, rancor, and enmities," according to one French bishop in

1440. In England, football (soccer)—which may have derived from *la soule*—had a long legacy, propped up by a myth that the game was invented in the eleventh century with Englishmen kicking a Dane's severed head among themselves. Stool ball, which enjoyed a hoary and somewhat pagan association in England, is said to have begun among milkmaids who threw (and later with bats, hit) balls toward their milking stools, attempting to knock them over. By the Renaissance the game was associated with courtship and the Easter season and later evolved into the games of rounders and cricket, though the sixteenth-century enclosure movement restricted the fields on which peasants and others could play. Finally, in piazzas across Italy the Easter season brought on games, in this case the game of *calcio,* in which uniformed (and only highborn) players kicked and hurled a leather ball filled with animal hair, to the cheers of spectators.

The possibility of disruption and violence in sports—and the problems with related gambling and dice games—had always been of concern to the authorities, and in the Renaissance new voices began to assert themselves in condemning the "devilish pastimes," especially when played on the Sabbath. Among the Protestant leaders, Martin Luther was a rarity in his approval of sports and especially bowling (*Kegels*), which allegorically reminded him of the Christian "knocking the devil out of his ground." In general, however—and especially in John Calvin's Geneva and in Puritan England—such amusements as maypoles, bearbaiting, and cockfighting were placed under the sin of idleness and heavily restricted, if not prohibited. Enforcement was uneven, however, since peasants especially refused to end their seasonal play in the fields, where, according to one seventeenth-century poem,

> The beauteous maids and willing swains
> In scenes of frolic crowd the plains;
> And to the Spring their honours pay
> In rites of customary play.

BIBLIOGRAPHY

Baker, William J. *Sports in the Western World.* Totowa, N.J., 1982.

Henderson, Robert W. *Ball, Bat, and Bishop: The Origin of Ball Games.* New York, 1947.

SARAH COVINGTON

STAGES OF LIFE. *See* **Life Stages.**

STAMPA, GASPARA (c. 1523–1554), Venetian poet and musician. A leading and influential female poet-singer of the first half of the sixteenth century in Venice, Stampa produced the largest and most varied *canzonieri* (poetic song books) in Italian literature. Stampa was born in Padua to a Venetian mother, Cecilia, and an impoverished Milanese noble, Bartolomeo Stampa, a jewel merchant. Her father educated his three children, Cassandra, Baldassare, and Gaspara in Greek and Latin, modern languages, and music. When he died in 1531, Gaspara's mother moved the family back to her native Venice to promote her daughters' careers as musical performers. A *virtuosa* (musician and singer), Stampa improvised on stock melodic formulas for poetic recitation and entertained fellow poets and artists on the lute in informal salon gatherings.

A lauded poet, she was closely tied to the Venetian poet Domenico Venier (1517–1582) and his literary academy and private salon in Venice. Her sonnets and *capitoli in terza rima* (story-poems in three-line stanzas) are highly musical and were often used in musical improvisation. A member also of the Accademia dei Dubbiosi and dubbed "Anasilla" (from Anaxum, Latin for the river Piave), Stampa wrote love poetry employing pastoral motifs to point out and criticize the fact that women were not allowed to arrange social and erotic relations for themselves.

Stampa's *Rime* were published posthumously in 1554 by her sister, Cassandra, and are dedicated to the poet Monsignor Giovanni Della Casa. Stampa had arranged the poems as a chronological diary in the style of a *canzoniere*. In it, 311 poems describe the psychological status of the woman lover, inspired in part by her unreciprocated love relationship with a nobleman of the feudal elite from the countryside north of Venice, Count Collaltino di Collalto, who she met in the Venier salon on Christmas Day in 1548. The unbridgeable social gap between them led to their final break in 1550; after Stampa's death in 1554 Collaltino married a woman of his own rank. Abdelkader Salza, the 1913 editor of Stampa's poems, rearranged the original structure of the book, dividing it into love poems and occasional poems. The first section includes 245 poems, most of them sonnets. Some of the love poems are addressed to Bartolomeo Zen, a Venetian patrician with whom she had a relationship. The second section includes poems for male and female friends and literati and concludes with religious sonnets. Although the revised sequence of poems suggests that Stampa addresses her poems only to two male lovers, the book as a whole seems to be directed at a large audience whose sympathy she hopes to gain.

Stampa's adherence to the poetic theories of Pietro Bembo (1470–1547) influenced her choice of Petrarch as her principal poetic model. She adopted Petrarch's method of symbolic representation: Collaltino was represented as a *colle altro* (high hill), a reference to his unreachable, noble qualities and to the sacred Parnassus of art. Stampa also adopted the Petrarchan lyric style to describe a woman's experiences of ecstasy and sorrow, jealousy and anxiety, and passion and erotic feelings of love. Her repeated imitations of Ovid's tales of Echo and Philomela allowed her to explore the issues of speech mutilation and female oppression. These myths permitted Stampa to compare herself to mythical victims of masculine cruelty.

BIBLIOGRAPHY

Primary Works

Stampa, Gaspara. *Rime.* Edited by Rodolfo Ceriello. Milan, 1976.

Stampa, Gaspara. *Rime di Gaspara Stampa e di Veronica Franco.* Edited by Abdelkader Salza. Bari, Italy, 1913.

Stampa, Gaspara. *Selected Poems.* Edited and translated by Laura Anna Stortoni and Mary Prentice Lillie. New York, 1994.

Secondary Works

Bassanese, Fiora A. *Gaspara Stampa.* Boston, 1982.

Borsetto, Luciana. "Narciso ed Eco. Figura e scrittura femminile del Cinquecento: esemplificazioni ed appunti." In *Nel cerchio della luna: Figure di donna in alcuni testi del sedicesimo secolo.* Edited by Marina Zancan. Venice, 1983.

Jones, Ann Rosalind. "Feminine Pastoral as Heroic Martyrdom: Gaspara Stampa and Mary Wroth." In *The Currency of Eros:*

Women's Love Lyric in Europe, 1540–1620. Bloomington, Ind., 1990. Pages 118–154.

Jones, Ann Rosalind. "New Songs for the Swallow: Ovid's Philomela in Tullia d'Aragona and Gaspara Stampa." In *Refiguring Woman: Perspectives on Gender and the Italian Renaissance.* Edited by Marilyn Migiel and Juliana Schiesari. Ithaca, N.Y., 1991.

MARGARET F. ROSENTHAL

STARKEY, THOMAS (c. 1495–1538), English humanist and political thinker. Starkey was born to a family of relatively minor gentry in Cheshire and was educated at Magdalen College, Oxford (B.A. 1516; M.A. 1521). There he made lifelong friends, most important among them Reginald Pole (1500–1558). Probably along with Pole, Starkey went to Padua, where he completed his education during the 1520s.

While acting as secretary to Pole in Paris in 1529–1530 and for several years thereafter, Starkey wrote his most important work, *Dialogue between Pole and Lupset.* He stayed with Pole during his visits to the University of Avignon and to Padua once more. At that time, in common with Pole and his circle, Starkey moved in the direction of a more "evangelical" religion, which marks the later parts of the *Dialogue.* In late 1534 Starkey returned to England. His extensive contacts with Englishmen and Italians in Italy soon earned him Thomas Cromwell's notice, and early in 1535 he entered royal service.

In addition to gathering intelligence from Italy and engaging in a protracted correspondence with Pole about Henry's divorce, on his own initiative Starkey wrote domestic propaganda for Cromwell in the form of *An Exhortation to the People Instructing Them to Unity and Obedience* (1536). Starkey also wrote Cromwell a set piece on his specialty, Aristotelian political science. He wrote a remarkable letter of advice to Henry on how to capitalize on the opportunity presented by the execution of Anne Boleyn in 1536. That year represented the crisis of Starkey's career. Temporarily disgraced when Pole sent Henry his inflammatory *Pro ecclesiasticae unitatis defensione* (Defense of the unity of the church) condemning Henry's break with Rome, Starkey yet received a valuable preferment in the form of the mastership of the collegiate church of St. Lawrence Pountney in London.

The final two years of Starkey's life were largely spent writing, although he finished neither of two big projects. The first was a set of notes on the Old Testament that may have been meant to underpin a defense of Pole, and the second was a refutation of the Dutch controversialist Albert Pighe's *Hierarchiae ecclesiasticae assertio* (Ecclesiastical hierarchy), which had argued an uncompromising case for papal supremacy. This combination of support for Pole's evangelical Catholicism and opposition to Roman pretensions to political headship of the church in England typified English conservatives and helps to explain Starkey's continued association with them. His ties were so close that only death allowed him narrowly to escape indictment in the wake of the Exeter conspiracy of 1538.

Long thought one of the principal followers of Marsilius of Padua, a major contributor to the creation of the Anglican via media (middle way), and the first modern politician, Starkey was in fact thoroughly rooted in the ideas of Aristotle, especially in the idea that a mixed constitution (composed of elements of aristocracy, monarchy, and democracy) is necessary; this he combined with his experience in Padua and Venice to fashion a new order for England, laid out in his *Dialogue.* Almost exactly as in Venice's government, just then being carefully described by two of Starkey's and Pole's friends, Donato Giannotti and Gasparo Contarini, interlocking councils were to restrict the monarch's power in a system designed to promote the common good, the Aristotelian end of civil life. Starkey defined the "common good," as he did other key phrases, in a very playful, constantly changing way, as might be expected of a humanist writing one of the first dialogues in English. Nevertheless, the serious purpose behind his play is unmistakable. Starkey meant to restore the high nobility to its proper place at the head of the commonwealth by adding to its claims of lineage those of virtue. The nobility was to be educated in civil law, which was to replace the barbaric legal system left behind by the Normans. The *Dialogue's* original dedicatee was almost certainly Pole, cousin of Henry VIII. That Starkey saw no problem in redirecting the work to the king after Pole let him down, even while proposing an elective monarchy, offers striking testimony to the fluidity of English politics in the mid-1530s. Starkey also put forward a plan for the church, which was also to have an aristocratic constitution, a plan he drew in part from his knowledge of Parisian and Paduan conciliarism. Starkey had no more need of Marsilius's ideas about ecclesiastical government than he did of Marsilius's secular ideas.

Starkey preserved more or less this basic program throughout his career. In his other major work, the *Exhortation,* he grounded his case on the Aristotelian notion of the mean, while adding, under Cromwell's direction, a new argument from *adiaphora,* things indifferent (and therefore of no significance to salvation), which he nevertheless thought the prince could command, thereby justifying the religious changes Henry and Parliament had made. This case was identical to that developed earlier by much more authoritative advisers to the king, among them Archbishop Cranmer. Starkey drew somewhat more radical conclusions than Cranmer had, conclusions that likely would have appealed to Henry, especially the claim that only a minimum of doctrine was necessary: the Nicene Creed was plenty. The pope's power was severely curtailed, most of it going to the prince and the kingdom of England, "a whole congregation and perfect."

None of Starkey's works had any influence. The *Dialogue* remained unpublished until the nineteenth century, and the *Exhortation,* although originally issued by the royal printer, disappeared from both Elizabethan and late Stuart discussions of the ecclesiastical constitution, despite marked similarities between some of Starkey's ideas and those of Richard Hooker, for example. It was not until the *Dialogue* was first published in London in 1878 that Starkey attracted attention, almost immediately becoming a major figure in interpretations of Henry's reign and Tudor political thought. Yet Starkey's thought is "Tudor" only by the accident that he was an Englishman. Virtually all the significant content of the *Dialogue,* which makes Starkey appear an aberration in his native circumstances, was common coin in his Italian circles. Starkey made good use of his cross-cultural experiences and cast England in the mold of Venice.

BIBLIOGRAPHY

Primary Works

Starkey, Thomas. *A Dialogue between Pole and Lupset.* Edited by T. F. Mayer. London, 1989.

Starkey, Thomas. *An Exhortation to the People Instructing Them to Unity and Obedience.* London, 1536. Reprint, Amsterdam, 1973.

Secondary Work

Mayer, T. F. *Thomas Starkey and the Commonweal: Humanist Politics and Religion in the Reign of Henry VIII.* Cambridge, U.K., 1989.

THOMAS F. MAYER

STEPHANUS. *See* **Estienne Press.**

STOICISM. Renaissance authors learned about ancient Stoicism primarily from two Latin sources, both known to the Middle Ages: the letters and moral treatises of the Roman Stoic philosopher Seneca; and the philosophical works of Cicero, who, although not a Stoic, summarized many of their doctrines. In the fifteenth century new Greek sources were translated into Latin: Diogenes Laertius's biographies of famous ancient Stoics in his *Lives of the Philosophers;* and the *Enchiridion* (Manual) of the Greek slave turned Stoic philosopher, Epictetus.

Although Stoicism was originally a full-scale philosophical system, including logic, physics, and cosmology, later interest concentrated on ethics. The Stoics regarded virtue as the supreme and only good, vice, the only evil. They classified other goods, such as health and honor, and evils, such as illness and disgrace, as morally "indifferent." Virtue consisted in living in agreement with nature, the guiding principle of which was reason; vice was defined as disobeying reason and following harmful emotions (desire, fear, pleasure, and distress), which in the wise are extinguished.

The compatibility of Christianity and the virtue-centered ethics of Stoicism had been emphasized by many church fathers. Ambrose (339–397), for instance, took over its scheme of four cardinal virtues (courage, justice, prudence, and temperance), which featured prominently in the Christian moral philosophy of the Middle Ages and Renaissance. Other early theologians, such as Augustine (354–430), rejected as unchristian the Stoic belief that emotions such as fear were to be eradicated rather than redirected toward God. Both points of view found advocates during the early Renaissance. Petrarch (1304–1374) saw Stoicism and Christianity as broadly in agreement, while Coluccio Salutati (1331–1406) condemned the Stoic beliefs that virtue was the only good and that emotions were harmful as psychologically ineffective, if not impious.

The Flemish humanist Justus Lipsius (1547–1606) was the first to adapt Stoicism systematically to the needs of contemporary Christians, regarding it as bringing inner peace and tranquillity to those suffering from the upheavals of the religious wars in the late sixteenth century. Drawing on Seneca, whose works he edited in 1605, Lipsius recommended steadfastness (*constantia*) in the face of adversity. Lipsius's ideas were popularized and developed by Guillaume du Vair, a French bishop and political figure, who blended the Stoic doctrines of Epictetus with Christian beliefs to produce his *Sainte philosophie* (Holy philosophy) of 1584.

Ancient Stoicism held that everything happens according to the preordained and inexorable course of fate, a position Lipsius carefully distinguished from Christian faith in divine providence. The Italian Aristotelian Pietro Pomponazzi (1462–1525), in his *De fato* (On fate), written in the 1520s but not published until 1567, had supported Stoic determinism on philosophical grounds, while preserving free will with theological arguments.

Stoic cosmology holds that the universe is permeated by *pneuma* or *spiritus* (breath), a divine but material substance composed of air and fire, which regulates all events, including the internal functions of plants, animals, and human beings. This notion played a role in Renaissance astrological theory: the fifteenth-century Florentine Platonist Marsilio Ficino postulated a cosmic *spiritus* as the channel through which astral influences reach our world. In the sixteenth century, the concept of *spiritus* is found in the sense-based natural philosophy of Bernardino Telesio, who used it to explain virtually all human activities, both physical and mental.

See also **Moral Philosophy** *and biographies of Lipsius and Ficino.*

BIBLIOGRAPHY

Primary Work
Kraye, Jill, ed. *Cambridge Translations of Renaissance Philosophical Texts.* 2 vols. Cambridge, U.K., 1997. Vol. 1, *Moral Philosophy.* Part 5, "Stoic Ethics," pp. 179–225. Contains texts by Coluccio Salutati, Angelo Poliziano, Justus Lipsius, and Francisco de Quevedo.

Secondary Work
Morford, Mark. *Stoics and Neostoics: Rubens and the Circle of Lipsius.* Princeton, N.J., 1991.

JILL KRAYE

STRAPAROLA, GIANFRANCESCO (c. 1480–
after 1557), Italian writer. What we know about Straparola's life comes from the frontispiece of his works: he came from Caravaggio. His family was not prominent and he survives only through a volume of poetry (primarily sonnets) first published in 1508 and a collection of tales, *Le piacevoli notti* (The merry nights; 1550–1553). Although modern readers may find the tales lacking in psychological penetration and character development, the almost twenty editions in the second half of the sixteenth century and the several translations guarantee him a place among Renaissance storytellers. Straparola's extensive use of Oriental fables was rediscovered in the eighteenth century by French authors when folktales and fairy tales became subjects of major interest.

Le piacevoli notti is set in a contemporary adaptation of the famous Boccaccian frame: thirteen consecutive nights of narration by ladies and gentlemen, guests of Ottaviano Maria Sforza, bishop of Lodi, on the island of Murano, the fictional court assembled to escape political upheavals and persecutions. Straparola is thus able to shift the responsibility of the multiple meanings (one is usually obscene) in the final riddle of the stories to his storytellers. The historical perspective is vague, as it is in many Oriental folktales and animal fables. Characters live immersed in ancient societies often in a fabulous geography and a timeless era lacking specific social reference. The intervention of supernatural forces capable of stifling heroic efforts results in narrative and characters outside the realistic tradition. The cautious use of the pathetic and the moralizing gesture did not spare Straparola's work from the wrath of the Counter-Reformation; it was placed on the Index of Prohibited Books in 1624.

BIBLIOGRAPHY

Primary Works
Straparola, Giovanni Francesco. *The Facetious Nights of Straparola.* Translated by W. G. Waters. London, 1898.
Straparola, Giovanni Francesco. *Italian Renaissance Tales.* Edited and translated by Janet Smarr. Rochester, N.Y., 1983.

Secondary Work
Mazzacurati, Giancarlo. "La narrativa di G. F. Straparola: Sociologia e struttura del protagonista fiabesco." *Studi mediolatini e volgari* 17 (1969): 49–88.

GIUSEPPE CANDELA

STRASBOURG. Two important facts characterized the Renaissance in Strasbourg: it arrived during the early sixteenth century and, as a result, developed hand-in-hand with the Reformation. Strasbourg's Renaissance was almost solely a literary and intellectual movement. Its most prominent figures were Jacob Wimpheling (1450–1528) and Sebastian Brant (1457 or 1458–1521), who mirrored northern humanism by virtue of their preoccupation with social, and in particular religious, criticism. Wimpheling is the more complicated of the two. He adopted humanist literary forms, sharply criticized the clergy, became first a lecturer on poetry and rhetoric at Heidelberg and then cathedral preacher at Speyer, but utterly rejected the civic virtues of Cicero and the Roman Republic. He even declared that the scholastic theologians were better sources for Christian reading than the Fathers or the classical authors. One of his former students, Jacob Sturm, who was the city's leading politician until his death in 1533 and a decided force for the Reformation, nonetheless declared, "If I am a heretic, it is you who have made me one."

Brant was a purer case. His best-known work was *The Ship of Fools,* a harsh attack on Germans' lack of good morals and wisdom. He was so committed to social reform that he lacked the light touch of humor found in, for example, Thomas More's *Utopia.* Above all, Brant was one of the earliest to turn to an idiom that Martin Luther and his followers later used to great advantage. He wrote in the vernacular. Like Ulrich von Hutten (1488–1523), his intense patriotism provided the fire from which antipapal sparks flew; Hutten may indeed be regarded as having followed Brant's lead. Together, they illustrate the cultural patriotism and fascination with German history so common at the time, but they remained loyal sons of the church.

Sturm and Wimpheling to one side, humanism came to Strasbourg from the Basel circle that gathered around Erasmus and the press of Johannes Froben. Each former member—Wolfgang Capito, Martin Bucer, and Caspar Hedio—became better known as reformers of the southwest German and Swiss type, who brought with them deep training in and commitment to the humanistic disciplines. Capito began as a student at Freiburg in Breisgau, was briefly in Bruchsal, and then became cathedral preacher and professor at Basel, and a renowned Hebraist. Hedio, who had been Capito's student and successor as cathedral preacher in Basel, followed him to Mainz and thence to Strasbourg, where he served in the same positions and pursued the history of the patristic period. Bucer celebrated his ordination by visiting the Basel group, secured release from his vows as a Dominican through Capito, and then, after brief terms as a preacher with Franz von Sickingen and in Wissembourg, came to Strasbourg, where he pursued biblical studies. The fourth member of the group, Matthias Zell, was also educated at Freiburg and became a preacher in one of the side chapels of the cathedral. According to Capito, he was not among Freiburg's ablest students, but he was instrumental in converting Capito to active support for Luther's views. All four decided on theological grounds that Luther was correct and Rome wrong.

Fiery preaching, iconoclasm, and popular anti-intellectualism are most commonly associated with the reform movement. Strasbourg did experience brief, contained, and perhaps even controlled outbursts of each, but educational programs using humanist pedagogy were essential parts of the city's Reformation. As early as 1524, much in the manner of Luther's *Open Letter to All Municipalities on the Founding of Schools,* Capito began two series of theological lectures in the provost's chambers at St. Thomas. One employed the vernacular for the literate laity, which probably corresponded to the city's ruling classes. The other, "where we treat everything somewhat more fully" was held in Latin for the clergy. This preparatory work bore fruit in late 1524 and early 1525, when the group of reformers faced the crises of clerical marriage, the disciplinary authority of the bishop, a lawsuit from a few of the canons of St. Thomas, the Peasants' War, and a municipal decree that all the clergy must become citizens (and pay taxes). But by then, the reformers' biblical lectures had brought most of the noncloistered clergy and enough of the politicians to decide that Luther was right and Rome was wrong, and to act on this decision.

This same alliance between humanist education and evangelical theology led naturally to the calling in 1534 of Johann Sturm (no relation to Jacob) and the founding of Strasbourg's famous *Gymnasium.* Strasbourg had no university and, in spite of Wimpheling's urgings, its municipal schools taught only reading, writing, and arithmetic. The reformers' first petition to the government called for the founding of a Latin school to educate both the citizenry and a new clergy, just as Luther urged in his *Open Letter.* The realization of this dream also led to the establishment of special funds to support students from families that could not afford to send their children to the *Gymnasium.* By the early 1540s the alliance between humanism and the Reformation seemed both firm and productive, as the school became famous throughout northern Europe.

During the 1570s a dispute arose over who was responsible for education: church or school authorities. At the core of the dispute was the relationship between humanism and the Reformation, a question that had already found expression in the famous polemic between Erasmus and Luther over free will and the clarity of Scripture. In Strasbourg, the dispute came to a head with the publication of the Formula of Concord in 1578 and its inclusion in the *Book of Concord,* which was published in 1581. The *Book,* which also contains, among other documents, the Augsburg Confession and Luther's two catechisms, remains the one official statement of doctrine for most Lutheran churches to this day, and Strasbourg adopted it formally in 1598. But the problem was the *condemnamus,* in which the authors rejected teachings contrary to those presented in the Formula. The debate continued, but by its end, the question had come full circle. Sturm held that all well-educated people could ascertain and teach religious truth on their own, while Johann Pappus, then president of the Company of Pastors of Strasbourg, insisted that matters of doctrine were the preserve of theologians. Sturm was released from his post and Pappus was seconded by Lutheran theologians throughout the empire. Consequently, the Reformation reduced the *studia humanitatis* to a necessary preparation for theological studies, and Strasbourg's Renaissance humanism survived chiefly in the pastors' growing interest in the new discipline of church history.

See also **Brant, Sebastian**; **Capito, Wolfgang**; **Humanism**, *subentry on* **Germany and the Low Countries**; **Sturm, Johann**; **Wimpheling, Jacob**.

BIBLIOGRAPHY

Brady, Thomas A., Jr. *Protestant Politics: Jacob Sturm (1489–1553) and the German Reformation.* Atlantic Highlands, N.J., 1994.

Chrisman, Miriam Usher. *Bibliography of Strasbourg Imprints, 1480–1599.* New Haven, Conn., 1982.

Chrisman, Miriam Usher. *Lay Culture, Learned Culture: Books and Social Change in Strasbourg, 1480–1599.* New Haven, Conn., 1982.

Kittelson, James M. *Wolfgang Capito from Humanist to Reformer.* Leiden, Netherlands, 1975.

Rott, Jean. *Investigationes Historicae: Églises et société au 16e siècle.* 2 vols. Strasbourg, France, 1986.

JAMES M. KITTELSON

STROZZI, ALESSANDRA MACINGHI

(c. 1407–1471), Florentine letter writer. Alessandra Macinghi Strozzi was both typical and unusual for an upper-class woman in fifteenth-century Florence. Born in 1407 or 1408 to the small, elite lineage of the Macinghi, Alessandra received a rudimentary education common for women of her position. She learned how to read and write in the Tuscan vernacular, and how to keep household accounts. In June 1422, at the age of fourteen, Alessandra married Matteo Strozzi. Matteo was twenty-five years old, a merchant of good birth but modest wealth. Alessandra's father Filippo provided her with a dowry of 1,600 florins, a large sum by the standards of the day. Between 1426 and 1436 the couple produced three daughters and five sons, of whom only two daughters and three sons survived to adulthood.

In November 1434 Alessandra's husband Matteo was exiled to Pesaro as a political opponent of the Medici faction. Shortly after the household went into exile, Alessandra's husband and three of her children died of plague in 1435. Upon Matteo's death, Alessandra returned to Florence with her remaining children, bearing her last child a few months later. She remained in Florence until her death in 1471. As a widow who never remarried, Alessandra spent much of her energy trying to establish her sons in business and arrange suitable marriages for her children. In these pursuits Alessandra resembled many other upper-class Florentine women.

What sets Alessandra apart is the survival of seventy-three letters written to her sons living abroad as exiled merchants in Naples and Bruges; few other extensive collections of letters written by women survive from this period. These often lengthy letters, dating from August 1447 to April 1470, provide a window onto the social and political landscape of fifteenth-century Florence, as well as onto Alessandra's inner life. A keen observer of the world around her, Alessandra wrote frequently, if cautiously, about the political situation in Florence, describing new events and circumstances to her sons. She noted mundane but important details such as the price of food, and often discussed the family's financial situation. She discussed marriage prospects for her sons and daughters extensively and expended considerable effort to secure suitable wives for her exiled sons. Above all, Alessandra's letters portray her as a mother concerned with the welfare of her children, offering advice, consolation, occasional scoldings, and a deep, conventional piety.

Alessandra's letters also indicate that her sons occupied a more central place in her emotional life than did her daughters. This difference may be explained in part by the fact that, after daughters married, they became more active in the practical affairs of their new families. By contrast, a mother and her sons could and often did spend much of their adult lives together. Alessandra's married daughters continued to play a regular part in her daily life but, as women and members of another lineage, they could not recoup the Strozzi family's lost fortunes to the same extent as could her sons.

Given their unusual detail and wide range of subject matter, the letters of Alessandra Strozzi provide a rich, intimate glimpse into the experiences of Florentine women and their families that few other sources can match.

BIBLIOGRAPHY

Primary Works

Strozzi, Alessandra. *Una lettera della Alessandra Macinghi negli Strozzi in aggiunta alle settantadue pubblicate da Cesare Guasti nel 1877* (A letter by Alessandra Macinghi Strozzi in addition to the seventy-two published by Cesare Guasti in 1877). Edited by Cesare Guasti. Florence, 1890.

Strozzi, Alessandra. *Selected Letters of Alessandra Strozzi: Bilingual Edition.* Translated by Heather Gregory. Berkeley, Calif., 1997. Partial translation of *Lettere di una gentildonna fiorentina del secolo quindici ai figliuoli esuli* (1877).

Secondary Works

Crabb, Ann Morton. "How Typical Was Alessandra Macinghi Strozzi of Fifteenth-Century Florentine Widows?" In *Upon My Husband's Death: Widows in the Literature and Histories of*

Medieval Europe. Edited by Louise Mirrer. Ann Arbor, Mich., 1992. Pages 47–68.

Martines, Lauro. "A Way of Looking at Women in Renaissance Florence." *Journal of Medieval and Renaissance Studies* 4 (1974): 15–28.

SHARON T. STROCCHIA

STUART DYNASTY. The Stewarts governed the Kingdom of Scotland from 1371; restyling themselves the Stuarts, they also governed the Kingdom of England and Wales, with its dependent kingdom of Ireland, from 1603. Some authorities treat the flight and abdication deposition of James II in 1689 as the terminal date for the dynasty; others include the reign of his Dutch nephew (and son-in-law) William III (1689–1702) and the reign of his younger daughter Anne (1702–1714) as continuations of Stuart rule.

Origins of the House of Stewart.

The Stewarts came to the throne of Scotland after a half century of civil war between the Balliols and the Bruces. The death of David II without legitimate issue (1371) led to the uneasy accession of Robert II, whose claim lay with the marriage of Walter the Steward to Marjory, daughter of Robert the Bruce. This lineage made Robert II heir by a uterine succession and not a Salic one (mediated only through and to males) and was therefore against Scottish convention. Fortunately, Robert II had twenty-one children: twelve of the males became earls, and seven females married into established noble families; they created a vast dynastic network that brought more ballast to the Stewarts' hold on power. By the accession of James I (1406) it was secure.

A British Ruling House.

The Stewarts inherited the thrones of England and Ireland (and changed the spelling of their name to Stuart) through a kind of dynastic roulette. In 1503 the Tudors were in the process of securing their claims in England and wished to obtain guarantees that the Scots would cease to support pretenders to their throne. Henry VII of England therefore entered into a "treaty of perpetual peace" with James IV of Scotland, a peace sealed by a marriage alliance between James IV and Henry's elder daughter Margaret. The childlessness of Henry's elder son Arthur and of the three legitimate children (Edward VI, Mary I, and Elizabeth I) of his younger son (Henry VIII) brought the great-grandson of James IV and Margaret Tudor to the English throne exactly a century after the "perpetual peace."

The fact that an act of Parliament and the will of Henry VIII expressly forbade the Scottish line from inheriting the English throne was an important reason for James I's outspoken support for the theory of divine right monarchy: his claim by divine and natural law had to take precedence over the positive laws of particular kingdoms. So effectively did James I settle things that his son Charles I had the most uncontested accession to the English throne since Henry VIII in 1509 or perhaps since Henry V in 1413. Charles's divisive policies and lack of political skills destroyed the strong position he inherited and led to the most bloody of all British civil wars within and between his three kingdoms, in the aftermath of which he was put on trial and executed. The Scots refused to accept the unilateral action of the English and proclaimed his son Charles II king of Britain and Ireland, and he was crowned as such at Scone on 1 January 1651. However, the armies of the English Commonwealth crushed the Scottish armies, and Scotland was incorporated into an enlarged English state. In 1660 monarchy was restored and Charles II's lazy pragmatism appeared to have restored the House of Stuart's fortunes. But Charles II had no legitimate issue, and the throne passed to his Catholic brother James, whose policies destroyed the House of Stuart if not the monarchy itself.

Problems of Security.

The Stuarts lived dangerously. Of the eight Stuart monarchs to reign between 1406 and 1649, no fewer than six died by acts of violence. Two were judicially executed (Mary, queen of Scots, and Charles I of England); one was murdered (James I of Scotland); three died in battle (James II, III, and IV); and a seventh (James V) died as an indirect consequence of the defeat of his army in battle. No wonder James II of England fled to France rather than face his bitter enemies in December 1688. The violent deaths in the Stuart family led to an astonishing series of royal minorities in the fifteenth and sixteenth centuries: of the Scottish Stewarts, James II came to the throne at the age of seven, James III at the age of eight, James IV at the age of fifteen, and James V, Mary, and James VI all before their second birthdays.

Rivalry with the Tudors.

Anglo-Scottish rivalry was omnipresent in the later Middle Ages, and the English royal house regularly claimed feudal sovereignty over Scotland and therefore the right to arbitrate disputes concerning the title to the Scottish throne, the right to appoint regents, and the right to approve royal marriages. The Scots reciprocated by taking sides in the English dynastic wars of the later fifteenth century. To protect themselves against the stronger nation to the south, however, Stewart kings

Five Children of Charles I. Portrait by Anthony van Dyck, 1637. From left: Princess Mary; James, duke of York (later James II); Charles (later Charles II); Princess Elizabeth; and Princess Anne. NATIONAL PORTRAIT GALLERY, LONDON/SUPERSTOCK

formed close military ties with the kings of France ("the Auld Alliance"). This twice led them into disastrous attacks on northern England in the first half of the sixteenth century. In the first reckless attack, culminating in the Battle of Flodden on 9 September 1513, one-third of the Scottish nobility (and James IV himself) were killed, while in the second—the Battle of Solway Moss on 25 November 1542—a quarter were killed or taken prisoner. In the aftermath of this second disaster, and the consequent death of James V, Henry VIII compelled the Scottish nobles he had taken prisoner to agree to the marriage of the infant Mary (James's week-old heir) to Edward, Prince of Wales. When the Scots reneged on this agreement, he sent an army to intimidate them into honoring the treaty ("the Rough Wooing").

These experiences polarized the Scots into those who saw the long-term future of Scotland as a province of England and those who saw it as a colony of France. Eventually this difference of opinion became a religious divide too, with the pro-English nobility becoming Protestant and the pro-French nobility remaining Catholic. If Mary, queen of Scots, had had a son by Francis II before he died, that child would have inherited the crowns of France and Scotland and been (in French and Scottish eyes) the rightful ruler of England or, at the very least, the heir apparent to Elizabeth. After Francis's death, however,

Mary returned to Scotland, where her actions provoked civil war and her deposition. She fled to England, where Elizabeth kept her in prison for eighteen years and eventually colluded in her trial and execution.

Religious problems. The dynastic issue was complicated by religious issues. The personal faiths and public religious policies of Mary, queen of Scots, Charles I, and James II were primary causes of the first two losing their heads and all three losing their thrones. From 1559 (in England) and 1560 (in Scotland) the kingdoms were formally Protestant, but Mary, queen of Scots, Charles II, and James II died as Catholics, and Charles I's personal religion drew more on the spiritual and pastoral theology of Catholic humanism than on the Anglo-Swiss Protestantism of his official church. Only James I, brought up in Scotland by the severest of Calvinist tutors, had any reverence for the *via media* that was the Church of England's guiding principle. Charles I's determination to bring a Counter-Reformation style of worship and regiment (rooted in a strong clerisy and a reversal of the sixteenth-century plunder of the wealth and jurisdiction of the church), together with an authoritarianism that he acquired directly or indirectly from the continental absolutists (and especially Jean Bodin), plunged his three realms into interlocking civil wars and led eventually to his

95

Stuart Dynasty

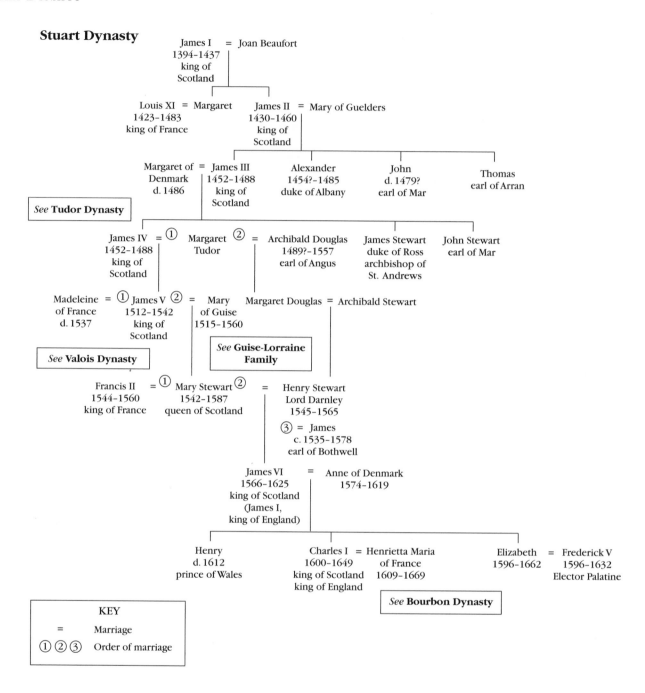

deposition and execution and to the failed eleven-year experiment in republicanism known as the Interregnum, or the Commonwealth and Protectorate.

Marriage Policies. Scotland is far smaller than England, with a population that was never more than a quarter the size of that of England and with fewer natural resources, a less mature economy, and a less developed political system. The Scots felt under constant threat from their southern neighbor in the island of Britain. The Stewarts were therefore an outward-looking dynasty, always seeking to avoid acculturation by the English and absorption into an enhanced English realm.

Royal marriages were dominated by these considerations, and all the marriages contracted by Scottish kings before 1603 were with royal continental brides, with two exceptions: at the time of James I of Scotland's accession he was a prisoner of the English in London, and he married Henry VI's cousin Joan Beaufort before his return to Scotland; James IV married Margaret Tudor. James II, James V, and

Mary married into the royal families of Burgundy and France, and James III and James VI into the Danish royal families.

After the accession of the Stuarts to the throne of Britain, they looked to Catholic Europe for their brides: Charles I married the sister of the king of France; Charles II married a daughter of the king of Portugal; and James II (after a forced marriage to the daughter of Charles II's lord chancellor whom he had made pregnant) married an Italian princess. On the whole these were prudent marriages designed to prevent their realms from being drawn into binding international commitments, although the marriage of Charles I and Henrietta Maria did lead unexpectedly to an Anglo-French war occasioned in some part by the failure of the English to honor the secret religious clauses of the marriage treaty and of the French to pay the dowry.

But if the marriages had limited international ramifications, they did complicate matters at home; for it is a striking fact about the Stuart kings that all their wives and all their children (with the exception of those who died young and, ironically, the exception of the daughters of the Catholic James II) died as Roman Catholics. When the Parliament of 1701 set out to regulate the succession, it had to pass over forty-eight Catholic descendants of James I to find the first Protestant claimant (the electress Sophia of Hanover and her son George, in due course King George I of Britain and Ireland [1714–1727]). This unilateral action by the English Parliament created a constitutional crisis in relations with the Scots, who were not bound by it and who threatened to dispose separately of the Scottish crown. This threat created the leverage the Scots needed to initiate the union of the kingdoms in 1707. The Scots surrendered legislative and executive separation in return for cast-iron guarantees protecting their own legal system and church and granting them free trade with England and English colonies. A union of crowns finally became a union of kingdoms.

The End of the House of Stuart.   James II was a zealous Catholic and, having only Protestant daughters, proved an old man in a hurry, seeking to force through constitutional changes that would secure full civil and religious equality for his coreligionists on a long-term basis. The unexpected birth to his aging wife of a son and heir in 1688 produced a crisis resolved by the arrival of his nephew and son-in-law William of Orange with a large army. James's flight led to the transfer of the title to William jointly with his wife, Mary, the elder of James's

daughters. For decades after 1689 one can speak of an intermittent war of the two dynasties as James II, his son James ("the Old Pretender"), and grandson Charles Edward ("the Young Pretender") sought to reestablish themselves on the thrones of Britain. They had much latent support throughout the three kingdoms and much active support in the Scottish Highlands and in parts of Ireland, and the enemies of the English state (at various times the French, the Spanish, the Swedes, and others) were willing to support the Jacobite cause with money, ships, and expeditionary forces. The Jacobite threat remained a very real one in the minds of most of those who governed in Britain and Ireland until at least 1746 and possibly until the early 1760s. But occupation of the throne passed to Dutch William, Protestant Anne, and then to the electors of Hanover.

See also biographies of monarchs mentioned in this entry.

BIBLIOGRAPHY

Primary Work
James I. *King James VI and I: Political Writings.* Edited by Johann P. Sommerville. Cambridge, U.K., 1994. An excellent modern edition of the works of the most scholarly and academic of the Stewarts/Stuarts, which reveals the nature and extent of Renaissance influences on the mental world of this most *British* of rulers.

Secondary Works
Bradshaw, Brendan, and John Morrill, eds. *The British Problem: State Formation in the Atlantic Archipelago.* London, 1996. Focuses on the problems of multiple or composite monarchy.
Grant, Alexander, and Keith J. Stringer, eds. *Uniting the Kingdom? The Making of British History.* London, 1995. Part 3 (chapters 7–10) is relevant to the major themes of this entry.
Kenyon, John P. *The Stuarts: A Study of English Kingship.* Rev. ed. London, 1977. Classic Anglocentric pen-portraits of the seventeenth-century rulers of Britain.
Lynch, Michael. *Scotland: A New History.* London, 1991. The most recent and liveliest of several excellent general histories of Scotland with strong portraits of all the Stuarts.
Macdonald, Alasdair A., Michael Lynch, and Ian B. Cowan, eds. *The Renaissance in Scotland.* New York, 1995. Strong on literary aspects of the court.
Morrill, John S., ed. *The Oxford Illustrated History of Tudor and Stuart Britain.* Oxford, 1996. Two chapters devoted to the court, but much discussion of dynastic issues throughout.
Nenner, Howard A. *The Right to Be King: The Succession to the Crown of England, 1603–1714.* Chapel Hill, N.C., 1995. A careful study of a troubled pattern of dynastic inheritance.
Smuts, R. Malcolm, *Court Culture and the Origins of a Royalist Tradition in Early Stuart England.* Philadelphia, 1987. A model study of continental influences at a crucial stage of English state formation.

JOHN S. MORRILL

STUDIA HUMANITATIS. *See* **Renaissance, Interpretations of the,** *subentry on* **Paul O. Kristeller.**

STUNICA, JACOBUS LOPIS (Diego López de Zúñiga; c. 1470–1531), Spanish churchman. Stunica's career involved both support of and opposition to monuments and figures of the European Renaissance. Stunica's academic genealogy can be traced back to the most acute Italian humanist, Angelo Poliziano, for he studied Greek under one of Poliziano's pupils, Ayres Barbosa. Stunica was adept in Latin, Greek, and Hebrew; he was acquainted with Aramaic and Arabic. He undoubtedly worked on the Complutensian Polyglot Bible (printed 1512–1517); he himself reported that his responsibilities in that enterprise included the collection and comparison of New Testament manuscripts in Greek against manuscripts in Latin. His peers also credited him with producing the Polyglot's interlinear Latin translation of the Septuagint, which was the oldest Greek rendition of the Old Testament.

Stunica's fame—for both his colleagues and modern scholars—lies in his relentless polemic against Erasmus's textual criticism, particularly with regard to the New Testament. The dispute began after Erasmus printed his Greek and Latin New Testament, entitled *Novum instrumentum,* in 1516. Stunica saw Erasmus's versions of that text, and critical commentary on the same, and became outraged over the potential insult to St. Jerome, the alleged translator of the Vulgate; he quickly published his *Annotationes contra Erasmo* (Annotations against Erasmus), a series of 212 annotations, which appeared in Alcalá in 1520. Eventually Stunica and Erasmus exchanged eleven published attacks and rebuttals. Even as late as 1527—after Erasmus published the fourth edition of the *Novum instrumentum*—Stunica drew up critical notes on that text's latest printing, though in this particular instance he never had them printed.

Stunica's polemics against Erasmus have never been critically edited or translated and a reliable bibliography of his work does not exist. Modern scholars have focused instead on Erasmus's replies to his antagonist. Stunica's criticism seems to have alternated between objections to Erasmus's philological decisions, and protests against Erasmus's violations of church custom, at least as Stunica himself construed that tradition. We know that Stunica eventually moved beyond the censure and annotation of Erasmus's *Novum instrumentum,* and indicted his editions of the church fathers as well. We also know

that Stunica tied Erasmus openly to Martin Luther in his Alcalá publication of 1520. The fact that he was a respected intellectual in Spain may have heightened the weight of that connection for his Spanish contemporaries. Notably, Stunica's chastisement of Erasmus had no significant impact on his career. After 1521 he lived in Rome, where he lectured on Greek poetry and enjoyed the patronage of the dean of the college of cardinals, Bernardino de Carvajal. By the end of his life, he moved in the retinue of Cardinal Francisco de Quiñones, the papal ambassador to the Holy Roman Emperor and Spanish king, Charles V. He died in Naples in 1531.

BIBLIOGRAPHY

Primary Work
Erasmus, Desiderius. *Apologia respondens ad ea quae Iacobus Lopis Stunica taxaverat in prima duntaxat Novi Testamenti aeditione.* Edited by H. J. de Jonge. In *Opera omnia.* Vol. 9, Part 2. Amsterdam and Oxford, 1983. The introduction by de Jonge, pp. 3–49, is the best overview of Erasmus's and Stunica's debates.

Secondary Works
Bentley, Jerry. *Humanists and Holy Writ.* Princeton, N.J., 1983.
Rummel, Erika. *Erasmus and his Catholic Critics.* 2 vols. Nieuwkoop, Netherlands, 1989.

LU ANN HOMZA

STURM, JOHANN (1507–1589), German educator. Sturm made a major contribution to German humanism as a pedagogue and an editor of Greek and Latin texts. He also introduced Cicero as the base of secondary education. Born in Schleidan, the Rhineland, his early education in Louvain followed the new methods of the Brethren of the Common Life. At the University of Louvain he and his professor of Greek, Rutger Regius, prepared and published Greek texts for students, thus establishing a pattern for Sturm's life. In 1529 he went to Paris to study rhetoric and dialectic. Drawn into Cardinal du Bellay's effort to ally Francis I with the German Protestants (1534–1535), Sturm's position in Paris became precarious. In 1536 he was asked to teach rhetoric and dialectic in Strasbourg.

The Strasbourg reformers and the magistrates had begun to reform the schools in 1524. Their eagerness led to the establishment of two private Latin schools under the humanists Otto Brunfels and Johann Sapidus, two theological schools, and elementary schools in every parish. In 1538 the Latin schools and the lower theological classes were combined into one institution, the Strasbourg Gymnasium. Sturm was appointed rector.

The goal of the gymnasium was to create a Christian citizen, but Sturm believed the curriculum must also provide the knowledge of nature and of the mind so fully cultivated by the ancients. The primary method of the school was to surround the students with Latin. Sturm's techniques were innovative. Each student compiled his own dictionary, carrying the accumulated pages from home to school for eight years. Similar journals were kept for grammar, for Greek and Latin examples illustrating the principles of grammar, and for poetry. Students declaimed the speeches of the great orators before the assembled school every Friday. The full repertoire of the Latin and major Greek dramatists was presented annually.

Sturm described his methods in a treatise *De literarum ludis recte aperiendis* (A correct description of a school for literary learning; 1538, reprinted four times between 1539 and 1557). His letters to the teachers of the school, *Classicae Epistolae sive Scholae Argentineses* (Letters for the classes of the Strasbourg school; 1565, 1573), explained his philosophy of education and outlined a precisely defined order of study that each faculty member was to follow. Each student's task, each step in the learning process, was placed in a sequence so that students proceeded from the simpler problems and concepts to the more complex as they moved from class to class.

Between 1538 and 1542 Sturm edited and published fourteen Latin and Greek texts for the gymnasium. These included texts of classical authors, collections of orations and poetry, and specialized treatises on dialectic and rhetoric. The foundation of all of this work was Cicero. There were four volumes of his orations, two volumes of his letters, two volumes of his philosophical essays, and the *De Officiis* (On duties). In addition Sturm published two volumes on dialectics: Aristotle's *De moribus ad Nicomachum* (Nichomachean ethics) and a collection of Plato's dialogues. A major contribution to humanist education, they were widely adopted in gymnasiums and other secondary schools and were reprinted six or eight times by presses across Europe, in Prague, Paris, London, Basel, Augsburg, and Cologne.

Between 1547 and 1576 Sturm published eight texts on rhetoric based on the Greek authors Hermogenes, Dionysus of Hallicarnasus, and Aristotle. In 1551 and 1552 with Michael Toxites, a faculty member, he published seven commentaries on Cicero's orations. He also wrote three treatises on the education of elites: *Nobilitas literata* (On the literate nobility), *De educatione Principum* (On the education of princes), and, from his correspondence with Roger Ascham, *Epistolae duae, de nobilitate anglicana* (Two letters on the English nobility; 1551). These treatises on education, as well as his collections of poetry and Cicero's letters, appeared in new editions throughout the seventeenth century.

Sturm's emphasis on rhetoric had a moral purpose. He perceived rhetoric as a civilizing force that could solve conflicting interests, disorder, and violence that plagued urban society. The skilled orator could bring together merchants, artisans, noblemen, and lawyers to work for the common good. The gymnasium trained young patricians for their future role as magistrates and civil servants.

Ironically, after 1552 the gymnasium was embattled. Johann Marbach, the leader of the Strasbourg clergy, believed that Luther's Confession of Augsburg should supersede Bucer's Articles of Faith. Marbach was opposed by Sturm and the faculty of the Upper Classes, and a bitter controversy ensued. Politically necessary, the new orthodoxy prevailed. In 1581 Sturm was dismissed as rector.

See also **Education**; **Humanism**, *subentry on* **Germany and the Low Countries.**

BIBLIOGRAPHY

Primary Work

Spitz, Lewis W., and Barbara Sher Tinsley. *The Reformation and Humanist Learning: Johann Sturm on Education.* St. Louis, Mo., 1995. English translations of the later pedagogical treatises and a biographical essay.

Secondary Works

Rott, Jean. "Bibliographie des oeuvres imprimées du recteur Strasbourgeois Jean Sturm (1507–1589)." In *Investigationes Historicae.* Vol. 2. Edited by Marijn de Kroon and Marc Lienhard. Strasbourg, France, 1986. Pages 461–559.

Schindling, Anton. *Humanistische Hochschule und freie Reichstadt: Gymnasium und Akademie in Strassburg 1538–1621.* Wiesbaden, Germany, 1977.

MIRIAM USHER CHRISMAN

SUÁREZ, FRANCISCO (1548–1617), Spanish theologian, scholastic philosopher. Born in Granada, Spain, Francisco Suárez pursued some study of canon law at Salamanca. He entered the Society of Jesus in 1564 and devoted himself to studying philosophy and theology. After being ordained in 1572, he was sent to teach philosophy and later theology at Ávila, Segovia, and Valladolid. He then spent five years, from 1580 to 1585, as professor at the Collegio Romano in Rome, the Jesuit flagship school, but poor health forced his return to Spain, where he taught at Alcalá (1585–1593) and Salamanca (1593–1597), the leading universities of Spain. His most productive years were 1597–1615, while he held the chair of theology at the University of Coimbra in Portugal.

The center of Suárez's life was writing massive studies in philosophy and theology, which fill twenty-eight volumes in the 1856 Paris edition of his works. Almost all his works are in a prolix Renaissance Latin. He has been seen as both the last of the great medieval Scholastics and a precursor of modern philosophy. Certainly he was the last great philosopher-theologian of the second Scholasticism, one of the major achievements of Spain's golden age. Among his works were a commentary on Thomas Aquinas's *Summa theologiae,* a four-volume study of religious orders that the superior general of the Jesuits encouraged him to write, and treatises on law and on grace. His treatise *De legibus* (On law; 1612) is his greatest contribution to the modern world because it encouraged the development of international law. The Renaissance interest in the church fathers clearly influenced Suárez's writings, but he was mainly a disciple of Aristotle and Aquinas, although a very independent one. He rejected the cornerstone of Thomistic metaphysics, the real distinction between essence and existence. His theology of grace allowed greater human freedom than did those of most Protestant and Catholic theologians of his era. His works on metaphysics enjoyed great popularity, not only in Spain but also in Protestant Europe, in the half century after his death.

Suárez was less engaged in controversial writings than most theologians of his time, but he did write a treatise, *Defensio fidei catholicae et apostolicae adversus anglicanae sectae errores* (A defense of the Catholic and apostolic faith against the errors of the Anglican sect; 1613), in which he attacked Anglicanism and the oath of loyalty that James I required of his Catholic subjects. The king was so angered that he had it burned and encouraged his own theologians to reply. Suárez's treatise contained a defense of papal power that angered Gallicans, who defended the special rights of the Catholic Church in France.

Jesuits in Spain cultivated a school of Suarezian philosophy and theology well into the twentieth century, but interest in his works lagged after the Second Vatican Council of 1962–1965, and few of his works have been translated into English.

BIBLIOGRAPHY

Primary Works

Suárez, Francisco. *Francisci Suarez opera omnia.* 28 vols. Paris, 1982.

Suárez, Francisco. *Selections from Three Works of Francisco Suárez, S.J.* Edited by Gwladys L. Williams and Henry Davis. Oxford, 1944.

Secondary Works

Fichter, Joseph Henry. *Man of Spain: Francis Suárez.* New York, 1940.

Gracia, Jorge, ed. *Francisco Suárez.* Special issue of *American Catholic Philosophical Quarterly* 65 (summer 1991).

Mullaney, Thomas U. *Suárez on Human Freedom.* Baltimore, 1950.

JOHN PATRICK DONNELLY, S.J.

SÜLEYMAN I (the Magnificent; 1494–1566), Turkish sultan (1520–1566). Unlike his father, Selīm I (the Grim; 1470–1520), who neglected European affairs in favor of consolidation of Ottoman power in the Muslim Near East, Süleyman devoted himself to the conduct of the *jihad* (holy war) in Europe. The impressive expansion of the Ottoman Empire during his reign, mostly through military successes, gained him the sobriquet of "Magnificent" in non-Ottoman Europe. In the empire itself, however, he was known as *kanuni* (lawgiver).

Süleyman did achieve resounding military successes at a time of rapid expansion of the Holy Roman Empire of the Habsburgs under the emperor Charles V (ruled 1519–1556), of the Franco-Habsburg confrontation in Europe, and of the Protestant Reformation. His successes were most striking, however, during the early years of his reign, principally in Hungary and in the eastern Mediterranean, areas of secondary interest to Charles V. Süleyman's forces defeated the armies of King Louis II of Hungary (ruled 1516–1526) at the celebrated battle of Mohács in 1526. Responding in part to the urgings of the anti-Habsburg Magyar nobility opposed to a Habsburg succession, Süleyman made repeated military incursions into Hungary, which resulted, despite the unsuccessful siege of Vienna in 1529, in the acquisition of central Hungary and the establishment of Turkish suzerainty over Transylvania. In the Mediterranean, the conquest of Rhodes in 1522 was followed by constant raids by the Turkish fleet headed by the famous corsair Khayr ad-Dīn (Barbarossa) and lesser successors after his death in 1546.

Of perhaps greater significance than military successes was the impact of these conflicts on the German Reformation. The entry of the Ottoman Empire into European history through Süleyman's alliance with Francis I of France in 1536 was directed against Habsburg hegemony, a position that became the cornerstone of Ottoman foreign policy for over three centuries. Ferdinand's need of Protestant financial support while pursuing his claims to the Hungarian crown, and Charles's need to avoid civil war in Germany while pursuing the Habsburgs's imperial goals—both pursuits involving military confrontations with the Turks—were successfully exploited by the German princes in their quest to establish Lutheranism in Germany in 1555.

Süleyman's reputation as a lawgiver is somewhat exaggerated. Most of the laws were designed to eliminate corruption and to restore the fundamental principles of the Kanoun Namé, the basic Ottoman legislation handed down by Mehmed II the Conqueror (ruled 1444–1446, 1451–1481). Ultimately, Süleyman's place in history is that of the last sultan whose efforts to maintain and even enlarge the size and importance of a conservative Islamic empire met with a considerable degree of success. Shortly after his death, however, the forces of change, both internal and external, were to undermine the stability and power of the Ottoman sultans and start the period of the empire's territorial retrenchment, internal crises, and general decadence.

BIBLIOGRAPHY

Inalcik, Halil. *The Ottoman Empire: The Classical Age, 1300–1600*. New York, 1973.

Merriman, Roger B. *Suleiman the Magnificent, 1520–1566*. Cambridge, Mass., 1944.

STEPHEN FISCHER-GALATI

SULLY, MAXIMILIEN DE BÉTHUNE, DUC DE

(1559–1641), French statesman. Sully is best known for his work as chief minister of Henry IV of France, between the mid-1590s and 1610, when he eventually combined offices controlling the finances, communications, artillery, fortifications, and navy. He had grown up in the Protestant court of that king, then only prince of Navarre; and both had been formed in a distinctively Protestant humanism, with outstanding teachers like the poet Florent Chrestien (1451–1596). Their studies were especially strong in mathematics, ancient literature, and history. These disciplines would mark Henry and Sully for life.

The mathematical aspect of Sully's education found full expression in his work as director of budgets, where he personally worked out complicated mathematical calculations. Ancient literature and history remained inspirations for the whole of his life, though to judge by our fragmentary knowledge of the contents of his library, he was more interested in the historical than the literary aspects of classical antiquity; he was particularly interested in the works of Plutarch. When he wrote his memoirs, he frequently compared the events of his own time to those of

Greece and Rome. His literary style in no way resembled that of the spare and elegant masters of antiquity, but was rambling and convoluted to a fault. Often, in the titles of his works and in the names of his characters (he also wrote a novel, *Gelastide*), he composed riddle-names based on Greek and Roman words.

He also liked to use Roman mottoes on the coins that he had struck each year, on the emblems that adorned the walls of his country houses, and on the decorative bindings of some of his books. One of his favorite mottoes, appropriate for his grand mastery of the artillery, was "quo jussa Jovis," meaning "I (the thunderbolt) fly whither Jupiter sends me."

In his public life, Sully does not seem particularly to have encouraged humanists through his patronage; indeed, he seems to have taken pleasure in rebuffing great scholars like Isaac Casaubon (1559–1614), who pleaded with him in vain for his pension. In charge of finances, fortifications, the artillery, and the navy, Sully did not have much occasion to demonstrate his humanist tastes. In his many building projects, he seems to have leaned more toward Netherlandish than Italian examples. He had never been to Italy, unlike many of his contemporaries, and so had been unable to taste the Renaissance at its source.

Still, even if he had nothing of the Italianizing taste of kings like Francis I and Henry II, his early education had imparted a great appreciation for classical literature and history. Surprisingly, since he was commonly viewed as an austere and withdrawn person, he was very fond of dancing—an echo, perhaps, of the Renaissance idea that physical exercise and dexterity complemented intellectual accomplishments.

BIBLIOGRAPHY

Barbiche, Bernard, and Ségolène de Dainville-Barbiche. *Sully*. Paris, 1997.

Buisseret, David. *Sully and the Growth of Centralized Government in France, 1598–1610*. London, 1968.

DAVID BUISSERET

SUMPTUARY LAWS.

The term "sumptuary laws" as used in the Renaissance describes regulations intended to prevent extravagance in food, dress, and other commodities. The laws were justified on moral, religious, or social grounds. Sumptuary laws were a feature of many feudal regimes that flourished in rich diversity during the Renaissance. They regulated conspicuous consumption, particularly of clothing, ornamentation, and jewelry, and expenditure on weddings, christenings, and funerals. The laws most persistently included a moral discourse against luxury, but they also cited economic motives of both protection and taxation. Luxury was considered sinful because it gave evidence of the cardinal sin of pride. This objection was mixed with the more mundane motive of attempting to prevent people from squandering their wealth. This mixture is revealed in an English sumptuary law, the Act for the Reformation of Excess of Apparel of 1533, that referred to "the utter impoverishment and undoing of many inexpert and light persons inclined to pride, mother of all vices."

Sumptuary laws changed little over time and did not differ significantly in Protestant or Catholic countries. France and Spain, centralized absolutist states, had sumptuary laws from the early thirteenth century into the eighteenth century. Even the Puritan settlers in New England took the tradition of sumptuary laws with them.

Many such laws provided markers of social boundaries. Laws that governed the wearing of furs were common, with royalty preserving the most sumptuous for themselves. The mix of discourses of religion, luxury, and economics is typical. In England, there were sixteen statutes and proclamations taking a hierarchic form between 1463 and 1597, with significant shifts in the degree of extravagance allowed to urban merchants. From 1547 English law regulated women's dress.

The Italian cities had diverse sumptuary laws. Most of the statutes sought to restrain luxury through price limits on clothing materials and jewelry; Venice limited expenditure on interior decoration and upholstery of gondolas. Doweries were limited out of concern that large dowries led to late marriage and thus low fertility. In Florence the sumptuary dress rules permitted greater latitude to unmarried girls than to married women to facilitate their prospects of marriage.

Innovation in fashion frequently came under attack. In 1512, when the League of Cambrai gathered to attack Venice, the Senate debated the design of sleeves, fringes and, ornaments. Here and elsewhere throughout Europe women's décolletage was closely regulated.

Sumptuary law was closely imbricated with class competition in the Italian cities. In Florence sharp struggles occured between merchants and the nobility. Limits were imposed on expenditures for funerals and weddings since such events were occasions of conspicuous consumption by the old aristocratic families that were the enemies of the city fathers. Weddings were also occasions on which the well-to-do provided entertainment to the lower orders, often ending in disorder.

The general style of Florentine sumptuary law can be gleaned from the ordinance of 1373, the preamble of which read: "Considering the Commune's need for revenue to pay current expenses it is enacted that: First, all women and girls, whether married or not, of whatever age, rank and condition who wear any gold, silver, pearls, precious stones, bells, ribbons of gold or silver, will be required to pay each year the sum of 50 florins." This fiscal tactic tied sumptuary rules closely to the existing consumption taxes on salt and wine. Women were ordered to register all dresses above a certain value and the enforcement of sumptuary legislation was placed in the hands of *ufficiali delle donne* (magistrate for women). Inspectors were appointed to examine domestic clothes chests; items in contravention of the sumptuary code might continue to be worn if they were taxed and marked with a special lead seal.

In Switzerland early laws focused on expenditures for weddings and funerals. Later the Swiss shifted their attention to dress with laws organized around a mix of economic and moral considerations. Swiss laws were a mix of attempts to prevent waste of personal wealth or conspicuous consumption and strict regulation of young women (concerning, for example, décolletage and bans on sleighriding with men other than their fathers or husbands). During John Calvin's twenty-four years in power in Geneva (1541–1564) there were eight hundred to nine hundred arrests, seventy-six banishments, and fifty-eight death sentences for sumptuary and moral offences, but, perhaps surprisingly, there was no new sumptuary legislation until after Calvin's death in 1564.

German cities had a long tradition of sumptuary laws. The Germans were much concerned with maintaining distinct dress codes for mistresses and their maids and for masters and apprentices. Throughout Europe dress codes were imposed on prostitutes. Paradoxically, some regulations required conspicuous costume, often in the form of color-coded hoods, while others banned any display of luxury.

Most penalties for violations of sumptuary laws took the form of fines. Enforcement of the laws varied widely. In England there are few records of punishment, while in Switzerland enforcement was strict. In Italy enforcement, while often rigorous, varied considerably over time.

BIBLIOGRAPHY

Baldwin, Frances Elizabeth. *Sumptuary Legislation and Personal Regulation in England*. Baltimore, 1926. Detailed history of English sumptuary laws.

Greenfield, Kent R. *Sumptuary Law in Nürnberg: A Study in Paternal Government*. Baltimore, 1918. A study of sumptuary regulation in Reformation Germany.

Hughes, Diane Owen. "Sumptuary Laws and Social Relations in Renaissance Italy." In *Disputes and Settlements*. Edited by John Bossy. New York and Cambridge, U.K., 1983. Pages 69–99. A detailed account of Italian laws, with particular reference to Florence.

Hunt, Alan. *Governance of the Consuming Passions: A History of Sumptuary Regulation*. New York, 1996. A comprehensive study of sumptuary law.

Vincent, John M. *Costume and Conduct in the Laws of Basel, Bern, and Zurich 1370–1800*. Baltimore, 1935.

ALAN HUNT

SUPERNATURAL WORLD IN RENAISSANCE ART.

Renaissance artists represented, and on occasions attempted to harness, the hidden or supernatural forces of nature as part of the wider project to recover nature's secrets lost to humankind at the time of the Fall. The witches, devils, and beasts characterized in masques and paintings made manifest the dark side of this supernatural world just as the Renaissance "type" of the benevolent magus embodied its benign side.

The Apocalypse.

The vision of the Apocalypse of St. John the Divine as recorded in the last book of the Bible, Revelation, with a new earthly Jerusalem as its conclusion, was a common prophetic theme in Renaissance art and a biblical counterpart to the promised return of both the golden age of antique legend and the magical paradise recorded in Hermetic texts. An essential stage in the triumph of the new Jerusalem was thought to be humankind's rediscovery of the means to harness the hidden, or occult, power of nature and thereby connect with the uncorrupted harmony of the heavens. These supernatural forces had, according to initiates such as the Neoplatonic philosophers Giovanni Pico della Mirandola (1463–1494) and Marsilio Ficino (1433–1499), once been controlled by Adam before the Fall, and it was his knowledge of creation that was thought to be recorded in the esoteric principles of white magic, Christian kabbalism, and Neoplatonism.

During the Renaissance, this arcana came to be identified with the figure of the magus (or alchemist), as famously characterized by Shakespeare's Prospero. Despite traditional superstition, Neoplatonists held that, if properly controlled, supernatural forces would necessarily eventually triumph over the black arts symbolized by the devil, witches, and the like and thereby perfect humankind's post-Fall condition. Furthermore, the biblical narrative upon which this expectation was based—as the inevitable course toward which history was directed—naturally informed the temporal aspirations of the Renaissance Christian prince—Philip II in Spain, Rudolf II at Prague, James I in Britain—and the court art that expressed his dynastic claims.

Two of the most powerful interpretations of this biblical vision were offered by Albrecht Dürer, who published his series *Apocalypsis cum figuris* (Apocalypse in pictures) in 1498 (comprising fifteen woodcuts), and by Jean Duvet, who followed with his own visualization of this theme in 1555. Sandro Botticelli's *Mystic Nativity* (1501) underlined the millenarian expectations of the new century in an inscription that reads,

> I Sandro painted this picture at the end of the year 1500 in the troubles of Italy in the half time after the time according to the eleventh chapter of St. John in the second woe of the Apocalypse in the loosing of the devil for three and a half years. Then he will be chained in the twelfth chapter and we will see him trodden down in this picture. (Burke, p. 234)

The Magus in Art.

Imagery from pagan mysticism and Neoplatonism, symbolizing magical control over nature, is common in the works of Botticelli, Michelangelo, and Raphael. At the court of Ferrara, Dosso Dossi (Giovanni Lutero) painted the enchantress of the *Odyssey,* Circe (c. 1516–1518), popularly considered a witch, while in the Stuart court masque Merlin was presented as foreshadowing the king in his command of supernatural forces (apparently confirmed by the British monarch's traditional power to heal by touch).

Indeed, following Adam, the biblical heroes were thought to have been possessors of such powers—as most clearly evidenced by Christ's miracles—and the magicians of antiquity were necessarily integrated into the Christian scheme. Hence Hermes Trismegistus, the father of occult arts who—like Prometheus and Daedalus, had created magical statues animated by spirits—was represented in the medieval pavement of Siena Cathedral and in the frescoes painted by Bernardino Pinturicchio for Pope Alexander VI in the Appartamento Borgia in the Vatican (1492–1494). In the guise of the Roman god Mercury, Hermes looks upward to the clouds, the realm of divine light, in Botticelli's *Primavera* (c. 1478).

Supernatural Forces. David exorcises Saul by playing his lyre. Fresco by Pellegrino Tibaldi (1527–1596) in the library of the Escorial Palace, Spain. Painted 1587–1592. The fresco illustrates the text of 1 Samuel 16:23. ESCORIAL LIBRARY/INSTITUT AMATLLER D'ART HISPÀNIC, BARCELONA

The Persian magus Zoroaster, accompanied by Plato, Pythagoras, and Euclid, is represented in Raphael's *School of Athens* (1509–1511), while Pellegrino Tibaldi's frescoes in the Escorial Library, Spain (1587–1592), feature the astrologer Alchabitius, the Egyptian priests, Daniel instructed by the Chaldean Magi, and Dionysius the Areopagite observing the eclipse at Christ's Passion. The efficacy of supernatural forces was here celebrated in the fresco representing the legend of David exorcising Saul by means of his harp.

Through the influence of Saturnian melancholy, artists were themselves thought subject to supernatural forces. This state of inspired enchantment was represented by Dürer in *Melencolia I* of 1514 and more ominously by Lucas Cranach in *The Melancholy Witch* of 1528. Supposedly born under the influence of Saturn, the Renaissance artist and magus thus became jointly inspired agents of the Saturnian golden age.

Alchemy and Art. Much like the alchemists, Renaissance artists studied the forces of nature in order to represent them. Leonardo da Vinci (1452–1519) had sought to decipher the magical forces of nature, while according to Vasari, both Cosimo Rosselli (1439–1507) and Parmigianino (Francesco Mazzola; 1503–1540) neglected painting to study alchemy. During the Renaissance alchemy influenced the development of the elaborate picture-language of emblematics, which sought to symbolize the supernatural world: a fountain could stand for the purification of metals, Christ for the philosopher's stone, and a dragon for regeneration or, on occasion, the devil.

Alchemical emblematics informed the *Hypnerotomachia Poliphili* (Dream of Poliphilus) traditionally attributed to Francesco Colonna, an esoteric romance published with woodcut illustrations by an unknown artist in Venice in 1499, and more directly influenced Salomon Trismosin's *Splendor solis* (Splendor of the sun; 1598). During the sixteenth century the moral emblems of Achille Bocchi (1488–1562) and Piero Valeriano (Bolzani; 1477–1558) sought to picture the entire hidden order of nature and the secrets of creation understood by Adam before the Fall.

The Stuart Court Masque. In England the use of supernatural imagery informed much Stuart court art, in which the king was presented as the embodiment of the celestial order. In Gerrit van Honthorst's emblematic painting *Apollo and Diana* (1628), the duke of Buckingham is cast as Hermes and introduces to Charles (Apollo) and Henrietta Maria (Diana) the liberal arts. These arts are presented in the form of allegorical figures, each with instruments of their magic art, such as globes, armillary spheres (an astronomical instrument), and the original alphabet.

In the court masque, with stage designs and costumes by Inigo Jones (1573–1652), images of the court as a paradigm of celestial order were contrasted by those of hell presented as a disharmonious collection of supernatural forces personified by witches and popular magicians—all ultimately banished by the king. The masque was indebted to the Italian intermezzi (performances of theatrical illusion), whose staging of supernatural forces had been recorded by the architectural theorist Sebastiano Serlio (1475–1554) in his second book of architecture (1545). In order to distinguish the Stuart masque as a white art, the spells of hags and witches characterized a section of the drama known as the antimasque, which was exorcised by the Stuart monarch's command over the natural forces. In Ben Jonson's *The Masque of Queens* (1609), for example, the black magic of witches was symbolized by Jones's stage set of "an ugly hell," which, at the sound of loud music and the appearance of "Virtue," was replaced by its antithesis in the form of "a glorious and magnificent building figuring the House of Fame." The white powers of the monarchy and their perfect emblem of harmony, the court, could thus banish black magic, which was identified with the imperfect country at large as the harbinger of witchcraft and, later, the dark forces of revolution. The aspiration of the Stuart monarchy was toward the promised new Jerusalem; hence the final masque of their rule, William Davenant's *Salmacida spolia* (1640), closed with a "celestial prospect" that "filled all the whole scene with apparitions and harmony."

Architecture and Magic. The role of the Renaissance artist in amending, reforming, and perfecting the terrestrial world in the image of the celestial, through a harnessing of supernatural forces and a close imitation of divine nature (and of the human body in particular), had been made clear by Ficino in *Theologia platonica* (1482).

The Neoplatonic aspiration toward harmony and perfect proportion in human works informed the subsequent treatises on art and architecture, most notably those published by John Dee (in 1570), Giovanni Paolo Lomazzo (in 1584), Daniele Barbaro (in 1556 and 1568), and Vincenzo Scamozzi (in 1615). Of all the arts, architecture came to have a central role for the Neoplatonist as the setting for the reunification of man-the-microcosm with the world macrocosm. The perfect numbers and proportions that according to the Roman theorist Vitruvius governed both the antique columns and the geometric lines, or *linee occulte* (occult lines), as Serlio called them, of a building's ground plan were all ultimately traceable in the human body as the uncorrupted pattern of perfect proportion and divine influence.

The most striking evocation of the dark forces of the Last Judgment and Apocalypse are to be found in the paintings of Hieronymus Bosch (c. 1450–1516), with their landscape of diabolical creatures. Bosch's hell scenes inspired paintings such as *Landscape with a Magical Procession* (1525), attributed to Benevenuto Garofalo, and reflected the developing taste for grotesque beasts as represented, for example, in the ceiling of the Cambio in Perugia painted around 1500 by Perugino (Pietro Vannucci; c. 1450–1523) or in the fresco works by Giovanni da Udine (1487–1564). In the 1546 engravings of Cornelis Bos (c. 1510–1566), monsters and satyrs are presented as bound up with hermetic learning (symbolized by Egyptian motifs), and they conceal its profound wisdom and power behind their distorted masks. From these unnatural, or rather supernatural forms, the art and architecture of mannerism and rococo was but a small step away.

See also **Alchemy; Architecture,** *subentry on* **Architectural Treatises; Bible,** *subentry on* **Christian Interpretation of the Bible; Drama, English,** *subentry on* **Jacobean Court Masque; Emblem; Hermetism; Magic and Astrology; Paganism; Plato and Platonism.**

BIBLIOGRAPHY

Primary Works

Ficino, Marsilio. *Théologie platonicienne de l'immortalité des âmes*. Translated by Raymond Marcel. 3 vols. Paris, 1964–1970. Translation of *Theologia platonica* (Florence, 1482).

Serlio, Sebastiano. *Sebastiano Serlio on Architecture*. Vol. 1. Translated by Vaughan Hart and Peter Hicks. New Haven, Conn., 1996. Translation of books 1–5 of *Tutte l'opere d'architettura et prospetiva* (1537–1547).

Secondary Works

Burke, Peter. *The Italian Renaissance: Culture and Society in Italy*. Cambridge, U.K., 1987.

Hart, Vaughan. *Art and Magic in the Court of the Stuarts*. London and New York, 1994.

Hersey, George L. *Pythagorean Palaces: Magic and Architecture in the Italian Renaissance*. Ithaca, N.Y., 1976.

Patrides, C. A., and Joseph Wittreich, eds. *The Apocalypse in English Renaissance Thought and Literature*. Manchester, U.K., 1984.

Wind, Edgar. *Pagan Mysteries in the Renaissance*. Harmondsworth, U.K., 1967.

Wittkower, Rudolf. *Born under Saturn; The Character and Conduct of Artists: A Documented History from Antiquity to the French Revolution*. London and New York, 1963.

Yates, Frances. *The French Academies of the Sixteenth Century*. London, 1947.

Yates, Frances. *Giordano Bruno and the Hermetic Tradition*. London, 1964.

Yates, Frances. *The Occult Philosophy in the Elizabethan Age*. London, 1979.

Yates, Frances. *Theatre of the World*. London, 1969.

VAUGHAN HART

SWEDEN. *See* **Scandinavian Kingdoms.**

SWITZERLAND. The Swiss Confederation as a political entity and Switzerland as a distinct region in Europe both emerged during the Renaissance. Al-

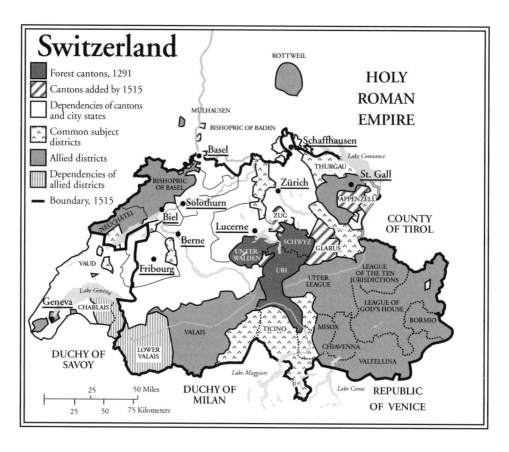

Switzerland

Forest cantons, 1291
Cantons added by 1515
Dependencies of cantons and city states
Common subject districts
Allied districts
Dependencies of allied districts
— Boundary, 1515

HOLY ROMAN EMPIRE

ROTTWEIL

MÜLHAUSEN
BISHOPRIC OF BADEN
Basel
BISHOPRIC OF BASEL
NEUCHÂTEL
Biel
Solothurn
VAUD
Fribourg
Berne
Lucerne
Lake Geneva
Geneva
CHABLAIS
DUCHY OF SAVOY
LOWER VALAIS
VALAIS

Schaffhausen
Lake Constance
THURGAU
St. Gall
Zürich
APPENZELL
ZUG
SCHWYZ
UNTER-WALDEN
URI
GLARUS
UPPER LEAGUE
COUNTY OF TIROL
LEAGUE OF THE TEN JURISDICTIONS
LEAGUE OF GOD'S HOUSE
BORMIO
MISOX
CHIAVENNA
VALTELLINA
TICINO

Lake Maggiore
Lake Como

25   50 Miles
25   50   75 Kilometers

DUCHY OF MILAN
REPUBLIC OF VENICE

though early leagues among towns and rural valleys in the region dated to the thirteenth century, the Confederation consolidated only after the Battle of Sempach in 1386, and created its main political institutions during the fifteenth century. The Confederation consisted of a fabric of alliances, which by the early sixteenth century included thirteen sovereign cantons along with subject territories and allies. It reached its final premodern form by the 1530s, under the pressure of three major conflicts: war with the Habsburg dynasty and with Burgundy; engagement in the Wars of Italy after 1494, which brought the Confederation its Italian-speaking subject territories as well as European attention; and the Protestant Reformation after 1520, which divided the Confederation between Catholics and Protestants. The Confederation's legal separation from the Holy Roman Empire began after the Swiss War of 1499, but was complete only in 1648, as the Renaissance gave way to the baroque in northern Europe.

During the same period, Switzerland became a distinct region in the minds of Europeans, thanks partly to the efforts of humanist geographers who reintroduced the classical Roman designations "Helvetia" and "Rhaetia." The two church councils held in the region—in Constance from 1414–1418 and in

Basel from 1431–1449—also increased Europeans' familiarity with Switzerland. The role of Swiss mercenaries in wars in Italy and later France produced a rather different picture, one emphasizing the wildness but effectiveness of Switzerland's soldiers. Economic and political ties with Italy, meanwhile, assured that Renaissance impulses found their way across the Alps during the fifteenth and sixteenth centuries, though their reception was uneven in a region that remained oriented primarily to the Holy Roman Empire.

Humanism in Switzerland. Renaissance humanism began to influence Swiss intellectuals late in the fifteenth century. Local writers seeking to describe the political system of the emerging Confederation mixed humanist-style historiography and geography with more traditional forms of chronicle. Albrecht von Bonstetten (c. 1445–1509) praised the Confederation in his *Superioris Germaniae Confoederationis Descriptio* (Description of the Upper German Confederation; 1479), whereas Felix Hemmerli (c. 1388–c. 1458) criticized it harshly for usurping noble power. Later Swiss humanists wrote histories in more refined Latin, notably the two Glarus scholars Heinrich Loriti ("Glareanus"; 1488–1563) and Aegidius Tschudi (1505–1572). Glareanus's "Helvetiae Descriptio" (1514) gathered classical references within a frame of Latin verse, as did Tschudi's *De prisca ac vera Alpina Rhaetia* (The ancient and true Alpine Rhaetia; 1538).

Glareanus, like many Swiss humanists, spent considerable time in Basel, where he settled after studying in Cologne and receiving the accolade of Imperial Poet Laureate in 1512. As head of a student residence and member of the university faculty, he provided humanist-influenced education to many young Swiss men while composing learned works, notably on music theory (*Dodekachordon*, 1547). Indeed, the confluence of Basel's printing industry, its university, and the city's trade links ensured Basel's distinctive role, after it joined the Confederation in 1501. It was the only canton where humanism really flourished, illustrated most vividly by Erasmus of Rotterdam's choice to live there.

The Reformation profoundly changed the situation of humanist intellectuals after 1520. Humanist-influenced Huldrych Zwingli of Zürich and Johannes Oecolampadius led the Protestant movement in Switzerland, yet the resulting divisions eventually forced every thinker to choose between the Catholic and Protestant faiths. The most accomplished Swiss humanist of his generation, Joachim Watt (Vadianus), joined the movement by returning to his native St. Gall to help move it toward Protestantism. In Basel, too, the Reformation divided the humanist community after the city joined the Protestant camp in 1529. Both Erasmus and Glareanus chose to leave, but the city's intellectual community was also enriched by learned Protestant refugees throughout the sixteenth century. Humanism's influence persisted in Switzerland, nevertheless, especially on teaching: for example, the village preacher and chronicler Bartholomäus Anhorn the Elder (1566–c. 1644) called on Cicero and Livy as his models when composing local histories around 1600.

Artistic Production. The artistic impulses of the Renaissance received a more piecemeal reception in Switzerland. The most lasting influence may have occurred in the valleys south of the Alps, where Italian-speaking populations lived under Swiss rule after 1512. There, village churches and local palaces were often decorated in popular versions of the Renaissance style. Elsewhere, the late Gothic style of the north continued to predominate. Only in Basel was a series of artists strongly influenced by Italian models. During the Council of Basel, Konrad Witz painted for Italian patrons works that combined local and Italian approaches to artistic representation; in the sixteenth century, Hans Holbein the Younger painted portraits and facades in Basel and throughout Switzerland before moving to England. Urs Graf (c. 1485–c. 1527), a Basel goldsmith and mercenary, forcefully celebrated secular individualism in his drawings, though without adopting many Italian techniques. Niklaus Manuel of Bern (c. 1484–1530) was another many-sided figure, who depicted medieval themes like the "Dance of Death" in paintings influenced by Albrecht Dürer and Matthias Grünewald, but also flourished as a Reformation propagandist and politician.

Many scholars note that the autonomy of the Swiss cities promoted a self-awareness similar to that found in Renaissance Italian city-states; it found expression in decorated town halls in Bern, Basel, and Lucerne during the sixteenth century. Still, the artistic innovations of the Renaissance entered the artistic vernacular of Switzerland more as features of individual works than as a coherent artistic movement.

Outside Perceptions of Switzerland. As the Swiss Confederation grew it attracted attention from European thinkers, most notably Niccolò Machiavelli, who admired the Swiss combination of military effectiveness and republican government. In *The Prince* (1513) he praised the Swiss with his observation that "Rome and Sparta remained armed and free for many centuries; the Swiss are most armed, and thus most free." Later, monarchist authors such as Jean Bodin (1530–1596), observing the Confederation's division after the Reformation, argued that the Swiss Confederation showed how popular participation in politics inevitably led to anarchy. Rulers all around Switzerland, however, worried that their own peasantry would "turn Swiss" and throw off their lords.

The Renaissance has not been a major theme for historians of Switzerland, who have focused more on the Reformation. Nevertheless, Renaissance ideas shaped the cultural environment in which a distinct Swiss state and identity emerged, and consequently left their imprint on aspects of Swiss culture including education, artistic production, and political theory.

See also **Basel**; **Oecolampadius**; **Vadianus, Joachim**; **Zwingli, Huldrych**.

BIBLIOGRAPHY

Aschmann, Rudolf, et al. *Der Humanist Heinrich Loriti, genannt Glarean 1488–1563: Beiträge zu seinem Leben und Werk.* Mollis, Switzerland, 1983.

Major, Emil, and Erwin Gradmann. *Urs Graf.* London, 1947.

Muralt, Leonhard von. "Renaissance und Reformation." In *Handbuch der Schweizer Geschichte*. Zürich, Switzerland, 1972. Vol. 1, pp. 391–431.

Reinle, Adolf. *Die Kunst der Renaissance, des Barock, und des Klassizismus*. Vol. 3 of *Kunstegeschichte der Schweiz*. Edited by Joseph Gantner. Frauenfeld, Switzerland, 1956.

Sablonier, Roger. "The Swiss Confederation." In *The New Cambridge Medieval History*. Vol. 7, *c. 1415–1500*. Edited by Christopher Allmand. Cambridge, U.K. 1998. Pages 645–670.

RANDOLPH C. HEAD

SYMONDS, JOHN ADDINGTON. *See* Renaissance, Interpretations of the, *subentry* on John Addington Symonds.

SZYMONOWIC, SZYMON (Szymonowicz; Simon Simonides; Szymon Bendoński; 1558–1629), Polish humanist poet. Szymon Szymonowic's father, Szymon of Brzeziny, a humanist with a university degree, was a member of the city council of Lwów (now the Ukrainian town of Lvov), then one of the most significant centers of Polish literary culture in the Ruthenian territory of the Polish Commonwealth. Szymonowic attended the University of Cracow from 1575 to 1577, where he received his B.A. and worked as a lecturer. Later he probably studied in France or Belgium.

Back in Poland he was introduced to the circle of friends of Jan Zamoyski (1542–1605), an eminent humanist and politician and a patron of artists. In Zamość (in southeastern Poland) Zamoyski founded a center of intellectual culture and later a high school, the Akademia Zamojska (1593). Szymonowic quickly gained Zamoyski's friendship and thus was made responsible for organizing the Akademia, a library, and a local printing house. As a reward for his merits as well as for his earlier poetic works, Szymonowic, a plebeian, was made a nobleman in 1590 and given the title of *poeta regius* (royal poet) by King Sigismund III. As a nobleman he used the surname Bendoński. He owned Czarnięcin, a village near Zamość given to him by Zamoyski, where he settled toward the end of his life and eventually died.

Szymonowic began his literary work in Cracow with poems in Latin. It was there that he composed *Divus Stanislaus* (Saint Stanislas; written 1575–1582), the hero of which was the eleventh-century patron of the town and its university, Stanisław of Szczepanów, a bishop of Cracow who was killed as a result of a disagreement with King Bolesław Śmiały. Modeled on the form of Pindar's lyrics, the poem consists of eighty-four stanzas. Szymonowic's lyrical poems, published in one volume, *Flagellum livoris* (A whip for envy; 1588), exemplify the influence of Horace among Polish poets at that time. Both in that volume and in the panegyric poem *Aelinopaean* (Threnody; 1589), Szymonowic praised Jan Zamoyski's abilities as an army commander. For his biblical poem *Joel proheta* (Joel the prophet; 1593), dedicated to Pope Clement VIII, Szymonowic is said to have received a laurel wreath from the pontiff. The poem made his name known throughout Europe, as the Netherlandish edition of his poems *Poematia aurea* (Golden poems; Leiden, 1619) and his foreign correspondence indicate.

Szymonowic is known as the author of a collection of twenty pastorals written in Polish in thirteen-syllable verses, which were published in 1614 under the title *Sielanki* (literally "country girls," derived from the word *sioło,* countryside; the term entered Polish permanently as the Polish equivalent for "idyll"). *Sielanki* is an example of the liveliness of the Polish Renaissance culture at the beginning of the seventeenth century and represents a synthesis of European tradition (pastorals by Theocritus, *Bucolics* by Virgil, eclogues by Jacopo Sannazaro) and the local tradition (Polish and Ruthenian folklore, realism in describing the country life, and the poetic patterns inherited from Jan Kochanowski). *Sielanki* also served as a model for the further development of pastorals in Polish literary culture.

See also Neo-Latin Literature and Language; Poland.

BIBLIOGRAPHY

Primary Work

Heck, Korneli. *Szymon Szymonowicz (Simon Simonides): Jego żywot i dzieła*. Cracow, 1901–1903.

Secondary Works

Mikulski, Tadeusz. *Rzeczy staropolskie*. Wrocław, Poland, 1964. See "Z badań nad Szymonowiczem," pp. 452–458.

Pelc, Janusz. Introduction to *Sielanki i pozostałe wiersze polskie,* by Szymon Szymonowicz. Wrocław, Poland, 1964.

ANDRZEJ BOROWSKI

TANSILLO, LUIGI (1510–1568), Neapolitan poet. Luigi Tansillo hailed from an aristocratic family of Venosa. In 1535 he entered the court of the Spanish viceroy don Pedro di Toledo, where he had diplomatic and military duties. From 1561 until his death, Tansillo was governor of Gaeta.

Tansillo began his literary career with the publication of the pastoral drama *I due pellegrini* (The two pilgrims) in 1527. The "rustic" poem *Il vendemmiatore* (The grape harvester; 1532) combines a celebration of carnal love and enjoyment of life with elegiac evocations of the golden age and fleeting youth. *Stanze a Bernardino Martirano* (Stanzas for Bernardino Martirano; 1540) recounts the vicissitudes of a sea journey that Tansillo took with Toledo's son, don Garzia. The mythological poem *Clorida* (1547) uses the story of a nymph who inhabits the country villa of Tansillo's protector as a pretext for descriptions of the natural setting and praise of don Garzia's military prowess. Other works of interest include the didactic poem *La balia* (The wet nurse; 1552), which encourages mothers to nurse their own children, and *Il podere* (The farm; 1560), an idyll celebrating serene country life.

Tansillo's fame depends principally on the sacred poem *Le lagrime di San Pietro* (The tears of Saint Peter; 1585), the first example of a genre that became popular over the next century, and his Petrarchan sonnets (first anthologized in 1551, though not published in their entirety until 1711).

Tansillo's original reelaboration of Petrarchan and classical models expressed itself most significantly through his intensely sensual descriptions of natural landscapes, the musicality of his verse, and his virtuosic shows of technical ability, often through the use of unusual conceits. Tansillo was esteemed by later poets such as Torquato Tasso, Giordano Bruno, and Giambattista Marino, and critics have often seen in his descriptive sensibility an anticipation of the baroque aesthetic.

BIBLIOGRAPHY

Primary Works

Tansillo, Luigi. *Il canzoniere edito e inedito*. Edited by Erasmo Pèrcopo. 2 vols. Naples, Italy, 1996. Tansillo's shorter poetic works, with an extensive philological introduction.

Tansillo, Luigi. *Poemetti*. Edited by Carmelo Cappuccio. Florence, 1954. Longer narrative poems.

Secondary Work

Toscano, Tobia R. "Due 'allievi' di Vittoria Colonna: Luigi Tansillo e Alfonso d'Avalos." *Critica letteraria* 16 (1988): 739–773. Discussion of Tansillo in the context of Renaissance Petrarchism.

NANCY L. CANEPA

TAPESTRY. *See* **Decorative Arts.**

TARABOTTI, ARCANGELA (born Elena Cassandra; pseudonyms, Galerana Baratotti, Galerana Barcitotti; 1604–1652), Venetian advocate of women's liberty and equality, critic of contemporary patriarchy, social satirist, polemicist. Tarabotti's indignation sprang from bitter experience: as a young girl she was sent to the Benedictine convent of Sant' Anna in Castello, where she was pressured into taking vows at sixteen that bound her for life. She died in Sant' Anna, probably of tuberculosis.

Tarabotti's own father dictated her state in life solely because she was lame and consequently not a good prospect in the harsh climate of the Venetian marriage market. She never forgave him for treating her as a social reject. Significantly, in most of her writings she does not refer to herself as a nun (*suora*), but as a layperson (*signora*) who has close acquaintance with the monastic way of life. Indeed, she describes herself repeatedly as a prisoner held against her will.

Tarabotti had no formal education; she was assisted by members of the libertine Accademia degli Incogniti (academy of the disguised, a predominantly literary academy many of whose members hid or disguised opinions considered immoral and irreligious), founded in 1627 by the wealthy and gifted Venetian patrician Gian Francesco Loredan, senator and member of the highest governing body in Venice, the Council of Ten. They brought her books and corresponded with her. Loredan was a patron, helping her publish, and Tarabotti dedicated her *Lettere familiari e di complimento* (Familiar and complimentary letters) of 1650 to him (no other Venetian woman writer enjoyed his support).

Tarabotti's first book in print, *Il Paradiso monacale* (Monastic life as paradise), appeared when she was almost forty. It was a public act of reparation and rehabilitation for the scandal already aroused by two previous works that had gone the rounds in manuscript, *La tirannia paterna* (Paternal tyranny) and *L'Inferno monacale* (Monastic life as hell). The latter was not published until 1990, and the former, her very first composition, was published posthumously in 1654 with a less accusatory title and a changed prologue, *La semplicità ingannata* (Innocence betrayed).

Tarabotti refers to *La tirannia paterna* as a major testament of her philosophy and theology of women's liberty and equality, deriving its power from traumatic experiences reflected upon for years. For Tarabotti, male and female were created equal by God, who not only gave the same gifts of rationality and free will to both sexes but also intended husband and wife to have equal rights and responsibilities. Tarabotti interprets the controversial word used for Eve, "helpmeet" (Latin, *adiutorium*), to mean companion and friend rather than to indicate that Eve was subject to Adam, the contemporary view of civil and canon law.

Besides giving a feminist reading of the Old and New Testaments, Tarabotti draws on Dante's *Divine Comedy*, adopting Dante's exaltation of free will as God's greatest gift to the human race in order to condemn those who would take it away from women. Like Dante, she wrote not only an *Inferno* and *Paradiso* but also a *Purgatorio* (of which there is no trace), which addressed the sufferings of wives at the hands of abusive husbands. In all three polemical satires, the greatest sin of contemporary patriarchy is to deny women education. Ignorance, she is sure, is a form of social control to subjugate women and deny them, as unqualified, a public role. A natural debater, she longed to attend a proper school, not to mention one of the numerous universities that were a feature of male European intellectual life.

When Francesco Buoninsigni, a member of the Incogniti, published a satire, *Contro il lusso donnesco* (Against women's love of luxury; 1638), blaming women's imbecility for gross expenditure on dress and grooming, Tarabotti countered with an *Antisatira* exposing the vanity that drove men's extravagance in dress, cosmetics, and wigs. She further argued that women had every right to adorn themselves as it gave them some kind of social dignity they otherwise did not have. If only men allowed women to be educated, they would turn their minds to other things.

Her final, most philosophical satire, *Che le donne siano della spetie degli huomini* (Women are of the same species as men), published in 1651, a year before her death, rebutted paragraph by paragraph a satire of 1647, in turn based on a Latin tract of 1595. These earlier satires aired deeply offensive opinions about women not having a rational soul, not being capable of virtue or vice, and so not being eligible for salvation. Although claiming to be "paradoxical," these kinds of intellectual casuistry, Tarabotti recognized, were at the expense of ignorant women who could not answer. Like a lawyer in court, she took up their defense, and won.

Tarabotti's works trod the paths of underground, clandestine literature. The most outspoken writer about women's social and cultural subordination was consigned to almost total oblivion. She has been vindicated only in the last half of the twentieth century by feminist appraisals that at last have given her pleas for women's rights a voice.

BIBLIOGRAPHY

Primary Works

Buoninsegni, Francesco, and Suor Arcangela Tarabotti. *Satira e antisatira*. Edited by Elissa Weaver. Rome, 1998.

Medioli, Francesca, ed. *L'Inferno monacale di Arcangela Tarabotti*. Turin, Italy, 1990.

Tarabotti, Arcangela. *Che le donne siano della spezie degli uomini*. Edited with notes and introductory essay in English by Letizia Panizza. London, 1994.

Tarabotti, Arcangela. *Paternal Tyranny*. Translated with notes and introductory essay by Letizia Panizza. Chicago, forthcoming. Translation of *La tirannia paterna*.

Secondary Works

De Bellis, Daniela. "Arcangela Tarabotti nella cultura veneziana del XVII secolo." *Annali del Dipartimento di Filosofia, Università di Firenze* 6 (1990): 59–110.

King, Margaret. *Women of the Renaissance*. Chicago, 1991.

Labalme, Patricia. "Venetian Women on Women: Three Early Modern Feminists." *Archivio Veneto* 5th series, no. 197 (1981): 81–109.

Odorisio, Ginevra Conti. *Donna e società nel Seicento*. Rome, 1979. Extracts and discussion.

Weaver, Elissa. "Suor Arcangela Tarabotti." In *Italian Women Writers*, edited by Rinaldina Russell. Westport, Conn., 1994.

Zanette, Emilio. *Suor Arcangela, monaca del Seicento veneziano*. Venice, 1960.

LETIZIA PANIZZA

TARTAGLIA, NICCOLÒ (1499–1557), Italian scientist. Although Niccolò's real name was probably Fontana, he was known as Tartaglia (stammerer) because of a speech defect caused by face wounds he received during the Sack of Brescia in 1512. Losing his father in early childhood, Tartaglia grew up in poverty, and his education was largely the fruit of his own intelligence and love of study, particularly mathematics. Between 1516 and 1518 he moved to Verona, earning his living as a teacher of the abacus (i.e., commercial arithmetic), and thence in 1534 to Venice, where—apart from a period in Brescia in 1548–1549—he lived the rest of his life as a teacher of mathematics.

Tartaglia studied the mathematics of the ancient Greeks through the Latin translations of the time and early grew aware of the need to recover this classical heritage. To this end he produced his editions of the ancient mathematicians. His *Opera Archimedis* (Archimedes's works; 1543)—a collection of medieval translations by William of Moerbeke (c. 1215–c. 1286)—contained, among other works, the first book of *On Floating Bodies*. For the next twenty years or so this text, which proved fundamental to the gradual emancipation from Aristotelian physics culminating in Galileo, was available only in Tartaglia's editions. This same text lies behind the hydrostatic treatment of falling bodies Tartaglia gave in his *Travagliata inventione* (Hard-won discovery; 1551), on the raising of sunken vessels, and in his commentary on his own Italian version of Archimedes's treatise (published as the first treatise in *Travagliata inventione*). The text is also the basis for the first experimental table of specific gravities of certain materials, published posthumously in 1565 as an appendix to Jordanus Nemorarius's *De ratione pon-deris* (On the theory of weight; mid-thirteenth century) edited by Tartaglia. His Italian translation of Euclid's *Elements* (1543)—the key, he believed, to all science—was also something quite new: for the first time he gave craftsmen, mechanics, and engineers access to the geometrical construction in all its rigorous deductive logic, a theoretical quality he considered Euclid's claim to fame.

The emulation of Euclid distinguishes an important part of Tartaglia's own work. *Quesiti et inventioni diverse* (Various questions and inventions; 1546) improves on many propositions in medieval statics, drawn mainly from Jordanus, by supplementing the principles, redefining the order of the propositions, and reelaborating the proofs. Among these propositions, that of the equilibrium of bodies on an inclined plane is particularly significant for the development of the science of movement. One of Tartaglia's innovations in his *Nova scientia* (New science; 1537), the work that makes him the founder of ballistics, lies in his axiomatic-deductive approach. Beyond the results it achieved (demonstrating, for instance, that a forty-five-degree elevation gives a cannon its greatest range of fire), which were long used in military treatises, *Nova scientia* is also important as marking the transition toward a thoroughly modern outlook on mechanics, even though some Aristotelian concepts (like the impossibility of mixing natural and violent motions and the notion of impetus) are still at work.

By abstracting from certain conditions of movement in reality, like air resistance, and considering bodies as materially simplified, Tartaglia found a way of reconciling the empirical complexity of reality with the conceptual simplicity of mathematical theory—an approach he later developed in his *Quesiti*. In this work the normative function he gave to mathematical reasoning in dealing with material reality had a dual outcome: first, it produced more rigorous results in the science of ballistics, especially in the definition of the trajectory of a projectile as entirely curvilinear, which overcame the incompatibility of natural and violent motions; second, it prefigured the modern concept of scientific experiment, in which mathematical reasoning establishes the conditions for verifying a theory.

We also owe to Tartaglia the solution of numerous arithmetical, geometrical, and algebraic problems, published in his *Quesiti* and in his last work, *General trattato di numeri e misure* (General treatise on numbers and measures; 1556), which was to be an encyclopedia of pure and applied mathematics. In this field, however, his greatest achievement was the solution for cubic equations, a discovery dating from his stay in Verona and which he shares with Scipione dal Ferro (1465–1526). Though not immediately applicable to equations in which the quadratic term is present, and inadequate in solving the so-called "irreducible case," in which square roots of negative numbers appear, this discovery broke through a centuries-old barrier. It also gave rise to a bitter dispute when Girolamo Cardano (1501–1576) published Tartaglia's formula in his *Ars magna* (The great art; 1545) after it had been entrusted to him in secret. Cardano's pupil, Ludovico Ferrari, replied to the accusation of plagiarism Tartaglia made against his former friend. The antagonists' dispute, which rang through the world of science for two years (1547–1548) in the twelve *Cartelli di matematica disfida* (Notices of mathematical challenge), was a powerful stimulus to progress in algebraic theory.

BIBLIOGRAPHY

Primary Works

Drake, Stillman, and Israel E. Drabkin, eds. *Mechanics in Sixteenth-Century Italy: Selections from Tartaglia, Benedetti, Guido Ubaldo, and Galileo.* Madison, Wis., 1969. Pages 61–143. Lengthy excerpts from *Nova scientia* and *Quesiti et inventioni diverse,* translated and annotated by Stillman Drake.

Tartaglia, Niccolò. *La nova scientia, con una gionta al terzo libro.* Venice, 1550. Reprint, Sala Bolognese, Italy, 1984.

Tartaglia, Niccolò. *Quesiti et inventioni diverse.* Venice, 1546. Reprint, with commentary by Arnaldo Masotti, Brescia, Italy, 1959.

Tartaglia, Niccolò, and Lodovico Ferrari. *Cartelli di sfida matematica.* Reprint, with commentary by Arnaldo Masotti. Brescia, Italy, 1974.

Secondary Works

Bortolotti, Ettore. "I contributi del Tartaglia, del Cardano, del Ferrari, e della scuola matematica bolognese alla teoria algebraica delle equazioni cubiche." In *Studi e Memorie per la storia dell'Università di Bologna* 10 (1926): 55–108.

Carugo, Adriano. "Tartaglia, Benedetti, Galileo, e le origini della dinamica moderna." In *Giovanni Battista Benedetti. Spunti di storia delle scienze.* Venice, 1985, pp. 61–83.

Favaro, Antonio. "Per la biografia di Niccolò Tartaglia." *Archivio storico italiano* 71 (1913): 335–372.

Gabrieli, Giovanni Battista. *Nicolò Tartaglia: Invenzioni, disfide e sfortune.* Siena, Italy, 1986.

Koyré, Alexandre. "La dynamique de Nicolo Tartaglia." In *Études d'histoire de la pensée scientifique par Alexandre Koyré.* Paris, 1973.

Masotti, Arnaldo. *Studi su N. Tartaglia.* Brescia, Italy, 1962.

ANNA DE PACE

TASSO, BERNARDO (1493–1569), Italian poet. Born into a Bergamasque family known for having established a European postal service, Bernardo Tasso was educated in both law and literature. He began his courtly career sometime before 1525, and in 1532 he entered the service of Ferrante Sanseverino, prince of Salerno, performing secretarial and ambassadorial duties. A generous patron, Sanseverino allowed Tasso at one point to retire to Sorrento to work full-time on his chivalric romance *Amadigi.* But the association also brought great sadness to Tasso's life. Sanseverino's political fortunes led in 1551 to Tasso's permanent separation from his beloved wife, Porzia de' Rossi, as well as from his daughter, Cornelia (b. 1536 or 1537). His son, Torquato (1544–1595), one of the greatest poets of the late sixteenth century, later joined him in Rome, but Porzia died in 1556 without ever seeing her husband again.

Tasso began his literary career as a lyric poet, publishing over his lifetime five volumes of poetry covering amorous, religious, classical, and encomiastic themes. He also published two successful volumes of letters, combining themes of compliment and courtiership, problems with the postal system, and financial worries; many address the composition of the *Amadigi.* Tasso is perhaps best known today for this lengthy poem, published in Venice in 1560. It is based on the Spanish prose romance *Los quatro libros del virtuoso caballero Amadís de Gaula* and combines typical Renaissance themes of courtesy, love, and battle. Tasso originally wanted to write an epic in blank verse, narrating the single action of a single hero, Amadis of Gaul, according to contemporary neo-Aristotelian standards. He scuttled this plan when he realized that it would not find favor with a court audience so used to poems like Ludovico Ariosto's *Orlando Furioso* (3d ed., 1532), which mixed multiple narratives and was written in octaves. Editions of Tasso's poem appeared as late as the nineteenth century, but by the late 1990s it no longer enjoyed critical favor.

Other works by Tasso include a lost *Guidone Selvaggio,* based on a minor character in *Orlando Furioso,* as well as some lost comedies. A *Ragionamento della poesia* (Discourse on poetry), combining Aristotelian and Horatian ideas about poetry, was published in 1562. In 1563 Tasso began to compose *Il floridante,* a shorter poem that was to contain substantial material from the *Amadigi.* Unfinished at the time of his death, it was edited and published by Torquato.

Tasso had hoped that the publication of the *Amadigi* would reverse his financial fortunes, which had flagged in part thanks to an ongoing dispute with his wife's brothers over her dowry. But the poem did not bring him wealth. During his final years his health failed, and upon his death on 5 September 1569 his son buried him in the church of Sant'Egidio in Mantua. The body was later transferred to Ferrara.

Tasso belongs to a group of secondary Renaissance poets whose works, while little read today, reflect the prevailing trends of their age, and whose careers, both courtly and literary, tell a story of financial concerns and surrender to conformity.

BIBLIOGRAPHY

Primary Works

Tasso, Bernardo. *Delle lettere accresciute, corrette, e illustrate con la vita dell'autore.* Padua, Italy, 1733.

Tasso, Bernardo. *L'Amadigi del S. Bernardo Tasso, colla vita dell'autore e varie illustrazioni dell'opera.* Bergamo, Italy, 1755.

Tasso, Bernardo. *Rime.* Edited by Vercingetorige Martignone and Domenico Chiodo. Turin, Italy, 1995.

Secondary Work

Williamson, Edward. *Bernardo Tasso.* Rome, 1951.

MICHAEL SHERBERG

TASSO, TORQUATO

(1544–1595), Italian poet and dramatist. Torquato Tasso was the last major poet of the Italian Renaissance. His life, a mixture of glory and misfortune, of genius crippled by mental illness, illustrates the decay of the vigorous civic and courtly culture that had made Italy the creative center of Europe. The high measure of creative freedom and self-confidence that Jakob Burckhardt describes in *The Civilization of the Renaissance in Italy* (1860)—a portrait of the age that has been challenged but not displaced—was giving way to pressures for conformity derived from the increasing domination of Italian affairs by Spanish interests, and by the currents of severe piety promoted by the Counter-Reformation. At its best, Tasso's work incorporates the tensions that marked this decay and transmutes them into great art.

Life. Tasso was born in Sorrento. His father, Bernardo (1493–1569), a typical Renaissance courtier poet, was at the time secretary to the prince of Salerno, one of the great barons of the Kingdom of Naples, which was part of the Spanish empire. In 1547 both Salerno and Bernardo became involved in resistance to the introduction of the Spanish Inquisition into Naples, and eventually had to flee the kingdom.

Early travels and education. Young Tasso followed his father, leaving his mother and sister behind, and spent the years from 1551 to 1560 moving from court to court in central and northern Italy as his father sought new patrons, first in Rome, then in

Torquato Tasso. Anonymous portrait. GALLERIA PALATINA, FLORENCE/SCALA/ART RESOURCE

Urbino, Venice, and Mantua. In the course of these peregrinations, Tasso acquired an excellent education as well as the high literary and intellectual ambitions that were still fostered in those brilliant centers of Renaissance culture. At the same time, however, he gained his first taste of the peculiar insecurities attendant on the life of a courtier and poet in the second half of the sixteenth century.

In 1560 Tasso entered the University of Padua. His father wanted him to study law in order to free himself from dependence on patronage, but Tasso's interests lay in poetry and philosophy. He was already at work on a narrative poem about the First Crusade that was ultimately to turn into his masterpiece, *Gerusalemme liberata* (Jerusalem delivered), and he soon abandoned his legal studies in order to attend lectures in philosophy and pursue his literary interests. In 1562 he published *Rinaldo,* a chivalric romance that established him at the age of eighteen as a poet of great promise, and it was probably at Padua that he wrote the first draft of the *Discorsi dell'arte poetica* (Discourses on the art of poetry; Venice, 1587), his first effort to develop a coherent theory of literature as a basis for his own practice. In 1565, after two years at the University of Bologna, he forsook the university altogether, never having taken a degree, and traveled to Ferrara to join the household of Cardinal Luigi d'Este, brother of the duke, Alfonso II (1533–1597). Thus he committed himself to the life of courtly dependence that his father had wanted him to avoid.

Protégé of the Este. In the cardinal's household, and later in the duke's, which he joined in 1572, Tasso had no regular duties. His role was to amuse, instruct, and glorify his patrons by writing, which he did copiously, producing numerous lyrics, orations for special occasions, his pastoral drama *Aminta,* a prose account of a trip to France, the first two acts of a tragedy, and other works. In 1575, moreover, he completed *Gerusalemme liberata,* which was eagerly awaited by a large audience throughout Italy, and especially by Duke Alfonso, whom the poem celebrated much as Ludovico Ariosto's *Orlando furioso* (1516) had celebrated an earlier Este prince, the cardinal Ippolito. Before Tasso would publish, however, he insisted on having the poem reviewed by five eminent critics, whose opinions he wanted about the poem's literary qualities and its theological and political orthodoxy.

Tasso's motive in inviting criticism before publication was to protect himself, but the suggestions of his critics proved more numerous and troublesome than he had anticipated, and he soon found himself embroiled in exhausting debates over a multitude of details. He responded to his critics in long and carefully argued letters, agreeing to some changes but resisting others, and he produced a prose "Allegory" to be published with the poem emphasizing its edifying and orthodox purposes. Nevertheless, the debates continued, and in the midst of them Tasso seems to have suffered a nervous breakdown. The facts remain obscure. What we know or can reasonably surmise is that he grew quarrelsome and suspicious at court, on one occasion even coming to blows with another courtier; that he feared he was being denounced to the Inquisition; that he sought to counter the accusations of his enemies by going to the inquisitors of his own accord to seek absolution; and that in the summer of 1577 he tried to stab a servant whom he suspected of spying on him.

Placed under strict guard, Tasso nevertheless managed to escape and make his way south to his sister in Sorrento, leaving the precious manuscript of the *Gerusalemme liberata* behind in Ferrara. He spent the next two years wandering from one refuge to another, seeking in vain the return of his poem.

A brief visit to Ferrara in 1578 was unsuccessful, but he returned in 1579 hoping for a reconciliation. Alfonso, however, was preoccupied with preparations for his wedding to Margherita Gonzaga and had little time for Tasso, who felt neglected. Worse, he was unable to obtain his manuscript. In the end, apparently, Tasso's fears and anger overwhelmed him. He denounced Alfonso and the court publicly and had to be restrained by force. Taken to the nearby hospital of Sant'Anna, he was chained as a madman. Although the chains were soon removed, his imprisonment lasted seven years.

The extraordinary length of this imprisonment has never been satisfactorily explained. The legend that his breakdown and imprisonment resulted from a forbidden love for the duke's sister Leonora, celebrated by Johann Wolfgang von Goethe in his play *Torquato Tasso* (1790), by Lord Byron (1788–1824), and by many other poets and painters, has been discredited. On the other hand, the explanation offered by apologists for Alfonso that his only concern was Tasso's welfare is also hard to accept. While in Sant'Anna, Tasso continued to suffer periods of emotional instability. In sixteenth-century terms, he was a melancholic, suffering from what we might call paranoia or manic depression, but the testimony of his many visitors and the evidence of his literary activity during his confinement suggest that most of the time he was essentially sane.

From prison Tasso conducted a voluminous and learned correspondence on many subjects; he returned to revising *Gerusalemme liberata,* which was restored to him and which finally appeared, together with the "Allegory," in 1581; he continued to write prolifically in shorter, lyric forms; he contributed two essays to the great literary quarrel of the mid-1580s over the relative merits of his own epic and Ariosto's *Orlando furioso;* and he produced eighteen dialogues, many of them lengthy and complex, as well as *Discorso dell'arte del dialogo* (Discourse on the art of the dialogue). In 1586 Alfonso released him into the custody of Vincenzo Gonzaga of Mantua.

Last years. Tasso's last years were ones of continued productivity and restless wandering. Mantua, Florence, Rome, and Naples were the centers to which he gravitated without ever stopping for long. He finished the tragedy, *Il re Torrismondo* (King Torrismondo; 1587), that he had begun before his imprisonment in Ferrara, and composed a major new religious poem, *Le sette giornate del mondo creato* (The seven days of the creation of the world, 1594), as well as many other works in verse and prose, including more dialogues, a reworking of the *Discorsi dell'arte poetica,* and a second theoretical treatise entitled *Discorsi del poema eroico* (*Discourses on the Heroic Poem;* 1594). His major project, however, was a revision of *Gerusalemme liberata* along lines that would make it even more consistent with the theology of the Counter-Reformation, with history, and with the epic practices of Homer and Virgil. The result, published in 1593 with a new title, *Gerusalemme conquistata* (Jerusalem conquered), and dedicated to a new patron, Cinzio Aldobrandini, nephew of Pope Clement VIII, may be seen as the poet's ultimate effort to accommodate to the new age. Although interesting and not without poetic power, the changes, on the whole, weakened rather than strengthened the poem. *Gerusalemme conquistata* has never supplanted *Gerusalemme liberata* in critical favor or in popularity. Tasso died in Rome.

Work. Tasso's work exhibits the ambition of the Renaissance writer to master as much of the intellectual tradition and as many of the literary genres as possible. In Tasso's case, this meant trying his hand at pastoral, epic, lyric, tragedy, a long theological-philosophical poem, philosophical discourses, letters, and dialogues. Of the principal genres, only comedy never engaged him. His work reflects in varying ways the two sides of his artistic personality: intense, emotional sensuousness on the one hand, and equally intense moral and intellectual seriousness on the other. In his greatest work, these elements combine in complex ways, often full of tension and irony.

Aminta. Tasso's brilliant contribution to the late-Renaissance vogue of pastoral drama, *Aminta,* was written in 1573 and performed during the same year at the Belvedere, an Este villa on an island in the Po. The play at once confirmed the promise of Tasso's early poems and rapidly spread his fame throughout Italy and Europe. It tells the story of the love of Aminta, a youthful shepherd poet, for the reluctant Silvia, a love that leads him to despair and attempted suicide before he and Silvia are happily united at the end. Tasso's portrayal of young love is both psychologically subtle and poetically beautiful. The pastoral setting recalls the golden age, a commonplace of Renaissance classicism, and Aminta seems to represent the kind of love that might have flourished in such an age, a natural love, unselfish, delicate, and intuitive. Similarly, Silvia's reluctance is presented not as sophisticated coyness but as the aversion to erotic experience that is natural in a certain kind of spirited young woman, another Renaissance commonplace.

Tasso's *Gerusalemme liberata.* Title page of the 1590 Genoa edition.

A kind of Diana at first, like the goddess Silvia prefers hunting to men until Aminta's persistent devotion melts her virginal chilliness. That the pastoral world in which the young lovers eventually find happiness is a poetic fiction as unrealistic as it is beautiful Tasso makes clear through the melancholy irony that throughout the poem balances the idealism. Against Aminta and Silvia, Tasso contrasts the older Tirsi and Dafne, who remind us of the corruptions of the urban and courtly world—specifically the world of Ferrara—and the fact that true love provides at best a fleeting refuge from its sorrows.

Gerusalemme liberata (*Jerusalem delivered).* In the Renaissance, the highest kind of poetry was epic, the genre that most completely fulfilled the classical prescription that poetry should both delight and instruct. In choosing the First Crusade as the subject for his epic, Tasso signaled a shift from the epic practice of his most illustrious Italian predecessors in the field—Ariosto (1474–1533), Luigi Pulci (1432–1484), and Matteo Maria Boiardo (1441–

1494)—who, he felt, had emphasized delight at the expense of instruction. *Gerusalemme liberata* was intended to redress the balance. Without wholly abandoning the complex plots, the erotic adventures, the marvelous devices, and other fantastic elements that had become the stock-in-trade of the earlier romantic epic, Tasso subdued them to his higher moral and religious purposes and to his sterner aesthetic, based more closely on Homer, Virgil, and other classical models.

Love and heroism are *Gerusalemme liberata*'s great themes, and the poem presents as rich and complex an account of the tensions between them as Tasso deemed consistent with epic dignity. So the seduction of Rinaldo, the poem's Achilles, by the beautiful witch Armida, expresses both the undeniable attraction of sensual escape from heroic duty and the equally undeniable moral degradation that results from self-indulgence. Rinaldo's journey to Armida's mountain paradise in the Fortunate Isles represents a kind of return to the golden age, a desirable goal, which *Aminta* celebrated. In *Gerusalemme liberata,* however, the return serves the purposes of a witch and must be rejected by the hero in spite of its charm. In another of the poem's great love stories, heroic duty dictates that the Christian hero Tancredi's love for the pagan heroine Clorinda can never be consummated except spiritually. When she makes a particularly damaging attack on the Christian camp, he attacks and wounds her fatally, discovering too late what he has done. As she dies, all he can do is baptize her (at her request) with water from a nearby spring.

In imitation of both classical and earlier Renaissance epics, *Gerusalemme liberata* contains many battle scenes. Although they have attracted little critical attention, they contain some of Tasso's most carefully wrought writing. He is especially good at combining violent action with delicate psychological analysis. The combat between Tancredi and Clorinda with its disturbing mixture of eroticism, wrath, violence, and religion is famous—it was set to music by Claudio Monteverdi in 1624—but there are other descriptions of combat that are comparable in subtlety and force. Like Virgil, Tasso expresses the melancholy aspect of warfare, but his celebration of military heroism, both Christian and pagan, appears to have engaged his complex imagination as fully as his representations of love. The last three cantos, describing the final battle for Jerusalem, are among the most exciting and successful.

Lyric poetry. After *Aminta* and *Gerusalemme liberata,* the works for which Tasso was best known in his own day were the lyrics, of which he wrote a large number. Employing forms that the age favored—especially the sonnet and madrigal—and covering the range of standard subjects—love, religion, and tributes to patrons—Tasso's lyrics contain many elegant variations on the conventional themes and conceits of the Renaissance lyric, whose traditions go back to Petrarch (1304–1374) and the classics. Autobiographical references to his early separation from his mother, to his years of youthful wandering with his father, to his troubles in Ferrara, and to other personal events, add poignancy to many of the lyrics. Their verbal inventiveness and the musicality of their verses commended Tasso's lyrics to later poets looking for models and to composers looking for texts to set to music.

Il re Torrismondo. Inspired on the one hand by Sophocles's *Oedipus Rex,* Renaissance literary theory, and Aristotle's *Poetics,* and on the other hand by medieval romance and chivalry, Tasso's tragic drama is a complicated tale of incest and betrayed friendship in northern Europe. Torrismondo and Alvida's incestuous love is an emblem of stark human misery, of a destructive fate that the lovers cannot understand and cannot resist. *Il re Torrismondo,* which Tasso began in the 1570s but did not complete until 1587, failed to achieve the immediate success of *Aminta* and has never been popular. Nevertheless, it contains some powerful poetry and, taken as a whole, constitutes a compellingly grim vision of a courtly world with no exits, a world devoid of religious or heroic consolations.

Le sette giornate del mondo creato *(The creation of the world).* The most ambitious poem of Tasso's final years, *Le sette giornate* is a long meditation on the opening verses of Genesis, on nature in both its pristine and its fallen states, on man, on God, and on all things heavenly and sublunar. Designed to organize Tasso's vast learning into a complex demonstration of piety in the spirit of the Counter-Reformation, the poem impresses but fails to come to life except now and then in isolated passages of fanciful learning or religious feeling. The central themes of his greatest poetry—love and war—are absent, and the result seems sometimes more an intellectual exercise than an expression of his deepest imaginative impulses.

Discourses and dialogues. The works in which Tasso displays most impressively the philosophical interests that he developed as a student at Padua are his discourses on poetic theory and his dialogues. The former—*Discorsi dell'arte poetica,* printed in 1587 but written much earlier, and *Discorsi del poema eroico* (Discourses on the heroic poem), probably begun in the late 1580s and published in 1594—are among the most interesting and important contributions to the vast outpouring of Renaissance theorizing about literature. Both works are fundamentally Aristotelian, but they are also eclectic, incorporating material from Plato, Horace, and numerous other sources. Both may be read as commentaries on, and justifications of, Tasso's own poetic practice, but they are not mere apologies; they are both learned and intellectually impressive, entering into the central questions of Renaissance literary theory with intelligence and discernment. Above all, they demonstrate the intense seriousness of Tasso's commitment to poetry; his desire to cut through the debates of his own time, to clear away confusion, and to find a firm intellectual ground on which to base his work. The later discourse is essentially an expansion of the earlier, ampler in argument and illustration, demonstrating more fully Tasso's love of philosophy.

In his twenty-six dialogues, a large number of which were written in the sixteen years from his incarceration in Sant'Anna to his death, Tasso gave even wider scope to this love. Mostly Platonic in form and Aristotelian in substance, the dialogues range over a wide variety of subjects—beauty, the court, the family, emblems—presenting fictional discussions among real people, whom Tasso's readers would have recognized, in familiar settings. Tasso himself appears in many dialogues, either in his own name or disguised as a "Neapolitan Stranger." Perhaps the most interesting way to read the dialogues today is as a commentary on Tasso's own life and times. From the relationships between ideas, characters, and settings emerges a witty and highly critical portrait of the late Renaissance courtly world in which Tasso lived.

Letters. Tasso's letters, which number over fifteen hundred, make fascinating reading for anyone interested in his life and times, but must be taken with great caution. Some of them quite clearly reflect Tasso's exaggerated fears. Others may be distorted by self-justifying efforts to win sympathy or help. Many were furnished to early editors by the recipients themselves and may have been censored before they were released; in most cases the originals have disappeared. Nevertheless, the letters reveal aspects of Tasso's personality—his taste for playful and ironic humor, for example—that are not as evident elsewhere in his work, and they can be both elo-

quent and moving. The letters that have survived from his debates with the critics about *Gerusalemme liberata* shed valuable light on the development of his critical views.

Reputation and Influence. By the late 1570s, as *Aminta* and the early lyrics became widely known, and as parts of *Gerusalemme liberata* began to circulate in manuscript, Tasso was recognized as one of the greatest poets of the age. In the 1580s a fierce debate arose in Italy over the respective merits of Tasso's epic and Ariosto's *Orlando furioso:* the latter was praised for its inventiveness and variety, its liveliness, its innovation, its modernity; the former for its clear and unified structure, its moral and religious seriousness, its respect for tradition, its conformity to ancient models.

Outside Italy, the terms of the debate were less important than its clear implication that Tasso had already, in his own lifetime, seen his work elevated to the status of a classic. In Spain, France, England, and elsewhere, recognition of this status was almost immediate, and translations of his works soon followed. Tradition has it that Elizabeth I committed passages of *Gerusalemme liberata* to memory and expressed envy of the Este because they had such a poet to glorify their dynasty. In the seventeenth century, the rise of neoclassicism, with its emphasis on rules and reason, produced a reaction against certain features of *Gerusalemme liberata*—its use of the supernatural, its mingling of lyric and epic style—but the poem's general popularity endured and Tasso's eminent reputation, fortified by romantic interest in him as a type of suffering genius, continued unshaken well into the nineteenth century. Today his popular reputation has diminished, even in Italy, but he remains a significant figure in the history of literature, studied both for the intrinsic interest of his greatest works and for the light that his career sheds on the waning years of the Renaissance.

See also **Chivalry,** *subentry on* **Romance of Chivalry;**
   Literary Theory, Renaissance.

BIBLIOGRAPHY

Primary Works

Tasso, Torquato. *Aminta.* In *Three Renaissance Pastorals.* Edited by Elizabeth Story Donno. Binghamton, N.Y., 1993. Pages 1–54. A seventeenth-century translation of *Aminta* by Augustine Mathews.

Tasso, Torquato. *The Creation of the World.* Edited by Joseph Tusiani. Binghamton, N.Y., 1982. Translation of *Le sette giornate del mondo creato.*

Tasso, Torquato. *Discourses on the Heroic Poem.* Edited by Mariella Cavalchini and Irene Samuel. Oxford, 1973. Translation of *Discorsi del poema eroico.*

Tasso, Torquato. *Jerusalem Delivered*. Edited by Ralph Nash. Detroit, Mich., 1987. Translation of *Gerusalemme liberata*.

Tasso, Torquato. *King Torrismondo*. Edited and translated by Maria Passaro. New York, 1997. Translation of *Il re Torrismondo*.

Tasso, Torquato. *Opere*. Edited by Bruno Maier. 5 vols. Milan, 1963–1964.

Tasso, Torquato. *Tasso's Dialogues*. Edited by Carnes Lord and Dain A. Trafton. Berkeley and Los Angeles, 1982. Translations of selected dialogues and *Discorso dell'arte del dialogo*.

Tasso, Torquato, and Edward Fairfax. *Godfrey of Bulloigne: A Critical Edition of Edward Fairfax's Translation of Torquato Tasso's* Gerusalemme liberata, *Together with Fairfax's Original Poems*. Edited by Kathleen M. Lea and T. M. Gang. Oxford, 1981.

Secondary Works

Brand, C. P. *Torquato Tasso*. Cambridge, U.K., 1965. The best comprehensive study of the life and work in English.

Getto, Giovanni. *Interpretazione del Tasso*. Naples, Italy, 1951. The starting point for contemporary criticism.

Solerti, Angelo. *Vita di Torquato Tasso*. 2 vols. Turin, Italy, 1895. Still the authoritative biography.

DAIN A. TRAFTON

TAXATION.   *See* **Finance and Taxation.**

TECHNOLOGY.

Mechanical and material processes and techniques, including craft production of all kinds, building construction, and the manufacture and operation of machines, were called "mechanical arts" during the Renaissance. The mechanical arts, usually learned through apprenticeships or informal hands-on practice, were sharply distinguished from the natural philosophy taught at universities and based on the study of authoritative texts. By the seventeenth century experimental philosophers attempted to validate claims about the natural world through experiments based on the manipulation of instruments, such as the telescope and the barometer, and apparatuses, such as the air pump. The mechanical arts and natural philosophy had come to be closely allied. In part, the origins of such a development lie in the changing role of the mechanical arts in the prior two centuries.

Yet for most crafts and technologies, despite significant developments, it would be a mistake to suppose a sharp break in practices or techniques from the medieval period. Arts and practices such as farming, cloth manufacture, leather tanning, carpentry, stonework and other aspects of building construction, metalwork, ceramics, glassmaking, and food production utilized traditional procedures and techniques. Innovation and change should be seen against the background of a broad stream of continuity from previous centuries.

Agriculture.   A significant number of new foods were added to the European diet in the sixteenth century as a result of European colonization of the Americas. Some new crops, most importantly the potato from the Andes region of South America and maize (corn), came to be cultivated extensively in Europe. Other products, such as coffee, cocoa, chocolate, and tobacco, became staples of consumption but remained primarily imports. New crops and new items of consumption influenced agricultural practices. The relative balance of animal husbandry and cereal crops, the nature of field rotation, irrigation and hydraulic technologies, and horticulture and gardening practices influenced one another and varied on a regional basis. Notable regional developments included for England "convertible husbandry," a system of land use in which cultivation and pasturage were alternated on the same field, and "floating meadows," in which complex irrigation systems submerged entire fields in water for certain periods (protecting them from frost and depositing silt). Both techniques emerged in the 1580s and resulted in the significant improvement of English agricultural productivity.

Yet for most regions agriculture was grounded primarily in long-standing traditional practices rather than innovation. An example from southeastern Spain is the irrigation agriculture of Valencia. Thomas F. Glick (*Irrigation and Society in Medieval Valencia,* 175–188) shows that irrigation practices survived political and cultural changes over centuries. Examples of very long-range technological continuity in Valencia include the dam as a device to raise water into irrigation canals; the *noria*, a waterwheel equipped with buckets to lift water; the *ganat*, a hydraulic system made by sinking a series of wells and connecting them underground to tap groundwater; and the irrigation cultivation of orange trees. Other areas of continuity include methods of apportioning water, ways of assigning responsibility for the upkeep of canals, and techniques of policing.

Hydraulic Engineering.   Hydraulic engineering and land-drainage projects developed as a response to geographic conditions. In the Netherlands dike construction had been carried out systematically from the eleventh century to protect the land from encroachments by the sea. By the sixteenth century the dikes were regulated by local and state authorities. Construction techniques varied according to local conditions. The earth core of the dike was protected on its slopes by clay and straw, seaweed, or bundles of reeds. Other arrangements, in-

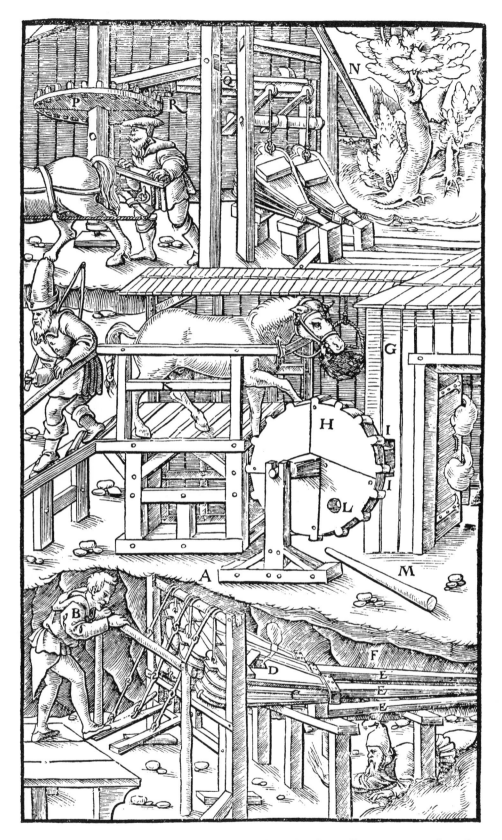

Mining Technology. Three ways to power the bellows that draw off noxious vapors from deep mine shafts. *Top,* a horse turns a shaft connected to a cog wheel that turns a lantern gear that turns an axle that works bellows; *middle,* a horse turns a wheel that works bellows inside a hut; *bottom,* a man uses treadles to work bellows. Illustration from *De re metallica* by Georgius Agricola (1494–1555).

cluding palisades of piles, came into use in the fifteenth century.

Laying dry the many inland *meers,* or lakes, became an important activity in sixteenth-century Netherlands. Dike workers constructed an earthen bank around the *meer* and encircled the bank with a canal. Drainage mills pumped the water out into the canal, where it flowed by gravity or through sluices into a river or main canal. These large drainage projects put a significant amount of new land into cultivation and contributed to the technical development of the drainage mill. An adaptation of the windmill, the drainage mill was created by the invention of a rotary cap, which enabled its sails to be turned to the wind without turning the whole mill. Netherlandish land-drainage projects also led to the development of various kinds of pumps and other drainage technologies.

In Italy hydraulic engineering centered on controlling the turbulent and flood-prone Italian rivers, constructing navigable canals, and draining marshes. Controlling the rivers of Italy required technologies entirely different from those of the Netherlands, including pile dikes, masonry walls, stone pitching, protection by various forms of mattress (structures of logs tied with willow sprigs thrown over eroding banks), and fascine work. The regulation of rivers was carried out in part through the construction of canals, which also served transportation needs. The earliest navigable canals constructed in Italy were in Lombardy. Carried out by the Sforza rulers in the second half of the fifteenth century, Lombard canal building was made difficult by a highly irregular topography characterized by steep slopes. The problem was solved by developing an extensive system of locks.

Italian efforts to drain marshes centered on several problem areas, including the malaria-infested Pontine Marshes covering three hundred square miles in the papal state southwest of Rome. Engineers working on the project included Leonardo da Vinci (1452–1519), who proposed recutting the ancient Roman canal that had run parallel to the Appian Way and constructing an additional canal at right angles as a cutoff channel for waters flowing down the Lepini Mountains. Actual work was not undertaken until Sixtus V (pope, 1585–1590) authorized it decades later in 1585. Completed in 1589, the work fell into disrepair after the death of Sixtus shortly thereafter.

In England a major drainage project centered on an area of about 700,000 acres in four eastern counties—Lincolnshire, Cambridgeshire, Huntingdon-shire, and Norfolk. In the sixteenth century drainage projects focused on about 302,000 acres of this area, which was called "the Great Level." The first comprehensive plan for drainage was presented in 1589 to the lord high treasurer, William Cecil (1520–1598), by the Netherlandish engineer Humphrey Bradley of Brabant (fl. c. 1584–1625). Although the plan was sound, will and resources were lacking. Effective drainage of the area was a seventeenth-century development. Bradley himself went on to assist the French king Henry IV (ruled 1589–1610) in draining marshlands in France.

Textiles. The manufacture of cloth was fundamentally important to the economy of the Renaissance. Woolen cloth of various types was most significant, but the production of cotton, linen (made from flax), and luxury cloths such as silks, including velvets and brocades, became increasingly important. Cloth manufacture was a complex process that varied according to the fiber being used and involved numerous steps carried out by specialists. The manufacture of wool cloth, for example, involved shearing sheep and cleaning the wool, either combing or carding (separate techniques), spinning, weaving, dyeing, fulling (beating the cloth in a mixture of water and other substances to thicken and strengthen it), tentering (drying and stretching on a tentering frame), napping (raising the nap with a tool equipped with teasels made from the spiny flower of a plant), and shearing (clipping the raised nap close to the weave).

Spinning, weaving, and fulling constituted separate crafts. Spinning was often done by women in a putting-out system; weaving was done by master weavers and their assistants at central locations; fullers often worked at a fulling mill near a fast river outside of town. The process of spinning (consolidating short fibers of wool, cotton, or flax into a single strand) was transformed during the Renaissance in that hand spinning was replaced by the use of the spinning wheel. Having entered Europe in the late thirteenth century, the spinning wheel was subsequently improved. Early spinning wheels required two separate actions—spinning the fibers and then winding on the yarn. The flyer, introduced about 1480, allowed these two actions to occur with one continuous operation of the wheel. Another innovation, the treadle, appeared in the early sixteenth century. It allowed the seated spinner to turn the wheel by treading with her feet, thereby freeing her hands to draw out the fibers for the yarn. Weaving was usually accomplished with a horizontal frame loom or treadle loom. Patterned cloth was woven with a two-harness loom in which the figure harness created the design and a second harness did the detailed weaving of the cloth. Fulling, usually mechanized in this period, was done at fulling mills in which the hammers for beating the cloth were powered by waterwheels.

Building Construction and Architecture.

Building construction in the Renaissance involved the utilization of traditional building crafts, such as stonemasonry, carpentry, and brickwork, while at the same time it produced important changes in style. Interest in classical forms, part of the broad humanist interest in antiquity, prompted detailed investigation of ancient buildings, ruins, and artifacts, as well as extensive study of the ancient architectural treatise *De architectura* (On architecture), by the Roman architect and military engineer Vitruvius (fl. 27 B.C.E.). *De architectura* treated the subjects of ancient architecture, which were more inclusive than its modern counterpart and included the design of public and private buildings, hydraulics, time measurement, and machines, including military machines.

Yet the structure considered to mark the beginning of Renaissance architecture, the dome of the Santa Maria del Fiore cathedral in Florence, was not primarily a product of classical inspiration. Designed by Filippo Brunelleschi (1377–1446) and constructed between 1420 and 1434, the famous structure dominates the city to this day. One of the largest masonry domes ever built, it represents a brilliant technical solution to the problem of spanning the huge space of 140 feet (42 meters) of the octagonal drum of the cathedral, a space too large for the utilization of traditional timber armature. Brunelleschi's technical solution involved three components. First, the stresses of the dome were distributed on eight major and sixteen lesser vertical ribs that joined at the top. Second, the dome was built as a double-shelled structure with an inner and an outer shell (a stair between the two shells leads to the lantern at the top). Third, the brickwork of the shells was built up in a herringbone pattern that enabled them to be self-supporting during construction. Brunelleschi also designed scaffolding and innovative hoisting machines to carry out the work.

Renaissance Europe experienced a building boom with the construction of palaces and villas, town houses, public buildings, loggias, churches, cathedrals, and bridges. Richard A. Goldthwaite, in *The Building of Renaissance Florence,* explains that pal-aces were built by the elite classes motivated by a desire for more spacious and comfortable living and by a new ethos of conspicuous consumption. Construction fueled the trades that provided materials, such as bricks, stone, lime, and timber. Brick making was an important industry that involved digging clay and tempering it, putting it into molds, and firing it in a kiln. Some cities, such as Bruges, maintained permanent brickyards with large kilns that produced thousands of bricks a day. Kilns were also used to produce lime from limestone, an essential ingredient of mortar. Other important building materials included stone (cut from quarries and dressed and sometimes made into capitals, window moldings, and other decorative pieces), gravel for foundations, and timber.

Bridge construction involved specialized techniques, including laying foundations. In some cases foundations could be laid in the water by sinking rubble in large wicker containers or dumping it into an underwater enclosure of piles that had been driven into the riverbed with a pile driver. This operation created islands that provided foundations on which to build the masonry piers that held up the bridge. Alternatively, pier foundations were sunk into the ground below the riverbed. To accomplish this task, the river had to be diverted or a watertight cofferdam had to be built. Cofferdam construction was difficult and involved building an enclosed dam with piles sealed with a mixture of sand and clay. The water inside the cofferdam was then pumped out, and the area was excavated down to the firm ground on which the bridge foundation was built.

Power and Machines.

Humans and animals remained important sources of power for hauling, lifting, and other tasks. Cranes and mills powered by treadmills worked by humans were common, as were mills turned by mules and horses. In addition, however, many known devices and machines were improved or modified. Mills were constructed in a variety of ways, some powered by waterwheels (including overshot, undershot, and horizontal types) and some by wind. Mills were constructed for various purposes, such as grinding grain, making paper, and fulling cloth. Various kinds of pumps also evolved significantly, as did cranes and other lifting devices. Modifications of machines often centered on specific parts, such as gears and screws. An important fifteenth-century invention was the combined crank and connecting rod that was able to convert continuous rotary motion to reciprocating motion.

Certain kinds of machinery developed as a result of changes in industries. For example, the great expansion of the mine industry led to the digging of deep mine shafts, which presented the serious problem of water removal. One result was the improvement of various kinds of suction pumps, with their pistons and valves, and experimentation with other kinds of pumps as well. Mining and ore processing brought many other innovations, including enlarged furnaces with air supplied by huge bellows operated by waterwheels (the blast furnace) and the earliest rails, along which ran solid-wheeled carts carrying ore. In other cases, inventions led to new industries and new kinds of production. The screw and machines that used the screw, such as the lathe, developed significantly. New applications of the screw press, an old technology, included the printing press and die stamping metals for seals and coins.

Everyday Objects and Luxury Goods. Numerous specialized artisanal crafts flourished in the fifteenth and sixteenth centuries to satisfy increased demand for a multitude of objects ranging from ordinary household articles, to tools of all kinds, to luxury goods. Carpenters and smiths fashioned tools for farming and for use by specialized artisans, such as wheelwrights and coopers, who made wooden vessels, such as barrels, from staves and hoops. Tanners and leather workers produced numerous items, from saddles and harnesses to leather containers to shoes. Potters created everyday items, such as plates, and luxury ceramics, including painted majolica. Glassmakers produced vessels, window glass (including the stained glass of churches and cathedrals), vases, and numerous other items that involved complex processes that varied regionally. Glassmaking required as many as three furnaces and used coloring and other decorative techniques. The most famous glassware came from Venice, where glassmakers jealously guarded their techniques (or took them elsewhere in exchange for patents). Crystal glass was a Venetian invention of the fifteenth century.

Numerous other objects were produced by complex craft processes—terra-cotta tiles, furniture, paintings, tapestries, jewelry, relief sculpture, inlaid-wood surfaces, cast-bronze equestrian statues, and books. The printing press, invented around 1450, created a whole new industry along with its allied crafts of papermaking, ink manufacture, typefounding, construction of presses, and bookbinding.

Precision Instruments. Instruments for navigation, astronomical observation, gunnery, and surveying developed significantly. Oceanic explorations required navigational aids beyond those used in traditional coastal sailing. To the medieval invention of the magnetic compass were added new position-finding instruments, often adopted from astronomy. The sea astrolabe, the cross staff, and the quadrant helped the sea captain establish latitude by measuring the position of celestial objects, such as the North Star. Versions of some of these instruments also were used for surveying. An instrument known as the *polimetrum* for taking bearings and altitudes and for leveling was an early prototype of a theodolite. (The theodolite combined a bearing dial with a sight rule turning on a vertical scale for measuring altitudes.)

The specialized craft of instrument makers developed from the fifteenth century. Traditional astronomical instruments, such as quadrants, astrolabes, and armillary and other spheres, as well as timekeepers, such as sundials and clocks, were constructed with great attention to accuracy. Other instruments were developed for military purposes, such as the gunner's quadrant and the military compass. An improved version of the latter was invented by Galileo Galilei (1564–1642). Optical instruments, the most significant early example of which was Galileo's telescope of 1609, became important near the end of the period.

Writings on the Mechanical Arts. Books on crafts and mechanical arts proliferated from the early fifteenth century, at first in manuscript form and after the invention of printing in both manuscript and print. Fifteenth-century books on the mechanical arts include German writings on gunpowder artillery, the machine books of the Sienese notary Mariano Taccola (1382–c. 1453), engineering treatises by the engineer and architect Francesco di Giorgio Martini (1439–1501), and writings on machines by Leonardo da Vinci. Renaissance architectural writings begin with *De re aedificatoria* (On the art of building; c. 1450) by Leon Battista Alberti (1404–1472). In addition, books appeared on painting, sculpture, military technology (including gunpowder artillery), and artist's perspective.

Authored by both learned humanists and skilled practitioners, such writings were often dedicated to wealthy patrons, princes, and rulers. In the sixteenth century treatises appeared on mining and ore processing, including *De re metallica* by Georgius Agricola (1494–1555), a humanist treatise famous for its spectacular technical illustrations. Books appeared on military technology and fortification, ceramics, painting, sculpture, navigation, dike building and hydraulics, glassmaking, animal husbandry and crop cultivation, and painting and sculpture. They include the "Theaters of Machines," of which the best known is the *Various and Ingenious Machines* (*Le diverse et artificiose machine*) by Agostino Ramelli (1531–c. 1608), a book of complex, beautiful illustrations accompanied by textual explanations.

Most books on the mechanical arts cannot be considered primarily as instructional books for practitioners. They played a more complex role of representing the power of the princes and rulers to whom they were often dedicated and of catering to a new interest in material techniques, a delight in the products of construction, design, and artisanal craftwork, and an interest in the processes required to make such objects. Many such books are beautiful objects in themselves, often with impressive drawings and illustrations. These books helped to raise the status of the mechanical arts, in part by explicating them and in part by rationalizing their subject matter. Many authors advocated the value of handwork and articulated the ideal of a close interaction between theory and practice.

The extent to which the mechanical arts influenced the development of experimental philosophy has been a contested issue among historians of science. Early views included that of Edgar Zilsel (1891–1944), who argued that artisans made a significant contribution to the development of experimental science, and the opposite view of Alexandre Koyré (1892–1964), who believed that scientific innovations were theoretical in nature and therefore not influenced by the mechanical arts. At the end of the twentieth century the role of the mechanical arts in the development of science was still being debated, although in somewhat different terms. Aspects of relevant scholarship include the status of practitioners and of disciplines, issues of authorship and of patronage, and the role of instrumentation.

See also **Agriculture; Architecture,** *subentry on* **Architectural Treatises; Brunelleschi, Filippo; Ceramics; Communication and Transportation; Decorative Arts; Fortifications; Industry; Jewelry; Mining and Metallurgy; Printing and Publishing; Printmaking; Science.**

BIBLIOGRAPHY

Primary Works

Agricola, Georg. *De re metallica.* Translated by Herbert Clark Hoover and Lou Henry Hoover. New York, 1950. English translation of *De re metallica* (1556). Humanist treatise on mining and metallurgy with famous illustrations.

Hall, Bert S., ed. *The Technological Illustrations of the So-called "Anonymous of the Hussite Wars": Codex Latinus Monacensis 197, Part 1.* Wiesbaden, Germany, 1979. A facsimile edition of a German manuscript with an excellent technological commentary that serves as a basic introduction to fifteenth-century technological developments.

Leonardo da Vinci. *The Madrid Codices.* Edited by Ladislao Reti. 5 vols. New York, 1974. Facsimile edition, transcription, and translation of Leonardo's mechanical treatise and notebook.

Piccolpasso, Cipriano. *The Three Books of the Potter's Art.* 2 vols. Translated and introduced by R. W. Lightbown and Alan Caiger-Smith. London, 1980. Translation of *I tre libri dell'arte del vasaio* (1557). Includes useful introduction.

Ramelli, Agostino. *The Various and Ingenious Machines of Agostino Ramelli: A Classic Sixteenth-Century Illustrated Treatise on Technology.* Translated and edited by Martha Teach Gnudi and Eugene S. Ferguson. New York, 1976. Translation of *Le diverse et artificiose machine* (1588). Includes a useful pictorial glossary of machine parts.

Secondary Works

Blair, John, and Nigel Ramsay, eds. *English Medieval Industries: Craftsmen, Techniques, Products.* London, 1991. Extremely valuable detailed studies of specific crafts.

Galluzzi, Paolo, ed. *Leonardo da Vinci: Engineer and Architect.* Montreal, 1987.

Glick, Thomas F. *Irrigation and Society in Medieval Valencia.* Cambridge, Mass., 1970.

Goldthwaite, Richard A. *The Building of Renaissance Florence: An Economic and Social History.* Baltimore, 1980.

Heller, Henry. *Labour, Science, and Technology in France, 1500–1620.* Cambridge, U.K., 1996.

Long, Pamela O. "Power, Patronage, and the Authorship of *Ars*: From Mechanical Know-how to Mechanical Knowledge in the Last Scribal Age." *Isis* 88 (March 1997): 1–41. Detailed discussion of fifteenth-century writings on the mechanical arts.

Mazzaoui, Maureen Fennell. *The Italian Cotton Industry in the Later Middle Ages, 1100–1600.* Cambridge, U.K., 1981.

Pacey, Arnold. *The Maze of Ingenuity: Ideas and Idealism in the Development of Technology.* 2d ed. Cambridge, Mass., 1992. Relevant chapters provide an excellent short introduction to Renaissance technology.

Parsons, William Barclay. *Engineers and Engineering in the Renaissance.* Baltimore, 1939. Classic, still useful study, especially good on canals and hydraulic engineering.

Prager, Frank D., and Gustina Scaglia. *Mariano Taccola and His Book* De ingeneis. Cambridge, Mass., 1972.

Rossi, Paolo. *Philosophy, Technology, and the Arts in the Early Modern Era.* Translated by Salvator Attanasio. Edited by Benjamin Nelson. New York, 1970. Translation of *I filosofi e le macchine* (1962). An important and accessible study of the relationships of early modern science and technology.

Saalman, Howard. *Filippo Brunelleschi: The Cupola of Santa Maria del Fiore.* London, 1980.

Singer, Charles, et al. *A History of Technology.* Vol. 2, *The Mediterranean Civilizations and the Middle Ages, c. 700 B.C. to c. A.D. 1500,* and vol. 3, *From the Renaissance to the Industrial Revolution, c. 1500–c. 1750.* London, 1956–1957. The relevant volumes of a multivolume work, a fundamental reference.

PAMELA O. LONG

TELESIO, BERNARDINO (1509–1588), Italian natural philosopher. Telesio was born in Cosenza, Italy, where he received his early training from his uncle, a classical scholar, who taught him both Greek and Latin. He studied philosophy and mathematics at the University of Padua, obtaining his doctorate in 1535. Aristotle and Galen were still the reigning authorities there, but as interpreted in the Latin tradition of Averroes (1126–1198). Telesio reacted against his teachers at Padua as well as the medieval scholastic tradition on the basis of his reading of Aristotelian and Galenic texts in the original Greek.

Primarily interested in nature as presented in these sources, Telesio attempted his own synthesis of their teachings in what has come to be known as a new nature philosophy as opposed to what was then taught in the universities. He first developed his system in a Benedictine monastery and began writing in Naples under the patronage of the Carafa family. In 1563 he visited Brescia to consult with Vincenzo Maggi, an expert on Aristotle's Greek text. Encouraged by his conversations with Maggi, in 1565 Telesio published at Rome the first version of his major work, *De rerum natura iuxta propria principia* (On the nature of things from proper principles). This was augmented by two later editions at Naples (2d ed., 1570; 3d ed., 1586). Despite the title's similarity to the *De rerum natura* of Lucretius, no atomist or corpuscularian teachings are proposed in this work. In his later years, which he passed in Cosenza, Telesio founded the Accademia Cosentina to promote study of natural philosophy according to the principles and methods he had taught. Other of Telesio's treatises on natural subjects remain in manuscript and were edited by his disciple Antonio Persio with the title *Varii de naturalibus rebus libelli* (Brief treatises on natural subjects; Venice, 1590).

Although usually characterized as an anti-Aristotelian, Telesio took inspiration from Aristotle's treatment of heat and cold in the *De generatione et corruptione* (On generation and corruption), while rejecting Aristotle's doctrine on matter and form in the *Physics*. The principles of nature he favored as accessible to the senses, which matter and form are not, were three: two natural agents (*agentes naturae*), heat and cold, and bodily bulk (*corporea moles—De rerum natura*, 3d ed., 1.5). For Telesio, wetness and dryness were not primarily qualities, as they were for Aristotle, but derivative qualities. Thus his system required new explanations for the new "mediums," water and air, which for Aristotle were explained by primary quality pairings of wet-cold and wet-dry, respectively. In further opposition to Aristotle, Telesio introduced concepts of space and time that anticipated later notions of absolute space and time, allowed for the possibility of a void (*vacuum*) and dissociated time from motion rather than seeing it as motion's measure (ibid., 1.25). Other distinctive teachings were that the soul (*spiritus*) is corporeal and derived from seed enclosed in the body, and that sensation is simply the perception of actions of things, impulsions of air, and the soul's own passions rather than the reception of forms without matter, as Aristotle had defined it (ibid., 7.2). Reasoning was not stressed in Telesio's thought, since for him sense knowledge is primary and reason leads quickly to metaphysical entities that have no explanatory role in his system. Being subsidiary to sensation, reason for Telesio is restricted to supplying for the deficiencies of sense when nature's qualities are not directly observable (ibid., 8.3).

From foundations such as these Telesio developed a naturalistic ethics in which virtues were powers that ensure the conservation and perfection of spirit (ibid., 9.4). His discussion of virtues and vices, associated as they were with a self-interested creature pursuing its own conservation, anticipated in some ways the seventeenth-century views of René Descartes, Thomas Hobbes, and Baruch Spinoza. Otherwise, claims that have been made for the modernity of Telesio's thought are difficult to justify on the historical record. He was not interested in the logic of Aristotle's *Organon*, nor was his empiricism, if one may call it that, methodically grounded. He did not make use of experiment, as did Jacopo Zabarella and Galileo Galilei, nor did he make controlled observations, as did his contemporary Francesco Patrizi. Telesio had little realization of the importance of measurement, nor was he a mechanist, despite his rejection of action at a distance on the grounds that it was caused by an "occult" quality. It is true that he rejected much of Aristotle, but the type of argument Telesio employed was not much different from that of the Aristotelians of his day, nor did it achieve results in his study of nature that were clearly superior to theirs.

BIBLIOGRAPHY

Delcorno, Carlo. "Il commentario 'De fulmine' di Bernardino Telesio." *Aevum* 41 (1967): 474–506. A treatise on lightning.

Deusen, Neil Van. *Telesio, The First of the Moderns*. New York, 1932. The most complete work in English.

Fiorentino, Francesco. *Bernardino Telesio*. 2 vols. Florence, 1872–1874. The basic secondary source.

Gilbert, Neil W. "Telesio, Bernardino." In the *Dictionary of Scientific Biography*. Edited by Charles C. Gillispie. Vol. 13. New York, 1976. Pages 277–280.

Kristeller, Paul O. *Eight Philosophers of the Italian Renaissance.* Stanford, Calif., 1964. Pages 91–109.

WILLIAM A. WALLACE

TERENCE (Publius Terentius Afer; 193 or 183–159 B.C.), Roman comic playwright. All six of Terence's comedies are extant: *Andria* (The girl from Andros), *Hecyra* (The mother-in-law), *Heautontimorumenos* (The self-tormenter), *Eunuchus* (The eunuch), *Phormio,* and *Adelphoe* (The brothers). Typically, the plight of one or two sets of lovers is resolved in marriage after much scheming and a recognition scene. Terence followed his Greek models of the Attic New Comedy more closely than did his Roman predecessor Plautus, but he is generally thought to be more sophisticated. While his plays did not all gain popular success in their own day, they were admired by later Roman writers, such as Cicero and Horace. In late antiquity his plays were recited in schools and aroused the interest of grammarians, including the fourth-century commentator Aelius Donatus.

Manuscripts and Editio Princeps.

The survival of Terence, unlike that of some ancient authors, is not due to a sudden discovery. Both the age and proliferation of the manuscript material, which includes fragments on papyri and a manuscript in Visigothic script, testify to his continuing appeal. Nearly all of the 650 extant manuscripts present versions of an inferior text that goes back to a lost common ancestor designated as Σ. The single most important manuscript, offering a superior though not flawless text, is A. Dating from the fourth or fifth century, it is known as the *Codex Bembinus* after its owner Bernardo Bembo (d. 1519), who described it as a *codex mihi carior auro,* "a manuscript dearer to me than gold." His son Pietro, Cardinal Bembo (1470–1547), put the manuscript at the disposal of the humanist scholar Angelo Poliziano in 1491 for collation with an early printed edition of 1475. Poliziano's annotated copy, which has survived, contributed in turn to the edition of Benedictus Philologus (Florence, 1505). The editio princeps (first printed edition), however, had appeared by 1470 at Strasbourg; by 1600 the number of printed editions, often with ample commentaries, would run to several hundred, if not a thousand.

Popularity and Dissemination of Works.

Better known than Plautus (but not as well as Virgil), Terence was read and commented on in the Middle Ages, though not performed; in the tenth century he was imitated by Hrosvitha von Gandersheim (whose "comedies" Conrad Celtis would publish in 1501).

From the earliest years of the Renaissance, however, there was a lively humanistic interest in Terence. Petrarch copied, studied, and quoted Terence, and composed a *Vita Terentii* (Life of Terence), which corrected the erroneous medieval identification of the African-born poet with the Roman senator Q. Terentius Cullio. Terence was further copied by Giovanni Boccaccio, cited by Coluccio Salutati, praised by Guarino da Verona, and imitated by Enea Silvio Piccolomini in his *Chrysis.* The discovery of Donatus's commentary, prefaced by Suetonius's *Life of Terence* and two theoretical treatises on drama, at Mainz in 1433 and at Chartres in the 1440s kept the interest alive, as did the recovery by the Italian poet Porcelio (Giannantonio Pandone, 1405–1485) of the aforementioned *Codex Bembinus* in or around 1453. The first of Terence's plays to be staged since antiquity was *Andria,* produced at Florence in 1476. From then on, Terence would be performed quite regularly, as his plays became a popular school text from Italy to England.

Some educators did object to Terence's joyous treatment of lust, avarice, and deceit, but many others (including Philipp Melanchthon) stressed the moral utility of his comedies, as well as their stylistic elegance. Together with Horace, Terence was the favorite author of the northern humanist Desiderius Erasmus, who edited Terence's plays and recommended them (with some cautions) for school use, finding in Terence an ideal source for learning conversational Latin—even though the comedies were written in verse. Certainly, Terence's capacity to turn a phrase provided lasting maxims such as "*quot homines tot sententiae*" (as many opinions as there are men) and "*fortis fortuna adiuvat*" (fortune favors the brave), both from *Phormio.* The adage "*homo sum: humani nil a me alienum puto*" (I am a man: I think nothing human to be foreign to me; from *Heautontimorumenos*) famously adorned Michel de Montaigne's study.

Influence on Genres or Concepts.

Together with Plautus, Terence forms the basis of Italian, and European, comedy, providing tone, intrigues, structure, and stock characters such as the miserly old man, the young son eager for love, the boastful soldier, and the parasite. While the world of Plautus is a harsh one and his jokes are often coarse, the happy endings of Terence's plays and the greater urbanity of sentiments and language evidently made him the more assimilable of the two. On the other hand, the widespread practice of *contaminatio,* or the combination of various source plays (for which

Terence himself had been criticized in his own day), make it difficult to fathom the precise extent of his overall influence. In individual texts or authors, this influence can range from overt allusion and close imitation to borrowed names and entire reworkings.

In sixteenth-century Italy, the imitation of Plautus and Terence found expression in the *commedia erudita* (erudite comedy), such as Ludovico Ariosto's *Cassaria* (The casket comedy), performed at Ferrara in 1508, to which *Heautontimorumenos* contributed. In England as in France, the influence of Terence worked both directly and indirectly, often through Italian comedy. Nicholas Udall, headmaster of Eton and then Westminster, imitated *Eunuchus* in *Ralph Roister Doister* (c. 1554), the earliest known "regular" English comedy. Through George Gascoigne's translation (1566) of Ariosto's *I suppositi* (The masqueraders), *Eunuchus* also provided material for Shakespeare's *Taming of the Shrew,* while *Hecyra* is significant for *All's Well That Ends Well*. In Neo-Latin theater, Gulielmus Gnapheus (Wilhelm de Volder) drew on Terence for his internationally renowned piece on the prodigal son, *Acolastus* (Antwerp, 1529), while Christophorus Stymmelius adopted a Terentian intrigue in his *Studentes* of 1545. In the second half of the sixteenth century, Cornelius Schonaeus, a schoolmaster from Haarlem, enjoyed unequaled success with his *Terentius Christianus,* a collection of plays based on biblical stories. The influence of Terence could be felt until well into the seventeenth century: according to Jean de La Fontaine (whose own French adaptation of *L'Eunuque* [The eunuch; 1654] had flopped), it was Molière who brought to France "le bon goût et l'air de Térence," the good taste and manner of Terence.

See also **Drama,** *subentry on* **Erudite Comedy; Drama, English,** *subentries on* **Elizabethan Drama** *and* **Jacobean Drama; Neo-Latin Literature and Language.**

BIBLIOGRAPHY

Herrick, Marvin T. *Comic Theory in the Sixteenth Century.* Urbana, Ill., 1964.

Lawton, Harold W. *Térence en France au seizième siècle.* 2 vols. Geneva, 1970–1972.

Miola, Robert S. *Shakespeare and Classical Comedy: The Influence of Plautus and Terence.* Oxford, 1994.

Villa, Claudia. *La "Lectura Terentii."* Padua, Italy, 1984.

INGRID A. R. DE SMET

TERESA OF ÁVILA (original name Teresa Sánchez de Cepeda y Ahumada; name in religion Teresa de Jesús; 1515–1582), Spanish mystical writer, religious reformer.

Teresa Sánchez was born into a merchant family in the Castilian city of Ávila in 1515. Her father was the son of converted Jews persecuted by the Inquisition in the 1480s; her mother's family was of Old Christian origin. Although she had no formal education and never learned Latin, Teresa was an avid reader from childhood and a prodigious writer in adulthood. In 1535, against her father's wishes, she entered a Carmelite convent, taking the veil in 1537. Around the age of forty she began to hear voices and experience visions of the divine. Her alarmed confessors initially recommended exorcism. Through a series of written confessions, she eventually assuaged their fears and won their support.

Teresa's mysticism, with its most immediate source in Franciscan recollection (a movement emphasizing affective piety and mental prayer) and possibly deeper, though indirect, roots in syncretic Judeo-Muslim mysticism, complied with the Catholic Reformation insistence on the sacramental life of the church while affirming the possibility of an immediate and subjective experience of the presence of God. In 1562, motivated by the desire to save Protestant souls through prayer, Teresa founded Saint Joseph's of Ávila, a small convent based on the Discalced (primitive, literally "unshod") Carmelite rule. The monastic reforms she instituted included strict enclosure, austerity, social egalitarianism, the rejection of racial prejudice, and dedication to mental prayer. In 1567 she met the Carmelite priest who was to become Saint John of the Cross, a great poet and mystic, and collaborated with him in extending her reforms to Carmelite monasteries. Denounced to the Inquisition on at least six occasions for alleged heterodox beliefs and irregular religious practices, she was never formally tried for heresy. Teresa died in 1582 in Alba de Tormes, shortly after founding her seventeenth convent. Canonized in 1622, she was declared Doctor of the Church in 1970, the first woman accorded this honor.

Teresa's significance as a religious and literary figure has varied enormously over the centuries. Although in her writing and her monastic reform she frequently challenged women's exclusion from a magisterial and apostolic role in the Church, she was canonized as an exemplar of feminine obedience. In the wake of her election as Doctor of the Church, her contributions to mystical theology and Christian feminism have been reexamined. Long thought to be a simple, artless writer who wrote as she spoke, contemporary literary historians have elucidated her mastery of a wide array of sophisticated rhetorical strategies that allowed her to subvert prohibitions

Teresa of Ávila. Portrait by Juan de las Miserias. Oil on canvas; 1562. LAURIE PLATT WINFREY, INC.

against women's roles as religious teachers. Her most famous works include her *Libro de la vida* (Life; 1562–1565), a confessional autobiography; *Camino de perfeccion* (The way of perfection; 1562–1564); a guidebook to mental prayer and an impassioned defense of women's rights to pursue the mystical path; and *Castillo interior* (trans. *The Interior Castle;* 1577), an allegory of the soul's progress toward mystical union. Sequestered by the Inquisition, these works were approved for publication posthumously in 1588.

BIBLIOGRAPHY

Primary Works

Teresa of Ávila. *The Collected Works of St. Teresa of Ávila.* Translated with introductions by Kieran Kavanaugh and Otilio Rodríguez. 3 vols. Washington, D.C., 1976–1985. Translation of all extant works except the letters.

Teresa of Ávila. *The Letters of Saint Teresa of Jesus.* Translated and edited by Edgar Allison Peers. 2 vols. London, 1951. Reprint, London, 1981.

Secondary Works

Ahlgren, Gillian T. W. *Teresa of Ávila and the Politics of Sanctity.* Ithaca, N.Y., 1996.

Bilinkoff, Jodi. *The Ávila of Saint Teresa: Religious Reform in a Sixteenth-Century City.* Ithaca, N.Y., 1989.

Weber, Alison. *Teresa of Ávila and the Rhetoric of Femininity.* Princeton, N.J., 1990.

ALISON WEBER

TEUTONIC KNIGHTS. *See* **Baltic States.**

THEATERS. Few permanent theaters were built in medieval Europe, but with changing political and social conditions during the sixteenth century, notable but widely different structures appeared in Italian and Spanish cities, together with an unparalleled concentration in London. Even in England a great many—perhaps most—theatrical performances were offered by troupes of actors who were either fully itinerant or spent long periods on the road, away from their home base. There were far more temporary theaters than permanent ones, set up in public halls, the halls and sometimes courtyards of great houses, and the assembly rooms of inns. Too little is known about these occasional conversions, or fit-ups, with the result that the permanent houses enjoy most modern attention.

Temporary Theaters. Documents do exist to give an idea of some fit-up theaters. At Whitehall Palace, for example, outside London, the Great Hall was frequently prepared for the actors, with a demountable set of bleacherlike seating and possibly a stage and some galleries, the whole arrangement called the "frame" and capable of being taken apart and stored between events. In 1635 the architect John Webb made a plan of such a scheme which is extant; in 1621–1622 Inigo Jones's new Banqueting House had been provided with a similar kit, with a broad scenic stage at one end of the room, seven rows of stepped seating to either side of a central area, and a gallery of four rows above. A fit-up theater for the hall at the queen's palace in Somerset House was stored at the headquarters of the King's Works in Scotland Yard. But these were all elaborate court provisions; the humbler arrangements made at town halls and inns were seldom documented.

Oxford and Cambridge colleges sometimes set up theaters in their halls. The fullest scheme for which records survive was that at Christ Church, Oxford, in 1605, where the Royal Works intervened to design a fit-up in the hall with scenes by Inigo Jones and an auditorium deriving from one published by the Italian architect Sebastiano Serlio.

In a part of Serlio's *Architettura* that was originally published in Paris in 1545, he described and illustrated a temporary theater scheme based on one he had designed years before in Italy. His aim was to compress as much as he could of an ancient Roman theater within the confines of a modern hall or courtyard, the whole adapted to modern scenic stage conditions, which he saw as a branch of the science of perspective. Similar preoccupations governed the design at Christ Church and influenced the court theaters of the seventeenth century, though these were also shaped by the old tradition of the "frame."

Italian and Spanish Theaters.

Theaters like Serlio's were common as temporary structures in the ducal palaces of Italy, as at Ferrara in the Sala Grande in 1565 or at an academic auditorium by Giovanni Battista Aleotti in the same city forty years later. One or two permanent theaters were constructed along the same lines, most notably Vincenzo Scamozzi's Teatro Olimpico at Sabbioneta (1588–1590), with its semicircular *cavea* (or rounded auditory) of degrees facing a Serlian raked and scenic stage. Similar houses were built at Piacenza (1592), and Aleotti's vast theatrical interior, the Teatro Farnese at Parma (1617–1618), derived from the same sources. This and the Sabbioneta theater are partly extant.

Also extant is an academic theater in Vicenza built by Andrea Palladio and finished by Scamozzi in 1588. The Teatro Olimpico took Serlio's ancient Roman theme and expressed it more fully than before, with a semielliptical *cavea* of stepped degrees backed by an architectural "portico" of columns and facing a five-entrance, two-storied "front" (or *scenae frons*) lavishly enlivened with neoclassical statuary. Within the entrance doorways Scamozzi—perhaps contradicting Palladio's original intentions—provided deep three-dimensional perspectives of street scenes.

In Spain rather different theatrical conditions obtained. Where Italian theaters were built by courts and academies, in Spain charitable brotherhoods ran some of the more important houses as sources of finance for their hospitals. Theaters such as the Corral de la Cruz and the Corral del Príncipe in Madrid were open to the public (the women separated from the men in a special screened gallery). Begun in 1579 and 1582, respectively, they were developed piecemeal over some decades, starting as simple courtyard auditoriums and ending as roofed-in and partly galleried playhouses of some complexity. Specific architectural influences were therefore less formative than the daily business of the playhouse, but by the second decade of the seventeenth century, theaters in Seville and Valencia were showing a considerable integration of design, especially in the former

city's Coliseo (built 1607 and rebuilt in 1614 and 1622). Parts of two corral theaters survive, buried within the fabric of later structures, at Almagro and Alcalá de Henares, outside Madrid.

London Public Theaters.

In England the earliest public theaters sprang up in the London neighborhood when local entrepreneurs saw that there was money to be made from the provision of permanent stages on which itinerant troupes of players could be invited to appear. For political (and possibly financial) reasons the new houses were located in the suburbs, beyond the jurisdiction of the City proper.

Early theaters. The earliest theater of which we have notice—in 1567—is the Red Lion, a set of galleries erected in the yard behind a farmhouse in Whitechapel, enclosing a stage thirty feet by forty feet and five feet high. Apparently mounted on the stage was a turret thirty feet high, possibly for use as dressing rooms as well as an upper acting area. This remarkable and massive structure seems to have been without precedent. There is no record that it lasted long, but nine years later its commercial-minded owner, John Brayne, joined with the actor James Burbage to build a playhouse in Shoreditch. This theater is shown in a contemporary view as a polygonal three-storied frame with a turret apparently rising above its stage in the manner of the Red Lion. Brayne and Burbage called it simply the Theater, perhaps to show that its design was yet another modernized version of the ancient Roman *theatrum*, a connection often recognized in Elizabethan theaters by contemporary Londoners and visiting tourists. The three levels of the Roman rounded auditory, or *cavea*, were interpreted as three superimposed galleries, surrounding a raised stage with formal doors of entrance for the players. Performances were by daylight.

Several more playhouses built to a similar scheme now followed, beginning with the Curtain, not far from the Theater, in 1577. On Bankside, to the south of the Thames, Philip Henslowe and John Cholmley erected the Rose, generally like the others but apparently rather smaller. Its remains were excavated in 1989, showing it to have been a timber-frame structure raised on a low brick plinth, its main frame a fourteen-sided polygon seventy-four feet in diameter. There were no signs that the original building had a stage turret, or even a roof over the stage, though people who sat in the galleries were protected by a thatch roof over them. At ground level the galleries were about twelve feet, six inches deep

A Palladian Theater. Teatro Olimpico, Vicenza, Italy, designed by Andrea Palladio (1508–1580) and completed in 1588 by Vincenzo Scamozzi (1552–1616). ALINARI/ART RESOURCE

from front to back and seem to have extended even behind the wide tapered stage, where they were doubtless fitted as dressing ("tiring") rooms.

In 1592 Philip Henslowe had the stage half of this structure pulled down and rebuilt a few feet further north, so that what had been a more or less regular polygonal plan now became **D**-shaped, with the stage at the flat end. The new platform differed little from the original in size and shape, but now there was a roof over it, partly supported by columns placed at the front corners, so that for most of the audience performances were framed as if by a late Victorian proscenium arch. Three years later Henslowe paid for a descent machine to be built in the stage roof.

The Swan. A little upstream at Paris Garden, the Swan was built around 1595, its interior the only one of the great pre-Restoration public auditoriums to be illustrated by a contemporary, the Dutch humanist traveler Johannes de Witt. (The original sketch, now lost, has come down to us in a copy by Aernout van Buchell.) De Witt was particularly struck by the Swan's neo-Roman form and remarked too on the illusionism of the decor, which used painted wood to imitate richer materials, especially marble.

The form of the Swan seems to have been a transitional one, with a stage turret of the Red Lion type supplemented by a small stage roof built against it, lean-to fashion. The front of the roof was supported by giant Corinthian columns which rose, not from the stage front as at the 1592 Rose, but halfway back toward the tiring house, with the result that much of the stage remained exposed to the elements and inevitable decay. The actors may have felt the need to position themselves clear of these columns, between them and the mass of the audience located in the yard and galleries: that, at any rate, is where de Witt placed them in his sketch. Giant columns (columns that rose through more than one story) were a novelty in Elizabethan London and seem to have flagged the Romanness of the building for observers like de Witt.

Nevertheless, great public auditoriums like the Swan were not necessarily the most profitable theater enterprises in the London region. The Swan itself seems never to have succeeded, and even James Burbage, the proprietor of the Theater, sank all his capital into fitting out an enclosed "private" theater at Blackfriars within the boundaries of the City, aiming at a richer audience. As it turned out, Burbage and his successors (he died in 1597) were frustrated by the neighbors' objections to a noisy playhouse in their midst, and the opening was postponed. At the same time, the site landlord of the Theater was making such difficulties over the renewal of the lease that the Burbage family, along with the Lord Chamberlain's Men, the acting company then in residence, hired the carpenter Peter Street to supervise the dismantling of their building. He took its useful parts across the river to Bankside, where during 1599 he pieced them together again on a site close to the Rose. This renewed playhouse was called the Globe. It was presumably much the same in size and plan as the Theater.

The Globe and the Fortune. Across the way at Henslowe's rebuilt Rose of 1592, the stage roof seems to have been constructed integrally with the main frame of the galleries. Its front was supported by columns, but at the back it was tied into the main frame. This scheme marked a radical advance on the stage-turret type and for the first time provided a complete coverage of the stage. John Norden's 1600 view of London shows such integrated roofs on both the Rose and the new Globe: presumably at the latter the old turret of the Theater had been replaced by the new Rose type of stage roof, though like the Globe's galleries it was covered economically in thatch.

The economy was false, for the Globe burned down in 1613 when its roof caught fire. It was immediately replaced by a similar building, its roof tiled but its main frame set on the old foundations. A small part of these—little more than one bay—was excavated late in 1989, just enough to suggest that the likeliest plan of the main frame was a twenty-sided polygon ninety-nine feet in diameter, with galleries twelve feet, six inches deep from front to back. However, slight and ambiguous evidence from a ground radar survey of other parts of the site may indicate that the Globe was irregularly planned and slightly smaller than the Rose, about seventy-two feet in diameter.

Soon after the new Globe opened, the chief actor at the Rose, Edward Alleyn, financed a new and competitive theater to the north of London, the Fortune. Through his partner, Henslowe, he hired Peter Street to do the work, and subsequently retained not only the original contract but daily accounts of the building process. The Fortune is therefore better documented than any other London public theater of the time. Its design was to copy that of the Globe in most respects, though its plan was different: an eighty-foot square, with a courtyard fifty-five feet square centrally located within, so that the ranges of galleries which constituted most of the main frame were all twelve feet, six inches deep front to rear (as

at the Rose and Globe). Within the yard was a raised stage forty-three feet wide, extended forward to the halfway point and covered by a "shadow" or stage roof. The three levels of galleries were twelve, eleven, and nine feet high.

The accounts show that the main frame was built of oak, freshly felled in the late winter of 1599/1600 and barged down the Thames to London. Presumably at Street's wharf in Bridewell the timbers were worked into the members of the great square frame; they were then transported to the building site and erected in May on foundations already prepared for them. During the summer the more refined internal work was carried forward, using deal boards imported from the Baltic. The Globe had been thatched, presumably to save money; Alleyn could afford tile, but that did not prevent his theater from burning down in 1621. It was then replaced by a brick structure, probably round in plan.

It seems likely that the stage at the Globe was similar in size to that at the Fortune, and that its covering roof was supported toward the front by giant columns like those of the Swan but so positioned as to allow the roof to cover the entire stage, as it did at the Rose.

Inn-yard theaters. Except for the Globe, all these theaters were purpose-built from scratch, each to a deliberate plan. But at the Boar's Head, in Whitechapel, an existing inn yard was converted into a permanent theater in 1599, with a stage rather oddly located at the center of the yard, reached by a kind of catwalk from some rudimentary tiring rooms in the western range of the building. This arrangement was altered in the following year, the stage being lifted bodily to abut the western range, more galleries being built around the yard, and a roof provided to cover the stage.

A similar inn-yard conversion at the Red Bull in 1605 created an important theater of which very little is known, and in 1613 the bearbaiting arena on Bankside was rebuilt as a dual-purpose theater-cum-baiting ring, its frame modeled on that of the Swan, but with a removable stage of unknown dimensions entirely covered by its own roof.

Public theater decor. In all the open "public" theaters performances were staged by daylight. Their decor combined elements of almost courtly interiors with others more often associated with the street. At the Fortune carved satyrs appeared on every forward post, whereas the Hope and its model the Swan were fitted with expensive turned columns, delicately painted. Stage roofs, painted underneath to resemble marble, were decorated with signs of the zodiac and possibly other cosmic motifs; but down below the yard surface at the Rose and Globe was made of industrial slag imported perhaps from a local soap yard, a material commonly used to pave streets. At the Fortune, as presumably at its model the Globe, iron spikes defended the lower gallery from the yard, a fearsome barrier across which the players had to project. Even the giant columns supporting the stage roofs were redolent of outdoor architecture.

London Private Theaters. Another class of London playhouse, the so-called private houses, provided interior spaces for performance. They were fully roofed-in and lit by candles, with the result that they were smaller than the public houses and needed to charge more for a place (generally sixpence against the public theaters' penny or two). They therefore served a more exclusive audience and did away with the standing room of the yard, offering instead a seated pit directly in front of the stage, with two or three levels of galleries surrounding it on three sides.

Little is known of most of the eight private theaters active in London between 1576 and 1642. The most important was the Blackfriars, mentioned above. In its earlier years it was the home of child actors, but in 1609 it became a sister theater of the Globe, where the King's Men (Shakespeare's company) performed during the winter months. It was in a splendid upper room, once used as a Parliament Chamber, forty-six feet wide by sixty-six feet, approached at the northern end by a wide stair. It appears to have had a U-shaped auditorium of two or possibly three galleries, with a raised stage at the south end equipped with three doors of entrance, a balcony, a stage trap, and a descent machine. After 1616 it was rivaled by the Cockpit Theater in Drury Lane, which may be shown in an otherwise unidentified set of drawings by Inigo Jones. They show a U-shaped auditorium of two levels of gallery with perilously steep steppings, arranged so that much of the audience face each other rather than the stage. The space available to each person is eighteen inches fore and aft, and because the seats are armless benches, people must have been in close physical contact with each other when the theater was full. Ventilation is by a series of small windows, offering far less air displacement than in later theaters. Both auditorium and stage were lit by candles (and possibly by torches). During a long five-act play the atmosphere must sometimes have been uncomfortable.

The Jones drawings show the gallery fronts with turned posts, proportioned as Doric below and Corinthian above, and the *frons* adorned with statuary. Further details of the decoration of these theaters are largely speculative, but all playhouses, public and private alike, seem to have been elaborately painted according to the latest architectural fashions. Thus both the Globe and the Blackfriars may well have used details similar to those of the well-known contemporary Southwark school of funerary sculptors, with paint laid to imitate colored marbles, hardstones, and gilded details such as gadroon moldings, terms, and obelisks.

BIBLIOGRAPHY

Allen, John J. *The Reconstruction of a Spanish Golden-Age Playhouse: El Corral del Príncipe 1583–1744.* Gainesville, Fla., 1983. Much useful documentation.

Bentley, Gerald Eades. *The Jacobean and Caroline Stage.* 7 vols. Oxford, 1949–1968. Standard history.

Chambers, E. K. *The Elizabeth Stage.* 4 vols. Oxford, 1923. Standard history, still unsurpassed.

Cox, John D., and David Scott Kastan, eds. *A New History of Early English Drama.* New York, 1997. Wide-ranging survey.

Foakes, R. A. *Illustrations of the English Stage, 1580–1642.* London, 1985. Thorough discussion of all the main pictorial evidence.

Foakes, R. A., and R. T. Rickert, eds. *Henslowe's Diary.* Cambridge, U.K., 1961. Essential source material.

Gandolfi, Vittorio. *Il Teatro Farnese di Parma.* Parma, Italy, 1980. Includes documents and illustrations of many Italian Renaissance theaters.

Gent, Lucy, ed. *Albion's Classicism: The Visual Arts in Britain, 1550–1660.* New Haven, Conn., and London, 1995. Full survey of contemporary aesthetic issues.

Gurr, Andrew. *Playgoing in Shakespeare's London.* Cambridge, U.K., 1987. Fully documented account.

Orrell, John. *The Theatres of Inigo Jones and John Webb.* Cambridge, U.K., 1985.

Serlio, Sebastiano. *The Five Books of Architecture: An Unabridged Reprint of the English Edition of 1611.* New York, 1982.

Shergold, N. D. *A History of the Spanish Stage from Medieval Times until the End of the Seventeenth Century.* Oxford, 1967. Standard work.

JOHN ORRELL

THEOLOGY. *See* **Bible,** *subentries on* **Christian Interpretation of the Bible, Jewish Interpretation of the Bible; Christian Theology; Patristics.**

THIRTY YEARS' WAR (1618–1648). Fought over much of central Europe, the Thirty Years' War is best characterized as a conflict within the Holy Roman Empire between territorial particularism—advocated most forcefully, but not exclusively, by the most radical segment of political Protestantism—and the revived, ardently Catholic, imperial authority

Thirty Years' War. An allegorical print showing the Elector Palatine Frederick V (represented by the lion) and the Holy Roman Emperor Ferdinand II (eagle) climbing stairs to attain the crown of Bohemia. The war began as a struggle for the crown of Bohemia in 1618. BILDARCHIV, ÖSTERREICHISCHE NATIONAL BIBLIOTHEK, VIENNA

under the direction of the Austrian house of Habsburg. The principle of particularism eventually triumphed, in part because the conflict in the empire became enmeshed in long-standing international antagonisms. The war fits with the Dutch revolt (1576–1609) and the French Wars of Religion (1560–1598), as a pivotal moment in the long-standing conflict over the location of legitimate political and religious authority in the era. The importance of the war as a transitional moment has been underscored by the frequent use of the date 1648 as a dividing line in western civilization and European history courses.

The Thirty Years' War began as a religious and constitutional conflict in the kingdom of Bohemia, which crystallized when two ministers of the Catholic King Ferdinand (1526–1564; Emperor Ferdinand II, 1556–1564) were tossed from a window of Prague Castle by an angered mob of Lutheran and Calvinist noblemen, an act which became known as the "defenestration of Prague." The conflict then escalated in stages, each of which is conventionally known by the name of the primary opponent of the emperor and his allies: a Bohemian phase (1618–1621), which ended in the defeat of the Protestant nobility; a Dutch-Palatine phase (1621–1625), which brought the subjugation of the Palatinate; a Lower Saxon–Danish phase (1625–1629), in which the Danish in-

vaders were eventually defeated, which moved the main theater of war to northern Germany and resulted in the exclusion of Denmark from German affairs after the Peace of Lübeck (1629) and the promulgation of the Edict of Restitution (1629), overturning Protestant control of ecclesiastical territories occupied since 1552; a Swedish phase (1629–1635), which abruptly turned the tide for the Protestants through the military triumphs of King Gustavus Adolphus (reigned 1611–1632), but which began to unravel after his death in the battle of Lützen (1632) until almost all of Sweden's German allies deserted at the Peace of Prague (1635); and a French-Swedish phase (1635–1648), in which the French minister Cardinal Richelieu moved from covert diplomacy to open warfare in order to further weaken his Spanish and Austrian enemies and which continued until virtually all the parties were exhausted.

Some historians view these stages, and the ancillary conflicts that flowed into them, such as the War of the Mantuan Succession (1628–1631), as discrete conflicts rather than a single war. But the term "thirty years' war" was coined during the war. Consciousness about the duration and unity of the conflict was already apparent in commentaries from the 1630s. The long, drawn-out, and comprehensive negotiations that resulted in the Peace of Westphalia (1648) reinforced the sense that the war was a single unified conflict.

Much ink has been spilt over the relative weight to be given to religion, reason of state, and defense of tradition as motivations for the belligerents in the conflict. There is ample evidence that all three motives played important roles (often for the same belligerent), which is one of the reasons the war lasted so long. The threads of religion, state-building, internal social conflict, and international interests were so tangled up in one another that signal triumphs in one area could have unexpected repercussions in a different area. Thus, even though there were a number of seemingly decisive battles during the war, the war was not ultimately decided on the battlefield, but at the negotiating table.

The Thirty Years' War is also notable for the ferocity and destructiveness with which it was fought. The social impact of the war was seared on the memory of both political leaders and the general populace. The sufferings of the peasants and townspeople reinforced the notion that the war was a cataclysmic event and a moment of transition. This suffering was combined with the perception that no clear victory ever emerged out of the military campaigns and helped promote a general mood for peace.

The Thirty Years' War marks a political end to the age of the Renaissance, because it accelerated and began to harden several developments that had characterized the previous century. First, the contours and content of sovereign state authority became sharpened in the conflict between the Holy Roman Emperor and rulers of individual territories within the empire. Second, the links between state-building and confessionalization were first tightened and then significantly weakened as a result of the long period of indecisive religious warfare. Third, a long period of economic expansion came to an end (either as a prelude to the war or as a result of the war). And fourth, the international dimension of the development of state sovereignty was also expanded by the conclusion of an international peace treaty at the end of the war. The treaties that made up the Peace of Westphalia of 1648 were a milestone of international relations that set the stage for post-Renaissance diplomacy.

BIBLIOGRAPHY

Asch, Ronald G. *The Thirty Years' War: The Holy Roman Empire and Europe, 1618–1648.* New York, 1997. The best recent study in English for assessing the Central European aspects of the conflict.

Parker, Geoffrey, ed. *The Thirty Years' War.* 2d ed. London, 1997. The standard English-language survey. Manages a balanced treatment of central European and international aspects of the conflict.

Sutherland, N. M. "The Origins of the Thirty Years' War and the Structure of European Politics." *English Historical Review* 107 (1992): 587–625. Focuses on the international dimension of the conflict. Weak on central European aspects, but valuable for situating the war in the context of Renaissance politics.

JOHN C. THEIBAULT

TIME.   *See* **Calendars; Clocks.**

TINÓDI, SEBESTYÉN   (1505/10?–1556), Hungarian songwriter, the first significant representative of a Hungarian genre, the battle chronicle, a by-product of the anti-Turkish wars. A wandering lutist, Sebestyén Tinódi came from the emerging social stratum of peasant burghers. His parents were prosperous enough to send their sons to a Latin school. Tinódi spent some years in the service of Bálint Török, a famous warlord. After his mentor fell into Turkish captivity in 1541, Tinódi lived in the courts of various aristocrats. He later settled in Kassa (Košice, Slovakia), where he lived with his wife and children. From there he visited and wrote about the battle scenes.

While he tried his hand at all contemporary epic genres, Tinódi's favorite subjects were the battles fought on Hungarian soil and their heroes, the soldiers who challenged the dreaded Turks. Although he was supported mostly by feudal lords, his poetry reflects a plebeian stance.

The war Tinódi described was actually a mosaic of many, often simultaneously fought battles for individual fortresses or outposts. In the manner of present-day war correspondents, Tinódi provided his readers (or listeners) with eyewitness reports. He told about the events in songs, accompanied by music of his own composition. It is of particular interest to analyze the work of Tinódi because he narrates like a medieval bard, but his poetry is informed by the cultural preferences of the Renaissance, relying on scholarly histories and the classics. That Tinódi considered himself more than a songster is implicit in his self-description: "Sebastianus Literatus de Tinod, Lutinista" (Sebastian of Tinod, Latinist and lute player).

The final profile of his oeuvre was probably developed in collaboration with his printer, Georg Hoffgreff. Unfortunately, Tinódi chose an archaic format: his *Cronica* consists of unending sets of rhyming quatrains (*aaaa, bbbb, cccc,* and so on) that make for tiresome reading. Yet *Cronica* was considered of such import that Johannes Sambucus (János

Zsámboky, 1531–1584) decided to make the work widely available by translating the section about the battle of Eger (1553) into Latin verse. Sambucus's translation, divided into four sections, contains close to 1,800 lines. Although not an outstanding poet, Sambucus was a significant humanist on the European scene (imperial historian and librarian of the Vienna court), and his translation validated Tinódi's work as historically accurate and of poetic value. Indeed, in 1553, Emperor Ferdinand ennobled Tinódi for his literary achievements and excellence.

In the same year, Tinódi visited Transylvania, where his *Cronica* was published by the famous press of Gáspár Heltai in 1554. This journey yielded another of his main works, *Erdéli historia* (Transylvanian history; 1553), chronicling the years 1540 and 1541, in five parts.

Tinódi considered himself a teacher of history in the service of Hungary, which he hoped to see again victorious and united. It was probably for this reason that he stayed away from the partisan political and religious disputes that were so frequent in Europe during his career. Most probably a Protestant, Tinódi never voiced any religious preferences in his writings. Yet he died while visiting the Sárvár estate of one of his earliest mentors, the outstanding patron of Protestant humanists Tamás Nádasdy (1498?–1562), by then palatine of Hungary.

BIBLIOGRAPHY

Klaniczay, Tibor. "Tinódi Sebestyén emlékezete." In *A reneszánsz és a barokk, Tanulmányok a régi magyar irodalomról.* Budapest, Hungary, 1961. Pages 39–53.

MARIANNA D. BIRNBAUM

TINTORETTO (Jacopo Robusti; 1518–1594), Venetian painter. Tintoretto was the only one of the dominant Venetian painters of the sixteenth century who was actually born in Venice. More than those of Titian or Veronese, his career was essentially based in Venice, and his major works remain in the churches and confraternities of that city.

Early Career. Tintoretto's sobriquet, meaning "little dyer," derives from his father's profession as a cloth dyer. Little is known of his training as a painter. One tradition (Ridolfi, Boschini) places him briefly as an apprentice with Titian, who is said to have expelled the youngster, being jealous of his talent. Tintoretto's earliest paintings suggest study in the busy, conservative workshop of Bonifazio de' Pitati, whereas his more ambitious figural style may have found inspiration in the art of Pordenone. By 1539

he is recorded as an independent master: "mistro Giacomo depentor."

In 1548 he very publicly declared himself with a canvas for the meeting hall of the Scuola Grande di San Marco (a confraternity) representing *St. Mark Rescuing a Slave* (Venice, Gallerie dell'Accademia). The painting caused a sensation; celebrated in a letter of the writer Pietro Aretino, it was initially rejected by the brothers of the *scuola*. In this composition acutely foreshortened figures define a dynamic spatial structure and break the tableau flatness of the canvas, a flatness that had been traditional in Venetian mural decoration. Possibly even more disturbing to contemporaries was the evident speed of execution, the rapid brushwork that disturbed even Aretino. Radical foreshortening and an energetic brush remained two of the defining characteristics of Tintoretto's style. Indeed, the speed of his brush led critics like Giorgio Vasari to claim that Tintoretto made a mockery of the art of painting, passing off unfinished canvases as completed works of art.

Tintoretto was said to have painted a motto over the door to his studio: "The Drawing [*disegno*] of Michelangelo and the Coloring [*colorito*] of Titian." Such personified reconciliation of basic aesthetic alternatives actually found published form precisely in 1548, in Paolo Pino's *Dialogo di pittura* (Dialogue on painting). Tintoretto was an avid student of Michelangelo's art, drawing after small casts of the Florentine's sculpture and studying graphic copies of his pictorial inventions; he adapted those models to the active economies of his own compositions—for example, in *St. Mark Rescuing the Slave* and on the facade frescoes of Ca' Gussoni (lost, known through graphic copies).

Between 1562 and 1566 Tintoretto executed three more paintings for the Scuola di San Marco, further scenes of the life and miracles of the patron saint of Venice: *The Carrying of the Body* (Venice, Gallerie dell'Accademia), *The Finding of the Body* (Milan, Pinacoteca di Brera), and *The Miraculous Rescue of the Saracen by St. Mark* (Venice, Gallerie dell' Accademia). The first of these is quite thinly painted on a brownish toned canvas, with long strokes of white painting defining spectral figures and architecture in the background, just the kind of rapid execution that left doubt as to its state of finish. But the carping of central Italian critics did not hinder the painter's local success. Tintoretto set out to fill the available walls of Venice with his work, and his business strategies proved as unconventional as his art.

The Scuola di San Rocco. Thus, in 1564, did he gain the commission for the ceiling painting in

Tintoretto. *Miracle of Saint Mark.* Also called *Rescue of the Slave from Torture.* Painted c. 1548. ACADEMIA, VENICE/
ANDERSON/ALINARI/ART RESOURCE

the board room (*albergo*) of the Scuola Grande di San Rocco: rather than submit a small model to the competition, he had a quickly executed painting of *The Apotheosis of St. Roch* installed and presented it as a gift, an offering to the saint that could not be refused. Despite criticism of his tactics, he managed to extend his control of the decorations of the room, executing next a monumental *Crucifixion* (1565), generally considered his grandest painting, and in the following two years representations of Passion scenes leading up to that event. The radical foreshortening and precipitous spaces that mark Tintoretto's compositions are subject to more certain pictorial control by the larger chiaroscuro patterns—overall distribution of light and dark values—that establish a dominant pictorial organization. Such dynamic contrast is fundamental to Tintoretto's art.

Tintoretto became a brother of the Scuola di San Rocco and arranged to continue his decorative ef-

forts. In 1575–1576 he painted the central ceiling canvas of the large meeting hall of the *scuola,* representing *The Brazen Serpent,* and in the following two years he completed the project with further Old Testament scenes: *Moses Striking Water from the Rock* and *The Gathering of Manna,* smaller ovals of *The Fall of Man* and *The Paschal Feast,* and flanking images of prophets. On the walls below he then painted a cycle dedicated to the life of Christ (1579–1581), continuing on the ground floor with scenes from the infancy (1583–1587). The pictorial decorations of the Scuola di San Rocco thus trace the development of Tintoretto's art over the course of two decades; the building itself stands as the most important monument to that art.

Venetian Patronage. Although he did receive commissions from beyond the lagoon—such as the cycle celebrating the Gonzaga triumphs

Tintoretto. *Crucifixion.* Oil on canvas; 1566–1567; 5.35 × 1.22 m (17.5 × 4 ft.). SCUOLA GRANDE DI S. ROCCO, VENICE/ ALINARI/ART RESOURCE, NY

(1578–1580; Munich, Alte Pinakothek)—Tintoretto's primary patronage came from within Venice. His early work in the Sala del Maggior Consiglio (Hall of the Great Council) of the Ducal Palace was destroyed by fire in 1577; in the major campaign of redecoration, however, he and his workshop played a dominant role, including the central ceiling panel of a celestial Venice receiving Doge Nicolò da Ponte and the Signoria (1580–1584) and the enormous canvas, *Paradise,* behind the ducal throne (1588–1592), as well as many of the votive pictures of the doges and portraits of Venetian officials.

In addition to such state commissions and the patronage of the *scuole grandi,* the great confraternities, Tintoretto worked extensively for the lesser confraternities of Venice, the smaller *scuole,* many of which maintained chapels dedicated to the Holy Sacrament in churches throughout the city. For these groups he produced a number of representations of the Last Supper, often paired with a scene of the Washing of the Feet; the earliest of these are canvases for the church of San Marcuola (1547). His conception of the Last Supper, in contrast to that of Paolo Veronese, is characterized by a modesty of setting and person; his iconography is essentially humble, appealing to a more popular congregation—although his last, most luminous rendition of the theme was for the Benedictines of San Giorgio Maggiore (1592–1594).

Many of these late canvases represent the collective work of the master and assistants. Tintoretto directed a family workshop; his chief assistant and heir was his son Domenico (1560–1635), after whom the Tintoretto shop continued for another generation. Such collective enterprise and professional continuity were typical of artistic production in Venice, sustained by a guild system that lasted well into the eighteenth century.

Tintoretto's bold brushwork did indeed effect a union of *disegno* (design) and *colorito* (color): long, directional strokes of light paint over a darker ground charge the surface with a graphic energy. It is especially in the brilliance of his brush that Tintoretto brings to a climax an essential component of sixteenth-century Venetian painting.

[For Tintoretto's *St. George and the Dragon,* see the frontispiece to this volume.]

See also **Venice**, *subentry on* **Art in Venice**.

BIBLIOGRAPHY

Primary Works

Aretino, Pietro. *Lettere sull'arte di Pietro Aretino* (Pietro Aretino's letters on art). 3 vols. in 4. Edited by Ettore Camesasca. Commentary by Fidenzio Pertile. Milan, 1957–1960.

Boschini, Marco. *La carta del navegar pitoresco* (The chart of pictorial navigation; Venice, 1660). Edited by Anna Pallucchini. Venice and Rome, 1966. Includes *Le ricche minere della pittura veneziana* (The rich mines of Venetian painting; Venice, 1576), the introduction to which contains Boschini's appreciation of Tintoretto's art.

Pino, Paolo. *Dialogo di pittura* (Dialogue on painting; Venice, 1548). In *Trattati d'arte del Cinquecento.* Edited by Paola Barocchi. Bari, Italy, 1960. Vol. 1.

Ridolfi, Carlo. *The Life of Tintoretto and of His Children Domenico and Marietta.* Translated and with an introduction by Catherine Engass and Robert Engass. University Park, Pa., and London, 1984. From *Le maraviglie dell'arte* (The marvels of art). Venice, 1648. Edited by Detlev Freihernn von Hadeln. 2 vols. Berlin, 1914–1924.

Vasari, Giorgio. *Lives of the Painters, Sculptors, and Architects*. 2 vols. Translated by Gaston du C. de Vere, with an introduction and notes by David Ekserdjian. New York and Toronto, 1996. Translation (1912) of *Le vite de' più eccellenti pittori, scultori ed architettori,* 2d ed. (1568).

Secondary Works

Lepschy, Anna Laura. *Tintoretto Observed: A Documentary Survey of Critical Reactions from the Sixteenth to the Twentieth Century.* Ravenna, Italy, 1983.

Pallucchini, Rodolfo, and Paola Rossi. *Tintoretto: Le opere sacre e profane* (The sacred and secular works). 2 vols. Venice, Italy, 1982. The basic catalogue raisonée.

Rosand, David. *Painting in Sixteenth-Century Venice: Titian, Veronese, Tintoretto.* Rev. ed. Cambridge, U.K., 1997.

DAVID ROSAND

TITIAN (Tiziano Vecellio; c. 1488–1576), Venetian painter. Titian was the leading master of the Venetian school of painting and enjoyed the greatest international renown in sixteenth-century Europe. From his base in Venice, where he was a dominant cultural figure, serving as official painter to the state, he worked for a wide range of aristocratic and ecclesiastic patrons throughout Italy and beyond. Titian transformed the art of oil painting, and for subsequent generations of artists his name came to personify the art of painting.

Early Career and Training. Titian was born in Pieve di Cadore, in the Dolomites, of an important local aristocratic family. Although his precise date of birth is undocumented and remains a point of contention among scholars, the legend of his dying at the age of 99, or even 103, based in part on the old artist's own exaggerations, may be discounted. The more reliable primary sources suggest a birthdate about 1488 (the calculation in Lodovico Dolce's *Dialogo della pittura* [Dialogue on painting; 1557]; a less convincing date of 1480 is given by Giorgio Vasari in his *Lives* [2d ed. 1568]). Dolce's *Dialogo della pittura,* published during Titian's lifetime and presumably with his own direct participation, was a Venetian response to the absence of a biography of the artist in the first edition of Vasari's *Lives* (1550).

Dolce, through the character of Pietro Aretino, offers an apology for Titian's art as well as the fullest early account of his development. According to this account, Titian was sent to Venice at the age of nine to live with an uncle, who was an engineer in the service of the republic; the youngster was apprenticed to Sebastiano Zuccato, the artist overseeing the mosaic decorations of the ducal basilica of San Marco and directly responsible to the procurators who oversaw San Marco, which was the church of the state. Zuccato thus enjoyed a privileged position within the Venetian artistic community, and Titian's apprenticeship to a mosaicist should be understood in this context. Evidently recognizing the extraordinary talent that had been entrusted to him, Zuccato sent the youth on to the workshop of Gentile Bellini, the painter in charge of the murals of the Ducal Palace. The young Titian was clearly moving in the highest circles of official patronage.

Impatient with Gentile's dry and archaic methods, Dolce reports, the apprentice challenged the master with the boldness and speed of his own drawing. Such generational confrontation evidently led to Titian's departure; from Gentile's shop he went to study briefly with that master's brother, Giovanni Bellini, and from there the young painter soon went to work with Giorgione.

Dolce thus has the boy traversing a full art historical arc from the most conservative to the most advanced painters then practicing in Venice. If the account sounds rather too neat, it nonetheless fits the officially mandated pattern of workshop training in Venice. Titian would have served his required apprenticeship with Gentile Bellini and then worked as assistant to Giovanni. Finally, the young painter—now presumably enrolled as a master in the Arte dei Depentori, the Venetian painters guild—appears as assistant to Giorgione on a major fresco project, the external decorations of the recently rebuilt Fondaco dei Tedeschi, the German warehouse on the Rialto, which had been destroyed by fire in 1505. There, in 1508, and not yet twenty, according to Dolce, Titian won greater public acclaim for his work than did the commissioned master Giorgione.

The oil medium. Although Titian's early stylistic development continues to be debated, it is possible to track his progress from the relatively crisp delineation of a manner formed in the ambience of Gentile Bellini (*Christ Carrying the Cross;* Venice, Scuola Grande di San Rocco)—but also revealing an awareness of Bellini's brother-in-law, Andrea Mantegna—through the tonal and formal softening of the art of Giovanni Bellini (*St. Mark Enthroned with Sts. Cosmas and Damian, Roch and Sebastian;* Venice, Santa Maria della Salute) to the radically new manner of Giorgione. Indeed, the so-called *Concert Champêtre* (Paris, Musée du Louvre; see the color plates in volume 5), a major expression of the new style established by Giorgione, has been attributed to Titian himself by some modern scholars.

Giorgione's transformation of the oil medium involved the exploitation of the canvas support, a support especially developed in Venice where the constant humidity challenged the stability of fresco painting on plaster. Traditionally, the oil medium had been applied in a sequence of translucent glazes over a light gessoed panel, enabling the deeply luminous effects to be seen in the art of Giovanni Bellini. The new technique, however, built upon the opacity of the oil medium, a greater density of pigment suspended in the binder. Working up from a darker ground toward lighter forms, reserving glazes for the final layer, the painter could cover over previous forms or scrape off paint. Painting technique itself thus became a more open, flexible process. Working on the rougher weave of canvas, the new art respected the broken touch, the individual stroke of the brush. Lighter forms emerged from a darker ground, and clear contours were lost in a surrounding ambient shadow. Poetic suggestion rather than sharp delineation set the expressive tone of this new art.

Giorgione died young, during a plague in 1510, but the implications of his art were realized by his two celebrated followers, Sebastiano del Piombo and Titian. It may have been the same plague that led Titian to move in 1510 to Padua, where the following year he executed three frescoes in the decorative cycle of the confraternity of St. Anthony, the Scuola di Sant'Antonio. Representing scenes of the life and miracles of Padua's patron saint, these murals are Titian's first essays in monumental narrative composition. In Padua the young artist was challenged by the grand models of past tradition: the frescoes of Giotto in the Arena Chapel, of Mantegna in the Ovetari Chapel, and Donatello's reliefs on the high altar of the basilica of Sant'Antonio. The year in Padua proved a crucial experience in the development of the young Titian; there he came to maturity.

Return to Venice. Back in Venice, Titian asserted his professional position with aggressive self-confidence. Citing an invitation to join the papal court, an invitation evidently arranged by the humanist cardinal Pietro Bembo, Titian presented himself to the Venetian Council of Ten on 31 May 1513, offering his services in the decoration of the Sala del Maggior Consiglio (Hall of the Great Council) of the Ducal Palace. Specifically, he volunteered to replace the decaying fourteenth-century fresco by Guariento representing the Battle of Spoleto, a task, he wrote, "so difficult that no one has yet dared to undertake it." Declaring rhetorically that his art was a means to

honor rather than gain, he asked only for payment for the colors and other necessary expenses and the promise of the next *senseria,* a lucrative broker's patent, to fall vacant at the Fondaco dei Tedeschi. Such a request, however, was tantamount to requesting recognition as heir apparent to the official state painter, for a *senseria* and its attendant profit and privileges were generally reserved for the painter in charge of the Ducal Palace decorations, who was also ducal portraitist and responsible for executing the votive picture of each newly elected doge. The incumbent was the aged Giovanni Bellini, who is said to have resisted the claims of his former pupil. Titian began work on the battle piece by the end of 1514, and two years later, upon the death of Bellini, he inherited the *senseria* and with it the position of premier painter to the republic.

Although it was only in 1538, after much procrastination and official reprimand, that Titian completed *The Battle of Spoleto* (the canvas was destroyed by fire in 1577), his early thoughts for the composition are reflected in the twelve-block woodcut of the *Submersion of Pharaoh's Army in the Red Sea,* published about 1515 by Bernardino Benalio with a copyright privilege (a later edition from the same blocks was published by Domenico dalle Greche in 1549). Conceived as a cheaper surrogate for painting, this great print effectively records the boldness of Titian's draftsmanship; the sweeping lines of his pen and the intricate systems of crosshatching are rather loosely translated by the cutters' knives, yielding irregular graphic patterns of great power—an aesthetic quite different from the closer control and linear refinement of Albrecht Dürer's influential model.

During these early years, even as he was assuming major painting commissions, Titian was evidently involved with the publishers of Venice, producing designs for other monumental woodcuts, including a long processional *Triumph of Faith* (possibly published as early as 1508) and a *Sacrifice of Abraham* (c. 1515), which went through many subsequent editions. Somewhat later, his design of the author portrait for the definitive edition of Ludovico Ariosto's *Orlando furioso* (Ferrara, 1532) established a model for such printed portraits. Toward the end of his career, in 1566, Titian took more direct advantage of Venetian publishing laws and conventions; acting as his own publisher, he obtained a copyright privilege for the prints executed after his work by the Netherlandish engraver Cornelis Cort, thereby maintaining control of the production and distribution of his inventions.

Titian. *Assumption of the Virgin.* The painting is in the church of S. Maria Gloriosa
dei Frari, Venice. Painted c. 1516–1518. ANDERSON/ALINARI/ART RESOURCE

Altarpieces. On 19 May 1518 Titian's first great public work in Venice was unveiled on the high altar of the Franciscan church of Santa Maria Gloriosa dei Frari, an *Assumption of the Virgin (Assunta)*. Over twenty-two feet in height, unprecedented dimensions for a painting on wood panel, the *Assunta* fits into a monumental marble frame, a triumphal arch dated 1516 and very probably conceived by Titian himself. The painter sited the work scenographically within the space of the church; viewed down the nave through the aperture of an earlier choir screen, the painting commands the architectural experience of the Frari.

The *Assunta* confirmed Titian's artistic dominance in Venice. Through a series of commissions he continued to explore the pictorial challenge of the altarpiece, radically revising conventions as he adapted composition to context. Between 1519 and 1526 he received payments for an altarpiece for the Pesaro family to go on a side altar in the Frari. Acknowledging the diagonal visual access to a viewer approaching the painting down the nave, Titian rotated the traditional *sacra conversazione,* the figural structure of enthroned Madonna and Child with attendant saints, creating an asymmetrical composition: the perspective of the painted architecture is adapted to an oblique view, whereas the dynamic interaction of the figures, uniting saints and Pesaro family members in common adoration of Virgin and Child, is calculated to engage a worshiper kneeling directly before the altar.

Culminating Titian's creative transformation of the altarpiece was a painting for the Dominican basilica of Santi Giovanni e Paolo, a representation of *The Martyrdom of St. Peter Martyr,* completed in 1530 (destroyed by fire in 1867). Also intended for a side altar and therefore visually accessible on angle from the nave, the Peter Martyr altarpiece accommodates its internal space to an oblique approach. Here, however, the setting is not architectural but rather a monumental landscape, in which the heavens open in a blaze of glory as angels bring the martyr's palm to the murdered saint below. The painting of the landscape, the pathos of the saint, the terror of the fleeing companion, whose shrieking voice seemed almost audible: these were elements singled out for special praise by Pietro Aretino (letter of 1537), by Lodovico Dolce, and by Giorgio Vasari. Often copied, the Peter Martyr altarpiece was Titian's most celebrated painting, establishing a model of figural affect and of eloquent aggrandized landscape.

Landscapes. Landscape had played a significant role in Venetian painting for several generations. Na-ture had been accorded a luminously religious aura in the art of Giovanni Bellini in particular, and that poetic sensibility had been secularized by Giorgione, in part by casting nature into deeper shadow. Heir to both achievements, Titian infused landscape with the energy of his own brush, so that the organic processes of nature, its constant flux, found expression in painterly technique. Leonardo da Vinci had recognized the affinities of creative process, observing the dynamics of creation and comparing the artist to God. Titian, in turn, taught a knowing public to view nature in terms of the painter's brush, as attested in Aretino's famous description of a sunset over the Grand Canal: "Oh with what beautiful strokes of nature's brush was the atmosphere pushed back, clearing it away from the palaces, just as Titian does in painting landscapes!" he wrote in 1544 to the painter, whose "brush is filled with the very spirit of nature."

Even as he invested landscape with new pictorial substance, Titian gave fuller articulation to the significance of natural form, realizing its symbolic as well as dramatic potential. In the marriage picture known as *Sacred and Profane Love* (1514; Rome, Galleria Borghese; see the color plates in this volume) he modified the conventions of the moralized landscape, distinguishing the morally demanding road to virtue on the earthly side from the celestial openness on the spiritual side of the dialectically structured composition. In the woodcut of the *Red Sea* he gave powerful graphic shape to the Shekinah, "the pillar of cloud" in which God manifested himself to the Israelites (Exodus 13:22). In *The Presentation of the Virgin in the Temple,* painted between 1534 and 1538 for the Sala dell'Albergo of the Scuola Grande di Santa Maria della Carità (in situ, now the Gallerie dell'Accademia in Venice), Titian set the light of nature as a foil to the golden aureole radiating from the Virgin, and the mountain peaks rising in the landscape stand as witness to the words of the Marian liturgy, celebrating the Immaculate Conception: "The Lord possessed me in the beginning of his ways. . . . The mountains with their huge bulk had not as yet been established: before the hills I was brought forth" (Proverbs 8:22–25). In the same painting—the composition of which revives the archaic processional format of the narrative canvases of the Bellini and of Vittore Carpaccio—the Temple is set before the Palace of Solomon, which Titian paints with clear reference to the Ducal Palace in Venice, itself a palace of justice. Like his landscapes, Titian's architectural naturalism carries particular significance, here confirming the Solomonic wisdom and justice of the Venetian state.

Courtly Commissions. Having secured his position as successor to Giovanni Bellini in Venice, Titian succeeded as well in establishing his reputation at centers of courtly culture throughout Italy, beginning with the Ferrarese court of Alfonso I d'Este, which he visited first in 1516. In the course of the next two decades, following the intermarital network of the Italian courts, he developed close ties with the Gonzaga at Mantua and with the della Rovere of Urbino, painting the portraits of these princes, their consorts and mistresses, and establishing himself as the most sought-after portrait painter in Italy.

Portraiture. As a portraitist, Titian built upon traditions developed by Giovanni Bellini and then by Giorgione: a bust-length image seen behind the framing barrier of a low parapet. Titian revised the intimacy of that formula, endowing his sitters with a greater degree of physical presence and more calculated classical composure. Extending the figure to half or three-quarter length, he created a more monumental high Renaissance effigy, one that allowed a fuller corporeal expression to aristocratic status. Titian's sitters present themselves and the necessary defining attributes of rank and person with little of the self-conscious elegance and artifice characteristic of Florentine court portraiture. Rather than proclaiming their function with heraldic clarity, accompanying symbols and attributes are absorbed into a larger phenomenological context, becoming part of the world and presence of the sitter—like the cannon so casually caressed by Alfonso d'Este, symbol of his expertise in artillery and statecraft (New York, Metropolitan Museum of Art; copy of lost original?), or the rosary and faithful dog in the portrait of Federico Gonzaga (Madrid, Museo del Prado). The armored posturing of a series of Roman emperors Titian was painting for the Mantuan court in the later 1530s (now lost) was readily translated in his portrait of Francesco Maria della Rovere (Florence, Galleria degli Uffizi), conferring upon the duke of Urbino the aura of ancient imperial leadership.

Pictorially, in his portraits Titian subdued Giorgione's romantic chiaroscuro, subjecting it to a more precise control and seeking a more deliberate balance between tonal softening and the substantial reality of surfaces—of flesh, cloth, fur, armor. It is just this naturalistic dimension that distinguishes Titian's court portraits from those of his contemporaries in Florence and Rome. And that naturalism became a

topos in the literary celebration of Titian's art, finding its most influential voice in Pietro Aretino, in whose poetry and prose the life-giving power of Titian's brush became a leitmotif. A portrait by Titian (see the entry on Aretino in volume 1) breathes more naturally than nature, its pulse is more vital; it undermines the reasons for believing in death. And the painter himself encouraged such belief by working from older portraits by lesser artists and restoring youth to subjects no longer young (Isabella d'Este; Vienna, Kunsthistorisches Museum) or pictorial life to the already deceased (Empress Isabella; painting destroyed). Such rhetorical resonance in turn conditioned response to the images themselves, alerting an audience to the vibrancy of painted surface.

Ancient Paintings Revived. In 1514 Giovanni Bellini completed and signed *The Feast of the Gods* (Washington, National Gallery of Art), a painting that Titian subsequently revised, expanding the landscape to a more monumental scale. Bellini's painting was to be part of a series of mythological subjects commissioned by Alfonso d'Este for a small room (*camerino*) in the castle at Ferrara, the conception of which may have been inspired by the *studiolo* of his sister Isabella d'Este in Mantua (see the painting of Bacchus and Ariadne in the color plates in this volume). Other pictures were to be by Raphael and by Fra Bartolommeo della Porta, both of whom died, however, before completing their work. One by one, the commissions passed to Titian. Between 1518 and about 1525 he painted three narrative pictures of classical mythological subjects, each based upon an *ekphraseis,* a literary description of an ancient painting (now lost or merely imagined). Two of these were based on such descriptions in the *Imagines* of Philostratus the Elder, an Italian translation of which Alfonso had in fact borrowed from his sister: one is a representation of *Cupids,* more generally known as *The Worship of Venus,* the other a *Bacchanal of the Andrians* (both Madrid, Museo del Prado). The third painting, *Bacchus and Ariadne* (London, National Gallery; see the color plates in this volume), draws upon several descriptive accounts by Catullus (*Carmina*) and by Ovid (*Ars amatoria*).

Titian realized the *ekphraseis* of Philostratus following the ancient author's descriptions quite faithfully; literally, he fleshed out the text, giving a carnal reality to the cupids and an appropriately measured pace to the drunken dance and song of the Andrians, whose island was blessed by Bacchus so that its stream ran not with water but with wine. The encounter of Bacchus and the abandoned Ariadne on

Naxos, however, offered a more dramatic challenge; here the emotional stakes were different, the outcome more cosmic. Titian responded by inventing a moment of the most calculated poignancy that is best epitomized in the poetic lines it inspired centuries later: "the swift bound / Of Bacchus from his chariot, when his eye / Made Ariadne's cheek look blushingly" (John Keats, "Sleep and Poetry").

In reconstructing antique pictorial compositions known only through literary sources, Titian was participating in an activity central to the *rinascita dell'antichità,* the rebirth of antiquity that gave name to the epoch itself. The re-creation of that lost pictorial culture had effectively been part of Renaissance aesthetic ambition at least since Leon Battista Alberti had recommended such *ekphraseis* in his three books *On Painting* (1435). The Renaissance painter faced a double challenge in reviving those ancient compositions: to surpass the art of the past and, in so doing, to demonstrate his own powers by matching the evocative model of the literary sources.

Although the paintings of the ancients were no longer extant and could be known only through verbal descriptions, writers such as Pliny the Elder had left much tantalizing information concerning the fame of those lost works and of their makers, and especially of the fourth-century B.C. painter Apelles. Already in fifteenth-century Italy celebrated painters were accorded the title of "the New Apelles." Nor was the rhetoric of such an honor entirely empty, for the Renaissance painters themselves invited the comparative equation by the very act of re-creating the paintings of the ancient Greek master. And no artist was more seriously compared with Apelles than Titian himself.

Habsburg Patronage. Titian was first introduced to Charles V in 1529 by Federico Gonzaga in Mantua and again in 1532, when he was commissioned to paint the emperor's portrait. This was completed the following year in Bologna, the site of Charles's papal coronation as Holy Roman Emperor. Titian executed several paintings of the emperor in armor, for which he was rewarded richly with 500 *scudi* and, even more significantly, with new honors. On 10 May 1533 the emperor conferred upon the painter the title of "Count Palatine and Knight of the Golden Spur." In the patent of nobility Charles explicitly recognized both the cause of this extraordinary award and its cultural context:

> Your gifts as an artist and your genius for painting persons from life appear to us so great that you deserve to be called the Apelles of this age. Following the example of our forerunners, Alexander the Great and Octavius Augustus, of whom one would only be painted by Apelles, the other only by the most excellent masters, we have had ourselves painted by you, and have so well tested your skill and success that it seemed good to us to distinguish you with imperial honors as a mark of our opinion of you, and as a record of the same for posterity. (Quoted in Ridolfi, *Le maraviglie dell'arte*)

Titian came to enjoy a relationship with Charles that did indeed seem comparable to the fabled intimacy between Apelles and Alexander the Great. Called to the imperial court then at Augsburg in 1548, he painted the image of the emperor in his moment of greatest public triumph, his recent victory at Mühlberg (24 April 1547) over the forces of the Protestant League (see the color plates in volume 1). In a monumental equestrian portrait (Madrid, Museo del Prado) that established a model for the genre, Titian faithfully recorded the armor worn by the emperor on that occasion, as well as the particular horse and its caparison. Drawing on a number of sources—including Pliny's reference to Apelles's "portrait of Antigonos in armor advancing with his horse" (*Natural History* 35.96), ancient imperial representations in Roman art, the Renaissance tradition of equestrian monuments, as well as Dürer's engraving *Knight, Death, and the Devil*—he created a richly allusive image that celebrates the triumphant Holy Roman Emperor as *Miles Christianus,* the Christian knight, defender of the Catholic faith. Following his abdication in 1556, when Charles retired to the Hieronimite monastery at Yuste, he took with him the heavenly vision of the Trinity, the painting known as *La Gloria* (Madrid, Museo del Prado), in which Titian had represented the shrouded praying emperor and his deceased empress among the blessed.

Charles's son, Philip II, succeeded him as monarch of Spain and ruler of the Netherlands; he also succeeded him as Titian's most prominent patron. If Philip's patronage proved to be a most significant force in Titian's later career, it is also true that the painter himself was responsible for guiding the aesthetic education of the Spanish monarch, who seems not to have initially appreciated the relative openness of Venetian brushwork. Of a portrait of himself in armor (see the entry on Philip II in volume 5), Philip complained in 1551 to his aunt, Mary of Hungary: "It is easy to see the haste with which it was executed, and had there been time it would have been redone." The picture in question may be the full-length portrait of Philip that Titian painted during his second trip to Augsburg in 1550–1551 (Madrid, Museo del Prado).

Titian. *Self-portrait*. Painted c. 1550. STAATLICHE MUSEUM, BERLIN/BILDARCHIV FOTO MARBURG/ART RESOURCE

Poesie. For Philip, Titian painted a series of Ovidian mythologies that the painter referred to as *poesie*. These were indeed poetic celebrations of the female nude, sensual representations of amorous encounters of mortal and immortal. The project, a triumph of Titian's engagement of the nude in paint, seems to have been initiated by the artist himself, beginning with a *Danaë* (Madrid, Museo del Prado; see the entry on Myth in volume 4) that he sent to Philip, possibly as early as 1550. This picture was a more mature variation of one he had painted for Cardinal Alessandro Farnese in 1544–1545 (Naples, Museo di Capodimonte)—itself a variation on the reclining nude of the *Venus of Urbino* delivered to Guidobaldo II della Rovere in 1538 (Florence, Galleria degli Uffizi; see the color plates in this volume). When, in September 1554, Titian delivered a second *poesia*, a *Venus and Adonis* (Madrid, Museo del Prado), he explained that whereas Danaë was "seen from the front" he wanted to vary the pose in this *poesia* and "show the figure from a different view" so as to increase the appeal of the room (*camerino*) in which they were to hang. Subsequent *poesie* offer still other views of the figure: *Diana and Actaeon* and *Diana and Callisto* (both Edinburgh, National

Gallery of Scotland) belong to the pictorial category of bathing scene (*bagno*), the occasion for the display of the female nude in a natural setting. Two others set the figure against the perils of the sea: *Perseus and Andromeda* (London, Wallace Collection) and *The Rape of Europa* (Boston, Isabella Stewart Gardner Museum).

In shipping canvases to Philip, Titian was evidently hoping to gain royal favor and aid in collecting the pensions that had been granted to him by Charles V. Later, he complained of having received no compensation for the paintings he had sent to the Spanish monarch. It is not at all clear that Philip ever actually commissioned these *poesie*. The *camerino* in which Titian imagined them installed seems never to have existed, except in the painter's own mind. Such a situation frustrates efforts at interpreting the series in a particular key, political or dynastic; although mythological subjects were of course always open to such interpretation, no such intentional iconographic program seems to have guided the artist in this case.

Social Status. With titles, privileges, benefices, and—despite the difficulty in collecting his due—wealth, Titian enjoyed a status beyond that of other Renaissance painters, with the single exception of Michelangelo. Although he remained very much a Venetian painter, the head of a family workshop, he increasingly distanced himself from that craftsman's world, in which the guilds were regulated and supported by the state. In 1531, two years before he was ennobled by the emperor, Titian was still an active member of the Arte dei Depentori (painters guild), serving on a commission that awarded very modest dowries of twenty ducats to the daughters of five poor brothers of the guild. By contrast, for the marriage of his own daughter in 1555 he was able to provide an impressive dowry of 1,400 ducats.

Also in 1531 he moved into a grander house at Birri Grande, on the northern edge of Venice; set within garden grounds and overlooking the lagoon, it became the scene for gatherings with friends, especially Aretino and the architect and sculptor Jacopo Sansovino; these gatherings became internationally famous through the published letters of Aretino. As a man of aristocratic pretension, Titian assumed for himself an *impresa,* a device carrying the motto *Natura Potentior Ars* (Art more powerful than nature) and illustrated by the image of a bear licking her unformed cub into shape: thus did the artist also improve upon nature by giving form to its raw material.

The Roman Challenge. That Titian had been able to produce something as monumentally grand as the *Assunta* without having seen the artistic marvels of ancient and modern Rome offered, in Dolce's account, a measure of his natural genius. Indeed, by the middle of the century, the comparison between Titian and Michelangelo had come to personify the essential aesthetic alternatives of Italian art. These contrasted Venetian *colorito,* a painterly colorism that stressed natural appearances through open brushwork, with the formal qualities of central Italian *disegno,* with its stress on firm drawing and clear contour.

In the second edition of his *Lives,* Vasari dramatized the conflict in his report of Titian's Roman sojourn of 1545–1546. Having visited Titian's studio in the Belevedere where the painter was completing the *Danaë* for Alessandro Farnese, Michelangelo is said to have praised the naturalism of the image, declaring Titian unsurpassed in the imitation of nature through coloring; however, he added (according to Vasari), it was a pity that painters in Venice never learned to draw properly and had to hide that fundamental failure under the superficial appeal of coloring. This basic contrast, between the blended naturalism of Venetian *colorito,* considered essentially feminine, and the more secure *disegno* of central Italian art, harder and more masculine, conditioned academic discourse through the following centuries.

Although he had certainly been fully aware of the famous models of ancient art before his trip to Rome and of the achievements of rivals like Michelangelo and Raphael, Titian's direct encounter with Roman art came at a moment in his career when he had indeed been moving toward more monumental and ambitious figural design. His engagement with such formal problems may be seen, for example, in the paintings for the ceiling of Santo Spirito in Isola (in the Venetian lagoon) representing *Cain and Abel, The Sacrifice of Isaac,* and *David and Goliath* (now in the sacristy of Santa Maria della Salute in Venice)—a commission inherited from Vasari, who had visited Venice in 1541. Completed by 1544, these paintings display a radical foreshortening that responds to the particular placement of the canvases but also to the challenge of Michelangelo's art, celebrated for the difficulty of its figural design.

Titian's primary activity in Rome was painting the portraits of his Farnese patrons, especially Pope Paul III, whom he had already portrayed in Bologna in 1543 (Naples, Museo di Capodimonte; see the entry on Nepotism in volume 4). The grandest and most moving of these is the image of the aged pope with his two grandsons, Ottavio Farnese, who became duke of Parma, and Cardinal Alessandro Farnese (Naples, Museo di Capodimonte; see the entry on Nepotism in volume 4). Left unfinished, the canvas has seemed to many critics a penetrating representation of psychological tension, a pictorial revelation of political intrigue and treachery at the papal court. Whether or not such an interpretation can be historically sustained, this triple portrait, with its dramatic economy of glance and gesture, stands as full testimony to Titian's skill as a portraitist, his ability to create dynamic personality.

An Art More Powerful Than Nature. Despite his criticism of Venetian *colorito,* Vasari was nonetheless appreciative of Titian's achievement and sensitive to his particular development of the art of oil painting. Revisiting Venice in 1566, he observed the difference between Titian's early and late styles, noting that whereas "the early paintings are executed with a certain fineness and incredible diligence and can be viewed from close up and from afar," the later works "are carried out in bold strokes, broadly applied in great patches [*macchie*], in such a manner that they cannot be looked at closely but from a distance appear perfect."

The fullest and most satisfying account that has come down to us concerning the old Titian's working methods was published a century after the painter's death by Marco Boschini, an artist, poet, and passionate critic. Boschini was a true spiritual heir to the artistic traditions of the Venetian Renaissance, and his writings provide an eloquent exposition of Venetian *colorito.* Crediting his account to Jacopo Palma il Giovane, a painter who claimed to have studied with Titian, Boschini describes the way in which the old master began by blocking in his pictures broadly "with a mass of colors." Applying the paint with a loaded brush, he would build up forms with "pure red ochre, which would serve as a middle ground; then with a stroke of white lead, with the same brush then dipped in red, black, or yellow, he created the light and dark areas of the relief effect. And in this way, with four strokes of the brush he was able to suggest a magnificent figure." Then Titian would turn the canvas to the wall, leaving it there for weeks or months; when he took it out again he would scrutinize it, seeking out deformities or faults, whereupon, "like a surgeon treating a patient he would remove some swelling or excess flesh, set an arm if the bone were out of joint, or adjust a foot if it were misshapen, without the slightest pity for the victim. . . . And he gradually covered with living flesh those bare bones, going over them repeatedly until all they lacked was breath itself."

Confirming what one senses in Titian's late paintings, Boschini declares that "in the final stages he painted more with his fingers than with the brush." Boschini's descriptive language effectively captures the visceral quality of Titian's painting, the sense in which paint seems to transcend its metaphoric or correlative relation to flesh and appears instead a convincing substitute for it. Molding carnal effigies out of oily pigment, Titian extended the direct tactile experience of his painting by even abandoning the mediating implement, the brush, to work directly with his hands. "Wishing to imitate the operation of the Supreme Creator," the account concludes, Titian "used to observe that he too, in forming this human body, created it out of earth with his hands."

Perhaps no painting better validates this account than *The Flaying of Marsyas,* one of the last of Titian's works (Kromeříz, Státní Zámek). For all the remarkable looseness of its brushwork, the canvas is clearly signed, affirming authorial intention and responsibility; the signature also suggests the readiness of a late sixteenth-century public to accept such a radical pictorial structure as a finished picture. Here, Titian's brush creates a fabric of the world, moving from figure to ground to establish a fully mimetic continuum; the viewer is invited not merely to complete suggested form but rather to participate in the energies that so self-evidently and literally inform the scene. And the body of Marsyas, hanging upside down like a martyred saint, reveals the modeling touch of the painter's hand, creating flesh out of paint.

Titian left final testimony to this creative relationship in the canvas he originally intended to grace his own tomb, which he had planned to be at a side altar in the Frari: a *Pietà* (Venice, Gallerie dell' Accademia). At the core of this composition an aged Virgin Mary supports the body of Christ in her lap; approaching that body, reaching out with both hands and touching it, is the figure of St. Jerome, in which guise Titian portrayed himself. The painter projected an image of himself in touch with the body of his savior, in perpetual prayer for salvation, a prayer that depends upon the incarnation of paint as flesh. Just behind Jerome is a small votive panel that repeats this pictorial prayer; in it, kneeling before a vision of the Pietà, are the painter himself and his son Orazio, his chief assistant and heir.

Titian died on 27 August 1576, during—but possibly not because of—a devastating plague, which shortly thereafter claimed the life of Orazio. The Vecellio family workshop suddenly ceased to exist. The *Pietà,* like other works similarly abandoned in the studio, was acquired by another painter, Palma il Giovane in this case, who put some final touches on it and an inscription: "What Titian left unfinished Palma reverently completed and dedicated to God." Although Palma claimed to have been his pupil, Titian had no immediate followers. Many young painters came to work and learn in the studio, but, as Vasari wrote, the master offered no actual instruction; instead, his assistants learned what they could by studying the works themselves. This was the case with Titian's true heirs, the great painters of the following century: Rubens, Rembrandt, and Velázquez certainly learned important lessons in the art of oil painting by studying the works of the Venetian.

See also **Aretino, Pietro; Bellini Family; Giorgione; Venice,** *subentry on* **Art in Venice.**

BIBLIOGRAPHY

Primary Works

Aretino, Pietro. *Lettere sull'arte di Pietro Aretino* (Pietro Aretino's letters on art). 3 vols. in 4. Edited by Ettore Camesasca. Commentary by Fidenzio Pertile. Milan, 1957–1960.

Boschini, Marco. *La carta del navegar pitoresco* (The chart of pictorial navigation; Venice, 1660). Edited by Anna Pallucchini. Venice and Rome, 1966. Includes *Le ricche minere della pittura veneziana* (The rich mines of Venetian painting; Venice, 1576), the introduction to which contains Boschini's account of Titian's working method.

Dolce, Lodovico. *Dialogo della pittura, intitolato l'Aretino* (Dialogue on painting, titled Aretino; Venice, 1557). Translation by Mark W. Roskill in *Dolce's "Aretino" and Venetian Art Theory of the Cinquecento.* New York, 1968.

Pino, Paolo. *Dialogo di pittura* (Dialogue on painting; Venice, 1548). In *Trattati d'arte del Cinquecento.* Edited by Paola Barocchi. Bari, Italy, 1960. Vol. 1.

Ridolfi, Carlo. *The Life of Titian.* Translated by Julia Conaway Bondanella and Peter Bondanella. University Park, Pa., 1996. From *Le maraviglie dell'arte* (The marvels of art; Venice, 1648). 2 vols. Edited by Detlev Freiherrn von Hadeln. Berlin, 1914–1924.

Tiziano: Le lettere (The letters of Titian). Edited by Celso Fabbro. Cadore, Italy, 1976.

Vasari, Giorgio. *Lives of the Painters, Sculptors, and Architects.* 2 vols. Translated by Gaston du C. de Vere, with an introduction and notes by David Ekserdjian. New York and Toronto, 1996. Translation (1912) of *Le vite de' più eccellenti pittori, scultori ed architettori.* 2d ed. (1568).

Secondary Works

Chiari Moretto Wiel, M. Agnese. *Titian Drawings.* New York, 1990.

Crowe, J. A., and G. B. Cavalcaselle. *The Life and Times of Titian* 2 vols., 1877, 2d imp. London, 1881. The classic biography, richly documented and eminently readable.

Freedman, Luba. *Titian's Portraits Through Aretino's Lens.* University Park, Pa., 1995.

Goffen, Rona. *Piety and Patronage in Renaissance Venice: Bellini, Titian, and the Franciscans.* New Haven, Conn., and London, 1986.

Goffen, Rona. *Titian's Women.* New Haven, Conn., and London, 1997.

Hope, Charles. *Titian.* London, 1980.

Manca, Joseph, ed. *Titian 500.* Washington, D.C., 1993. Symposium papers on a range of topics.

Panofsky, Erwin. *Problems in Titian, Mostly Iconographic.* New York, 1969.

Rosand, David. *Painting in Sixteenth-Century Venice: Titian, Veronese, Tintoretto.* Rev. ed. New York, 1997.

Rosand, David. *Titian.* New York, 1978.

Rosand, David, ed. *Titian: His World and His Legacy.* New York, 1982. Papers on Titian and his Venetian context and colleagues.

Rosand, David, and Michelangelo Muraro. *Titian and the Venetian Woodcut.* Washington, D.C., 1976.

Le siècle de Titien: L'âge d'or de la peinture à Venise (Titian's century: the golden age of painting in Venice). Paris, 1993. Catalog of an exhibition.

Tietze, Hans. *Titian.* London, 1950.

Tietze, Hans, and E. Tietze-Conrat. *The Drawings of the Venetian Painters in the Fifteenth and Sixteenth Centuries.* New York, 1944. An important introduction to creative procedures and workshop production in Venice.

Titian, Prince of Painters. Venice, Italy, 1990. Catalog of an exhibition.

Tiziano e Venezia (Titian and Venice). Vicenza, Italy, 1980. Papers on a range of topics from an international conference held in Venice in 1976.

Wethey, Harold E. *The Paintings of Titian.* 3 vols. London, 1969–1975. The standard catalogue raisonné.

Wethey, Harold E. *Titian and His Drawings, with Reference to Giorgione and Some Close Contemporaries.* Princeton, N.J., 1987.

David Rosand

TOLEDO. For much of the Renaissance period, Toledo was one of the foremost cities of the crown of Castile. Strategically located at the center of the Iberian Peninsula, the city served as a hub for the exchange of merchandise, men, and ideas. It was one of eighteen urban centers that sent deputies to the Castilian Cortes, and the peripatetic monarchs frequently visited and convened meetings of the Cortes in Toledo. An unrivaled ecclesiastical capital, Toledo was the seat of the primate of the Spanish church, the site of church councils, and home to numerous clergymen.

During the first three-quarters of the sixteenth century, a period of prosperity and demographic expansion for many Castilian cities, Toledo's population increased dramatically from about 30,000 in 1528 to 60,000 in 1571, making Toledo the second largest city in Castile (only Seville was larger). But when Philip II established his court in Madrid, only seventy kilometers to the north, Toledo began to lose population and prestige to the new capital. Emigration was not the only cause of a shrinking population; a decreasing birthrate and the economic malaise that struck much of the nation in the seventeenth century also contributed. By 1639, the population of Toledo had dwindled to 24,000 inhabitants.

Before its decline, the city's life was dynamic and varied. From 1519 to 1522, Toledo was at the center of resistance to the new Habsburg dynasty, leading the Comunero Revolt. Many inhabitants were involved in the manufacture of wool and silk cloth. In 1562, the master silk weavers numbered 423, and they were but a few of the many people employed in this labor-intensive industry. Toledo was home to a sizable group of conversos (Jewish converts to Christianity)—estimated at nearly 20 percent of the 1486 population—whose activities were closely observed by the Inquisition, installed in Toledo in 1485. As merchants and money managers, conversos dominated the city's economy, and they largely controlled the procurement of raw silk and wool as well as the distribution of finished products. One family of converso origin, the Toledo Zapata, or the Counts of Cedillo, was responsible for founding the University of Toledo in the mid-sixteenth century.

The new university was but one example of the city's cultural vitality; Toledo's several printing presses were another. In the early 1500s the works of Erasmus enjoyed some diffusion, although this popularity was tempered in later years by the Inquisition, which condemned many of his works and some of his followers. One of those condemned in 1535 was the cathedral canon and theologian Juan de Vergara, a translator of Aristotle and a collaborator of the Complutensian Polyglot Bible subsidized by Cardinal Francisco Jiménez de Cisneros. Vergara belonged to a literary group that included the famed poet Garcilaso de la Vega. Other literary circles emerged in later years, but overshadowing local poets and dramatists were the *arbitristas,* who proposed reforms of the excessive and unfairly distributed tax system, schemes to reverse depopulation and the diminution of local cloth industries, and a reduction in the vast number of secular and ecclesiastical offices, all in an effort to resolve the ills besetting the nation in the early seventeenth century. Without a doubt the Toledan artist who has attained the greatest fame in modern times is the painter El Greco (Domenikos Theotokopoulos; 1541–1614), who immortalized the city and some of its prominent citizens in his paintings.

The many surviving Renaissance buildings give some idea of the city's prosperity in its heyday. One example is the Hospital of Saint John the Baptist, or Tavera, founded in 1541 outside the city walls by the cardinal-archbishop of Toledo, Juan Tavera. Today this sizable building houses a museum, an archive, and a school. The medieval *alcázar* (fortified palace) of the monarchs in Toledo was remodeled substantially in the sixteenth century by the architects Alonso de Covarrubias and Juan de Herrera. Heavily damaged during the civil war of the 1930s, the *alcázar* has since been rebuilt. In the 1570s, work began on a new *ayuntamiento* (city hall), designed by the architects Juan de Herrera and El Greco's son, Jorge Manuel Theotokopoulos. This graceful building, with some later additions, stands opposite the main entrance to the cathedral.

See also Comuneros, Revolt of the; El Greco; Garcilaso de la Vega; Vergara, Juan de.

BIBLIOGRAPHY

Martz, Linda. *Poverty and Welfare in Habsburg Spain: The Example of Toledo.* Cambridge, U.K., and New York, 1983. Includes information about the politics and economy of the city in the sixteenth and early seventeenth centuries.

Toledo Museum of Art, et al. *El Greco of Toledo.* Boston, 1982. A lavishly illustrated collection of essays dealing largely with cultural topics.

LINDA MARTZ

TOLERATION. When applied to religion, "toleration" refers to the public recognition of the right to exercise faiths other than the official one. In late medieval Christian Europe, this right existed in practice where Jews and Muslims had long survived as minorities, especially in Spain and Portugal, parts of eastern Europe, and southern Italy. Toleration never implied equality; the minority faith might enjoy full autonomy (domestic worship, specialized butchers) but was seldom allowed public worship and was denied any possibility of its members enjoying civic integration (holding public office) in the dominant society. The option of granting toleration was normally reserved to local lords and communities, whether ecclesiastical or secular, and not to national rulers; some lords used the power even to tolerate dissenting Christians, a policy that had always provoked major problems (such as with the lords who tolerated Cathars in Languedoc). Pressure against tolerated Jews and Muslims, when it occurred, tended to develop less from religious "intolerance" than for social, cultural, and political reasons. The Spanish Inquisition was a typical case of an intolerant institution brought into existence not because of actual heresy but because of community and political conflicts.

The Protestant Reformation created a completely new scenario in which extensive dissent ("heresy") arose not among minority groups but within the majority Christian faith and therefore forced a closer examination of the relationship between dissenters and nondissenters. For a long time effective toleration on the late medieval model continued to be practiced, thereby allowing dissenting groups to coexist in peace. Over wide areas of Transylvania and Poland, for example, Catholics, Lutherans, Orthodox, Uniates, and Calvinists lived side by side in their own communities without conflict. In southern France nobles protected their Reformed subjects and coexisted with Catholics. The persecution and execution of "heretics" throughout the Continent continued, incongruously, along with a significant degree of tolerance.

Two main factors provoked a reassessment of the need for legislation on "toleration." First, the nascent political state was obliged to seek stability for itself by resolving religious differences among the nobility. The situation did not arise in states such as Spain, where the Reformation never took root. By contrast, it was a vital problem in one of Spain's dependent territories, the Netherlands, to an extent that eventually led to the split of the country (1579) between two confessions, Catholic and Calvinist. The most notorious case was France, where provincial particularism together with religiously motivated noble factions threatened to destroy a country that had never enjoyed political unity. Many with experience of the problem in France (the Politiques) opted for a secularist solution, namely, that the state should remain indifferent to the religious orientation of its subjects. They were denounced by a leading Catholic, Marshal Tavannes, as people "who would rather that the realm be at peace without God than at war for him." Second, the indiscriminate execution of religious radicals (especially Anabaptists) obliged a rethinking of the reasons for persecution. What was gained by executing heretics? The first cogent examination of this question was formulated by the humanist Sébastien Castellio (1515–1563) in the wake of the 1553 execution by Calvin of Miguel Servet. Castellio's work *De haereticis* (On heretics; 1554) appealed for a rejection of the concept of "heretic." Others, especially in the Netherlands and France, reiterated that mutual tolerance was the solution to indiscriminate persecution. The argument from mutual goodwill, however, was an inadequate response to the gravity of religious civil war. Toleration, it became obvious, would have to be imposed by law.

One undeniable fact made a measure of toleration inevitable by about 1600—"heresy" could not be physically exterminated, since entire populations were involved. The problem was solved in different ways in different countries. In England the Reformation church imposed an outward conformity (Elizabeth Settlement; 1559) but, apart from subsequent short periods of repression (directed in particular at supporters of papal authority), did not seriously penalize the discreet activities of Catholics or Puritans. The first nationwide toleration settlement was achieved in Poland with the Warsaw Confederation (1573), which, however, did little more than protect the rights of those communities patronized by the higher nobility. In France successive compromises by warring nobles were accepted by the crown and given the force of law. The peace of Monsieur (1576), in particular, conceded unprecedented freedom to dissenting Calvinists within a Catholic state. A more broadly based national settlement, the Edict of Nantes (1598), brought the French wars to an end. This had substantial weaknesses—its observance was not universally binding (the church neither accepted nor implemented it)—and the effective relegation of Calvinism to a secondary position as a "tolerated" rather than an "equal" religion dissatisfied many Huguenots, who continued to wage war against the government until 1622.

In contrast to these significant practical advances in coexistence between people believing differently, the theory of toleration made slow progress before 1600. It is now recognized that in late medieval and early modern times, including much of the Reformation period, those who were believing Christians and sought tolerance tended to exclude dissidents and non-Christian confessions from their program. The various writers who spoke up for the rights of the individual conscience offered only partial solutions to how the rights of many conflicting consciences could be reconciled. The first Anabaptists, like Balthasar Hubmaier (burned 1528), based their claim for liberty on a rejection of the role of the state; this branded them as social anarchists, as later demonstrated in the events of Münster in 1536. Other radicals, like Sebastian Franck (c. 1499–c. 1549) and Kaspar Schwenckfeld (1489–1561), held to a more mystical concept of an "invisible" body of believers; Menno Simons (1469–1561) accepted, in contrast, the role of the state, but not in religious matters. Very many other thinkers, Catholics and Protestants, firmly supported a degree of toleration, but on dif-

fering premises. The Catholic Erasmian George Cassander (1513–1566), for example, appealed for charity as the basis of toleration; he was also among the first to suggest that there should be common agreement among Christian faiths on "essentials," with toleration of nonessentials. Some radical sectarians had little positive to offer, since they claimed rights for their own conscience but denied similar rights to consciences that disagreed with them. The lack of precision over political and social obligations during the Renaissance and Reformation period made it difficult to find an acceptable basis for concepts of toleration.

See also Inquisition; Protestant Reformation; Wars of Religion.

BIBLIOGRAPHY

Bainton, Roland H. *The Travail of Religious Liberty*. Philadelphia, 1951.

Grell, Ole Peter, and Bob Scribner, eds. *Tolerance and Intolerance in the European Reformation*. Cambridge, U.K., 1996.

Kamen, Henry. *The Rise of Toleration*. New York, 1967.

Lecler, Joseph. *Toleration and the Reformation*. Translated by T. L. Westow. 2 vols. New York, 1960.

HENRY KAMEN

TOLETUS, FRANCISCUS (1532–1596), philosopher, theologian, and first Jesuit cardinal, important for his influence in the Collegio Romano, founded by Ignatius Loyola (1491–1556) in 1551. Born in Cordova, Spain, Toletus obtained an M.A. in philosophy from the University of Zaragoza, then taught philosophy and studied theology at the University of Salamanca, where he was the favored student of Domingo de Soto (1494/95–1560). Already a priest, he entered the Jesuit novitiate at Toledo in 1558. In 1559, while still a novice, he was sent to teach at the Collegio Romano—philosophy until 1562, then theology until 1569. In 1569 he was appointed preacher at the papal court, an office he held until 1593, when he was made a cardinal by Pope Clement VIII. Highly regarded for his learning and diplomacy, Toletus was sent on many papal missions, including one to Louvain in 1580 to promulgate the bull of Pope Gregory XIII against the teachings of Michel de Bay (Baianism). In his last years he played an important role in the revision of the Vulgate (the Latin text of the Bible).

Toletus's many expositions of Aristotle grew out of his philosophy courses at the Collegio Romano, where he taught logic, physics, and metaphysics, including the tract on the soul. These were soon published as *Commentaria, una cum quaestionibus*

(Commentaries, together with questions) on the respective books of Aristotle, went through many editions, and formed the core of teaching notes for Jesuit philosophers at the Collegio to the end of the sixteenth century. In logic, Toletus gave abbreviated treatment to summulist questions and concentrated instead on Aristotle's *Categories, Perihermenias,* and *Posterior Analytics.* In his exposition of the *Analytics* he discussed the demonstrative regress and also opposed his Jesuit colleague, Benedictus Pererius (1535–1610), by maintaining that mathematics is a science in the Aristotelian sense. The Venice 1597 edition of Toletus's *Logica* is important for its incorporating additions (*Additamenta*) by Ludovico Carbone of Costacciaro (d. 1597), which Carbone plagiarized from the logic course taught at the Collegio by Paolo della Valle (1561–1622) in 1587–1588—the same set of notes from which Galileo earlier appropriated his *Logical Treatises.* In his physics course Toletus manifested considerable knowledge of the Merton tradition in kinematics and dynamics, analyzed reaction in detail, and treated the problem of quantifying qualities. He moved the discussion of natural minima (the smallest parts of a natural substance) from the theoretical plane to explaining how compounds are formed from their constitutive elements, and offered experimental evidence against the existence of a void. In his psychology he had distinctive views on the object of cognition and the role of the agent intellect in conceptualization. He also defended the teaching that the soul's immortality can be demonstrated by reason. Like most scholastics of his day, he was intent on reconciling Aristotle with Christian revelation, showing that the truths of philosophy do not contradict divine truth.

In theology Toletus composed a commentary on the *Summa theologiae* of St. Thomas Aquinas (1224–1274), in which he contested many interpretations of that work by Thomas de Vio Cajetan (1469–1534). In his commentary, Toletus also discussed predestination in view of foreseen merits, the first Jesuit at the Collegio Romano to do so.

BIBLIOGRAPHY

Galilei, Galileo. *Galileo's Logical Treatises: A Translation, with Notes and Commentary, of his Appropriated Latin Questions on Aristotle's* Posterior Analytics. Translated and annotated by William A. Wallace. Dordrecht, Netherlands, and Boston, 1992.

Lewis, Christopher. *The Merton Tradition and Kinematics in Late Sixteenth- and Early Seventeenth-Century Italy.* Padua, Italy, 1980.

Wallace, William A. *Galileo and His Sources: The Heritage of the Collegio Romano in Galileo's Science.* Princeton, N.J., 1984.

WILLIAM A. WALLACE

TOMBS. Renaissance sculptors continued a medieval tradition of producing numerous memorial tombs honoring prominent figures of the era. Renaissance tomb monuments are considered to be Italian in origin and fundamentally classical in design. From a strictly chronological point of view, however, the Gothic style—particularly in architecture—persisted well into the fifteenth century in Italy and into the sixteenth in much of northern Europe. But even a definition of Renaissance that excludes the Gothic would encompass thousands of memorials in a seemingly infinite variety of designs, whether Italian or Italianate and whether convincingly classical or superficially so. Nevertheless, it is possible to single out major sepulchral types that were used throughout the period and that are distinguished from their predecessors more by style than by genre: the tomb slab; the *arcosolium;* the wall tomb, raised or set at floor level; and the freestanding memorial.

The preferred sites for these monuments were those favored in previous centuries, but only those within churches (generally the most significant examples) have survived in sufficient quantity to convey a reasonable picture of tomb development. Church burials and their accompanying memorials were often situated in private chapels, but most were placed as close to the high altar as allowed by the available space and the wealth and importance of the deceased. Though these monuments served various functions, all performed a few fundamental tasks. First, and most obviously, they marked the location of the interred body (or bodies), and gave the name of the deceased (or at least the family name) and usually the date of death. Commonly a family coat of arms adorned the marker, and larger memorials (almost always for a single individual) often indicated his (or, rarely, her) social status by an inscription and, when an effigy was supplied, by the figure's attire. Also frequent were inscribed appeals to the Deity for the salvation of the subject's soul and laudatory descriptions of his or her virtues and accomplishments.

Tomb Slabs. Aside from the least expensive tomb markers—a relatively small inscribed plate set into the church floor—the most common Renaissance sepulchral memorial was the tomb slab, a stone cover approximately the size of the grave beneath it, set into the church pavement. Usually marble, but sometimes bronze for wealthy or prominent individuals, these works customarily carried only inscriptions and family coats of arms. Many, however, were also supplied with recumbent effigies in relief,

Figure 1. Tomb of Doge Pietro Mocenigo. Sculpture by Pietro Lombardo (c. 1435–1515) and his studio in the church of SS. Giovanni e Paolo, Venice. COURTESY OF ROBERT MUNMAN

often presenting the figure within a niche-like enclosure and occasionally on a bier, as if lying in state. This can be seen, for example, in the bronze slab for Bishop Giovanni Pecci (Cathedral, Siena, 1426–1428) by Donatello (c. 1386–1466), which uses linear perspective, only recently invented, to create an illusion of the bier's three-dimensionality. The use of the tomb slab diminished significantly by the sixteenth century, partly because of changes in taste and partly because of diminished floor space within preferred churches.

Wall Tombs. In spite of (or perhaps because of) their expense, Renaissance wall tombs, whether reliefs, *arcosolia,* or larger architectural structures, were produced in significant numbers. A monument raised on brackets often created an impressive effect and had the further advantage of not taking up

scarce floor space. Roman-inspired *arcosolium* tombs, consisting of a sarcophagus set within an arched recess, also were usually elevated but were relatively small and simple in design. The *arcosolium* enjoyed some popularity in the second half of the fifteenth century in Florence (a typical example is the tomb of Francesco Sassetti, S. Trinita, c. 1485–c. 1488, attributed to Giuliano da Sangallo [c. 1445–1516]).

The more frequently used wall tomb set at floor level has come to typify the Renaissance sepulchral monument. Among the best-known examples are two Florentine tombs (both in S. Croce) for the humanists Leonardo Bruni (c. 1448–1450), by Bernardo Rossellino (1407/10–1464), and for Carlo Marsuppini (c. 1453–1454), by Desiderio da Settignano (c. 1430–1464). [See the biography of Bruni in volume 1 for an illustration of his tomb.] Both works contain effigies atop Roman-inspired sarcophagi set within slim frames like triumphal arches, and in both the delicate carving of the portraits and surface details was originally complemented by a discreet use of polychromy and gilding. This emphasis on classical elements, with a corresponding reduction of religious imagery (largely that of the Madonna and Child, now relegated to the upper zone below the arch), was underscored by the Latin epitaph detailing each man's humanistic accomplishments rather than presenting the traditional petitions for salvation. Many variations of this tomb type were produced throughout the fifteenth century, both in Florence and elsewhere, though not always with the same reduction of sacred symbolism.

A number of wall tombs incorporating the motif of a triumphal arch appeared in Venice. Many of these monuments were extraordinarily large, multilevel structures with numerous life-size, freestanding niche figures accompanying a recumbent effigy and/or a naturalistic portrait (standing or kneeling) of the deceased. The niche figures usually represented virtues, saints, or warriors, or a combination of such figures, as in the tombs of Doge Niccolò Tron (S. Maria Gloriosa dei Frari, 1476–1479), by Antonio Rizzo (1430/1440–c. 1499) and Doge Pietro Mocenigo (SS. Giovanni e Paolo, 1476–1481; fig. 1), by Pietro Lombardo (c. 1435–1515). The religious imagery of these monuments, as in Florence, tended to appear on the uppermost levels. Toward the end of the fifteenth century, these large Venetian tombs had fewer figures and greater emphasis on architectural elements, as can be seen in the tombs for the doges Andrea Vendramin (early 1490s–c. 1505?) and Giovanni Mocenigo (c. 1505–1510?, both SS. Giovanni e Paolo) by Tullio Lombardo (c. 1455–1532) and his shop. By the mid-sixteenth century this preference was carried even further, as in the monument of Doge Francesco Venier (S. Salvatore, 1555–c. 1560), by Jacopo Sansovino (1486–1570), a work that exemplifies the monumental intent of high Renaissance classicism.

In Rome the long medieval tradition of elaborate ecclesiastical tombs continued throughout the Renaissance. As a rule these structures contained a sarcophagus supporting an effigy within a tabernacle-like architectural frame or a classical triumphal arch. In both cases the central arch usually contained reliefs of the Madonna and Child or saints, and was usually flanked by pilasters or wider piers containing niche figures of saints or virtues. The abundant variations on these types are too numerous to delineate here, but the high Renaissance monuments for cardinals Ascanio Sforza (fig. 2) and Girolamo Basso Della Rovere (both Santa Maria del Popolo, 1505–1509), by Andrea Sansovino (c. 1467–1529), can be singled out as among the most formally and technically impressive. These twin tombs are also noteworthy for the poses of their "living effigies," which show the cardinals reclining, each supporting his head with one hand, as if the figure were asleep rather than dead.

This motif eventually was widely utilized by both Italian and northern sculptors, as in the tomb of Sebastian Echter von Mespelbrunn (Würzburg Cathedral, 1577/78), by Peter Osten (fl. 1571–1589), a work also representative of the kind of overlaying of Renaissance detail on a Gothic foundation so frequently found in northern memorials. Such a mixture of styles is, in fact, typical of sixteenth-century Germany, where the sepulchral monuments (usually of modest size) often combined a Gothic naturalism in portraiture and decorative detail with idiosyncratic interpretations of classical architecture as filtered through Italian Renaissance derivations (as for example, the tomb of Bishop Lorenz von Bibra, Würtzburg Cathedral, finished 1522, by Tilman Riemenschneider). Significantly, these works (and northern tombs generally) also employed the medieval "transi" effigy—a figure of a partially decomposed corpse (or a skeleton)—as a memento mori (reminder of death) far more often than did Italian examples.

Undoubtedly the most celebrated wall tombs of the period were—and remain—the memorials by Michelangelo (1475–1564) for Giuliano and Lorenzo de' Medici, young princes of the controlling family of Renaissance Florence. [The tomb of Lorenzo is illustrated in the Michelangelo entry in volume 4.]

These twin monuments, on opposite walls of the Medici Chapel (in the New Sacristy) of S. Lorenzo in Florence (1521–1534), lack effigies but instead contain seated, idealized portraits of the deceased in shallow niches over their sarcophagi; reclining on the latter are the four famous (and incomplete) figures personifying Day and Night, Morning and Evening. Though neither the chapel nor the tombs were finished to Michelangelo's original designs (at the very least, four reclining figures of river gods were to be placed at the bases of the raised sarcophagi), these beautiful and dignified memorials represent the great sculptor's most complete statement in funereal design. Iconographically complex, the Medici Chapel's full meaning (or even its often assumed Neoplatonic symbolism) has yet to be definitively established.

The Freestanding Monument. Few freestanding tombs were created in the fifteenth century

Figure 2. Tomb of Cardinal Ascanio Sforza. Sculpture by Andrea Sansovino (c. 1467–1529) in the church of Sta. Maria del Popolo, Rome. COURTESY OF ROBERT MUNMAN

in Italy, and fewer have survived. The type, however, at least in the form of a simple sarcophagus and effigy, was common during the Middle Ages in northern Europe and continued throughout the Renaissance, usually in a Gothic style. Among the most impressive early Italian examples is the Burgundian-inspired tomb of Ilaria del Carretto (cathedral, Lucca, c. 1406/07), by Jacopo della Quercia (1374?–1438), well known for the charming countenance of the youthful Ilaria, as well as for what may be the earliest postclassical appearance (on the sarcophagus's sides) of full-size, classical, swag-bearing putti (nude baby boys). But while the freestanding tomb monument was not an Italian specialty, one example, had it been built as conceived, would have been unprecedented in size and grandeur: Michelangelo's first design (1505) for the tomb of Pope Julius II. This work was to have been a three-tiered mausoleum-like structure with some forty more than life-size figures and numerous reliefs. The renowned statue of Moses, now the centerpiece of the tomb as it was completed some forty years later (S. Pietro in Vincoli, Rome), was originally only a corner figure on the structure's second level.

Absent Michelangelo's original tomb for Julius, the freestanding Renaissance monument is perhaps best represented today by memorials dedicated to German and French royalty, specifically those for Emperor Maximilian I (Hofkirche, Innsbruck, 1502–1584, by Gilg Sesselschreiber [fl. 1496–after 1520] and a large contingent of designers and sculptors), and three French kings and their queens: Louis XII and Anne de Bretagne (c. 1515–1531, by Antonio and Giovanni Giusti); Francis I and Claude de France (begun 1547, by Philibert de l'Orme [Delorme; 1505/10–1570] and Pierre Bontemps [c. 1512–c. 1570]); and Henry II and Catherine de Médicis (1559–1573, by Francesco Primaticcio [1504/05–1570] and Germain Pilon [c. 1525–1590]; all at St.-Denis). The latter three monuments are characterized by classical architecture and the typically French motifs of portrait figures kneeling at prie-dieux atop the structure and recumbent "transi" effigies directly below. But Maximilian's monument (actually a cenotaph; his body is buried in Wiener Neustadt) is unique in its inclusion of the twenty-eight bronze, life-size "ancestors" (both real and adopted) that flank the tomb between the columns of the Hofkirche's nave. The effect of these figures, simultaneously startling and moving, gives the monument an air of medieval grandeur that somewhat belies its Renaissance origins.

See also Sculpture.

BIBLIOGRAPHY

Butterfield, Andrew. "Social Structure and the Topology of Funerary Monuments in Early Renaissance Florence." *Res* 26 (autumn 1994): 47–68. Interesting case study.

Cohen, Kathleen. *Metamorphosis of a Death Symbol; The Transi Tomb in the Late Middle Ages and the Renaissance.* Berkeley, Calif., 1973. In-depth study of this specific symbol.

Crossley, Fred. H. *English Church Monuments* A.D. *1150–1550: An Introduction to the Study of Tombs and Effigies of the Mediaeval Period.* London, 1921. Out-of-date but useful presentation of English memorials; many illustrations.

Davies, Gerald S. *Renascence: The Sculptured Tomb of the Fifteenth Century in Rome, with Chapters on the Previous Centuries from 1100.* London, 1910. Out-of-date but still useful detailed catalog of Roman Renaissance tombs.

Munman, Robert. *Sienese Renaissance Tomb Monuments.* Philadelphia, 1993. Discussion and catalog of a specific regional memorial practice; large bibliography.

Olson, Roberta J. M. *Italian Renaissance Sculpture.* London, 1992. Condensed, general study; a good introduction to the subject.

Panofsky, Erwin. *Tomb Sculpture: Four Lectures on Its Changing Aspects from Ancient Egypt to Bernini.* New York, 1964. Also ed. H. W. Janson, New York, 1992. Classic, erudite study of tomb and tomb sculpture iconography and development.

Poeschke, Joachim. *Donatello and His World.* Munich, 1990. English translation by Russell Stockman. New York, 1993. Authoritative, up-to-date catalog of major artists and works. Extensive bibliography.

Poeschke, Joachim. *Michelangelo and His World.* Munich, 1992. English translation by Russell Stockman. New York, 1996. Authoritative, up-to-date catalog of major artists and works. Extensive bibliography.

Pope-Hennessy, John. *Italian High Renaissance and Baroque Sculpture.* New York, 1985. Standard, authoritative study; detailed catalog of major artists and major works.

Pope-Hennessy, John. *Italian Renaissance Sculpture.* New York, 1985. Standard, authoritative study; detailed catalog of major artists and major works.

s'Jacob, Henriette. *Idealism and Realism: A Study of Sepulchral Symbolism.* Leiden, Netherlands, 1974. Informative iconographic study; large bibliography.

Smith, Jeffrey Chipps. *German Sculpture of the Later Renaissance, c. 1520–1580: Art in an Age of Uncertainty.* Princeton, N.J., 1994. Excellent, detailed study of somewhat neglected material.

ROBERT MUNMAN

TORNABUONI, LUCREZIA (1425–1482), Florentine writer and patron. Born to Francesco Tornabuoni around 1425, Lucrezia was wedded to Piero de' Medici in 1444, in a union that cemented the political and commercial ties of the two banking clans and placed Lucrezia at the center of Florentine political and cultural life.

Tornabuoni's correspondence and her double-entry account book reveal much about the Medici household and its associates. The tasks entrusted to Lucrezia varied from the supervision of her children's education and marriage settlements to the administration of the family's farms and shops. Hers was a multifarious activity of patronage and charity, with significant political implications and consistent with the support of the middle and lower ranks of society by the Medici. Tornabuoni's sponsorship of writers active in the popular vernacular genres attests to an analogous literary taste and indicates that she supported the aspects of Lorenzo de' Medici's cultural policy that encouraged the literary bent of the Florentine artisan class.

What remains of Tornabuoni's literary output consists of nine hymns, or religious lauds (*laudi*), and five narrative poems. The hymns were songs addressed to God, the Virgin Mary, and the saints, which had been sung since the thirteenth century by members of spiritual movements and religious confraternities. Tornabuoni's songs present one unifying theme, the glory of Christ the Redeemer and his appearance on earth, and are marked by a joyous exaltation at the news of universal redemption. Corollaries to the message of salvation are the main episodes of Christ's life, from the Nativity and the acceptance of his mission to Judas's betrayal and the contemplation of the cross. Other poems dramatize human history from the loss of Paradise to the coming of the Savior. At times, the presence of Mary, whose subdued lamentations evoke scenes of her own life, provides a tender accompaniment to the stark episodes of her son's passion. The most famous of these hymns is "Here Comes the Powerful King!" in which arrival of the Savior is celebrated with a jubilant description of the ancient patriarchs and prophets being awakened to eternal life and taking a seat in the Redeemer's court in Heaven.

Tornabuoni's longer poems are adaptations of the biblical narratives about Hester, Judith, Susannah, and Tobias, and of the evangelical story of John the Baptist. They belong to the genre of *cantari,* which can be religious narratives, fictionalized histories, or chivalric romances, sung by storytellers at public events and in the homes of wealthy citizens. Lucrezia's stories are distinctive for their vivid descriptions of domestic interiors, walled gardens, and ceremonies and banquets, as well as for their sharp assessment of military forces and battles. Characterizations are vividly drawn, and confrontations between different classes of people and the power struggle engaging the protagonists are brought vividly to light. Overall, Tornabuoni's presence in the history of the Renaissance is valued for the light that it sheds on Florence and the Medici, on a significant chapter of Italian literary history, and, not least, on the prerog-

atives that upper-class women retained for themselves in the private and public sectors.

BIBLIOGRAPHY

Primary Work

Tornabuoni, Lucrezia. *Lettere.* Edited by Patrizia Salvadori. Florence, 1993.

Secondary Works

Pezzarossa, Fulvio, ed. *I poemetti sacri di Lucrezia Tornabuoni.* Florence, 1978.
Russell, Rinaldina. "Lucrezia Tornabuoni." In *Italian Women Writers.* Edited by Rinaldina Russell. Westport, Conn., 1994. Pages 431–440.

RINALDINA RUSSELL

TORRES NAHARRO, BARTOLOMÉ DE (c. 1485–after 1520), Spanish poet and playwright. His probable New Christian origin (descent from converted Jews) would have posed social difficulty in early-sixteenth-century Spain and may explain why his most productive years were spent in Italy. *Propalladia* (First fruits of Pallas), which brings together his collected poems and nine plays, was first published in 1517 and became a respectable editorial success (nine editions in slightly over fifty years). It was through the printed editions of his plays that Torres Naharro's considerable influence on later, albeit considerably less gifted, playwrights was felt.

The *Propalladia* contains a *Prohemio* (Prologue) that is one of the first theoretical statements on the theater to emerge from Renaissance Spain. Torres Naharro distinguishes between the *comedia a noticia* (a play based on the observation of a concrete social milieu) and the *comedia a fantasía* (a fictitious romantic comedy). His notions on the theater blend classical precept and practical experience, and, strikingly for his time, he insists on performance as an essential element of drama. Torres Naharro defined what would become the conventional way of beginning a play throughout the first part of the sixteenth century in Spain: the *introito* (generally a comically aggressive shepherd's monologue) followed by the *argumento* (a plot summary of the play proper).

Torres Naharro's bold originality is evident in the two *comedias a noticia, Comedia tinellaria* (The servants' dining room comedy) and *Comedia soldadesca* (The military comedy), which deal with the goings-on in the servants' dining room of a cardinal's household and the raising of a papal army, respectively. Both plays can be read as satires, and Stanislav Zimic sees *Comedia soldadesca* as an indictment of Julius II's bellicose foreign policy. Although

Comedia Ymenea was once read as a precursor of seventeenth-century plays on the theme of female honor, Torres Naharro provides for a commonsense solution: the marquis is persuaded by rational arguments and by Ymeneo's offer of marriage not to kill the sister he suspects of having compromised her family's honor. Here, as in his other plays, Torres Naharro separates the world of the play from the world of the audience, creating a theater that is illusionistic rather than ritualistic.

BIBLIOGRAPHY

Primary Work

Torres Naharro, Bartolomé de. *Propalladia and Other Works of Bartolomé de Torres Naharro.* 4 vols. Edited by Joseph E. Gillet. Bryn Mawr, Pa., 1943–1961.

Secondary Work

Zimic, Stanislav. *El pensamiento humanístico y satírico de Torres Naharro.* 2 vols. Santander, Spain, 1977–1978.

RONALD E. SURTZ

TORTURE. *See* **Crime and Punishment.**

TOSCANELLI, PAOLO DAL POZZO (1397–1482), Florentine astronomer, mathematician, and cartographer. A prominent member of the Florentine intelligentsia of the fifteenth century, Paolo dal Pozzo Toscanelli was one of the most renowned mathematicians of his age. His accomplishments as an astrologer, astronomer, and geographer earned the respect of the architect Filippo Brunelleschi, the philosopher Nicholas of Cusa, the mathematician Regiomontanus, and the humanists Giovanni Pico della Mirandola and Marsilio Ficino. Toscanelli's most famous (and most contested) relationship is his association with Christopher Columbus. The navigator sought the aging mathematician's advice when gathering support for his proposed westward journey to Asia.

As a young man, Toscanelli studied mathematics at the Studio Fiorentino and medicine at the University of Padua, where he formed a lifetime friendship with Nicholas of Cusa. Toscanelli returned to his native Florence in 1424 and set up a medical practice. Like many physicians, Toscanelli was skilled in astronomy and mathematical arts, and these became his primary avocation. Astrology was a prognostic tool for physicians; Toscanelli practiced the art, although as Pico reports, he admitted the uncertainty of its use. Toscanelli left few writings, but the artifacts he left behind attest to his lively interest above all in cosmography and cartographic techniques.

Toscanelli observed six comets between 1433 and 1472 and was one of the first astronomers to treat comets as properly celestial objects. (Traditional Aristotelian accounts treated comets as a meteorological phenomenon, sudden illuminations below the orb of the moon that do not disturb the changeless perfection of the heavens.) Toscanelli also developed clever and accurate ways of mapping the course of these comets. Around 1468, he made a gnomon (a device for measuring the height of the sun) in the cathedral of Florence. He pierced a slot in the dome nineteen meters above the floor so that the sun would shine through it and illuminate a stone slab below at high noon at the summer solstice. This allowed accurate measurement of the solstice, which was important to calendrical calculation and cartographic projection.

Toscanelli came from a family of spice merchants, and his interest in new routes to India and east Asia apparently sharpened after the expansion of the Ottoman Turks obstructed traditional spice routes in 1453 and Portuguese navigators began to explore Atlantic routes around Africa. He began considering whether a western sea-route to Asia would be possible. Although Eratosthenes of Cyrene (third century B.C.) had made a relatively accurate estimation of the circumference of the earth of about 250,000 stadia (or roughly 25,000 miles), Toscanelli accepted the narrower ancient approximations of the size of the globe at about 180,000 stadia. The smaller approximation was the one adopted by Ptolemy (second century A.D.), whose geographical treatise had been recovered earlier in the fifteenth century to the great excitement of European scholars finally able to access the Alexandrian's methods for constructing world maps. Toscanelli believed the smaller estimate of the earth's circumference was more consistent with the contemporary travelers' accounts that he so avidly elicited as a basis of his own map. Toscanelli constructed a nautical map of the Atlantic that placed China and Japan more than one hundred degrees to the east, and therefore some 6,500 miles closer to Europe. This map apparently came into the possession of Christopher Columbus after a short correspondence around 1480–1482. Toscanelli's long life, however, would come to its close a decade before the Genoese mariner may have set his course in accordance with the Florentine's projections.

BIBLIOGRAPHY

Abetti, Giorgio. "Toscanelli dal Pozzo, Paolo." *Dictionary of Scientific Biography.* New York, 1971. Vol. 13, pp. 440–441.
Apfelstadt, Eric. "Christopher Columbus, Paolo da Pozzo Toscanelli, and Fernao de Roriz: New Evidence for a Florentine

Connection." *Nuncius* 7, no. 2 (1992): 69–80. An article on the debate on Toscanelli's correspondence with Columbus.

Jervis, Jane L. "Toscanelli's Cometary Observations: Some New Evidence." *Annali del Istituto e Museo di Stori della Scienza* 2, no. 1 (1977): 15–20.

Uzielli, Gustavo. *La vita e i tempi di Paolo da Pozzo Toscanelli: Richerche e studi, di Gustavo Uzielli, con un capitolo (VI) sui lavori astronomici del Toscanelli, di Giovanni.* Rome, 1894. The classic Italian study.

Vignaud, Henry. *Toscanelli and Columbus. The Letters and Charts of Toscanelli on the Route to the Indies by Way of the West.* London, 1902. A critical study on the authencity and value of these documents.

M. HENNINGER-VOSS

TOURNAMENTS. Although war games are recorded in antiquity, for example in the *Aeneid,* and neoclassical theorists like Claude François Ménestrier (*Traité des tournois,* 1669) sought ancient origins for the tournament, it seems to date in characteristic form only from the eleventh century. Like other manifestations of the chivalric tradition, however, it enjoyed great prosperity in the Renaissance, as it was generally complementary to rather than opposed to the movement of classical revival.

Medieval Origins.
Early tournaments had entailed *mêlées,* that is, fights between groups. Various weapons were used, with little quarter (mercy) given and frequent casualties. Later, *mêlées* became rare, and the usual combat was between two mounted knights charging at each other with the new couched lances, which were less likely to be lost after each use. Such encounters, properly called jousts, became less dangerous with the introduction of blunted weapons, and from the early fifteenth century, barriers called tilts were erected to keep the horses of charging knights from colliding. As late as 1559, however, King Henry II of France was fatally wounded while jousting in Paris. Tournaments were prohibited at times by both ecclesiastical and civil authorities but remained tremendously popular, in part for their value as martial training (at least until the Thirty Years' War), in part as sport, and in part as glorious spectacles.

The sporting element was strong from the beginning, and champions, like the Englishman William Marshal in the twelfth century and Peter I of Cyprus in the fourteenth, went jousting from country to country in search of fame and prizes. The theatrical element in tournaments, always present, became much more prominent during the Renaissance.

Tournaments as Pageantry and Theater.
Tournaments were increasingly held to celebrate dynastic marriages, births, or christenings, or for state visits and encounters of princes like the meeting of Francis I of France and Henry VIII of England at the Field of Cloth of Gold in 1520. During the reigns of Elizabeth and James I in England, tournaments came to be given annually to celebrate the sovereign's Accession Day. With the civic connection, the costumes

Tournament. Presentation of banners of knights taking part in a tournament. Illustration by Barthélemy d'Eyck from *Le livre des tournois* by René of Anjou, c. 1460. CLICHÉ BIBLIOTHÈQUE NATIONALE DE FRANCE, PARIS. FR 2695, FOL. 67v–68

of contenders grew in magnificence and were often shown off in elaborate preliminary parades called *comparse*. Tournaments also took on fictional frameworks, usually loosely inspired by the vast chivalric literature of the time.

Knightly contests were, of course, an essential part of this literature. In the twelfth century Chrétien de Troyes had described tournaments in romances such as *Érec et Énide* (c. 1170). In the next century Ulrich von Lichtenstein supposedly recounted his own tourneying experiences in a poem with the supremely chivalric title of *Frauendienst* (The service of ladies). Sir Thomas Malory's popular late compilation *Le Morte d'Arthur*, printed by Caxton in 1485, includes a tournament anachronistically organized by Sir Lancelot in the fifteenth-century style. Joustings in various circumstances are also featured in the Spanish *Amadís de Gaula* (1508) and in the new Italian romances of chivalry, including Ludovico Ariosto's *Orlando furioso* (1516).

In turn, real tournaments imitated situations, realistic or fantastic, from romances. For example, a well-documented *passo honroso* held on a riverside near the Spanish city of León in 1434 centered on a knight's feigned efforts to free himself from enslavement to a lady, and more plot development of this sort soon took place under the sponsorships of the dukes of Burgundy and Duke René of Anjou (1409–1480). In contests called *pas d'armes,* such as the *Pas de l'arbre de Charlemagne* near Dijon in 1443, knights emulated heroes of romances by declaring their intention of defending a certain place against all comers. In the 1468 celebrations for the marriage of Charles the Bold to Margaret of York, a Knight of the Golden Tree, serving the Lady of the Secret Isle, set up a challenge tree in the market square of Bruges and defended it for several days. René of Anjou distinguished himself not only by arranging and participating in "literary" jousts (also called *tournois à thème*) at Nancy, Chinon, Saumur, and Tarascon, but also by writing around 1460 a detailed, illustrated treatise on how tournaments should be staged. During the later Renaissance, very much more was written on this subject, and there were also many works on horsemanship.

In the sixteenth century, fictional frameworks became usual for tournaments. Thus, to Henry VIII of England's celebrations for the birth of an heir in 1511, a queen from the allegorical land of Ceure Noble had sent four challenging knights with equally allegorical names (one of whom, Ceure Loyall, was played by Henry himself). Sometimes, as at Vienna celebrations in 1571, the plot included some person-

Knight at a Tournament. Escutcheons and mounted knight from a German manuscript. ©BIBLIOTECA APOSTOLICA VATICANA. ROSS 711, FOL. 40

ages drawn from classical mythology, who moved easily into the chivalric setting. Decor grew extremely elaborate, as in the 1549 tournament of the *Château Ténébreux* arranged at Binche by Queen Mary of Hungary for the visit of Charles V and his son Philip, and, soon thereafter, in several chivalric spectacles at the Este court in Ferrara, beginning with a much admired *Castello di Gorgoferusa* in 1561. The theatrical element in tournaments was most evident when the results of their contests seem to have been preordained. Thus Philip of Spain is not likely to have won out over other contenders at Binche by superior skill, while at Whitehall in 1581, Sir Philip Sidney and three other knights apparently acted out a prearranged failure to capture the Fortress of Perfect Beautie, which symbolized the Queen's virginity and moral integrity.

In the time when the martial purpose of tournaments had been paramount, nearly all participants had been genuine knightly warriors (although the Florentine republic had arranged several chivalric contests for its burghers not long before 1400). In the late Renaissance and the following baroque period, many tournaments were programmed like other entertainments to glorify a reigning dynasty, and participants, noble or not, were more like actors than martial contenders. The spectacles themselves were often moved from public squares into palace courtyards or gardens. With the increased importance of music and fancy horsemanship, some tournament performances became equestrian ballets, and others, with sophisticated musical compositions and elaborate stage settings, may have contributed to the early development of the opera.

See also **Arms and Armor; Chivalry; Duel; Honor; Parades, Processions, and Pageants.**

BIBLIOGRAPHY

Anglo, Sydney. *Spectacle, Pageantry, and Early Tudor Policy.* 2d ed. Oxford, 1997. Detailed attention to tournaments, including that at the Field of the Cloth of Gold, in the general context of English royal pageantry from the accession of Henry VII to the beginning of Elizabeth's reign. Excellent bibliographical essay on relevant scholarship since the 1969 edition.

Barber, Richard, and Juliet Barker. *Tournaments: Jousts, Chivalry, and Pageants in the Middle Ages.* Woodbridge, U.K., 1989. A handsomely illustrated study with much about fifteenth- and sixteenth-century tournaments as well as earlier ones.

Béhar, Pierre, and Helen Watanabe-O'Kelly, eds. *Spectaculum Europaeum: Theatre and Spectacle in Europe from the End of the Sixteenth to the Middle of the Eighteenth Century: A Handbook.* 2 vols. Hamburg, Germany: forthcoming. In the series Wolfenbütteler Arbeiten zur Barockforschung. Sections either in English or in French. To include a long section (in English) by Watanabe-O'Kelly on tournaments in various European countries during the late Renaissance and the baroque, with illustrations and much bibliography.

Watanabe-O'Kelly, Helen. *Triumphall Shews: Tournaments at German-speaking Courts in Their European Context 1560–1730.* Berlin, 1992. Substantial introductory chapter on the Renaissance tournament throughout Europe. Useful bibliographies and a chronological register.

Young, Alan. *Tudor and Jacobean Tournaments.* London and Dobbs Ferry, N.Y., 1987. An illustrated survey of tournaments in the whole period of the English Renaissance, with a valuable bibliographical chronology.

BONNER MITCHELL

TOURNON, FRANÇOIS DE (1489–1562), French statesman and churchman. The second son from a prominent family of the Vivarais, François de Tournon rose rapidly in the church, becoming archbishop of Embrun in 1517 and a cardinal in 1530. He was a good example of the pluralist Renaissance prelate, holding numerous benefices that included four archbishoprics. He was active in the government of Francis I from his succession in 1515, and supervised the ransom of Francis's two sons sent to Spain for their father after Francis's capture at Pavia in 1525. In 1532 the king dispatched him to Rome to support Henry VIII's request for a divorce from Catherine of Aragon. Returning to France in 1533, he served as a key royal adviser, especially in financial matters, until the succession of Henry II in 1547. Tournon lacked favor with Henry, who sent him back to Rome. After Henry's death in 1559 the cardinal served Francis II and Charles IX until his own death in 1562.

Early in his career he was an active patron of humanists and artists. He corresponded with Erasmus and conveyed to him Francis I's invitation to lead the College of the Three Languages, which Francis was organizing. Among the French humanists to whom Tournon extended patronage were Nicolas Bourbon and Jean de Boysonné. While supportive of the moderate humanists' program of church reform, he was orthodox in doctrine and turned sharply against the reform movement when he deemed it going too far. He sought to have Rabelais condemned as a Zwinglian in 1536. Tournon became an advocate for the Jesuits and established them at the College of Tournon in 1561.

BIBLIOGRAPHY

François, Michel. *Le cardinal François de Tournon.* Paris, 1951. The only full biography of the cardinal.

Knecht, R. J. *Renaissance Warrior and Patron: The Reign of Francis I.* New York, 1994. Shows Tournon's role in government at the time when he was most active.

FREDERIC J. BAUMGARTNER

TOYS. *See* **Material Culture.**

TRAGEDY. *See* **Drama.**

TRANSLATION. [This entry includes three subentries, an overview, a discussion of translation in Elizabethan England, and a discussion of Jewish translators.]

Overview

Translation was a very important means of communicating knowledge in the Renaissance, despite the humanist emphasis on reading texts in their original languages. Renaissance translations were of several kinds and intended for different groups of readers.

Greek-to-Latin Translations.

Few Europeans knew ancient Greek before Manuel Chrysoloras of Constantinople came to Florence in 1397 to teach it to local humanists. In the following decades, other Greeks also came to Italy, especially after the fall of Constantinople in 1453, and a handful of Italian humanists went to Constantinople to learn Greek.

The acquisition of Greek enabled scholars to read, and to translate into Latin, Greek texts previously unavailable and to make new and improved Latin translations of Greek texts available only in medieval translations. The humanists frequently attacked medieval translations (which were sometimes Greek-to-Arabic-to-Latin translations) for their mistakes and lack of understanding of the content. The humanists wanted to replace medieval word-for-word translations with "meaning of the text" translations. And because the humanists had a better understanding of ancient Latin and Greek works in their historical contexts, and knew more ancient texts than did their medieval predecessors, they were able to produce better translations.

The most prolific of the first generation of Greek-to-Latin translators was Leonardo Bruni (c. 1370–1444), who translated some of Demosthenes's speeches, many of Plutarch's *Lives,* the pseudo-Aristotelian *Economics,* St. Basil of Caesarea's *Letter to Young Men to Study Pagan Literature,* and other works. The greatest fifteenth-century accomplishment of the acquisition of ancient Greek was to make possible a complete Latin translation of Plato's works. Several humanists, including Bruni, translated more or less successfully parts of Plato's corpus in the first half of the fifteenth century. Marsilio Ficino (1433–1499) then produced a good humanistic Latin translation of the *opera omnia* of Plato (prepared 1463–1469; published in 1484). This made Plato completely available and accessible for the first time in western Europe.

The next most important Greek-to-Latin translation was of the works of the medical scholar Galen (probably 130–200), whose treatises were at the center of European medicine. Various north Italian medical scholars with humanistic training in Greek, plus the Belgian Andreas Vesalius, then teaching at the University of Padua, produced a folio-size, ten-volume Latin translation of almost all the works of Galen. The Giunti Press of Venice published it in 1541. The new Latin edition replaced medieval trans-

lations and also included translations of a few works previously unavailable in Latin. Frequently reprinted, the new Latin Galen led eventually to a rejection of Galenic medicine, when scholars compared his views with what they found through anatomical dissection.

The humanists produced new Latin translations of Aristotle as well. But the medieval Latin translations still dominated, because it was difficult to discard medieval Latin philosophical vocabulary coined by the medieval translators of Aristotle. Ciceronian Latin, so loved by humanists, did not offer good substitutes for such words as *anima* (soul) and *intellectus* (intellect). A greater consequence of the application of Greek expertise to the Aristotelian corpus was the editing, then translation into Latin, of some previously inaccessible ancient Greek commentaries on Aristotle.

Latin-or-Greek-to-Vernacular Translations.

Renaissance readers lacking Latin or Greek hungered for information about the ancient civilizations that they so admired. However, few vernacular translations of ancient texts appeared in the fifteenth century. The expansion of the vernacular presses in every part of Europe in the sixteenth century made possible an abundance of translations of ancient works in grammar, history, moral philosophy, rhetoric, and even some philosophical texts, such as Plato's dialogues. Some writers made careers out of translating Latin and Greek classics into vernacular languages, while others earned supplementary income doing so. Latin and Greek texts imparting professional knowledge, such as the medical works of Galen, legal works, and Aristotle's scientific works, were seldom translated into vernacular languages. But ancient works that taught Renaissance men and women how to live and speak were translated into vernacular languages. Aristotle's *Nicomachean Ethics, Poetics, Politics,* and *Rhetoric* were examples.

New Latin works that attracted wide interest were often translated into vernacular languages. Thomas More's *Utopia* (1516), which illuminated contemporary social problems and human nature by means of a fictional society set in an exotic locale, was an example. Desiderius Erasmus's *Encomium moriae* (Praise of folly; 1511) and other works excoriating clerical vice and exhorting men and women to live according to the example of Christ were often translated into vernacular languages. Such works focused on topics of great interest: ecclesiastical corruption and personal salvation. The Latin *Imitatio Christi* attributed to Thomas à Kempis (c. 1379–1471) was translated into most European vernacular languages because it was a popular devotional work and was even employed as a school text.

Vernacular-to-Vernacular Translations.

Highly esteemed vernacular works of literature were often translated into other vernacular languages. Castiglione's *Il cortegiano* (*The Book of the Courtier;* 1528) was translated into English, French, Spanish, and Latin because it lovingly evoked the setting and values of a courtly society. Other works were translated because they were viewed as literary classics. Sir John Harington (1560–1612) published an English translation of Ludovico Ariosto's *Orlando furioso* (1516) under the same title in 1591. Edward Fairfax (c. 1575–1635) published an English translation of Torquato Tasso's epic poem *Gerusalemme liberata* (1581) under the title *Godfrey of Bulloigne* (1600). Such translations helped spread the influence of the translated works.

Less lofty vernacular works were also translated. In 1528 the Spanish humanist Antonio de Guevara (c. 1480–1545) published his *Libro aureo de Marco Aurelio: emperador y eloquentissimo orador* (The golden book of Marcus Aurelius: emperor and most eloquent orator; expanded edition 1529). It purported to be a newly discovered ancient biography of the emperor Marcus Aurelius. Within a fictional ancient setting, Guevara delivered humanistic moral advice based on the classics. The book became a European best-seller and school text, with Dutch, English, French, German, Italian, and Latin translations in the sixteenth and seventeenth centuries.

Translators of literary texts for popular and/or general readerships added, deleted, or rearranged material. They altered names and places in order to bring the work to readers in another language. At times it is difficult to distinguish between material added in translation and original writing, a distinction that did not greatly trouble Renaissance translators. For example, Garci Rodrìguez de Montalvo, about whom little is known, published in 1508 the first surviving version of a Spanish chivalric romance called *Amadís de Gaula*. Although derived from medieval French material, it was an original Renaissance romance. English, French, Italian, and other translations followed, as did sequels. But determining where translation ended and new material began, in the various versions, would be a very difficult task.

Nor did Renaissance authors always draw a line between translation and plagiarism. Vernacular authors commonly included in their works unacknowledged translated material from ancient Latin and Greek sources. Perhaps these authors considered the plagiarized and translated material such an accepted part of Renaissance culture that the original author did not need to be named.

See also **Plato, Platonism, and Neoplatonsim; Galen; Castiglione, Baldassare; Ficino, Marsilio; Guevara, Antonio de.**

BIBLIOGRAPHY

Burke, Peter. *The Fortunes of the Courtier: The European Reception of Castiglione's Cortegiano.* University Park, Pa., 1996.

Copenhaver, Brian. "Translation, Terminology and Style in Philosophical Discourse." In *The Cambridge History of Renaissance Philosophy.* Edited by Charles B. Schmitt, Quentin Skinner, Eckhard Kessler, and Jill Kraye. Cambridge, U.K., 1988. Pages 77–110. Good discussion of the translation issues for philosophical texts.

Grendler, Paul F. *Schooling in Renaissance Italy: Literacy and Learning, 1300–1600.* Baltimore, 1989. See pp. 300–304, 422–424, for Italian translations of Guevara.

Hankins, James. *Plato in the Italian Renaissance.* 2 vols. Leiden, Netherlands, and New York, 1991. Deals with translation and reception of Plato before Ficino.

Wilson, N. G. *From Byzantium to Italy: Greek Studies in the Italian Renaissance.* Baltimore, 1992. Deals with many Greek translators in fifteenth-century Italy.

PAUL F. GRENDLER

Elizabethan Translations

From its inception the English book trade relied heavily on translations. William Caxton's first publication was his own version of a French history of Troy (1473–1474); similar efforts loom large in his subsequent list. The appetite for such works secured the services of writers not otherwise minded to appear in print; the only significant work of Thomas Wyatt's published during his lifetime was his translation of Plutarch's *Quiet of Mind* (1528). With Elizabeth's accession the enterprise of offering foreign texts in native attire was rejuvenated and became more systematic; by 1603 all of Plutarch was so dressed. Some substantial literary careers were composed almost wholly of translations: notably those of Arthur Golding (1536–1606), translator of some thirty works from Latin and French, and Philemon Holland (1552–1637), the most industrious translator of classical prose, including Livy, the elder Pliny, and Plutarch's moral works. Several individual translations became important works of Elizabethan literature in their own right; their influence can sometimes be traced with remarkable specificity in the poems and plays of the time.

From a contemporary viewpoint, the most consequential translation was of the Bible. Only in Elizabeth's reign did an English Bible become widely and legally available; the most popular was the Geneva Bible, prepared by Protestants exiled during the reign of Queen Mary and published in 1560. The Protestant commitment to congregational singing led to numerous rhymed translations of the Psalms; a collection of versions by Thomas Sternhold, John Hopkins, and others (1562) became one of the most widely reprinted books of its age. Contemporary works of religious instruction and controversy were much in demand; Calvin's sermons and commentaries were the mainstay of Golding's career. Foreign religious texts were also sought out and fitted opportunistically to a strong market for moral edification; in a typical instance, George Gascoigne translated a supposititious (spurious) sermon of Augustine's and made it the centerpiece of his *Delicate Diet for Daintymouthed Drunkards* (1576).

Translation from classical Latin and Greek was an important pedagogical tool in humanist education, and could become a lifelong habit; we have examples from Elizabeth herself. Published classical translations were predominantly of history, biography, and moral philosophy (Lucretius conspicuously absent). Even by sixteenth-century standards Greek was underrepresented (no Plato, not much Aristotle), though among the more influential achievements was Thomas North's version of Plutarch's *Lives* (five editions, 1579–1631). Shakespeare's Roman plays would not exist without it; his devotion to North's very phrasing solves a crux in the text of *Coriolanus.* Of classical poetry, epic was best served, usually in the fourteener couplets (rhymed lines of seven iambic feet) that until the 1590s were taken to be the equivalent of dactylic hexameter. A version of Virgil's *Aeneid* by Thomas Phaer and Thomas Twyne went through six editions (1573–1620); Golding's translation of Ovid's *Metamorphoses* went through seven (1567–1612), and was another book that Shakespeare kept to hand. Under James these were joined by George Chapman's translations of the *Iliad* (complete in 1611) and the *Odyssey* (1615)—the former unfashionably still in fourteeners, the latter not. Two translations of classical prose fiction proved popular and influential: Apuleius's *Golden Ass* by William Adlington (five editions, 1566–1636) and Heliodorus's *Egyptian History* by Thomas Underdown (five editions, 1569–1617). Translations of drama were sparse: a translation of Lodovico Dolce's reworking of Euripides's *Phoenissae* (performed 1566, published 1573), prose versions of Plautus's *Menaechmi* (1595) and of Terence (1588, 1598), the latter meant as a school text.

Verse translations of Seneca's tragedies appeared individually from 1559 on and were gathered into a complete collection in 1581; the volume was not reprinted. Translations of most of Ovid's elegiac poems were published—Christopher Marlowe's version of the scandalous *Amores* (first printed c. 1597) survived an attempted suppression to become quite popular—but other elegiac and lyric poets received only scattered attention.

Translation of contemporary secular texts favored the practical and informative: medical and scientific works, herbals, travel literature. There was a particular appetite for guides to courtly behavior—most famously Baldassare Castiglione's *The Courtier* (Englished by Thomas Hoby in 1561), but also similar works by Giovanni della Casa, Stefano Guazzo, and Giambattista Gelli (a Latin translation of Castiglione was also published). Niccolò Machiavelli's *Art of War* appeared in English (three editions, 1560–1588), as did his *Florentine History* (1595); manuscript translations of *The Prince* existed, but none was printed until 1640. John Florio's translation of Michel de Montaigne's *Essays* (1603, though there may have been earlier editions) appears to have been on Hamlet's shelf. Italian *novelle* were represented in a number of influential anthologies, beginning with William Painter's *Palace of Pleasure* (1566–1567); some longer works of prose fiction were also translated, the most popular being the Iberian romances of Amadis and Palmerin (beginning c. 1572). Three substantial sixteenth-century poems received ambitious verse translations: Guillaume Du Bartas's *Divine Weeks and Works,* by Josuah Sylvester (in installments from 1598 on); Ludovico Ariosto's *Orlando furioso,* by John Harington (1591); and Torquato Tasso's *Gerusalemme liberata,* by Edward Fairfax, under the title *Godfrey of Bulloigne* (1600). Edmund Spenser translated two French sonnet sequences in their entirety as *Ruins of Rome* and *Visions of Bellay* (1591); elsewhere a good deal of lyric poetry was translated as individual poems. Richard Tottel's *Songs and Sonnets* (1557) brought into print the Petrarchan translations and imitations of Thomas Wyatt; Henry Howard, earl of Surrey; and others (including some sonnets in fourteeners), and inaugurated the public phase of English Petrarchism; miscellanies and sequences over the next half century were spangled with often unacknowledged versions of the lyrics of Petrarch and his Continental followers.

The translators often wrote with a strong sense of mission for the spread of learning, sometimes with a sharply patriotic edge (introducing his translation of Pliny, Holland calls for conquest of Latin by English to requite Rome's military conquest of Britain). The translations were an important site at which a significant enhancement of the literary word-hoard was negotiated. Most of the open polemics were in favor of colloquial diction and against inkhorn terms; some translations, such as Golding's Ovid, experimented with a heightened nativism that can now seem almost antic ("gripple," "orped," "queachy"). A fair number of foreign, especially Latinate words were nevertheless imported by translators and became effectively naturalized ("despicable," "ponderous," "prodigious"). The level of scholarship was uneven (most Greek works are translated from Latin or French intermediaries), and some translators made deliberate alterations and interpolations in the interests of contemporary effectiveness; their unusually open pursuit of such effectiveness supplied a vigor and sense of enterprise that later, more scrupulous translations often lack.

See also **Bible,** *subentry on* **The English Bible.**

BIBLIOGRAPHY

Jacobsen, Erik. *Translation, a Traditional Craft: An Introductory Sketch with a Study of Marlowe's Elegies.* Copenhagen, 1958.

Lathrop, Henry Burrowes. *Translations from the Classics into English from Caxton to Chapman, 1477–1620.* Reprint, New York, 1967.

Matthiessen, F. O. *Translation: An Elizabethan Art.* Cambridge, Mass., 1931.

Whibley, Charles. "Translators." In *Prose and Poetry: Sir Thomas North to Michael Drayton.* Vol. 4 of *The Cambridge History of English Literature.* Edited by A. W. Ward and A. R. Waller. Reprint, Cambridge, U.K., 1970. Pages 1–25.

Winny, James. *Elizabethan Prose Translation.* Cambridge, U.K., 1960.

Wright, Louis B. *Middle-Class Culture in Elizabethan England.* Chapel Hill, N.C., 1935.

GORDON BRADEN

Jewish Translators

By the middle of the fourteenth century a considerable corpus of scientific and philosophical texts was available in Hebrew translation. Jewish scholars in the Renaissance continued to augment this corpus. The great majority of the works selected for translation were written in Latin; during the medieval period, the most important source had been Arabic writings. Almost all of the translations were executed in Spain, Provence, and Italy. In general, the Iberian translators concentrated on philosophy and Provençal translators on medicine. The Italian translators worked in many fields but evinced a special interest in the exact sciences.

Iberian Peninsula. Baruch (Benedictus) ben Isaac ibn Ya'ish, scion of an important Spanish scholarly family, translated a number of Aristotelian works toward the end of the fifteenth century. Ibn Ya'ish complains about distortions in the Hebrew versions that were prepared from the Arabic. However, it seems that his difficulties were with the Arabic language rather than the Islamic philosophers, for not only does he rely heavily upon Ibn Rushd (Averroes), whose comments (along with those of Thomas Aquinas and others) are included in the translation, but he also follows the advice of Ibn Rushd in dividing the text into small chapters, something Aristotle had not done. Elijah Habillo, who worked in Monzon in Aragon in the 1470s, translated more than a dozen short treatises by Aquinas, William of Occam, and others. The Catalan Abraham Shalom (d. 1492) translated a few books, including *Philosophia pauperum* (Philosophy of the indigent), attributed to Albertus Magnus. In addition to the translations inspired by interest in Latin Scholasticism, others were driven by the increasingly aggressive efforts to convert Jews to Christianity. The Hebrew translation of the Gospel of Matthew, which forms part of Shem Tov ibn Shaprut's *Even Bohan* (Testing stone), was meant to help in resisting missionary pressures.

France. Abraham Avigdor, who flourished in the second half of the fourteenth century, is the first Jew known definitely to have studied at the medical college of Montpelier. He translated a number of logical and medical texts, including Gerard de Solo's book on fevers (based on the ninth book of Rhazes's *Almansor,* a medieval work dedicated to the ruler al-Manṣûr). The same work was translated in 1394 by Leon Joseph of Carcassonne, who introduced it with a lengthy and informative translator's preface. Leon also translated Pseudo-Hippocrates's *De esse aegrotorum secundum lunam* (On the sick, in accordance with the moon); that work of prognostication was translated again in 1406 by Tanchum ben Moshe of Beaucaire.

In the 1350s Judah ben Nathan, a Provençal physician, prepared a Hebrew version of Abu Hamid al-Ghazali's *Intentions of the Philosophers.* His version, the most frequently copied of several Hebrew renditions, became a standard text during the Renaissance. There is some irony in this development, insofar as al-Ghazali's purpose was to set up Avicennian philosophy for the blistering attack delivered in his *Incoherence of the Philosophers.* Though that work was also translated into Hebrew, as was Averroes's rebuttal, neither had an impact close to that of *Intentions*.

Azariah ben Joseph, also known as Bonafoux Bonfil Astruc, was born in Perpignan but, like the rest of his coreligionists, was forced to leave Provence. He eventually settled in Italy where, in the 1420s, he translated Boethius's *Consolation of Philosophy* (he seems to have identified with Boethius's plight) and a medical book of al-Zahrawi.

Italy. Italian Jews seem to have worked under fewer pressures and restrictions than their coreligionists elsewhere. Some figures carried on extensive and varied contacts with Christian scholars, with whom they collaborated in their translation activities. In the mid-fifteenth century Mordecai Finzi of Mantua translated the Oxford Tables (a set of astronomical tables drawn up by John Batecomse for the meridian of Oxford) "with the help of a non-Jew"; and he studied with Bartolomeo dei Manfredi, whose work on the *celidario* (an astronomical instrument) he rendered into Hebrew. Finzi translated two key works on algebra, a branch of mathematics which Jews had largely neglected during the medieval period. In his translation of the book on algebra by Abu Kamil, Finzi employs a number of Romance terminologies; this fact, together with the lack of any supporting evidence that Finzi knew Arabic, led some scholars to suggest that Finzi worked from a putative Spanish or Italian version. Finzi's Hebrew version of *Algebra* of Dardi of Pisa is the most complete copy of that work. Finzi gives precise details of the circumstances of his translation, and the Latin manuscript with Finzi's writings in the margin is still extant.

Italy should be seen as the center for Jewish interest in Georg Peurbach's *Theoricae,* even though none of the Hebrew translations of that key astronomical text (which include a translation of the commentary of Francesco Capuano) can be located there. In particular, the Hebrew commentaries on Peurbach and on Joannes de Sacro Bosco's *Sphere* by Moses Almosnino (1515–c. 1585) contain many snippets from Latin and Italian writings, which Almosnino translated with the assistance of a certain Aaron Afia.

Italian Jews were also quite active in translating a broad range of texts into Latin. Abraham de Balmes (c. 1440–1523), physician to Cardinal Domeníco Grimani, translated for his patron the writings of Ibn al-Haytham, Averroes, and others. Elijah Delmedigo (c. 1460–1497), an associate of Giovanni Pico della Mirandola, translated a number of Averroean books.

Both translators relied on Hebrew versions rather than the Arabic originals. Through the work of these and other Jewish intellectuals, Christian readers were familiarized with much material that would otherwise have been unavailable to them. The impact of this activity on a number of key thinkers, not the least of whom is Nicolaus Copernicus, should not be overlooked.

BIBLIOGRAPHY

Langermann, Y. Tzvi. "Peurbach in the Hebrew Tradition." *Journal for the History of Astronomy* 29 (1998): 137–150.

Langermann, Y. Tzvi. "The Scientific Writings of Mordekhai Finzi." *Italia* 7 (1988): 7–44.

Levey, Martin, ed. *The Algebra of Abu Kamil.* Madison, Wis., 1966.

Roth, Cecil. *The Jews in the Renaissance.* New York, 1965.

Shatzmiller, Joseph. *Jews, Medicine, and Medieval Society.* Berkeley, Calif., 1994.

Steinschneider, Moritz. *Die hebraeischen Uebersetzungen des Mittelalters und die Juden als Dolmetscher.* Berlin, 1893.

Y. TZVI LANGERMANN

TRANSPORTATION. *See* **Communication and Transportation.**

TRAVEL AND TRAVEL LITERATURE. The passion for travel and exploration in a world in rapid expansion is one of the most distinguishable phenomena of the Renaissance. For centuries, among other European countries, Italy had been the object of curious visitors due to its special ties with Christianity and classical history. During the Renaissance wanderers and explorers went beyond well-charted boundaries "for there is no sea unnavigable, no land uninhabitable" (Robert Thorn, a British merchant, 1527). Ship logs, letters and memoirs, guidebooks and travel accounts, maps and broadsheets rapidly documented their findings and spread the news of recently discovered worlds and the vast possibility of gathering the wealth they contained. Discovering diversity is a complex process that involves finding the other in ourselves and encourages suspicion, fears, and crises of one's own values. While the medieval Dante, "whose country is the entire world," could find in Latin a common denominator that linked him with all the world's scholars, Montaigne, a man of the Renaissance, undertook his travels abroad to exercise his spirit "to notice unknown things."

Travel as Atonement: Pilgrimages and Wandering. Travel is a painful chore (travel and travail have the same etymology, associating travel with hardship and pain), a journey that implies an uprooting, an alienation, an exile of sorts. Penitential journeys, mimicking the human voyage through life, with their components of calling and atonement, were common in both Western and Eastern religions. All journeys start with a departure that is ultimately the uprooting of the traveler, a painful experience akin to death ("To leave is to die a little," according to a French proverb), a folly of some sort, implying separation, loneliness, exile. A corollary to biblical narratives, the Christian pilgrimage attempts to reenact the exodus of one's ancestors to their promised land or the individual's voyage back to God. While Desiderius Erasmus and François Rabelais ridiculed pilgrimages as contrary to the most basic laws of household propriety, the fascination with them continued in the Renaissance. In 1434 King Henry VI granted permission to more than two thousand of his subjects to go to Santiago de Compostela; one of the first books to be printed in England by Wynkyn de Worde was *Informacion for Pylgrymes unto the Holy Londe* (1498); out of 528 travel books published in sixteenth-century France, forty-two were related to pilgrimage.

In the Renaissance the urbanization of a mass of disenfranchised, rambling rogues found its literary representation in a wealth of novels whose plots pivot around the adventures of peripatetic pícaros, or rogues. Two centuries of picaresque literature, from *Lazarillo de Tormes* (1554) to *Don Quixote* (1605), Fielding's *Tom Jones* (1749), and Voltaire's *Candide* (1759), bespeak the success of the "road novel" in most European languages. Although the contents are mostly fictional, these novels nonetheless describe real itineraries with great accuracy. Mateo Alemán's *Guzmán de Alfarache* (1599; continued by Juan José Martí in 1602) is a characteristic travel adventure, and a woman wanderer, *La pícara Justina* (1605) by Francisco de Úbeda, follows her male counterparts on the roads of Spain. Some titles explicitly connect novels with travel: *Viaje entretenido* (Entertaining voyage; 1603), *Viaje del mundo* (World voyage; 1613), *El pasajero* (The passenger; 1617). Literature, travel, and autobiography meet in the *Vida y sucesos de la Monja Alférez* (The life and times of Monja Alférez; 1625), the story of Catalina de Erauso, a Spanish nun turned soldier in South America, or the *Vida* (Life; 1899) of a soldier and navigator, Alonso de Contreras. The literary success of the rambler cuts across regional borders: Thomas Nashe's *Unfortunate Traveller* (1594) and numerous translations of the Spanish novels mentioned above are followed by Richard Head's *The English Rogue* (1665) and Daniel Defoe's *Moll Flanders* (1722). Sev-

enteenth-century France saw Charles Sorel's *Francion* (1622), Paul Scarron's *Roman comique* (Comic novel; 1651–1659), and Antoine Furetière's *Roman bourgeois* (Novel of the middle class; 1666). Pierre-Augustin Caron de Beaumarchais's Figaro, a resourceful and philosophical hero, and Giacomo Casanova, who traveled aimlessly around Europe, owe much to their literary ancestors of Renaissance Spain. Travel can be, indeed, "a fool's paradise," according to Ralph Waldo Emerson, for "the rage of traveling is a symptom of deeper unsoundness."

Travel and Intellectual Formation: The "Moving Academy" of the Grand Tour. Plato was one of the few discordant voices in the Western tradition to fear the bad influence of foreign experiences on young people. The majority of traditional authorities, however, while underscoring the "discommodities" of journeying, agree with Turner that "traveilynge ensueth verie great commoditie in every kind of lyfe" (*Travailer;* 1575).

These descriptions have inspired and motivated the art of traveling. If the Renaissance did not introduce travel as a pedagogical tool, it surely assigned to it a fundamental role in the formation of the honest man. The lesson of Homer's Ulysses ("Many were the men whose cities he saw and whose minds he learned," *Odyssey* I), are echoed in Dante (*Inferno.* 26. 98–99). Personal experience became the touchstone of the Renaissance pedagogy for the ruler-to-be as in Machiavelli's *Dell'arte della guerra* (The art of war; 1520), or the young aristocrat, as in Castiglione's *Il cortegiano* (*The Book of the Courtier;* 1528). The traditional distrust for anything foreign displayed by Tudor England gave way to the grand tour, described by Shakespeare as "a course of learning and ingenious studies" (*The Taming of the Shrew,* I). A *curriculum studiorum,* or course of study, in Italy's renowned universities made it "the most direct and personal means of diffusing humanism" through Europe (Peter Burke), a way to bridge intellectual gaps and bring much-needed refinement to one's provinciality. The scholars William Grocyn, Thomas Linacre, John Colet, and Thomas Hoby all spoke highly of it. Wandering northern scholars matriculated in European universities. They sought information in treatises on travel and travel guides before joining and following a stale, circular itinerary (the so-called *giro d'Italia,* or circuit of Italy) through Milan, Florence, Rome, and Venice, often stopping in Naples to enjoy its wild celebration of the carnival. The home of refinement and civilization, and the background of youthful readings, Italy is what Percy

Bysshe Shelly described as the "Paradise of exiles," from Thomas Hoby to Montaigne, from Baltasar Gracián to Inigo Jones, in spite of the censure often leveled at Italian mores by various notable Renaissance scholars. The grand tour was the glamorous goal of many scions of the British aristocracy, who followed John Raymond's words: "to Italy we owe our civility." Serious students, like John Evelyn in 1652, "having mastered the tongue, frequented the courts, looked into their customs, [were] present at pleadings, observed their military discipline, contracted acquaintance with their learned men, studied their arts, and [were] familiar with their dispositions." The frivolous traveler, however, wasted his time abroad and returned to England transformed into an "Italianfyd Inglischemane," as Thomas Howard sarcastically implied, an "affectate traveller," speaking English through "his teeth, like . . . Monsieur Mingo de Moustrap" (Thomas Nashe).

Conditions of Travel.

The journey of the students of this "moving Academy," as Samuel Purchas defined the grand tour, was a painful chore. The physical comfort and speed of travel had changed little from Roman times, for the "great road revolution" was to take place only at the end of the seventeenth century. The overland journey consisted of a long series of tiresome days spent horseback riding through unknown territories on barely marked roads that suddenly became rivers in the rainy season, and restless nights in flea-infested inns, three or more people to a bed, often in the company of bandits or semiregular soldiers ready to rob the incautious traveler. The traveler to Italy could either "post" (that is, travel using rental horses stationed at suitable distances along the main roads) or hire the service of a *procaccio,* the director of a convoy that was sometimes accompanied by soldiers to protect travelers in dangerous areas. At the end of the sixteenth century the first coaches replaced horses on the most traveled and leveled roads.

Sea voyages from England to Livorno were still uncommon, because Barbary corsairs and European privateers roamed the Mediterranean. Whenever the voyager ventured to try ship travel, he could be tossed for forty days by the "most furious Levanters," as Jonathan Skelton complained in 1757, and risk being enslaved by Muslim corsairs or robbed by French pirates; he often ended his journey quarantined in a squalid Italian lazaretto, a hospital for poor people suffering from contagious diseases. Money was also a problem; the traveler had to take letters of credit in his own country and cash them abroad because severe monetary restrictions existed in most countries to protect local currency.

Travel as a Profession and Mission: Merchants, Ambassadors, and Missionaries.

The happy time in Eden or in Saturn's golden age was also a period of stasis. Humanity was content and did not need to move about in search of outside happiness: "the same land gave people a cradle and a grave," noted Luigi Tansillo, a sixteenth-century Italian writer. John Milton observed that "the world was all before them, where to choose / Their place of rest." Travel is the undertaking of unhappy humans, dissatisfied with their lot. Merchants and soldiers began carrying goods or voyaging to "forraine shores or warres or wares ill sought" (Samuel Daniels), even as they sometimes questioned whether the effort was worth the pain and danger they experienced. ("Now am I in Arden: the more fool I; / When I was at home I was in a better place," Shakespeare.) The voyages to the New World by Spanish and Portuguese sailors were undertaken to find new sources of riches. "To search for gold and precious stones" is a goal that Christopher Columbus mentioned multiple times in his diary. Such greed did not conflict with the admiral's goal of spreading Christianity; he said that a man with gold would "succeed in bringing souls to Heaven." Indeed, religion, gold, and, inevitably, politics have been precariously symbiotic reasons for travel from the time of thirteenth-century Franciscan friars (William of Rubruck, John of Plano Carpini, Odoric of Pordenone) who followed Marco Polo on his eastern route to the missionaries who plied the ocean aboard the same ships that carried the conquistadores to New Spain or the Far East.

Religious travelers and official envoys wrote about their voyages more frequently than did merchants. John Whethamstede (d. 1465), the energetic abbot of St. Albans, detailed his continental adventures on his way to attend the Council of Pavia (1423); Jacques Sirmond, a Jesuit theologian, composed a long Latin travelogue of his hard trip from Paris to Rome in 1590. The chronicles of pious travel literature and the letters of missionaries to their superiors in Europe are rife with provocative descriptions of the discovery of new peoples and their chances for conversion or proclivity to create new martyrs out of their European visitors. Among ambassadors' writings, the numerous Venetian *relationi,* their formal reports to the Senate, are models of sharp and realistic analysis of foreign life. Among the merchants, Amerigo Vespucci sailed west soon after Columbus, and Antonio Pigafetta accompanied

Magellan around the world, followed by a host of Italian adventurers, Francesco Carletti (c. 1573–1636), Pietro della Valle (1586–1652), and Giovanni Francesco Gemelli Careri (1651–1725). The detailed accounts of their journeys around the world deeply influenced the Renaissance imagination.

Travel as Exploration and Conquest: A Male Activity.   Travel as a conquest is traditionally a male activity, "an excellent ornament for gentlemen" (Samuel Purchas); "Any city and the entire world is the homeland for the strong and intelligent man" (Marcellus Palingenius, an Italian humanist, in his *Zodiacus vitae,* 1528). In the earliest travel chronicles, it is the male, Odysseus (Ulysses), who leaves his home to go to war and eventually to wander throughout the world, leaving Penelope to keep intact the household and its economy. The history of exploration, justified by a series of religious, commercial, political, and military considerations, is also dominated by men, affected and embroiled in stereotypes such as passion for honor, zeal to serve God and the king, or hunger for wealth. As early as the fifteenth century Portuguese sailors went far south of the Pillars of Hercules, along the western coast of Africa, into uncharted waters and without the guidance of the polestar. They followed the path of Ugolino and Vadino Vivaldi, Genoese brothers who sailed out of the Mediterranean in 1291 and were never seen again, and fourteenth-century French navigators who had rediscovered the Canary Islands, the mythical "Fortunate Islands" of Pliny the Elder, Plutarch, and Ptolemy. The age of reconnaissance was born. Immediately after the voyages of Columbus (1492–1504) and Vasco da Gama (1497–1499), bold seamen from various European nations, backed by international financiers and expecting honors and recognition, embarked on voyages of discovery: to South America and the first sight of the Pacific Ocean (Vasco Núñez de Balboa, 1513; Hernán Cortés, 1519) or the Amazon River (Francisco de Orellana, 1541; William Davies, 1608), Central America (Juan Ponce de León, 1513), and inland exploration (Alvar Núñez Cabeza de Vaca, 1528–1536; Francisco Vásquez de Coronado, 1539–1540; Hernando de Soto, 1540), to the northeastern coast of the new continent (John Cabot, 1497–1498; João Fernandes, 1500–1536; the brothers Gaspar and Miguel Côrte-Real, 1501; Giovanni da Verrazzano, 1524–1528; Jacques Cartier, 1534–1536; Sir Humphrey Gilbert, 1583; Samuel de Champlain, 1609); in search of the Northwest Passage (Sir Martin Frobisher, 1576–1578; John Davies, 1586); following

Magellan across the Pacific (Sir Francis Drake, 1577–1579). Their inexhaustible thirst for the unknown and boundless desire for glory had an extraordinary impact on the European imagination; "if there had been more of the world, they would have attained it" (Camoens).

Women were traditionally considered homebound. Few braved the dangers and embarked on pilgrimages: in the fifth century, Egeria left an extraordinary account of her travels through the Middle East, and Chaucer mentions a few traveling nuns in the prologue to his *Canterbury Tales.* According to Georgius Loysius's *Pervigilium Mercurii* (1598), only "a poor, lecherous, or insolent woman" would dare to travel for other reasons than pilgrimages. Even Teresa of Ávila (1515–1582), a saint and doctor of the Catholic church, who made extensive journeys to found convents and settle controversies, was called "a restless and wandering woman." Lady Whetenall, the first, perhaps, of the few courageous women who joined the grand tour in progress, died in childbirth in Padua in 1650.

Travel as Leisure: Petrarch and Renaissance Tourism.   Cross-cultural contacts among travelers create a sense of self-awareness and an understanding of how people differed from one another. In a body of narrative about toilsome journeys, happy travelers are unusual. One such is the person who in the *Thousand and One Nights* "sings the joys of wandering," for

> even the moon-colored pearl must forsake the deep
> green levels
> And be drawn across the beaches
> Where the waiting merchants are,
> Ere it shows and glows and reaches
> . . . the white neck of a girl!
>
> (256th Night)

Among endless reports of dejected travelers, Petrarch's 1336 account of his excursion to Mount Ventoux stands out as one of the rarest and earliest records of pleasure in travel. Like modern mountaineers, he climbed that mountain solely because it was there, admitting that it was indeed a frivolous activity for a scholar. He made a timid apology for his waste of time, noting that Livy had observed that King Philip of Macedonia had climbed Mount Hemus for no specific reason other than viewing two seas from the top. Not until the end of the seventeenth century, however, did mountain climbing become an activity favored by German travelers, according to Saint-Évremond's comedy *Sir Politick Would-Be* (c. 1664).

A few decades after Petrarch, Gilles Le Bouvier underscored "the pleasure of seeing the world," yet his enjoyment of travel was still the exception. Francesco Vettori, a sixteenth-century Florentine ambassador to Germany, called travel "the best of all honest pleasures humanity can take"; his manner of traveling was quintessentially aristocratic, for it was, as he asserted, without financial worries, at a leisurely pace, accompanied by pleasant friends. Thomas Coryate wrote a rare optimist's account of a walking tour of the Continent (*Crudities;* 1611), defining it as "the sweetest and most delightful of all pleasures in the world." Like Vettori, Benvenuto Cellini, on his way to France (1540) where Francis I had requested his services, reminded the king that the artist deserved the same traveling comforts available to the aristocracy. Still, the journey was painfully slow, even for the rich and powerful, such as Leo of Rozmital, a German baron whose European travels (1465–1467) are among the earliest fully documented voyages.

An emerging, wealthy bourgeoisie was ready to search abroad for its intellectual roots. Renaissance Italy was the ultimate goal of learned foreigners. The grand tour was also a moment of leisure and pride ("he is nobody that hath not travelled," Thomas Nashe); these travelers wanted to see and be seen, although they often avoided their fellow countrymen to take unbeaten paths. Hoby, Montaigne, Nicolas Audebert, Nicolas Peiresc, Jean-Jacques Bouchard, John Evelyn, Isaac Basire, and many others visited famous sites, met with local scholars, maintained a regular correspondence with them, and wrote about their experiences. Their journals were published much later, as the public's interest in private lives increased: Montaigne's *Journal* appeared in 1774, Bouchard's *Voyages* in 1897, Audebert's travelogue in 1981–1983, John Evelyn's *Diary* in 1818, and Isaac Basire's *Travells* in 1987.

Travel as a Metaphor: Life's Journey.

Accounts of the human voyage through life, common in the Western canon, from Plato's apocryphal *Axiochus* to William Langland's *Piers Plowman* and Alciati's *Emblemata* inspired many allegorical writings of the Renaissance. Teresa of Ávila's momentous *Camino de perfección* (1583) is surrounded and followed by several texts in various languages: *Peregrination spirituelle* (Jan Pascha, 1576), *Viaggio spirituale* (Cornelio Bellanda, 1578), *Pilgrimage to Paradise* (Leonard Wright, 1591), *De sacris et religiosis peregrinationibus* (Jakob Gretser, 1606), *Pilgrim's Journey towards Heaven* (William Webster,

1613), *Duyfkens ende Willemykens pelgrimagie tot haren beminden binnen Ierusalem* (Boetius Bolswert, 1627), *Pilgrim's Passe to the New Jerusalem* (M. R. Gent, 1659), and *The Pilgrim's Progress* (John Bunyan, 1678).

Travel and Travel Literature. The relationship between travel and writing dates from the early days of human history. Akkadian and Sumerian tablets record the fantastic journey of Gilgamesh (c. 2000 B.C.): "He had left for a long voyage. When he came back, tired and broken by fatigue, he rested and engraved his entire story on a stone."

Traditionally, travel writing has been a hybrid genre, mixing travel with other material, including history, geography, and even fiction. Many of the Renaissance poets reported on their travels in Latin (Jacques Sirmond). Real travel narrative seeped into literary works as well, as in Miguel de Cervantes's *Don Quixote.*

The age of reconnaissance blossomed in Europe from 1450 to 1550, spurred by multiple economic interests. These interests included opening trade with Asian countries that had provided Europe with much-needed spices, as well as the knowledge of new territories, human races, and exotic fauna and flora. This knowledge spread rapidly by way of printed books and upset long-accepted philosophical tenets. Returning wayfarers shared their experiences with others to obtain fame, the ultimate source of pride of Renaissance travelers. Their reports were carefully collected by learned scholars, as, for example, in Thomas Elyot's *The Governour* (1531): "I cannot tell what more pleasure shulde happen to a gentil witte than to beholde in his own house every thinge that within all the worlde is contained." The voyages of discovery directed by Prince Henry "the Navigator" of Portugal (1394–1460) were chronicled by Gomes Eanes de Azurara (1453); the journey of Bartolomeu Dias was narrated by Alvise da Mosto (1507) and Duarte Pacheco Pereira (1505–1508); Vasco da Gama's report survived through the *Décadas de Asia* of João de Barros, while Lodovico de Varthema's *Itinerario* (1510) to the East Indies, translated into several languages, enjoyed an immediate success. Columbus's journal of his voyage to the New World was abstracted by his friend and historian Bartolomé de Las Casas. Peter Martyr of Anghiera shrewdly chronicled the new discoveries, followed by Amerigo Vespucci's forged letters to Lorenzo di Pierfrancesco de' Medici (*Mundus novus;* 1504), which caused the German geographer Martin Waldseemüller to name the new continent after him.

Lively controversies between Renaissance travelers and geographers continued, a struggle between practice and theory, between mariners who had learned their lessons, in the words of André Thevet "on a ship under the teaching of the winds" and others who were more at ease in "scholarly debates in the Sorbonne."

The body of Renaissance travel literature is extensive and cumbersome; it defies neat categorizations and precise schemes. If the essence of nature is constant motion, the pervasiveness of travel literature is not surprising. Travel writing is directly related to autobiographical literature. Narrator and subject are often one and the same; their story begins not with their birth, but with their departure, and is concluded with their return home.

The categories of travel narrative (hodoeporics) proposed here are limited to journeys really undertaken. Apart from the mass of fictional travels, epics, and utopian journeys, true travel literature ranges from the guidebook, where the writer's presence is minimal, to personal narratives, journals, poems, and letters. Perhaps, the best example of objective report, devoid of personal involvement, is the "itinerary," at times no more than a barren list of place-names and distances, such as Estienne's *Guide des chemins de France* (Guide to the byroads of France; 1553), Villuga's *Reportorio de todos los caminos de España* (Account of all journeys through Spain; 1546), Rowland's *The Posts of the World* (1576), and Codogno's *Itinerario delle poste per tutto il mondo* (1608). Similar tools for seafarers were Alvise da Mosto's *Portulano* (1490) and Contreras's *Derrotero universal* (c. 1630). Objective descriptions of towns for the perusal of fifteenth-century travelers (such as Flavio Biondo's *Roma instaurata* or Maffeo Vegio's *De amplitudine civitatis Ravennae*) evolved by the end of the sixteenth century into literary portraits of the major European cities, disguised as accounts of real visits (Hieronymus Turles, Just Zinzerling, and Theodor Zwinger). Some travelers, such as Louis Coulon (*L'Ulysse françois;* 1643) and Pierre Bergeron (*Voyage d'Italie;* 1611) combined in one report the observations they made during several trips, interspersing personal narrative with information taken from guidebooks, for the sake of completeness. The individual's interpretation of the events appeared in the *Antiquités de Rome* (1558) written by a dejected Joachim du Bellay and a real trip through Germany and Italy in 1580–1581 by Montaigne (*Journal de voyage*), emphasized the author's personal interpretation of the facts.

Nearly 150 manuscripts of Marco Polo's *Milione* (thirteenth century) and numerous editions of John Mandeville's *Travels* (fourteenth century) illustrate how the true portrayal of the foreign reality was often deformed by the "marvelous." Nonetheless, the fascination with faraway lands and peoples produced a series of successful compilations: Giovanni Battista Ramusio's *Navigationi e viaggi* (1550–1559), Richard Hakluyt's *Principal Navigations* (1589), Samuel Purchas's *Hakluyt Posthumus* (1625), and Pierre Bergeron's editions of *Travel to the New World* (1629). These exotic encounters with people around the world strongly stimulated the imagination of poets, from Tasso to Shakespeare and Milton, while Luíz Valdes de Camões wrote his *Lusiadas* (1572) after his own voyage around the world. Álvar Nuñez Cabeza de Vaca left a gripping account of his epic journey from Florida to Mexico (1528–1536). Later on, Francesco Carletti, Pietro della Valle, and Giovanni Francesco Gemelli Careri dealt with their discovery of differences in detailed accounts of their journeys around the world. Jean Marot described in poetry military expeditions (*Voyage de Gênes;* 1507; *Voyage de Venise;* 1509); Erasmus wrote lively accounts of his wanderings through Europe in many letters to his friends.

Around the middle of the sixteenth century the popularity of the grand tour gave rise to a sequence of personal travel narratives to Italy, starting with Sir Thomas Hoby's *Booke of Travaile,* published before 1566, and Roger Ascham's *Scholemaster* (1570), and continuing through the next century with the memoirs of Thomas Coryate (1611), William Lithgow (1614), George Sandys (1615), Fynes Moryson (1617), Peter Mundy (c. 1615), Isaac Basire (1647–1649), and John Raymond (1648).

Letters and journals usually underwent major rewriting before publication. For example, an Italian priest, Sebastiano Locatelli, wrote the *Viaggio di Francia* and transcribed it three times in thirty years, each time adding more fabulous elements, and finally transforming his travel account into what more resembles a novel than a travel narrative.

Eventually, the end of the sixteenth century witnessed the development of the *methodus apodemica,* a technique of formulating a precise picture of a foreign land. Just as Venetian ambassadors were routinely given a set of rules on how to write their *relationi,* or formal reports, to the Senate, scholars created a scientific method of jotting down their observations: how to scrutinize a new land, what order to follow in observing and reporting, and what questions to ask the locals. It was the dawn of a new science that produced through the eighteenth century a huge body of travel literature.

See also **Grand Tour; Pilgrimage**.

BIBLIOGRAPHY

Selecting among the numerous translations in English of the journals written by Renaissance explorers and travelers is a difficult task. Fortunately, many of them have been published in English by the Hakluyt Society of London, in scholarly editions that for the most part are still available. Several of the authors quoted in the article are found in this collection.

Primary Works

Anghiera, Pietro Martire d'. *The History of Travayle in the West and East Indies*. Introduction by T. R. Adams. New York, 1992. Facsimile edition.

Pigafetta, Antonio. *The First Voyage Around the World (1519–1522): An Account of Magellan's Expedition*. Edited by Theodore J. Cachey. New York, 1995.

Polo, Marco. *The Travels of Marco Polo*. Translated and with an introduction by Ronald Latham. New York, 1958.

Waldseemüller, Martin. *The Cosmographiae Introductio, . . . Followed by the Four Voyages of Amerigo Vespucci*. New York, 1907.

Secondary Works

Fuller, Mary C. *Voyages in Print: English Travel to America, 1576–1624*. New York, 1995.

Haynes, Jonathan. *The Humanist as Traveler: George Sandys's "Relation of a Journey Begun A.D. 1610."* Rutherford, N.J., 1986.

McPhail, Eric. *The Voyage to Rome in French Renaissance Literature*. Saratoga, Calif., 1990.

Monga, Luigi. *L'odeporica/Hodoeporics: On Travel Literature*. Annali d'Italianistica 14, 1996.

Penrose, Boies. *Travel and Discovery in the Renaissance, 1420–1620*. Cambridge, Mass., 1952.

Sells, A. Lytton. *The Paradise of Travellers: The Italian Influence on Englishmen in the Seventeenth Century*. Bloomington, Ind., 1963.

LUIGI MONGA

TRAVERSARI, AMBROGIO (Ambrose of Camaldoli; 1386–1439), Florentine monk, leading patristic scholar among Italian humanists. Born in Portico, a village near Florence in the Romagna, Traversari went to Florence in 1400, entering the Camaldolese monastery of Santa Maria degli Angeli. There he learned Greek without a teacher (according to his own account), although he was probably later aided by the Greek Demetrius Skaranos, who had become a fellow monk at the Angeli and who served as Traversari's Greek amanuensis.

Traversari's expertise in Greek and his cultivation of classical Latin literature brought him to the attention of Niccolò de' Niccoli (c. 1364–1437), a Florentine patrician and bibliophile, who remained a close, lifelong friend. Niccoli's family fortune and his zeal for book hunting made it possible for Traversari to gain access to rare and ancient manuscripts as sources for his patristic scholarship. Through Niccoli, Traversari also developed contacts with the wider world of Italian humanism. During the 1420s Traversari's cell at the Angeli became an informal meeting center for a number of Florentine humanists, including the mathematician Paolo dal Pozzo Toscanelli (1397–1482), the poet Carlo Marsuppini (1399–1453), and Cosimo de' Medici (1389–1464), the future Florentine leader. Later, toward 1430, they were joined by Giannozzo Manetti (1396–1459), who began his Greek studies under Traversari.

Traversari read extensively in Latin patristics, particularly Jerome, a favorite of many humanists. He also worked on texts of Lactantius, widely admired among humanists for his elegant Latin and his support for classical studies, and on Tertullian. Traversari's most important contribution to the patristic revival, however, was in his study of the Greek church fathers. Over the last two decades of his life he produced more than twenty humanistic Latin translations of the orations, sermons, letters, saints' lives, and treatises of such Greek Fathers as Basil, Gregory Nazianzus, Ephraem, Pseudo-Dionysius (the Areopagite), and especially John Chrysostom. Like other humanists, Traversari regarded these patristic texts, which embodied classical rhetorical and literary qualities, as superior to the "quibbles" and "arid sterilities" of scholastic theology in inspiring the pursuit of moral virtue. He also approved the patristic emphasis on the moral exposition of scripture, especially the biblical homilies of Chrysostom. His most important venture outside of patristics was to translate Diogenes Laertius's *Lives of the Philosophers,* which became a key source of humanist knowledge of the philosophical traditions of antiquity.

In 1431 Traversari was named general of the Camaldolese, and he spent the next three years making reform visitations to the houses of his order. His account of these journeys is preserved in his *Hodoeporicon,* which along with his voluminous correspondence from these years affords insights into the condition of the monastic vocation during the early Renaissance. He also served as papal legate to the Council of Basel in 1435 and was a principal member of the Latin delegation attending the Council of Ferrara-Florence (1438–1439). There his knowledge of Greek and his expertise in patristics proved fundamental to the efforts to resolve the long-standing doctrinal conflicts that had divided Eastern and Western Christianity.

BIBLIOGRAPHY

Primary Work

Mehus, Laurentius, ed. *Ambrosii Traversarii generalis camaldulensium . . . latinae epistolae.* 2 vols. Florence, 1759. Reprint, Bologna, Italy, 1968.

Secondary Works

Ambrogio Traversari nel sesto centenario della nascita. Florence, 1988. A volume of conference proceedings.

Stinger, Charles. *Humanism and the Church Fathers: Ambrogio Traversari (1386–1439) and Christian Antiquity in the Italian Renaissance.* Albany, N.Y., 1977.

CHARLES L. STINGER

TRENT, COUNCIL OF. Reckoned by Roman Catholics as the nineteenth ecumenical council in the history of the church, this assembly of bishops and theologians met at the northern Italian city of Trent in three distinct periods—1545–1547, 1551–1552, and 1562–1563. The council was convoked by Pope Paul III (reigned 1534–1549) to respond to the doctrinal challenges raised by the Protestant Reformers, especially Martin Luther, as well as to deal with demands from both Catholics and Protestants for the reform of the church.

Emperor Charles V emerged in the early 1520s as the great Catholic champion of a council as the most equitable way to proceed, but for political reasons other leaders like Francis I, king of France, and especially Pope Clement VII (reigned 1523–1534), successfully delayed its convocation. Even the relationship between Paul III and the emperor was marked by distrust and conflicting aims. The protracted length of the council and the long delays between its three periods were due to political, military, and ecclesiastical factors that persistently threatened the very life of the council. When the council opened in 1545 only thirty-one prelates were present, and the number never exceeded two hundred.

Although papal legates presided over the council, the popes, who never set foot in Trent during these years, were only partially successful in controlling the agenda and the course the council took. Far from being a smoothly functioning organization following a clear blueprint, the council was often marked by turmoil and sharp debate, leading many observers to believe that it could never be successfully concluded.

By the time the council met, moreover, any real possibility of healing the religious divisions was past, and for all practical purposes the council, by clarifying the Catholic position on disputed issues, set a seal upon a situation already beyond repair. The importance of Trent for the subsequent history of the Roman Catholic Church can hardly be overestimated, although research has shown how distorted have been some interpretations of it and how limited the success of certain attempts to implement it.

Doctrine. Trent did not attempt a full statement of Catholic belief but intended to respond only to questions raised by the Reformation, which fall under three headings. First, Luther's interpretation of "scripture alone" as the basis for all teaching led the council at the very beginning of its deliberations in 1546 to establish the canon of scripture from which it would argue, which included the so-called deuterocanonical books like Judith and Wisdom, and to decree that apostolic traditions also had to be taken into account along with scripture. With that matter settled, the council after a brief statement on Original Sin next moved to the doctrine of justification, over which it labored for seven months. Stung by Luther's criticism that Catholics were Pelagians in that they believed their "works" rather than grace would save them, the council sedulously insisted that justification was accomplished always and everywhere under the inspiration of grace. It also taught, however, that in some mysterious way human responsibility was not absent, which the council believed Luther denied.

Finally, the council addressed the sacraments, for Luther had not only reduced their number to two from the traditional seven but had also redefined them. The council began this task at the end of the first period and continued it through the next two. It reasserted the sevenfold number of the sacraments, taught with new urgency that they were all instituted by Christ, and for the most part validated the sacramental teaching elaborated by scholastic theologians of the Middle Ages.

Notable by its absence is a statement on papal primacy, a doctrine repudiated by Protestants of every type. All bishops present at the council of course believed in the doctrine, but they very much disagreed on what practical prerogatives it entailed and especially on the relationship between the papacy and the episcopacy and between the papacy and the council itself. Whenever these issues surfaced, they sent the council into such crisis that they could not be pursued.

Reform. The council had from the beginning a clear focus in that it hoped to reform three ecclesiastical offices: the papacy, the episcopacy, and the pastors of parishes. It was consistently frustrated in its attempt at the first but vigorously pursued the other two. These reforms were aimed at assuring a

Council of Trent. The council meeting in the specially constructed amphitheater in the church of Sta. Maria Maggiore in Trent. The cardinal legates sit on a raised platform at the left as a speaker addresses the assembly. The representative of Philip II of Spain sits in the center in front of the scribe. ©THE BRITISH MUSEUM, LONDON

better quality of pastoral care. The last period of the council was when, under the skilled leadership of Cardinal Giovanni Morone, most of the pertinent decrees were formulated.

For bishops the council was finally able to issue a strong decree insisting on residence in their dioceses and forbidding their holding more than one bishopric at the same time. This was the foundation stone of the reforms at Trent. The council also required bishops to hold regular synods with their clergy, visit and oversee the parishes and other institutions of their dioceses, show greater stringency in admitting candidates to priestly ordination, assure that confessors be properly qualified, and promote preaching on Sundays and feast days, setting an example themselves.

The council implicitly tried to establish a closer relationship between bishops and the local clergy than was common earlier, even though this relationship was articulated principally in juridical and disciplinary terms. The council gave new prominence to the parish as the site where pastoral activity properly took place. In decreeing every diocese was to establish a seminary for the training of poor boys for the priesthood, it set in motion a process of regular-

ization that over time was taken as normative and finally eliminated alternatives.

The council was thus concerned almost exclusively with codifying and enforcing the discipline proper to the pastoral functions of bishops and diocesan clergy, and practically all its reform decrees in some way or other fall under this rubric. This means that the council had hardly a word to say about many other important aspects of Catholic life, such as confraternities and the missionaries being sent in such great numbers from Europe to the Spanish and Portuguese dominions overseas.

The Council and the Renaissance. The council was symptom and cause of a shift in cultural and religious sensibilities in society at large that differ from those usually attributed to the Renaissance. It signaled and exemplified, for instance, a more effective concern with surveillance and with enforcement of codes of conduct, which affected almost all segments of society and aspects of culture. In this way its relationship to the Renaissance was, though powerful and pervasive, for the most part indirect.

The council made no pronouncement about "the new learning"—humanism—but especially after the first period the language in which the decrees were formulated came to be dominated by theologians trained in scholastic theology and canon law. Moreover, the early decision to accept the Vulgate, the traditional Latin text of the Bible attributed to St. Jerome, as an authentic text for use in theological debate was interpreted as a caution against radical application of the new humanist philology to the biblical text. For a humanist like Erasmus the reading of the Bible was at the center of Christian piety; the failure of the council to make any pronouncement favoring the publication and reading of vernacular Bibles opened the way afterward to successful campaigns to suppress these activities as dangerous to faith. Yet the decision to retain Latin as the language for the public liturgy of the church certainly fell in line with the desires of many humanists and in the long run helped promote among Catholics the study of classical languages. As with so many other phenomena of the era, however, the council made no statement concerning the new humanistic schools.

High on the agenda of many humanists was a revival of preaching through application to it of the principles of classical rhetoric. Although the council said relatively little about this ministry, its admonition in the Fifth Session (1546) that preaching was the "chief duty" (*munus praecipuum*) of bishops and its insistence in the Twenty-Fourth Session (1563) that bishops and pastors preach every Sunday and feast day were taken seriously. These statements directly contributed to the great outburst of preaching activities in Catholicism in the post-Tridentine period and indirectly contributed to the writing and publication of the many "ecclesiastical rhetorics," treatises on how to preach inspired by humanistic principles.

The council reacted to the iconoclastic tendencies of some Protestant reformers by asserting in the Twenty-Second Session (1562) the legitimacy in rites and ceremonies of lights, candles, vestments, "and many other things of this kind," and by insisting in the Twenty-Fifth Session (1563) on the "great profit derived from all holy images." In so doing the council reaffirmed a tradition that antedated the Renaissance by many centuries but that at the same time gave support to that outpouring of art, much of it religious in nature, that marked the Renaissance.

In the latter decree the council, besides in general fostering the use of art in churches, helped promote a more self-conscious use of images for purposes of instruction and indoctrination. Its warning about removing all superstition and lasciviousness from painting, though more restrained in its language than

was that of even a humanist like Erasmus, led especially in Italy to treatises on what was appropriate to "sacred art" and to attempts to censor it.

See also Catholic Reformation and Counter-Reformation; Conciliarism; Preaching and Sermons, *subentry on* Christian Preaching and Sermons.

BIBLIOGRAPHY

Primary Works

Tanner, Norman P., ed. *Decrees of the Ecumenical Councils.* Vol. 2: *Trent to Vatican II.* London and Washington, D.C., 1990. Pages 655–799. Original text established by Giuseppe Alberigo et al. Texts of the council's decisions in Latin with English translation.

Secondary Works

Jedin, Hubert. *Crisis and Closure of the Council of Trent.* Translated by N. D. Smith. London, 1967.

Jedin, Hubert. *A History of the Council of Trent.* Translated by Ernest Graf. 2 vols. St. Louis, Mo., 1957–1960.

Jedin, Hubert. *Papal Legate at the Council of Trent: Cardinal Seripando.* Translated by Frederic C. Eckhoff. St. Louis, Mo., 1947.

Mozzarelli, Cesare, and Danilo Zardin, eds. *I tempi del concilio: Religione, cultura e società nell'Europa tridentina.* Rome, 1997.

Prodi, Paolo, and Wolfgang Reinhard, eds. *Il concilio di Trento e il moderno.* Bologna, Italy, 1996.

Tallon, Alain. *La France et le Concile de Trente (1518–1563).* Rome, 1997.

JOHN W. O'MALLEY

TRISSINO, GIAN GIORGIO (1478–1550), Italian man of letters. Born of an aristocratic family, Trissino was a noteworthy figure in the culture of the first half of the sixteenth century. He undertook humanistic studies, studying Greek in Milan with Demetrius Calcondila. After returning to the Venetian Republic in 1508, he was exiled from it in 1512 as a sympathizer of the Habsburg Empire. He passed his years in exile first at the Este court in Ferrara and then in Florence (1513–1514), where he frequented the gatherings of scholars and literary figures in the gardens of the Rucellai family palace, the Orti Oricellari. After moving to Rome in 1514, he was given diplomatic assignments in Italy and Germany by Popes Leo X (who obtained the restitution of his assets and the revocation of his exile), Clement VII, and Paul III. During this period he was in contact with the greatest literary men of his era, from Niccolò Machiavelli to Pietro Bembo, expressing positions that were often in radical opposition to the dominant linguistic and literary theories.

Trissino's fame is tied to his proposal, hard-fought but defeated, for an integral classicism in both the linguistic and literary fields. He expressed these principles in the six "divisions" of his *La poetica* (1529–1562), a monumental attempt to systematize all literary genres in the vernacular according to Aristotelian norms. He worked for the concrete realization of such a program, contributing repeatedly to the much-debated question of the vernacular language. In this field he argued unsuccessfully for a reform of the alphabet by means of the introduction of vowels and consonants from the Greek alphabet in *Epistola de le lettere nuovamente aggiunte ne la lingua italiana* (Letter concerning the new letters added to the Italian language; 1524). In his dialogue *Il castellano* (The lord of the castle; 1529) he also proposed, on the basis of a tendentious reading of Dante's *De vulgari eloquentia* (On vernacular eloquence), which he rediscovered, translated, and published (1529), the adoption of a "courtly" language, formed by mixing all the Italian dialects. In the literary field, beyond a conspicuous collection of *Rime volgari* (Vernacular rhymes; 1529) interesting for their metric experimentation, he achieved with *Sofonisba* (written in 1514–1515 and published in 1524) the first "regular" tragedy of the Renaissance, faithful to the Greek models and to Aristotelian unities, and with the comedy *I simillimi* (The look-alikes; 1548) a condensation of Plautus's *Menaechmi*.

Trissino's cultural battle in the name of the heroic poem against the "romance" model incarnated in Ludovico Ariosto's *Orlando furioso* (Mad Roland) and its numerous imitators inspired the twenty-seven books of *Italia liberata dai Goti* (Italy liberated from the Goths), over which he labored for about twenty years, publishing the first nine books in Rome (1547) and the other eighteen in Venice (1548). Rejecting the chivalric octave for the unrhymed hendecasyllable (which meant to imitate classical hexameter), Trissino narrates the events in the reconquest of the Italian peninsula on the part of Justinian's Byzantines and his general, Belisarius, against the Ostrogoths (A.D. 535–539), with the intention of restoring the classical model of Homer according to norms derived from Aristotle's *Poetics*. The poem is dedicated to the Emperor Charles V, who is prefigured in the poem by a Justinian of Dantesque wisdom and whom an old and infirm Trissino pursued in vain throughout Germany in order to render personal homage to him. Frustrated in his ambition and exhausted by his efforts, Trissino died immediately following his return to Rome in 1550. His failed poetic endeavor (opposed by his contemporaries for its pedantic, descriptive, and prosaic Homerism) was criticized by, among others, Torquato Tasso, who nevertheless kept the "errors" of his predecessor in mind

when fashioning his own way to the Christian heroic poem in *Gerusalemme liberata* (Jerusalem delivered; 1581).

See also **Aristotle and Cinquecento Poetics; Italian Literature and Language.**

BIBLIOGRAPHY

Primary Works

Trissino, Gian Giorgio. *La poetica.* Vol. 1, *Trattati di poetica e retorica del Cinquecento.* Edited by Bernard Weinberg. Bari, Italy, 1970.

Trissino, Gian Giorgio. *Rime.* Edited by Amedeo Quondam. Vicenza, Italy, 1981.

Trissino, Gian Giorgio. *Scritti linguistici.* Edited by Alberto Castelvecchi. Rome, 1986.

Trissino, Gian Giorgio. *La Sofonisba.* In *La tragedia classica dalle Origini al Maffei.* Edited by Giammaria Gasparini. 2d ed. Turin, Italy, 1976.

Trissino, Gian Giorgio. *Tutte le opere . . . non più raccolte.* Edited by Scipione Maffei. 2 vols. Verona, Italy, 1729.

Secondary Works

Atti del convegno di studi su G. G. Trissino. Vicenza, Italy, 1980.

Zatti, Sergio. "L'imperialismo epico del Trissino." In *L'ombra del Tasso.* Milan, 1996. See chapter 3, pages 59–110.

SERGIO ZATTI

TRITHEMIUS, JOHANN (1462–1516), German Benedictine theologian, humanist; also known as Johannes Heidenberg. Adopting his Latin name from his birthplace of Trittenheim on the Mosel River, Johann Trithemius completed his education at Heidelberg, where he joined a humanist circle that included Conrad Celtis and Johann Reuchlin. After assuming the abbacy of St. Martin at Sponheim in 1482, he transformed the obscure cloister under his charge into a renowned seat of Christian learning with a library of over two thousand volumes. In 1505 a dispute with his monks prompted his move to Saint Jacob at Würzburg, where he was abbot from 1506 to 1516. Among his patrons was Emperor Maximilian I, to whom he personally presented several writings.

Trithemius's scholarly output is divisible into six main categories: monastic instruction, mystical theology, ecclesiastical history, Christian humanism, demonology, and magic. In his monastic role Trithemius penned numerous homilies and sermons advocating learned piety, and in his *De laude scriptorum* (In praise of scribes; 1492) he rationalized keeping the scriptorium busy even as the art of printing was rapidly making hand-copying anachronistic. In his mystical role, influenced by Nicholas of Cusa among others, Trithemius theorized about the stages of spiritual ascent. In his historiographical role he composed a number of chronicles, catalogs, and biographies, in the course of which, out of an eagerness to forge links between contemporary Germans and the ancient Trojans and Druids, he did not demur at fabricating primary sources. In his humanist role—in truth, better realized in theory than practice—Trithemius advocated the union of eloquence with knowledge, in the furtherance of which he encouraged expertise in the language triad of Latin, Greek, and Hebrew. In his demonological role Trithemius composed several treatises, which, although placing greater emphasis on exorcism than on the incrimination of alleged sorcerers, helped justify the witch persecutions.

Finally, in his most controversial role, Trithemius, his demonological warnings aside, argued for the compatibility of Christian theology with magic. In his *De septem secundeis* (Concerning the seven secondary intelligences; 1508), setting forth a vision of historical cycles corresponding to successive reigns by planetary intelligences, Trithemius established an astrological backdrop for his occult theory. Specializing in the art of cryptography, first explicated in his *Stenographia* (published 1606), which expressly invoked angelic assistance in the transmission of secret messages, and then in his angel-free *Polygraphia* (published 1518), Trithemius furnished his cryptic applications with theoretical buttressing derived from ancient hermetic, Pythagorean, and kabbalistic principles. In this way he effectively transformed his mystical theology into magical theology.

Having modeled himself on his German predecessor Albertus Magnus (c. 1200–1280), Trithemius claimed among his own more notable disciples Heinrich Agrippa of Nettesheim, who dedicated the first edition of his *De occulta philosophia* (On occult philosophy; 1510) to the abbot. To the detriment of his posthumous reputation, Trithemius fell subject to the same kinds of attacks he leveled against wicked sorcerers in his demonological writings. While expressly distinguishing his arcane methods from what he deemed to be the disreputable ones of his younger contemporary Faust, Trithemius ironically accrued a magical legend of his own that eventually merged with the Faust legend.

BIBLIOGRAPHY

Arnold, Klaus. *Johannes Trithemius (1462–1516)*. 2d ed. Würzburg, Germany, 1991.

Brann, Noel L. *The Abbot Trithemius (1462–1516): The Renaissance of Monastic Humanism*. Leiden, Netherlands, 1981.

Brann, Noel L. *Trithemius and Magical Theology: A Chapter in the Controversy over Occult Studies in Early Modern Europe*. Albany, N.Y., 1999.

                                        NOEL L. BRANN

TUDOR DYNASTY. Five members of the Tudor family ruled England, Wales, and Ireland between 1485 and 1603: Henry VII, Henry VIII, Edward VI, Mary I (or Mary Tudor), and Elizabeth I. This was a remarkable achievement for a period in which dynastic politics was driven by the need for a legitimate male heir, and diplomatic relationships with other kingdoms depended, to some degree, on successful marriage ties with other royal families. Henry VII became king during a period of civil conflict and consolidated his position. His son and grandchildren managed to survive rebellions, counterclaims to the throne, and the religious upheaval of the Reformation in Europe. In some ways, the long Tudor century was unusual. The ideal monarch in the sixteenth century was adult and male: between 1547 and 1603—nearly half of the Tudors' 118 years on the throne—England, Wales, and Ireland were governed by a boy and two women.

Henry VII (1457–1509; ruled 1485–1509).

The Tudors claimed Welsh descent through the grandfather of Henry VII, Owen Tudor. From the very beginning, Henry VII was keen to cultivate a sense of history and dynasty. The Welsh poet Dafydd Llwyd maintained that Henry Tudor and his brother Jasper were "of the stock of Cadwalader," the ancient Welsh king, "the bright ray." Other authors wrote less independently. Polydore Vergil and Bernard André were encouraged by the crown to write histories of the kingdom and lives of the king that reflected the belief that Henry was the true heir of the ancient British kings. Royal propagandists explained that Tudor victory against Richard III at the battle of Bosworth (1485) had been foretold in an angelic visit to Cadwalader.

The reality was less inspiring. Henry VII had to work hard to maintain and consolidate his position after 1485. Henry was the son of Edmund Tudor and Margaret Beaufort, the great-granddaughter of John of Gaunt, duke of Lancaster and son of Edward III. So when King Richard III's subjects rose up against him after 1483, in a rebellion led by Henry Stafford, duke of Buckingham, Henry Tudor became the senior candidate with a Lancastrian claim to the throne. Henry was in exile in Brittany in 1485 but returned to England at the beginning of August and defeated Richard III at Bosworth.

This military victory was not the end of the matter. His marriage in January 1486 to Elizabeth of York, the daughter of Edward IV, was crucial. It was also important for Henry to legitimize his claim through parliament, and this is what the Lords and Commons

Tudor Dynasty

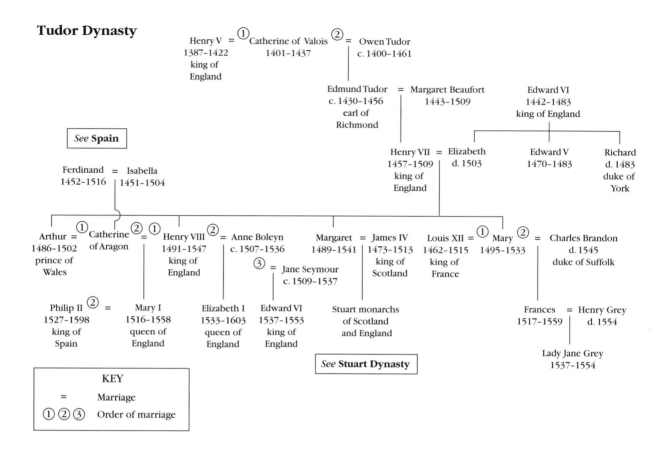

Henry V = ① Catherine of Valois ② = Owen Tudor
1387–1422   1401–1437   c. 1400–1461
king of
England

Edmund Tudor = Margaret Beaufort   Edward VI
c. 1430–1456   1443–1509   1442–1483
earl of   king of England
Richmond

See Spain

Henry VII = Elizabeth   Edward V   Richard
1457–1509   d. 1503   1470–1483   d. 1483
king of   duke of
England   York

Ferdinand = Isabella
1452–1516 1451–1504

Arthur = ① Catherine ② ① Henry VIII ② = Anne Boleyn   Margaret = James IV   Louis XII = ① Mary ② = Charles Brandon
1486–1502   of Aragon   1491–1547   c. 1507–1536   1489–1541 1473–1513   1462–1515 1495–1533   d. 1545
prince of   king of   ③   king of   king of   duke of Suffolk
Wales   England   = Jane Seymour   Scotland   France
  c. 1509–1537

Philip II ② =   Mary I   Elizabeth I   Edward VI   Stuart monarchs   Frances = Henry Grey
1527–1598   1516–1558   1533–1603   1537–1553   of Scotland   1517–1559 d. 1554
king of   queen of   queen of   king of   and England
Spain   England   England   England   Lady Jane Grey
  See Stuart Dynasty   1537–1554

KEY
= Marriage
① ② ③ Order of marriage

did in 1485 when they declared that the powers of the English crown rested in "the most royal person of our now sovereign Lord King Harry VII" and, crucially, "in the heirs of his body lawfully come."

One of the ironies of the first Tudor reign is that although Henry and Elizabeth produced male heirs in 1486 (Arthur, who died in 1502) and in 1491 (Henry, later Henry VIII) the new dynasty still faced external challenges. The parliamentary act confirming Richard III's title was repealed in 1485 and Pope Innocent VIII (reigned 1484–1492) confirmed the union between Henry and Elizabeth. Nevertheless, Henry VII faced a serious revolt in 1487 when Lambert Simnel posed as Edward Plantagenet, earl of Warwick, the imprisoned nephew of Edward IV. Similarly, Perkin Warbeck impersonated Edward IV's younger son, Richard Plantagenet, before he was captured in 1497 and hanged in 1499. The exiled Yorkist heir, Edmund de la Pole, earl of Suffolk, was finally handed over to Henry VII by Archduke Philip of Austria (King Philip I of Castile, brother-in-law of Catherine of Aragon and father of the emperor Charles V), imprisoned in the Tower of London, and executed by Henry VIII in 1513.

Henry VIII (1491–1547; ruled 1509–1547).

Henry VII's younger son and surviving heir, Henry,

had two sisters, Margaret (1489–1541) and Mary (1496–1553), both of whom helped to promote England's relationship with its neighbors. Margaret married James IV of Scotland in August 1503 and, in effect, secured the Anglo-Scottish peace negotiated in 1502. Similarly, Mary Tudor's marriage to Louis XII of France in 1514 sealed an Anglo-French treaty engineered by Cardinal Thomas Wolsey. When Henry VII died in 1509, he was succeeded by his son Henry.

Henry VIII's reign was the most complex and dynastically driven of the Tudor century. He married six wives: Catherine of Aragon (1509), the mother of Mary I; Anne Boleyn (1533), the mother of Elizabeth I; Jane Seymour (1536), the mother of Edward VI; Anne of Cleves (1540); Catherine Howard (1540); and Catherine Parr (1543). During his marriage to Catherine of Aragon, Henry fathered an illegitimate son, Henry Fitzroy, born around 1519 and created duke of Richmond and Somerset in 1525; Fitzroy died in 1536. Henry VIII may also have had a son by Mary Boleyn, the sister of Anne, but the king desperately wanted a legitimate male heir.

Part of the problem for Henry was Catherine of Aragon's apparent inability to produce an heir, but the difficulties of the king's relationship with Catherine were complicated by Henry's complex psychological reaction to the failure of their union and, from the early 1530s, his determination to marry Anne Boleyn. In 1501 Catherine of Aragon had married Henry VII's eldest son Arthur, but he died less than a year later. In order to fulfill England's treaty obligations with Spain, Henry VIII married his brother's widow on his accession to the throne in 1509. Four of Catherine's children died soon after birth. This convinced Henry of the significance of a biblical text from Leviticus (20:21): "If a man shall take his brother's wife, it is an impurity. He hath uncovered his brother's nakedness; they shall be childless." The fact that there was a contrary text (Deuteronomy 25:5) made little difference to Henry but it did complicate the contemporary debate. The king became convinced that his marriage to Catherine was forbidden by divine and natural law, but Pope Clement VII (reigned 1523–1534) refused to overrule the bull of Pope Julius II (reigned 1503–1513) confirming Henry's and Catherine's union.

The effort that went into securing the end of Henry's first marriage—a coordinated attempt by researchers to prove that the English king was an emperor over whom the pope had no jurisdiction—and the king's need to have a male heir began a pattern of marriage and separation (by divorce or execution), which lasted until Henry's union with Catherine Parr in 1543. An important part of this pattern was parliamentary legislation. Henry married Anne Boleyn in 1533, and his first Act of Succession (1534) annulled the marriage to Catherine of Aragon and disinherited their daughter Mary. The act declared that Henry's and Anne's children "shall be your lawful children and be inheritable and inherit."

Anne Boleyn gave birth to Elizabeth 1533, but in 1536 her fortunes changed. After she miscarried in January 1536, Henry declared that the marriage was damned; Anne's position was not helped by the fact that she was a prominent religious reformer, and conservative Catholics were keen to use an opportunity to neutralize her influence at court. Their candidate for Henry's hand was Jane Seymour. Once again, a parliamentary statute confirmed the new queen's position. The second Act of Succession (1536) repealed the first (1534) and declared that the king's marriage to Anne Boleyn "shall be taken, reputed, deemed, and adjudged to be of no force, strength, virtue, nor effect." Both Mary and Elizabeth were declared illegitimate. The succession would pass to Henry's heirs by Jane Seymour, and Jane did indeed give birth to a son, Edward, in October 1537.

Jane Seymour died following childbirth. Henry VIII married again in 1540 in a match that was, for the king, unhappy and mildly repulsive. Henry had commissioned a portrait of Anne of Cleves and, in the brush of Hans Holbein, she looked attractive; in the flesh, he found her profoundly unappealing. There was a political dimension to the Cleves marriage—England's developing relationship with the Protestant German League of Schmalkalden—but Henry married Anne under protest. The union contributed to the political downfall of its architect, Henry's chief minister Thomas Cromwell; immediately after Cromwell's execution in July 1540 the king divorced Anne and married Catherine Howard, a renowned court beauty.

Evidence of Catherine Howard's multiple adulteries was presented to her husband at the beginning of 1542 and she was beheaded that February. Henry married his sixth and final wife, Catherine Parr, in July 1543, but Catherine—like Anne of Cleves and Catherine Howard—did not provide children for the king and his realm. The year 1537 had been the crucial one: with the birth of Edward, his last legitimate child, the dynastic context of the rest of the Tudor century had been established. Henry had three heirs, two of them girls, and some female relatives through his sister Mary and her marriage in 1515 (following the death of Louis XII) to Charles Brandon, duke of Suffolk. One dynastic marriage that failed to move beyond betrothal was union between Edward Tudor and Mary Stuart, queen of Scots (1542–1587), the granddaughter of Margaret Tudor (Henry VIII's sister): the Scots rejected the match, which led to Anglo-Scottish war and Mary's removal to France.

Henry VIII's third Act of Succession (1544) set the pattern of royal succession for the whole of the later Tudor period, 1547–1603, although it was clearly imagined that Edward, Mary, or Elizabeth would have children of their own. The statute established that if both Henry VIII and Edward Tudor died "without heir of either of their bodies lawfully begotten" the crown would pass to Mary and then to her lawful heir or, if Mary was childless, Henry's second daughter Elizabeth. Henry VIII's will of December 1546 confirmed this arrangement and added that if Elizabeth died without a legitimate heir the crown would pass to Frances Brandon, duchess of Suffolk, and her heir, or, again, if Frances died without a legitimate child, to her sister Eleanor.

Edward VI (1537–1553; ruled 1547–1553).

Henry VIII died in January 1547. He was succeeded by his son Edward VI who, according to the provisions of his father's will, would be supported by a regency council of sixteen until his eighteenth birthday. But almost immediately after Henry's death, Edward's uncle, Edward Seymour, earl of Hertford (the brother of Jane Seymour, and later duke of Somerset) maneuvered himself into the position of protector of the realm. Seymour's power collapsed in 1549 in a bloodless coup coordinated by his colleagues in the council. The year 1549 demonstrated the fragility of personal monarchy: control of the physical person of the monarch was crucial to political success and this was a problem many of Edward's senior subjects were very conscious of—male minority and female monarchy were potentially unstable in a system designed for adult men.

By the spring and early summer of 1553, it was becoming increasingly clear to Edward's councillors that the king was ill and that the succession, as it stood, would fall to his sister. Because Mary's Catholicism was considered unacceptable—Edward and most of his senior councillors were strongly Protestant—an attempt was made to update the provisions set down by Henry VIII. One surviving draft of this new plan was written by Edward himself, but it seems clear that the new royal will was engineered by John Dudley, duke of Northumberland. The evidence does present some problems. The main text of the will was copied in 1611 apparently from the original. This copy has Edward's name at the top of it, although, like his father, the king had a "dry stamp" of his signature which left an impression on paper and could be filled in with ink. The document was signed by Edward's senior subjects and dated 21 June 1553, just under a fortnight before the king's death on 6 July. The succession would pass to Jane Grey, the daughter of Frances, duchess of Suffolk, bypassing and bastardizing Edward's sisters Mary and Elizabeth.

Jane Grey and Mary.

Jane Grey (1537–1554; ruled 6–19 July 1553) was the best option Edward's Protestant councillors could find: she had, after all, been mentioned in Henry VIII's third Act of Succession (1544) and his will (1546), and had married into the Dudley family in May 1553—her husband was Guildford, the son of John Dudley, duke of Northumberland. Jane lasted long enough to sign some official documents as "Jane the Queen" but Dudley's experiment ultimately failed: Mary Tudor (1516–1558; ruled 1553–1558), generally recognized as the legitimate heir to her brother, gathered military forces in East Anglia, marched on London, and seized power. Edward VI's most senior councillors were imprisoned for treason. John Dudley, Jane Grey, and her father, Henry Grey, duke of Suffolk, were beheaded in 1554.

Mary I was declared legitimate by her first parliament but the future of the crown was an issue even

by November 1553. Mary realized that the rival claimants to the English succession were Mary Stuart, queen of Scots, Frances Brandon, duchess of Suffolk, and Elizabeth Tudor. Mary's preferred option was Margaret, the wife of Matthew Stewart, earl of Lennox, and, through her mother, a granddaughter of Henry VII. Mary seems to have hoped that the form of the succession would be established in the treaty of her marriage to Philip, king of Naples (ruled from 1554; king of Spain, ruled 1556–1598).

During the reign of Edward VI, Bishop Hugh Latimer had preached about the potential danger to England of foreign marriages for Mary and Elizabeth. Mary married Philip in July 1554 in a match that cemented relations with Spain, England's traditional ally in Europe, but left the queen open to charges of foreign influence at her court. Philip played a small part in the government of the kingdom, but spent most of the reign out of England. Nevertheless, Mary became involved in Spain's war against France and the queen herself failed to produce an heir.

Elizabeth (1533–1603; ruled 1558–1603).

When Mary I died in November 1558, she was succeeded by her sister Elizabeth. Mary had disliked Elizabeth's illegitimacy and Protestantism but there were no serious or practical alternative candidates. One claim to the English crown was, in theory, dangerous: that of Mary Stuart, queen of Scots, the granddaughter of Henry VIII's sister Margaret. During the negotiations at Cateau-Cambrésis in 1559, the French representatives argued that Mary was the rightful heir to the English throne. This claim worried Elizabeth's councillors, but the threat posed by Mary did not become a practical problem for the English until the middle of Elizabeth's first decade as queen.

Elizabeth's subjects expected her to play by the rules of dynastic politics: marry and produce (preferably male) heirs. There were a number of early marriage candidates for the queen. Elizabeth's main suitor was Lord Robert Dudley, but his candidacy was made more difficult by his position as the queen's subject and by questions about his possible complicity in the death of his wife, Amy Robsart (1560). Foreign possibilities were Philip II of Spain (out of a sense of duty to his wife's sister), Eric XIV of Sweden (a monarch of questionable mental stability), and the Scot, James Hamilton, earl of Arran (who was equally unstable). Elizabeth seemed resolutely determined not to marry—in part, perhaps, because of her limited options but mainly because marriage for a female monarch in the sixteenth century meant the effective surrender of political power.

Tudor Dynasty. An allegorical representation by Lucas de Heere (1534–1584) of the family of Henry VIII: Philip II of Spain, the husband of Mary; Mary; Henry VIII; Edward VI; Elizabeth. Painted c. 1570–1575. SUDELY CASTLE, GLOUCESTER-SHIRE, U.K./THE BRIDGEMAN ART LIBRARY

Parliament pressed for the queen's marriage in 1559, and continued to petition throughout her reign.

The future of the succession became the main concern of Elizabeth's subjects. Although other potential matches were mentioned and negotiated—with Archduke Charles of Austria in the 1560s and Francis, duke of Anjou of France in the 1570s—Elizabeth was past thirty years of age even by the end of her first decade, and, biologically and politically, marriage and children were beginning to seem like a vain hope. Parliament encouraged the queen to declare a successor but she refused. So when, in 1562, Elizabeth became seriously ill with smallpox, her realm faced the serious prospect of losing its monarch. This was particularly dangerous at a time when continental Europe was dividing itself in civil and religious conflict.

Mary Stuart, queen of Scots, became an Elizabethan obsession. She had a good claim to the English crown and most contemporaries recognized her position. In addition, she represented the main Catholic families of France and, in the eyes of Elizabethans, she was supported by the pope and England's enemies in Europe. In France she posed no real problem. But after the death in 1560 of her first husband, Francis II of France, she returned to her realm of Scotland and became a more immediate threat. A key dynastic event was Mary's marriage in 1565 to Henry Stewart, Lord Darnley, the grandson of Margaret Tudor by her second marriage to Archibald Douglas, earl of Angus—Mary and Darnley presented a strong and joint dynastic threat to Elizabeth.

The marriage between the queen of Scots and Lord Darnley ended with the murder of Darnley in 1567, and the power of Mary Stuart's claim was severely damaged a year later by her deposition and flight to England. But although Mary was imprisoned by Elizabeth until her execution, she still had the potential to cause trouble for the English regime. The European powers were profoundly interested in Elizabeth's treatment of Mary, and there were rumors of continental conspiracies to free her. The queen of Scots conducted secret marriage negotiations with England's premier peer, Thomas Howard, duke of Norfolk, which led eventually to Howard's execution and call in the parliament of 1572 for a final and fatal solution to the problem of Mary. Elizabeth at last yielded to pressure from her councillors and executed the queen of Scots in 1587.

Elizabeth I was the last Tudor monarch. During her final illness, in February and March 1603, Elizabeth's councillors contacted James VI, king of Scotland, and son of Mary, queen of Scots, and Darnley. Supported by royal councillors and the English nobility, James was recognized as the heir to the English throne and became the kingdom's first Stuart (the English version of Stewart) monarch as James I.

The Tudors in English History. The Tudors ruled England, Wales, and Ireland during a period of important change in western European history. The sixteenth century was marked by war between monarchs on the Continent and by exploration and expansion outside Europe. The Reformation of religion fractured the ecclesiastical monopoly of the Roman Catholic Church, and the Tudor dynasty was responsible for the development of a Church of England separated from Rome, which, during the reign of Edward VI and his successors, became distinctively Protestant.

The Reformations in England, Wales, and Ireland affected the relationship between the Tudor monarchs and their subjects. The pilgrims of grace protested against the dissolution of the monasteries (1536) and some subjects in the south of England rebelled in 1549, reflecting concern over the introduction of a radical Protestantism. In 1569 the northern English earls of Northumberland and Westmorland raised armies against Elizabeth I in an effort to reestablish Catholicism. Although these uprisings were serious—particularly because in the second half of the century the Elizabethan government imagined that Catholics in England and on the Continent were conspiring to overthrow Elizabeth I— the kingdom gradually accepted Protestantism as the national faith.

Constitutional historians of the nineteenth century associated the Tudors with England's transition from a medieval kingdom into a modern state. The king's council was interpreted as the forerunner of the prime minister's cabinet, and two of Henry VIII's most prominent servants, Cardinal Thomas Wolsey and Thomas Cromwell, seemed to exercise prime ministerial power. By the end of the sixteenth century, Parliament appeared more influential than it had been at the beginning, and for some historians this change set the scene for the crisis between Charles I and Parliament in the 1630s and 1640s. Aspects of this interpretation have been revised since the 1950s. Even the late Tudor polity was not a modern bureaucratic state, but a system of government based very much on the person of the monarch and the royal court, in which Parliament wanted to advise and counsel, rather than oppose, the crown.

But it is hard to ignore the fact that political life did change over the century. The concept of political power as something that could be separated from the physical body of the monarch—in the effect, the notion of the state—developed in the second half of the century. Some writers considered the relationship between subject and monarch in radical terms, and by the reign of Elizabeth I there was an important literature on the resistance of authority and even the deposition of kings. It is arguable, too, that the ideologies of Catholicism and Protestantism replaced the traditional pattern of wars between foreign dynasties, and that as a result the Tudor polity must be considered a European kingdom.

See also **England**; **Scotland**; **Stuart Dynasty**; *and biographies of monarchs mentioned in this entry.*

BIBLIOGRAPHY

Primary Works

Elton, G. R., ed. *The Tudor Constitution*. Cambridge, U.K., 1982. This edition includes selections from the parliamentary acts of succession.

Hargrave, Francis, ed. *The Hereditary Right of the Crown of England Asserted*. London, 1713. Prints major documents.

Levine, Mortimer. *Tudor Dynastic Problems, 1460–1571*. London and New York, 1973. Prints documents covering the whole period, introduced by commentaries.

Secondary Works

Alford, Stephen. *The Early Elizabethan Polity: William Cecil and the British Succession Crisis, 1558–1569*. Cambridge, U.K., 1998. Considers the impact of Mary Stuart, queen of Scots's claim to the English crown on Elizabethan politics.

Doran, Susan. *Monarchy and Matrimony: The Courtships of Elizabeth I*. London and New York, 1996.

Guy, John. *Tudor England*. London and New York, 1988. The standard history of the Tudor dynasty.

Jordan, W. K. *Edward VI: The Threshold of Power*. Cambridge, Mass., 1970. Discusses the attempts in 1553 to alter the Tudor succession.

Jordan, W. K. *Edward VI: The Young King*. Cambridge, Mass., 1968.

Loades, David. *Mary Tudor: A Life*. Oxford, 1989.

MacCaffrey, Wallace. *Elizabeth I*. London, 1993.

Scarisbrick, J. J. *Henry VIII*. London, 1968; New Haven, Conn., and London, 1997.

STEPHEN ALFORD

TURKEY. *See* **Ottoman Empire.**

TURNÈBE, ADRIEN (1512–1565), French classicist. The humanist scholar Adrien Turnèbe was born in Les Andelys, Normandy, and died in Paris. Master of Arts in 1532, he became professor at the University of Toulouse, then occupied a chair of Greek and Latin literature at the Collège des Lecteurs Royaux in Paris, switching to the chair for Greek and Latin philosophy in 1561. From 1552 to 1556 he was director for Greek books at the Imprimerie Royale (royal press). He edited, translated, and wrote commentaries on various Greek authors, such as Aeschylus, Aristotle, Plutarch, Sophocles, and Synesius. His Latin editions and commentaries include works by Ausonius, Cicero, Horace, Juvenal, Lucretius, Martial, Persius, Quintilian, and Varro. He was the editor of Hermes Trismegistus, and defended Plato against Aristotle. His son Odet de Turnèbe (1552–1581) wrote a celebrated comedy in French (*Les contens,* 1581). Adrien Turnèbe's reputation as a scholar was widespread in Europe, and he was praised in France by Étienne Pasquier and Michel de Montaigne. His own works include a compendium of emendations and scholia of classical authors, the *Adversaria,* the three parts of which appeared successively in 1564, 1565, and 1580. His commentaries, translations, orations, poems, dedicatory works, and treatises (on topics such as method, heat, and wine) were assembled in his *Opera* in 1600.

BIBLIOGRAPHY

Lewis, John. *Adrien Turnèbe (1512–1565): A Humanist Observed*. Geneva, 1998.

ULLRICH LANGER

TUSCANY. *See* **Florence.**

TYNDALE, WILLIAM (also Hychyns; c. 1491–1536), Bible translator, first English Reformer. Born in Gloucestershire to an affluent farming family, Tyndale took his bachelor's degree in 1512 (Magdalen Hall, Oxford) and his master's degree in 1515, the year of his ordination. Thereafter, he was tutor and chaplain for John Walsh at Little Sodbury. Interested in Lutheran ideas and in translating the Bible into English, Tyndale offered his services to Cuthbert Tunstall (1474–1559), the bishop of London. Rebuffed, he found support among London merchants, but by 1524 left for the safety of northern Europe to translate the Bible.

Perfecting his linguistic skills, Tyndale began translating and publishing the Bible, probably supported by merchants who smuggled into England large numbers of his publications. A Reformer influenced first by Martin Luther (1483–1546), he entered into various debates and wrote at least ten tracts, the most significant being his politically conservative *The Obedience of a Christian Man* (1528) and *A Pathway into the Holy Scripture* (1531). Because of his writings, he was pursued by authorities for ten years until his arrest as a Lutheran heretic in 1535. Tyndale was executed 6 October 1536 in Vilvorde.

In translating the New Testament from the Greek, Tyndale was inspired by Erasmus's Greek edition (1516) and by Luther's German translations. In 1526, he published his first New Testament, later revised for a 1534 translation. Following Luther, some of whose works he was the first to translate into English and incorporate into his own texts, he attacked the ecclesiastical establishment and argued for justification by faith and a self-authenticating, vernacular scripture as the sole source, unmediated, of faith and morality. He may also have been influenced by Huldrych Zwingli (1484–1531) on the nature of the priesthood and sacraments. Once he began translating the Pentateuch, he broke with Luther in suggesting that salvation produced good works and obedience to the law. Tyndale translated the Pentateuch (1530) and Jonah (1531). Evidence indicates that Tyndale's translation of Joshua through 1 Chronicles was incorporated into the 1535 Bible of Miles Coverdale (1488–1568) and into Matthew's Bible (1537), prepared under the pseudonym "Thomas Matthew" by John Rogers (c. 1500–1555).

Tyndale's fusion of faith and law, his debt to Luther, and his sense of covenant remain areas of inquiry, as does his achievement as a translator. Like other Reformers, Tyndale redefined the nature of the church, a redefinition that underscored his confrontation with Thomas More (1478–1535). After the appearance of Tyndale's New Testament, More responded for the English ecclesiastical establishment with his *Dialogue Concerning Heresies* (1529). Tyndale produced *An Answer unto Sir Thomas More's Dialogue* (1531) which More challenged in *Confutation of Tyndale's Answer* (1523–1533).

Tyndale was primarily a linguist and translator, benefiting from new humanistic textual tools without which he could not have done his pioneering work. Although critical of classical writers, he saw in the new learning implications for translating and interpreting the scriptures. In his polemical tracts, he demonstrated a humanist interest in rhetoric and linguistic strategies. Like Erasmus, he stressed morality and humility while condemning clerical ignorance. With his humanist philological approach and his knowledge of Greek and Hebrew (his translation of the Pentateuch was the first Hebrew translated into English), he embraced the humanist textual enterprise. His translations are marked by his extraordinary knowledge of Hebrew, his sense of the Aramaic behind the gospel Greek, and his ability to translate both languages in a direct and colloquial style. Because much of Tyndale's translation was incorporated into the 1611 Authorized (King James) Version, Tyndale had a significant influence on English style and the development of the language.

See also **Bible,** *subentry on* **The English Bible;** **Translation,** *subentry* **Overview.**

BIBLIOGRAPHY

Primary Works

An Answer to Sir Thomas More's Dialogue: *The Supper of the Lord after the True Meaning of John 6 and 1 Cor. 9; And Wm. Tracy's* Testament *Expounded.* Edited by Henry Walter. New York, 1968.

Doctrinal Treatises and Introductions to Different Portions of the Holy Scriptures. Edited by Henry Walter. New York, 1968.

Expositions and Notes on Sundry Portions of the Holy Scriptures, together with The Practice of the Prelates. Edited by Henry Walter. New York, 1968.

Tyndale's New Testament. Edited by David Daniell. New Haven, Conn., 1989.

Tyndale's Old Testament. Edited by David Daniell. New Haven, Conn., 1992.

Secondary Works

Daniell, David. *William Tyndale: A Biography.* New Haven, Conn., 1994.

Day, John T., Eric Lund, and Anne M. O'Donnell, eds. *Word, Church, and State: Tyndale Quincentenary Essays.* Washington, D.C., 1998.

Dick, John A. R., and Anne Richardson, eds. *William Tyndale and the Law.* Kirksville, Mo., 1994

RUDOLPH P. ALMASY

TYPOGRAPHY. The essentials of printing did not change from the time of Johann Gutenberg's invention until the arrival of radical technical improvements toward the end of the eighteenth century. In the era of the handpress, every printer faced the same problem as Gutenberg of how to apply a limited number of characters in infinitely various combinations to a sheet of paper to give a visible impression of the text those characters represented. Short of the laborious and short-lived method of cut-ting the words onto wooden blocks for transfer to paper, every printer adopted Gutenberg's solution of inked movable metal types, cast in quantity in a type mold and impressed onto paper by a hand-powered press. The Gutenberg Bible, published at Mainz in 1455, aimed to reproduce the appearance of contemporary German manuscript Bibles. Nearly all early printed books took on forms inherited from the scribal culture from which they sprang and with which they coexisted for many decades, until the economic advantages of print for most purposes replaced handwriting as the main medium of transmission of recorded information. These forms responded to national, social, and functional traditions in book production as they had become established in the later Middle Ages.

The look of a printed book was determined by its layout and type. Large books, with leaves consisting of a sheet of paper folded just once in folio format, tended to be reserved for the library shelf, church lectern, or scholar's desk. Quarto books, with the sheet folded twice, or octavo books, with the sheet folded three times, were more portable. Such categories as speeches delivered at the papal court, prayer books, and popular vernacular literature were almost invariably printed in these and smaller formats. Certain types of books, such as the Bible or the breviary, were printed in both large and small formats. The former was designed for church or monastic reading. The small format was intended for individual use, providing readers with portable volumes. Scholarly or professional books in the fifteenth century were generally printed in folio or large quartos. Even very brief legal texts of a few leaves were printed in folio and often bound with other similar tracts.

Tradition also prescribed how the printed text was placed on the page. The conservative professions of law and theology, and to some extent of medicine and philosophy, tended to favor conservative-looking books, with two columns of gothic type on a folio page. Academic books such as these were soon equipped with indexes, printed foliation (numbered pages), rubrics in larger type, headlines giving guidance to the content, and commentary, often disposed around an island of text in the middle of the page in accordance with manuscript layouts. Certain texts or types of text were for decades linked to a particular style of typeface: the Latin Bible was printed a hundred times in the fifteenth century but only once in roman type, and that misjudgment contributed to putting its printers out of business. Books of hours came from the press in new editions almost

ue maria
gr̄a plena
dominus
tecū bene
dicta tu in mulierib'
et benedictus fruct'
uentris tui : ihesus
christus amen.

Gloria laudis resonet in ore
omniū Patri genitoq̄ʒ proli
spiritui sancto pariter Resul
tet laude perhenni Labori
bus dei vendunt nobis om
nia bona. laus:honor:virtus
potétia: ᷔ gratiaʒ actio tibi
christe. Amen.

Uiue deū sic ᷔ vi͞es per secula cun̄
cta. Prouidet ᷔ tribuit deus omnia
nobis. Proficit absque deo null'in
orbe labor. Illa placet tell' in qua
res parua beatū. Øse facit ᷔ tenues
luxuriantur opes.

Si fortuna volet fies de rhetore consul.
Si volet hec eadem fies de cõsule rhetor.
Quicquid amor iussit nõ est cõtédere tutū
Regnat et in dominos ius habet ille suos
Uita data é vréda data é sine fenere nobis
Mutua: nec certa persoluenda die.

Usus ᷔ ars docuit quod sapit omnis homo
Ars animos frangit ᷔ firmas dirumit vrbes
Arte cadunt turres arte leuatur onus
Artibus ingenijs quesita est gloria multis
Principijs obsta sero medicina paratur
Cum mala per longas conualuere moras
Sed propera nec te venturas differ in horas
Qui non est hodie cras minus aptus erit.

Non bene pro toto libertas venditur auro
Hoc celeste bonum preterit orbis opes
Precunctis animi est bonis veneranda libertas
Seruitus semper amettis quoque despicienda
Summa petit liuor perflant altiffima venti
Summa petunt dextra fulmina missa iouis
In loca nonnunqu am siccis arentia glebis
De prope currenti flumine man at aqua

Quisquis ades scriptis qui mentem forsitan istis
Ut noscas adhibes protinus istud opus
Nosce: augustensis ratdolt germanus Erhardus
Litterulas istos ordine quasqʒ facit
Ipse quibus veneta libros impressit in vrbe
Multos ᷔ plures nunc premit atqʒ premet
Quiqʒ etiam varijs celestia signa figuris
Aurea qui primus nunc monumenta premit
Quin etiam manibus proprijs vbicunqʒ figuras
Est opus:incidens dedalus alter erit

Nobis benedicat qui ī trinitate viuit
ᷔ regnat Amen: Hono: soli deo est tribuendu
Aue regina celo ᷔ mater regis angelo
rum o maria flos virginum velut rosa
vel ilium o maria : Tua est potentia tu
regnuʒ domine tu es super omnʒ gen
tes da pacem domine in dieb' nostris
mirabilis deus in sanctis suis Et glori
osus in maiestate sua orb panthon kyr

Quod prope face diem tibi iam conuina futurus
forsitan ignoras atque ne dubites
Ergo para cenam non qualem stoicus ambit
Sed lautam sane more cirenaico
Namque duas mecum florente etate puellas
Adducam quarum balsama cunnus olet
Pernula sola domi sedeat quam nuper habebas
Si nondum cunnus vepribus horruerit
Sunt qui simulent ᷔ auari crimen amici
O dicant facto ramor ut ille cadat Hec Philelphus

Nunc adeas mira quicunqʒ nomina queris
Arte uel ex animo poesia fuisse suo
Seruet ille tibi:nobis iure sorores
Incolumen seruet usqʒ regare licet

Est homini uirtus fuluo preciosior auro: ænæas
Ingenium quondam fuerat preciosius auro.
Miramurqʒ magis quos munera mentis adornãt:
Quam qui corporeis emicuere bonis.
Si qua uirtute nites ne despice quenquam
Ex alia quadam forsitan ipse nitet

Nemo suç laudis nimium lętetur honore
Ne uilis factus post sua fata gemat.
Nemo nimis cupide sibi res desiderat ullas
Ne dum plus cupiat perdat ᷔ id quod habet.
Ne ue cito uerbis cuiusquam credito blandis
Sed si sint fidei respice quid moneant
Qui bene proloquitur coram sed postea praue
Hic erit inusus bina qʒ ora gerat

Pax plenam uirtutis opus pax summa laborum
pax belli exacti præcium est præciumque penclî
Sidera pace uigent confistunt terrea pace
Nil placitum sine pace deo non munus ad aram
Fortuna arbitris tempus dispensat ubi
Illa rapit iuuenes illa ferit senes

κΛιω Τευτέρτη τέ θαλεια τέ μελπομενη τέ
Πεϕμχοϕη τεϕατω τε πολυμνεια τούρανιυ
τε καλλιόπη θέΔη προφέρεϛτη εϛίναπα
σαωϕ ιϵσυσ Χρισουά μαρια τέλοσ.

Indicis characteʒ diuersaʒ mane
rierū impressioni parararū: Finis.

Erhardi Ratdolt Augustensis viri
solertissimi:preclaro ingenio ᷔ miri
fica arte:qua olim Venetijs excelluit
celebratissimus. In imperiali nunc
vrbe Auguste vindelicoʒ laudatiñi
me impressioni dedit. Annoqʒ salu
tis.M.CCCC.LXXXVI.Kalē.
Aprilis Sidere felici compleuit.

Typography. Type specimen sheet printed in April 1486 by Erhard Ratdolt, a printer at Augsburg, Germany. Four styles of typefaces are included: a decorated initial, rotunda (in ten sizes in the left column and the top half of the right), roman (three sizes in the middle of the right column), and Greek. At the bottom of the right column, the title ("Indicis character[um] diuersar[um]," sample of various typefaces) and colophon (beginning "Erhardi Ratdolt Augustensis viri") are printed in rotunda.

every week from the 1490s onward, but not until 1525 did any printer dare to issue one in roman type.

These conservative traditions were not the only ones at work in the fifteenth century. Had printing arrived fifty years earlier, it would have taken longer to liberate itself from manuscript models. The beginning of the fifteenth century saw the first stirrings of the humanist reform of script. The humanists sought to recover the classical virtues of clarity and purity. The Florentines Poggio Bracciolini (1380–1459) and Niccolò de' Niccoli (c. 1364–1437) were central to the rapid development of humanist handwriting, basing their hands on late Carolingian minuscule scripts (rather than ancient Roman lettering, which was known to them in inscriptions but lacked lowercase letters). The result was a round, upright, formal book hand characterized by spaciousness and the avoidance of abbreviation and of fusion of letters. In the first half of the fifteenth century, this *littera antiqua* script became almost de rigueur, especially in the hands of professional scribes, for the sort of works in which the humanists took an interest, preeminently the Latin texts of classical and patristic antiquity, and increasingly of their own writings. The gothic handwriting to which they opposed the *antiqua* was spurned as *littera moderna*.

The Germans Konrad Sweynheym and Arnold Pannartz, who introduced printing to Italy in about 1464, adapted themselves to this local taste. Their press at Subiaco and then at Rome printed Latin works of classical and patristic authors in a version of humanistic script, as well as quotations of Greek in a greek type, another innovation in printing. The style of font that we now call roman, a direct descendant of Poggio's formal *antiqua* book hand, was perfected at Venice in 1469–1470 by another German, Wendelin of Speyer, and by the Frenchman Nicolas Jenson. By 1470 humanist handwriting was fixed in roman type of a beauty and regularity that few scribes could match. Jenson's type became a point of comparison and departure for all the great roman type cutters of the next century, notably Francesco Griffo, who cut all the types for Aldo Manuzio at the end of the century, and Claude Garamond, who supplied designs for Paris printers from the late 1520s onward.

A development of great importance for the sixteenth century took place in the last year of the fifteenth. Alongside the upright *antiqua* that he had devised with Poggio, Niccoli had adopted a cursive form of humanist handwriting, essentially a more rapid, sloping version of the same script. This hand, as practiced and transmitted by such influential scribes as the Roman Pomponio Leto and the Paduan Bartolomeo Sanvito, was eventually fixed in type by Griffo. The italic font first appeared in a woodcut adorning a book that Manuzio published in 1500, the *Letters* of St. Catherine of Siena. Thereafter the type came to be as widely used as roman, and often in combination with it, for most of the succeeding century, in Griffo's style or in the more refined model introduced at Rome by the writing master Ludovico degli Arrighi in the 1520s.

The adoption of roman and italic as the vehicles of scholarly works—and many other sorts of books—was assured in the opening decades of the sixteenth century, not least by the widely admired example of Manuzio's scholarly publications. But this outcome was by no means certain in the early period. Faltering beginnings in roman type, for classical and humanist texts, were made by the first printers of France and Spain. Both countries soon reverted to the gothic types more familiar to their citizens and to the German printers who introduced printing there. Germany itself, though it can claim one of the earliest roman types, became ever more wedded to the varieties of gothic type known as Schwabacher and (somewhat later, its predominance dating from the second half of the sixteenth century) Fraktur. The latter was the German national script for four hundred years until the National Socialists decided it was un-German on 3 January 1941. And Jenson himself, as he retreated from the overproduced classics to the safer fields of law and liturgy, printed many more books in the graceful rounded gothic types of Venice (called now *rotunda*, but known then all over Europe as *litterae veneticae*) than in his better-known romans. The Dutch showed a special attachment to spiky gothic *textura* types, and England too was firm in its preference for this type, which they called black letter. Nearly all printing in the vernacular was carried out in these national gothic styles, except in Italy, where popular literature appeared indifferently in gothic or roman types for a public by now habituated to the humanist *antiqua*. Italian translations of the Bible almost always appeared in roman type from the very first in 1471, but Luther's Bible in German, and German Protestant literature as a whole, produced in vast quantities during the Reformation, was just as exclusively set in gothic. No work in English was printed in roman types until the 1550s.

The decisive change was that Italian taste came to prevail among the printers of Paris in the first three decades of the sixteenth century. The new learning was initially carried in books of such scholar printers as Josse Bade and Henri Estienne. Henri's successors, Simon de Colines and his son Robert Estienne, along with the type designer Garamond and the book decorator Geofroy Tory, together evolved a distinctively French style of Renaissance book in the 1520s. Garamond took over and developed the romans, italics, and greeks as cut by Griffo for the Aldine press. Garamond's greeks became famous as the *grecs du roi,* which set the style of Greek typography for many subsequent generations. Colines and the Estiennes, as well as many Lyonnese printers, copied the small format in which the Aldine classics had appeared. By mid-century even scholarly works often appeared as octavos in roman and italic types. More imposing folio volumes were graced with elaborate woodcut borders on the title page, framing an ever more designed title, usually in a considerable variety of types.

The Renaissance style of bookmaking was by now widespread throughout Europe, with Johann Froben at Basel (Erasmus's printer of choice) in the early decades of the sixteenth century and Christophe Plantin at Antwerp in its second half just as accomplished as the Paris printers in the production of high-quality works of scholarship for an international public. For national literatures, national types continued to be used until well into the seventeenth century and beyond. Yet even the most conservative professions yielded their traditional forms of book before the tide of the modern. Legal texts continued to be printed in gothic types till 1550 or so but not thereafter; it was a sign of the times that the great 1550–1552 Latin Aristotle with Averroes's commentary published in eleven volumes by the Giunti Press at Venice was set in roman and italic, not the *rotunda* type, which was traditionally used for works of philosophy and for commentaries. The educated, Latin-reading public of Europe was henceforth served books in a uniform modern style, set in roman, italic, and greek types, that endured essentially unchanged for the next two hundred years.

See also **Calligraphy; Printing and Publishing.**

BIBLIOGRAPHY

Bühler, Curt F. *The Fifteenth-Century Book: The Scribes, the Printers, the Decorators.* Philadelphia, 1960.

Goldschmidt, Ernst Philip. *The Printed Book of the Renaissance: Three Lectures on Type, Illustration, Ornament.* Cambridge, U.K., 1950.

Johnson, A. F. "The Sixteenth Century." In *A History of the Printed Book.* Edited by Lawrence Counselman Wroth. New York, 1938. Pages 121–156.

Steinberg, S. H. *Five Hundred Years of Printing.* New ed. Revised by John Trevitt. London, 1996.

MARTIN DAVIES

TYRANNICIDE. Theories of tyrannicide became the subject of much discussion during the Renaissance as people confronted the problem of what to do when a ruler went morally astray. The word tyrant came from the sixth-century B.C.E. Greek term for usurper (*tyrannos*), though in time it also included legitimate rulers who oppressed their people. Thereafter, tyrants by usurpation and by oppression remained a fundamental distinction in all discussions of tyrannicide. Assassination became a common political weapon in the Renaissance, though not always as a case of tyrannicide. Victims included Giuliano de' Medici (d. 1478), William the Silent (1533–1584), Gaspard II de Coligny (1519–1572), Francis, second duke of Guise (1519–1563), and his sons Henry I, third duke of Guise (1550–1588), and Louis, second cardinal of Guise (1555–1588), Henry III (1551–1589) and Henry IV of France (1553–1610), George Villiers, duke of Buckingman (1592–1628), and Albrecht von Wallenstein (1583–1634).

Judeo-Christian and Classical Traditions. Judeo-Christian and classical commentary on the legitimacy of tyrannicide deeply informed Renaissance debates on the subject. Numerous exceptions to the sixth commandment prohibition of murder can be found in Hebrew Scripture. Examples include Ehud's slaying of Eglon, king of Moab, who had enslaved the Israelites (Judges 3), Judith's killing of Holofernes (Apocrypha), and Jehu's murder of the tyrant Jehoram, king of Israel (2 Kings 11). David's refusal to lay his hands on Saul because he was God's anointed served as exemplar for obedience to a tyrant, however. Overall, Jewish tradition justified tyrannicide in cases of both usurpation and oppression if the individual believed that he or she had a special mission from God.

Early Christian writers, such as St. Paul and Tertullian, held much more firmly to the sixth commandment, arguing that resisting a legitimate ruler was the equivalent of opposing God's will. They instead exhorted the faithful to emulate Christ by enduring tyranny patiently, even to the point of martyrdom, since vengeance belonged to God alone. Nevertheless, for church fathers such as St. Augustine, exceptions against a blanket prohibition of tyrannicide could be made if the individual again had a mission directly from God or if public magistrates carried out the act. The source of this second line of reasoning sprang from classical pagan writers who, in general, approved of tyrannicide. Plato considered the tyrant to be an enemy of virtue, a philosopher-king corrupted by base desires and naked self-interest. Aristotle defined tyranny as an unnatural perversion of monarchy wherein the ruler only acts out of egoism, not the public good. In his seminal work *Politics* he drew out additional distinctions: unlike monarchy, tyranny sought to dominate citizens not protect them, to steal rather than safeguard their wealth, to foment factionalism rather than strengthen unity, to pursue war rather than peace, and to encourage vice rather than virtue. In such cases, citizens could rightfully resist a tyrant, since evil rule was anathema to freedom that was, in turn, the very lifeblood of the *polis*. This emphasis on secular political criteria to justify tyrannicide resurfaced in Roman writings, such as Livy's commentary on the murder of the Gracchi, the praise heaped by Cicero on Julius Caesar's assassins, and Seneca's aphorism that no sacrifice pleased the gods more than the blood of a tyrant. Even the legendary founder of Rome, Romulus, killed his brother Remus in order to protect the city.

Medieval Traditions. In the universities during the twelfth century, Catholic theologians reexamined theories of tyrannicide from a scholastic point of view. In his book *Policraticus* (1159) John of Salisbury reasoned that any ruler who violated his sacred duty to uphold law and justice committed treason against God. Anyone could kill him since consecration no longer protected him.

A century later St. Thomas Aquinas unhesitatingly called for the death of tyrants by usurpation, since Christians only had a duty to obey rulers set over them by God. Tyrants by oppression, however, posed more delicate problems to which he turned to Aristotle for guidance. Initially Aquinas argued that resistance to a legitimate ruler was a mortal sin; Christians should instead patiently bear the yoke of tyranny, praying to God to end their suffering. Yet obedience to any ruler cannot exceed the demands of the rule of law. For this reason Aquinas eventually conceded that sedition against a tyrant was licit if initiated by recognized leaders of the community.

This position became known as the *melior pars* argument and exerted a considerable influence on the views of the Italian jurist Bartolo of Saxoferrato (1314–1357), who invoked Roman legal precedents to justify resisting tyrants by usurpation as well as oppression. The radical position of the French lawyer Jean Petit, who in 1409 argued in court that private individuals, "without any order or command," could commit tyrannicide, was condemned as heretical a few years later by Jean de Gerson (1363–1429), whose views on the subject the Council of Constance upheld in 1415. Medieval scholastics thus stressed the importance of elite leadership and formal procedures when dealing with a tyrant by oppression, though God—as always—reserved the right to command a private individual to put a tyrant to death without recourse to a trial.

Renaissance and Reformation Theories of Tyrannicide. Given their classical training humanists in general looked favorably upon acts of tyrannicide if motivated to protect the public good. In *Discorsi sopra la prima deca di Tito Livio* (Discourses on the first ten books of Livy) Niccolò Machiavelli (1469–1527) praised Brutus as a paragon of civic virtue for helping to kill Caesar. To republican idealism he added the stark political realism of *Il principe* (1513; trans., *The Prince*), arguing that conventional moral restraints had little effect when it came to the political murder of usurpers. Francesco Guicciardini (1483–1540), in his *Storie fiorentine* (History of Florence), suspected the self-interested motives of individuals who championed the cause of resisting evil governments, arguing from historical example that the usual result was the establishment of an even more severe tyranny. The French humanist Étienne de La Boétie (1530–1563), in his *Discourse on Voluntary Servitude,* discussed the subject's complicity in governmental acts of oppression, arguing that a ruler's authority ceased the moment a subject withheld his obedience.

In general humanists only considered the problem of tyrannicide indirectly in their political writings. The advent of the Reformation in the early sixteenth century quickly focused the attention of both political theorists and theologians on the burning question of what to do about a ruler's alleged offenses against "true" religion. Theories of tyrannicide steadily became more radical as conflict over religion persisted from 1540 to 1648. John Calvin (1509–1564) agreed with Martin Luther (1483–1546) that God sent tyrants to punish his people, and that only He could depose or convert evil rulers. Yet Calvin did allow disobedience to irreligious commands by a tyrant if sanctioned by magistrates or elected representatives of the community. Like Augustine and Aquinas he reserved room for God to send private individuals on special missions, including the murder of a tyrant.

As religious conflict escalated after 1550, Protestant writers later known as monarchomachs went much further than Calvin. In his *A Short Treatise of Politic Power* (1556), for example, the English reformer John Ponet (1516?–1556) declared that God delegated authority to rulers via the consent of the people, who may revoke that authority if it becomes tyrannical. The Scotsman George Buchanan (1506–1582) built a radical case for resistance on contract theory in *De jure regni apud Scotos* (The laws of the kingdom of the Scots; 1579). If a ruler violated any terms of his contract, Buchanan argued, then he became a tyrant at war with his people. In a state of war anyone could then kill the tyrant out of a legitimate right of self-defense.

In France, in the wake of the St. Bartholomew's Day massacre (1572), Théodore de Bèze's (1519–1605) *De jure magistratum* (On the rights of magistrates; 1574) reiterated the longstanding argument that justified tyrannicide by individuals appointed by God or public magistrates. The estates general in France, moreover, exercised constitutional prerogatives in overseeing the contract between a ruler and the people. The *Vindiciae contra tyrannos* (Defense of liberty against tyrants; 1579), probably written by Philippe de Mornay (1549–1623), contributed the theory of the double covenant. The first covenant existed between God, the ruler, and the people in matters of faith; in matters of secular governance, however, a second compact between only the ruler and the people prevailed that could be revoked by magistrates or representative assemblies for acts of oppression. The German political theorist John Althusius (1557–1638) echoed these views in his *Politica methodice digesta* (Politics methodically ordered; 1603).

Catholic writers associated with the Holy League in France embraced these same theories of resistance in the 1580s and 1590s. The pseudonymous *De justa reipublicae christianae in reges impios authoriate* (The just authority of a Christian commonwealth against impious kings; 1590) invoked a radical theory of tyrannicide based on popular sovereignty.

Most Leaguer writers, such as Jean Boucher in his tracts *De justa Henrici tertii abdicatione e Francorum regno* (The just deposition of Henry III from the kingdom of the French; 1589) and *Apologie pour Jehan Chastel* (Apology for Jean Chastel; 1595), embraced more conventional arguments authorizing political murder should a ruler overturn the rule of law, encourage heresy, or persecute the church. In such cases both the papacy and representative assemblies may authorize resistance and ultimately tyrannicide. Other Catholic theologians, such as the Dominican friar Domingo de Soto (1494–1560), offered more moderate solutions based on the teachings of Aquinas. Most Jesuit theologians, such as Cardinal François Tolet and Emmanuel de Sâ, agreed on the need for formal procedures to authorize resistance. Yet Juan de Mariana (1536–1624), the Spanish Jesuit who wrote *De rege et regis institutione* (1598; trans., *The King and the Education of the King*) went much further when he invoked the people's right to self-defense against tyrants who stole their wealth, overturned the rule of law, or threatened religion.

Renaissance theories of tyrannicide continued to inform discussions of rightful resistance against oppressive governments from the English Civil War down to the French Revolution.

See also **Resistance, Theory of;** *and biographies of figures mentioned in this entry.*

BIBLIOGRAPHY

Ford, Franklin L. *Political Murder: From Tyrannicide to Terrorism.* Cambridge, Mass., 1985. A scholarly introduction to the subject that includes a long list of major political murders and executions in the age of the Wars of Religion.

Boesche, Roger. *Theories of Tyranny from Plato to Arendt.* University Park, Penn., 1996. Examines the problem of tyranny by looking closely at the writings of major political theorists.

Mousnier, Roland. *The Assassination of Henry IV: The Tyrannicide Problem and the Consolidation of the French Absolute Monarchy in the Early Seventeenth Century.* Translated by Joan Spencer. London, 1973. A probing case study of political murder set in the context of contemporary political events and ideas about tyrannicide.

MICHAEL WOLFE

UMBRIA, ART IN. Landlocked, earthquake prone, hilly, and mountainous, with only six percent plain, Umbria is the heart of central Italy. The name Umbria, Augustan in origin, was not current in the Renaissance, but was a nineteenth-century revival. Trapezoid in shape, the region is some fifty miles at its broadest, about sixty at its longest. Perugia is at the center, and during the Renaissance was the one sizable city, with about twenty thousand permanent residents in 1551 (there were fluctuations in part because of university students); around it were twenty small cities, likewise walled, of approximately two thousand to nine thousand inhabitants, with Gubbio and Città di Castello to Perugia's north, Orvieto and Spoleto to its south. Uniquely, Sansepolcro in the far north was pawned in 1440 by the pope to the Florentine republic, and eventually in 1581 consigned by a later pope to the grand duke of Tuscany.

Influence of the Papacy. By the end of the fifteenth century the pope's claim to the entire region as part of the Papal States had been largely realized, the culmination of a century and a half of sporadic warfare to that end. Assumption of papal authority over a city normally truncated rule by its princely dynasty; this was so for the Trinci of Foligno (ruled 1310–1439), and for the Baglioni of Perugia (ruled 1479–1522, 1531–1535, 1540). There were exceptions: the Vitelli of Città di Castello dominated that city's government in the sixteenth century; the Baglioni controlled Spello until 1583; first the Montefeltro (until 1508), then the della Rovere (until 1631) remained papal vicars of Gubbio; the Orsini held Narni throughout the Renaissance.

In the fifteenth century while the ruling dynasties of the region enhanced their "magnificence" by building sumptuous residences and by lavish patronage to demonstrate civic duty and Christian devotion, many artistic commissions testified to the religiosity of the commune and of wealthy families, individuals, religious institutions, and confraternities (the latter commissioning in particular religious processional banners). The region's people favored Christian mysticism, particularly as associated with their saints Francis and Clare of Assisi. With a few outstanding exceptions, the rebirth of antiquity in painting and fresco tended to be limited to its trappings, such as classical columns, in an otherwise Christian subject. In architecture the Renaissance was more evident, for instance in Federico da Montefeltro's Gubbio palace, built by the architect Francesco di Giorgio Martini (1439–1502) of Siena in 1474–1478. In the 1480s Sixtus IV, a Franciscan, paid for extensive rebuilding of the friary of Saint Francis at Assisi, a feature being a two-tiered cloister of classical columns and arches.

Apart from time's usual transmogrification of buildings and their contents, the region has suffered much inadvertent devastation: for instance Norcia was virtually destroyed by a series of earthquakes in 1567, 1703, 1730, and 1859. There has also been conscious destruction: in 1540, after Perugia's revolt, the pope had the Baglioni palace razed to be replaced by a fortress, its wing extending toward the present-day *Stadio;* Foligno was much damaged by bombs in World War II. Moreover, under papal authority a city's prized movable art tended to be transferred to

Rome, and Napoleon had transported to Paris cartloads of treasures; few items were returned to their original location. The compilation of a list of the region's artistic work, with an indication of the original location, would be invaluable. Without this guide generalizations remain somewhat tentative. Yet it seems self-evident that in the fifteenth century commissions for religious art predominated; these embraced all decorative forms, with painting in the forefront.

During most of the Renaissance there were in Perugia fifty-one Christian institutions, comprising monasteries, friaries, and convents (each with a church), and the cathedral, parish, and confraternity churches or chapels; every small city had a similar diversity and commensurate number of institutions. One can suppose, therefore, that the region had some six hundred such institutions in all, and hence the scope for artistic commissions was considerable. Furthermore it appears likely that in the fifteenth century many of these bodies acquired one or more religious paintings—rooms of the National Gallery of Umbria, Perugia, and those of the Vatican Pinacoteca are testimony. Striking are the large traditional-style polyptychs that focus on the Madonna and Child.

Artistic Highlights of Perugia. The nuns of the aristrocratic convent of Saint Anthony commissioned probably in 1467 a polyptych from Piero della Francesca (c. 1415–1492) of Sansepolcro; perhaps the link was Flavia Baglioni (certainly the convent's prioress in 1477), as Piero had painted frescoes for the Baglioni palace in 1437–1438, when first built. In 1468 Bartolomeo Caporali (c. 1420–c. 1503) of Perugia painted the *Assumption* for the lower-class convent of Santa Giuliana; between 1466 and 1468 he had assisted Benedetto Bonfiglio (active 1445–1496) of Perugia in painting *Madonna and Child with Four Saints,* and the *Annunciation* for the Church of Saint Dominic. In 1486 Caporali painted for Santa Giuliana the *Pietà;* this subject had been commissioned from him in 1477 by Perugia's cathedral. The ornate tomb of Bishop Gianandrea Baglioni (d. 1451), which is attributed to Urbano da Cortona (1426–1504), likewise enhances the cathedral.

In 1507 the painting *Madonna and Child with Saints Francis and Jerome* was ordered from Perugino (Pietro Vannucci; 1450–1523) of Città del Castel for the altar of a yet to be built chapel in Santa Maria de' Servi (demolished in 1540). Perugino and Raphael (1483–1520) of Urbino probably collaborated in 1507–1508 on the fresco *Trinity and Saints* for the tiny Camoldolese Church of San Severo. Probably in 1507 Raphael painted *Madonna and Child* for the Ansidei family chapel in the Church of San Fiorenzo, and certainly that year he painted *Deposition* (also called *Entombment*) for the Baglioni chapel in the Church of Saint Francis al Prato. The latter was commissioned by Atalanta Baglioni to record the murder in 1500 of her eldest son by his brother; set over this panel was *God and Angels,* while below were three small panels of the *Cardinal Virtues.*

A late fifteenth-century description of the Great Hall of the Baglioni palace reveals it was then decorated with portraits; along one wall were those of Perugian *condottieri,* on the facing wall were scholars, with each subject's name and achievements indicated by a painted inscription. Dominating the hall was a portrait of *Perusia,* the mythological foundress of the city. Perugia's *Collegio del Cambio* (office of the money changers) was built in 1452–1457, and the wall of its elaborately decorated interior audience chamber was outstanding: facing the entrance were two bas-relief lunettes, each with Perugia's device of a griffin; a niche between contained the terracotta figure of seated Justice. The contract to complete the work of decorating the other walls and the ceiling went to Perugino in January 1496. The scheme, devised by the Perugian humanist Francesco Maturanzio (1443–1518) sought to harmonize antiquity and Christianity. Here, unusually in the region, were abundant classical themes.

Smaller Cities. As papal control advanced north in the region in the fifteenth century, often the lesser cities suffered a decline in population and a deterioration in prosperity, which meant a dearth of artistic patronage in the following century. During the sixteenth century the pope spent enormous sums in the region on fortresses and on making churches conform architecturally to post-Tridentine concepts. There were, though, striking examples of artistic patronage in the fifteenth century beyond Perugia.

The Trinci palace in Foligno, begun in 1389, was structurally complete by 1408. One of the original ceilings is in situ painted with the arms of Pope Sixtus IV, who renovated the entire palace. Much of the original decoration remains. In one room the wall-frescoes depicted *Heroes of Roman History,* assigned to the school of Ottaviano Nelli (active 1400–1444) of Gubbio; another room was frescoed with representations of the *Liberal Arts* and the *Planets,* attributed to a follower of Gentile da Fabriano (active 1408–1427). A small chapel was frescoed with scenes from the *Life of Mary,* probably by Ottaviano Nelli himself. Justly famous is the fresco series *The Renaissance Antichrist* by Luca Signorelli (1441–1523) of Cortona in the Cappella Nuova of Orvieto's cathedral. The work occupied the artist for four years, beginning in 1500, and completed work begun and abandoned in 1447 by Fra Angelico (c. 1387–1455). Introducing portraits of famous men of the classical and Christian worlds, the frescoes were in effect a damning indictment of papal tyranny, as opposed to penitential Christianity. Often even the smallest communities of the region could boast one work of artistic merit: for instance Perugino's last work was the *Nativity* (1523) for the Confraternity of the Annunciation of Fontignano.

The Umbrian school of painters—a concept now rather disfavored—was a nineteenth-century convenience popularized by Bernard Berenson's *Central Italian Painters* (1897), though in use by other art historians as well. The first significant exhibition of paintings associated with the school was in Perugia in 1908, followed two years later by one entitled "Pictures of the Umbrian School" (Burlington Fine Arts Club, London). There were artists born in the region, often prolific in output, such as the Nelli family of Gubbio, Niccolò Alunne (c. 1430–1502) of Foligno, Perugino, and those of Perugia itself: Caporali, Bonfiglio, and Pinturicchio (Bernardino di Betto; c. 1454–1513), but there was very little homogeneity. Their styles reflected various local traditions and diverse influences from beyond the region's border. Moreover, many commissions, particularly those for what today are reputed masterpieces, went to artists from the neighboring states of Florence and Siena, and from the Marches and Romagna.

See also **Trent**, **Council of**; *and biographies of figures mentioned in this essay.*

BIBLIOGRAPHY

Berenson, Bernard. *Italian Pictures of the Renaissance: Central and North Italian Schools.* 3 vols. London, 1968. This provides a list of existing paintings and the location for each by artist; there are illustrations of some paintings.

Castellaneta, Carlo. *L'opera completa del Perugino.* Milan, 1969.

De Vecchi, Pierluigi. *The Complete Paintings of Raphael.* Rev. ed. Harmondsworth, U.K., 1987.

Garibaldi, Vittoria, ed. *Piero della Francesca: Il polittico di Sant'Antonio.* Perugia, Italy, 1993.

Marle, Raimond van. *The Renaissance Painters of Umbria.* Vol. 14 of his *The Development of the Italian Schools of Painting.* The Hague, Netherlands, 1933.

Riess, Jonathan B. *The Renaissance Antichrist: Luca Signorelli's Orvieto Frescoes.* Princeton, N.J., 1995.

Rowdon, Maurice. *The Companion Guide to Umbria.* London, 1969.

Santi, Francesco. *The National Gallery of Umbria, Perugia.* 2d ed. Rome, 1965.

Touring Club Italiano. *Guida d'Italia: Umbria.* 4th ed. Milan, 1966.

CECIL H. CLOUGH

UNIVERSITIES. The Renaissance university taught students at an advanced level and provided the institutional setting in which scholars did research.

New Universities. Renaissance Europe inherited from the Middle Ages twenty-nine functioning universities in 1400, then proceeded to create forty-six more universities, for a total of sixty-three by 1601. The foundation dates given reflect when two conditions were met: a charter authorizing the granting of degrees and the beginning of significant teaching. The new Italian universities established in the Renaissance were Ferrara (founded 1391, deteriorated in the early fifteenth century, and refounded in 1442), Turin (1411), Catania (1445), Macerata (1540), Salerno (c. 1592), Messina (1596), and Parma (1601). There was one loss: the University of Florence moved to Pisa in 1473, effectively terminating the University of Florence, but revivifying Pisa. Although not a university teaching law and medicine, the Collegio Romano founded by the Society of Jesus in Rome in 1551 taught the humanities, philosophy, theology, and mathematics at a university level. New Spanish universities were Barcelona (1450), Huesca (founded 1354, declined, then reestablished in 1464), Palma in Majorca (1483), Sigüenza (1489), Valencia (1500), Alcalá (1509), and Saragossa (1583).

The new universities of France were Aix (1409), Dôle (1422), Poitiers (1431), Caen (1439), Bordeaux (1441), Valence (1452), Nantes (1461), and Bourges (1464). Louvain (1426) became the sole university in the Low Countries. Copenhagen (1475) was the Danish university, and Uppsala (1477) the Swedish university. The British Isles added Saint Andrews (c. 1410), Glasgow (1451), and Aberdeen (c. 1500).

Central Europe added numerous universities in the Renaissance. They were Leipzig (1409), Rostock (1419), Greifswald (1460), Freiburg im Breisgau (1456), Basel (1460), Ingolstadt (1472), Mainz (1476), Tübingen (1477), Wittenberg (1502), Frankfurt an der Oder (1506), Marburg (1527), Königsberg (1544), Jena (1558), Helmstedt (1575), and Würzburg (1561–1582). Cracow was founded in 1364, dwindled to nothing, then was resurrected in 1400.

The fundamental reason for founding new universities was demand, which came from several directions. Above all, increasing numbers of men wanted to learn. But society needed more trained

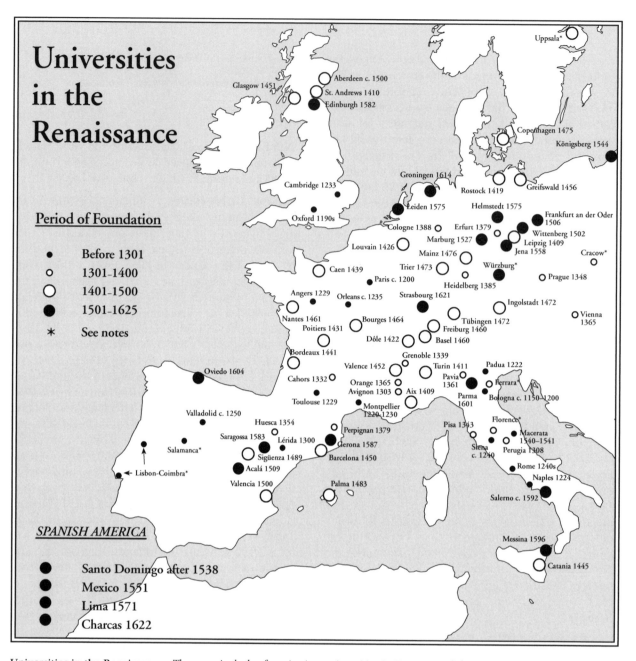

Universities in the Renaissance. The map includes functioning universities in Europe and the Americas during the Renaissance. A functioning university began when two conditions were met: (1) the pope or the emperor conferred on a city or school the right to confer degrees recognized throughout Christendom and (2) a minimum of six to nine professors taught arts, law, medicine, and/or theology at an advanced level. The date at which these conditions were met is sometimes difficult to determine. Some towns had the right to confer degrees, but offered little or no advanced instruction. Some institutions, such as Catholic and Protestant religious schools, offered extensive advanced instruction, but not necessarily in university subjects beyond theology; they often also lacked the authority to confer degrees.

Notes

Cracow   Founded in 1364; ceased operations about 1370; reestablished in 1400.

Ferrara   Probably founded in 1391, but ceased operations within a decade; reestablished in 1442.

Florence   Ceased operations and moved to Pisa in 1473.

Lisbon-Coimbra   Founded at Lisbon in 1290; in Coimbra, 1308–1338; in Lisbon, 1338–1354; in Coimbra, 1354–1377; in Lisbon, 1377–1537; in Coimbra after 1537.

Salamanca   Founded between 1218 and 1254, but the date at which it became a full university granting degrees is not clear.

Uppsala   Founded in 1477; ceased operations in 1515; reestablished in 1595.

Würzburg   Founded in stages between 1561 and 1583.

190

professionals as well. Monarchs, princes, and cities required civil servants, preferably with law degrees. The adoption of Roman law in central Europe created a demand for lawyers and judges trained in this field, which meant that numerous Germans studied in Italian universities, the center for the study of Roman law. A medical degree enabled the recipient to become a private physician, a court physician, or one employed by a town. Numerous clergymen earned theology degrees and then taught novice clergymen, especially in the schools of the large traditional mendicant orders, the Dominicans, Franciscans, and Augustinians.

Sometimes princes and city councils founded universities for economic reasons. If a local university existed, the young men of the state could study at considerably less cost than if they had to go elsewhere. And fathers could keep a closer eye on their sons. A university also conferred prestige on the host city or ruler. Just as artists created works of art to grace a court, and writers praised a city, so the presence of eminent professors at the local university proclaimed that the prince or the city encouraged learning.

Most governments sometimes sought to guarantee a large student body for the local university by forbidding subjects from studying elsewhere. But these laws were seldom enforced. At the same time, civic leaders often dreamed that the local institution would attract students from afar, as did Paris and Bologna. Wealthy foreign students who purchased lodging, food, servants, and sometimes tutors brought considerable additional income into a town. But they also brought more violence and increased danger to the virtue of local women.

Renaissance universities were more closely linked to the state than their medieval predecessors. Princes and cities exercised control by appointing and paying professors and heads of colleges. They added or eliminated subjects. After Europe divided into Catholic and Protestant lands, they imposed religious requirements on faculty and students, with varying degrees of success. University graduates, in turn, often played major roles in ruling the state.

Structure. All universities shared a common structure. Students attended lectures on texts stipulated by the university statutes for several years before presenting themselves for degree examinations. Professors lectured on the books of Aristotle for logic, natural philosophy, and metaphysics; the works of Hippocrates, Galen, and Avicenna for medicine; the *Corpus juris civilis* and *Corpus juris ca-*

nonici for law; and Peter Lombard's *Sententiarum libri 4* (Sentences) and the Bible for theology. All texts were written in Latin; lectures, disputations, and examinations were also conducted in Latin. Students were required to attend lectures for one to three years for a bachelor's degree in arts, five to seven years for doctorates in law and medicine, and twelve or more years beyond the master of arts degree for the doctorate of theology. In practice, these requirements were sometimes shortened. Professors and students participated in academic exercises, such as disputations, which were formal debates conducted according to the rules of logic.

When he (all students were male) felt prepared, the student submitted himself to a degree examination. A college of doctors, composed of professors and graduates of the university in the degree subject, examined the candidate. If he satisfied the examiners, the student received one or more degrees recognizing him to be an expert in a subject and authorizing him to teach it anywhere in Christendom. The universal acceptance of degrees came from papal and imperial charters authorizing universities to grant degrees.

Although all universities shared common characteristics, the subjects emphasized and the level of instruction varied greatly from institution to institution. Paris and Oxford emphasized instruction in arts and theology. Medicine and law were much less important; indeed, Paris did not teach civil law. Paris and Oxford had many teenage students and awarded numerous bachelor's degrees. Universities in central Europe tended to follow the Parisian model.

But Italian universities began as centers for instruction in civil law, canon law, and medicine at the doctoral level, and continued on this path. They taught arts subjects, such as logic and natural philosophy, as preparation for medicine, and taught little theology until the second half of the sixteenth century. Students obtained doctoral degrees, while the master's degree, with the right to teach, normally accompanied the doctorate. The bachelor's degree had disappeared from Italian universities by the early fifteenth century. Hence, students at Italian universities were typically laymen eighteen to twenty-five years of age. Spanish universities, and French universities outside of Paris, tended to concentrate on law.

The size of universities varied greatly. Paris had several thousand students and several hundred teachers at various levels during the Renaissance. This was because Paris had numerous younger students and older clergymen who both studied and taught. The latter taught arts to teenage students while studying for advanced degrees themselves. Bologna, the largest Italian university, had 75 to 100 professors and 1,500 to 2,000 students in the fifteenth and sixteenth centuries. Other universities were smaller. A typical university had 30 to 40 professors who taught 300 to 500 students. Some universities had only 10 to 20 professors teaching 200 to 300 students. But even the smallest provincial university was immensely important to the intellectual life of a region.

It is likely that the number of university students and degrees awarded increased in Europe as a whole between 1400 and 1600, despite numerous wars, which temporarily closed universities, and the Protestant Reformation, which produced a sharp enrollment drop in German universities. The increased number of degrees argues that society valued learning, or perhaps only the degree, more than it had in earlier centuries.

Students could easily attend more than one university, because the texts were the same and all instruction was in Latin. Students sometimes traveled from one university to another because of the appointment or departure of a famous professor. Aware of this, universities competed for a few famous professors, especially in civil law. These fortunate academics moved from one university to another, attracted by higher salaries. But the majority of professors spent their entire careers at a single university.

As in the Middle Ages, university students organized themselves into "nations" corresponding to their homelands, then elected student leaders to represent them to the host city. In the Middle Ages, student organizations militantly asserted student rights against local governments and helped choose professors. Student organizations retained their ceremonial prestige in the Renaissance but lost much of their power. Civil governments appointed professors and increasingly dominated other aspects of the university.

The Influence of Humanism. The most important change was the introduction of humanistic studies into the Renaissance university. Professors teaching the ancient Latin and Greek literary texts began to appear in Italian universities in the first half of the fifteenth century. Major humanists, such as Francesco Filelfo and Angelo Poliziano, plus many lesser humanists, became professors of rhetoric, poetry, and Greek in the second half of the fifteenth century. Humanists began to assume university posts in northern European universities in the early six-

teenth century, sometimes in the face of strong opposition from the theologians already there.

The linguistic and critical historical skills of humanistic studies had a major impact on teaching and research. Humanists taught a better understanding of ancient Latin and Greek. Most important, they read texts critically within a historical context. Humanistically trained professors sometimes also communicated to students their contempt, not always justified, for medieval scholarship.

By the late fifteenth century, and especially in the sixteenth century, professors of philosophy used humanistic skills to read Aristotle in Greek, rather than in medieval Latin translations. They also read the ancient Greek commentaries on Aristotle, which had been neglected for linguistic reasons. The results were strong criticism of medieval commentators and new interpretations of Aristotle's works. Professors of medicine used their newly acquired humanistic skills to examine the medical texts of Galen in Greek and to find medieval Latin translations wanting. They produced new Latin translations based on a better understanding of the original Greek. This process is sometimes called medical humanism.

Other changes in university medical research included greater emphasis on anatomy as a result of more frequent and more detailed dissection of human bodies. Padua and Pisa simultaneously established the first university botanical gardens in 1545 in order to improve the study of the medicinal properties of plants. Clinical medicine began in the 1540s when a Paduan professor took students to hospitals in order to lecture on a disease at the bedside of an ill patient. These innovations, in combination with medical humanism, produced a revolution in teaching and research of medicine at the University of Padua by 1550. Other universities quickly followed Padua's lead.

The application of humanist criticism to the study of law produced humanistic jurisprudence, which meant the attempt to reconstruct philologically and historically the social context of Roman law and then to base commentaries on the law within that context. Sixteenth-century French universities welcomed humanistic jurisprudence, while Italian universities remained aloof.

Overall, professors in Renaissance universities taught the same subjects and texts as did their medieval predecessors, but approached both in innovative ways. Although only a tiny fraction of the male population taught or studied in universities, institutions of higher learning made an immense contribution to Renaissance learning and trained the leaders of society.

See also articles on specific universities.

BIBLIOGRAPHY

Cobban, Alan B. *The Medieval Universities: Their Development and Organization*. London, 1975. Especially good on Bologna and Paris as the prototypical northern and southern universities.

A History of the University in Europe. Vol. 1, *Universities in the Middle Ages*. Edited by Hilde De Ridder-Symoens. Cambridge, U.K., 1992. Vol. 2, *Universities in Early Modern Europe (1500–1800)*. Edited by Hilde De Ridder-Symoens. Cambridge, U.K., 1996. Comprehensive information on all aspects of universities with emphasis on general patterns and the university in society. Particularly good on northern European universities.

History of Universities. Avebury and Oxford, U.K., 1981–. Annual volume founded by the late Charles B. Schmitt. Includes articles, bibliographical surveys of recent research, and reviews. Best place to find new research on Renaissance universities.

McConica, James K., ed. *The Collegiate University*. Vol. 3 of *The History of the University of Oxford*. Oxford, 1986. Best and most recent study of all aspects of Oxford between 1485 and 1603.

Schmitt, Charles B. *Aristotle and the Renaissance*. Cambridge, Mass. and London, 1983. Short survey describing how Renaissance scholars approached Aristotle in new ways.

Thorndike, Lynn. *University Records and Life in the Middle Ages*. New York, 1944. Collection of university documents (c. 1150–c. 1650) in English translation. Particularly good for students and daily life.

Wear, A., R. K. French, and I. M. Lonie, eds. *The Medical Renaissance of the Sixteenth Century*. Cambridge, U.K., 1985. Excellent collection of studies on medical humanism, anatomy, and other aspects of the medical Renaissance.

PAUL F. GRENDLER

URBANISM.

URBANISM. The Renaissance cultural orientation toward antiquity also left its imprint on the theory and reconceptualization of urban space and of cities more generally. With the move toward the establishment of absolute monarchies across Europe, interest in the city both as commercial-administrative center and as representative of its ruler's identity and power grew apace. The experience of ancient Rome even in its ruinous state taught generations of architects and patrons to value the creation of monumental urban ensembles. Moreover, ancient written sources, such as Vitruvius's *De architectura* (On architecture) and historical accounts of the city and of emperors' lives (Suetonius's *De vita Caesarum;* Lives of the Caesars), underscored the building activities of princely patrons and offered insights into the connections between rulership, religious ritual, military display, crowd control, sound husbanding of the economy, and the design of cities. Nevertheless, although straight, paved roads, city gates, triumphal arches, and fora could be discerned among the rubble, little was preserved of Rome's urban glory. As a result, in this, as in so many other instances, Renaissance architects were thrown back upon their own imaginations and interpretive skills.

Design and Governance. Much of Renaissance attention to urban design was a consequence of the growth of cities into commercial, administrative, and political centers and therefore also into powerful symbols of governance. Both capitals of important secular and ecclesiastical states (such as Paris, Rome, Madrid, and London) and those of smaller yet equally significant republics or principalities (such as Florence, Venice, Augsburg, and Munich) became natural sites for innovation in town planning and patronage. Despite vital growth, however, existing cities offered little latitude for major urban reconfiguration other than on their peripheries, because in addition to the natural topography of their sites, many of these cities inherited their constituent parts from the Middle Ages. Indeed, the fourteenth century had known a substantial economic boom in many parts of Europe that had led to major building campaigns (as in, for example, the Palazzo Vecchio and Piazza della Signoria in Florence). Moreover, complex land ownership, existing fortification walls, gates, street patterns, gardens, waterways, and canals, as well as the basic repertoire of urban forms and materials, were so many obstacles in the path of large-scale urban renewal.

Because both building technology and economic and administrative systems changed little in this period, building types also remained much the same. Notable exceptions were related to fortification design (especially of bastion and citadels on the rings of larger cities), the growth of military architecture being a direct result of the virtual revolution in warfare that the introduction of the cannon and gunpowder had caused. Similarly, in the Protestant north, as the administration of schools, almshouses, and hospitals passed from the church to the government and the patriciate, new buildings were built, monasteries and convents were converted to new uses, and traditional formats were changed. The development of social housing—for the old, the poor, the widowed—a new phenomenon in this period, also affected conceptions of urban form (in Venice, the Casa delle vedove for widows, 1399, and the Marinarezza for retired and disabled sailors, 1395; in Augsburg, Fugger housing [the "Fuggerei"] for indigent and pious Catholics, 1516). A rising housing market also provided an impetus to property development. Landowners such as monasteries, hospitals, and confraternities shifted uses of land from agricul-

An Exemplar of Urbanism. Piazza del Campidoglio (Capitol), Rome. Michelangelo designed the square and the buildings surrounding it after 1546. The view is northwest, with the Senate House behind the viewer. ALINARI/ART RESOURCE

ture to housing. The resulting mixed-use buildings, composed of repeatable, plain units that created uniform "walls" to new, straight streets, also contributed to the move toward more regularized cityscapes (as with the via Leonina, Rome).

Theory. The difficulty that architects encountered in their attempts to realize large-scale changes within existing cities made theory, ideal designs, and painting important outlets for their ideas and for the development of a discourse on the subject. Renaissance literature on town planning was largely based on the ancient Roman Vitruvius. He had not dealt with the issue of the city at length, but he had covered building types from palaces and temples to theaters and fora and thus offered a model for the components of the ideal, classical city. Although his recommendations on city design were pithy, his precepts on architecture were general enough to be transferable and constituted the basis upon which Renaissance city theory was developed. These included the emphasis on commensurability, on ideal geometrical figures (circle and square), on body-based ratios, on the harmonious resolution of utility, and on firmness and beauty. Ancient texts on warfare, agriculture (Varro, *De re rustica*), politics and government (Aristotle, *Politics;* Plato, *Republic*), or simply guidebooks (*Mirabilia urbis Romae*) were used to fill in the gaps of his text.

Much of the Renaissance literature on city design focused on three principal topics: the ideal fortified city (for example, Filarete's Sforzinda in his *Trattato,* 1461–1464, and Albrecht Dürer's *Etliche Unterricht zu Befestigung der Stett, Schloss, und Flecken,* 1527); the ideal port city (for example, Pietro Cataneo's *Architettura,* 1556); and the establishment of a hierarchical system of facade treatments that covered the range from church to the "meanest hovel" (for example, Sebastiano Serlio, Book 6, *On Domestic Architecture*). In all instances, true to their classical convictions, architects and theoreticians sought to establish visual order and control through various means: geometrically derived ground plans (circle, star, etc.), attention to the visual apprehension of public space, proportional relationships governing components of buildings and open spaces, a gridded system of streets, and a consistent use of classically derived forms.

Few, if any, cities were realized based on these principles. Rather, fortified military posts like Palmanova (1593) on Venetian territory, Klundert (1583), Coeworden (1597) and Willemstad (1583) in the Netherlands, and Freudenstadt (1599) in Württemberg represent the applications of these conceptual models. However if the ambitions behind these ideal designs were unrealistic, the impulse was not. In a period of significant political strife and religious war across Europe, the concentration on blending architecture with military engineering was eminently sensible (see designs for the port of Naples, Claudio Tolomei's proposals for a Sienese port city on Monte Argentario, and Francesco de Marchi's *Della architettura militare libri tre* [1599]). Moreover, the emphasis on visual discipline and standardization, with its implications of a controlling power, served the purposes of colonization, as illustrated all too well in the *Royal Ordinances for New Towns* (1573) drafted for Philip II of Spain for the settlement of the New World.

Perhaps the most celebrated (virtually) new city created in the Renaissance was Pienza (1459–1464), the birthplace of Pope Pius II Piccolomini, a small Tuscan village transformed into an urban monument to himself and his family. Its trapezoidal square, located at the heart of the little town and surrounded by palaces and the cathedral, was laid out with specific sightlines in mind (toward the distant hillside view and toward the town itself) and exemplifies the kinds of urban interventions that such theoreticians as Leon Battista Alberti proposed in their treatises. The architectural background to paintings, intarsia panels, and stage sets are the only other surviving documents of the urban vision of Renaissance architects (for example, the painting *Ideal City,* Urbino, Palazzo Ducale). Free from the real constraints of the site, they illustrate a world of *varietas* (variety) in a classical key, organized according to strict geometrical and perspectival grids that obtain a harmonious, unified environment suited for the life *all'antica* (in the classical style) that Renaissance patrons wished to enact.

Practice. Although military architecture offered most scope for the realization of ideal towns, and the representational arts a virtual context for it, real, large cities did nevertheless provide rulers and architects with significant opportunities for urban renewal. Rome is perhaps the most important such example, for during the Renaissance it rose from a nearly abandoned and derelict city of 17,000 inhabitants to become the real capital of Catholic Christendom. A series of popes (Julius II, Leo X, Sixtus V) and architects (Raphael, Michelangelo, Domenico Fontana, Giacomo della Porta) left their collective mark on the shape of the city. Straight streets were cut into its fabric (via Giulia); important squares (Piazza del Campidoglio, Piazza Farnese) were refurbished and connected to major arteries (via Papale); a sophisticated system of water supply and fountains punctuated significant intersections and squares and became urban furniture alongside loggias, porticoes, steps, balustrades, and sculpture; and most impor-

tant, a network of axial connections between the principal churches effectively unified the city around its pilgrimage sites (1585–1589).

Such a rationalization of the urban plan set a precedent for later developments both in Italy and throughout the rest of Europe. The nucleus for the transformation of Madrid by Philip II—the reconfiguration of the Plaza Mayor (Juan de Herrera and others, 1580–1590)—shows the directions in which the Roman example could be taken. Transforming a traditional Castilian square as he had done at Toledo and as Francisco de Salamanca had done at Valladolid (1562), Herrera sought to achieve as effective an urban setting as Rome's, but he used different means to do so. Rather than creating vistas and relying on key, opulent monuments, to heighten their impact he made architecture out of the streets themselves, standardizing facades and extending simple, utilitarian construction infinitely to create a monumental civic space.

The early-seventeenth-century squares in Paris (Place des Vosges) and London (Covent Garden), with their monumental effect achieved by the repetition of large-scale pattern, could not have existed without such predecessors in southern Europe. Indeed, on the whole in the north, Renaissance urbanization had meant a more refined architectural style, rational town improvements and town extensions (Brussels, Grande Place; extensions to Haarlem, Amsterdam, and Leiden), and the strictly formal layout of the classical ideal city had found little favor. Popularized through illustrations (as in Étienne Dupérac's late-sixteenth-century engravings of the Piazza del Campidoglio), in surrogate form through garden layouts and experienced through travel, the classical model nevertheless achieved common currency and was ultimately transformed to suit local tastes, customs, and rituals.

See also **Architecture,** *subentry on* **Architectural Treatises; Rome,** *subentry on* **The City of Rome.**

BIBLIOGRAPHY

Ackerman, James S., and Myra N. Rosenfeld. "Social Stratification in Renaissance Urban Planning." In *Urban Life in the Renaissance.* Edited by Susan Zimmerman and Ronald Weissman. Newark, Del., 1989. Pages 21–49.

Adams, Nicholas, and Laurie Nussdorfer. "The Italian City, 1400–1600." In *From Brunelleschi to Michelangelo: The Representation of Architecture.* Exhibition catalog, Palazzo Grassi, Venice, 1994. Milan, 1994. Pages 205–232.

Adams, Nicholas, and Simon Pepper. *Firearms and Fortifications: Military Architecture and Siege Warfare in Sixteenth-Century Siena.* Chicago, 1986.

Barry, Jonathan, ed. *The Tudor and Stuart Town, 1530–1688.* New York, 1990.

Burke, Gerald L. *The Making of Dutch Towns.* London, 1956.

Friedrichs, Christopher. *The Early Modern City, 1450–1750.* New York and London, 1995.

Lotz, Wolfgang. "Sixteenth-Century Italian Squares." In *Studies in Italian Renaissance Architecture.* Cambridge, Mass., 1977. Pages 74–92.

Pollak, Martha. *Turin, 1564–1680: Urban Design, Military Culture, and the Creation of the Absolutist Capital.* Chicago, 1991.

Thompson, David. *Renaissance Paris.* London, 1984.

Trachtenberg, Marvin. *Dominion of the Eye: Urbanism, Art, and Power in Early Modern Florence.* New York, 1997.

Wilkinson Zerner, Catherine. *Juan de Herrera: Architect to Philip II of Spain.* New Haven, Conn., and London, 1993.

ALINA A. PAYNE

URBINO. The name Urbino may derive from the Latin words *urbs bina,* meaning a city on twin hills; its Roman origins were prior to the fourth century B.C. On 21 December 1375 Count Antonio da Montefeltro, head of the recently exiled dynasty that had ruled the city and its associated territory for some two centuries, was acclaimed lord by the city's citizens. The city had been the administrative center of an imperial county, which became a papal vicariate (and in the fifteenth century a papal duchy); it was also the center of an ecclesiastical diocese.

Urbino's walls, largely extant, mark its boundaries in the fifteenth and sixteenth centuries, when entry was restricted to seven gates, which were closed at night. The area within the walls, as well as the city's land extending some five miles beyond (the *contado*), was divided into quarters (*quadre*), each with its official notary and its militia. Localization of allied crafts within a quarter further fostered its identity, as did affiliations by quarter to churches and to religious orders and confraternities. The quarters converged at the main square, which was fronted by the principal civic and religious edifice. An index to the communal tax for 1496 and 1497 (now held at the Biblioteca Universitaria, Urbino) indicates assessment was by quarter, with three categories of affluence assigned to individuals and corporations. The document also listed communal property and the city's nobles (eleven, headed by the Montefeltro prince), who by statute were excluded from citizenship.

In 1598, within the walls and *contado,* there were 18,335 men, women, and children, presumably including the religious of both sexes and Jews. A population-return to the prince in 1591 (preserved at the Biblioteca Apostolica Vaticana) specified 2,146 men and 2,411 women in the city, totals which may exclude the religious. Certainly the city's population had declined during the sixteenth century, after increasing in the fifteenth, when settlement near the city walls grew. Throughout this time most of the *contado*'s population remained land-workers. Urbino's Jews were never confined to a ghetto; in the fifteenth century there were some five families, and the city's first Jewish bank dates from 1433. After the expulsion of the Jews from the Iberian Peninsula in 1492, the number of Jews residing in Urbino increased to a total of about a hundred by the 1550s. Already by 1500 the Jewish community had its small synagogue, whose ark is now displayed in the Jewish Museum, New York City. The Jews helped develop the city's commercial interests but had no citizenship rights.

The city's confined area and small population ensured strong social cohesion. There were more citizens in proportion to total residents than in large cities, and accordingly factionalism was constrained. In 1375 Count Antonio, like his forebears and successors who ruled, promised to uphold the city's statutes. This promise perpetuated outward signs of communal self-rule. The council, elected from citizens, though subject to the prince, dealt with the city's internal affairs. Citizenship usually was restricted to sons of a citizen residing in the city. Citizenship lapsed on non-payment of civic and guild dues, and on conviction of serious crime. As elsewhere, Urbino's guilds had an established order of precedence, headed by that of judges and notaries. The most broad-based was the traders guild (*mercanzia*). Some guilds may have admitted women, and some guilds may have had only a few members (just enough to serve this relatively small city). The guilds were represented on the council and took part in religious and civic functions.

Justice was dispensed by a judge (podestà) chosen by the council. Possibly because of a backlog in the 1490s, Duke Guidobaldo obtained papal authority to establish a college of thirteen doctors of law based in Urbino to deal with both civil and ecclesiastical disputes of lesser importance within the vicariate. Subsequently individuals with nonlegal qualifications became associated with the college and, along with the lawyers, taught within the city. In consequence, in 1564 Pope Pius IV authorized the college to award degrees in law, medicine, and other subjects, thereby granting it university status, although it was not effective as such a *studium generale* until more than a century later. Already from the mid-fifteenth century the city had paid a teacher to instruct boys in the humanities.

Arbitrary rule could be checked only by revolt, as in 1444, when Duke Oddantonio was assassinated. As the city's captain-for-life, the prince was granted by the commune a modest salary, paid yearly in two

Urbino. The Palazzo Ducale extends across the right half of the photograph, below and to the right of the dome. SCALA/
ART RESOURCE, N.Y.

installments. Princes also received dues of all kinds, and every town within the vicariate granted a salary. Since most Montefeltro and Della Rovere princes were mercenaries, they were usually able to supplement their civic income. For holding the vicariate, the prince was liable for an annual papal tax (*censo*), which was often either withheld or remitted. The prince, or his deputy, held public audience frequently, normally in his Urbino palace, known as the court (*corte*), adjudicating in matters such as disputes between citizens and claims of unjust administration. The entire vicariate was administered from the chancery in his palace, important in the city's life not least because of the large staff employed: several hundred in the 1470s. Moreover, as a military commander the prince required armorers, smiths, and veterinarians, usually based in Urbino.

In September 1375 the newly found supposed remains of St. Crescentius, Urbino's patron saint, were placed for viewing in the cathedral's high altar; Montefeltro coins bore a symbolic representation of this fourth-century martyr. There were various lay con-

fraternities to which men and women of the city belonged irrespective of social status. The Montefeltro princes sought to identify with these institutions by participating in social, charitable, and devotional activities. Count Guidantonio apparently commissioned frescoes from the Salimbeni brothers for the oratory associated with the Confraternity of St. John the Baptist (1416), and Count Federico contributed generously to Justus of Ghent's altarpiece for the Confraternity of Corpus Domini (1473–1474). Christian devotion was required of a good Christian prince, while his wealth, testimony of God's favor, was to be channeled into religious and civic buildings. Federico extensively renovated Urbino during the years from 1465 to 1482, when the city's wealthy families were inspired to rebuild their palaces in Renaissance style.

The exceptional prosperity of Urbino associated with Federico's rule proved transitory. During the fifteenth century the military reputation of the Montefeltro princes had brought to the city wealth and reflected glory. Following the death of the last Montefeltro in 1508, the vicariate passed to his adopted nephew, Francesco Maria Della Rovere. As the Della Rovere state expanded (incorporating Pesaro, Senigallia, and Camerino), Urbino was no longer a suitable administrative center. With the court and administration transferred to Pesaro in the 1520s, Urbino's ducal palace became redundant, with serious consequences for employment. The creation of a university in 1564 only marginally alleviated the city's decline, though it was responsible for the introduction of printing in 1575 (previously, in 1493, three books had been printed there).

See also **Montefeltro Family.**

BIBLIOGRAPHY

Beloch, Karl Julius. *Bevölkerungsgeschichte Italiens*. 3 vols. Leipzig and Berlin, 1937–1961. See vol. 2 (1939), pp. 78–84.

Benevolo, Leonardo, and Paolo Boninsegna. *Urbino*. Bari, Italy, 1986.

La libera università di Urbino. Urbino, Italy, 1963.

Mazzini, Franco. *Guida di Urbino*. Vicenza, Italy, 1962.

Mazzini, Franco. *I mattoni e le pietre di Urbino*. Urbino, Italy, 1982.

CECIL H. CLOUGH

URFÉ, HONORÉ D' (1568–1625), French writer. Honoré d'Urfé, author of the multivolume pastoral novel *L'Astrée* (Astrea), spent his early years in the culturally rich Forez region of southeast-central France. Raised at the family château among artists and writers, d'Urfé was formally educated at the Jesuit College of Tournon in the philosophy, history, literature, and art of the ancient world.

An activist in the Catholic League during the late 1580s and the 1590s, d'Urfé began writing *L'Astrée* at about the same time, although he did not publish the first part until 1607. (The second part followed in 1610, the third in 1617, and the fourth, published posthumously, in 1627. D'Urfé's secretary, Balthazar Baro, published this fourth part and later added a fifth part.) While its underlying structure derives from late-sixteenth-century Spanish pastoral novels and Italian pastoral theater, *L'Astrée* also incorporates the romance tradition inherited from ancient Greek and medieval texts. In the work, d'Urfé places his shepherds and shepherdesses (former aristocrats tired of court life) in an Edenic but geographically accurate fifth-century Forez, where they experience the interminable dilemmas of love.

The Renaissance convention of disguise ensures a freewheeling atmosphere, as cross-dressing and d'Urfé's linguistic and grammatical toying permit the widest exploration of romance, regardless of gender. The expression by d'Urfé of Renaissance Platonic doctrine, advocating the most perfect pure love between the two most perfect lovers, is undercut by the novel's narratives, many of which are recounted in episodic fashion, sustaining the erotic suspense.

Other works by d'Urfé include his philosophical meditations in the form of letters, *Epistres morales* (1598, 1603, 1608); pastoral poetry and theater; and an unpublished epic poem, *La savoysiade* (1599–1606). *L'Astrée* is his undisputed masterpiece.

BIBLIOGRAPHY

Primary Works

Urfé, Honoré d'. *Astrea*. Part 1. Translated by Steven Rendall. Binghamton, N.Y., 1995.

Urfé, Honoré d'. *L'Astrée*. Edited by Hughes Vaganay. Geneva, 1925.

Secondary Works

Gaume, Maxime. *Les inspirations et les sources de l'oeuvre d'Honoré d'Urfé*. Saint-Étienne, France, 1977. Classic study of the vast erudition underpinning d'Urfé's work.

Henein, Eglal. *Protée romancier*. Fasano, Italy, and Paris, 1996. Analyzes the many aspects of disguise, transformation, and transposition.

Horowitz, Louise K. *Honoré d'Urfé*. Boston, 1984. A general study (in English) of the author and his works, with primary chapters devoted to close textual analysis of *L'Astrée*.

LOUISE K. HOROWITZ

USURY. Usury was a precisely defined crime against God's law. In canon law and secular law it was codified as lending for guaranteed return over and above the principal of the loan without risk to the lender. This definition rested squarely on a series of biblical injunctions. Exodus 22:25 forbids oppressing one's poor neighbor with usury. Deuteronomy 23:20–21 says one cannot charge a brother usury. Ezekiel 18:7–8, 13 makes it clear that the righteous do not lend at usury, and that usurers "shall not live." Leviticus 25:35–36 instructs that if a brother is poor, do not charge him usury. The final Old Testament word on the issue came from the psalmist, who charged the godly to aid their neighbors, not lending to them at interest. The strongest rejection of loans at interest came from Christ in Luke 6:35, where he says "lend, hoping for nothing in return."

Medieval Attitudes. Given biblical prohibitions on usury, it is hardly surprising that Christian theologians from the fourth century on defined lending for gain as a sin. Aquinas and his fellow scholastics amplified authors like St. Jerome on the subject, and Gratian of Bologna incorporated condemnations of usury into the code of canon law. Aquinas must have been gratified to find that Aristotle shared his hostility toward usury, declaring it to be an unnatural thing to charge rent for money.

By the late Middle Ages there was a consensus among theologians that lending at interest for guaranteed return was illegal and damnable. They also agreed, however, that if the lender shared in the risk of the venture, the loan was legal. Consequently, laws against usury seldom interfered with merchant capitalism. Businessmen could always get loans if their contracts made them partners in risk. Theologians and canonists distinguished between usury that is forbidden by divine and human law, and factors or circumstances external to the loan that justified the taking of interest as compensation. These "extrinsic titles," as they were called, included such things as "an emerging injury" or "cessation of profit," or even a custom or civil law allowing, for the sake of the common good, the charging of modest interest. The difference between the amount lent and the profit it might have made was paid as *interesse* (interest). One had to prove the potential loss, however, to charge *interesse*. It was also possible to write contracts that specified *poena conventionalis*, a penalty for late payment that did not demand proof of potential loss. Merchant bankers like the Medici did not charge interest per se, but they often received gifts from grateful clients.

There were many legal ruses, too, that allowed illegal interest to be charged invisibly. A contract for a false sale, in which an inflated price was paid for a good, might be constructed. Or the appearance of risk might be incorporated in a contract by conditioning the payment on an eventuality such as the length of someone's life. Only the poor, lacking personal credit, were forced to pledge collateral to get money.

The oppression of the poor by usurers offended many good Christians. To counter the monopoly of Jewish money lenders who charged high interest rates and were outside the canon law's prohibitions, the Council of Priors, backed by the papal governor of Perugia, Ermolao Barbaro, introduced the *mons pietatis* (poor men's bank) in 1462, which was implicitly approved by Paul II in 1467. These nonprofit banks lent to the deserving poor at very low rates of interest and, by the late fifteenth century, they began to accept deposits. By the sixteenth century these banks were spread by the Franciscans all over Europe, though not in England, where Parliament refused to legalize them.

Renaissance and Reformation Attitudes.

As the demand for capital increased theologians became increasingly aware that lending at interest was not always theft. In the fifteenth century Jean de Gerson (1363–1429) in Paris, Conrad Summenhardt (1465–1511) and Gabriel Biel (c. 1420–1495) in Tübingen, and Johann Eck (1486–1543) in Ingolstadt argued that usury occurred only when the lender intended to oppress the borrower. Eck, supported by the Fugger banking family, became famous for his book *Tractatus de contractu quinque de centum* (Treatise on contracts at 5 percent; 1515), which defended 5 percent as a harmless and therefore legal rate of interest as long as the loan was for a legitimate business opportunity.

Eck's position horrified more conservative people, who continued to see usury as an antisocial crime. Not surprisingly, Eck's great enemy Martin Luther (1483–1546) refused to accept the idea that intention was a proper test for usury. Luther insisted that anyone who charged interest was a thief and murderer and should not be buried in consecrated ground. He allowed only one exception: if money was lent at interest to support orphans, widows, students, and ministers, it was good.

Reformers like Martin Bucer (1491–1551) and John Calvin (1509–1564) were much more sympathetic to Eck's argument. John Calvin's letter on usury of 1545 made it clear that when Christ said "lend, hoping for nothing in return," he meant that we should help the poor freely. Following the rule of equity, we should judge people by their circumstances, not by legal definitions. Calvin argued that one could lend at interest to business people who would make a profit using the money. To the working poor one should lend without interest, but expect the loan to be repaid. To the impoverished one should give without expecting repayment.

Calvin's arguments were amplified in Charles du Moulin's *Tractatus commerciorum et usurarum, redituumque pecunia constitutorum et monetarum* (Treatise on trade, usury, and returns on money by agreements and coining; 1546). Du Moulin (Molinaeus; 1500–1566) developed a utility theory of value for money, rejecting Aquinas's belief that money could not be rented because it was fungible.

This attack on the Thomist understanding of money was taken up by Spanish commentators. Domingo de Soto (1494–1560) suggested that Luke 6:35 was not a precept, since it has no relation to the justice of lending at interest. Luis de Molina (1535–1600) agreed. He suggested that there was no biblical text that actually prohibited usury.

By the second half of the sixteenth century Catholics and Protestants alike were increasingly tolerant of the idea that the legality of loans at interest was determined by the intentions of the parties. Theologians were often reluctant to admit much latitude for usury, but secular law and commercial practice embraced the idea that loans at interest, made with good intentions, were legitimate. In the Dutch republic and England the state ceased to control usury unless it was antisocial, leaving individuals to decide for themselves whether their actions were sinful. At about the same time the image of the usurer in literature changed from a sinister, grasping sinner to a socially inept fool. The medieval concept of usury was replaced by its modern definition, unjust rates of interest.

See also **Banking and Money; Poverty and Charity.**

BIBLIOGRAPHY

Divine, Thomas F. *Interest: An Historical and Analytical Study in Economics and Modern Ethics.* Milwaukee, Wis., 1959.

Gordon, Barry. *Economic Analysis before Adam Smith: Hesiod to Lessius.* London, 1975.

Jones, Norman. *God and the Moneylenders: Usury and the Law in Early Modern England.* Oxford, 1989.

Nelson, Benjamin N. *The Idea of Usury: From Tribal Brotherhood to Universal Otherhood.* 2d ed., Chicago, 1969.

Noonan, John T. *The Scholastic Analysis of Usury.* Cambridge, Mass., 1957.

Thireau, Jean-Louis. *Charles du Moulin (1500–1566). Étude sur les sources, la méthode, les idée politiques et économiques d'un juriste de la Renaissance.* Geneva, 1980.

NORMAN L. JONES

UTOPIAS. Sir Thomas More (1478–1535) invented the word "utopia" early in the sixteenth century as a pun on Greek roots (*ou topia,* no place; *eu topia,* the place where things are well). More's *Utopia* was the first of several Renaissance treatises to explore imaginatively the possibility of depicting a perfect society. Renaissance utopias shared a preference for rational, even geometric, organization of the physical environment, and a highly regimented life for their inhabitants. They were frequently isolated, located in remote regions of the known world. Residents of many utopias held property in common, raised children collectively, and shared other aspects of a communal life. Government structures were often authoritarian and inflexible. Utopias offered both a critical reflection on the imperfections of contemporary European societies and the vision of a more perfectly organized and just form of social organization.

More's *Utopia*. More's "Truly Golden Handbook," depicting the best state of a commonwealth and published under the title *Utopia* in 1516, was novel in two respects. First, it broke with the pattern of medieval portraits of the ideal society, which had focused on moral or material perfection. *Utopia* was not premised on divine intervention, nor on the absence of imperfections in human nature or the natural environment. Instead, it envisaged the overcoming or containment of deficiencies in humanity and nature through laws, institutional arrangements, education, and bureaucratic control. In this respect it contrasted with medieval visions of social perfection via divine intervention (the millennium), moral exhortation (the perfect moral commonwealth), natural beneficence (arcadia), or abundance (Cockaigne). More's handbook was a "talking picture," an attempt to reach beyond prescription to visualization, evoking an imaginative experience of life inside the perfect society. From the sharply critical commentary on contemporary society in book 1 to the depiction of utopian marriage and foreign policy in book 2, *Utopia*'s play on reality and imagination is subtle and complex. Similarly, the location of Utopia ("nowhere" as well as "the place where all is well") both built on and fictionalized the voyages of discovery. Later utopian writings often but not always incorporated the fictional strategies of More's work.

Utopia was novel, because it reinaugurated a genre of social speculation and idealization, but like many Renaissance works it was also deeply influenced in content, form, style, and language by selected classical models. The fifteenth-century "rediscovery" of Plato and Plutarch stimulated a revival of the "best state" exercise. Erasmus's Christian humanism and his exploration of Pythagorean notions of friendship added both a concrete social context and a sense of moral urgency to such exercises. But *Utopia* was a device in the realm of ideas, not of practical action. It was created as a means of restating an intellectual problem of the late Renaissance. To give coherence, if not synthesis, to the currents of neo-Stoic, scholastic, and humanist thought, which the northern humanists sought to reconcile with the reawakening of Christian social aspirations, More depicted a "best state" that both offered "solutions" and restated the dilemma.

That restatement had two dimensions. The Renaissance exercise in fusing the Scholastic and the humanist hinged, in one critical respect, on finding a suitable institutional context for virtue. In *Utopia* More ruthlessly exposed the limits of satire and moral exhortation (typical of the work of his humanist friends) within the existing social and institutional

Utopia. Frontispiece of *Utopia* by Thomas More. Engraving by Ambrosius Holbein, 1518.

framework. He presented a society in which wealth, status, work, dress, food, leisure, marriage, and the household are prescribed and maintained, at a high level of uniformity, by an institutional framework that embodies and, to a great extent, predetermines virtue. More's book also addresses the question of the social meaning of virtue. On the one hand, the Christian humanist saw virtue as the realization of the *philosophia Christi,* the observation of a given moral code by acting in charity to God and fellow

201

individuals. If all acted in accordance with their social obligations as laid down in the code, the ideal society of the perfect moral commonwealth might be realized; such a vision, however, implied victory in this world over original sin.

On the other hand, civic humanism took from Aristotle and Boethius the idea that virtue was a quality defined in action by the operation of human will in a civic setting. But following this line could open up the dilemma, which many saw epitomized in the writings of Machiavelli, of the potential disparity between the good individual and the good citizen. In *Utopia* More resolved these issues by depicting a society of imperfect people, in which the pursuit of rational self-interest, including the pursuit of (a carefully defined) pleasure, and the pursuit of virtue could be reconciled. Central to the design of this society was the reconciliation of private and public through community of property and the definition of personal pleasure as moral and intellectual enlightenment. Given this social and ethical context, a matrix of institutional regulation, bureaucratic surveillance, and educational socialization programmed the people, both rulers and ruled, for virtue, and dealt with them when they malfunctioned.

Other Utopias. Almost a century later Tommaso Campanella's *La città del sol* (1623; trans. *The City of the Sun*) sought a similar reconciliation of private reason and public good, based on the premise that private property destructively raises the personal above the communal and therefore should be abolished: "When self-love is destroyed, only concern for the community remains." As with More, Campanella's model had cenobitic, or monastic, overtones, but in Campanella's case community ownership and control extended beyond physical property to sexuality and to personal attributes such as generosity, fortitude, and diligence. Here Campanella's vision differed in degree and detail, rather than character, from More's, but in terms of knowledge of the natural world the difference was more substantial. Residents of More's *Utopia* believe in miracles, "which occur without the assistance of nature" and therefore remained incomprehensible. For Campanella's Solarians, nature is not only entirely comprehensible but already fully comprehended. All scientific knowledge is carved on the seven concentric walls of the city, forming a huge memory system or database. Scientific knowledge is already complete and is kept in "only one book," the city itself. Campanella associated science with astrology, the knowledge of natural law, and regularity. In his uto-

pia there is no room for miracles and, since knowledge is complete, no role for scientific research.

Knowledge, like virtue to which it was closely related, presented problems if it was too violently contested or so dynamic as to destabilize the foundations of society. Francis Bacon's *New Atlantis* (1627) contrasts with *The City of the Sun* in this respect, since it depicts a society in which science remains a continuing and powerful activity. Scientific research could reshape the relationship between society and its natural environment, thus changing the nature of the utopia itself. Bacon addressed this by setting freedom, contingency, and the power of scientific discovery loose within a social framework that eliminated moral contingency by controlling potentially aberrant individuals. The scientists of New Atlantis are ambiguously pictured as moral paragons charged with distinguishing the immediate works of God and those mediated through nature, but also as men capable of cheating and lying and therefore subject to the same controls and scrutiny as other citizens. The Baconian dilemma has dogged the scientific utopia ever since; either utopia controls science, or scientific discovery subverts utopia. The degree to which utopian writing, more than any other form of late-Renaissance political or social theorizing, confronted the problem of scientific power is striking.

Millennial Utopias. Many of Bacon's followers escaped the central problem of his utopia by relocating his scientific aspirations to a millennial, rather than a utopian, context. The pansophist aspirations of a sequence of social idealists who looked to an alliance of science and religion in the reconquest of humanity's dominion over fallen nature—from Giordano Bruno, through Christopher Besold, Johann Heinrich Alsted, and Johann Valentin Andreae, to Gottfried Wilhelm Leibniz—shared this tendency. This millennial element, presuming divine intervention, was more evident than utopia in the wake of the Reformation and commonly led to depictions of a postmillennial perfect moral commonwealth or arcadia (presuming natural beneficence). However, when the emphasis shifted to premillennial godly discipline this could lead to utopian outcomes (in the sense of organizational changes), especially on the Protestant side of the Reformation divide.

Johannes Eberlein von Gunsburg's *Wolfaria* (1521), with its draconian regulations enforced by ferocious punishments, illustrates this at its crudest; Andreae's *Christianopolis* (1619) does this as well, in more sophisticated form. Andreae, a prominent Lutheran pastor, addressed the problems (typical of a maturing religious movement with a long-term agenda) of how a godly community could be built in a fallen world. His answer incorporates some of the features of enclosed monastic households and some of those, as Andreae saw it, of Geneva under the discipline of John Calvin. But above all, Andreae placed elaborate emphasis on the socially integrative capacities of education. "The College" is both physically and socially central to his ideal city.

Under the influence of the great educational theorist Johann Amos Comenius (Jan Komenský), the idea of education as a principal instrument in building the ideal society flourished again in mid-seventeenth-century England. In *Nova Solyma* (1648), a Latin work intended for a European audience, Samuel Gott described an ideal society of christianized Jews located in the Holy Land. In part an attempt to reconcile millenarian and utopian aspirations, Gott's utopians hesitate between the self-rule appropriate to the saints and the godly discipline necessary to the natural man. His vigorous attempt to devise an educational theory, and to describe a practical pedagogy that would free self-rule while restraining discipline, ended in debate rather than conclusion.

Emphasis on Law and Institutions. In its scholastic form the "best state" exercise emphasized law and institutions over education. The pursuit of an ideal education for the prince and his advisers, as in Antonio de Guevara's *Relox de los principes* (Mirror of princes; 1529) or Erasmus's *The Education of a Christian Prince* (1516), gave way to a concern with constitutional constraints on his power. Similarly, the ideal aristocracy, frequently a feature of portraits of idealized republics, such as those of Venice, were exchanged for balanced governmental forms designed, after the model in Polybius's second-century B.C. history of Rome, to prevent aristocracy's degeneration into oligarchy. If utopians in their aspiration to social perfection must constrain imperfect individuals from constituting an imperfect society, they must also develop means of controlling the relationship between imperfect rulers and imperfect subjects. Hence their engagement with constitutionalism and, in this sense, with the impersonalization of politics. For Paolo Paruta, a Venetian writing in the late sixteenth century, an ideal government was that "by which people living in peace and union, may work righteously and obtain civil felicity." This could only be achieved if custom could be overcome and the subject's second nature be re-

modeled by "good institutions of life." Paruta's *Discorsi* (1599) were analyses of the problems of an institutionally well-balanced Polybian state. The ultimate extension of this development, and an exercise in overt constitutional architecture, came with James Harrington's *Oceana* in 1656.

The search for the ideal commonwealth also produced constitutional surveys or political gazetteers of more or less fictional states. Examples are Francesco Sansovino's *Del governo et amministratione di diversi regni et republiche* (The government and administration of diverse realms and republics; 1578) and Bartolomeo Cavalcanti's *Trattati . . . sopra gli ottimi reggimenti delle repubbliche antiche e moderne* (Treatise . . . on the best government of republics ancient and modern; 1571). The ideal constitution could resist the closure of utopian perfection by stabilizing the framework in which politics might be pursued, thus exposing the commonwealth to the possibility of corruption. Utopian designs embraced not only the machinery of state but also the fabric of society, so that there was no longer any role for politics or policy.

The fusing of the social and the constitutional, with the attendant termination of politics, is perhaps best exemplified in Harrington's *Oceana,* the last great flowering of the late-Renaissance utopia. Alongside the elaborate civil arrangements of *Oceana*'s government at local, regional, national, and imperial levels, were set equally detailed military arrangements covering all men between the ages of eighteen and thirty. The path to citizenship was through military service. Just as the utopias of More, Campanella, Anton Francesco Doni, Eberlein, and Andreae had taken monastic institutions as an initial model, so, in the aftermath of a century of religious warfare, utopian writers turned to military models. The anonymous French utopia, *Histoire du grand et admirable Royaume d'Antangil* (History of the great and admirable Kingdom of Antagil; 1616) describes the military organization, as well as the constitutional, judicial, and educational arrangements of an ideal society, set south of Java, in enormous detail.

Utopias in the Americas. Accounts of the discovery and conquest of "new worlds" fed not only the "discovery" of ideal societies but also a sense of the tabula rasa on which such societies might be depicted or even created. Frequently, the initial formulation was arcadian. Christopher Columbus, Peter Martyr Vermigli, and Bartolomé de Las Casas all anticipated encounters with golden-age societies populated by noble savages whose innocence and simplicity of life were to be contrasted with European sophistry and decadence. When *Utopia* was published in 1516, Las Casas was planning the perfection of Cuba, Hispaniola, San Juan, and Jamaica. In the 1530s Vasco de Quiroga recommended the implementation of More's utopian design in the New World since European customs were not appropriate for the golden age. Almost a century later the *reductiones* of the Jesuits in Brazil, Uruguay, Argentina, and Paraguay sought to sustain the innocence of the natives through a paternalistic and morally controlled communism.

Colonies formed without regard to indigenous peoples presented more complex challenges and sometimes harsher responses. In 1606 Virginia was described as "Earth's only Paradise," but by 1609 conflict, disease, and famine had reduced the colony to anarchy. William Strachey's codification of the subsequent lawmaking, published in 1612 as *Lawes Divine, Morall, and Martiall,* laid down a framework of strict discipline and control over time, speech, behavior, work, trade, and hygiene. Peter Cornelius Plockhoy made similar proposals for the Dutch colony of the New Netherlands in the 1660s, but by then English colonial utopias were moving in the direction of aristocratic, Harringtonian commonwealths.

Immortal Republics. The Renaissance utopia was a startling and provocative phenomenon that challenged the political imagination to transcend time and place in new ways. In its liberation from custom it required a lawgiver to rise above normal limitations. More's Utopus was a system designer, not primarily a lawgiver or a pronouncer of moral maxims. He had not only to legislate but also to design social arrangements, institutional mechanisms, bureaucracies, and means of enforcement that would contain and reshape the impulse to ignore, break, or undermine codes of conduct or the rule of law. In eliminating social ills it became necessary to do more than articulate rules and rely on the exercise of human free will. So the moral code that Christianity provided was in itself insufficient,

and in that sense the Renaissance utopia could suggest a dangerous impiety.

Owing little to God, nature, or tradition, utopia could appear a kind of sacrilege. A pre-Christian fictional setting was frequently used to avoid this appearance. On the other hand, in utopia unexpected twists of fate were banished by the establishment of predictability and moral certainty. Citizens lost their individual capacity to cope with adversity, but the republic was rendered immortal, immune to corruption. Once the founding legislator had done his work, princes were reduced to functionaries. Utopia ended both politics and the play of particular providence. It could absorb the classical aspirations of humanism and the desire for a godly community on both sides of the Reformation divide, just as it later absorbed the military aspirations of the neo-Stoic state born out of the warfare engendered by those divisions.

See also **Bacon, Francis; Campanella, Tommaso,** *subentry on* **Campanella the Philosopher; More, Thomas; Political Thought.**

BIBLIOGRAPHY

Primary Works

Campanella, Tommaso. *The City of the Sun: A Poetical Dialogue.* Translated with introduction and notes by Daniel J. Donno. Berkeley, Calif., 1981. Translation of *La città del sol* (1623).

Harrington, James. *The Commonwealth of Oceana and A System of Politics.* Edited by J. G. A. Pocock. Cambridge, U.K., 1992.

More, Thomas. *Utopia.* Edited by George M. Logan and Robert M. Adams. Cambridge, U.K., 1989.

Secondary Works.

Alexander, Peter, and Roger Gill, eds. *Utopias.* London, 1984.

Bann, Stephen, and Krishan Kumar, eds. *Utopias and the Millennium.* London, 1993.

Davis, J. C. "Science and Utopia: The History of a Dilemma." In *Nineteen Eighty Four: Science between Utopia and Dystopia.* Edited by Everett Mendelsohn and Helga Nowotny. Dordrecht, Netherlands, 1984.

Davis, J. C. *Utopia and the Ideal Society: A Study of English Utopian Writing 1516–1700.* Cambridge, U.K., 1981.

Manuel, Frank E., and Fritzie P. Manuel. *Utopian Thought in the Western World.* Oxford, 1979.

J. C. DAVIS

VADIANUS, JOACHIM (Vadian; Joachim von Watt; 1484–1551), humanist scholar, poet, physician, and reformer of St. Gall, Switzerland. Born in St. Gall into a respected family of moderate means and active in civic affairs, Joachim attended the University of Vienna in 1501 and was soon captivated by the new humanist learning, acquiring his M.A. in 1508 and adopting the humanistic name of Vadianus. Influences on his academic life included the famous poet Conrad Celtis, who had established a school of poetry and mathematics alongside the university, the humanist Johannes Cuspinianus, the linguist Angelo Cospus, and the Italian theologian John Camers (Varino Favorino).

While based in Vienna, he traveled in Italy, and published poems, orations, and a treatise on poetry, *De poetica*. On a visit home in 1509, he found in the abbey library Walahfrid Strabo's *Hortulus*—a work combining poetry and botany—on which he lectured and subsequently published.

Alongside his humanistic studies he began what became a lifelong fascination with geography, stimulated by travels in northern Italy and emphasizing direct observation rather than book knowledge. His edition of Pomponius Mela demonstrated a willingness to discard traditional authorities such as Aristotle and Pliny when they were contradicted by empirical observation. Ever the empiricist, he supplemented his scholarly activity by geographical expeditions, scaling Mount Pilatus in Switzerland and descending Polish salt mines to examine the structure of rocks.

His ascent of the academic ladder was swift—poet laureate of the Holy Roman Empire (1514), pro-fessor of poetry and university rector (1516), and doctor of medicine (1517). A wide circle of correspondents had extended his reputation far beyond Vienna, and an influential future based in that city beckoned. But in 1518 he cut his ties with the university and returned to St. Gall.

There he was appointed town physician, a scholarly sinecure rather than a practical vocation. He became a member of the small council (the highest council of government) when his father died in 1521 and showed increasing preoccupation with the Reformation cause, initially with the biblical humanism of Erasmus, and subsequently with the writings of Huldrych Zwingli, Martin Luther, and Philipp Melanchthon. He studied the church fathers in new printed editions and formed a learned study group to which he lectured on the Creeds (*Brevis indicatura symbolorum*) and the Book of Acts (*Collectanea acta apostolorum*).

In 1526 Vadianus became *Bürgermeister* (mayor), and for the remainder of his life held one or another of the three leading public offices in the city. The Reformation in St. Gall was legislated at the end of 1526 and the abbey was secularized in 1529 (only to revert to Catholic control in 1531). Vadianus saved numerous manuscripts when the abbey was dissolved and exercised a moderating influence on the Reformation in St. Gall.

During the last two decades of his life, he remained in demand as a consultant on political and religious matters and traveled widely, but much of his time was devoted to historical research and writing. Based largely on the abbey manuscripts, his writings included chronicles of the abbey, the city, and Lake Constance, as well as a history of monasticism and an account of the Roman emperors and Frankish kings. The abbey history appeared a quarter century after his death, while other works remained unpublished. He also contributed to a new edition of Glareanus's *Helvetiae Descriptio* (Description of Switzerland).

As his death approached in 1551, he arranged for his library and manuscripts to be presented to the town. Some four thousand letters have survived from his extensive correspondence.

See also **Switzerland.**

BIBLIOGRAPHY

Primary Work
Vadian (Joachim von Watt). *Die Vadianische Briefsammlung der Stadtbibliothek St. Gallen.* 7 vols. Edited by Emil Arbenz and Hermann Wartmann. St. Gall, Switzerland, 1890–1913.

Secondary Works
Bonorand, Conradin. "Stand und Probleme der Vadian-Forschung." *Zwingliana* (1954–1958). Pages 586ff.
Bonorand, Conradin. *Vadians Weg vom Humanismus zur Reformation und seine Vorträge über die Apostelgeschichte (1523).* St. Gall, Switzerland, 1962.
Näf, Werner. *Vadian und seine Stadt St. Gallen.* 2 vols. St. Gall, Switzerland, 1944–1957.
Rupp, E. Gordon. *Patterns of Reformation.* Philadelphia and London, 1969. Pages 357–378.

JOHN TONKIN

VALDÉS, ALFONSO DE (d. 1532), Spanish humanist. Alfonso de Valdés is considered the foremost follower of the work of Erasmus in Spain. During his life he served as the Latin secretary to Emperor Charles V. The exact date of Valdés's birth is not known. His father, Hernando de Valdés, was *regidor* (alderman) of the Castilian city of Cuenca. Both of Valdés's parents were of converso stock, that is, they were Jews who converted to Christianity to avoid persecution. His uncle, Fernando de la Barrera, a priest, was burned at the stake by the Inquisition in 1491 for the secret practice of the Jewish faith; in the Spain of the time the potential consequence for the family in terms of social ostracism and economic ruin was considerable. Not very much is known about Valdés's education. It is generally thought that he studied with Pedro Mártir of Angleria, perhaps at the court of Valladolid. He may even have undertaken further studies in the new school founded by Cardinal Francisco Jiménez de Cisneros in Alcalá de Henares. Valdés was among those secretaries in the imperial court listed by Mercurino Gattinara in 1522. Valdés carried out numerous diplomatic tasks for the

court. Although the exact date of his death is not known, according to two allusions, he must have died between 2 and 4 October 1532 in Vienna, a victim of the plague.

Valdés is the author of two major texts of the Spanish Renaissance: *Diálogo de las cosas ocurridas en Roma* (Dialogue of the happenings in Rome; 1527) and *Diálogo de Mercurio y Carón* (Dialogue of Mercury and Charon), written between 1528 and 1530. Of the former, when a copy of the work fell into the hands of Baldassare Castiglione, papal nuncio at the imperial court, a veritable polemic occurred with Castiglione furiously attacking Valdés.

The intellectual basis of both works is the difference between the teachings of the New Testament and the actual behavior of the Roman church. Both works document from the emperor's point of view the history, religious questions, and diplomatic policies of that era, and especially in *Dialogue of Mercury and Charon,* the relations between Charles V, Francis I of Angoulême, and Henry VIII.

The spiritual and religious content of his works could be best described by the phrase *monachatus non est pietas* (the cassock does not the priest make). Valdés emphasizes inner spirituality over external forms of religiosity. He follows the Erasmian *philosophia Christi* (the philosophy of Christ as enunciated in the doctrines of the New Testament) and inveighs against the lax morality of the clergy, the trafficking in church offices, the cult of relics and indulgences, and other targets.

Valdés's *Dialogue of Mercury and Charon* is considered by scholars to be the best Renaissance example of nonfiction prose. Its use of language is of the highest and best type of Castilian prose of the sixteenth century, and its content documents a particularly critical moment in the spiritual state of affairs of Spain at that time.

BIBLIOGRAPHY

Primary Work
Valdés, Alfonso de. *Dialogue of Mercury and Charon.* Translated by Joseph V. Ricapito. Bloomington, Ind., 1986.

Secondary Work
Bataillon, Marcel. *Erasme et Espagne: Recherches sur l'histoire spirituelle du XVIᵉ siècle.* Paris, 1937.

JOSEPH V. RICAPITO

VALDÉS, JUAN DE (1509?–1541), Spanish humanist, religious writer. Juan de Valdés came from a family of converso origin in Cuenca, Castile; his brother Alfonso was a Latin secretary to the Emperor Charles V (Charles I of Spain). In 1523 Juan came into contact with some heretical *Alumbrados,* or Illuminated Ones, of Toledo. He attended the University of Alcalá, a center of humanism and religious reform, from 1525 to 1529. In the latter year he published his first work, *Diálogo de doctrina cristiana* (Dialogue on Christian doctrine), which led the Inquisition to charge him with heresy. He fled to Rome in 1531 and finally settled in Naples in 1535, where he served in various diplomatic and official capacities.

In Naples, Valdés became the leader of a covert religious reform movement involving humanists, aristocrats, and humble friars, and it was there that he wrote most of his works. His Spanish works circulated in manuscript, but none of the surviving manuscripts are in his hand. His followers published most of his works in posthumous Italian translations.

His *Diálogo de la lengua* (Dialogue on language; c. 1535) manifests his humanistic and linguistic concerns. Translations and biblical commentaries on Old and New Testament texts followed. Valdés also wrote the short *Instrución cristiana para los niños* (Catechism for children; c. 1540s) and other religious treatises, the best known of which are *Sul principio della dottrina cristiana: Cinque trattatelli evangelici* (On the principles of Christian doctrine: Five theological treatises; 1545), *Alphabeto christiano* (The Christian alphabet; 1546), and *Le cento e dieci divine considerazioni* (A hundred and ten divine considerations; 1550). Although written by others, *Trattato utilissimo de beneficio di Giesú Christo* (The benefits of Christ; 1543), the first widely read Italian Protestant work, is dependent on ideas put forth by Valdés.

Although he was influenced by Erasmus, *alumbrado* doctrines, and perhaps by Luther, the religious views held by Valdés were unique and original. His first work, *Diálogo de doctrina cristiana* appeared to be Erasmian, but also masked the heretical doctrines of the *Alumbrados.* As he refined *Alumbrado* ideas that went back to 1509, Valdés brought them closer to the terminology of the Protestant Reformation. Indeed, the book contains views on justification by faith and rejection of good works as a path toward salvation similar to those found in Martin Luther's shorter *Catechism* published four months later. Valdés based his views on experience and his concept of knowledge, and on a doctrine of atonement. But Valdés was not a mystic, nor did he make use of the terms "union with God" and the "threefold mystical way." Hence, his doctrine of illumination is typologically closer to the magisterial Reformation of Luther and John Calvin, rather than to the more radical Reformation of the Anabaptists.

The combination of spiritual force, focus on the inner spiritual life, and a lack of concern for religious ceremonies that Valdés evinced inspired important Italian religious figures to seek their own religious paths. Pietro Martire Vermigli became a Calvinist, Bernardino Ochino an anti-Trinitarian, although there is nothing in the extant works of Valdés to support anti-Trinitarianism. Pietro Carnesecchi remained in Italy and was executed as an unrepentant Valdesian in 1567. But the humanist cardinals Reginald Pole and Gasparo Contarini remained Catholic, while holding to a version of justification by faith. Celio Secondo Curione, another Italian disciple of Valdés, who in exile became Protestant, produced an Italian translation of *Consideraciones divinas* (1550) that was highly influential. John Wesley read an English translation two centuries later.

Valdés remains an enigmatic figure, a bridge between Spain and Italy, between Renaissance and Reformation.

BIBLIOGRAPHY

Primary Works

Valdés, Juan de. *Comentario a los Salmos* (1–41). Edited by Manuel Carrasco. Madrid, 1885.

Valdés, Juan de. *Commentary upon the Gospel of St. Matthew.* Edited by Eduard Boehmer and John T. Betts. London, 1882. Translation of *El evangelio según San Mateo.*

Valdés, Juan de. *Commentary upon St. Paul's Epistle to the Romans.* Edited by John T. Betts. London, 1883. Translation of *Comentario de la epístola de San Pablo a los Romanos* (1556).

Valdés, Juan de. *Commentary upon St. Paul's First Epistle to the Church at Corinth.* Edited by John T. Betts. London, 1883. Translation of *Comentario dela primera espístola de San Pablo a la iglesia en Corintio* (1557).

Valdés, Juan de. *Life and Writings of Juan de Valdés, Otherwise Valdesso, Spanish Reformer in the Sixteenth Century.* Edited by Benjamin B. Wiffen. London, 1865. Includes a translation of *Le cento e dieci divine considerazioni* (A Hundred and Ten Divine Considerations; 1550).

Valdés, Juan de. *Valdés's Two Catechisms: The Dialogue on Christian Doctrine and The Christian Instruction for Children.* 2d ed., enlarged. Edited by José C. Nieto. Translated by William B. Jones and Carol D. Jones. Lawrence, Kans., 1993.

Secondary Works

Nieto, José C. *Juan de Valdés and the Origins of the Spanish and Italian Reformation.* Geneva, 1970.

Williams, George H. *The Radical Reformation.* 3d ed. Kirksville, Mo., 1992. Pages 47–52, 819–829.

JOSÉ C. NIETO

VALLA, LORENZO (1407–1457), major theoretician of Renaissance humanism. Lorenzo Valla was born in Rome to a family of lesser nobility from the Lombard city of Piacenza. Both his father and his maternal uncles were jurists in the employ of the papal Curia. Such employment was typical of the new professional class from which many humanist scholars emerged. Lorenzo was educated privately and received important guidance from a number of these Greek and Latin scholars in the employ of Pope Martin V gathered in Rome. Leonardo Bruni was a "corrector" of Valla's Latin, and Giovanni Aurispa and Rinuccio di Castiglione Fiorentino were tutors of Greek for Valla.

Grammar and Religious Thought.

Despite the powerful influence of many leading humanists at the time of his youthful education, Valla from the beginning showed an indomitable independence of study and judgment. In 1416 and 1417 Poggio Bracciolini discovered two manuscripts of Quintilian's *Institutio oratoria* (Institutes of oratory) at Saint Gall in Switzerland and in France, and restored this major Roman handbook of rhetoric to scholarly study. Valla, a young self-educated scholar at the age of twenty, engaged in the study of this work of Quintilian and wrote *De comparatione Ciceronis et Quintilianis* (A comparison of Cicero and Quintilian) strongly favoring Quintilian as the proper Latin guide to humanistic study—this despite the highly favored Ciceronianism of leading humanists at the Curia including both Leonardo Bruni and Poggio Bracciolini. Poggio became a lifelong critic of Valla, and had an immediate influence in dissuading the pope from employing Valla in the Roman Curia after the deaths of his uncle and his father.

In 1430 Valla went to his ancestral environs of Piacenza to take care of his family's properties. By the next year, 1431, he had written the first version of another provocative and challenging work: his *De voluptate* (On pleasure), later reissued as *De vero bono* and *De vero ac falso bono* (On true good, 1433; and, On true and false good; 1448). There are minor changes, mainly stylistic corrections, but the work remained essentially as he first wrote it. *De vero bono* challenged the highly favored Stoicism and the occasional Epicureanism of the humanist movement with an assertion of a Christian vision of earthly and heavenly joy derived in part from Epicurus but more substantially from Saint Augustine.

With the promotion of Quintilian's *Institutio oratoria* and his religio-ethical vision in *De vero bono*, Valla established the two basic directions of his entire corpus of writings: restoration of the grammatical character of language and thought, and the transformation of many elements of late-medieval religious institutions as well as other aspects of the Christian life. A powerful voice in his own days, he became a major influence in the age of Erasmian humanism and ecclesiastical reform in the later fifteenth and early sixteenth century. In his efforts to accomplish these aims Valla became a persistent critic of all the contrary views he encountered, and he considered himself a *miles Christianus,* a Christian soldier. In a letter, in which he explains why he criticized so many ancient, medieval, and contemporary authors, he said: "Whoever wrote anything about science or art who did not criticize his predecessors? Otherwise what reason would there be for writing, except to correct the errors, omissions and redundancies of others?" (*Epistole,* no. 13). The list, particularly of medieval authors he criticized, is long. But among the ancients two, Aristotle and Boethius, stand out because of their surviving powerful influence on Scholastic philosophy and culture. He does not criticize Cicero, though he was charged with doing so by his powerful humanist critic, Poggio Bracciolini. Rather he sought to focus the interests of the humanists onto Quintilian's more grammatically based and detailed textbook-style formulation of rhetoric as a more effective guide to literary theory and practice in his own age. In this sense he may be called the founder of philology.

In Valla's first version of *De vero bono* he had chosen three humanists whose character reflected the roles of Stoic, Epicurean, and Christian: Leonardo Bruni, Antonio Beccadelli, and Niccolò Niccoli, all of whom he had known in Rome. Bruni was in historical actuality an Aristotelian with Stoic learnings, and the fictitious character did indeed assume certain positions of Aristotelian moral philosophy. The Epicurean was made to mock the purity of the Vestal Virgins and offer other shockingly daring opinions, such as preferring whores to nuns. In the subsequent versions Valla changed the names of the interlocutors to those of scholars and figures of the Lombard region. Although there was some role-playing intended to shock the reader, Valla's purpose was serious and never abandoned. He says,

> the pleasures of the body are generated with the aid of the soul and the pleasures of the soul with the collaboration of the body. Do we ponder anything in our mind which is not quasi-corporeal, that is, in accordance with the things we have seen, heard, perceived with some sense, from which contemplation is born. . . . contemplation is nothing except the progress of learning, that is, what we call reflection as well as invention.

There is a strongly empirical element in Valla's speculations. A little later, speaking of divine providence, he says,

Not only such things as heaven, earth and sea but universal mankind also, and those whom I have called participants, were made on account of you, that is on account of individuals. In the Book of Moses God said, "It is not good for man to live alone, let us make a helpmate for him similar to him." Although this was said about a woman, nevertheless it must also be applied to a man. For as the wife to the husband, so the husband is a helpmate to the wife, and likewise other men among themselves, in which the meaning of charity consists.

These views he never changed and considered his later works consistent with them.

In 1431 Valla was appointed to teach rhetoric at the University of Pavia. But in February 1433 he was forced to flee the university because of the indignation of the jurists over his criticism of Bartolus of Sassoferrato, a leading late-medieval legal scholar, for a faulty reading of the *Digest*. After a brief stay in Milan, where he taught privately, a year in Genoa teaching rhetoric, and some time in Florence, he joined the court of Alfonso of Aragon, the king of Naples and Sicily, in 1435. But he was soon back in Milan, captured along with Alfonso in the naval battle of Ponza. There he wrote a letter to his friend, the Milanese humanist Pier Candido Decembrio denouncing Leonardo Bruni's *Laudatio urbis Florentiae* (Praise of the city of Florence) on the grounds that Florence was founded under the despotic auspices of Sulla and, thus, was not the heir to republican Rome.

Philology and Philosophy. Returned with Alfonso to the kingdom of Naples in 1437, Valla completed his second masterwork, *De elegantiis linguae latinae* (The elegances of the Latin language; 1471). He had begun this work in Milan in 1433 and was also busy translating during these years Aesop's *Fables,* Xenophon's *Cyropedia,* and Homer's *Iliad* (completed only to the sixteenth book and finished by another). Lorenzo Valla's *Elegantiae,* as it came to be known, was the first of the great philological works of the Renaissance and showed the way not only to a scientific understanding of the Latin language but also to a deep appreciation of its richness and resourcefulness. Valla showed by his analysis of a long series of Latin terms the precision and subtle differentiation of its vocabulary and how infinitely refined Latin was through its syntax and great variety of ways of expressing thoughts differentially. He also argued in the prefaces to its six books the importance of the spread of Latin by the Roman conquests. The establishment of a high level of civilization in Europe was far more important than its temporally

Lorenzo Valla. CULVER PICTURES

limited military conquests. Thus the recovery of classical Latin would contribute to a resuscitation of the degraded medieval cultures and would beautify religion and life.

In 1439 Valla completed the first version of his third great masterwork, his *Repastinatio philosophiae et dialecticae* (The reconstruction of philosophy and dialectic). This first version survived in only two manuscript copies and has only recently been subjected to study. More elaborate second and third redactions of 1448 and 1452 formed the basis of the Renaissance and early modern printed editions entitled *Retractatio philosophiae et dialecticae,* and commonly known as *Dialectical Disputations,* or *Dialectica.* The first version is bolder, more fiery, and challenging, like Valla's other works, but his points are more literally spelled out in the *Retractatio* or "Redrafting" of a few years later. The central purpose of the work is to undermine Aristotle's categories and metaphysics, as transmitted to the medieval west in Boethius's writings, and hence the prevailing scholastic mode of theology, philosophy, and dialectic.

This then is a work of major theoretical importance and has much in common with late twentieth-century studies of language. The objects of knowledge and of language are reduced to the single class: "thing," or *res*. There are no transcendentals such as "the good," "the true," or "the one," only a thing, or things. Only three of Aristotle's ten categories of things exist: substance, quality, and action; these categories correspond to the grammatical parts of speech: nouns, verbal modifiers called adjectives or adverbs, and verbs. This comes straight out of Quintilian, who called them "statuses," or "bases" distinguished by the Latin questions *An sit, Quid sit, Quale sit:* Does the thing (or *res*) exist? What thing is it? What are its qualities or peculiarities? On this basis Valla explores the whole range of things determined to exist, in their genuses and species, and in their individual differences and qualities. But this, of course, required an extensive argument and analysis. This was his reformation of philosophy into philology. Of course it was not only about words or the things that words stood for, it was about *verba et res* (words and things), the heart of grammatical and rhetorical theorizing. The consequence was to establish the theoretical basis of humanism and give humanists the intellectual tools to study and practice their art. His successors took it up where he left off, beginning with Angelo Poliziano and, most important, Desiderius Erasmus of Rotterdam.

This reconstruction of philosophy is set forth in book 1 with detailed examination of the qualities of things determined by the five senses and the constructions of the mind. Valla also addresses dialectic, under which he includes the variable use of language (book 2) and the methods of proof: syllogisms and induction (book 3). Syllogism is the deduction from an established principle of a conclusion concerning a matter to be determined, and its results are certain. Hence it is the established method of philosophy, particularly scholastic philosophy. Induction is the attainment of a probable conclusion from the collection and ordering of facts, and therefore is less than certain, but probable; it is the traditional domain of rhetorical argumentation. These two mental operations, the subject matter of book 3, are claimed now for rhetoric by Valla, so that there is no longer a need for dialectic as a branch of philosophy. In this work the humanist and humanism are elevated as replacements of the philosopher and philosophy and become central to the art of rhetoric.

In this same year, 1439, Valla completed his *Dialogus de libero arbitrio* (Dialogue on free will). Side by side with his writings and study on rhetorical theory Valla was concerned with religious and ecclesiastical affairs. This dialogue takes the position that man, through observation and reasoning, can determine the outcome of his earthly affairs, but he cannot determine his salvation by his own free will. For that he must trust in God. But this theological argument is linked to his critique of Scholasticism by his rebuke of both Boethius and Aristotle, the pagan mentors of Scholasticism. (He denies in the dialogue that Boethius was a Christian.) The *Dialogue on Free Will* was remarked upon favorably more than once by Martin Luther in his *Tischreden (Table Talk)*. It was also mentioned by Erasmus in his *De libero arbitrio diatribē sive collatio* (*Discussion of Free Will;* 1424) as not to be regarded seriously. But Valla, who did not write in the context of the Reformation, would not have denied that a man can perform good works out of the affect of love with which he is endowed— a stronger power than human reason. Salvation, however, was a divine, not a human power.

The Donation of Constantine. In a letter of 1441 to his close friend Giovanni Tortelli, who advised against issuing "new opinions," he says:

> But when I consider with reason the works that I have composed, what is it that I should fear? I, who overturn all the wisdom of the ancients in my works, should not freely express extraordinary opinions in lesser things? . . . I show that philosophers are dreaming in natural matters; metaphysics consists in a few little words and is not present in any things but only in words, and those words from Aristotle are ignored in a marvellous laziness.

There is more. This proud scholar was not afraid and knew his worth. But trouble lay ahead, and his desire to return to Rome was at stake.

In 1440 Valla issued two works attacking powerful ecclesiastical institutions: his *De falso credita et ementita Constantini donatione declamatio* (On the falsely believed and fictitious donation of Constantine) and his *De professione religiosorum* (On the profession of the religious). The first was an attack on the legendary gift of the Roman emperor, Constantine (ruled 306–337), on his deathbed, of the temporal rule of the empire to Pope Sylvester. Valla demonstrated that this was an eighth-century forgery concocted to bolster the power of the papacy in its struggle with the Carolingian emperors. It is a brilliantly written, ironic attack on the secular pretensions of the papacy, produced at the time that Valla's

VVM SAEPE ME
CVM NOSTRORᵌ
MAIORVM RES GE
STAS ALIORVMQᵌ
VEL POPVLORVM
VEL REGVM CON
SIDERO VIDENTV
R MIHI NON MODO DITIONIS
NOSTRI HOMINES VERVMETIAM
LINGVAE PROPAGATIONE COETE
RIS OMNIBVS ANTECELLVISSE
NAM PERSAS QVIDEM MEDOS
ASSYRIOS GRAECOS ALIOSQVE
PERMVLTOS LONGE LATEQVE RE
RVM POTITOS ESSE QVOSDAM
ETIAM VT ALIQVANTO INFERIVS
QVAM ROMANORVM FVIT I
TA MVLTO DIVTVRNIVS IMPERI
VM TENVISSE CONSTAT NVLIᵒS
TAMEN ITA LINGVAM SVAM AMP
LIASSE VT NOSTRI FECERVNT Q
VI VT ORAM ILLAM ITALIAE Qᴁ
MAGNA OLIM GRAECIA DICEBA

Valla's *De elegantis*. Opening page of a manuscript of *Elegantiae* (Elegances). The initial letter depicts Valla writing. Portraits of Roman emperors appear in the medallions in the margins. Mid-fifteenth century. UNIVERSITY LIBRARY, VALENCIA

mentor, King Alfonso, was engaged in war with Pope Eugenio IV over territory. This work is much admired by modern scholars for its critical analysis of the texts concocted and utilized for defense of the papacy. It is important to note that Valla was not the only scholar aware of this error. The canonist and future cardinal, Nicholas of Cusa, was another.

The other work, on the profession, or vow, of the regular clergy—monks, nuns, friars, and other orders—who had acquired the title of *religiosi* (religious), attacked the notion that they were more entitled to salvation than lay Christians. It is again a sprightly work in dialogue form between a "Frater" (brother) and "Lorenzo." Both of these works aroused immediate indignation among the clergy at the very time Valla was seeking to negotiate permission from Pope Eugenius to return to Rome.

In addition to this ecclesiastical offense, in the first redaction of his *Dialectica* Valla defended the position of the Greek Orthodox, at the Council of Florence on the Trinity, that the Holy Spirit proceeded only from the Father, not also from the Son, as the Latin Church held. As an aftermath of these judgments, Valla was brought before the Inquisition of Naples in the winter of 1444 and charged with questioning the existence of the Apostolic Council of Jerusalem and even questioning Aristotle's ten categories. Although he knew Eugenius IV and several cardinals were suspicious of him, he arranged through King Alfonso a visit to his relatives in Rome in the fall of 1444 and was forced into a hurried escape to avoid apparent prosecution. Valla prepared an *Apologia* to the Pope, retracting or explaining some of his positions, and negotiated for a permanent return to Rome that occurred in the spring of 1448, at which time Eugenius died and Nicholas V, himself a humanist, welcomed Valla, gave him a teaching post at the revived University of Rome, and made him a curial official and a canon of the Basilica of St. John Lateran. In 1455 he became *Secretarius Apostolicus* (Apostolic secretary). In all of these roles he was handsomely rewarded financially.

Later Career. Before he returned to Rome, Valla had written a first version of a commentary or *Collatio* on the New Testament, which he later revised into his *Adnotationes in Novum Testamentum* (Annotations on the New Testament) while in Rome. Erasmus published this work in 1505 and was influenced by it to produce his own *Annotations* in 1516. In 1445–1446, while still at Naples, Valla wrote *Historiarum Ferdinandi Regis Aragoniae libri* (Books on the history of King Ferdinand of Aragon), about

King Alfonso's ancestor. Bartolomeo Facio, another humanist at the Neapolitan court, attacked this work in a series of invectives. Valla replied in his *Antidotum in Facium* (Antidote to Facio). Besides his comments on historiographical methodology, this work is notable for Valla's reconstruction of the text of Livy in its book 4, one of Valla's more venerated philological accomplishments.

During his stay in Rome, Valla translated Herodotus's and Thucydides's histories. In the preface to the latter he compared translation to commerce as a way of entering into another culture. He also replied to Poggio's *Invectives* against him in two *Antidotes in Poggium* and two satirical dialogues called *Apologus*. He wrote three discourses notable for their content: an inaugural oration to his course of lectures in which he stressed the importance of the Church in keeping Latin culture alive; *Sermo de mysterio Eucharistiae* (Sermon on the mystery of the Eucharist; 1456 or 1457); and *Encomium Sancti Thomae Aquinatis* (Encomion on Saint Thomas Aquinas; 1457). The last work was notable in expressing both his admiration for the saint and his rejection of Aristotelian-based scholastic theology. Instead he favored the theology of the church fathers such as Jerome and Augustine. Valla died, unexpectedly, on 1 August 1457 at the age of fifty, after only nine and a half years in his beloved Rome.

Lorenzo Valla, with his intellectual brilliance, historical farsightedness, and militant stubbornness undoubtedly made an impact on his time and hastened the transformation we know as the Renaissance into its irreversible maturity.

BIBLIOGRAPHY

Primary Works

Valla, Lorenzo. *Dialogue on Free Will*. Translated with an introduction by Charles Trinkaus. In *The Renaissance Philosophy of Man*. Edited by Ernst Cassirer, Paul Oskar Kristeller, and John Herman Randall, Jr. Chicago, 1948.

Valla, Lorenzo. *Epistole*. Edited by Ottavio Besomi and Mariangela Regoliosi. Padua, Italy, 1984.

Valla, Lorenzo. *On Pleasure: De Voluptate*. Translated by A. Kent Hieatt and Maristella Lorch. New York, 1977.

Valla, Lorenzo. *The Profession of the Religious*. Translated and edited by Olga Zorzi Pugliese. Toronto, 1985.

Valla, Lorenzo. *The Treatise of Lorenzo Valla on the Donation of Constantine*. Translated by Christopher B. Coleman. Toronto, 1993.

Secondary Works

Besomi, Ottavio, and Mariangela Regoliosi, eds. *Lorenzo Valla e L'umanesimo italiano*. Padua, Italy, 1986.

Camporeale, Salvatore I. *Lorenzo Valla: Umanesimo e Teologia*. Florence, 1972.

Fois, Mario. *Il Pensiero Cristiano di Lorenzo Valla nel quadro storico-culturale del suo ambiente*. Rome, 1969.

Gaeta, Franco. *Lorenzo Valla: Filologia e storia nell'umanesimo Italiano*. Naples, 1955.

Lorch, Maristella di Panizza. *A Defense of Life: Lorenzo Valla's Theory of Pleasure*. Munich, 1985.

Setz, Wolfram. *Lorenzo Vallas Schrift gegen die konstantinische Schenkung*. Tübingen, Germany, 1975.

Trinkaus, Charles. *In Our Image and Likeness: Humanity and Divinity in Italian Humanist Thought*. Chicago and London, 1970; Notre Dame, Ind., 1995. See chapters 3, 12, and 14.

CHARLES TRINKAUS

VALLE, FEDERICO DELLA. *See* **Della Valle, Federico.**

VALOIS DYNASTY. A cadet line of the Capetian dynasty (not in the direct line of succession), the house of Valois gained the French crown in 1328 and held it until 1589. Philip of Valois (Philip VI, ruled 1328–1350) was crowned after the death of his childless cousin, Charles IV, despite the rival claim of another cousin, Edward III of England. Nine years after appearing to accept Philip's legitimacy, Edward declared war on the "so-called king" of France in 1337,

A Valois King. Anonymous portrait of Charles VIII (ruled 1483–1498). GALLERIA DEGLI UFFIZI, FLORENCE/ALINARI/ART RESOURCE

beginning the Hundred Years' War. In the course of the war the French kings John II (ruled 1350–1364), Charles V (ruled 1364–1380), Charles VI (ruled 1380–1422), and Charles VII (ruled 1422–1461) several times nearly lost the throne.

Outward Expansion. After 1453, when the English were driven from all of France except Calais, the attention of the Valois kings turned to their rivals and cousins, the Burgundian dukes. Louis XI (Valois, ruled 1461–1483) succeeded in turning the Swiss against Duke Charles the Bold of Burgundy, who was killed at the Battle of Nancy in 1477. Charles's heiress, Duchess Mary, sought help against Louis by marrying Maximilian of Habsburg. This began a series of marriage alliances that eventually passed a vast range of lands surrounding France and hatred of the Valois to their grandson, Holy Roman Emperor Charles V, ensuring that hostility marked relations between Valois and Habsburg for the duration of the Valois dynasty.

A French claim to the kingdom of Naples occupied the reign of Charles VIII (ruled 1483–1498). In 1494 he led the first French invasion of Italy, beginning the long French involvement there until 1559. When he died childless, his cousin succeeded as Louis XII (ruled 1498–1515). Having also a claim to the duchy of Milan through his grandmother Valentina Visconti, Louis sought to make good his Italian rights in the second French invasion. Pope Julius II, objecting to Louis's pretensions to Italian lands, organized the Holy League in 1509, which expelled the French by 1514.

Louis's cousin and successor, Francis I (ruled 1515–1547), returned to Italy to reclaim Milan from the Swiss. His victory at Marignano in 1515 restored Milan to French rule and cowed Pope Leo X into agreeing to the Concordat of Bologna, which gave the king the right to fill the major benefices in the French church, with papal oversight. With access to the church's wealth assured, the French monarchy had little interest in supporting Protestantism when it appeared during Francis's reign. His reclaiming of Milan provided Emperor Charles V with a pretext for war. At the Battle of Pavia in 1525, Francis was captured and held for ransom. Exchanging his two older sons for freedom, he continued the war until 1529, when he agreed to give two million crowns and sovereignty over Naples, Milan, and Flanders to Charles to retrieve his sons, while Charles conceded Burgundy. The peace remained a dead letter, however, as warfare continued between the Valois and the Habsburgs.

Valois Dynasty

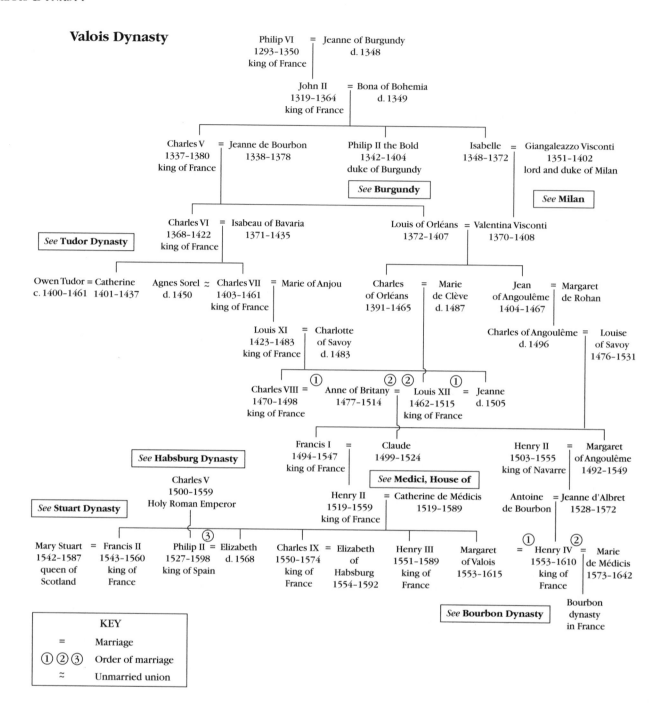

Philip VI = Jeanne of Burgundy
1293–1350   d. 1348
king of France

John II = Bona of Bohemia
1319–1364   d. 1349
king of France

Charles V = Jeanne de Bourbon   Philip II the Bold   Isabelle = Giangaleazzo Visconti
1337–1380   1338–1378   1342–1404   1348–1372   1351–1402
king of France   duke of Burgundy   lord and duke of Milan

See **Burgundy**

See **Milan**

Charles VI = Isabeau of Bavaria   Louis of Orléans = Valentina Visconti
1368–1422   1371–1435   1372–1407   1370–1408
king of France

See **Tudor Dynasty**

Owen Tudor = Catherine   Agnes Sorel ≈ Charles VII = Marie of Anjou   Charles = Marie   Jean = Margaret
c. 1400–1461 1401–1437   d. 1450   1403–1461   of Orléans   de Clève   of Angoulême   de Rohan
king of France   1391–1465   d. 1487   1404–1467

Louis XI = Charlotte   Charles of Angoulême = Louise
1423–1483   of Savoy   d. 1496   of Savoy
king of France   d. 1483   1476–1531

①   ② ②   ①
Charles VIII = Anne of Britany = Louis XII = Jeanne
1470–1498   1477–1514   1462–1515   d. 1505
king of France   king of France

Francis I = Claude   Henry II = Margaret
1494–1547   1499–1524   1503–1555   of Angoulême
king of France   king of Navarre   1492–1549

See **Habsburg Dynasty**

Charles V   *See* **Medici, House of**
1500–1559
Holy Roman Emperor   Henry II = Catherine de Médicis   Antoine = Jeanne d'Albret
1519–1559   1519–1589   de Bourbon   1528–1572
king of France

See **Stuart Dynasty**

③   ①   ②
Mary Stuart = Francis II   Philip II = Elizabeth   Charles IX = Elizabeth   Henry III   Margaret   = Henry IV = Marie
1542–1587   1543–1560   1527–1598   d. 1568   1550–1574   of   1551–1589   of Valois   1553–1610   de Médicis
queen of   king of   king of Spain   king of   Habsburg   king of   1553–1615   king of   1573–1642
Scotland   France   France   1554–1592   France   France

See **Bourbon Dynasty**   Bourbon
dynasty
in France

	KEY
=	Marriage
① ② ③	Order of marriage
≈	Unmarried union

Renaissance culture captivated Francis, and numerous Italian artists, architects, and humanists came to France under his patronage, among them Leonardo da Vinci, Benvenuto Cellini, Rosso Fiorentino, and Francesco Primaticcio. The latter two helped make his château of Fontainebleau the center of Renaissance art in northern Europe. He provided patronage to humanists such as Guillaume Budé and organized the College of the Three Languages to teach the classical languages. His reign was the era of several luminaries of French literature, including François Rabelais, Clément Marot, and Marot's sister, Margaret of Angoulême. Francis was sympathetic to the humanists' program of moderate church reform, but when he was confronted with Protestantism in the Day of the Placards in 1534, he responded with an outburst of persecution. John Calvin was among those who fled the realm. Calvin's publication of the

Institutes of the Christian Religion in French in 1541 provided direction to previously disorganized French Protestantism and made it a powerful force in France for the next century.

Francis's son, Henry II (ruled 1547–1559), was married at age fourteen to Catherine de Médicis in order to forge an alliance with the Medici pope, Clement VII. Catherine's presence increased the number of Italians at the court, but Henry preferred native artists and architects using Italianate forms, among them Jean Goujon, Pierre Lescot, and Philibert de L'Orme. He also patronized French writers, especially the poets known as the Pléiade, who included Pierre de Ronsard. He returned French forces to Italy, and Philip II of Spain responded by invading northern France in 1557. When Philip failed to attack Paris, Henry used the army he had assembled to defend the city to take Calais in 1558. With the spread of Protestantism worrying both, they agreed to the Peace of Cateau-Cambrésis in 1559.

Civil Strife and Decline.   When Henry was mortally wounded in a tournament celebrating the peace, his fifteen-year-old son, Francis II (ruled 1559–1560), took the throne. Control of the monarchy fell to the Guise, uncles of Francis's wife, Mary, queen of Scots. The Bourbons and other nobles resented their exclusion from power, and they joined forces with the French Protestants against the Guise, who were leaders of the ardent Catholics. The drift to civil war did not end with Francis's death in 1560 and the accession of his brother, Charles IX (ruled 1560–1574). The four decades of civil war produced the worst blemish on the Valois—the Saint Bartholomew's Day massacre of Huguenots in Paris and other towns in 1572. Stricken with guilt over his role in the massacre, Charles died in 1574. The fiscal crisis confronting the monarchy in this era prevented extensive patronage of Renaissance culture, although Catherine de Médicis gained notoriety supporting astrologers, including Nostradamus.

Charles's brother Henry III (ruled 1574–1589) returned from Poland, where he had been elected king the previous year, to take the throne. The best educated of the Valois kings, he created a Palace Academy to discuss intellectual developments, such as heliocentrism. Although he earlier had led the Catholic forces, he now sought compromise. Angry Catholics led by Henry of Guise opposed his concessions to the Huguenots. When the king's brother, the duke of Anjou, died in 1584, making the Huguenot prince Henry of Bourbon his successor, the Catholic League was organized to prevent Bourbon's becoming king.

Henry III opposed the League, and it forced him out of Paris during the Day of the Barricades in 1588. Henry ordered the deaths of Guise and his brother, and the League exacted revenge by assassinating Henry in 1589. His death marked the end of the Valois, as Henry IV began the Bourbon dynasty. Despite a dismal last three decades for the Valois, the dynasty had done a great deal to define the French nation, state, and monarchy. The Bourbon kings built royal absolutism on the foundations laid by the Valois.

See also **Burgundy**; **Dynastic Rivalry**; **France**; **Wars of Italy**; **Wars of Religion**; *and biographies of monarchs mentioned in this entry.*

BIBLIOGRAPHY

Baumgartner, Frederic J. *Henry II, King of France, 1547–1559.* Durham, N.C., 1988.

Baumgartner, Frederic J. *Louis XII.* New York, 1994.

Bridge, John. *A History of France from the Death of Louis XI to 1515.* 5 vols. Oxford, 1921–1936. Especially strong on war and diplomacy during the era 1483–1515.

Cameron, Keith. *Henri III: A Maligned or Malignant King?* Exeter, U.K., 1978.

Holt, Mack. *The French Wars of Religion, 1562–1629.* Cambridge, U.K., 1995.

Kendall, Paul. *Louis XI: The Universal Spider.* New York, 1970. Reprint, New York, 1986.

Knecht, R. J. *Renaissance Warrior and Patron: The Reign of Francis I.* New York, 1994.

Potter, David. *A History of France, 1460–1560: The Emergence of a Nation State.* New York, 1995.

Vale, M. G. A. *Charles VII.* Berkeley, Calif., 1974.

FREDERIC J. BAUMGARTNER

VARCHI, BENEDETTO   (1503–1565), Florentine humanist, historian, and philologist. Varchi studied law at Pisa but, upon receipt of a sizable inheritance, dedicated himself to letters, mastering Greek and Provençal and traveling widely throughout northern Italy. In Padua he immersed himself in Aristotelianism, a philosophy which had a lasting impact on his outlook, and gained admission to the Accademia degli Infiammati. Having supported the expulsion of the Medici from Florence in 1527, he followed his political allies, members of the Strozzi family, into exile. Nonetheless, after the loss of his wealth Varchi accepted the invitation of Cosimo I de' Medici, ruler of Florence, to return home in 1543, and became a courtier. He joined the Accademia Fiorentina (Florentine academy) and lectured for many years on Dante and Petrarch. Cosimo I continued to afford Varchi generous treatment, commissioning him in 1547 to compose a modern history of the city. In his later years Varchi increased in religious devotion and, immediately before his death, was named provost of Montevarchi, his ancestral home. An individual of great intelligence and broad learning, possessed of a prodigious memory and pragmatic flexibility, he was held in high esteem by the leading figures of his day.

Varchi was a prolific writer of both verse and prose. In the first category are eclogues and numerous sonnets in the Petrarchan mold, as well as compositions in Latin and others written in the vernacular but employing classical meter. Among components of the second group are commemorative orations, lessons on literary criticism, a comedy entitled *La suocera* (The mother-in-law), and a grammar of Provençal (adapted from extant descriptions). The *Storia fiorentina* (Florentine history) prepared for Cosimo I, not published until 1721, is perhaps his best-known work. Beginning with the reestablishment of the republic in 1527 and covering up to 1538, it comprises sixteen books that reveal the care with which its author utilized historical documents in a constant search for realism and truth. This text offers a fascinating portrait of early sixteenth-century Florence and makes patent Varchi's dispassion and independence of thought: never reluctant to condemn Pope Clement VII and other Medici, he is also restrained in the praise of his patron.

Varchi contributed significantly to the language debates in Italy, controversies known collectively as the *Questione della lingua* (Question of the language), through his authorship of a treatise entitled *L'Ercolano* (The Ercolano; first edition 1570). This document allegedly was composed in support of Varchi's friend, Annibale Caro (1507–1566), whose attention to spoken Tuscan had been censured by Lodovico Castelvetro (1505–1571). Defending a reliance on contemporary Florentine as the basis for sound linguistic expression, *L'Ercolano* affirms the essential oral nature of language and the primacy of usage over authority and reason. Nevertheless, Varchi believed that familiarity with established models from previous centuries is mandatory for the attainment of stylistic beauty. As a response to competing views of acceptable Italian language practice, the disquisition offers a valuable compendium of concepts espoused by previous authors accompanied by Varchi's replies, and contains a wealth of information regarding the colloquial Florentine of that era.

BIBLIOGRAPHY

Primary Works

Varchi, Benedetto. *L'Ercolano: Dialogo di Messer Benedetto Varchi nel quale si ragiona delle lingue, ed in particolare della toscana e della fiorentina.* 2 vols. 1804. Reprint, Milan, 1979.

Varchi, Benedetto. *Opere di Benedetto Varchi ora per la prima volta raccolte.* Edited by Antonio Racheli. 2 vols. Trieste, Italy, 1858–1859.

Varchi, Benedetto. *Storia fiorentina di Benedetto Varchi.* Edited by Gaetano Milanesi. 3 vols. Florence, 1857–1858.

Secondary Works

Manacorda, Guido. *Benedetto Varchi: L'uomo, il poeta, il critico.* 1903. Reprint, Rome, 1978.

Pirotti, Umberto. *Benedetto Varchi e la cultura del suo tempo.* Florence, 1971.

MICHAEL T. WARD

VARTHEMA, LODOVICO DE (c. 1472–c. 1517), Italian traveler to Asia. Little is known of Varthema other than what he tells us in his immensely popular description of his journeys, the *Itinerario,* which he first published in Italian in 1510. He was born perhaps in or near Bologna between 1470 and 1472, perhaps of Genoese or Modenese origin, and his father may have practiced medicine. His brisk and engaging prose style suggests humanist training. His only occupation known with certainty, however, was as a soldier, possibly serving under Federico da Montefeltro, duke of Urbino. He left Venice for Alexandria, Egypt, in 1502, and then embarked on his extensive travels—disguised as a Muslim in order to make the hajj, the pilgrimage to Mecca required of Muslims, and to visit Medina. (He was probably the first European whose claim to seeing those cities was genuine.) He continued on to Yemen, Ethiopia, India, and perhaps as far as the Moluccas, the spice islands. Knighted in 1507 by the Portuguese viceroy Almeida for bravery at the siege of Cannanore, India, he then returned to Italy in 1508. He cultivated friendships with high-ranking prelates and aristocrats in Rome, where he published his *Itinerario,* and where he died between 1511 and 1517.

Varthema was one of the best known and most successful travel writers since Marco Polo and John Mandeville. For several decades, his *Itinerario* served as a primary modern authority on the Portuguese discoveries in the East, as well as being an overnight international literary success. The first Roman edition was followed in the sixteenth century by thirteen other Italian editions, six in Latin, four in Spanish, seven in German, two in Flemish, and one edition each in English and French. At least another ten editions date from the seventeenth century.

Varthema's work is the best example of a new literary tradition that would shape the genre of travel writing for centuries: the "tales of the curious and adventurous traveler." He typifies the traveler as an independent character, a person who defines himself by a desire to know other places and peoples, rather than traveling primarily with a fixed purpose—as a pilgrim, missionary, merchant, conqueror, spy, or ambassador. Thus, while much of Varthema's journey followed the same pattern (dressing as a Muslim and following the trade routes) as the tale of Niccolò Conti (1395–1469), *Historiae de varietate fortunae,* which was edited by Poggio Bracciolini a century earlier, it differs from such older accounts by its emphasis on travel for the sake of travel. Polo and Conti will always be remembered as merchant-patricians from Venice, but Varthema is simply the man from Bologna who went to see the East. This self-conscious fashioning of his own persona has parallels not only in travel literature, but also in the new forms of autobiographical and prescriptive treatises of the Renaissance. Varthema appeals to the knowledge attained through practical experience in much the same way as a Macchiavelli, Guicciardini, or Castiglione appeals to experience over authority.

While some parts of his trip remain open to question (especially the interior of Persia and any of his observations beyond India), Varthema's lasting legacy is to elevate the role of the traveler to that of the independent and skillful observer, and to liberate the genre of travel-writing from its ties to pilgrims and traders.

See also **Travel and Travel Literature**.

BIBLIOGRAPHY

Primary Work

The Travels of Ludovico di Varthema: In Egypt, Syria, Arabia Deserta and Arabia Felix, Persia, India, and Ethiopia, A.D. *1503 to 1508.* Translated from the original Italian edition of 1510 with a preface by John Winter Jones: edited with notes and an introduction by George Percy Badger. London, 1863 [and many subsequent editions]. Translation of *Itinerario de Ludovico de Varthema Bolognese nello Egypto, nella Surria, nella Arabia deserta & felice; nella Persia, nella India & nella Ethiopia. La fede, el uiuiere, & costumi de tutte le prefate prouincie con gratia & privilegio infra notato.* Rome, 1510.

Secondary Works

Barozzi, Pietro, *Ludovico de Varthema e il suo* Itinerario. Rome, 1996.

Rubiés, Joan-Pao. *South India through Foreign Eyes: Ethnography and Travel in Renaissance Europe, 1200–1600.* Cambridge, U.K., forthcoming.

LANCE G. LAZAR

VASARI, GIORGIO. *See* **Renaissance, Interpretations of the,** *subentry on* **Giorgio Vasari.**

VATICAN LIBRARY. One of the world's great collections of Renaissance manuscripts and early printed books, the Vatican Library is a Renaissance creation. Around 1450 Pope Nicholas V (1447–1455) conceived the idea of a public library in the Vatican Palace. Popes had had an archive for documents and books dating from the first century. In the Middle Ages, they frequently carried the collection around with them on trips, including to Avignon, where they resided for most of the fourteenth century. Only a portion of the Avignon documents and manuscripts ever found their way back to Rome. After the turmoil of the Great Schism (1378–1415), Martin V (1417–1431) and Eugenius IV (1431–1447) traveled a great deal. Nicholas V, on the other hand, firmly established the tradition of popes staying put in Rome. He also launched a series of construction projects, including the public library. Nicholas V wanted a library "for the common convenience of the learned," as he explained in a letter to the humanist Enoch of Ascoli, and not the old hodgepodge of books and documents. With his own books serving as its core, Nicholas V established the library in three connected rooms underneath what is today the Borgia Apartments: one room for Latin books (800 manuscripts), another for Greek (353 manuscripts), and a third (*bibliotheca secreta*) for documents and books reserved for the pope. Nicholas saw to the decoration of the *biblioteca graeca* before he died.

However, the library languished until Pope Sixtus IV (1471–1484), the builder of the Sistine Chapel, took up Nicholas V's project. Sixtus IV added a fourth room, hired artists such as Melozzo da Forlì to fresco the walls, greatly increased the number of books (the library held more than thirty-six hundred books by the time he died), and clearly separated the library from the archive, although a complete physical and institutional separation of the archive from the library was not achieved until the seventeenth century. Sixtus IV appointed the humanist Bartolomeo Sacchi ("Platina") as the first librarian of the transformed library, an appointment memorialized in the celebrated fresco by Melozzo on the wall opposite the entrance to the first room of the library (transferred to Pinacoteca of the Vatican Museums in 1820). A hundred years later, when the space under the Borgia Apartments had become woefully inadequate for the by now tremendously enlarged collection, another great Renaissance builder, Sixtus V (1585–1590), became the "third founder" of the library. Sixtus V commissioned his architect Domenico Fontana to bisect the middle of Donato Bramante's Cortile del Belvedere with the imposing structure that today still houses the library. Sixtus V also endowed the library with a staff of eight resident

Vatican Library. Vestibule of the Sistine Library. Portraits of cardinal librarians line the walls above the display cases.
©BIBLIOTECA APOSTOLICA VATICANA, VATICAN CITY

scholars called *scriptores,* expanding upon a practice begun in the 1540s, when three experts (one in Latin, another in Greek, and a third in Hebrew) were assigned to the library. During the Renaissance a good number of leading scholars served at one time or other as Vatican librarians or *scriptores.*

Unfortunately, the openness that had characterized the library in the early Renaissance (even frequently letting its manuscripts out on loan) ceased in the second half of the sixteenth century. The suspicious atmosphere generated by the Reformation effectively made the library inaccessible to almost all except Vatican insiders. By the early seventeenth century the library allowed consultation by special permission only for a few hours on those days that were not one of the many feast days requiring closure. Moreover, after 1566 visitors were not permitted to consult the inventories, thus making genuine exploration of the collection impossible. But in 1883, after two hundred years of these severe restrictions,

Pope Leo XIII (1878–1903) opened up the library to all qualified researchers, just as he had done for the papal archives in 1881. Americans played a role in modernizing the library. From 1927 to 1939 the Carnegie Endowment for International Peace paid for the installation of a modern stack system using steel shelves from Snead of Jersey City and for the implementation of a modern cataloging system under the direction of Americans and American-trained librarians.

The Vatican today is the single largest depository of Renaissance Latin manuscripts (they form the largest block of its more than seventy-five thousand manuscripts in Latin, Greek, Hebrew, Arabic, Syriac, Persian, Coptic, and other languages). It has over eight thousand incunables (that is, books printed before 1501) and one of the largest collections in the world of sixteenth- and seventeenth-century books.

[For a portrayal of Pope Sixtus IV inaugurating the Vatican Library, see the color plates in volume 3;

for a portrayal of the pope's visit to the library see the illustration in **Libraries,** in volume 3.]

See also Libraries; Papacy.

BIBLIOGRAPHY

Bignami Odier, Jeanne, and José Ruysschaert. *La Bibliothèque vaticane de Sixte IV à Pie XI.* Vatican City, Italy, 1973.

Boyle, Leonard E., O.P. "Sixtus IV and the Vatican Library." In *Rome: Tradition, Innovation, and Renewal.* Victoria, B.C., Canada, 1991. Pages 65–73.

Grafton, Anthony, ed. *Rome Reborn: The Vatican Library and Renaissance Culture.* Washington, D. C., and Vatican City, Italy, 1993.

Müntz, Eugène, and Paul Fabre. *La Bibliothèque du Vatican au quinzième siècle.* Paris, 1887.

The Vatican Library: Two Papers by Monsignor Eugène Tisserant and Thedore Wesley Koch. Jersey City, N.J., 1929.

JOHN MONFASANI

VEGA, GARCILASO DE LA. *See* **Garcilaso de la Vega.**

VEGA, INCA GARCILASO DE LA (1539–1616),

Peruvian mestizo and creole chronicler. The Inca Garcilaso de la Vega is recognized primarily for his historical works, which present from both the American Indian and European perspective a valuable body of information about the traditions and way of life of pre-Columbian Peru.

Vega was born in Cuzco to the Incan princess Isabel Chimpu Ocllo and the Spanish captain Sebastián Garcilaso de la Vega. Later, in Spain, the chronicler added the title "Inca" to demonstrate pride in his Indian heritage. He spoke Quechua along with Castilian, and he learned Latin in school. His earliest education occurred in his father's house in Peru, where he was exposed to Spanish and indigenous traditions. Vega went to Spain in 1560 at the age of twenty-one to complete his education and to petition the Spanish crown for monies he believed were owed to his father for his service in Peru. After serving in the Spanish army he settled into a life of writing.

Vega's first work, appearing in 1590, was a translation from Italian into Spanish of Leone Ebreo's Neoplatonic dialogues, *The Philosophy of Love,* which set forth the nature, origin, essence, and universality of love. He claimed that he undertook it to pass his time productively and because it was a work highly regarded by the humanists of his day.

In 1605 he published *La Florida del Inca* (The Florida of the Inca), an account of Hernando de Soto's ill-fated expedition to what is now the southeastern United States. His most reliable source was the personal testimony of his friend, the old conquistador Gonzalo Silvestre, who had participated in the adventure. The *Florida* honored the heroes of the expedition and encouraged the Spanish to complete the conquest of the land.

The *Comentarios reales* (Royal commentaries), published in Lisbon in 1609, are the hallmark of Vega's production. In its nine books Vega explores the origins of the Incas; their religion, laws, and government; and the lives of important Inca before the arrival of the Spanish. Vega saw Incan civilization as being almost on a par with that of ancient Rome. In his view the Incan empire, like the Roman, prepared the way for acceptance of Christianity. Vega's history, while entertaining, is tinged with nostalgia and fantasy.

The second part of the work, published posthumously in 1617, is the *Historia general del Perú* (General history of Peru). Its eight books deal with the Spaniards' discovery of Peru, the conquest, the civil wars between the Pizarros and the Almagros, and the revolt and punishment of tyrants. Vega, dedicating the work to the Virgin Mary, proposed to honor the memory of his father; to encourage the Indians, mestizos, and creoles of Peru to live up to their potential for greatness; and to celebrate the heroism of some of the Spanish conquistadors.

In the seventeenth century, Vega was regarded as the final authority on the Incan empire. His works continued to enjoy a favorable opinion in the eighteenth century, especially among the French rationalists, who saw Vega's histories as a precursor of social studies. Eighteenth-century Spaniards, however, prohibited the *Comentarios,* fearing that the work might inspire rebellion among the Indian population of the Andes.

See also **Americas.**

BIBLIOGRAPHY

Primary Works

Vega, Inca Garcilaso de la. *The Florida of the Inca.* Edited and translated by John Grier Varner and Jeannette Johnson Varner. Austin, Tex., 1951. Translation of *La Florida del Inca* (1605).

Vega, Inca Garcilaso de la, trans. *The Philosophy of Love.* Translated by F. Friedeberg-Seeley and Jean Barnes. London, 1937. Translation of *La traduzión del Indio de los tres diálogos de amor de León Hebreo* (1590).

Vega, Inca Garcilaso de la. *Royal Commentaries of the Incas and General History of Peru.* Translated by Harold V. Livermore. 2 vols. Austin, Tex., 1996. Translation of *Primera parte de los comentarios reales de los Yncas* (1609) and *Historia general del Perú* (1617).

Secondary Works

Castanien, Donald G. *El Inca Garcilaso de la Vega.* New York, 1969.

Pupo-Walker, Enrique. *Historia, creación y profecía en los textos del Inca Garcilaso de la Vega.* Madrid, 1982.

Varner, John Grier. *El Inca: The Life and Times of Garcilaso de la Vega.* Austin, Tex., 1968.

Zamora, Margarita. *Language, Authority, and Indigenous History in the* Comentarios reales de los Incas. Cambridge, U.K., and New York, 1988.

JAMES C. MURRAY

VEGA CARPIO, LOPE FÉLIX DE (1562–1635),

Spanish playwright, poet, and novelist. Called by his contemporaries "*monstruo de la naturaleza*" (prodigious monster of nature) and "*fénix de los ingenios*" (intellectual phoenix), Lope de Vega's dramatic and poetic output was unequaled among writers in any language for sheer quantity and lyricism. He was recognized in his own time for his innovative role in transforming Spanish theater into the immensely popular *comedia nueva* (new theater) that drew crowds to the *corrales* of Madrid, open-air patios adapted for theatrical use. Of the 1,800 plays claimed for Lope after his death by his protégé Juan Pérez de Montalbán, around 314 have survived that are definitely by Lope, and another 187 have been attributed to him with varying probability of authorship. Except for the picaresque novel, Lope cultivated all the literary genres of his time: sonnets, *romances* (ballads), epic, Byzantine and pastoral romance, the Italianate novella, and prose fiction mixed with poetry.

Life and Times. Son of a master embroiderer, Lope was a child prodigy who composed verses before he could write and was able to read Latin as well as Castilian when he was five. He stated that he wrote his first play at the age of twelve, possibly in connection with the Jesuit school he attended for two years. At fourteen he entered the service of Jerónimo Manrique de Lara, bishop of Ávila, and began to attend the University of Alcalá. He may have also attended the University of Salamanca while serving in the household of Pedro de Dávila, marquis of Las Navas. At twenty-one he enlisted in a military expedition to the Azores. In 1588 he was banished for eight years from Madrid and for two years from the entire kingdom of Castile as punishment for malicious libel against the family of a producer-director, Jerónimo Velázquez, with whose married daughter, Elena Osorio, Lope had a five-year affair. When Elena broke off the affair in favor of a wealthier lover, Lope circulated satirical verses attacking her and her family. This incident was the basis for numerous sonnets and ballads in which Elena appears in pastoral and Moorish disguises, and most notably as the central plot of *La Dorotea,* published three

years before Lope's death. His activities during the years of exile before being pardoned in 1595 were typical of Lope's passionate and patriotic character: he returned to Madrid illegally and married Isabel de Urbina in 1588, joined the Armada at Lisbon, lived with his wife in Valencia until 1590, moved to Toledo to serve the marquis of Malpica, and then to Alba de Tormes to serve as secretary to the powerful duke of Alba until 1595. Isabel died in childbirth in 1590, and Lope, pardoned before his sentence was completed, returned to Madrid. He began a long term as secretary to the duke of Sessa in 1605.

Perhaps the most important influence of Lope's exile on his literary career was his acquaintance with Valencian dramatists. Upon his return to Madrid, he introduced several innovations that challenged classical dramatic precepts and enriched theatrical activity there. Lope enumerated these innovations in the *Arte nuevo de hacer comedias en este reino* (New art of playwriting in this kingdom; 1609), addressed tongue-in-cheek to the Academia de Madrid, whose erudite objections he countered with the more persuasive authority of the popular audience whom he acknowledged as his decisive authority. Lope's crucial passage regarding tragicomedy uses Giovanni Battista Guarini's defense of *Il pastor fido* (The faithful shepherd; 1590) to justify comic relief, scenes, characters, and subplots in serious theatrical works. In addition to disregarding the classical unities of time and plot, Lope reduced the number of acts to three, introduced metrical variety that enlivened the performance (in contrast to the ponderous *octava rima* used by earlier Spanish playwrights and the uniformity of the twelve syllable alexandrine in French classical theater), drew his plots from the rich Iberian historical and legendary traditions as well as religious and mythological material, introduced subplots involving lower-class characters, and developed the comic figure of the *gracioso,* usually a witty servant. Other popular features of his plays were the figures of the peasant protagonist and the *mujer varonil,* the woman dressed as a man. Scholarly controversy continues over the interpretation of these figures' crossing of class and gender boundaries and their affirmation, respectively, of their personal honor and autonomy, and the social conservatism or subversive potential of Lope's theater.

The richness of Lope's lyric gift was shown to greatest effect in the variety of poetic forms employed in the *comedia nueva:* lively eight-syllable *romances* (ballads) for narrative, *redondillas* (eight-syllable verses rhyming *abba*) for the speech of servants and women characters, eleven-syllable *octava*

Lope Félix de Vega Carpio. CULVER PICTURES

rima in eight-line stanzas rhyming *abababcc* for solemn deliberation, and sonnets for moments of suspense while characters await the outcome of offstage action. In the afternoon performances on the sparsely furnished open-air apron stage of the *corrales* Lope's poetic gift created atmospheric effects and dramatic transformations in light, mood, and setting. Not surprisingly, he vehemently opposed the Italian influence that promoted stage machinery, moveable scenery, and props to create the illusions that he was so skilled at painting in words.

Lope's personal life defied social norms as emphatically as his theater did classical dramatic precepts. The women with whom he shared his life and who bore his children appeared in his poetry and fiction under pseudonyms: Elena Osorio as "Filis" and his first wife Isabel de Urbina as "Belisa." After Isabel's death he shared a household with an actor's wife, Micaela de Luján ("Camila Lucinda"), with whom he had a son, Lope, and a daughter, Marcela, while living elsewhere with his second wife, Juana de Guardo, whom he married in 1598. Juana de Guardo died in childbirth in 1613, three years after the couple had moved definitively to Madrid, and a year after their son Carlos Félix died at the age of

seven. In 1614, perhaps in response to these two losses, Lope was ordained a priest, despite his love affair with Jerónima de Burgos ("Gerarda"). The last great love of Lope's life was the wife of a businessman, Marta de Nevares Santoya ("Amarilis"), whom he continued to care for until her death in 1632, after she became blind and insane in 1628. Despite his obvious disregard for clerical celibacy, Lope wrote eloquent devotional poetry. He acknowledged and brought up his children, wrote of them with great affection, and was deeply moved by their loss. Of Micaela de Luján's surviving children, his son Lope was lost at sea, and the dramatist clearly missed the intellectual companionship of his daughter Marcela, a poet herself, who took orders and became Sor Marcela de San Félix in the neighboring trinitarian convent. Lope's humble family origins and seemingly facile gift for versification were targeted by his more erudite rivals. Some of them could claim noble genealogies, but none could challenge his theatrical and literary success. His death was the occasion of public mourning, and his name became synonymous with excellence in any field.

Theater. Scholars have grouped Lope's plays under chronological and thematic systems of classification. Since autograph manuscripts were discarded or lost in the process of revision for performance, and references to events in the early published texts, or "Partes," may not be reliable indications of the time of composition, versification has proved more reliable in dating Lope's early, middle, and late plays. Across those categories, his plays can be grouped by theme and source material: historical (drawing on chronicles but also on ballad traditions and legends), saints' lives, *autos* (religious plays for Corpus Christi), honor, mythological, and cloak-and-sword plays, although these groupings overlap. *Fuenteovejuna* (The sheep-well; 1612–1614) transports a well-documented fourteenth-century uprising of peasants against a tyrannical overlord to a fifteenth-century context, and further justifies the peasants' action by their loyalty to Ferdinand and Isabella, emblematic of political stability against rebellious nobles. Together with *Peribáñez y el comendador de Ocaña* (Peribáñez and the commander of Ocaña; 1612), this is the best-known of the "peasant honor plays" of Lope's middle period, celebrating vengeance as an effective means of resolving questions of honor. In another honor play from this middle period, *Los comendadores de Córdoba* (The commanders of Córdoba), an outraged husband kills not only his adulterous wife, but all the servants and even the animals in his household who might have witnessed his dishonor.

Much of Lope's most powerful theater dramatizes incidents from medieval Castilian history, drawing on chronicles, legends, and ballad traditions. The infamous revenge involving the princes of Lara figures in *El bastardo Mudarra* (The bastard Mudarra; 1612) and the Cid appears in *Las almenas de Toro* (The battlements of Toro; 1621). Lope's gift for adapting the emotional and musical flexibility of Castilian popular traditions is at its best in *El caballero de Olmedo* (The knight from Olmedo; 1620–1625), based on a few lines of a popular ballad about a murder of a young man from Olmedo by the servants of his rival in Medina. Lope added a go-between modeled after the bawd in *La Celestina* (1499) by Fernando de Rojas and created evocative language and songs to portend the tragic outcome. The violent plot of *El castigo sin venganza* (Punishment without vengeance; 1631) is based upon a novella by Matteo Bandello, but Lope's more complex characterizations give tragic dimensions to the murder of a young wife who yields to the temptation of adultery with her husband's illegitimate son.

Lope's *capa y espada* (cloak-and-sword) plays belong to a long tradition of comic intrigue that can be traced to Plautus and Terence. Many of these playfully ridicule the customs, taboos, and prejudices of Lope's social milieu, as *Los melindres de Belisa* (The fickleness of Belisa; 1606–1608) and *La discreta enamorada* (The prudent woman in love) and *Amar sin saber a quién* (Loving without knowing whom). *La dama boba* (The lady simpleton; 1613), contrasts the emotional naiveté of the erudite Nise with the wisdom and shrewdness that is awakened in her ignorant, frivolous sister under the influence of love. The *mujer varonil* (brave woman) whose refusal to marry must be overcome in *La vengadora de las mujeres* (The avenger of women; 1621) is also one of Lope's *damas doctas* (learned women). She protests the injustice of historical accounts written by men and is determined to write her own defense of women's virtue. One of Lope's most brilliantly written plays is set in Italy: the courtly action of *El perro del hortelano* (The dog in the manger; 1613–1614) involves the shifting emotions of love and jealousy and is resolved by the improbable "discovery" of the secretary Teodoro's aristocratic lineage, which makes it possible for him to marry Diana, countess of Belflor.

Epic Poetry. While Lope excelled at submitting his inventive facility to the discipline of a sonnet or the three acts of a *comedia,* his epic poems seem to have provided an opportunity for baroque excess. His experience with the Armada in 1588 inspired his epic poem *La Dragontea,* against Sir Francis Drake. *La hermosura de Angélica* (Angelica's beauty; 1602) is a continuation of Ariosto's *Orlando furioso* in a Castilian setting. His *Jerusalén conquistada* (Jerusalem regained; 1609) is a response to Tasso's *Gerusalemme liberata* (Jerusalem liberated). Lope's poem on the life of Mary Stuart, *La corona trágica* (The tragic crown; 1627), earned him the title of doctor of theology and the Order of Saint John; thenceforth he signed his works Fra Lope de Vega.

Lyric, Epic, and Prose. Lope's poetic gift is as evident in his theater as in his love sonnets and *romances* published in contemporary collections, including the *Cancionero general* (1600), and his own *Rimas humanas* (Human rhymes; 1602), *Rimas sacras* (Sacred rhymes; 1614), and *Rimas divinas y humanas de Tomé de Burguillos* (Divine and human rhymes of Tomé de Burguillos; 1634), one of Lope's poetic personae. Lope's ballads convey the elusive charm of the popular lyric in an artistic re-elaboration, for example in "Hortelano era Belardo" (Belardo was a gardener), "Mira, Zaide, que te aviso" (Look, Zaide, I'm warning you), "Pobre barquillo mío" (Poor little boat of mine), and "A mis soledades voy" (To solitude I go).

Several of Lope's extensive prose works include large portions of verse: *La Arcadia* (1598), the last significant Spanish pastoral novel; the mythological *La Filomena* (1621) and *La Circe* (1624); the Byzantine romance *El peregrino en su patria* (The pilgrim in his homeland; 1604); the pastoral allegory *Los pastores de Belén* (1612); and *La Dorotea* (1632), a dramatic dialogue modeled after *La Celestina,* narrating his youthful love affair with Elena Osorio. His *Novelas a Marcia Leonarda* (1621–1624), written for Marta de Nevares, are *novelas cortesanas,* courtly novellas involving social customs and love intrigues.

Many of Lope's plays have been translated into English, as has *La Dorotea.* The difficulty of poetic translation has limited the appreciation of his poetic gift among readers who do not speak Spanish.

See also **Drama, Spanish.**

BIBLIOGRAPHY

Primary Works

Vega Carpio, Lope Félix de. *La Dorotea.* Edited by Edwin S. Morby. 2d ed. Berkeley, Calif., 1968.

Vega Carpio, Lope Felix de. *La Dorotea.* Translated and edited by Alan S. Trueblood and Edwin Honig. Cambridge, Mass., 1985.

Vega Carpio, Lope Felix de. *Lírica*. Edited by José Manuel Blecua. Madrid, 1981.

Vega Carpio, Lope Felix de. *Obras*. Edited by Emilio Cotarelo y Mori. 13 vols. Madrid, 1916–1930.

Vega Carpio, Lope Felix de. *Obras escogidas*. Edited by Federico C. Sáinz de Robles. 4th ed. 3 vols. Málaga, Spain, 1962–1964.

Vega Carpio, Lope Felix de. *Obras poéticas*. Edited by José Manuel Blecua. Barcelona, 1969.

Secondary Works

Carreño, Antonio. *El romancero lírico de Lope de Vega*. Madrid, 1979.

Larson, Donald R. *The Honor Plays of Lope de Vega*. Cambridge, Mass., 1977.

Morley, S. Griswold, and Courtney Bruerton. *The Chronology of Lope de Vega's "Comedias." With a Discussion of Doubtful Attributions, the Whole Based on a Study of His Strophic Versification*. New York, 1940; reprint, 1966.

Rennert, Hugo A., and Américo Castro. *Vida de Lope de Vega*. 2d ed. Additions by Castro and Fernando Lázaro Carreter. Salamanca, Spain, 1968.

Trueblood, Alan S. *Experience and Artistic Invention in Lope de Vega: The Making of "La Dorotea."* Cambridge, Mass., 1974.

EMILIE L. BERGMANN

VENICE. [This entry includes two subentries, one on the history of the city and territory of Venice in the Renaissance and the other on artists active in Venice.]

Venice in the Renaissance

One of the principal cities of Renaissance Italy and perhaps the most beautiful, Venice was the only one to retain its independence amid invasion and occupation—and did so until the arrival of Napoleon in 1797. Venice was remarkable for its early acquisition of a maritime empire, its conquest of a mainland empire after 1400, its government (an aristocratic republic headed by an elected, and limited, monarch), its relative social harmony, and its brilliant cultural attainments.

The Maritime Empire. By 1300, Venice was the capital of a maritime empire and the center of one of the two major commercial networks in Europe (the other being that of the Hanse cities). Venice achieved this primacy as a result of its unusual site and the accidents of its early history, the energy and inventiveness of its merchants, and the competence of the state they created.

In the sixth and seventh centuries, mainland refugees fleeing Lombard invaders settled in fishing communities living precariously on a series of mudflats and sandbanks set in a lagoon off the Adriatic coast of northeastern Italy. Their island communities united by the year 1000 to form the unique and autonomous city of Venice, ruled by an elected doge (Latin *dux,* duke or leader) in consultation with merchant councils. Venetian merchants had already begun to trade in the commodities readily available to them—salt and fish—up the rivers that emptied into the lagoon and down the Adriatic coast. Soon they joined in Mediterranean trade as fierce competitors of the Genoese. Rivalry with Genoa peaked in 1379–1380 at Chioggia, just south of Venice, where the two naval powers struggled for primacy. The superb leadership of Venice's two admirals, Vettore Pisani and Carlo Zeno, prevented a direct assault on the city and assured its continued dominance of Mediterranean trade.

After 1453, the Ottoman seizure of Mediterranean lands presented the next significant challenge to Venetian supremacy at sea. Despite territorial losses and impediments to trade, Venetian diplomacy with Constantinople allowed the continued pursuit of commercial activity. In the late sixteenth century, when the Ottoman Turks had built up their fleet and began to seek control of the western Mediterranean, Venice joined with Habsburg Spain, the pope, and other Italian cities to win a stunning victory against the Ottoman navy at Lepanto on 7 October 1571—the last battle to be fought by rowed galleys in what was now the age of sail.

After Lepanto, Venice continued to figure in the community of European financial centers. As the appetite for spices gave way to one for sugar, tobacco, and cotton, and as the world trading system shifted from a Mediterranean to an Atlantic and then Pacific focus, Venice's importance declined. When Napoleon invaded Venice in 1797 and put an end to a republic that had endured for more than a millennium, its departure from center stage was little noticed.

The Territorial Empire. Scarcely had Venice triumphed in 1381 over its maritime rival Genoa than it turned its attention westward to the Italian terra ferma (solid land). Previously, Venice had stayed aloof from terra ferma politics. By 1400, Venetian merchants were interested in the security of overland trade routes. Adding to a foothold at tiny Treviso (1339–1381, and after 1389), Venice began to expand forcefully in the adjacent region of northeastern Italy.

From 1405 to 1454, Venice acquired a terra ferma empire by committing great energies, much wealth, and the services of skilled leaders. From 1405 to 1422, it added Verona, Vicenza, Padua, and Belluno, capitalizing on the dismemberment of the Milanese empire briefly established by the despot Gianga-

leazzo Visconti. By the latter date, Venetian dominion was also established along an arc to the northeast, including Friuli and Dalmatia. From the 1420s until the truce reached in 1454, Venice resisted the territorial ambitions of Milanese rulers Filippo Maria Visconti and his son-in-law and successor, the condottiere Francesco Sforza who passed from Venetian service to become duke of Milan. During these years, Venetian conquests extended across the grid formed by the vertical system of rivers that are tributaries to the Po: across the Adige to Brescia, across the Oglio to Bergamo and Crema, and across the Adda, briefly, with an eye to Milan.

The Venetian project of territorial expansion required a restructured military system. Previously, Venice had maintained a navy (officered by nobles) but not an army. Now it created an army led by condottieri (hired generals), and supervised by elected Venetian *provveditori* (supervisors), who led troops recruited from the mainland or maritime possessions (from Dalmatia, for instance). Created of necessity de novo, the structure of the Venetian army—consisting of condottieri and large numbers of recruited troops—anticipated the "military revolution" of the next century.

The competent and ambitious Venetian condottieri often included self-made men from the petty rural nobility who hungered to become rulers—as a few did (Francesco Sforza being the principal case). Others sought good salaries and lavish bonuses from the republic. One such man was the Paduan Erasmo da Narni, called Gattamelata, whose equestrian statue crafted by Donatello stands before the cathedral of Padua; another, Bartolomeo Colleoni (captain general, 1455–1476), lived out his years in wealth and luxury as a patron of the arts, and his statue, by Verrocchio, stands before the Venetian church of Santi Giovanni e Paolo. Less fortunate was Francesco Bussone, called Carmagnola, who, having deserted Visconti for Venice, was executed by the Venetians before he could desert them for Milan.

The Peace of Lodi (9 April 1454) settled the wars between Venice and Milan. Pope Nicholas V further urged the general agreement of 1455 called the Italian League. The Italian League, with a renewable term of twenty-five years, proposed to maintain peace by achieving a balance of power among the five principal states of Venice, Milan, Florence, Naples, and the Papal States. (Historians have noted its foreshadowing of the 1815 Congress of Vienna.)

Despite the solemn agreements of the Italian League, Venice still pressed for territorial and commercial advantages, thereby arousing the resentment of the other Italian powers. Venetian designs on Ferrara (under papal dominion) resulted in a destructive war in 1481–1484 that blackened the city's image. The peace treaty reaffirmed the principles of the Italian League. When French armies under Charles VIII invaded Italy in 1494, opening an era of the intervention in Italy of the great nation states of Europe that was not finally settled until the Treaty of Cateau-Cambrésis in 1559, Venice faced a perilous situation. Shifting their own alliances rapidly as opportunity dictated, the city's leaders found, in 1509, that all the major armies in the field were arrayed against the city.

By the League of Cambrai (1508), the pope, France, Spain, the Holy Roman Empire, and allied Italian cities united against Venice and seized its terra ferma cities. During the ensuing war (1509–1517), Venice's political fortunes were at their nadir. But the nobility gave sacrificially to support the military effort, and the people of the mainland colonies resisted the foreign takeover. Almost miraculously, it seemed, the city and empire were saved. When the Italian phase of the Habsburg-Valois wars limped to a close in 1530, an intact Venice was free to attend to its internal affairs, the only Italian city to maintain great power status.

The rest of the sixteenth century saw increased competition among a populous nobility for prestigious and lucrative positions (and a consequent increase in corruption), discussion about the role of the doge, and competition between traditionalists (*vecchi,* or old) and modernizers (*giovani,* the young), a group of nobles with a reform agenda. Early in the next century, the city withstood a papal interdict, presenting to Europe a model of an autonomous secular state.

The Venetian Republic. The doge presided over the Venetian commune, or republic. His election, a matter of enormous gravity, required an elaborate process (intended to prevent the operation of family or other special interests) of a series of nine committees of varying sizes chosen by lot or election. Once elected, the doge became a public person, adorned with special ornaments and ringed

about by ritual observances that elevated the ruler's position but masked his personality.

The dogeship was embedded in a republican system. During the eleventh and twelfth centuries, the powerful merchant patriciate of Venice limited dogal power through the creation of a series of councils with which the ruler was to consult and which themselves originated public policy. At the death of each doge, a committee drafted a *promissio* (promise), an oath his successor was obliged to take accepting specific restrictions on his powers. The unique relationship of doge and councils is concretely expressed in functions of the doge's palace. It is both a royal residence and series of meeting halls for the various councils of state, and above all for the huge Great Council, whose electoral function set the whole republican mechanism in motion.

The Great Council achieved definition in the first century of the Renaissance era, an evolution from medieval conciliar bodies. In 1297, those then present in an enlarged Great Council voted to limit to descendants of their own families the pool of candidates thereafter eligible for that body. The effect was to create a permanent noble caste, distinguished from the other nobilities of Europe by its merchant origins. At the time, the nobility consisted of about twelve hundred adult males from about 150 families. This pivotal decision of the Great Council, known as the *serrata* (closing), did not accomplish its end immediately. During the early 1300s, other major clans gained noble status. During the Chioggian War, a further thirty families that had contributed to the emergency call for funds were added to the circle of Venetian nobility. Thereafter, no new families were admitted to the nobility until the seventeenth century, when, as in other European states, the sale of titles was a prime source of fund-raising. The nobility was in effect coterminous with the Great Council, which enrolled all adult male nobles (except clerics).

In addition to the Great Council, which elected most officials (including the doge) and generated laws, several smaller bodies made policy and advised the doge. The most important state council was the Senate. Originally defined as a body of sixty members, it had by the fifteenth century acquired sixty adjunct members, as well as the forty members of the *Quarantia* (see below), and the ducal councillors sitting ex-officio. It elected and supervised ambassadors, *provveditori,* and other important magistrates, and oversaw the project of terra ferma expansion. The weightiness of the latter enterprise is reflected in the division of the Senate records, from about 1440, to those concerned with the land and sea empires—the former gradually outstripping the

225

Venetian Territories in the Eastern Mediterranean

latter in bulk. The *Quarantia,* or "Forty," also met apart from the Senate as a court of appeals, led by its three *capi* (heads). The *avogadori di comun* (state attorneys) also had important judicial functions. They prosecuted officials who abused their offices and intervened to preserve due constitutional process.

The Council of Ten was created after a faction of the nobility attempted revolution in 1310 (and acted promptly when, forty-five years later, the doge Marino Falier, attempting a coup, was captured, tried, and executed). The Ten's charge was to investigate treasonable activity. In time, it came to deal with policy matters of high importance construed as affecting the security of the state. Its three rotating *capi,* each holding office for only a month at a time, joined the doge's advisory council. The Ten became increasingly important from the late 1400s; by the seventeenth century outside observers and the "young" nobles viewed them as the tyrannical rulers of the city.

An advisory body called the *Signoria* (the "Lordship," or executive) consisted of six ducal councillors together with the three *capi* of the Forty. The *Signoria* met after 1400 with six *savi grandi* (great

sages, or chief ministers), to which were added after 1430 five *savi di terraferma* (sages for mainland affairs) and five *savi agli ordini* (sages for marine matters). All together they formed the *Pien Collegio* (Full College). Sometimes these members were augmented further by the attendance of the three state attorneys.

Finally, many lesser committees and councils formed the complex Venetian government, such as those in charge of the salt office, customs duties, or state ceremonies. Election to these positions was eagerly sought by nobles who had no chance of acquiring offices with higher prestige.

Although there was no set *cursus honorum* (sequence of honors) as in ancient Rome, frequently nobles destined for high position would enter the Senate early in their careers, and subsequently achieve the positions of state attorney, sage, ducal counselor, member of the Council of Ten, and eventually ducal candidate. Such a career was a full-time enterprise requiring a commitment of funds, as higher offices were unpaid and many required considerable expenditure. Nobles who pursued this career course constituted an inner core of Venetian rulers numbering perhaps one hundred to two hundred men. Lesser offices, in contrast, were not only easier to attain and open to the lesser strata of the nobility, but might also yield salaries, perquisites, or bribes.

The *serrata* of 1297 resulted in the exclusion of non-nobles from government office. A stratum of non-nobles, nevertheless, served in positions deeply involved with government affairs. These were the secretaries, literate and educated men, who sat in the government councils, who took the careful minutes that historians now study, and who drew up official state papers. Drawn mostly from an affluent middle-class of professionals and merchants, they acquired status as well as reliable salaries from their government service. By the sixteenth century, candidacy for the secretariat was limited to *cittadini originari* (original citizens), persons born in Venice and whose parents and grandparents had never practiced a trade or artisan craft. Secretaries acquired great prestige and occupied a position in the social order just below the nobility. Some secretaries were privy to high matters of state, and might act covertly as special emissaries or agents.

Venice was therefore both a city and a nation, at once a republic, an aristocracy, and a monarchy—a unique and almost unidentifiable identity among the nations of Renaissance Europe. Over the centuries, an elaborate set of civic rituals had developed by which Venice presented itself to the world and reinforced the commitment of its citizens. On various occasions, the doge, the noble magistrates, the state secretaries, and the heads of the *scuole* (philanthropic confraternities and guilds) all marched in procession through the great Piazza San Marco, the city's central square, in front of the basilica. On Ascension Day, the doge solemnly cast a ring into the waters, achieving symbolically the marriage of Venice with the sea.

The Myth of Venice. Ritual events were carefully scripted manifestations of Venetian political theory. In words as in ceremonies, Venice presented itself to the world as La Serenissima (the serene republic), divinely founded, ideally constituted, splendidly governed, harmonious, productive, and benevolent. Historians have called this self-concept the "myth of Venice." The myth dominated Venetian cultural life, as it has dominated much of what historians have written about Venice since the close of the Renaissance.

The myth of Venice first appeared in chronicles and letters of the thirteenth and fourteenth centuries. Over several centuries, the essential elements of the myth remained constant: the unique magnificence of the site of Venice, to whose quays ships carried the world's goods; the excellence of the city's constitution; the harmony among all social classes; the benevolence of the Venetian regime; the divine origin and enduring destiny of the city.

The myth was not wholly untrue. Venice was uniquely picturesque. Its distinctive appearance was the subject, indeed, not only of literary discussion but also of a good part of the city's magnificent artistic production. The notion of the superiority of the Venetian constitution commanded a wide audience. Florentine theorists urged their compatriots to imitate Venetian government structures when, having rid themselves of the Medici, they considered forming a republic of their own. English republicans listened attentively to what their observers had to say about the Venetian political process. Features of the Venetian constitution were known to the leaders of the American Revolution, and the United States Constitution owes some small debt to its Italian predecessor.

Yet the myth also masked a reality less glamorous than that presented by civic propagandists. The noblemen who ruled the city often descended to vote-selling, self-promotion, and embezzlement. They were sometimes incompetent or delinquent. They promoted the interests of the metropolis over those of the subject cities, and of the nobility over those of citizen merchants and workers. In relations with foreign states, they employed devious means to pursue selfish objectives.

In particular, the last form of misbehavior won for Venice a negative reputation that endured alongside the preeminent one engendered by the myth. Italian critics of Venetian expansion during the fifteenth century, and Enlightenment opponents of hereditary aristocracy in the eighteenth, propounded an "anti-myth" of Venice: a Venice that was greedy, opportunistic, and aggressive, a place of decadence and repression.

Over the last generation, historians have tested the myth and anti-myth alike with close studies of Venetian economy, society, and culture in order to understand just how Venice achieved its reputation for social cohesion and enduring, stable government.

Economy and Society. The nobility of Venice was a unique social caste that shaped civic life more than any other social group. It jealously limited the power both of the monarch chosen from its numbers and of the citizens who, however wealthy, could never aspire to political office. The adult male nobles numbered from 1,200 to 2,500 (reaching a maximum around the year 1500). With their families they constituted about 6 or 7 percent of the city's population. That population ranged between a low of about 50,000 after the plague struck in 1348 to a high of 190,000 around 1570. The epidemics of 1575–1577 and 1630–1631 resulted in great losses, after which the total fluctuated between 100,000 and 160,000 until the end of the republic. In contrast to other European elites, the nobles dressed soberly, presenting themselves as a corporation rather than as discrete individuals. Excessive individualism was discouraged in Venice.

In origin, the Venetian nobility was a merchant class. During the fifteenth century, with the increase in government activity because of the terraferma expansion, a subgroup of the wealthiest nobles committed themselves to political careers, leaving commercial activities to other family or clan members. Wealthy nobles owned grand palaces and patronized the arts. From the sixteenth century, many nobles purchased mainland estates and lived a leisurely life on the land, putting their mercantile past behind them.

Poorer nobles sought lesser political offices that yielded a salary, and bartered their influence or their vote to their richer colleagues. Occasionally, the government subsidized noblemen whose poverty impugned the dignity that was thought to be theirs by right. Poverty did not disqualify a nobleman from the privileges of rank. The high honor accorded the nobility within Venice extended to the noble (or patrician) elites of the subject cities of the terraferma.

Below the nobles was a stratum of citizens of whom the most privileged were the *cittadini originari*. Citizens who were not *originari* could still engage in commerce, the engine of the Venetian economy. Those born abroad might be granted prized mercantile privileges *de intus et extra* (the right to trade as a Venetian within its dominion or abroad), or merely *de intus* (only within the city). These entitlements were granted by decree to those who did not engage in a trade or artisan craft and who had been resident for certain terms of years.

Although non-noble citizens could not pursue political careers, they could freely acquire wealth and status. Often they belonged to the unique Venetian institutions called *scuole,* within which they could aspire to office (from which nobles were barred) and influence, display their wealth in conspicuous acts of patronage, find fellowship, and practice Christian piety. The *scuole* were voluntary, charitable organizations encompassing both rich merchants and poor workers. They performed works of charity and de-

votional exercises, spent lavishly to adorn their churches and their own meeting halls, and were represented in the processions and rituals that embodied the life of the city.

Craft guilds enrolled many of the city's workers and artisans. As elsewhere, they set standards for price and quality, and handled disputes. The revolutionary tendencies that characterized Italian guilds in the late Middle Ages and into the Renaissance were almost entirely absent in Venice. The guild presence was small even though the Venetian economy supported large groups of specialized workers. Among them were the craftsmen who worked in shipbuilding: caulkers, carpenters, and sail and rope makers. Many of these worked in the largest state-run factory before the modern age, the *Arsenale* (Arsenal, where ships were built). Silk- and glassworkers were also highly skilled artisans who joined in guilds.

More powerful than the guilds of workers or artisans were the associations among neighbors. Venice was organized around its sixty or seventy parishes (grouped in six *sestieri,* or districts), whose members identified strongly with their church. Neighborhood ties were strengthened by rituals, similar to the grand public ones that celebrated the state, but specific to the parish. They were also promoted by a network of women, including wealthy noblewomen and poor workmen's wives, whose conversation, charitable giving, church attendance, and birthings were all means for effecting social solidarity.

For most Venetian women, life was local, the life of the parish. Wives of noblemen and wealthy citizens rarely left their houses except to go to church. Women of lower status were freer to move about, but seldom strayed beyond their parishes. As elsewhere in Europe, women of the lowest status possessed the greatest freedom—poor women who worked as peddlers, servants, or prostitutes. Venetian prostitutes were numerous and carefully watched by officials. Courtesans, or high-status prostitutes who entertained noble and citizen clients, might attain wealth and prestige.

Crime, disease, and poverty did not spare the Venetians. The Venetian government fought crime with a regime of strict surveillance and prompt justice. Each neighborhood was supervised by officials called the *signori di notte* (gentlemen of the night). Malefactors were fined, banished, or executed as elsewhere in Italy. Justice was not equal. Crimes committed against nobles were often viewed with

Venice. View of the city by Erhard Reuwich from Bernhard von Breydenbach's *Peregrinatio in Terram Sanctam,* 1468.

special harshness. Those committed by nobles were often viewed with leniency.

As elsewhere in Italy, the relief of poverty was deemed the responsibility of charitable agencies, not of the state (although the state always kept the granaries well-stocked). In Venice, it was the particular province of the *scuole*. These provided money for orphans, widows, abandoned or deserted wives, and for reforming prostitutes. In addition, individuals made specific charitable bequests—to hospitals or dowry funds, churches or religious orders. Hospitals housed the impoverished or elderly as well as the seriously ill. The familiar scourge of leprosy, in addition to the more recent afflictions of the plague (after 1348) and syphilis (after 1494), encouraged the creation of special hospitals for their victims.

Among the many associations that made up Venetian society—political, artisanal, charitable— there also flourished those for foreigners, who were numerous in Venice. The Greeks and the Slavs each had their own churches, the social and spiritual center of their communities. German-speaking merchants from north of the Alps and Turks from Constantinople (after 1453) lived in their own *fondaci* (warehouses) near the city's commercial center in the Rialto. After 1516 (and until 1797), the Jews of Venice were confined to the *ghetto* (its original meaning was "iron foundry"), notoriously the first such gated, closed community. Within the ghetto, they too lived according to their own laws and customs.

Religion.   Religion permeated Venetian culture. Churches were everywhere, as were priests, friars, and nuns, the unwed daughters or widowed mothers of the citizens. Inspiring preachers aroused the enthusiasm of thousands, as did Giovanni Dominici and St. Bernardino of Siena, two of Italy's foremost preachers. From the confessional, the clergy guided the beliefs and behavior especially of women. Men and women of property left wealth to churches and religious orders and to the hospitals, schools, and orphanages that they superintended. The city boasted of the many relics it possessed, most importantly the body of St. Mark, the patron saint, enterprisingly recovered in the ninth century (according to legend) from distant Alexandria. The miraculous was everywhere.

Yet Venice remained aloof from the pope. The great basilica of San Marco, attached to the Doge's Palace and related architecturally to Byzantium rather than Rome, was considered the doge's chapel. It was not the city's cathedral, and Venice had no bishop to compete in authority with the clergy at San Marco. From 1451, the Patriarchate of Grado was transferred to Venice, which thereby acquired its own supreme ecclesiastical leader. The first incumbent was the capable administrator and saintly ascetic Lorenzo Giustiniani (1381–1456), whose two brothers were both politicians of first rank. The bishops and other major clerics of the subject terraferma cities were regularly named by the Venetian Senate, and not by the pope. Citizen clerics were barred from the secretariat and noble clerics from the Great Council and all political offices. Thus Venice maintained its autonomy in the religious sphere, while presenting itself as uniquely pious in its observance.

In the 1500s, reform movements affected Venice as they did the rest of Italy. Evangelical doctrines attracted several of its nobles. Gasparo Contarini, appointed a cardinal after a full secular career, was one of the authors of the *Consilium de emendanda ecclesia* (Proposal for the reformation of the church; 1537). He met with Philipp Melanchthon in 1541 in an attempt to work out a compromise between Rome and the Lutherans on the issue of justification by faith. The formula he arrived at was unacceptable to the papacy and to Martin Luther.

As heresies threatened the papacy, Venice was a home to many heretics. The city's location and size made it a center for the exchange of ideas and books. Protestant sympathizers existed among nobles, citizens, and artisans, who joined with their brethren to discuss heterodox notions at favored taverns. Intellectuals who wished to acquire copies of the works of Luther or Erasmus could do so easily in Venice. The Venetian government refused to give the Inquisition free rein to prosecute its citizens. Venice maintained its own magistracy on heresy, maintaining officially the strictest commitment to orthodoxy while insisting on having its own representatives present

at trials conducted by papal inquisitors. Venetian nonconformity climaxed in 1606, when the whole city was placed under the interdict in a jurisdictional matter, and the native-born friar Paolo Sarpi (1552–1623) championed its case to the world.

Culture. In ideas as in religion, Venice remained deeply traditional and yet tremendously original. Venice developed a rich historiographical literature, as medieval chronicles flowered during the Renaissance under the influence of humanism. Venetian humanism had distinctive characteristics, due mostly to the dominance within the intellectual elite of the same nobility that directed the state. Most of the Venetian humanists were themselves nobles, and these were almost entirely amateurs who also pursued political careers. Those who were not noble were nearly all linked to noble patrons. In consequence, Venetian humanism dealt heavily with political or historical themes. Almost entirely lacking were discussions of the dignity of man or of political liberty, which were staples of humanist discourse outside of Venice.

Whereas such discussions might have seemed threatening to the rulers of Venice, the studies of Aristotelian philosophy and theology they found congenial. Alongside the humanists, mostly noblemen, philosophers and theologians were drawn more often from the class of citizens or resident foreigners or clergy. The preeminence of these studies in Venice was also fostered by the proximity of the university at Padua, the only university that young nobles were supposed to attend, and most did. The effect was that intellectual life in Venice, especially in the fifteenth century, was greatly influenced by the university curriculum.

Venice had numerous schools that provided education below the university level. As elsewhere in Italy, these included both the grammar schools, which taught Latin, and schools that offered a vernacular curriculum and provided future merchants with the necessary business arithmetic. Among the grammar schools were two famous ones funded by the government: one at San Marco, which taught a secondary-level Latin curriculum to young noblemen as well as to future state secretaries; and one in the Rialto, which provided advanced lectures on philosophy. In addition, the children of wealthy citizens or nobles were often taught by humanist tutors. For advanced scholars, a public library was formed late in the fifteenth century around the collection bequeathed to Venice by the Greek immigrant Cardinal Bessarion (1403–1472). It still exists today as the Biblioteca Nazionale Marciana (National Marcian Library).

Foreign humanists who came to Venice in search of employment, if they did not teach, could work for one of the printing houses. Printing came to Venice around 1469. By 1500, Venice was Europe's major publishing center. From the 1490s, the printer Aldus Manutius developed Greek and italic fonts and the smaller, octavo book format. He produced exquisite and accurate editions (today's valued Aldine editions) of the Greek and Latin classics as well as contemporary works. During the 1500s, Venetian printshops were focal points for the spread of reform ideas. Cosmopolitan and free-spirited, Venice was a magnet for writers of all sorts, including the *poligrafi* (writers on many things)—the satirist and pornographer Pietro Aretino (1492–1556) among them—who wrote for profit and anticipated today's media writers.

By the 1500s, poetry and drama flourished in Venice (a departure from the fifteenth century, when Latin prose prevailed). Literati gathered in academies, or less formally in salons, to hear sonnets or discuss antiquities, science and mathematics, or political theory. The extraordinary freedom in literary conversation contrasts sharply with the measured and disciplined intellectual products of the previous century. Although there were no women writers active in Venice for most of the fifteenth century (apart from the brief stay of the Veronese humanist Isotta Nogarola), they became numerous thereafter. The Venetian humanist Cassandra Fedele was a celebrity from the 1480s well into the next century. During the sixteenth century, the poets Gaspara Stampa and Veronica Franco (the latter a courtesan, the former very likely one) gained great reputations from their erotic verse. From this century into the next, three women writers produced the most important works of the era on proto-feminist themes: Moderata Fonte (the pseudonym of Modesta da Pozzo), Lucrezia Marinella, and Arcangela Tarabotti.

Venice's great florescence in music and the visual arts is best told elsewhere. But a word must be said about Venice as a work of art in itself. Its cityscape, often painted by visitors, displays a horizon of buildings and towers of great beauty. Its hundreds of churches and palaces, constructed in styles ranging from Byzantine-Gothic to classical, faced with bare brick or glistening marble, create a brilliant mosaic of texture and color. Carved in niches, above doors and on paving stones, are reliefs of the winged lion, symbol of St. Mark and of Venice, his paw resting on the open book that signified the city was at peace.

See also **Italy**; **Mediterranean Sea**; **Ottoman Empire**; **Republicanism**.

BIBLIOGRAPHY

Brown, Patricia Fortini. *Venetian Antiquity: The Venetian Sense of the Past.* New Haven, Conn., 1996.

Chambers, David, and Brian Pullan, eds. *Venice: A Documentary History, 1450–1630.* Oxford and Cambridge, Mass., 1992. Collection of translated documents illustrating all areas of Venetian life.

Davis, James Cushman. *The Decline of the Venetian Nobility as a Ruling Class.* Baltimore, 1962.

Davis, Robert C. *Shipbuilders of the Venetian Arsenal: Workers and Workplace in the Preindustrial City.* Baltimore, 1991.

Finlay, Robert. *Politics in Renaissance Venice.* London and New Brunswick, N.J., 1980.

Gilbert, Felix. *The Pope, His Banker, and Venice.* Cambridge, Mass., 1980.

Grendler, Paul F. *The Roman Inquisition and the Venetian Press, 1540–1605.* Princeton, N.J., 1977.

Grubb, James S. *Firstborn of Venice: Vicenza in the Early Renaissance State.* Baltimore, 1988.

Hale, John R., ed. *Renaissance Venice.* London and Totowa, N.J., 1973.

King, Margaret L. *Venetian Humanism in an Age of Patrician Dominance.* Princeton, N.J., 1986.

Lane, Frederic C. *Venice: A Maritime Republic.* Baltimore and London, 1973.

Logan, Oliver. *Culture and Society in Venice, 1470–1790: The Renaissance and Its Heritage.* London and New York, 1972.

Lowry, Martin. *Nicholas Jenson and the Rise of Venetian Publishing in Renaissance Europe.* Oxford and Cambridge, Mass., 1991.

Mallett, M. E., and J. R. Hale. *The Military Organization of a Renaissance State: Venice c. 1400 to 1617.* Cambridge, U.K., and New York, 1984.

McNeill, William H. *Venice: The Hinge of Europe, 1081–1797.* Chicago, 1974.

Mueller, Reinhold. *The Venetian Money Market: Banks, Panics, and the Public Debt, 1200–1500.* Baltimore, 1997.

Muir, Edward. *Civic Ritual in Renaissance Venice.* Princeton, N.J., 1981.

Norwich, John Julius. *A History of Venice.* New York, 1982.

Pullan, Brian S. *The Jews of Europe and the Inquisition of Venice, 1550–1670.* Totowa, N.J., and Oxford, 1983.

Pullan, Brian. *Rich and Poor in Renaissance Venice: The Social Institutions of a Catholic State, to 1620.* Oxford and Cambridge, Mass., 1971.

Queller, Donald E. *The Venetian Patriciate: Reality versus Myth.* Urbana, Ill., 1986.

Romano, Dennis. *Patricians and Popolani: The Social Foundations of the Venetian Renaissance State.* Baltimore, 1987.

Ruggiero, Guido. *The Boundaries of Eros: Sex Crime and Sexuality in Renaissance Venice.* New York and London, 1985.

MARGARET L. KING

Art in Venice

The enchantingly beautiful city of Venice—already characterized by the fourteenth-century Tuscan poet Petrarch as "another world"—and the visual arts that flourished there reflect in numerous ways the city's special aspect: its unique geographical situation, maritime outlook, and mercantile affluence; its location as crossroads between Europe and the eastern Mediterranean world and status as luxury emporium; its role as colonizer and the hospitality it extended to foreigners; and the unparalleled long-term stability of its government and society. As had those of earlier ages, Venetian artists of the Renaissance blended influences from abroad with formal features established in deeply rooted traditions, achieving new artistic solutions whereby to honor and to perpetuate devotion to the city's primary patrons: the Virgin Mary and St. Mark. In so doing, they helped shape and glorify the republic's increasing self-definition as divinely protected and destined for greatness in world affairs. Consideration, here included, of tradition and of the artistic projects carried out or initiated during the fourteenth century provides a context for surveying the innovations and accomplishments in Venetian art during the fifteenth and sixteenth. In the course of this overview, artistic activity in other centers in the Veneto will be noted, as will the careers of major Venetian painters who worked elsewhere.

The City of Venice.

Founded in the northern Adriatic on an archipelago of mud flats and some hundred islets two miles off the Italian mainland, Venice had no need for conventional fortifications; its architecture is thus distinctive in its open and inviting character. The earliest extant residential structures, thought to date from the 1200s, conform to the basic, compact plan that remained characteristic of Venetian palaces: a large, central, axial room traverses the width of the building from the canal frontage on each floor and smaller rooms are arranged symmetrically to either side. The large room on the ground level (*androne*) is open at both ends to accommodate water traffic, and the corresponding room (*portego* or *salone*) on the upper floor (*piano nobile;* where the living quarters are situated) is amply fenestrated to provide light and air in the absence, initially, of a central courtyard. These domestic structures contributed—along with the sheer number of churches (137 in 1493) and church towers—to the impression of sumptuous splendor received by foreign visitors such as the French ambassador, Philippe de Commynes, who in 1494 declared Venice's shimmering, palace-lined Grand Canal to be "the fairest and best-built street in the world."

Three locations in Venice constituted the major foci of civic life. The Rialto, on the Grand Canal, which divides the city lengthwise, was the center of commerce; the Arsenale, to the north and east, housed the vast and all-important shipbuilding industry; and at the mouth of the Grand Canal, the Doge's Palace and St. Mark's Basilica define the seat of Venetian government and religious devotion. These areas received significant artistic attention up until the end of the sixteenth century; by that time, the appearance they bear today had already largely been determined.

Tradition and Major Projects of the Fourteenth Century.

Major sites of artistic activity in the fourteenth century included the basilica of St. Mark, the Doge's Palace, and the churches of Santi Giovanni e Paolo and Santa Maria Gloriosa degli Frari.

St. Mark's Basilica. Nowhere is Venice's long-term affiliation with the Byzantine Empire and characteristic love of splendor more conspicuous than at St. Mark's Basilica, built between c. 1063 and 1094. Varicolored marble columns and veneers and patterned floor pavings—often *spoglia* (spoils from earlier notable sites)—evoke a sense of awe and glory appropriate to worship, as does the extensive program of decorating the interior domes and their supports with holy images and narrative cycles in brightly colored mosaic against a shimmering background of gilt-glass tesserae, carried out by Greek or Greek-trained and local craftsmen during the next two centuries.

The wood cover (*pala feriale;* "everyday altarpiece") commissioned in 1345 by Andrea Dandolo (doge 1343–1354) for the high altarpiece depicted the legend of St. Mark and the translation of his relics from Alexandria to Venice. Executed by the prolific and influential Paolo Veneziano (active 1335–1358), the first important Venetian panel painter, this work is characterized by attenuated figures, lively storytelling, and lavish textural detail. Its brilliant color recalls local mosaic tradition and anticipates the coloristic interest of Venetian Renaissance painting. Gothic influence is merged with Veneto-Byzantine tradition in the figures of the mosaic cycle Dandolo commissioned for St. Mark's Baptistery (1343–1354). His wall tomb there (executed before 1354), however, breaks with Venetian tradition; in accordance with convention elsewhere in Italy for ruler tombs, it includes a sculptural effigy.

Intermingling of styles at St. Mark's Basilica continued with the addition atop the facade of slender, tall-roofed tabernacles and an elaborate late-Gothic cresting of figural and vegetal forms that pierces the sky. This project, employing Venetian, Lombard, and Tuscan stonecutters, was begun in 1384 and extended into the 1420s. In 1394 a new choir screen

Gentile Bellini. *Miracle of the True Cross.* In 1369 a reliquary containing a fragment of the True Cross fell into the canal beneath the Bridge of San Lorenzo as it was being presented to Andrea Vendramin; it remained miraculously suspended above the water until Vendramin dived in to rescue it. [For a depiction of a procession of the reliquary in St. Mark's Square, see the painting by Gentile Bellini illustrating the entry Parades, Processions, and Pageants in volume 4; for a depiction of the descendants of Andrea Vendramin venerating the reliquary, see the painting by Titian in the color plates in this volume.] GALLERIE DELL'ACCADEMIA DI BELLE ARTI, VENICE/ALINARI/ART RESOURCE

was commissioned from the Venetian brothers Pierpaolo (active 1383; died c. 1403) and Jacobello dalle Masegne (active 1383; died after 1409). Although the architectural forms harmonize with that of the venerable church interior, the apostle figures surmounting the screen are Gothic in their swaying poses and linear drapery; they are intensely animated in their facial expressions and interactions.

The Doge's Palace. Until the end of the Republic, the Doge's Palace housed government offices, meeting rooms, and the doge's apartments. Standing adjacent to the Basilica and along the waterfront, it succeeds two earlier buildings. In 1340 the Senate had voted considerable funds to enlarge the existing Sala del Maggior Consiglio (Great Council Chamber) so that it could accommodate the Council's sizable

membership. Possibly executed under the direction of Filippo Calendario (before 1315–1355), the structure is distinctive in supporting a flat, vast upper wall—veneered with an exotic diaper-pattern of pink and white stone—on a graceful double loggia of Gothic arches decorated with vibrant, naturalistic figurated capitals. Construction was begun in 1341 and progressed quickly over the next few years. To this period have been assigned the large, corner reliefs that feature deeply undercut and vigorously plastic vegetal forms and that skillfully and with great emotional sensitivity represent *The Fall of Man* and *The Drunkeness of Noah,* subjects appropriately relating to justice. On the west facade, also presumably executed under Calendario's supervision, is the relief roundel that introduces the later frequent allegorical representation of Venice as Justice seated on two lions.

By 1365 the Doge's Palace was sufficiently advanced for mural decoration of the Great Council Chamber to begin. Guariento di Arpo (active 1338; died before 1370) was invited from nearby Padua to fresco the huge end wall of the enormous room. Guariento was among the masterful practitioners of fresco technique active in Padua during the second half of the fourteenth century who carried forward the style of the Florentine painter Giotto in representing well-modeled, highly plastic figures clad in naturalistic, tactile drapery and set in a three-dimensional space. Others of note are the Veronese, Altichiero da Zevio (active 1369–1384), who in the 1370s painted the St. James Chapel in the Basilica of St. Anthony of Padua (known as the Santo); and the Florentine, Giusto di Menabuoi (c. 1320–1393), who carried out an extensive program (Padua, Baptistery), commissioned around 1378 by Fina Buzzacarini, wife of Francesco da Carrara, lord of Padua.

Guariento's work in Venice (damaged by fire but preserved beneath Tintoretto's *Paradise* executed to replace it) represents the *Coronation of the Virgin,* a favorite theme of the period that serves as theophany and depiction of assembled saints, who constitute the company of the blessed (the Church in Heaven) that will intercede on behalf of the Christian devout (the Church on Earth). This pictorial subject is not based in narrative but rather on belief in the incorruptibility of Mary's body and reflects the long-entrenched typology of Mary and the Church. Both Guariento and Altichiero departed significantly from Giotto's art by employing elaborate architectural structures of greater scale relative to the figures arranged within them. This tendency is impressively exemplified in Guariento's Council Chamber fresco by the intricate three-dimensional throne "complex" that seats the vast celestial assembly and simultaneously suggests the function of the room itself. Guariento's *Coronation* splendidly honors the Virgin, with whose purity the Venetian state identified. Reference to the legendary founding of the city on Annunciation Day (25 March) may be perceived in the inclusion of Mary and Gabriel to either side of the central scene.

Santi Giovanni e Paolo and Santa Maria Gloriosa dei Frari.

Other major structures of the fourteenth century and notable sites of future artistic activity are the vast, wide-naved Gothic churches of the Dominican and Franciscan orders respectively. The former, known locally as San Zanipolo, was begun around 1333 and served as burial place for twenty-five doges. The Franciscan church (the Frari), was also begun during the 1330s. Both are vaulted, using light-weight materials and tie-beams in consideration of the city's substructure. Another solution in Venice for roofing a Gothic-style church is the wood ceiling resembling a boat's keel at Santo Stefano (c. 1407).

Architecture and Sculpture of the Fifteenth Century.

Building continued apace in Venice during the fifteenth century as the Republic spread west onto the Italian *terraferma* (mainland) and forged new links with Florence. Architecture and sculpture were still generally carried out jointly by architect-masons sometimes working as families and often directing craftsmen brought in temporarily from various other centers to assist in large projects. Connecting names that appear in documents to individual extant works is tenuous, and the precise oeuvres of several masters are subject to wide debate.

That Giovanni Buon (Bon; c. 1360–1442) and his son Bartolomeo (c. 1400/10–1464/67) were the principal practitioners during the first half of the century is nevertheless clear, and one of their best-known buildings is the exceptionally well documented Ca' d'Oro (gold house; so named for the now-lost gilding of the sculptural decoration on the facade). Constructed between 1421 and 1436, the residence is distinguished by its airy, Venetian-Gothic window treatment. By 1424 the Senate had voted to demolish what remained of the twelfth-century Doge's Palace and began extending the west facade of the fourteenth-century building—following its design exactly—to St. Mark's Basilica. Bartolomeo Buon was commissioned to design, at the juncture, the palace's new ceremonial entrance (*Porta della Carta;* 1438–1442/4). Using red and white marble and white Istrian stone, the elaborate, crisply carved Gothic gateway comprises a strikingly lifelike, over life-sized portrait of the expansionist, long-tenured Doge Francesco Foscari (doge 1423–1457) kneeling before a figure of the winged lion of St. Mark (1885 replacement); personifications of virtues in niches; an elegant tripartite window; and a figure of Justice at the apex.

Classicizing elements of the Renaissance style developed in Florence began to appear in Bartolomeo Buon's later work, notably the rusticated lower order of the unfinished Ca' del Duca begun in 1457 (later so-named for Francesco Sforza of Milan). Most impressive is the Arsenale's land entrance, a structure that adapts the form of the ancient Roman Arch of the Sergii at Pula and includes a surmounting figure of the winged lion displayed against a pedimented Florentine-style tabernacle. Although the gateway (dated 1460) is often attributed to Bartolomeo, motivation to imitate the design of a Roman triumphal arch probably originated with humanist office-holders in the governmental branch that supervised the Arsenale.

Soon after, the first Renaissance church in Venice, San Michele in Isola (begun in 1469), was designed by Mauro Codussi (c. 1440–1504), who had come to Venice from the then subject-city of Bergamo. Its facade—reminiscent of the Florentine architect Alberti's designs—is articulated with classicizing pilasters, entablatures, and segmental pediment; the measured interior using Corinthian columns and round-headed arches generally recalls Filippo Brunelleschi's Florentine churches. Contributing to several notable on-going building projects, Codussi was the most gifted architect active in Venice during the second half of the century. His work demonstrates a remarkable sensitivity to the effects of light and space and to the early Christian interests of ecclesiastic patrons, as manifest in his small, domed, Greek-cross church, San Giovanni Crisostomo (begun 1497).

Contemporary activity at the Doge's Palace, where the Lombard-trained Antonio Rizzo (1430?–1499) was *proto* (foreman of works) from 1483 to 1498, centered on the courtyard and included construction of another monumental and thematically complex entranceway, the Arco Foscari. Begun by Bartolomeo Buon in 1438, it was completed in 1485 by Rizzo, whose animated, naturalistic marble statues of Adam and Eve were designed for its classicizing niches. In 1485 Rizzo began the ceremonial exterior staircase, embellishing its surfaces *all'antica* with reliefs of trophies, tritons, and nereids. Analogous repertories of classical decorative motifs recur in the bronze bases of the flagpoles in the Piazza San Marco by Alessandro Leopardi (1505–1506) and are used earlier by the Lombard, Pietro Solari generally designated Lombardo (c. 1435–1515; active in Venice, Padua, and Treviso) for the articulation of exquisitely worked classical architectural elements such as his additions to the church of San Giobbe (1470s).

The same high quality of marble carving is seen at Santa Maria dei Miracoli (1481–1489), Pietro's small barrel-vaulted church with marble-veneered surfaces enlivened by dark-colored encrustation. Commanding examples of the fusion of Romanizing form and content in early Renaissance Venice are

Rizzo's wall tomb of Doge Niccolò Tron (Frari, 1476–1480) and those of Doge Pietro Mocenigo (San Zanipolo, 1476–1481) and Doge Andrea Vendramin (San Zanipolo, c. 1488–1493) by Pietro Lombardo, assisted by his sons Tullio (c. 1455–1532) and Antonio (c. 1458–?1516). Mostly relegating Christian imagery to the top, these tall monuments—the first two of them including standing portraits of the doge—combine classicizing figures of virtues, warriors, and various Roman motifs—alluding to each doge's deeds and hence to the grandeur of the republic—within a progressively plastic and tightly integrated triumphal arch format.

Painting in the Fifteenth Century. Decoration of the Great Council Chamber in the Doge's Palace continued from the 1360s through the early 1400s with twenty-eight frescoes narrating events relating to the strategic diplomacy of Doge Sebastiano Ziani in reconciling, in 1177, the warring pope (Alexander III) and emperor (Frederick Barbarossa); above were placed portraits of the doges. The renowned painter from the Marches, Gentile da Fabriano (c. 1385–1427), worked on this project from 1408 to 1413, as did Pisanello (c. 1395–1455; later a distinguished court painter and medallist), between 1409 and 1415. Already in poor condition by mid-century, the frescoes were replaced by a new cycle representing the same scenes on canvas—a support more resistent to the humid, salt air of Venice—begun in 1474 under the direction of Gentile Bellini, joined in 1479 by his brother Giovanni. Eventually comprising works by Titian, Tintoretto, and Veronese, this second important "document" of painting in Venice was consumed by fire in 1577 and thereafter replaced by a third. Other major sites of artistic activity during this period were the meeting houses of the *scuole* (confraternities), often analogously decorated with painted narrative cycles.

Although their work in Venice is lost, the presence of Gentile da Fabriano and Pisanello was significant. The composition of one of Pisanello's history scenes is preserved in a drawing (British Museum) revealing affinities, in the relation of the figures to their architectural setting, not only with Guariento's and especially Altichiero's earlier treatment but also with that of Jacopo Bellini and later Venetian fifteenth-century narrative painters. Gentile da Fabriano's pioneering interests in the effects of light and his role as Jacopo Bellini's teacher may also be noted. Further, the two visiting painters are likely to have encouraged the embrace of the then widely popular International Gothic style by Venetian painters such as Jacobello del Fiore (active 1394–1439; president from 1415–c.1436 of the Venetian painters' guild) and Michele Giambono (c. 1395–1462). This style is exemplified in the curvilinear drapery of Jacobello's *Allegory of Justice* (Venice, Accademia), a work commissioned in 1421 for the law court in the Doge's Palace and representing Justice as both Venice and the Virgin crowned and seated on lions between the archangels Michael and Gabriel. The bright colors and decorative gold are also characteristic of traditional Venetian taste.

Throughout most of the century, painting in Venice was dominated by two families: that of Jacopo Bellini, the pioneer of the Renaissance style in Venice, and his sons Gentile and Giovanni; and that of Antonio Vivarini (c. 1418–1476/84), his brother-in-law Giovanni d'Alemagna (d. 1450), brother Bartolomeo (c. 1430–c. 1500?), and son Alvise (1446–1505). The Vivarini produced altarpieces not only for Venetian churches but also for export to cities on both Adriatic coasts. A large number are preserved and document the transition in Venetian painting from Gothic to Renaissance style. Early works include three polyptychs, for the Benedictine convent at San Zaccaria, Venice (now San Tarasio Chapel), dated 1443 and signed jointly by Antonio and Giovanni d'Alemagna. These depict richly ornamented fabrics and use gold leaf, jewel-like colors, and elaborately carved frames of gilded wood resembling contemporary Venetian-Gothic architecture. In the modeling, weight, and three-dimensionality of the painted figures, however, they reflect Florentine early Renaissance influence, possibly the specific influence of Filippo Lippi, who worked in Padua in 1434, and Andrea del Castagno, who is documented in Venice in 1442–1443; Castagno painted monumental figures in fresco in the San Tarasio Chapel and executed a cartoon for a program of narrative scenes in mosaic in the *Capella Nova* (new chapel; later "Mascoli Chapel"), commissioned by Francesco Foscari for St. Mark's Basilica, and to which Giambono and Jacopo Bellini likely contributed. The most progressive joint work of Antonio Vivarini and Giovanni d'Alegmagna is their triptych dated 1446 for the *albergo* (officers' meeting room) of the Scuola della Carità; perhaps also influenced by Lippi's work in Padua, they depict volumetric figures of the Madonna and Latin church fathers set in a unified three-dimensional space defined by perspectively rendered rectilinear walls.

The influence of artistic and intellectual currents in nearby Padua, seat of the university, continued to be felt. The humanist revival is reflected in Jacopo

Bellini's drawings that refer to ancient styles and the inclusion of fictive antique reliefs and references to ancient prototypes in numerous Venetian paintings as the century progressed. The impact of Donatello's work in Padua is evident in Giovanni Bellini's early compositions, and the impact of the linear, sculptural style of Andrea Mantegna on Gentile Bellini and Bartolomeo Vivarini during the 1450s is apparent. As had Mantegna in his San Zeno altarpiece of 1456–1459, Venetian painters increasingly employed classicizing architectural forms for altarpiece frames. The evolution in Giovanni Bellini's oeuvre of an altarpiece format combining saints with the Madonna seated on a high throne in an illusionistic chapel-like space had considerable longevity in Venice and the Veneto.

Bellini's adoption of the Netherlandish oil technique was of enormous importance to the course of Venetian painting. Long credited to the presence in 1475–1476 in Venice of the Sicilian painter Antonello da Messina (c. 1430–1479), Bellini's experimentation with oil as binding medium is now known to have began somewhat earlier, suggesting another source or that Antonello had made an earlier visit. The medium enhanced Giovanni's ability to render glowing, light-saturated color and to simulate the shimmering gold of Venice's mosaics. His influence on the next generation of painters in Venice and the Veneto was vast; one whose style is closely related is Giovanni Battista Cima (c.1459–1517/18), a native of Conegliano active in Venice from the 1480s. Another prolific painter of altarpieces and devotional works was the superb Venetian colorist Carlo Crivelli (active 1457–1493). Influenced by Jacopo Bellini and Paduanism at midcentury, Crivelli practiced from 1468 in the Marches. Active at this time in Venice was the Padua-trained Bolognese panel painter Marco Zoppo (1432?–?1478), who was highly regarded in humanist circles.

Giovanni Bellini, Alvise Vivarini, and Gentile Bellini were all exceptionally skilled portraitists, the latter often incorporating numerous portraits in large, narrative paintings commissioned to decorate the meeting rooms of the major confraternities. These works and those of Giovanni Mansueti (active 1485–1526/27) and the highly poetic Venetian, Vittore Carpaccio (c. 1460–1525/26)—who along with the Bellini brothers and Alvise Vivarini contributed to the Great Council Chamber cycle—are notable as documentation of the cityscape and of Venetian life and ceremony toward the end of the century. The last quarter of the 1400s also witnessed a flourishing printing trade in Venice and produced extraordinar-

Giovanni Bellini. Pesaro Coronation. Giovanni Bellini, *Coronation of the Virgin,* early 1470s (Pesaro, Museo Civico) seen reconstructed with the *Entombment of Christ* (Rome, Pinacoteca Vaticana). MUSEI CIVICI, PESARO

237

ily beautiful hand-illuminated books characterized by brilliant color, imaginative illusionistic effects, and classical motifs.

Architecture and Sculpture in the Sixteenth Century.

Despite war, plague, and the irrevocable diminution of Venice's maritime and economic status, building continued on a grander and more magnificent scale than ever. Monumental figures, huge wall tombs, and small decorative bronzes and marbles witness the ongoing importance of antique modes and styles of sculpture and of sumptuous visual effects.

Architectural elements of the Roman orders and Albertian motifs appear increasingly during the early decades to articulate the facades of the traditionally arranged Venetian palaces. An imposing example—capped by a substantial cornice bearing a classicizing frieze—is Mauro Codussi's Palazzo Loredan (later Vendramin-Calergi) begun c. 1502. The spacious domed church of San Salvatore (1507–1532) bespeaks a new emphasis on precise proportionality and the monumentality of ancient Roman architecture. Its design is in part the work of Tullio Lombardo, who also continued practicing sculpture as did his brother Antonio. Parallel to Giorgione, the two Lombardi and the Padua bronzist Andrea Riccio (1470–1532)—the originator of widely popular small bronzes and decorative objects *all'antica* whose masterpieces are the paschal candlestick in the Santo (1507–1516) and slightly later tomb monument of Girolamo and Marcantonio della Torre (Verona, San Fermo Maggiore)—embraced to a remarkable extent both classical sculptural models and nostalgically antique poetic subjects sympathetic to the literary taste of their humanist patrons. Both Lombardo brothers contributed to the cycle of marble reliefs in the tomb chapel of St. Anthony of Padua in the Santo. Before leaving Venice in 1506, Antonio designed the monumental bronze sculptural group of the Madonna and Child with Saints funded by Cardinal Giovanni Battista Zen (St. Mark's Basilica).

Change in both architecture and sculpture came with the arrival, following the Sack of Rome, of the Florentine sculptor Jacopo Tatti, generally designated Sansovino (1486–1570), who was named *proto* of St. Mark's Basilica in 1529 and remained in Venice until his death. Equipped with firsthand familiarity with ancient and high Renaissance buildings in Rome and the enthusiastic support of Andrea Gritti (doge 1523–1538), Sansovino initiated a period of urban renewal as Venice promoted its image as an undefiled "new Rome." Sansovino designed

numerous buildings including the churches of San Francesco della Vigna (begun 1534), San Martino di Castello (begun 1540), and San Giuliano (begun 1553) as well as residences on the Grand Canal: the Palazzo Dolfin (begun 1538) and the Palazzo Corner della Ca Grande (after 1545), the latter outstanding for its enormous size, rusticated lower story, and Vitruvian detail.

Sansovino's grandest contributions to the cityscape are the government commissions built opposite the Doge's Palace: the Mint (*Zecca*; 1535–1547) and the Library (*Libreria*; 1537–1591), erected to house the collection given the state in 1468 by Cardinal Bessarion. The Mint's fortified appearance, with rusticated lower arcade and distinctive, banded Doric columns, contrasts strongly with the open, luxurious character of the double-arcaded, elaborately ornamented Library, yet the two are harmoniously juxtaposed through the regularity of their classical orders. Adjacent to the Library, at the base of the bell tower, Sansovino's *Loggetta* (1538–c. 1542) exemplifies his talents as both architect and sculptor. Articulated as a Roman arch, the polychrome marble facade of this small state meeting house displays four graceful bronze figures of Olympian deities and Peace, constituting a classical counterpart to Bartolomeo Buon's Porta della Cartà opposite. Sansovino's sculptural legacy further includes bronze reliefs, completed in 1544, in the tribune of St. Mark's—once more narrating the patron saint's story—and the powerful, colossal *Mars* and *Neptune* that stand at the top of Rizzo's staircase in the courtyard of the Doge's Palace (1550s–1560s).

Two other outstanding architects were active in the Veneto during the sixteenth century: Michele Sanmicheli (c. 1484–1559), active in Rome and Orvieto before settling in his native Verona in 1526, and Andrea Palladio (1508–1580), born in Padua and based in Vicenza. Both contributed significantly to the Romanizing aggrandizement of the Venetian cityscape. Sanmicheli's facade of the Palazzo Corner at San Polo (designed c. 1550) employs rusticated-Doric, Ionic, and Corinthian orders; that of his majestic Palazzo Grimani at San Luca (begun 1556), a tightly integrated scheme of Corinthian orders. Three noble exponents of Palladio's hallmark application of interlocked temple facades are in Venice: his facade for Sansovino's San Francesco della Vigna (1568–1572) and those of his own magnificent and prominently situated churches of San Giorgio Maggiore (begun 1565) and Il Redentore (begun 1577). Other major works of the late sixteenth century are the high-arched Rialto Bridge (1588–1591; it replaced a wood structure), designed by the Venetian architect and engineer Antonio da Ponte (d. 1597) as was the prison beside the Doge's Palace, begun during the late sixteenth century and completed by Antonio Contino (1566–1600), architect of the Bridge of Sighs that connects them (c. 1600).

Sculpture during the second half of the century was dominated by the Trentine, Alessandro Vittoria (1525?–1608), who came to Venice in 1543 and worked with Sansovino. Vittoria's figural style departs from Sansovino's in its Michelangelesque musculature and pronounced torsion. Vittoria also contributed significantly to the contemporary building campaign through his design and execution of architectural stucco decoration. His many naturalistic portrait busts of Venetian patricians provide an analogy to Tintoretto's painted portraits. Sculptors of note active in Venice at the end of the century are the Veronese, Girolamo Campagna (1549–1625), who executed the dynamic, protobaroque bronze figural group for the high altar of Palladio's San Giorgio Maggiore (1592–1593), and the Paduan, Tiziano Aspetti (c. 1559–1606), who produced monumental figures for the Mint and Rialto Bridge and whose bronze reliefs further Sansovino's extraordinary luminous optical effects in this medium.

Painting in the Sixteenth Century. The sixteenth century witnessed the activity of many talented artists who together carried the international reputation of Venetian painting, established by Giovanni Bellini, to greater heights. Criticized by Giorgio Vasari for neglect of drawing, extolled by the Tuscan writer Pietro Aretino for the re-creation of visual effect, and eulogized by the Venetian writer Marco Boschini for the emotive power of expressive brushstroke, sixteenth-century Venetian painting continued with increasing self-awareness to adhere to the traditional commitment to color and optical splendor and to explore the rich potential of applying oil paint to canvas. Therein it established the groundwork for the greatest pictorial accomplishments in Europe in the following century. The history of the magnificent "Golden Age of Venetian Painting" is best learned from close discussion of its three major protagonists: Titian, Tintoretto, and Veronese. The following text notes broad trends and collaborative projects in the city of Venice and introduces other major painters working in Venice and the Veneto.

At the beginning of the century, the Bellini brothers, Cima, and Carpaccio continued to enjoy the status they each had attained during the fifteenth; Giorgione (Giorgio da Castelfranco) began the brief

career that was to revolutionize technique and subject matter; and the impact of visits of the Florentine, Leonardo da Vinci (1500), and the German, Albrecht Dürer (1505–1506), was felt. The pageantry and flavor for orientalizing detail that characterize many of Gentile Bellini's and Carpaccio's scenographic pictures is evident in the former's *St. Mark Preaching in Alexandria* (Milan, Brera). Whereas this composition was designed by Gentile, it was finished after his death by Giovanni (c. 1510); the light-filled atmosphere and broad planes of luminous color are characteristic of Giovanni's later paintings. Giovanni's signal picture from the first decade is the San Zaccaria altarpiece (1505), which, compared with his earlier work, reveals also a softer modeling and blurring of contours. The weighty figures are geometrically disposed within an illusionistic yet idealized space. Although these features, as well as the saints' quiet introspection, recall Giorgione's Castelfranco altarpiece, they also proceed logically from Giovanni's own previous development. Bellini's embrace of mythologies as subject during the sixteenth century, however, is likely to reflect Giorgione's oeuvre.

Influenced in his formation both by Bellini's luminosity and Giorgione's freedom of technique and subject, the Venetian painter Sebastiano Luciani later and generally designated del Piombo (c. 1485–1547) began a promising career in Venice, executing an altarpiece of compositional originality for San Giovanni Crisostomo and four organ shutters, showing volumetric figures in shimmering fictive golden niches, in the church of San Bartolomeo (c. 1509). Sebastiano moved permanently in 1511 to Rome. Under the influence of Michelangelo and ancient Roman sculpture, he achieved a unique and powerful synthesis of Roman high Renaissance sculptural form and Venetian color and luminosity, a synthesis first observed shortly after his arrival in the *Death of Adonis* (destroyed).

Giorgione's introduction of the sensuous female figure as subject matter—shown close-up at half-length, as a reclining nude, or in mythological scenes as in Sebastiano's picture—was taken up in Venice not only by the young Titian but also by Jacopo Palma (generally designated *il Vecchio* [the elder]; b. c. 1480–1490; d. 1528), who around 1510 arrived in Venice from his native Serina near Bergamo. Palma's extensive output of skillfully rendered and enticing female figures and inviting scenes of the Madonna seated with saints in a landscape is remarkable considering his early death and also surely indicates contemporary taste for these subjects among private collectors. A later noteworthy painter to supply the demand for them was Paris Bordone (1500–1571), who was born in Treviso, but trained in Venice under Titian. Bordone's monumental work includes the legendary Venetian subject *The Fisherman Delivering the Ring* (Venice, Accademia; 1530s or 1540s), commissioned for the *albergo* of the Scuola di San Marco.

Giovanni Gerolamo Savoldo (c. 1480/5–after 1548), a Brescian or of Brescian descent, had settled in Venice by 1521. Sensitive to the dramatic potential of light and author of night scenes, Savoldo reflects the influence of Giorgione's pastoralism and sense of mysterious psychological engagement in pictures of single figures such as the *Shepherd with a Flute* (1520s or 1530s, Los Angeles, J. Paul Getty Museum). Of great psychological fascination are both the personality and works of Lorenzo Lotto (c. 1480–1556). Born and trained in Venice, Lotto led a troubled life (as documented in his account books), spending much of his career in Treviso, Bergamo, and locations in the Marches. His portraits are often characterized by unusual off-balance poses, horizontal format, and emblematic or allegorical accessories as well as a disquieting confrontation of the sitter with the viewer [see the color plates in this volume for one of Lotto's portraits].

Titian's most important rival in the Veneto, in the realm of monumental narrative painting, was the prolific fresco painter Giovanni Antonio de' Sacchis (c. 1483–1539), generally designated Pordenone, the name of his native city in the Friuli. Pordenone, who traveled to Rome c. 1518, developed a muscular and distinctly personal figural canon; he heightened the drama of his scenes with daring experimentation in foreshortening. Working in the Veneto, Lombardy, and Emilia, Pordenone also executed commissions for Venice during the late 1520s and 1530s; he contributed a scene in 1537–1538 to the series of history paintings in the Great Council Chamber. Another prolific provincial master of the grand style was the Brescian, Alessandro Bonvicino, generally designated il Moretto (c. 1498–1554). Influenced by Titian and Savoldo, he produced coloristically sumptuous works often of profound religious feeling. Giovanni Battista Moroni (c. 1520/25–1578), native of Albino, was trained in Brescia by Moretto; active in Albino, Bergamo, and Trent, his oeuvre includes acutely observed, imposing portraits.

During the 1540s a taste for the central Italian mannerist style was introduced to Venice through visits and local commissions executed by the Tuscan painter Francesco Salviati and the painter and historian Vasari. This influence is most notable in the early Venetian works of Salviati's Tuscan pupil and namesake Giuseppe (Porta) Salviati (c. 1520–c. 1575), who remained in Venice; in those of Andrea Meldolla (c. 1510/15?–1563) generally designated Schiavone from his origins in Dalmatia; and in those of Lambert Sustris (c. 1510/15–after 1584?), probably a native of Amsterdam, who had been employed as Titian's assistant during the 1530s. By the 1560s, however, painting in Venice was dominated by the inventive and personal idioms of Tintoretto and Veronese, respectively. At the same time, Venetian collectors also patronized Jacopo Dal Ponte (c. 1510–1592), generally designated Bassano from Bassano del Grappa, his home-base in the Veneto. Similarly to Titian, Tintoretto, and Veronese, Bassano ran a large family workshop; together these masters were named by Boschini as the four greatest practitioners of the Venetian pictorial tradition. Bassano's *Flight into Egypt* from the early 1540s (Pasadena, Norton Simon Collection) represents the taste of his Venetian patrons as well as his technical and intellectual brilliance.

Two significant collaborative projects were carried out in sixteenth-century Venice at the city's heart. Under the direction of Titian and Sansovino, twenty-one roundels depicting allegories of learning were commissioned in 1556 from seven artists—including Giuseppe Salviati, Schiavone, and the newly arrived Veronese—to decorate the richly ornamented gilt ceiling of the reading room of the magnificent new Libreria. The second is the extensive campaign following the disastrous fire of 1577 to replace the decoration of the Great Council Chamber, to which not only Veronese and Tintoretto contributed but also Jacopo Bassano's son Francesco (1549–1592); Palma il Vecchio's great-nephew, Jacopo Palma il Giovane (the younger; c. 1548–1628), who was trained in Urbino and Rome but had returned to Venice in the early 1570s; and the eminent Federico Zuccaro (1540/41–1609) of Rome. The extant program, a "corporate" effort hospitable to the participation of outsiders, indicates sensitivity to the legacy of the history cycle that had previously adorned the room and reveals further effort to glorify the image of Venice. It documents once more the blending of artistic tradition and innovation in the service of the state.

See also **Bellini Family**; **Donatello**; **Giotto di Bondone**;
 Mantegna, Andrea; **Palladio, Andrea**; **Tintoretto**;
 Titian; **Veronese, Paolo**.

BIBLIOGRAPHY

Primary Works

Boschini, Marco. *Le ricche minere della pittura veneziana.* (The rich mines of Venetian painting). Venice, 1576.

Zanetti, Anton Maria. *Della pittura veneziana.* Venice, 1771.

Secondary Works

Aikema, Bernard, and Dulcia Meijers. *Nel regno dei poveri: arte e storia dei grandi ospedali veneziani in età moderna 1474–1797.* Venice, 1989.

Brown, Patricia Fortini. *Art and Life in Renaissance Venice.* New York, 1997.

Brown, Patricia Fortini. *Venice and Antiquity: The Venetian Sense of the Past.* New Haven, Conn., and London, 1996. Fundamental interdisciplinary study of the role of classical art and literature in shaping the "myth of Venice."

Brown, Patricia Fortini. *Venetian Narrative Painting in the Age of Carpaccio.* New Haven, Conn., 1988. Establishes historical context and important social function of the major narrative cycles commissioned by Venetian confraternities.

Chambers, David, and Brian Pullan, eds. *Venice: A Documentary History, 1450–1630.* Oxford, 1992.

The Genius of Venice 1500–1600. Edited by Jane Martineau and Charles Hope. London, 1983. Catalog of the exhibition held at the Royal Academy of Art, London, 1983–1984.

Goy, Richard. *Venice: The City and Its Architecture.* London, 1997.

Humfrey, Peter. *The Altarpiece in Renaissance Venice.* New Haven, Conn., 1993.

Humfrey, Peter. *Painting in Renaissance Venice.* New Haven, Conn., 1995.

Huse, Norbert, and Wolfgang Wolters. *Venedig: Die Kunst der Renaissance* (1986). English translation *The Art of Renaissance Venice.* Chicago, 1990.

Lazzarini, Lorenzo. "The Use of Color by Venetian Painters 1480–1580: Materials and Techniques." In *Color and Technique in Renaissance Painting.* Edited by Marcia Hall. Locust Valley, N.Y., 1987.

Lieberman, Ralph. *Renaissance Architecture in Venice 1450–1540.* New York, 1982.

Luchs, Alison. *Tullio Lombardo and Ideal Portrait Sculpture in Renaissance Venice, 1490–1530.* Cambridge, U.K., 1995.

McHam, Sarah Blake. *The Chapel of St. Anthony at the Santo and the Development of Venetian Renaissance Sculpture.* Cambridge, U.K., and New York, 1994.

Meilman, Patricia. *Titian and the Altarpiece in Renaissance Venice.* Cambridge, U.K., and New York, 1999.

Planiscig, Leo. *Venezianische Bildhauer der Renaissance.* Vienna, 1921. For several decades, the classic, comprehensive study.

La pittura nel Veneto. Edited by Mauro Lucco. *Il Trecento.* 2 vols. Milan, 1992; *Il Quattrocento.* 2 vols. Milan, 1989–1990; *Il Cinquecento.* 2 vols. Milan, 1996–1998.

Rosand, David. *Painting in Sixteenth-Century Venice: Titian, Veronese, Tintoretto.* Rev. ed. Cambridge, U.K., and New York, 1997.

Sinding-Larsen, Staale. *Christ in the Council Hall: Studies in the Religious Iconography of the Venetian Republic.* Rome, 1974.

Thomas, Martin. *Alessandro Vittoria and the Portrait Bust in Renaissance Venice: Remodeling Antiquity.* New York, 1998.

CAROLYN C. WILSON

VERGARA, JUAN DE (c. 1492–1557), priest, intellectual, foremost Spanish correspondent of Desiderius Erasmus. Scholars have consistently portrayed Juan de Vergara as a symbol of the Spanish Renaissance, if only because of his connections to Erasmus, Europe's most famous humanist. Vergara became an associate of the College of San Ildefonso—the centerpiece of the University of Alcalá de Henares—in 1514, and attained the doctorate in theology there in 1517. He read Greek and collaborated on the Complutensian Polyglot Bible (printed 1513–1517); he also translated Aristotle's *Physics, Metaphysics,* and *De anima.* His library contained works by ancient authors such as Cicero and Suetonius as well as ones by noted Italian humanists such as Lorenzo Valla and Angelo Poliziano.

Vergara moved in prestigious spheres for most of his life. As part of the entourage of the Holy Roman Emperor and king of Spain, Charles V, he witnessed Martin Luther's condemnation at the Diet of Worms in 1521. He eventually held at least eight ecclesiastical offices or benefices. One of those posts made him part of the governing body of the cathedral of Toledo, which was the richest church in Spain; but his most consequential position was the secretariat to three archbishops of Toledo between 1516 and 1533. Vergara turned his wealth to perilous ends after his half brother, Bernardino de Tovar, was arrested by the Spanish Inquisition in 1530: he tried to undermine the case by bribing witnesses, but when the Toledo inquisitors discovered the subornation, they arrested him in 1533. Vergara was held for two years but refused to mount a defense. In December 1535, he was sentenced to a heavy fine and one year of seclusion in a monastery. By June 1536, the ruling was commuted to allow him to fulfill the year of seclusion in the Toledo cathedral chapter.

Until the 1990s, historians believed that Vergara's arrest was caused by his support for Erasmus; they interpreted his ordeal as a blow for the Spanish Renaissance. Closer readings of the trial suggest the inquisitors only seized Vergara because they uncovered his extortion; they charged him with Lutheranism and Erasmianism in order to pursue his indictment as both an abettor of heretics and a heretic himself. Vergara's status as a Renaissance humanist is undeniable, but his interest to modern scholars now lies in the intricacy of his intellectual preferences and his role as a patron, as much as his correspondence with Erasmus.

BIBLIOGRAPHY

Bataillon, Marcel. *Érasme et l'Espagne.* Edited by Daniel Devoto and Charles Amiel. 3 vols. Geneva, 1991. A revised edition of

Erasme et Espagne: Recherches sur l'histoire spirituelle du XVIᵉ siècle. Paris, 1937.

Homza, Lu Ann. *Religious Authority in the Spanish Renaissance.* Baltimore and London, forthcoming. Chapter 1 features the closest reading of the Vergara trial thus far in historical scholarship.

Longhurst, John. "Alumbrados, erasmistas, y luteranos en el proceso de Juan de Vergara." *Cuadernos de la Historia de España* 27 (1957): 99–163; 28 (1958): 102–165; 29–30 (1959): 266–292; 31–32 (1960): 322–356; 35–36 (1962): 337–353; 37–38 (1963): 356–371. Includes substantial excerpts from Vergara's trial, with an interpretation that follows Bataillon's lead, and treats the ordeal as an assault on Erasmus's Spanish supporters.

LU ANN HOMZA

VERGERIO, PIERPAOLO (c. 1369–1444), Italian humanist, pedagogical theorist. Vergerio was born in Capodistria, a small town on the Gulf of Trieste ruled by the Venetians. His most vivid childhood memories were tied to his family's celebration of the feast of Saint Jerome. Jerome became for Vergerio a lifelong patron and an exemplar of virtuous living; he actually made a vow to deliver a panegyric every year on Jerome's feast. Basic studies in Latin grammar and stylistics instilled in Vergerio an enduring regard for classical Latin. Vergerio pursued a degree in the arts at the University of Bologna from 1388–1390. To finance his studies, Vergerio also taught dialectic to beginning students. He soon grew to dislike the rancorous debates of logicians, and he found greater inspiration in the moral persuasion of Seneca and Cicero. Cicero especially gave Vergerio a sense of the ways that one might harness persuasive oratory to the compelling example of an upright life.

At Bologna, Vergerio wrote a comedy entitled *Paulus,* inspired by the revolutionary ideals of the Roman playwright Terence. Terence had advocated flexibility and tolerance in dealing with an adolescent's discovery of his sexual powers after puberty. Vergerio likewise became interested in the question of how to educate an adolescent and used the comedy to explore his own convictions that a proper education in disciplines that emphasized the formation of character might well keep one from succumbing to lustful impulses.

Vergerio in Padua. From 1390 to 1397, Vergerio was in Padua, where he pursued degrees in medicine and law. He delivered his first sermons in honor of Saint Jerome and structured them as classical panegyrics according to the rules of rhetoric found in ancient handbooks. He also wrote speeches for specific political and judicial affairs at the court of Francesco Novello da Carrara, the ruling despot of Padua.

Vergerio's innovative techniques were nowhere more apparent than in his oration for the funeral of Francesco il Vecchio da Carrara, Padua's former despot, in November 1393. Unlike any of the other prominent orators who spoke on this occasion, Vergerio used no theme and no appeal to authorities to establish a theoretical proposition about Francesco da Carrara. Rather, he focused a classicizing oration upon the sadness aroused in the population by the death of their prince and the consoling character of his great deeds on their behalf. For the first time, a Renaissance orator broke with medieval conventions and modeled a funeral speech on classical norms for panegyric.

Vergerio's initial significant task as a humanist was a commission to prepare an edition of Petrarch's unfinished Latin epic, *Africa.* That commission is probably what brought Vergerio to Florence late in 1393; there he could discuss the edition with Coluccio Salutati, who had long urged the publication of *Africa* and had glossed the text. Vergerio completed his edition by November 1396. His editorial work became the occasion for wrestling with the legacy that Petrarch had left to humanists. Although Vergerio clearly admired the contributions of Petrarch and revered him as the father of humanism, he still felt that Petrarch had been too ambivalent about humanist involvement in politics. For Vergerio, such involvement was essential for a complete recovery of ancient rhetorical culture.

During these years Vergerio gathered notes for a treatise on the location and the constitution of Venice. He saw the Venetian republic as a potential employer, and he sought to communicate his admiration for the artistry of Venetians in choosing the location for their city and in building aristocratic political structures that mirrored the beauty and harmony of their physical structures.

Defense of Antiquity. Having failed to find employment at the Carrara court in Padua and the governmental chancery in Venice, Vergerio left Padua in 1397 and did not return until 1400. In 1397, Vergerio offered a stirring defense of humanism as a rhetorical culture when he denounced the mercenary general Carlo Malatesta for pulling down a statue of Virgil in Mantua. Not the only intellectual to respond to the destruction of the statue, Vergerio was the only one to add a defense of Cicero and oratory to his defense of Virgil and poetry. He was also the only one to emphasize the power of a visible monument to incite admiration and imitation of the individual portrayed.

A year later, Vergerio started writing a letter to denounce the degradation of Rome's antiquities. Myopic Christians, acting in the name of piety, had allowed Rome to fall into decay and were even destroying significant monuments from ancient times. Carlo Malatesta had likewise claimed to act in the name of true Christianity when he destroyed Virgil's statue. Vergerio was distressed by such frenzied zealotry. Through his devotion to Jerome, he had always seen the compatibility between classical and Christian cultures.

In 1398, he moved to Florence and participated in a Greek course offered until late in 1399 by Manuel Chrysoloras, a Byzantine exile in Florence. He then returned to Padua and again sought employment at the court of Francesco Novello da Carrara. By 1400, Vergerio had also completed his degree in civil law, most likely finishing his studies at Bologna.

A Humanist's Educational Program.

Hoping to be hired as a tutor for the despot's son, Vergerio composed a short treatise spelling out his program for an education in the humanities. *De ingenuis moribus et liberalibus studiis* (On the excellent habits and liberal studies appropriate to adolescence) was a synthesis of Vergerio's maturing convictions about humanist education and a watershed in the history of the movement. First copied in September 1403, it would be copied repeatedly for centuries thereafter, and would exert considerable influence on subsequent European theorists. As the title indicates, Vergerio sought to outline a program of liberal studies that would instill a sense of moral responsibility in adolescents. Among the most novel elements of the treatise, Vergerio elaborated a curriculum of three disciplines integral to the formation of ethical character and the development of political responsibility. To become a useful member of political society, an adolescent needed to master history, moral philosophy, and rhetoric.

According to Vergerio, those three disciplines comprised the core of the humanist program of studies. Moral philosophy was prescriptive, a source of sound values. History was illustrative, a source of convincing examples. And rhetoric was persuasive, the primary means to the end of ethical politics. Although Vergerio emphasized the importance of these disciplines for his stated aims, he also analyzed the value of virtually all disciplines then taught in Italian universities. While he advocated the adaptation of the curriculum to an individual student's needs and interests, he also saw the special value of oratory as a matrix in a curriculum designed to educate principled public servants.

From 1402 to 1406, Francesco Novello da Carrara engaged in a reckless policy of expansion, and his regime was eventually overthrown by Venice. Vergerio observed this process closely. For some years, he had been engaged in the writing of a series of biographies of the Carrara despots, *De principibus Carrariensibus* (On the Carrara princes), and he also wrote a short analysis of the ideal of monarchical government, *De monarchia*.

Admirer of Jerome.

With the demise of the Carrara, Vergerio looked elsewhere for employment. Perhaps anticipating that need, he had added to his list of degrees a further one in canon law. He set off for Rome in 1405, in search of work at the papal court. As he did, he took with him years of experience in delivering panegyrics for the feast of Saint Jerome. Vergerio saw Jerome as a scholar who epitomized the value of humanist learning for scriptural exegesis and for authentically catholic piety. He candidly discussed Jerome's famous dream, during which the saint had felt himself judged and punished by the Lord for being a Ciceronian. Vergerio did not see the dream as a condemnation of humanist studies but as a warning that Jerome should alter his scholarly priorities. In Vergerio's estimation, Jerome's writings were useful, his oratory ethical, and his degree of interior freedom remarkable. In the panegyrics, Vergerio transformed Jerome from the enemy of humanist learning to a proof of the value of those studies for believers. He presented his innovative perspective through the equally innovative medium of classicizing panegyric.

In Papal and Imperial Service.

In August 1406, before Pope Innocent VII (1404–1406), Vergerio preached a sermon that emphasized peace and reconciliation between the pope and his flock. A month later, he composed a poem to celebrate the idyllic life of humanists at the court of a generous ecclesiastical patron. On 30 September 1406, he preached his panegyric of Jerome before the papal court. He defended the value of humanist studies for believers and urged Pope Innocent to approach his rival in Avignon with the same kindness that Jerome had shown to a lion he had succeeded in taming.

After Innocent's death in November 1406, Vergerio was invited to address the gathering of cardinals who were about to elect a successor. He used the opportunity to urge the cardinals to postpone the election and seek an end to the schism that had disastrously divided Christendom. But the clerical nobility could not see beyond defense of their privileged position, and Vergerio's effort failed. The cardinals quickly elected Pope Gregory XII (1406–1415, d. 1417).

Although ambivalent, Vergerio continued to work for Gregory and the papal court. In September 1408, he again preached a panegyric on Jerome before the members of the court, now resident in Siena. When Gregory failed to resolve the schism, Vergerio left the papal court in 1409 and went home to Capodistria. He emerged from his brief retirement in 1411 to congratulate his friend Francesco Zabarella (1360–1417) on his appointment as a cardinal. A few years later, Vergerio joined Zabarella in Rome and then traveled with him to the Council of Constance (1414–1418).

At the council in 1414, Vergerio was appointed one of the examiners of the voting (*scrutator*). The next year, he traveled with the emperor Sigismund on a diplomatic mission to the kings of the Iberian peninsula. The long journey together became the grounds for the future association of emperor and humanist. In the summer of 1417, Vergerio offered theses in defense of the imperial position on matters of reform and the election of a new pope. Vergerio left Constance in 1418 in the company of Sigismund.

Vergerio spent his final years at Buda and Prague, putting all his training at the emperor's service. At Sigismund's behest, Vergerio acted as the imperial orator at a colloquy in 1421 between Hussites and Catholics. Vergerio translated from Greek into Latin the biography of Alexander the Great written in antiquity by Flavius Arrianus. Apparently, he retired from public service after Sigismund's death in 1437, and he died at Buda.

Vergerio's education, his work for court chanceries, his writings, and his circle of friends clearly placed him in the mainstream of early Italian humanism. He gave important new directions to the humanist movement and became one of the acknowledged leaders of humanism's third generation. Vergerio was especially creative in his educational program. He was the first intellectual in Western history to write a formal treatise on an education in the humanities. For Vergerio, the best way to form character in the adolescent children of a society's politically elite was to emphasize the disciplines of history, moral philosophy, and rhetoric. Skillful practice of public oratory was the shaping force of the entire program, and its mastery prepared one for a role in political culture. Vergerio himself often tried to use oratory as a passport to public responsibilities. His stress on the art of public speaking thereby permitted him to redefine the social role of a humanist intellectual.

BIBLIOGRAPHY

Primary Works

Vergerio, Pierpaolo. *De ingenuis moribus et liberalibus studiis adulescentiae.* Edited by Attilio Gnesotto. *Atti e memorie della R. Accademia di scienze, lettere, ed arti in Padova,* n.s., 34 (1917–1918). Pages 95–146.

Vergerio, Pierpaolo. *De principibus Carrariensibus et gestis eorum liber.* Edited by Attilio Gnesotto. *Atti e memorie della R. Accademia di scienze, lettere, ed arti in Padova,* 41 (1924–1925). Pages 327–475.

Vergerio, Pierpaolo. *De republica veneta* (On the Venetian republic). Edited by David Robey and John Law. *Rinascimento,* n.s., 15 (1975). Pages 38–49.

Vergerio, Pierpaolo. *Epistolario.* Edited by Leonardo Smith. Rome, 1934. The volume has 148 letters, including Vergerio's invective against Carlo Malatesta, his letter to Petrarch in the name of Cicero, his *De monarchia,* and his *Poetica narratio.*

Vergerio, Pierpaolo. *Paulus.* Edited by Alessandro Perosa. In *L'umanesimo in Istria.* Edited by Vittore Branca and Sante Graciotti. Florence, 1983. Pages 321–356.

Woodward, William Harrison. *Vittorino da Feltre and Other Humanist Educators.* Reprint, Toronto, 1996. Contains a condensed English translation of *De ingenuis.* Pages 93–118.

Secondary Works

McManamon, John M. *Pierpaolo Vergerio the Elder (ca. 1369–1444): The Humanist as Orator.* Medieval and Renaissance Texts and Studies 163. Tempe, Ariz., 1996.

Robey, David. "Humanism and Education in the Early Quattrocento: The *De ingenuis moribus* of P. P. Vergerio." *Bibliothèque d'humanisme et Renaissance* 42 (1980): 27–58.

Robey, David. "P. P. Vergerio the Elder: Republicanism and Civic Values in the Work of an Early Italian Humanist." *Past and Present,* no. 58 (February 1973): 3–37.

JOHN M. MCMANAMON, S.J.

VERGIL. *See* **Virgil.**

VERGIL, POLYDORE (1470?–1555), Anglo-Italian humanist and historian. Polydore Vergil was born in Urbino of a scholarly family. He was ordained by 1496 and probably entered papal service around this same date, where he met Adriano Castelli, himself a humanist as well as the agent at Rome of the English kings Henry VII and Henry VIII. Castelli was appointed collector of Peter's Pence in England in 1489; he made Polydore his deputy there in 1502. Six years later, Polydore also acquired the archdeaconry of Wells. He remained in England until 1553, when he returned to spend his last years in Urbino.

At the time of his arrival in England, Polydore had already established a scholarly reputation as the author of two important books: *Proverbium libellus* (Little book of proverbs; 1498) and *De inventoribus rerum* (Concerning the inventors of things; 1499). The first of these (also called *Adagia*) was a collection of ancient proverbs, identified and contextualized, which preceded Desiderius Erasmus's better-known work of the same name by a few months and went through many editions in the sixteenth century. The second, a series of very brief essays identifying the originators of all sorts of human activities and inventions such as religion, matrimony, letters and grammar, government, painting, and husbandry, down even to such recent developments as printing, was extremely popular and, in his own day, Polydore's most influential work.

Polydore's renown as a humanist made him welcome at Henry VII's court, and by 1506 the king had suggested that a history of England in the latest and best style would be welcomed. The first version was finished by 1514, although the first printed edition of *Anglica historia,* which ended with the death of Henry VII in 1509, did not appear until 1534, with a revision in 1546. Political wisdom suggested that the events of Henry VIII's reign be omitted until 1555, when Polydore had retired permanently to Italy; that edition carried the story to 1538. Polydore's long residence in England, and his excellent connections, made his book an important source for the history of the early Tudors, and historians from Edward Hall to Francis Bacon and beyond made full use of it.

The book had an even more important influence on Tudor historiography in general. Although Polydore's materials for most of the volume were drawn from the medieval chroniclers, his principles of organization came from the ancient Romans. The early history of England was compressed into eight books; thereafter, Polydore devoted one book to each reign and allowed the personality of the ruler to dominate—an idea taken up by Thomas More in his account of Richard III and, later, by Shakespeare and his fellow historical dramatists. Moreover, from the time of Richard II on, Polydore used a kind of providentialism to link the reigns: royal sins, and the retribution they brought in their wake, made for a coherent story. That story also allowed the book to serve as propaganda for the Tudors, as their arrival could be made to signal the end of the chaos of the Wars of the Roses. In addition, Polydore as a rational outsider found it possible to undermine such English nationalist legends as the story of King Arthur, though he recognized the danger in doing so, and protected himself by producing (in 1525) an edition of Gildas, the main source for post-Roman Britain. Nevertheless, the wrath of native historians like John Leland and John Bale led to a series of counterattacks

so vicious that Polydore's reputation took more than a century to recover.

BIBLIOGRAPHY

Primary Works

Vergil, Polydore. *The Anglica Historia of Polydore Vergil,* A.D. *1485–1537*. Edited by Denys Hay. London, 1950.

Vergil, Polydore. *Polydore Vergil's English History.* Edited by Sir Henry Ellis. London, 1846.

Vergil, Polydore. *Three Books of Polydore Vergil's English History, Comprising the Reigns of Henry VI, Edward IV, and Richard III.* Edited by Sir Henry Ellis. London, 1844.

Secondary Works

Hay, Denys. *Polydore Vergil: Renaissance Historian and Man of Letters.* Oxford, 1952. The essential study.

Levy, F. J. *Tudor Historical Thought.* San Marino, Calif., 1967. Useful for the historical context.

FRED J. LEVY

VERNACULAR LITERATURES AND LANGUAGES. *See entries on individual literatures and languages.*

VERNIA, NICOLETTO (c. 1420–1499), Italian Aristotelian philosopher. Vernia was born in Chieti and studied at the universities of Padua and Pavia. In 1468 he took over the chair of Gaetano da Thiene at the University of Padua, where he taught logic and natural philosophy. He wrote on medicine, logic, natural philosophy, philosophical psychology, and metaphysics. His early writings show a marked interest in defending the reading by Averroes (Ibn Rushd) of Aristotle, especially on the question of the "unity of the intellect," that is, that the human intellect is eternal and one for all humans. In 1489 the bishop of Padua, Pietro Barozzi, banned public disputations (debates) on the position of Averroes on the unity of the intellect. While Vernia is not mentioned by name in the decree, in a later letter to Vernia, Barozzi made it clear that Vernia was the target and held him responsible for making the views of Ibn Rushd known throughout Italy.

As early as 1487, however, Vernia was having second thoughts about the cogency of Averroes's interpretation of Aristotle on the human intellect. The impetus for this reevaluation was the recent translation of the writings of Greek commentators on Aristotle, especially Themistius, Simplicius of Cilicia, and Alexander of Aphrodisias. In addition, he showed a more sympathetic approach to such major Christian Latin thinkers as Albertus Magnus, Thomas Aquinas, and John Duns Scotus. He also was influenced in important ways by Giovanni Pico della Mirandola and Marsilio Ficino. As a result, by 1492 Vernia had completed his *Contra perversam Averrois opinionem* (Against the perverse view of Ibn Rushd; 1504), although his critique was not published until after his death. In this work he argued that there are as many human intellects as there are human bodies and that philosophy is capable of demonstrating personal immortality. Basing himself on Themistius and Simplicius as well as Albertus Magnus and recent translation of Plato, he also argued that Plato and Aristotle had the same basic position concerning human knowledge, namely that knowledge consists of a kind of "recollection" by the soul from its preexistent state.

BIBLIOGRAPHY

Primary Works

Vernia, Nicoletto. *Quaeritur utrum sint ponendae rationes seminales in materia respectu rerum quae ex ipsa generantur.* In Edward P. Mahoney. "Nicoletto Vernia's Question on Seminal Reasons." *Franciscan Studies* 38 (1978): 299–309.

Vernia, Nicoletto. *Quaestio est, an medicina nobilior atque praestantior sit iure civili.* In *La disputata delle arti nel Quattrocento.* Edited by Eugenio Garin. Florence, 1947. Pages 111–123.

Secondary Works

Mahoney, Edward P. "Nicoletto Vernia on the Soul and Immortality." In *Philosophy and Humanism: Renaissance Essays in Honor of Paul Oskar Kristeller.* Edited by Edward P. Mahoney. New York, 1976. Pages 144–163.

Mahoney, Edward P. "Philosophy and Science in Nicoletto Vernia and Agostino Nifo." In *Scienza e filosofia all'Università di Padova nel Quattrocento.* Edited by Antonino Poppi. Padua, Italy, 1983. Pages 135–202.

JAMES B. SOUTH

VERONESE, PAOLO

(Paolo Caliari; 1528–1588), Venetian painter. Born and trained in Verona, Paolo Caliari became, along with Titian and Tintoretto, one of the dominant painters in Venice of the second half of the sixteenth century.

Early Career. Coming from a family of stonecutters, Veronese turned to painting and studied with local masters, primarily Antonio Badile, whose daughter he later married. The family craft may have further introduced the young Paolo to a wider world of building, including the architect Michele Sanmicheli, whose classicism would have contributed to the painter's own sense of architectural form and space. Veronese was certainly aware of the ambitious mannerism of Giulio Romano, whose pictorial illusionism had transformed the choir vault of the cathedral of Verona. From his earliest work in Verona, datable to about 1546, Veronese's painterly style was marked by chromatic clarity and sensitively nuanced brushwork; his figures, inspired in part by the example of Parmigianino, carry themselves with elegance and move with an aristocratic confidence.

Two major commissions took the painter beyond the walls of Verona in 1551: the fresco decoration of Sanmicheli's Villa Soranzo (destroyed) on the mainland near Venice (surviving fragments preserved in the cathedral of Castelfranco and the Seminario Patriarcale in Venice) and his first Venetian commission, the altarpiece of the Giustiniani Chapel in San Francesco della Vigna (in situ), a Madonna and Child enthroned with accompanying saints that varies the asymmetrical composition of Titian's Pesaro altarpiece in the Frari.

Ceiling Paintings. In 1553 Veronese transferred to Venice to work on the ceiling decorations of the rooms of the Council of Ten in the Ducal Palace. These political allegories feature powerful foreshortened figures set against a heavenly background. This kind of painting set a pictorial challenge relatively new to Venice; the influential models for such illusionism were to be found in Rome or Mantua or Parma. Veronese's work stands out for its particular balance of spatial thrust and surface pattern, a balance achieved through both design and color.

His ability as a designer of ceiling paintings was further proved in his next major Venetian project, for the church of San Sebastiano. Canvases for the sacristy ceiling, featuring in the center a *Coronation of the Virgin,* were executed in 1555, and the following year Veronese turned to what was to be the most significant demonstration of his genius in the genre. The three pictures of the story of Esther that he painted along the nave ceiling articulate the central axis of the church with dynamic pictorial variation. Compositional structure here depends upon a foreshortening of architectural elements so acute that it effectively denies the spatial implications of perspective construction; orthogonals are aligned parallel to the picture plane, inflected to become nearly pure vertical lines, thereby articulating and affirming the surface of the canvas.

Veronese's mastery of ceiling painting received official recognition in 1557. For the ceiling of the Biblioteca Marciana (Library of St. Mark) seven artists had been commissioned to paint three roundels each of appropriately intellectual and moral allegories. His representation of *Music* earned Veronese the prize of a gold chain; the judges were Titian and Jacopo Sansovino, the architect of the library building.

Veronese. *The Wedding Feast at Cana.* Painted for the refectory of the Monastery of San Giorgio Maggiore, Venice. Oil on canvas; c. 1570; 6.66 × 9.9 m (21.5 × 32.5 ft.). MUSÉE DU LOUVRE, PARIS/SUPERSTOCK

Veronese's Feasts. The same control of perspective manifest on the ceiling of San Sebastiano informs the monumental architectural settings of Veronese's celebrated feasts, the great canvases for convent refectories for which he is most famous. The first of these in Venice, the *Wedding at Cana* (1562–1563; Paris, Musée du Louvre), was painted for the Benedictines of San Giorgio Maggiore. Set within a framework of classical architectural elements and against a bright blue sky—what Carlo Ridolfi calls a "maestoso Teatro" (majestic theater)—the colorful wedding feast is not to be read in a purely naturalistic key, as a slice of sumptuous Venetian life. Rather, Veronese structured the whole to bring out the meaning of the event: through costume, frontality, and axial placement, he distinguished Christ and his mother from the other guests, realizing pictorially the dialogue between the two and Christ's declaration that "mine hour is not yet come" (John 2:4).

The misunderstanding of Veronese's large feats, a function of their magnificence, has a long history going back to the *Last Supper* he painted for the Do-

minican refectory of Santi Giovanni e Paolo. For that picture, on 20 April 1573, he was summoned before the Venetian Inquisition to answer charges of indecorum—specifically, of having depicted "buffoons, drunkards, Germans, dwarfs and other such scurrilities" in a Last Supper. Although the most frequently recalled aspect of his response is his invocation of poetic license for painters, more important is his defense of decorum, in which he offered a compositional analysis of his picture: these servants of the rich host never enter the central space reserved for Christ and his disciples. The only change the painter made to his canvas was the addition of an inscription, retitling it a *Feast in the House of Levi.*

Modern critical scholarship continues to rescue Veronese from his reputation as a superficial decorator, finding in his brilliant paintings depths of significance that testify to their pictorial intelligence.

Patronage and Practice. Among Veronese's patrician patrons the most significant was Daniele Barbaro, patriarch elect of Aquileia, humanist, trans-

247

lator of Vitruvius's ten books *De architectura* (1556), and author of a treatise on perspective (1568). It was for Daniele and his brother Marcantonio that Palladio designed a villa at Maser, near Treviso. Veronese's frescoes (c. 1561) develop the harmonic meanings of the basic musical proportions that inform this villa *all'antica* (in the ancient manner). Iconographically, his paintings include allegorical and mythological subjects, portraits of the Barbaro family, and illusionistic views that continue actual vistas of the surrounding countryside. Veronese, who may have just returned from a trip to Rome, adapted the swift and fluid brushwork of ancient painting to achieve the most resonant re-creation of an ancient villa.

From the beginning of his career in Venice, Veronese was actively employed by the state in the continuing decoration of the Ducal Palace, most notably the Sala del Collegio (Hall of the College), one of the councils of the Venetian government, following a fire in 1574: the allegorical panels of the ceiling celebrate the Venetian Republic, its power and righteousness, and the canvas on the tribune wall represents an *Allegory of the Battle of Lepanto*. Following the fire of 1577 in the Sala del Maggior Consiglio (Hall of the Great Council) he designed one of the four main ceiling paintings, an *Apotheosis of Venice*. With Francesco Bassano, he also won the competition for the huge *Paradise* above the ducal throne, but at his death in 1588 the work remained unexecuted and the commission eventually passed to Tintoretto.

Veronese's style continued to be marked by chromatic clarity and supple brushwork. Toward the end of his career, partially inspired by the art of Jacopo Bassano, his manner deepened tonally, becoming in effect more Venetian. Light and color, still articulated by his inflected brush stroke, emerge from a darker ground, adding a new expressive weight.

Veronese was the master of a busy family workshop, in which his chief assistants were his brother Benedetto Caliari and his sons Carletto and Gabriele. They continued the family enterprise, signing themselves *Haeredes Pauli* (heirs of Paolo) after his death. Veronese was buried in San Sebastiano, the church he had turned into a monument to his own art.

See also **Venice**, *subentry on* **Art in Venice**.

BIBLIOGRAPHY

Primary Works
Boschini, Marco. *La carta del navegar pitoresco* (The chart of pictorial navigation; Venice, 1660). Edited by *Anna Palluc-chini*. Venice and Rome, 1966. Includes *Le ricche minere della pittura veneziana* (The rich mines of Venetian painting; Venice, 1576), the introduction to which contains an account of Veronese's technique.
Ridolfi, Carlo. *Le maraviglie dell'arte* (The marvels of art; Venice, 1648). 2 vols. Edited by Detlev Freihernn von Hadeln. Berlin, 1914–1924.
Vasari, Giorgio. *Lives of the Painters, Sculptors, and Architects.* 2 vols. Translated by Gaston du C. de Vere, with an introduction and notes by David Ekserdjian. New York and Toronto, 1996. Translation (1912) of *Le vite de' più eccellenti pittori, scultori ed architettori,* 2d ed. (1568).

Secondary Works
Cocke, Richard. *Veronese's Drawings.* Ithaca, N.Y., 1984.
Pignatti, Terisio, and Filippo Pedrocco. *Veronese.* 2 vols. Milan, 1995. The third edition of the standard catalogue raisonné.
Rearick, William R. *The Art of Paolo Veronese, 1528–1588.* Washington, D.C., 1988.
Rosand, David. *Painting in Sixteenth-Century Venice: Titian, Veronese, Tintoretto.* Rev. ed. Cambridge, U.K., 1997.

DAVID ROSAND

VERROCCHIO, ANDREA DEL (Andrea di Michele di Francesco Cione; c. 1435–1488), Florentine sculptor, painter, goldsmith, and draftsman whose workshop was the training ground for a whole generation of artists, including, most notably, Leonardo da Vinci. In his mature years Verrocchio became the leading sculptor in Florence and worked for the Medici and the Venetian state. Building on his interests in classical art and in the study of nature, he made some significant contributions to almost every category of sculpture.

Early Career and Sculpture, 1460s–1477. Verrocchio, the son of a *fornaciaio* (kiln worker), trained as a goldsmith with Antonio Dei (before 1457) and perhaps Francesco Verrocchio (not a relation). In a tax return of 1457 Verrocchio declared he could not find employment as a goldsmith, and it is believed that he subsequently spent some time in the workshop of an important Florentine sculptor, perhaps that of Antonio Rossellino. He evidently went through a period of rapid artistic development, and among his first major commissions was the monumental bronze group of the *Incredulity of Saint Thomas* (c. 1466–1483; Florence, Orsanmichele) ordered by the Tribunale di Mercanzia (merchant's court) to replace a statue by Donatello. Overcoming the problem of a niche designed for a single figure, Verrocchio worked out a dynamic composition that dramatically unites the two figures of Christ and Thomas. The group, furthermore, is characterized by an expressive use of drapery and an interest in physiognomy.

Andrea del Verrocchio. Equestrian Statue of Colleoni. Bartolomeo Colleoni (1400–1475) was a condottiere in the service of Venice and Milan. He was appointed general in chief of the armies of the Venetian Republic in 1454. The statue stands in the Campo SS. Giovanni e Paolo, Venice. ANDERSON/ALINARI/ART RESOURCE

Another of his great early sculptures was the tomb of *Piero I and Giovanni de' Medici* in the old Sacristy of San Lorenzo, Florence (1472). This monument, conceived almost like a freestanding tomb and lacking in overtly Christian imagery, is unlike the figurated tombs designed by his contemporaries. Verrocchio's training as a goldsmith is evident in his treatment of the decoration, especially the elegant designs of the bronze acanthus leaves and the fine plant forms carved in marble on the intrados.

The sculptor's brother Tommaso compiled an inventory in 1496 of works that Verrocchio completed for the Medici, and among the items listed are the *David* (Florence, Bargello) and the *Putto with a Dolphin* (Florence, Palazzo Vecchio), both generally

thought to date to the 1460s or early 1470s, though the *Putto* is sometimes given a later chronology of the 1480s. These freestanding bronze sculptures epitomize Verrocchio's concerns with classical statuary and realism, and they display perfectly chased (grooved or indented), finely detailed surfaces. In the design of his *David,* Verrocchio challenged Donatello, who, at an earlier stage, had worked on this same theme. In fact, Verrocchio replaced the androgynous forms and ambiguous air of Donatello's work with the confident expression of a young soldier-hero whose tunic tightly covers his firm torso. With the *Putto,* once part of a fountain at the Villa Medici at Careggi, Verrocchio designed a contrappostal pose that allows for the multiple viewpoint

Andrea del Verrocchio. *Baptism of Christ.* The painting was retouched by Leonardo da Vinci. GALLERIA DEGLI UFFIZI, FLORENCE/ALINARI/ART RESOURCE, NY

and results in what may be the first *figura serpentinata* in Renaissance sculpture.

Sculpture, 1477–1488. On winning a contest in 1477, Verrocchio received a commission from Pistoia city council to carve a marble cenotaph for *Cardinal Niccolò Forteguerri* (Pistoia Cathedral). Difficulties arose however, and the work remained unfinished at his death. Despite all the problems, the surviving elements of Verrocchio's monument to the cardinal are distinguished by a successfully worked out composition and a convincing naturalism in the treatment of the figures' movements and expressions.

In 1477 Verrocchio was also commissioned to execute a silver relief of the *Beheading of the Baptist* (Florence, Museo dell'Opera del Duomo) for the silver altar in the Florentine Baptistery. The small scale of the work does not undermine the dramatic tension in the composition, which is filled with an abundance of meticulously detailed elements. Verrocchio's capacity to carefully delineate physiognomic traits, as displayed in the silver relief, is utilized to even greater effect in the portrait busts that he is believed to have executed. The noble air of the *Lady Holding Flowers* (late 1470s; Florence, Bargello) is expressed not only in the exquisitely carved features but also in the delicate action of the arms and hands, the inclusion of which was an innovation for the Renaissance portrait bust.

Verrocchio's career as a sculptor culminated in the commission from the Venetian state of the bronze equestrian monument to Bartolomeo Colleoni (c. 1479–1492; Venice, Campo SS. Giovanni e Paolo), which occupied him until his death. The group was not cast in Verrocchio's lifetime, and consequently its surfaces do not reveal the precision of his fine chiseling. Compared to its predecessor, Donatello's *Gattamelata* (1447–1453) in nearby Padua, the *Colleoni* exhibits a greater sense of movement, especially in the vigorous contrapposto of the mercenary and the forceful turn of his horse's head. The menacing spirit of the work is further accentuated by Colleoni's ferocious expression and the horse's unsupported, raised hoof.

Painting. In his own time Verrocchio was a highly respected painter active from the mid-1460s at the latest. Today, however, the paintings that have been traditionally associated with him present serious problems of attribution. His most celebrated picture, the *Baptism of Christ* (c. 1475–1485; Florence, Uffizi), was executed for San Salvi, Florence, and is universally known for Leonardo's retouching and repainting to its surface. Verrocchio's contribution, characterized by a sculptural approach to form, is linked to the crisply delineated outlines of the robust central figures. The vigorous plasticity and imposing monumentality of the *Baptism* figures are also found in *Tobias and the Angel* (1470s; London, National Gallery), another work that is generally attributed to Verrocchio. This last picture contains a well coordinated pair of figures who are caught in a lively, stepping movement. The only known documented painting by Verrocchio, an altarpiece commissioned for Pistoia Cathedral in 1474, was executed mostly by his pupil Lorenzo di Credi.

In his capacity as teacher and painter Verrocchio exerted a powerful influence over many central Italian artists, including Sandro Botticelli, Luca Signorelli, Pietro Perugino, and Domenico Ghirlandaio, all known or thought to have had contact with his workshop. As a sculptor Verrocchio bridged the gap between Donatello's innovations of the fifteenth century and Michelangelo's creations of the high Renaissance.

BIBLIOGRAPHY

Adorno, Piero. *Il Verrocchio*. Florence, 1991.

Bule, Steven. *Verrocchio and Late Quattrocento Sculpture*. Florence, 1992.

Butterfield, Andrew. *The Sculptures of Andrea del Verrocchio*. New Haven, Conn., 1997.

Dolcini, Loretta, ed. *Verrocchio's Christ and Saint Thomas: A Masterpiece of Sculpture from Renaissance Florence*. New York, 1992.

Passavant, Günter. *Verrocchio: Sculptures, Paintings, and Drawings*. London, 1969.

Seymour, Charles. *The Sculpture of Verrocchio*. Greenwich, Conn., 1971.

FLAVIO BOGGI

VESALIUS, ANDREAS (1514–1564), Belgian anatomist. A physician-surgeon as well as an anatomist whose scientific work and experimental findings revolutionized the study of human anatomy, Andreas Vesalius is remembered principally for his master work, *De humani corporis fabrica* (*On the Fabric of the Human Body;* 1543). However, his primary contribution to the intellectual life of his time and to his successors was his use of more adequate data sampling than that used by his predecessors and its application to test their authoritative dicta, especially the findings of Galen, by more systematic and expert demonstration.

Family Background and Education. Born in Brussels, Vesalius was the son of Andreas Vesalius, an apothecary in service to the court of the Holy Roman Emperor Charles V, and Isabel Crabbe. After schooling in his native city and later in the nearby University of Louvain, Vesalius began to study medicine at the University of Paris, where he attended the lectures and demonstrations of the most important anatomists of the time. Their theoretical and detached presentations annoyed Vesalius, who, after returning for a time to Louvain, where he earned a bachelor of medicine degree in the spring of 1537, set out for the University of Padua, where in December of the same year he earned a doctor of medicine degree. The following day he was appointed to the faculty of the university as a professor of surgery, with the requirement that he do anatomical dissections. His first dissection in this post ended on Christmas Eve 1537, and the notes of a student who attended these procedures are still preserved.

Vesalius soon acquired an excellent reputation as a teacher who not only lectured expertly on anatomy but also performed his own dissections. In 1538, together with his countryman Jan Stephanus van Calcar, a student of Titian, Vesalius produced six large charts to illustrate his lectures. These *Tabulae anatomicae sex* (Six anatomical tables), were based mainly on Galenic precepts. Galen (129–c. 199 A.D.), a Greek anatomist who lived and worked in Marcus Aurelius's Rome, dissected only animals. His doctrines, which had become authoritative in many Eu-

Andreas Vesalius. Woodcut portrait by John Stephen of Calcar, 1542. The Granger Collection

ropean medical schools during the first half of the sixteenth century, are not correct when applied to human anatomy. Some of these errors, such as a five-lobed liver and an ovine vascular structure in the brain, appear in Vesalius's six anatomical tables, leading to the conclusion that in 1538 Vesalius was still a convinced Galenist. Several years later, however, after performing dissections before students in Bologna and acquiring more clinical material than had been available to him before, Vesalius denounced Galenic doctrines. A diligent German student took detailed notes recording this dramatic development firsthand, notes that went undiscovered until the mid-twentieth century.

A Renaissance Masterpiece. In 1540 Vesalius began working on his great illustrated anatomical text, *De humani corporis fabrica*. Draftsmen for these illustrations were recruited from Titian's studio in Venice. The finest block cutters from that city were employed, but strangely, though Venice was a center for the new art of printing, Vesalius chose to entrust the printing of his great work to the Basel humanist

and publisher Joannes Oporinus. Because of this decision, the woodblocks produced in Venice were loaded on mules and carried over the Alps, where Vesalius joined them to perform final editing and proofreading. While in Basel, Vesalius was asked to dissect the body of an executed criminal, and the articulated skeleton of that dissection remains in the Basel anatomical museum. The printing was completed in June 1543, and the first bound copy was available in August of that year. Virtually simultaneously, Vesalius produced a briefer work for the use of medical students and those with limited or no anatomical knowledge. Though known as *Epitome,* this work was not truly a digest of *Fabrica,* because that work's vast text could not be compressed into so few pages. In *Epitome* the illustrations are more important than the text. Though its page size is larger than that of *Fabrica* and it reproduces that work's famous title page, *Epitome* is arranged for the reader whom Vesalius described as wholly unskilled in dissection. An extremely popular work, *Epitome* was translated into German immediately; *Fabrica,* in contrast, was translated into modern languages only in the twentieth century.

To understand the magnitude of Vesalius's accomplishment, one must review the contents of *Fabrica*. Its folio format was among the largest available—only slightly smaller than that of a modern newspaper—and it runs more than 650 pages, some of quite small type. Its frontispiece depicts a dramatic presentation of a sixteenth-century anatomical dissection. Several pages later, the only authentic portrait of Vesalius appears. Detailed descriptive texts accompany the illustrations, and marginal references lead the reader from one subject to another. But the most striking feature of the work is the illustrations, best exemplified by the fourteen plates depicting the progressive dissection of a muscle. Such an integration of the whole human structure had never before been accomplished and was not to be attempted again until late in the seventeenth or even well into the eighteenth century.

As mentioned above, the scientific principles propounded in and exemplified by *Fabrica* made an even more lasting impact on Renaissance science than did its major increase in knowledge of the body's structure. Vesalius continually reiterated his belief that Galen's anatomy was unreliable because it was grounded in the study of animals and therefore could have no direct application to human anatomy. The only reliable authority was independent investigation of human structure. Moreover, because human structures tend to vary, one must study the same structure in a number of bodies before making a pronouncement. Thus, Vesalius propounded the essential scientific principle that an experiment must be repeated a number of times for verification.

Later Career. Returning to Padua when he was twenty-nine, Vesalius turned from the academic to the practical and, in keeping with a long family tradition, applied to Charles V for a position. He expected to spend most of his time treating the gluttonous emperor, whose gout, intestinal obstructions, and general physical deterioration were complicated by syphilis. Nevertheless, Vesalius always visited medical schools while accompanying the emperor on his travels throughout the empire. Occasionally, he was invited to participate in postmortem investigations. In consequence, during his employment in imperial service he developed several new techniques in surgery and continued to compile corrections for *Fabrica*.

In 1555, thirteen years after *Fabrica*'s initial publication, Vesalius published a second edition, which contains emendations and corrections on almost every page and expands some passages considerably. Just as he was about to publish this volume, his patron, Charles V, abdicated his imperial throne, dividing his empire between his brother, Ferdinand, and his son, Philip, who became the king of Spain and the Netherlands. Vesalius chose to join Philip's court in Spain. However, the cultural climate there did not prove conducive to Vesalius's scientific development. Illustrative of this atmosphere was Vesalius's participation in the case of Don Carlos, Philip's son and heir to the Spanish throne. Rejecting Vesalius's clinical advice, the Spanish court attributed the patient's recovery to the placement of the mummified body of a saint (Diego d'Alcala) in the bed of the ailing young man. In 1559, Vesalius consulted, along with the French surgeon Ambroise Paré, in the case of Henry II of France after his serious and ultimately fatal wounding in a tournament.

In 1564 Vesalius left on a long voyage, apparently a pilgrimage to the Holy Land. Before departing he gained reappointment to the medical faculty at the University of Padua. We may thus assume he planned to take up a research career once again, but unhappily, he did not live to do so. His return ship was damaged severely in a storm. It found shelter on the island of Zante (Zákinthos), off the western coast of Greece, where Vesalius, exhausted from the voyage, died in October 1564.

Following Vesalius's example, medical scholars of the later sixteenth and the seventeenth centuries made extraordinary advances in the understanding of the anatomy of the human body. Vesalius's anatomical findings laid the foundation for John Harvey's discovery and proof of the circulation of blood, which revolutionized research and teaching in human anatomy and physiology.

See also **Anatomy**; **Medicine**; **Padua, University of.**

BIBLIOGRAPHY

Primary Works

Cavanagh, George Stanley Terence. *The Panorama of Vesalius: A "Lost" Design from Titian's Studio*. Athens, Ga., 1996. A reproduction of the muscle plates of *Fabrica*, together with new findings concerning them.

Heseler, Baldasar. *Andreas Vesalius' First Public Anatomy at Bologna, 1540: An Eyewitness Report*. Translated by Ruben Eriksson. Uppsala, Sweden, 1959.

Saunders, J. B. de C. M., and Charles Donald O'Malley. *The Illustrations from the Works of Andreas Vesalius of Brussels*. New York, 1973. Includes a biographical sketch.

Vesalius, Andreas. *The* Epitome *of Andreas Vesalius*. Translated by L. R. Lind. Cambridge, Mass., 1969.

Vesalius, Andreas. *Vesalius on the Human Brain*. Translated by Charles Singer. New York, 1952.

Secondary Works

Cushing, Harvey. *A Bio-Bibliography of Andreas Vesalius*. 2d ed. Hamden, Conn., 1962.

O'Malley, Charles. *Andreas Vesalius of Brussels, 1514–1564*. Berkeley, Calif., 1964.

O'Neill, Ynez Violé, and Mark Infusino. *The Young Vesalius: The Bologna Dissections of 1540*. Los Angeles, 1993. A video essay.

Singer, Charles. *A Prelude to Modern Science: Being a Discussion of the History, Sources, and Circumstances of the "Tabulae anatomicae sex" of Vesalius*. Cambridge, U.K., 1946.

YNEZ VIOLÉ O'NEILL

VESPUCCI, AMERIGO (1454–1512), explorer and mapmaker. Born into a distinguished Florentine family of businessmen, Vespucci received a humanistic education that was overseen by his uncle, the Dominican Giorgio Antonio Vespucci. He served in a diplomatic mission to France and worked for the Medici bank before moving to Seville around 1492 to supervise Medici interests, especially the outfitting of ships. His interest in cosmography led him to undertake voyages of exploration relatively late in life to investigate Columbus's claims that he had found a westward route to Asia and to find whether particular lands were Spanish or Portuguese possessions according to the papal Line of Demarcation. Vespucci made at least two trips to the New World, the earlier for Spain under Alonso de Ojeda (May 1499–September 1500), where, representing the underwriters, he explored the north coast of South Amer-

Amerigo Vespucci. Portrait by Domenico Ghirlandaio (1448–1494). Fresco (detail) in the church of Ognissanti, Florence. ALINARI/ART RESOURCE, NY

ica, including the mouth of the Amazon. The second authenticated voyage was for Portugal under Goncalo Coelho (May 1501–July 1502), in which Vespucci explored the South American coast, perhaps as far south as Patagonia. After becoming a Spanish subject in 1505, Vespucci was appointed pilot-major of Spain, overseeing voyages and maintaining official maps, retaining the position until his death.

No single individual was responsible for the full realization that what Columbus had called the "Indies" was not part of Asia but of regions previously unknown to Europeans. Vespucci's efforts to determine longitude and his willingness to challenge Ptolemaic geography enabled him to realize that South America was distinct from Asia. In 1507 Martin Waldseemüller and other members of a learned society in St. Dié, Lorraine, declared that Vespucci had discovered a "previously unknown fourth part of the world" that should be named after him. Actually, this group was excited by what were probably fictionalized and sensationalized versions of Vespucci's own travel accounts that passed under his name— the *Mundus novus* (New world; 1504) and *Quatuor*

Americi navigationes (Four voyages of Amerigo; 1505). These accounts featured a perceptive emphasis on the novelty of the lands Vespucci visited; a questionable emphasis on the priority of his visits; and, using familiar discursive conventions, vivid use of traditional European themes about internal and external others—the primitive paradise on the one hand, sadistic cannibalism and lustful, dangerous women on the other. They became by far the most popular of the many writings on the New World (sixty editions were issued in many languages by 1520), and that popularity enabled the name "America" to stick. In his influential maps of 1538, Gerardus Mercator applied the name to both northern and southern continents. Vespucci's explorations have been hailed as a paradigm of scientific discovery, though the Eurocentrism of the Vespucci apocrypha shows that America was rather more invented than discovered.

See also **Americas.**

BIBLIOGRAPHY

Arciniegas, Germán. *Amerigo and the New World: The Life and Times of Amerigo Vespucci.* Translated by Harriet de Onis. New York, 1955. Translation of *Amerigo y el nuevo mundo.*

CHARLES WHITNEY *and* SUSAN STEIGERWALD

VICENTE, GIL (1465?–1536?), Portuguese playwright and poet. Gil Vicente was probably born in the province of Beira. Nothing certain is known about his life except that he married twice (around 1490 and 1517), and that he served in the royal courts of Manuel I and John III.

As can be deduced from his works, he was well read, had a good command of both classical and ecclesiastical Latin, and was intimately familiar with popular culture and iconography. Modern scholars generally believe that Gil Vicente, the playwright, and Gil Vicente, the goldsmith (creator of the celebrated Belém monstrance, 1506, and Master of the Royal Mint as of 1513), were one and the same person.

Vicente's dramatic career, initiated with *Monólogo do vaqueiro* (The herdsman's monologue; 1502) and concluded with *Floresta de enganos* (Forest of deceits; 1536), was inextricably associated with the Portuguese royal court, for which he was in charge of providing entertainment under the patronage of two monarchs, Manuel I (ruled 1495–1521) and John III (ruled 1521–1557). His complete works were published posthumously (1562), although several of his plays had been printed individually during his lifetime.

Of the forty-four plays Vicente wrote, eighteen are bilingual (in a mixture of Spanish and Portuguese), fifteen are wholly in Portuguese, and the rest in Spanish. His theater is characterized by a striking diversity of contents, themes, characters, and dramatic techniques. He composed pastoral and religious pieces, comedies, farces, and tragicomedies. He seemed to move from genre to genre with surprising ease. His early career betrays the influence of the rustic plays of his contemporary Salamancan playwrights, Juan del Encina and Lucas Fernández. Soon, however, he came to master the medium to the extent that he not only moved away from his models but surpassed them in dramatic conception, artistic versatility, character development, and manipulation of more complex subject matter.

Critics dwell on the "primitivism" of Vicente's theater in contrast to the "classicism" of the Renaissance. It should be remembered that in terms of structure his plays obey theatrical rather than dramatic canons, and that he had no direct knowledge of classical theater. Thanks to the careful scrutiny of modern scholars, more and more of his plays are shown to be informed by a logical structure and thematic unity. Examples include *Auto da Índia* (Play of India; 1509), *Auto de Mofina Mendes* (Play of Mofina Mendes; 1515), and *Comédia do viúvo* (The widower's comedy; 1524).

Vicente achieved in his theater an admirable synthesis of drama, poetry, and music. This can be best seen in two of his most intensely lyrical pieces, *Tragicomédia de Dom Duardos* (Tragicomedy of Dom Duardos; 1522) and *Auto da sibila Cassandra* (Play of the sibyl Cassandra; 1513). Even though the lyrical element is closely coupled with the dramatic, individual poems can stand on their own merit. In fact, many poems are found in virtually all anthologies of Hispanic poetry and also, in translation, in anthologies of world poetry.

Vicente appears to be in conflict with the social climate of his times: most of his plays, across the several genres, are imbued with a strong dose of satire. No one is immune to his caustic barbs, irrespective of social, vocational, or financial status. In such plays as *Auto da barca do inferno* (The ship to hell; 1517), *Auto da feira* (Play of the fair; 1526), *Farsa dos almocreves* (Farce of the carriers; 1527), and *Clérigo da Beira* (The priest of Beira; 1529 or 1530), Vicente bitterly rises in opposition to anything and anyone who may call the traditional values to question. His anticlericalism, though reminiscent of that

of Erasmus, was firmly rooted in the Iberian tradition. As a social critic, Vicente looks with melancholy at the present, pessimistically to the future, and nostalgically to the past.

Vicente is justly considered the father of Portuguese theater. What is more, he proved superior to all other playwrights of sixteenth-century Portugal, including his followers as well as such truly Renaissance dramatists as Francisco de Sá de Miranda and Luiz Vaz de Camoës. His influence was not confined to Portugal: it was felt in the religious drama of the Spanish golden age, in Felix Lope de Vega, Pedro Calderón de la Barca, and possibly even in the work of Fray Luis de León, Miguel de Cervantes, Shakespeare, and Molière. His poetic legacy survived into the twentieth century in the works of such celebrated poets as Federico García Lorca and Rafael Alberti.

BIBLIOGRAPHY

Primary Works

El Auto de la sibila Casandra. Edited and translated by Mary Borelli. Valencia, Spain, 1970.

A Critical Edition of Gil Vicente's "Auto da Índia." Edited by C. C. Stathatos. Barcelona, Spain, 1997.

A Critical Edition with Introduction and Notes of Gil Vicente's "Floresta de enganos." Edited by C. C. Stathatos. Chapel Hill, N.C., 1972.

Four Plays of Gil Vicente. Edited and translated by Aubrey F. G. Bell. Cambridge, U.K., 1920.

Gil Vicente: Farces and Festival Plays. Edited by Thomas R. Hart. Eugene, Oreg., 1972.

Lyrics of Gil Vicente. Edited and translated by Aubrey F. G. Bell. 2d ed. Oxford, 1921.

Three Discovery Plays: "Auto da barca do Inferno," "Exortação da guerra," "Auto da Índia." Edited and translated by Anthony J. Lappin. Warminster, U.K., 1997.

Tragicomédia de Amadís de Gaula. Edited by T. P. Waldron. Manchester, U.K., 1959.

Secondary Works

Bell, Aubrey F. G. *Gil Vicente.* Oxford, 1921.

Garay, René Pedro. *Gil Vicente and the Development of the Comedia.* Chapel Hill, N.C., 1988.

Hamilton-Faria, Hope. *The Farces of Gil Vicente: A Study in the Stylistics of Satire.* Madrid, 1976.

Hart, Thomas R. *Gil Vicente: "Casandra" and "Don Duardos."* London, 1981.

Keates, Laurence. *The Court Theatre of Gil Vicente.* Lisbon, Portugal, 1962.

Parker, Jack Horace. *Gil Vicente.* New York, 1967.

Suárez, José Ignacio. *The Carnival Stage: Vicentine Comedy within the Serio-Comic Mode.* Rutherford, N.J., 1993.

C. C. STATHATOS

VICTORIA, TOMÁS LUIS DE (Thomae Ludovici de Victoria Abulensis; c. 1548–1611), Spanish composer. Little is known of Victoria's life, education, and musical training prior to his entering the Colle-

gium Germanicum, a Jesuit institution in Rome, in 1565. A precocious youth, he issued in 1572, before he was twenty-five, a book of motets containing many of the works by which he is best known today.

Victoria is one of a group of five masters of the late sixteenth century that includes Orlando di Lasso, Philippe de Monte, William Byrd, and Giovanni Pierluigi da Palestrina, with whom he was associated during his early years in Rome. His Roman contemporaries include Luca Marenzio, Felice Anerio, Francesco Soriano, and Giovanni Maria Nanino. Along with his slightly older Spanish contemporary, Francisco Guerrero, Victoria carried on the sacred music tradition established by Cristóbal de Morales. Victoria was both a singer and an organist. He spent his final years as organist at the Convent of the Discalced Nuns of Santa Clara in Madrid.

Victoria's authenticated works include sixty-six motets, psalms, and Marian antiphons; twenty masses; thirty-five hymns; eighteen Magnificats; eighteen Holy Week responsories; nine lamentation lessons; two passions; and thirteen miscellaneous compositions. Research has uncovered seventy-one additional works attributed to Victoria in manuscript sources. Prominent in this group are ten polyphonic and twenty-five falsobordone (a harmonized recitation of a psalm or other simple liturgical piece) psalms, all for four voices.

In Rome from 1565 to 1587, Victoria never strayed far from his Spanish roots. His first position was as the director of music and organist at the national church in Rome of the Spaniards of Aragon, Santa Maria de Monserrato, and he incorporated Spanish melodies into several of his works. Most notable among these are those for the hymns "Pange lingua" and "Vexilla regis," as well as the Spanish lamentation tone—all three of which are found in his *Officium hebdomadae sanctae* (1585).

Victoria's music is at the stylistic crossroads between the Renaissance and the early baroque. Some works are imitative, for example, "Gaudent in coelis" (1585); some are homorhythmic, for example, "Vere languores" (1572); and some are polychoral, for example, his twelve-voice setting of Psalm 121, "Laetatus sum" (1583). Some works adhere to the modal system of the past and some, pointing to the future, are tonal in concept. That Victoria was in the forefront of stylistic change is evidenced not only by his use of a wide variety of vocal combinations and independent organ parts, but also by his extensive use of a period of silence in his works both to emphasize a portion of the text and to illuminate its structure. This penchant for pauses, as well as cadences, gives Victoria's works a sectional quality more characteristic of the cantatas and sonatas of his successors than the motets and madrigals of his contemporaries.

BIBLIOGRAPHY

Primary Works

Victoria, Tomás Luis de. *Officium hebdomadae sanctae.* 4 vols. Edited by Eugene Casjen Cramer. Henryville, Pa., 1982.

Victoria, Tomás Luis de. *Opera omnia.* 4 vols. Edited by Felipe Pedrell. Reprint, New York, 1965–1966.

Victoria, Tomás Luis de. *Opera omnia, nueva edición.* 4 vols. Edited by Higinio Anglés. Rome, 1965–1968.

Secondary Works

Cramer, Eugene Casjen. *Tomás Luis de Victoria: A Guide to Research.* New York, 1998. Contains a chronological listing of Victoria's publications with complete contents; the publication history of his printed works; a list of the works attributed to him and the manuscript sources in which they are found; and annotated lists of 278 secondary sources, 318 recordings, and 418 modern editions.

Hruza, Lucy. "The Marian Repertory by Tomás Luis de Victoria in Toledo Biblioteca Capitular *Mus. B. 30:* A Case Study in Renaissance *Imitatio.*" Ph.D. diss., University of Calgary, 1997. Discusses the versions of Victoria's masses: "Ave maris stella," "Gaudeamus," and "De beata Maria"; his psalm motet "Nisi dominus"; and his Marian antiphon "Salve regina" found in this unique source copied by the Vatican scribe Johannes Parvus. The author's discussion of the three Magnificats in this source appears in *Early Music* 25 (1997): 83–98, an article under the surname Wojcicka-Hruza, based on her M.A. thesis, "The Magnificats by Tomás Luis de Victoria in Toledo, Biblioteca Capitular *Mus. B. 30:* A Comparison with the Printed Editions (1576, 1581, and 1600)." University of Calgary, 1989.

Stevenson, Robert M. "Tomás Luis de Victoria (ca. 1548–1611): Unique Spanish Genius." *Inter-American Music Review* 12, no. 1 (1991): 1–100. See also his *La música en las catedrales españolas del siglo de oro* (Madrid, 1993), which contains this article in Spanish translation, with its bibliography, and is a revised (updated) version of the author's earlier *Spanish Cathedral Music in the Golden Age.* Berkeley, Calif., 1961.

EUGENE CASJEN CRAMER

VIENNA. Renaissance Vienna was more influential as a center of learning than of the visual arts. Its artistic and architectural significance lagged behind its political importance as the chief city in the Habsburg homelands and, at times, the imperial residence.

The Physical Environment. In the fifteenth and early sixteenth century Habsburg rulers, otherwise generous and discriminating patrons of the arts and learning, had little reason to undertake major building projects in the city. The emperor Frederick III (1415–1493) was altogether peripatetic; the emperors Maximilian I (1459–1519) and Ferdinand I (1503–1564) spent much time in Innsbruck. The court of Rudolf II (1552–1612) was a mecca of late Renaissance humanism and painting, but it was housed in Prague, not Vienna, which the monarch abandoned in 1583.

Ferdinand I did some remodeling of the shabby imperial Hofburg; the most prominent feature that remains is the strongly Italianate Schweizer Tor (Swiss gate) to the inner courtyard of the complex. He also expanded the tract with the construction of the gracefully colonnaded Stallburg, today the stable of the Spanish Riding School, but at the time intended as a residence for his eldest son, the future emperor Maximilian II (1527–1576). The latter had several ambitious building projects which he called upon Italian architects and builders to realize, most notably the Neugebäude on the outskirts of the city. This, however, like so many of this emperor's undertakings, was never finished. Thus, aside from some modest decorative features found on residential portals and columns, Vienna remained a medieval walled city.

Nor were the Viennese wealthy enough to underwrite the architectural transformations that the Renaissance brought to Florence or other European urban centers. While a hub of medieval commerce, Vienna had become a far less attractive place to do business by the beginning of the sixteenth century. The general shift of European trade patterns to the west and the increasing threat of Ottoman expansion had begun to take their toll on the city's economy. Its fortifications were substantially expanded during this time, necessary as a defensive measure in the military thinking of the time but a serious impediment to Vienna's physical growth.

Learning and Literature.

From the standpoint of the new learning in the Renaissance, however, Vienna played a more significant role, both in the German-speaking world and on the Continent. Its university, founded in 1365, was the second oldest in central Europe. From the late fourteenth century it was the site of important work in the natural sciences and in the development of instruments of measurement.

The first lay professor of any note was the mathematician and astronomer Georg von Peuerbach (1423–1461), the teacher of another outstanding member of the faculty, Johann Müller, also called Regiomontanus (1436–1476). Peuerbach's tables for the calculation of eclipses served as the basis for Johann Stoeffler's *Calendarium romanum* of 1518, which also incorporated later work of Regiomontanus. The text was of great use to contemporary navigators, among them Vasco da Gama and Christo-

Vienna. The Schweizer Tor (Swiss gate) in the Hofburg Palace, 1552. The inscription over the entrance to the quarters of the Swiss guard commemorates the emperor Ferdinand I, who was regent of Austrian Habsburg lands for his brother, Charles V, from 1521 and emperor in his own right from 1555 to 1564. ERICH LESSING/ART RESOURCE

pher Columbus. Toward the end of the fifteenth century, a second school of Vienna mathematicians and astronomers flourished under the patronage of the Collegium poeticarum et mathematicarum, established by Maximilian I for the humanist Conrad Celtis (1459–1508). Among its most illustrious names were the mathematician Johannes Stabius (d. 1522) and Georg Tannstetter (1482–1535), a mathematician, astronomer, and astrologer.

Partisans of the literary wing of the new learning had been welcome in the city from the middle of the fifteenth century. The emperor Frederick III had made Enea Silvio Piccolomini his chancellory secretary in 1442. An address by Piccolomini, the future pope, in 1445 on the meaning of the classical poets and their writings marked the beginning of intense humanistic activity in and around the university. In 1497 Maximilian I established a chair in rhetoric and poetry for Conrad Celtis. The latter created the Sodalitas litteraria danubiana (Literary society of the

Danube), to which he quickly brought friends and a group of talented and influential students. All were heavily influenced by the Neoplatonic thought of the erstwhile bishop of Brixen, Nicholas of Cusa (1401–1464), who had been an important voice in Austrian theological circles. In 1451 Cusa had preached at St. Stephen's Cathedral in Vienna on both the Lord's Prayer and the ties between the things of this world and the one beyond. *De possest* (On the possibility of being; 1460), a colloquy between Cusa and Bernhard von Kraiburg (d. 1477), a professor of canon law at the University of Vienna, examined the role that material reality played in man's understanding of Divine Truth.

Celtis himself had an exceedingly active personal publishing program. In 1502 he brought out his major poetic effort, *Quatuor libri amorum* (Four books of love). In preparation for a vast compendium, the *Germania illustrata,* to be based in part on the wide learning he accumulated in his many years as a wandering scholar, he and his students scoured monastic libraries, archives, and the literary artifacts of the German Middle Ages. Celtis himself also edited some central Latin works crucial to German history and culture. These included Tacitus's *Germania* and the Latin verse of the tenth-century nun Hrosvitha von Gandersheim. The successors to his chair in Vienna were at home both in Germanic and classical antiquity. Johannes Cuspinian (1473–1529) was a historian of Austria; Joachim von Watt (Vadianus; 1484–1551) lectured on German literature at the university in the winter semester of 1512–1513, a first in an academic setting. At least in central Europe, those lectures marked the beginning of the study of German literature as a university subject.

Music and Theater. Vienna became an important center of musical and theatrical life during the Renaissance as well. Maximilian I engaged some of the most prominent musicians and composers of his age for his court chapel. Both his grandson Ferdinand I and great-grandson Maximilian II followed in his path, the imperial chapel choir under the latter numbering around eighty singers. Maximilian I was also an enthusiastic patron of the secular stage. Celtis's students performed not only Terence (*The Eunuch*), Plautus (*Aulularia*), and Seneca (*The Enraged Hercules*), but also plays that their mentor himself had written. These productions could be very lavish; music, dance, and elaborate costuming were all part of the spectacle. In 1501, at the invitation of the emperor, Celtis and members of his circle traveled to Linz, where they put on a "Play of Diana"

in which Maximilian himself participated. Similar performances took place in Vienna. During the sixteenth century both Catholic and Protestant establishments of the city turned to drama to bring the message of moral reform to the citizens. Biblical stories were frequently given local twists, as in *The Marriage at Cana* by Wolfgang Schmeltzl, the schoolmaster of the Benedictine cloister of the city (Schottenstift). The wine of the scripture is clearly identified as coming from the Kahlenberg, one of the numerous vineyards that still dot the outskirts of the Austrian capital. The blending of the classical and the local that would characterize classical Viennese popular comedy of the nineteenth century had begun to take root.

See also **Celtis, Conrad**; **Humanism,** *subentry on* **Germany and the Low Countries.**

BIBLIOGRAPHY

Aschbach, Joseph Ritter von. *Die Wiener Universität und ihre Gelehrten.* 3 vols. Vienna, 1888. Standard work.

Geschichte der bildenden Kunst in Wien. 3 vols. Vienna, 1955–1973. Published under the auspices of the Verein für Geschichte der Stadt Wien. Vols. 2 and 3 cover the Renaissance.

Lietzmann, Hilda. *Das Neugebäude in Wien: Sultan Suleymans Zelt, Kaiser Maximilians II Lustschloss: Ein Beitrag zur Kunst-und-Kulturgeschichte der zweiten Hälfte des sechzehnten Jahrhunderts.* Munich, 1987.

Louthan, Howard. *The Quest for Compromise: Peacemakers in Counter-Reformation Vienna.* Cambridge, U.K., 1997. Late-sixteenth-century humanism at the court of Emperor Maximilian II.

Rommel, Otto, ed. *Wiener Renaissance.* Vienna, 1947. A classic anthology.

PAULA SUTTER FICHTNER

VIGNOLA, GIACOMO BAROZZI DA (1507–1573), Italian painter, architect, theorist. Born to a family of artists in the village of Vignola near Modena, Vignola was trained as a painter in Bologna, where he excelled as a draftsman and perspectivist and began to study architecture. His earliest teachers were probably Baldassarre Peruzzi and Sebastiano Serlio, who profoundly influenced his style. By 1538 Vignola was working at the Vatican as a painter and design assistant to Jacopo Meleghino, second architect of St. Peter's. In Rome he produced drawings of antiquities for the Accademia della Virtù. He also collaborated with Francesco Primaticcio on the making of bronze replicas of ancient statuary for King Francis I of France, an enterprise that took him to Fontainebleau in 1541–1543. Returning to Italy, Vignola became architect of the basilica of San Petronio in Bologna and redesigned the city's navigable canal.

Vignola. **Palazzo Farnese, Caprarola, Italy**. Caprarola is north of Rome near Viterbo. Vignola built the Farnese castle there between 1559 and 1572. ANDERSON/ALINARI/ART RESOURCE, NY

In 1550 he transferred to Rome to become architect to Julius III, beginning two decades of virtually continuous papal service, including direction of St. Peter's from 1565 until his death. At the same time he was house architect of the Farnese family and by 1558 he was living in the Palazzo Farnese, whose continued construction he supervised and augmented with interior decorations. After Michelangelo, Vignola was Rome's leading architect, and although he failed to establish a large workshop, his buildings and writings exercised considerable influence on architects in Rome and throughout Europe in succeeding centuries.

Vignola's familiarity with the architectural thought of Peruzzi and Serlio, coupled with his knowledge of the Roman buildings of Donato Bramante, Raphael, Giulio Romano, and Antonio da Sangallo the Younger, permitted him to formulate an authoritative style based on high Renaissance principles, but tempered with an austerity of ornament and a compositional clarity sought by later sixteenth-century taste. In domestic architecture he won fame with two Roman villas. The first is the Villa Giulia, built for Pope Julius III with significant contributions by Giorgio Vasari and Bartolommeo Ammannati in 1551–1555. Vignola designed the main building with a rus-

ticated front in the manner of Giulio Romano and a semicircular courtyard facade combining motifs from Bramante, Peruzzi, and the Pantheon. A copy of his master plan reveals that the villa was originally conceived with arcaded wings and an oval courtyard.

The second villa is the imposing Palazzo Farnese at Caprarola near Viterbo. Begun in the 1520s as a feudal castle, it rose to just above ground level until in 1558 Cardinal Alessandro Farnese determined to complete it as his summer residence. Caprarola is a summa of late Renaissance architectural thought, fusing three characteristic building types: polygonal fortress with bastions, moat, and drawbridge; urban palace with lavish interior decorations; and country villa with expansive vistas and landscaping. Below lies the town of Caprarola, partly rebuilt by Vignola to shoulder a long straight approach to the villa. Above arrowhead bastions loom the austere facades of the pentagonal palace, whose cylindrical courtyard facade was inspired by Bramante's Palazzo Caprini. The interior exhibits a masterful handling of space, circulation, and illumination, especially in the monumental spiral staircase.

Simultaneously Vignola planned the immense residence of Ottavio Farnese, duke of Parma and Piacenza, and his wife Margaret of Austria, natural daughter of Emperor Charles V, to overlook the Po River at Piacenza. Begun in 1558 or 1559 but left half-finished some three decades later, it was to have rivaled the other Farnese palaces in conception and scale. Its most novel feature was to have been a theater in the central courtyard.

Vignola's ecclesiastical designs rank among the most inventive and influential of the Renaissance. He began to explore elliptical church planning with Sant'Andrea in Via Flaminia, a chapel just outside Rome built for Julius III in 1551–1553. The exterior is informed by Roman tomb structures and a condensed reading of the Pantheon. From a rectangular plan the structure rises through warped pendentives to an oval cornice and dome. Drawing on centralizing and longitudinal planning traditions, the church combines spatial unity with liturgical focus. In 1559 Vignola produced an oval variation for the Madonna del Piano near Capranica by placing semicircular apses against two sides of a domed central space. His final elliptical project was Sant'Anna dei Palafrenieri at the Vatican, begun in 1565, where a rectangular structure encloses a domed oval nave ringed by Corinthian half-columns. Ultimately these oval churches derive from Peruzzi and Serlio, but their originality, integrity, and accessibility made them compelling models for baroque architects like Gianlorenzo Bernini and Francesco Borromini.

Vignola's best-known and most influential ecclesiastical work was Il Gesù, mother church of the Society of Jesus in Rome. The commission came in 1565 by way of Cardinal Alessandro Farnese, who funded construction. Vignola's contribution lies mainly in the Latin-cross plan that features a broad barrel-vaulted nave flanked by unobtrusive chapels, shallow transepts, and a semicircular apse. The design at once served Jesuit requirements and the self-promotional interests of Farnese. After Vignola's death the cardinal entrusted completion of Il Gesù to Giacomo della Porta, who heightened the nave vault and designed the dome and the facade.

Vignola's principal contribution to architecture was a tract on classical columnar decoration, *Regola delli cinque ordini d'architettura* (Rule of the five orders of architecture), first issued at Rome in 1562. Neither a humanistic exposition of principles nor a simple pattern book, the *Regola* is a practical manual intended for readers already acquainted with classical style. Using only thirty-two single-sided folio engravings, the author presents each order—Tuscan, Doric, Ionic, Corinthian, and Composite—proportioned according to a modular system encompassing all major and minor components. The conceptual clarity and elegance of the *Regola* gave it exceptional prestige in architectural education. During the last four centuries over five hundred editions have appeared in a dozen languages, surpassing the writings of all other Renaissance architects.

Vignola's second treatise, *Le due regole della prospettiva pratica* (Two rules of practical perspective), was prepared concurrently with the column book but appeared posthumously in an elaborately annotated volume published by Ignazio Danti in 1583. The text is a series of succinct theorems for perspective construction, demonstrating first the system of Leon Battista Alberti, then the "distance-point" method. For Vignola perspective was fundamental to design, and while *Le due regole* achieved only modest success in terms of publication, it remains the most authoritative summation of sixteenth-century perspective theory.

See also **Architecture**, *subentry on* **Architectural Treatises**.

BIBLIOGRAPHY

Primary Works

Vasari, Giorgio. *Lives of the Painters, Sculptors, and Architects.* Translated by Gaston du C. de Vere. 2 vols. London, 1996. Translation of *Le Vite de'più eccellenti Pittori Scultori e Architettori* (1568). Biography of Vignola in Life of Taddeo Zucchero.

Vignola, Giacomo Barozzi da. *Regola delli cinque ordini d'architettura.* Rome, 1562. Virtually all later versions modify text and illustrations. Best recent republication edited by Maria Walcher Casotti in Pietro Cataneo and Giacomo Barozzi da Vignola, *Trattati* (Milan, 1985), including exhaustive bibliography of editions to 1974.

Secondary Works

La vita e le opere di Jacopo Barozzi da Vignola, 1507–1573, nel quarto centenario della morte. Vignola, Italy, 1974. Best illustrated survey of buildings and drawings, with essays, documents, chronology, and bibliography.

Memorie e studi intorno a Jacopo Barozzi: Pubblicati nel quarto centenario della nascita. Vignola, Italy, 1908. Fundamental collection of essays with documents.

Thoenes, Christof. "Architecture and Society in the Work of Vignola." *Zodiac* 10 (1993): 14–35. Insightful interpretative essay.

Thoenes, Christof. "Vignolas *Regola delli cinque ordini.*" *Römisches Jahrbuch für Kunstgeschichte* 20 (1983): 345–376. Fundamental study of the first edition of the *Rule*.

Walcher Casotti, Maria. *Il Vignola.* 2 vols. Trieste, Italy, 1960. Latest full scholarly monograph.

RICHARD J. TUTTLE

VILLA I TATTI. I Tatti was the home of Bernard Berenson, the distinguished American art historian, for almost sixty years. Located on the eastern edge of urban Florence, the handsome sixteenth-century

Villa I Tatti. I Tatti, in Settignano, just east of Florence, was Bernard Berenson's house from 1905 until his death in 1959. He left the villa to Harvard University, which maintains its Center for Italian Renaissance Studies there. The villa also houses Berenson's personal collection of Italian Renaissance art. COURTESY OF VILLA I TATTI

villa is surrounded by seventy-five acres of gently undulant Tuscan farmland planted with olives and grapes, almond and fruit trees. Boccaccio's beloved stream, the Mensola, runs through the property; he himself lived for a time across the small country road from Corbignano, one of the late-medieval I Tatti farmhouses; Poggio Gherardo, where he claims the stories of the first three days of the *Decameron* were told, still crowns an adjacent hill. Upon Berenson's death in 1959 the villa, its contents, and its surrounding property were bequeathed to Harvard, his alma mater, and in the autumn of 1961 the Harvard University Center for Italian Renaissance Studies was opened there. However, the house itself, now a national monument, remains much as it did in Berenson's day, with his extensive collection of Italian and Asian art still in place and its celebrated gardens, designed for Berenson by Cecil Pinsent. Although the library has more than doubled in size since Berenson's day, it too retains much of its original character.

Villa I Tatti, as the center is officially known, is devoted to advanced study of the Italian Renaissance in all its aspects: the history of art, of literature, and of music; political, economic, diplomatic, and social history; and the history of science, of philosophy, and of religion. Each year, an international selection committee nominates from twelve to fifteen postdoctoral scholars in the early stages of their careers to become I Tatti fellows. In addition, I Tatti's scholarly community includes a dozen or more research associates from the Italian academic world, a number of visiting scholars and visiting professors, and the director.

Villa I Tatti offers the resources of its library (Biblioteca Berenson) of over 100,000 volumes and an archive of more than 300,000 photographs; the library also subscribes to more than 400 learned journals. In addition to a stipend, each fellow is given a study in which to work and the opportunity to associate daily with other members of the I Tatti community as well as with the many distinguished Renaissance scholars who regularly use the library. An annual series of lectures, seminars, and study days is sponsored by the center, and international conferences of an exploratory, usually interdisciplinary, nature are held there every year or so. There is also an active publication program, which includes the biennial journal, *I Tatti Studies: Essays in the Renaissance.*

The Harvard University Center for Italian Renaissance Studies was founded on the principle that maturing scholars working independently will profit from close association with each other, with leading senior scholars, and with other experts of various interests, ages, nationalities, and levels of achievement. Although the fellows at I Tatti represent a wide spectrum of discrete intellectual specialties, they all work on subjects within the Italian Renaissance and thus share, as it were, a common language, which makes possible an exchange of knowledge, interests, and scholarly discoveries. Not surprisingly, much of the scholarship done at Villa I Tatti is interdisciplinary in character.

Bernard Berenson's dream of a cultural center where the heritage of the past would be preserved and fruitfully studied has been realized at I Tatti to an extent even he could not have anticipated. The long list of important publications that have emanated from the center, the roster of world-renowned scholars who have been fellows, and the encomiastic, often moving, testimonials of those who have been involved with this institution combine to attest to the central position Villa I Tatti has come to occupy in Italian Renaissance studies throughout the world.

See also **Renaissance, Interpretations of the,** *subentry on* **Bernard Berenson.**

BIBLIOGRAPHY

Antichità viva 8, no. 6 (November–December 1969). Special issue dedicated to Bernard Berenson, containing an editorial and eight articles on Berenson, I Tatti, and related matters.

Lauritzen, Peter. "The Legacy of I Tatti: Bernard Berenson's Renaissance Villa near Florence." *Architectural Digest* (20 January 1990): 112–117+.

Samuels, Ernest. *Bernard Berenson: The Making of a Connoisseur.* Cambridge, Mass., 1979.

Samuels, Ernest. *Bernard Berenson: The Making of a Legend.* Cambridge, Mass., 1987.

Tassel, Janet. "Viva I Tatti . . . and the Ghost of Bernard Berenson Within." *Harvard Magazine* (March–April 1994): 34–41.

Weaver, William. *A Legacy of Excellence: The Story of Villa I Tatti.* New York, 1997.

WALTER KAISER

VILLALÓN, CRISTÓBAL DE (fl. 1525–1558), Spanish humanist. Very little is known about Villalón's life, aside from his educational career. He studied at Alcalá, Salamanca, and Valladolid, where he also taught logic and made a living as a private instructor in rhetoric from approximately 1530 to 1545. He was long best known for works whose attribution is now contested: *Viaje de Turquía* (Voyage to Turkey; c. 1557–1560), *El Crótalon* (The castanets; c. 1552–1553), and *Diálogo de las transformaciones de Pitágoras* (Dialogue on the transformations of Pythagoras; c. 1552–1553). The works known to have been written by him, however, place him among the more versatile prose writers of his day. The *Tragedia de Mirrha* (Tragedy of Mirrha; 1536), based on the Ovidian tale in book 10 of the *Metamorphoses,* is a piece of juvenilia, probably written as part of his rhetorical training. It shows a taste for storytelling that will be fully developed later in *El scholástico* (The scholar; c. 1542). The *Ingeniosa comparación entre lo antiguo y lo presente* (An ingenious comparison between antiquity and the present; 1539) is another rhetorical exercise, this time a double *declamatio,* or alternate defense of two opposite positions, without real dialogue and therefore without a resolution. More sophisticated dialogue (typically Ciceronian) and storytelling are combined in his most mature and important work: *El scholástico.* A utopia about the ideal university and its scholars, it includes academic as well as social education. Its immediate structural model is Baldassare Castiglione's *Book of the Courtier* (1528), but it incorporates many aspects of form and content derived from analogous classical works (Plato's *Republic,* Cicero's *De oratore*), as well as materials from recent sources such as Desiderius Erasmus's *Antibarbari* (Against the barbarians; 1520). Placing rhetorical and humanistic training at the core of a new, all-encompassing education, Villalón takes the opportunity to discuss topics as varied as speculation on love and friendship, the nature of pleasure, wonders of nature and art, the condition of women, the social role of different disciplines (law, painting, music, theology), freedom, the dignity of man, the art of government, and the art of good speech. Education becomes in fact the organizing principle of a miscellany of Renaissance lore, combined with a copious collection of short stories, some original, others gathered from folk and classical sources (Lucian, Plutarch).

El scholástico was banned from the press, probably for its Erasmian religious criticism, as well as for its allusions to political conflicts among the powerful real-life counterparts of two of its nine speakers.

Other works by Villalón are *El provechoso tratado de cambios y contrataciones de mercaderes, y reprobación de usura* (A profitable treatise on bartering and trade among merchants and a condemnation of usury; 1541); and *Gramática castellana* (Spanish grammar; 1558).

BIBLIOGRAPHY

Primary Work

Villalón, Cristóbal de. *El scholástico.* Edited by José M. Martínez Torrejón. Barcelona, Spain, 1997. The introduction is the only comprehensive study to this work. Includes a bibliography and heavy annotation.

Secondary Work

Kincaid, Joseph J. *Cristóbal de Villalón.* New York, 1973. A thorough description of all the works ever related to Villalón, supported by references throughout.

JOSÉ MIGUEL MARTÍNEZ TORREJÓN

VILLAS. In the Renaissance, the term "villa" referred to three things. The first was a physical structure (a building in the countryside); the second a social condition (agricultural property); and the third a literary and philosophical framework (the idea of rural retreat from city life). The several meanings of the term together encompassed the changing idea of rural life and its relationship to the city in this period.

The development of the villa as a building type was a Renaissance phenomenon linked to various economic, social, and artistic forces. By the end of the sixteenth century, a distinct type had emerged, yet there was no such uniformity in the desire to build on the part of patrons, the design influences for architects, or theoretical literature that identified an ideal of villa life. Rather, there was great variety throughout the Italian peninsula in both practice and theory. The one consistent thing in this period is that architects, patrons, and writers all saw country life as worthy and elevated the country house into the domain of conceptualized architecture.

Medieval Europe featured various levels of rural buildings. At the high end of the social scale was the fortified *rocca,* or castle, a seat of economic and political power for a seigniorial ruler or land owner. On the other end was the farm that provided agricultural goods for an owner who often resided primarily in the city. Renaissance villas continued these two types of residences and added another that was primarily intended to exploit the pleasure of the countryside and provide an escape from the density and pace of urban life.

In the sixteenth century the artist and author Sebastiano Serlio (1475–1554) described this taxonomy of housing as a system of building that progressed from the most humble structure to fortified palace for a tyrant prince. His treatise included rural and urban structures, organized into a sequence of buildings for different social and economic classes. All of his structures derive from the simplest building, and could be recombined and enlarged by using a system of components. Serlio's treatment of houses for the poor and villas for all levels of society was unique, though certainly influenced by Venetian architectural practice. His book embodies a self-consciousness in the Renaissance of the relationship between the expression of the house and the nature of its inhabitants.

Fifteenth-Century Traditions and Innovations. In the fifteenth century the Medici family consolidated their rural properties by building a series of new and renovated villas outside Florence that exploited the range of available types while also developing new variations on the available themes. Often these villas served as collection centers for local farms before goods were transported to the city. Cosimo de' Medici rebuilt villas of Trebbio (1427–1433) and Cafaggiolo (1443–1452), maintaining a fortified appearance with towers and machicolated passages around the main block that had been used on earlier buildings. The Medici thus ensured that their urban palaces with their extended families would have food and products from the countryside under all conditions.

Although these early fifteenth-century villas may not have been intended as defensive buildings, their architectural details often showed continuity with the existing castles or forts. This continuity with local tradition was an important aspect of the history of the villa during this period; style or form remained consistent while function shifted from feudal interests to agricultural and retreat.

The countryside was also a place of refuge in several senses. The Medici and other important families acquired country properties that allowed them to diversify their investments should their economic or political power wane. During times of plague, the country offered a refuge from the health risks in more populated areas.

The early Medici villas show an increased attention to the landscape and gardens that were intended as much for pleasure as production. The villa at Fiesole had no known connection with agriculture and was sited to emphasize the views across the river valley; Cosimo de' Medici commissioned this villa for his son Giovanni just before 1455. The building was

Villa del Trebbio. Painting of one of the Medici villas north of Florence by Giusto Utens, 1599. One of a series of lunettes originally in the Villa di Artimino. MUSEO DI FIRENZE COM'ERA, FLORENCE/SCALA/ART RESOURCE

not a reconstruction or adaptation but was new, with a massive substructure built into the hill that contained the kitchens, stables, and storage. The building was not built around a courtyard as at the earlier villas such as San Piero at Careggi (1430–1450), but open to the outside and oriented toward the garden and views. The simple and austere exterior eschews the language of fortification and confirms Leon Battista Alberti's disapproval of the "spires and battlements" of medieval buildings as inappropriate for the houses of private citizens.

Earlier traditions were carried on throughout the fifteenth century, but were generally subsumed within more individualized designs that elevated particular structures above others as unique examples. When Lorenzo de' Medici planned to build a villa at Poggio a Caiano he ordered numerous models from which to choose. The successful design by Giuliano da Sangallo (done in the early 1480s) demonstrated a new self-conscious evocation of the antique in the temple front inserted into the façade, and probably also reflected Lorenzo's involvement and knowledge of contemporary architectural thought.

Classicism and the Antique. Classical details appeared in villas before they did in urban pal-

aces. The use of post and beam construction (as both structure and ornament) may well have lent itself to the use of classical details and elements such as pilasters and columns that repeat the dominant and local building techniques.

In the sixteenth century, however, the design of villas underwent a change in scale, ornamental vocabulary, and a new level of associated meaning that connected rural building with ancient grandeur. Donato Bramante's design for the Cortile del Belvedere and adjoining structures for Pope Julius II (1505 ff.) connected the Vatican Palace with a villa which Innocent VIII had built on the north slope of the Vatican hill in 1485–1487. Through his architect, Julius aimed to outdo the ancients in their creation of architectural compositions on a grand scale that merged landscape with architecture. A series of terraces and long galleries created perspective. This was as much an earthwork as a building; the architecture framed the view from the stanze (rooms) painted by Raphael. Bramante also showed an understanding of the continuity of the interior and exterior space, which were connected through symbolism and references to the antique in scale and individual forms.

Roman antiquities profoundly affected the architects who came to Rome seeking patronage in the early sixteenth century. Raphael's design of a villa on Monte Mario for Cardinal Giulio de' Medici (later Pope Clement VII) was to rival ancient villas in its planning and decoration. The Villa Madama (as it was later called) was begun around 1516, and Antonio de Sangallo was the superintendent of works. The planning of the villa was based on surveys of many huge ancient villas that had been built on hillsides outside Rome, thus requiring enormous substructures. Raphael had studied Hadrian's villa at Tivoli outside Rome (as had Bramante), with an interest in both the architectural organization as well as the painted stucco in the ancient bath complex. The use of terraces at the Villa Madama had already been explored at Bramante's Belvedere, which this was clearly intended to rival. At the Belvedere, however, they were required to take into account other existing buildings whereas this was built in isolation, with a fusion of architectural and natural forms. Raphael's plan placed, at the center of the villas, a large round courtyard off of which were residential areas, a theater, stabling for two hundred horses, a hippodrome with gardens, and from the south a great open stairway to lead up from the Vatican. Each of these elements was visually discrete, and the complexity of the plan was impossible to understand from one point in the scheme. In a letter describing the villa Raphael related the scheme to one described in the ancient Pliny the Younger's letters. The garden loggia had Raphael's desire for a unity of the arts, architecture, sculpture, and painting, an ideal also taken from ancient art theory and known practice.

The Villa Giulia in Rome (begun in 1551) was built outside the city walls by Giacomo Barozzi da Vignola. The plain exterior recalls the tradition of fortified villas against which the rusticated entrance stands out in high relief and evokes the triumphal gates of antiquity. The plan moves through a sequence of courtyards, lined with niches for the placement of antique sculpture. On a lower level is a richly decorated *nymphaeum* (grotto dedicated to the nymphs) through which flows the waters of the Aqua Vergine, the ancient aqueduct restored by Julius III.

The villas of Andrea Palladio (1508–1580) exemplified this combination of elements from vernacular buildings and attention to the antique. Over the course of his long career Palladio designed a wide range of villas for the nobility of Vicenza, and published many of them in his *I quattro libri di architettura* (Four Books of Architecture; Venice; 1570). His popularity among this class and the promotion of his designs through his publication gave his designs a prominence both in his own time and for generations afterward. The villas vary in size, organization, siting, and interior decoration, based on the status of the owner and the intended function. Reclaimed land of the *terra firma* was a sound investment and, as in fifteenth-century Florence, villas ensured that urban owners would always have ample provisions and a refuge against the plague. Villas in the Veneto kept this agricultural connection, and Palladio's designs and theoretical writings paid special attention to the various needs of the farm and its management. He planned not only the main house but also residences for farm workers, stables for animals, sheds and outbuildings for equipment, and storage of produce, oil, grain, wine and hay (as in his design for Villa Thiene at Cicogna, 1556–1563).

After his trip to Rome in 1541 Palladio assimilated ideas from his study of ancient Roman baths into the plans and details of his villas, as at the Villa Valmarana at Vigardolo near Vicenza (1542). There he took the sequence of small, medium, and large rooms, use of cross vaults, and intersecting axes all from the planning of ancient baths. They became a feature of his subsequent designs. The Villa Almerico (more popularly known as the Villa Rotunda, completed by 1569) epitomizes Palladio's interest in symmetrical planning with four temple fronts facing the landscape on axis off a circular room. In contrast to the more agricultural villas, this is located just outside the city of Vicenza and is therefore more of a *villa suburbana* (like the Villa Farnesina in Rome, Baldassare Peruzzi, 1509–1511, and the Palazzo Te in Mantua, Giulio Romano, begun 1525). After Palladio's death Vincenzo Scamozzi based his own design for the Rocca Pisana (1576) on this villa, repeating the siting of the building on the hill, with beautiful views and healthy air.

BIBLIOGRAPHY

Primary Work

Serlio, Sebastiano. *Serlio on Domestic Architecture.* Text by Myra Nan Rosenfeld. New York, 1996.

Secondary Works

Ackerman, James S. *The Villa: Form and Ideology of Country Houses.* Princeton, N. J., 1990.
Bentmann, Reinhard, and Michael Müller. *The Villa as Hegemonic Architecture.* Translated by Tim Spence and David Craven. Atlantic Highlands, N. J., 1992.
Burns, Howard, with Lynda Fairbairn and Bruce Boucher. *Andrea Palladio 1508–1580: The Portico and the Farmyard.* London, 1975.

Coffin, David. *The Villa in the Life of Renaissance Rome.* Princeton, N. J., 1979.

Forster, Kurt. "Back to the Farm: Vernacular Architecture and the Development of the Renaissance Villa." *Architectura* 1 (1974): 1–12.

Heydenreich, Ludwig. "La villa: genesi e sviluppi fino al Palladio." *Bolletino Centro Internazionale di Studi di Architettura 'Andrea Palladio'* 9 (1969): 11–22.

Holberton, Paul. *Palladio's Villas: Life in the Renaissance Countryside.* London, 1990.

Lillie, Amanda. "The Humanist Villa Revisited." In *Language and Images of Renaissance Italy.* Edited by Alison Brown. Oxford, 1995. Pages 192–215.

Muraro, Michelangelo. *Venetian Villas: The History and Culture.* New York, 1986.

CHRISTY ANDERSON

VILLEROY, NICOLAS DE NEUFVILLE, SEIGNEUR DE

(1543–1617), secretary of state under four French kings. Villeroy's family began its ascent through municipal offices in Paris and by the sixteenth century began accumulating royal offices. Nicolas profited from his father's influence and entered royal employ in 1559 as a secretary of finances. By 1567, having caught the eye of Catherine de Médicis, he was made a secretary of state.

With the accession of Henry III (ruled 1574–1589), Villeroy became Henry's chief adviser and confidant. Despite his efforts, Villeroy could not persuade his weak and vacillating royal master to attend to the governance of his disintegrating realm. By September 1588 Henry repaid his servant's loyal service with an abrupt dismissal. Unwilling to serve a heretic king, Henry IV, Villeroy spent the next four years serving the Catholic League leader, the duke of Mayenne, while trying at the same time to reconcile Leaguers and Catholic royalists. When Henry IV finally converted to Catholicism (July 1593), Villeroy was willing to serve the crown again, and in September 1594 was reappointed a secretary of state. For the rest of Henry's reign (1589–1610), Villeroy was his secretary of state for foreign affairs and one of Europe's most esteemed statesmen. After Henry's death by assassination (May 1610), Villeroy served his widow and regent, Marie de Médicis, until his dismissal, engineered by the queen's favorite, Concino Concini. The assassination of Concini on Louis XIII's orders (April 1617) brought Villeroy's return to office until his death a few months later.

BIBLIOGRAPHY

Dickerman, Edmund H. *Bellièvre and Villeroy: Power in France under Henry III and Henry IV.* Providence, R.I., 1971.

Sutherland, N. M. *The French Secretaries of State in the Age of Catherine de Medici.* London, 1962.

EDMUND H. DICKERMAN

VILLON, FRANÇOIS

(1431–c. 1463), French poet. The last major poet of the French Middle Ages and author of the *Lais* (1456), the *Testament* (1462), and miscellaneous poems, among them the "Ballad of the Hanged," Villon was called the best Parisian poet there is by Clément Marot, the editor of the first critical edition of his works in 1533.

Villon was born François de Montcorbier or Des Loges into a poor family, about which little is known save his mother's faith and simplicity, according to the prayer which the poet bequeaths to her in the *Testament.* He was brought up by a church chaplain, Maître Guillaume de Villon, to whom the poet referred in the *Testament* as his "plus que père" (more than father) and whose name he used to sign all of his work from 1456. Thanks to this adoptive father, François Villon had access to the University of Paris, where he received his bachelor's degree in March 1449 and his license and master's in 1452.

Villon's poetic allusions to student pranks and to the Coquillards, a secret organization of ruffians, suggest that he was unable to find employment as a tonsured clerk in Paris, consorted with rowdy elements, and rapidly moved into the margins of society. In June 1455, wounded by a dagger-wielding priest, Villon killed his assailant. Six months later, judicial records indicate that he received a royal pardon. In December 1456 Villon participated in the theft of 500 *écus* from the Collège de Navarre and wrote the *Lais.* Following the belated discovery of the theft in March 1457, Villon left Paris for Angers and traveled widely in the provinces until 1461. While his whereabouts during that period remain the subject of speculation, it is known that he stopped at the court of Charles d'Orléans at Blois, to whose poetic competition he submitted his ballad "Je meurs de soif auprès de la fontaine" (I die of thirst next to the fountain). In the summer of 1461 he was imprisoned in Meung-sur-Loire by Thibaut d'Aussigny, bishop of Orléans, for an unidentified crime. His *Testament,* some ballads of which probably were composed in Thibaut's jail, begins with a virulent criticism of the bishop's cruelty and hypocrisy. On 2 October 1461, upon Louis XI's first entrance into Meung, Villon was freed; he then returned to Paris and completed the *Testament* by the end of 1462. In late November 1462, Villon was involved in a fatal brawl and, although not the murderer, was imprisoned at the Châtelet and sentenced to be hanged. He appealed his sentence to the Parlement of Paris, which commuted it to ten years of exile. Three days later, on 8 January 1463, Villon disappeared from Paris, never to resurface.

Villon's literary output is as enigmatic as his sparsely documented life, partly because of frequent, often acerbically comic allusions to contemporaries, which even his editor Marot admitted having difficulty understanding. The forty-stanza *Lais* parodies both legal discourse and the courtly *fin'amors* (refined love) ethic, which Villon subverts with double entendres of an often scatological nature. In his *Lais,* Villon interweaves reality (his departure for Angers) with fiction when he paints himself as a martyred lover who, because of unrequited affection, has no choice but to leave town and therefore bequeaths his friends and fellow citizens his paltry possessions, such as his trousers and hair clippings, his clerkly title, and window frames hung with cobwebs.

His *Testament,* a masterpiece of 158 eight-verse stanzas interspersed with sixteen ballads and three small poems, continues to mix fiction and reality as the poet-testator, just liberated from Bishop Thibaut's prison, makes his will while he is still of sound mind and reflects upon his spent, poverty-stricken youth, his spent promise, and a future that holds little hope. Often ironic, even bitterly comic (as when he wills his spectacles to the blind or criticizes ecclesiastical hypocrisy), the tone of this work is truculent when he settles scores with enemies. It is often contemplative as he considers both himself—namely, the injustices he suffered compounded by his self-destructive impulses—and other victims of poverty, love, or time. Occasionally, Villon can even be tender or sympathetic, particularly when he bequeaths his most potent gift, his own poetic voice, to figures who otherwise would not be heard, such as his mother or an aged prostitute called La Belle Heaulmiere.

The importance of his poetry was recognized in the Renaissance not only by his editor Marot but also by Rabelais, who has Panurge (in *Pantagruel,* 1532) cite Villon's famous refrain about evanescence, "Mais où sont les neiges d'antan" ("Where are the snows of yesteryear"), from the "Ballad of the Ladies of Yesteryear." Rabelais also introduces Villon into *Le quart livre* (Fourth book; 1552) as a poet who cites his own quatrain on his impending hanging in a conversation with Edward V of England.

BIBLIOGRAPHY

Primary Works

Villon, François. *The Poems of François Villon.* Translated by Galway Kinnell. New York, 1965. Translation of *Le lais* (1456), *Le testament* (1462), and *Poésies diverses.* See also *The Lyrical Poems of François Villon,* translated by A. C. Swinburne, D. G. Rossetti, William Ernest Henley, John Payne, and Leonie Adams (Reprint, New York, 1979). The most cited modern edition (in French) is *Le testament Villon; Les lais Villon et les poèmes variés,* edited by Jean Rychner and Robert Henry, 2 vols. Geneva, 1985.

Secondary Works

Dufournet, Jean. *Recherches sur le Testament de François Villon.* 2 vols. 2d ed. Paris, 1971–1973.

Dufournet, Jean. *Villon et sa fortune littéraire.* Bordeaux, France, 1970.

Hunt, Tony. *Villon's Last Will: Language and Authority in the Testament.* Oxford, 1996.

Peckham, Robert D. *François Villon: A Bibliography.* New York, 1990.

Siciliano, Italo. *François Villon et les thèmes poétiques du moyen âge.* Reprint, Paris, 1967.

Vitz, Evelyn Birge *The Crossroad of Intentions: A Study of Symbolic Expression in the Poetry of François Villon.* The Hague, Netherlands, 1974.

GRACE MORGAN ARMSTRONG

VINCI, LEONARDO DA. *See* **Leonardo da Vinci.**

VIOLENCE.

Renaissance society had a clear conception of violence, its origins, morality, and many manifestations. Defined as physical force that inflicted injury to persons or property, violence could be both socially sanctioned, as in judicial punishments and war, and prohibited, as in homicide and rape. There were, however, forms of violence about which Renaissance society displayed an ambivalent, conflicted, or changing attitude, especially vendettas and crimes of passion. Violence could also imply coercion short of bodily harm that involved the deprivation of freedom, such as abduction, kidnapping, and immurement, or that threatened injury, such as the characteristically Renaissance crime of verbal violence.

Renaissance society appears to have been notably violent. The countryside was more dangerous than the cities, which were protected with walls, armed guards at town gates, and internal policing. Merchants and others felt obliged to travel in convoys armed against highwaymen, unprotected peasants were vulnerable to bandits and predatory aristocrats, and undisciplined soldiers commonly looted and assaulted hapless civilians. Most men went about their daily business armed, and any woman without a male guardian or the protection of convent walls was vulnerable to sexual assault. The popularity of unfortified country houses and villas during the late sixteenth century may point to a decline in rural danger.

Morality of Violence. Despite its apparent ubiquity, violence in society at large does not seem to have been a matter of widespread moral concern. The clergy were obliged, of course, to refrain from acts of violence, including even hunting; confessional manuals advised priests to dissuade parishioners from quarreling; Franciscans, in particular, often served as peacemakers between feuding families; and churches were supposed to provide refuge for those pursued by enemies or the authorities. The official pacifism of the clergy, however, may have been more honored in the breach than in the promise: the legacy of the Crusades celebrated just war; feuds among monks sometimes broke out into violent confrontations within monasteries; and Pope Julius II's infamous appearance at the head of his army at the siege of Bologna hardly set an example of nonviolence for the rest of the church. Famous preachers condemned sexual sins, especially adultery and sodomy, far more than the pervasive violence of Christian society.

Many seem to have found inflicting and witnessing violence gratifying or even pleasurable. The public enthusiasm for watching judicial tortures and executions is only the most obvious example of a widespread psycho-sociological disposition. Diarists and chroniclers recounted numerous examples of ecstasy in causing pain to an enemy. Carnival sports, including bearbaiting, bull chases, and cat tortures, reveal not just an indifference to the suffering of animals but a certain sadistic enjoyment of it. Once free of the restraints of European law and social control, Christians abroad demonstrated a barbarous propensity for violence, from the systematic raping of African women to the extermination of entire populations in the Canary Islands and West Indies. As the famous case of Simon of Trent in 1475 reveals, Christians imagined that Jews ritually murdered children, which justified to them the quasi-judicial extermination of entire Jewish communities, a deed more widely celebrated than condemned. All these examples imply that in and of itself, violence was not necessarily viewed as immoral or undesirable, and yet Renaissance society was not without compassion toward orphans, the poor, vulnerable women, and the victims of Turkish raiders.

The systematic study of violence in the Renaissance has largely been conducted by tracing and classifying criminal prosecutions, a task that has emphasized the differences between Renaissance and modern assumptions about criminal violence. Certain nonviolent crimes, such as blasphemy and heresy, were considered more grievous than rape or assault, and many kinds of violence were tolerated or treated leniently. Punishments tended to be class and gender specific and subject to political considerations: lower-class men and women suffered mutilations and execution; upper-class criminals were usually fined or exiled; and murderous clergy were usually exempt from secular jurisdictions.

Individual Criminal Violence. One of the distinguishing characteristics of Renaissance violence is that individual actions often reflected family and collective animosities. During the Renaissance criminal justice began to abandon the principle of collective guilt, which punished an entire family for the crime of one of its members, in favor of a principle of individual responsibility. The collective solidarity of families and clans had traditionally made kin groups rather than the state the source of justice: the family killing together in revenge, in effect, regulated violence in society. During the fifteenth and sixteenth centuries the more frequent appearance of family renegades and incidents of domestic violence probably indicates the weakening of family solidarity and a rise of individual violence.

Violent speech. Renaissance judges were especially concerned about speech as a form of violence. Guido Ruggiero has shown that between 1349 and 1406 more than three-quarters of the cases heard by the Venetian Council of Ten involved allegations of verbal violence, indicating a belief that in violent words, violent deeds were born, including conspiracies against the state, assaults against public officials, factional fights, and vendettas. In some communities statutes outlawed specific insulting words and gestures. Punishments against crimes of speech could be quite severe, and threatening someone might be penalized more severely than physically assaulting him. The willingness of judges to criminalize speech was an important step toward supplanting the private justice of vendettas with the public justice of the state.

Assault and murder. Authorities tended to consider minor assaults and brawls as normal behavior and to punish them, if at all, with minor fines or summary justice at the scene, as long as the fighting did not draw blood, in which case the offense might be considered grave. During much of the period the distinction between violent and judicial redress of grievances remained incomplete, resulting in a significant number of assault cases in which the parties were also involved in litigation with each other. In evaluating assaults and murders, judges distinguished between crimes of passion and crimes of rational self-interest, which were punished with greater severity. The prevailing assumption was that

Violent Pastimes. *Gesellen-Stechen* (Apprentice-sticking) mayhem in Nürnberg, 3 March 1560. Painting by Jost Amman (1539–1591), 1561. BAYERISCHES NATIONAL-MUSEUM, MUNICH/AKG PHOTO

human beings were governed by their emotions, which sometimes led to unavoidable violence for which the assailant was not fully culpable, and the fear of punishment could not restrain impulsive violence because most people were not capable of coolly controlling their behavior. The objective of punishment was not to deter violence but to provide an institutionalized form of revenge, which would keep assaults and murders from escalating to vendettas. Those who demonstrated a self-interested emotional detachment from their violence, such as paid assassins, robbers, or mothers who exposed their babies, received more elaborate ritual executions than those who committed a senseless impulsive murder in the course of a domestic dispute, bout of drinking, or argument among gamblers. For Renaissance judges the crucial distinction was not so much between premeditated and unpremeditated murder as between rational self-interest and passionate emotions.

Sexual violence. Despite the rigidity of Christian moral strictures, sexual violence (sexual molestation, attempted rape, and rape) was understood as a minor form of assault and punished less severely than violent speech or robbery. Judicial authorities calculated the degree of criminality of the rapist by the age and status of the victim. While the rape of a young girl or boy was a serious crime, the rape of a married woman was less dire and of a widow less still. The rape of an unmarried woman of marriageable age was generally considered more an excess of youthful ardor than a crime, and such rapists could frequently escape punishment altogether. In the cities of southern France participation in gang rape seems to have been a rite of initiation for young artisans, whose victims were so shamed they were usually forced into prostitution. Needless to say, women did not share in this widespread reluctance of male authorities to take rape seriously, and by the late sixteenth century judicial records reveal women demanding a sterner official attitude.

Collective Violence. Except for the German Peasants' War (1524–1526), the French Wars of Religion (1562–1598), and other episodes associated with religious controversies, collective violence seldom had an ideological dimension during the Renaissance. Cities were often the locations for crowd demonstrations that became violent, but these were almost always short, spasmodic events in which groups of people agitated for specific economic or political outcomes or became involved in a struggle for power among competing elite families. Urban collective violence tended to have limited aims and limited destructiveness.

Markets or town squares, where large numbers of people gathered, provided the location for collective violence, and market days or festivals, especially carnival, provided the occasion. Both men and women participated in collective violence. The archetypical female action was the bread riot, given women's responsibilities for feeding their families. On such occasions official reluctance to subject women to counterviolence gave them a certain immunity, but these riots, which were usually limited to sacking bakeries and demonstrating for bread subsidies, had an inherent logic that contained the violence within defined limits. Only in extreme cases, such as in Naples in 1585, where the mayor clandestinely reduced the size of a loaf of bread in the public bakeries and was executed, did officials face serious physical harm. Guildsmen, particularly young journeymen, also followed a kind of implicit script in their riots over economic grievances. In the Ciompi Revolt in Florence in 1378, disfranchised guildsmen limited their protest to demanding the right to participate in the established guild political structure.

Rites of violence. Rather than riot in public places or harass public officials, youth abbeys—institutionalized gangs of young, unmarried men—had a nasty tendency to victimize vulnerable members of the community. Youth abbeys enforced sexual tyranny through ritualized violence, not just gang rape but charivari, which defamed a couple or individual who did not conform to the marital or sexual standards of the community. Consisting of mocking songs and banging pots and pans, a charivari could easily escalate into assault, arson, or even murder.

The performative masculinity of the youth abbeys was also manifest in other rites of violence, such as dangerous sports and staged combats. French, English, and Italian forms of football and Spanish and Italian bull chases represent just some of the most obvious examples of semi-regulated, officially tolerated violence. In the Venetian "bridge battles" (periodic fights by neighborhood gangs to gain possession of a bridge), combatants fought with fists and cudgels, resulting in serious injuries and sometimes deaths. Among aristocrats jousts continued well into the sixteenth century, also resulting in the occasional accidental death, including that of King Henry II of France in 1559.

Urban riots displayed a strongly ritual character that determined the course and nature of the violence. These rites of violence took many forms. There were ritual pillages that erupted after the death of a prince or pope. The assumption behind the pillage was that authority died with the ruler, creating an opportunity to sack his palace or to smash images of his rule. Ritual cannibalism appeared during popular revolts in Florence in 1343 and Romans (France) in 1580, when crowds killed public officials, dismembered them, paraded the body parts, and cannibalized the remains in a mood of manic celebration. During the Reformation ritual demonstrations involved iconoclasm, profanation of sacred objects, public humiliation of priests and nuns, and effigy burnings.

Feuds. One of the most highly ritualized forms of violence was feuding, which governments were at considerable pains to stamp out because feuds among prominent families so profoundly threatened the very foundations of the state. Venice eliminated feuding among its ruling families by the end of the thirteenth century. England was probably the most precocious kingdom, stamping out private feuds during the sixteenth. Feuding persisted during the Renaissance, especially in mountainous areas, regions distant from the political center of the country, and along borders between states.

Feuds tended to erupt in periodic bursts of violence in which the objects of attack were adult male members of an enemy family or clan. Boys and women were typically exempt from attack, and violence was carried out within implicit limits. Feuding murders were typically public assaults, rather than ambushes in the dark of night, and it was important to kill an opponent in certain prescribed ways in order to maximize the publicity of the murderer, who wanted to make himself known. The code of feuding violence borrowed from hunting customs, so that victims were sometimes treated as if they were hunted prey, butchered like meat, and fed to dogs. Feuds among aristocratic families could sometimes become the crystallizing agent for more widespread social violence, as in the devastating peasant revolt in Friuli in 1511. Feuding aristocratic families employed armed retainers or bravos, who were a major source of organized violence not just against their employer's enemies but against helpless peasants and citizens.

Since the principal means of combating feuding was through sentences of exile, feuds created outlaws—exiles who to survive habitually turned to brigandage, murder for hire, or smuggling. In Italy networks of exiles constantly agitated to return home, creating a potential rebel force that hovered along the borders of virtually every state. The persistent European warfare of the first half of the six-teenth century tended to siphon off some of these bandit-exiles, who found employment in the armies of warring princes. During the last half of the six-teenth century northern Italian states took advantage of the unusual period of peace to launch assaults on bandits and outlaws, largely through the criminali-zation of aristocratic violence.

During the same period the spread of the rapier sword and the pistol made combat much more deadly. Whereas before the mid-sixteenth century feuding families might indulge in brawling and street fights, afterward they were attracted to duels, which limited combat to the two duelists and controlled mayhem through a heavily ritualized code of con-duct. During the last half of the sixteenth century the fad for dueling spread from Italy to the rest of Europe as families and clans gradually abandoned collective violence in favor of the more limited and individu-alistic violence of the duel.

Legitimate and Illegitimate Violence.
During the Renaissance the difference between le-gitimate and illegitimate violence was often quite tenuous. The organized violence of the state easily shifted into illegitimate forms as knights became rob-ber barons, demobilized soldiers vagrants, sailors pi-rates, militiamen highway robbers, and policemen extortionists. The men who fulfilled the necessarily violent functions of the principalities and communi-ties, moreover, were often recruited from the crim-inal classes, a tendency that blurred any sociological distinction between those who perpetrated and those who prevented violence.

In making war or defending citizens against crime, all governments faced a critical shortage of manpower. No army was as big as the monarchs or cities who planned campaigns hoped. John Hale has estimated that only about 0.5 to 0.75 percent of the population ever served as combatants, and even field armies close to recruitment locales never suc-ceeded in drawing more than 5 percent of the eli-gible male population. As a result, recruiters relied on what they could get by emptying prisons, round-ing up paupers, or offering safe-conducts to outlaws. The recruitment gap was filled by mercenaries from specialized military economies, such as the moun-tain cantons of Switzerland, and local militia com-panies, expanding the access to weapons among ci-vilians without a noticeable increase in military efficiency. The aristocratic classes, which had tradi-tionally monopolized the officer corps and cavalry, showed an increasing disinclination to serve in wars

during the fifteenth and sixteenth centuries, resulting in the spread of professional soldiering, which cre-ated a rootless class of specialists in violence. Bands of roving ex-soldiers contributed to the sixteenth-century phenomenon of the underworld figure—the Spanish *pícaro,* the English rogue, the Italian *ribaldo* or *vagabondo.*

The confusion between legitimate and illegitimate uses of force was most evident in policing. No Re-naissance society developed a permanent, profes-sional police force. In cities where policing was most closely integrated into the community, understaffed officers, chosen from among the citizens or serving in elected judicial offices, relied on the community for detecting crimes, gathering evidence, and even capturing suspects. In some northern Italian cities the office of podestà provided some level of profes-sional competence to the job, but none of these men stayed in one place for very long, which meant that the podestà retained the taint of an outsider. In the countryside justice was often delegated to local aris-tocrats who held feudal jurisdictions, the very people responsible for some of the most rapacious violence. In rural jurisdictions the hand of legal coercion came from the aristocrat's retainers or perhaps an official enforcer (the English beadle, Italian *sbirro*), himself often recruited from among criminals.

At sea there was a similar blurring of the boundary between legitimate and illegitimate force. By the 1580s English, Dutch, and French vessels, calling themselves privateers but usually freelancers with-out any form of government authorization, preyed on enemy and neutral shipping. These pseudo-legal pirates can hardly be distinguished from the Muslim corsairs of North Africa, who at least maintained a consistently religious justification for their predation of Christian shipping. Christian ports such as Li-vorno, La Rochelle, Bayonne, and Dunkirk relied on licensed raiding to pursue violence at sea, and com-munities such as Senj on the Dalmatian coast were completely devoted to piracy.

All Renaissance states struggled with the tension between the necessary violence of war and policing, on the one hand, and the inability to contain that violence within the channels defined by government policy, on the other. During the last half of the six-teenth century governments in England, France, It-aly, Spain, the Netherlands, and Germany began to show an awareness of this problem by making at least tentative efforts to extend the authority of the state into the social and rural backwaters. Although the violence of the growing underworld—demobil-ized soldiers, vagabonds, and the urban poor—was hardly touched, the systematic attempts to criminalize the habitual violence of the provincial aristocracy were modestly successful, especially in England, Italy, and, later, France.

See also Crime and Punishment; Duel; Rape; Warfare.

BIBLIOGRAPHY

Billacois, François. *The Duel: Its Rise and Fall in Early Modern France.* Edited and translated by Trista Selous. New Haven, Conn., 1990. The best study of dueling violence.

Dean, Trevor, and K. J. P. Lowe, eds. *Crime, Society, and the Law in Renaissance Italy.* Cambridge, U.K., 1994.

Hale, J. R. *War and Society in Renaissance Europe, 1450–1620.* London, 1985. The most comprehensive examination of the relationship between war and violence in Renaissance society.

Martines, Lauro, ed. *Violence and Civil Disorder in Italian Cities, 1200–1500.* Berkeley and Los Angeles, 1972. An excellent collection of perceptive studies.

Maugain, Gabriel. *Moeurs italiennes de la Renaissance: La vengeance.* Paris, 1935. A neglected classic.

Muir, Edward. *Mad Blood Stirring: Vendetta in Renaissance Italy.* Baltimore, 1998. A study of vendettas and feuding in Friuli.

Muir, Edward, and Guido Ruggiero, eds. *History from Crime.* Baltimore, 1994. A collection of methodologically innovative studies based on criminal records.

Neveux, Hugues. *Les révoltes paysannes en Europe (XIVe–XVIIe siècle).* Paris, 1997. The best comprehensive survey of peasant violence.

Ortalli, Gherardo, ed. *Bande armate, banditi, banditismo e repressione di giustizia negli stati europei di antico regime.* Rome, 1986. The best comprehensive examination of brigandage throughout Europe.

Ruggiero, Guido. *The Boundaries of Eros: Sex Crime and Sexuality in Renaissance Venice.* Oxford, 1985. Chapter 5 presents a thorough discussion of rape.

Ruggiero, Guido. *Violence in Early Renaissance Venice.* New Brunswick, N.J., 1980. A pioneering work on the historical study of violence through criminal records.

EDWARD MUIR

VIRGIL (Publius Vergilius Maro; 70–19 B.C.), great poet of the Roman golden age. Virgil is the author of three major works that were widely read in the Renaissance: ten pastoral poems called the *Eclogues,* four books on farming called the *Georgics,* and the *Aeneid,* an epic that recounts the journey of Aeneas as he wandered through the Mediterranean world, founded Rome, and established the culture to which Renaissance Europe traced its origins. Disseminated in manuscripts and, after 1469, in printed books as well, Virgil's poetry lay at the center of Renaissance education, and from this position it exercised a profound influence on the literature, art, and values of the period.

Virgil and Humanism. By the fourteenth century, a group of avant-garde scholars known now as "humanists" were trying to recover a full, accurate understanding of the classical world as a foundation for cultural renewal. As humanism made its way into the schools, the works of Virgil took a central place in the curriculum of Renaissance Europe. By the end of the sixteenth century, almost everyone who had received a humanistic education—most of Europe's political and intellectual elite—knew at least some of Virgil's poetry.

The fact that Virgil's poetry was studied in the schools also determined how it was read. Renaissance teachers required their students to keep commonplace books, in which they recorded extracts from classical literature that they wanted to remember and reuse in their own writing. This encouraged Renaissance readers to approach Virgil as a source for well-turned phrases, rhetorical figures of speech, and stylistic embellishment on the one hand, and for sententious sayings with contemporary moral applicability on the other. On the most basic level, in other words, Virgil provided guidance in mastering Latin, the international language of the day, and in living a good life: "*audentes fortuna iuvat timidosque repellit*" ("fortune helps the bold and drives away the coward"; *Aeneid* 10.284), "*discite iustitiam moniti et non temnere divos*" ("be warned, learn justice, and do not scorn the gods"; *Aeneid* 6.620), and so forth. In this way Virgil's poetry was woven into the basic fabric of Renaissance intellectual life, so that Virgilian images, for example, entered the emblem books of Andrea Alciati (1492–1550) and his followers.

Of course, Renaissance readers also appreciated the finer points of Virgil's poetry, which provides the foundation for much of the literature of the Renaissance written in Latin. The *Eclogues* provided models for Petrarch (1304–1374), for example, as he fashioned his critiques of church and state in pastoral settings suffused with Virgilian language and moods. Generations of neo-Latin pastoral poets followed suit, beginning with Giovanni Boccaccio (1313–1375), Baptista Mantuanus (Giovanni Battista Spagnoli, c. 1448–1516), and Giacopo Sannazaro (c. 1456–1530) in Italy, and including Joachim Camerarius (1500–1574) in Germany, Daniël Heinsius (1580–1655) in the Low Countries, Joachim Du Bellay (1522–1560) in France, and a host of others. Neo-Latin poets wrote didactic literature as well, so that Virgil also shaped both the form and language of poems like the *Syphilis sive de morbo gallico* (Syphilis, or, Concerning the French disease; 1530) of Girolamo Fracastoro (1478–1553), a poem noteworthy as an early literary treatment both of Columbus's voyages and of the venereal disease that Renaissance medicine traced to those voyages.

The zenith of literary accomplishment, however, was the epic, and as humanist poets labored to produce a new *Aeneid,* they turned to Virgil for guidance. Again Petrarch provides the initial model: his copy of Virgil, now in the Ambrosiana Library in Milan, was lovingly annotated, and he set his hopes for literary immortality on his *Africa,* a Virgilian epic in praise of Scipio Africanus, the great hero of the Punic Wars against Carthage. This poem, along with other Virgilian epics like the *Sphortias* of Francesco Filelfo (1398–1481), makes difficult reading for us today, largely because Renaissance literary theory flattened the characters into moral absolutes, either pure good or pure evil. To fit the *Aeneid* itself into this critical framework, Maffeo Vegio (1407–1458) wrote a supplement in which the characters act with a moral consistency lacking in Virgil's original. This theory reached its logical conclusion in the *Christias* (1535) of Marco Girolamo Vida (c. 1490–1566), who made a morally perfect Christ his new Aeneas—a decision that seems reasonable enough when we recall that many Renaissance scholars continued to believe that Virgil's *Fourth Eclogue* prophesied the coming of Christ.

Virgil and Vernacular Culture. Virgil's influence, however, was not restricted to those who read Latin comfortably, for he found able translators, many of them excellent poets in their own right, throughout Renaissance Europe. Beginning around 1540 a number of poets rendered Virgil into Italian, with the version of Annibale Caro (1507–1566) finally achieving canonical status. In France, Clément Marot (c. 1495–1544) and Du Bellay included Virgil translations in their poetic oeuvre, while the translations of Louis de Masures (c. 1510–c. 1580), Richard Le Blanc (c. 1510–c. 1574), and Robert (1541–1590) and Antoine (1542–1591) Le Chevalier d'Agneaux were frequently reprinted. German translations were made by Thomas Murner (1475–1537), Stephanus Riccius (1515–1588), and Johannes Spreng (1524–1601); Spanish ones by Enrique de Villena (1384–1434), Fray Luis de León (1527?–1591), Diego López, and Gregorio Hernandes de Velasco; and English ones by Gavin Douglas (1474–1522), Thomas Phaer (1510–1560), Thomas Twyne (1543–1613), Richard Stanyhurst (1547–1618), and Henry Howard, earl of Surrey (1517?–1547).

Accessible, therefore, in translation as well as in the original Latin, Virgil's poetry influenced much of the great vernacular literature of Renaissance Europe, where it was adapted to a surprising variety of ideological and aesthetic positions. Both Ludovico Ariosto (1474–1533) and Torquato Tasso (1544–1595), for example, wrote long poems on the struggles of Christian armies against the infidels; both were deeply indebted to Virgil, yet Ariosto's *Orlando furioso* (Mad Roland; 1516–1532) creates a fantasy world in which nothing appears to be taken seriously while Tasso's *Gerusalemme liberata* (Jerusalem delivered; 1575) is intimately engaged with the affirmation of the values and goals of the Catholic Reformation. As a poet whose works were commonly mined for sententious expressions of traditional moral and religious values, Virgil was regularly appropriated by the politically powerful in the emerging absolutist states of Renaissance Europe.

Yet Marot's translation of *Eclogue* 1 (1532), and through Marot *The Shepheardes Calender* (1579) of Edmund Spenser (1553–1599), succeeded in using Virgil to create a poetic voice that was poised between accommodation and dissent as it explored questions of religion, power, and patronage. The *Georgics* in turn provided Spenser with a framework in *The Faerie Queene* (second installment published 1596) within which to advocate a revision of aristocratic ideals from a preoccupation with leisure, grace, and courtly nonchalance to what would become the middle-class virtues of diligence, care, and hard work. As a poem about exploration and colonization, finally, the *Aeneid* provided a literary model within which several generations of Europeans could come to terms with the discovery and settlement of the New World; Shakespeare's *The Tempest* (1611), however, uses its Virgilian sources to raise troubling questions about power and its proper limits. What is more, while the story of Dido (*Aeneid* 4), who kills herself when Aeneas leaves her behind for political reasons, was regularly used to support the traditional gender hierarchy in Renaissance Europe, Shakespeare's *Antony and Cleopatra* (1606–1607) can also be read as a reversal of the values generally assigned to *Aeneid* 4.

Virgil and the Arts. Virgil's influence in the visual arts of the Renaissance begins with the manuscripts and books in which his poetry was transmitted. Many of the dozens of Renaissance Virgil manuscripts were illuminated, and hand-painted illuminations are found in early printed books as well; a notable example is the frontispiece to the 1476 Venice edition painted by the master of the London Pliny (London, British Library). These hand-painted illuminations were gradually replaced by woodcuts, with the most famous Virgilian cycle being that in the Sebastian Brant edition, printed in Strasbourg in 1502.

The *Aeneid* forms the subject of a half dozen fresco cycles in the palaces of sixteenth-century Italy, the most interesting of which is perhaps the one in the Palazzo Spada in Rome; this *Sala dell'Eneide* (middle of the sixteenth century) presents Virgil's poem mediated by the Neoplatonic allegory of Cristoforo Landino (1424–1498), whose commentary was very influential during this period. Several other themes from the *Aeneid* proved to be perennial favorites with Renaissance artists. The death of Laocoön, for example, was depicted in several woodcuts by Marcantonio Raimondi (c. 1480–c. 1534), in a caricature by Titian (c. 1487–1576), and in a painting by El Greco (1541–1614), among others. The flight of Aeneas from Troy attracted special attention, with its inclusion in the Vatican fresco *Fire in the Borgo* of Raphael (1483–1520) and its rendering in the marble group of *Aeneas, Anchises, and Ascanius* (c. 1618–1619) by Gian Lorenzo Bernini (1598–1680). The story of Dido also proved attractive to artists working in several media, providing a subject for a grisaille by Andrea Mantegna (1431–1506), a wedding chest by Liberale da Verona (c. 1445–1526), and an oil painting by Jacopo Tintoretto (1518–1594). Even the minor arts like medals, ceramics, and tapestries embraced Virgilian themes.

Virgil also proved influential in Renaissance music. There are several motets based on *Aeneid* 4, including those by such masters as Josquin des Prez (c. 1440–1521), Orlando di Lasso (c. 1532–1594), and Adrian Willaert (1490–1562); this work culminated in one of the most famous of all Dido operas, Henry Purcell's *Dido and Aeneas* (1689).

See also Commonplace Books; Emblem; Epic; Neo-Latin Literature and Language; Translation; *and biographies of figures mentioned in this entry.*

BIBLIOGRAPHY

Bono, Barbara. *Literary Transvaluation: From Vergilian Epic to Shakespearean Tragicomedy.* Berkeley and Los Angeles, 1984. A thoughtful discussion of the treatment of Virgil by a number of Renaissance dramatists, culminating in Shakespeare.

Fagiolo, Marcello, ed. *Virgilio nell'arte e nella cultura europea.* Rome, 1981. Ostensibly the catalog of an exhibition held in Rome for the bimillennium of Virgil's death, this book is also the most complete source available on Virgil's role in Renaissance art.

Kallendorf, Craig. *In Praise of Aeneas: Virgil and Epideictic Rhetoric in the Early Italian Renaissance.* Hanover, N.H., 1989. Examines the role of the *Aeneid* in Renaissance literary theory and in the work of Petrarch, Boccaccio, Salutati, Vegio, and Landino.

Kallendorf, Craig. *Virgil and the Myth of Venice: Books and Readers in the Italian Renaissance.* Oxford, 1999. Describes moral, religious, and social strategies for reading Virgil, with a focus on Renaissance Venice.

Zabughin, Vladimiro. *Vergilio nel Rinascimento italiano.* 2 vols. Bologna, Italy, 1923–1925. The classic study of Virgil in Renaissance culture.

CRAIG KALLENDORF

VIRGINITY AND CELIBACY.

Virginity and celibacy are not the same. Virgins are usually celibate, but celibates are not necessarily virgins. Celibacy, the state of being unmarried, is a matter of public knowledge, whereas virginity is essentially private.

Virginity as a Christian Ideal.

Western Christianity put a high value on lifelong virginity. Like their medieval predecessors, many Catholic saints of the Renaissance period were men and women who zealously preserved their virginity. The new religious orders of the fifteenth and sixteenth centuries all provided an institutional setting for a lifetime of virginity, just as the earlier monastic and mendicant orders had done. Celibacy was the means to the preservation of virginity. Officially the requirement for monks and nuns was celibacy, not virginity per se, since those who had once been married were not excluded, but it was virginity that was praised and encouraged. The requirement of celibacy also applied to priests. Whatever the original reason, it strengthened the spiritual authority of the priesthood and the demarcation between priests and the laity.

For most Christians the way to observe the ideal of virginity was to remain a virgin until marriage. This applied especially to women. All single women were supposed to be virgins. The ranks of the saints continued to be filled with young women who resisted the loss of their virginity, whether to brutal attackers or to parentally approved bridegrooms. Joan of Arc (c. 1412–1431) had rejected at least one suitor in her native village and later fought off the advances of men guarding her in prison. The norm for more ordinary women was to be first a virgin and then a willing bride. Not to be a virgin was considered an obstacle to marriage and could justify rejection by a potential bridegroom. On the other hand, ecclesiastical courts made it possible for a man who had deflowered a virgin to rectify his fault by marrying her. A young woman whose family opposed her marriage to a man she preferred might force their hand by confronting them with the fact that she had lost her virginity to him.

Ideas about Celibacy. Desiderius Erasmus (c. 1466–1536), the illegitimate son of a priest and a celibate himself, had doubts about the value of clerical celibacy. The Protestant Reformers of the early sixteenth century called for its abolition, mainly on the grounds that the clergy should not be set apart from the laity. Martin Luther, John Calvin, and others made a point of getting married. Protestant treatises throughout the sixteenth and seventeenth centuries praised marriage as a spiritual institution of greater value than monasticism.

The Roman Catholic attitude toward marriage was ambivalent. While continuing to exalt celibacy the church regarded marriage as valuable. Over the course of centuries it had steadily increased its participation in the formation and regulation of marriage. This culminated in the inclusion of marriage among the sacraments at the Council of Florence in 1439 and the Council of Trent's requirement in 1563 that a priest had to be present at a wedding. Catholic writing on marriage stressed its value as a deterrent to illicit sexuality. For those who did not have the superior talent for virginity it was, in Saint Paul's words, "better to marry than burn" (1 Cor. 7:9).

Popular attitudes toward celibacy seem to have been almost as ambivalent as that of the Roman Catholic Church. People tended to regard celibacy with awe but assumed that marriage was a normal part of ordinary life. Luther's father expressed profound disappointment at his son's decision to become a monk and yet presented his monastery with a generous gift. Parents and other kin on almost all levels of society put the making of marriage alliances close to the center of their concerns. Elizabeth I of England, known as the virgin queen, used her presumed marital availability as an effective tool of diplomacy. Misogynistic literature, which often took the form of male complaints about the burdens of marriage, can be seen as a kind of praise of celibacy.

The Celibate Population. The western European marriage pattern, in contrast to what prevailed in much of the rest of the world, included a late age at marriage for most couples and permanent celibacy for a fairly large proportion of the population, although among patricians and nobles earlier marriage, especially of women, was common. Late-marrying adults, widows, and widowers formed a significant group of temporary celibates.

The largest category of celibates was the Catholic clergy, both secular and monastic. Secular clergy in minor orders did not take an absolute vow of celibacy but were not permitted to marry more than once or to marry widows, thus reinforcing the ideal of virginity before marriage. Many priests, celibates according to the letter of the law, were known to have concubines, who were wives in all but name. In the course of the Catholic Reformation priestly celibacy was more strictly enforced.

The main category of temporary celibates was servants. Many men and women in the middle and lower ranks of society spent several years as servants in the households of their masters. To be married was considered incompatible with being a household servant. Other occupational categories of the unmarried were soldiers and prostitutes. These represented the negative side of celibacy, rather than its link with virginity. If a prostitute married it was taken as a sign that she had reformed.

An important demographic feature of this period was the large number of widows, who remarried at a much lower rate than widowers, especially among the poor and less powerful. In the upper ranks of society the celibacy of young widows was generally not accepted. Older widows with sons, however, did not usually remarry.

One group of celibate men comprised younger sons of propertied families. Among the very wealthy, especially the landed nobility, younger sons were designated for careers that implied celibacy, such as the military and the Catholic clergy. Similarly, wealthy families would designate some daughters for the monastic life and splurge on dowries for one or two others. In Protestant countries wealthy families continued to use strategies that promoted celibacy for some of their offspring.

See also **Marriage**; **Religious Orders**; **Sexuality**.

BIBLIOGRAPHY

Primary Work

Les lamentations de Matheolus et Le livre de leësce de Jehan le Fèvre, de Resson (The lamentations of Matheolus and the book of joy of Jehan le Fèvre). Edited by A. G. Van Hamel. 2 vols. Paris, 1892, 1905. Vol. 1 contains the misogynistic attack by Matheolus on the miseries of marriage that was written in Latin in the early fourteenth century and translated into French by Jehan le Fèvre around 1370. Vol. 2 has an informative essay by the editor about its continuing influence into the sixteenth century.

Secondary Works

Flandrin, Jean-Louis. "Repression and Change in the Sexual Life of Young People in Medieval and Early Modern Times." In *Family and Sexuality in French History.* Edited by Robert Wheaton and Tamara K. Hareven. Philadelphia, 1980. Pages 27–48.

Hair, Paul, ed. *Before the Bawdy Court: Selections from Church Court and Other Records.* London, 1972.

Hajnal, John. "European Marriage Patterns in Perspective." In *Population in History.* Edited by D. V. Glass and D. E. C. Eversley. London, 1965. Pages 101–143. A groundbreaking work.

Laslett, Peter. *The World We Have Lost: Further Explored.* 3d ed. New York, 1984. An important overview of the lives and values of ordinary people, including their sexual morality. It first appeared in 1965.

Thomas, Keith. "The Double Standard." *Journal of the History of Ideas* 20 (1959): 195–216.

BEATRICE GOTTLIEB

VIRTÙ. *Virtù* is a term usually associated particularly with Niccolò Machiavelli, but it was used by him and by other Italian Renaissance writers (as were its cognates in other languages, such as French and English) in various senses. *Virtù* derives from the Latin *virtus* (from *vir,* man), and denotes the qualities that men, and human beings generally, should possess.

A common sense of *virtù* during the Renaissance (and the most common sense after) is that of "moral virtue," and it is opposed to *vizio* (vice). This sense, roughly equivalent to *bontà,* in the sense of moral "goodness," sometimes occurs in Machiavelli; thus, chapter 15 of *The Prince* discusses the qualities "for which men, and especially rulers, are praised or blamed," and lists various virtues or good qualities. When Machiavelli uses *virtù* in the plural (*le virtù*), it almost always denotes virtues or good qualities. *Virtù* in this sense denotes human qualities, considered with regard to their morality.

Virtù also frequently denoted natural "power," "faculty," or "talent," as well as "efficacy." This sense survives in references to the "virtues" of drugs, medicines, and precious stones. It is uncommon in Machiavelli, but he does say that skillful archers "know well the power (*virtù*) of their bows" (*The Prince,* chapter 6). *Uomini virtuosi* sometimes meant "talented men," those skilled in writing, painting, and sculpture; this sense still survives in "virtuoso" (now, especially, a skillful musical performer).

Machiavelli most often used *virtù,* however, in a political or military context, denoting primarily the "ability" to act effectively or successfully in politics or war. This use of *virtù* implies a certain unscrupulousness or ruthlessness, which are not characteristics of good men. Political *virtù* denotes skill in founding or ruling states, and military *virtù* denotes preparing for war sensibly and skillfully, fighting strongly and courageously.

Machiavelli contrasts political and military *virtù* with *ignavia* (indolence), *viltà* (baseness, weakness), *ozio* (sloth), and *debolezza* (weakness). He says that "those of our rulers who lost their principalities, after having ruled them for many years, should not lament their bad luck (*la fortuna*) but blame their own indolence (*ignavia*)" (*The Prince,* chapter 24). He ends this chapter thus: "Only those defences that are under your own control and based on your own ability (*virtù*) are effective, certain and lasting."

There is a frequent antithesis in Machiavelli between *virtù* and *fortuna.* If *virtù* here broadly denotes human capacity, *fortuna* denotes a more complex set of ideas: a nonhuman force that intervenes in human affairs, good and bad luck, favor or help, favorable or unfavorable conditions or circumstances, and success and failure. Machiavelli thought that able and enterprising men were best fitted to overcome unfavorable circumstances and hostile forces, and that in contemporary Italy (unlike in Spain, France, and Germany), there were few men of *virtù,* and that *fortuna* tended to dominate. There was much more *virtù* in the ancient world, especially in the Roman Republic (Machiavelli's ideal state), among the citizens generally, as well as the leaders. Whereas in principalities rulers tend to be suspicious of talented men active in public life, in republican Rome the laws and institutions (in short, the political culture) fostered the development of individual talents and of public spirit. Machiavelli thought that human beings need to be under pressure to work well, and there is an important connection between citizen *virtù,* public spirit, and a flourishing state.

See also **Machiavelli**, Niccolò, *subentry on* **The Political Theorist.**

BIBLIOGRAPHY

Price, Russell. "The Senses of *Virtù* in Machiavelli." *European Studies Review* 3 (1973): 315–345.

Seigel, Jerrold E. "*Virtù* in and since the Renaissance." In *Dictionary of the History of Ideas.* Edited by Philip P. Wiener. Vol. 4. New York, 1973. Pages 476–486.

Whitfield, J. H. *Machiavelli.* Oxford, 1947. Pages 92–105.

Wood, Neal. "Machiavelli's Concept of *Virtù* Reconsidered." *Political Studies* 15 (1967): 159–172.

RUSSELL PRICE

VISCONTI, GIANGALEAZZO (1351–1402), first duke of Milan. Visconti was one of Renaissance Italy's most effective rulers. His imperial investiture as duke in 1395 helped Milan rise to rank among Italy's five dominant states. Had he not died of the plague in 1402, Milan might even have conquered Florence. Instead, as soon as he died, the duchy began to shrink, and it never regained the full extent of his dominion.

Giangaleazzo's noble Visconti ancestors had played a leading role in the city-state of Milan for centuries. His father, Galeazzo II, was co-lord of Milan with two brothers, one of whom died young; together, they developed a potent Visconti dominion with connections throughout Europe. Ten-year-old Giangaleazzo received from the king of France both a noble title and a royal bride.

When his father died in 1378, Giangaleazzo joined his last surviving uncle, Bernabò, as co-lord of Milan. Both men were ambitious, intelligent, and ruthless, but they differed in temperament and policy. In 1385, the normally cautious Giangaleazzo captured and deposed Bernabò, imprisoned him, and possibly put him to death. Giangaleazzo then became sole lord of Milan.

In his last seventeen years, Giangaleazzo built a core state in western Lombardy through a precociously centralized princely administration. He regularized the dominion's finances and neutralized the corrosive effects of local feuds and privileges. He encouraged agricultural development and commercial expansion, recognizing the prosperity of his wealthy dominion as a foundation for success. Giangaleazzo established peace and security throughout the dominion, but his ambitions to dominate northern and central Italy undermined principled efforts to apply laws and policies evenhandedly.

A careful, penetrating thinker, Giangaleazzo shunned crowds and preferred to stay in his favorite castle at Pavia. He relied on well-chosen councillors to help conceive and execute policy. He also kept a network of intelligence agents throughout Europe. Although Giangaleazzo could afford to hire substantial armies, he favored reason, guile, and persuasion in achieving his ends. Ambitious but prudent, he avoided fighting battles he was unsure of winning, particularly against powerful Venice.

His preference for simplicity notwithstanding, Giangaleazzo maintained an elegant court, understanding the political value of princely hospitality and splendor. His monumental ambitions were also reflected in the architecture that he initiated, particularly Milan's huge Duomo (cathedral) and the Certosa di Pavia, an elegant monastery.

Giangaleazzo's 1395 purchase of the title duke of Milan from the Holy Roman Emperor was a personal and dynastic triumph that lifted Milan alongside Burgundy as an emerging princely power among the monarchies of early Renaissance Europe. His army's 1401 victory over German invaders at Brescia suggested that an Italian prince could best those monarchs even on the battlefield.

Giangaleazzo's overall ability to carry out his grandiose princely agenda led his Florentine enemies to identify him personally as "the Viper," which was the Visconti family emblem. As they watched him take over the surrounding city-states of Pisa, Siena, Perugia, and Bologna in 1398–1402, the Florentine humanist propagandists cast him as a cruel tyrant who was swallowing all of Italy through cunning and deceit. They saw his sudden death of plague on the apparent eve of his triumph over Florence as something of a miracle. For Giangaleazzo's Milanese subjects, however, his death was a disaster, and his achievements were never equaled.

See also **Milan**.

BIBLIOGRAPHY

Bueno de Mesquita, Daniel. *Giangaleazzo Visconti, Duke of Milan (1351–1402): A Study in the Political Career of an Italian Despot.* Cambridge, U.K., 1941. The only scholarly book-length treatment of Giangaleazzo in English.

Cognasso, Francesco. *I Visconti.* Milan, 1987. A useful Italian overview of Giangaleazzo and the Visconti dynasty.

GREGORY P. LUBKIN

VITORIA, FRANCISCO DE (Francisco de Arcaya y Compludo; c. 1486–1546), Spanish jurist and theologian. Vitoria was born in northern Spain, either in Vitoria or in Burgos, to Pedro de Arcaya and Catalina de Compludo, prosperous Basque parents. His mother may have been related to the famous Jewish converts Pablo de Santa María (1353–1435) and Alonso de Cartagena (1385/86–1456). Vitoria entered the Dominican Order at the Convent of San Pablo in Burgos around 1505. He was then selected to attend the Dominican College of Saint Jacques in Paris, where he studied and taught from about 1509 to 1522.

Although Vitoria was more a scholastic than a humanist, the humanist climate of Paris left a distinct mark on him; he read widely in Latin and Greek, attained a level of Latin eloquence that impressed even Erasmus and Juan Luis Vives, and became devoted to moral philosophy. His early studies were eclectic, guided mainly by Juan de Celaya, a nominalist, and Pierre Crockaert, a nominalist convert to Thomism whom Vitoria finally followed in embracing Thomas Aquinas's moral theology as the centerpiece of his own thinking.

After earning the licentiate and doctorate in theology in 1522 Vitoria was recalled to Spain and assigned to teach theology at the Dominican College of San Gregorio in Valladolid. In 1526 he was named to hold the highest-ranking chair in the theology faculty at the University of Salamanca. Vitoria held this post and resided in the Dominican monastery of

San Esteban until his death twenty years later. He became widely known for his moral teachings, particularly on the relationship between natural law and political justice.

An eloquent and compelling teacher, Vitoria profoundly influenced theological education in Salamanca, both through his own lecturing and by training generations of future professors. He brought to Salamanca one of the chief pedagogical innovations of the Parisian revival of Thomism by lecturing on Thomas Aquinas's *Summa theologica* instead of the traditional *Sentences* of Peter Lombard. His fellow Dominicans copied the practice and in 1561 the preference for Thomas was finally codified. Vitoria is also credited with importing to Salamanca the Parisian custom of dictation, or lecturing slowly enough to allow the students to copy the lecture down verbatim.

Vitoria's doctrines are known solely through somewhat imperfect notes that his students took on his lectures, which were first published in 1557. Surviving are commentaries on Thomas and Lombard that Vitoria delivered as ordinary lectures during the academic year, as well as thirteen shorter *relectiones,* more informal, popular lectures on specific practical moral or theological problems that he gave annually from 1528 to 1540. The latter covered subjects as varied as homicide, marriage and divorce, papal and conciliar authority, Spanish political rights in the Indies, and magic. He spoke out unreservedly on the political issues of his day, criticizing the Spanish crown's military ambitions, the conduct of the conquistadors in America, and papal resistance to ecclesiastical reform. Vitoria's academic progeny, who collectively are known as "the School of Salamanca," continued to publicize many of the central ideas of his moral theology throughout the sixteenth century. Some of its better known members include Domingo de Soto, Luis de Molina, Melchor Cano, Bartolomé de Carranza, and Diego de Covarrubias.

Vitoria's Political Theory and its Influence.

Vitoria is best remembered today for his application of Thomist natural-law theory to the problems of international politics. Although he has been called the "founder of international law," he did not share the modern concept of international law with such later thinkers as Hugo Grotius; for him the "law of nations" was part of a universal God-given order. He based his political theology on a four-part juridical hierarchy: divine law (the principles that God observed in creating the universe); natural law (the principles that rational creatures intuitively discern

by reason); the law of nations or *ius gentium* (the body of human law enacted by the common agreement of all human societies); and human positive law (the specific laws of individual human societies). From this starting point Vitoria argued, as had Aquinas, that political societies were natural organisms and political authority formed part of the natural order. He saw monarchy as the most natural form of government, but agreed that in theory other forms were legitimate. The power of monarchs was not simply God-given but also derived, in a crucial sense, from the community. Thus monarchs were themselves subject to the laws of nature and bound in conscience to obey them.

Vitoria did not intend this theory to provide legitimation for political resistance. His arguments had a sharp anti-Protestant edge; he thought that Luther and other Protestant theologians offered Christians an excuse to rebel against legitimate rulers. Protestants argued that people's depraved, sinful nature made them incapable of discerning or following natural law without the help of divine grace; political rights and political authority, therefore, depended on grace (which was not universally available), not on nature. Vitoria insisted that rights derived from nature, not from grace; thus the authority of any ruler was independent of his spiritual condition, and no one could claim a right to resist an unjust or ungodly ruler. Although political power derived from the community, it was transferred unconditionally to the ruler, and the subjects did not retain any right to withdraw their obedience.

Later Jesuit thinkers Francisco Suárez and Juan de Mariana, whose political ideas were certainly indebted to Vitoria, drew the more radical conclusion that since power derived from the community, the community could revoke it under extreme circumstances. Thus, ironically, Vitoria's ideas helped contribute in the long run to Catholic theories of popular sovereignty that converged with those of radical Protestants and ultimately with the resistance theory of John Locke.

Vitoria is most famous for his challenge to the Spanish crown's claims to dominion in the Americas. He argued in *Relectio de Indiis* (On the American Indians; 1537) that the law of nations gave the pagan tribes in America political sovereignty over their own affairs, and thus the right to reject Spanish dominion. As rational men, the Indians could not be denied their sovereignty on the mere grounds that (as Juan Ginés de Sepúlveda had argued) they were less civilized than the Europeans, or that (as many others argued) they were not Christians. Vitoria did not refute Spanish claims in America altogether, but he sternly denounced colonial atrocities. His judgments on this subject, which the Spanish crown greeted coolly, became the basis for further debate on Spanish policy in the Americas for more than a century to come.

See also **Americas; Political Thought.**

BIBLIOGRAPHY

Primary Works

Vitoria, Francisco de. *Comentarios a la Secunda Secundae de Santo Tomás.* Edited by Vicente Beltrán de Heredia. 6 vols. Salamanca, Spain, 1932–1952.

Vitoria, Francisco de. *Political Writings.* Edited by Anthony Pagden and Jeremy Lawrance. Cambridge, U.K., 1991.

Vitoria, Francisco de. *Relecciones teológicas del Maestro Fray Francisco de Vitoria: Edición crítica, con facsímil de códices y ediciones príncipes, variantes, versión castellana, notas e introducción.* Edited by Luis G. Alonso Getino. 3 vols. Madrid, 1993–1935.

Vitoria, Francisco de. *Relectio de Indiis.* Edited by Luciano Pereña and José M. Pérez Prendes. Madrid, 1967.

Vitoria, Francisco de. *Relectio de iure belli, o, paz dinámica.* Edited by Luciano Pereña et al. Madrid, 1981.

Secondary Works

Fernández-Santamaría, J. A. *The State, War, and Peace: Spanish Political Thought in the Renaissance, 1516–1559.* London and New York, 1977.

Hamilton, Bernice. *Political Thought in Sixteenth-Century Spain: A Study of the Political Ideas of Vitoria, De Soto, Suárez, and Molina.* Oxford, 1963.

Noreña, Carlos G. *Studies in Spanish Renaissance Thought.* The Hague, Netherlands, 1975.

Skinner, Quentin. *The Foundations of Modern Political Thought.* 2 vols. Cambridge, U.K., 1978.

KATHERINE ELLIOT VAN LIERE

VITRUVIUS. *See* **Architecture,** *subentry on* **Architectural Treatises.**

VITTORINO DA FELTRE (Vittorino Rambaldoni; 1378–1446), Italian humanist, scholar, educator. Born to a local notary in Feltre, Vittorino left home around 1390 and began a lengthy association with the University of Padua.

Education and Early Career. Vittorino enrolled in the arts faculty and pursued studies in dialectic, rhetoric, and philosophy, as well as canon law. While at Padua he dedicated himself in particular to the *studia humanitatis.* His first teacher was Giovanni Conversino da Ravenna (1343–1408) who himself had been a student of Petrarch. Later he studied under Gasparino Barzizza (1370–1431), widely considered the most outstanding Latin scholar of his generation and the holder of the university chair of rhetoric. Barzizza's influence on Vittorino was significant for two reasons. First, he introduced Vittorino to the latest humanist scholarship on Cicero. Second, Vittorino boarded with Barzizza and found in his teacher an example of hospitality that he later imitated in his own career. He received the doctorate in arts from Padua in 1410.

Vittorino's academic career was characterized both by financial need and an ongoing desire for study. As a student he supported himself by teaching Latin as a *magister puerorum,* that is, a teacher of beginning students. Even after completing his degree he continued his studies by taking up mathematics and Greek. As he could not afford the fees for studying mathematics with Biagio Pelacani da Parma (c. 1347–1416), he offered to act as a household servant for the professor to pay for his studies. This arrangement continued for about six months during which time he applied himself to Euclid's *Elements of Geometry* and possibly to algebra. These studies left their mark as he continued to tutor others in mathematics for the remainder of his career. In 1415 Vittorino left Padua for Venice, where he studied Greek with Guarino da Verona and George of Trebizond. Vittorino paid for this by offering Latin lessons in return. This experience of undertaking a broad curriculum while in difficult financial circumstances was not lost upon him when he began to operate his own school.

In 1419 Vittorino returned to Padua, became a highly successful teacher, and more fully developed his educational methods. He continued the practice of earlier university masters of taking students into his own home. He varied his fees depending on the financial status of the individual student. He refused to accept more students than he could responsibly instruct. Moreover, as a person of irreproachable character he also showed concern for the moral development of his students. He insisted on high ethical standards and did not hesitate to send away any student who did not meet them. He gained so much respect as a teacher that the university offered him the chair of rhetoric as Barzizza's successor in 1422. With that he set aside earlier thoughts of entering religious life and accepted the post. His association with Padua did not continue very long, however. He soon found that the tumultuous atmosphere of student life at Padua was not conducive to his classroom style nor to the close supervision of the adolescents in his charge that he believed necessary. This led Vittorino to resign the chair in April 1423 and leave Padua for Venice in order to operate his own school on his own terms.

The School at Mantua. In 1423 Vittorino received an invitation that not only changed the direction of his own career, but also had an enormous impact on the history of European education. Gianfrancesco Gonzaga, Marquis of Mantua, asked Vittorino to come to Mantua and establish a school for the education of his own children as well as those of other notable families of the region. Vittorino accepted this invitation largely on account of his hope of influencing the character of the future ruler of Mantua and consequently the well-being of his subjects. Nevertheless, he insisted that he enjoy the freedom to operate the school without interference from the palace. In subsequent years he showed great loyalty to the house of Gonzaga, but never felt restrained from frank criticism of the marquis when that was necessary to uphold the standards of the school. He remained in Mantua until his death more than twenty years later.

The school that Vittorino established at Mantua was called the Casa Giocosa, or "Pleasant House." In this former urban villa of the Gonzaga family he offered instruction to a limited number of students from the Gonzaga family, local nobles, and promising students from families of slender means. The house was stripped of its opulent furnishings but retained a bright and pleasant atmosphere. The total student population rose to about seventy, of whom about half were scholarship students. His young charges included boys and a few girls ranging in age from four to twenty years of age. The majority were adolescents, however, and so the Casa Giocosa functioned largely as a secondary school. This was a boarding school in which the students lived apart from the distractions of the ducal court and its courtiers.

In this setting Vittorino institutionalized the ideas for educational reform that humanists had expressed since the late fourteenth century. The rediscovery of ancient pedagogical manuals such as Quintilian's *Institutio oratoria* and Cicero's *Orator* stood at the heart of this reform. He also instituted practices based on his own earlier experiences as a student and teacher. The curriculum included not only those subjects most associated with the humanist program, that is, grammar, rhetoric, history, poetry, and moral philosophy based on Latin and Greek authors; it also included mathematics, music, philosophy, and religious instruction. Most prominent among the authors read by the students of Vittorino were Cicero and Virgil. The readings also included Livy, Homer, Demosthenes, Xenophon, Aristophanes, Sophocles, Aeschylus, St. John Chrysostom, and St. Augustine.

This list points to the role of Greek in the curriculum. While it did not stand as the equal to Latin, it was offered regularly to those students who were capable of studying it. For this purpose Vittorino brought Greek scholars to Mantua to assist him in this work, including George of Trebizond and Theodore of Gaza.

Vittorino's methods also included attentiveness to the physical and psychological needs of his pupils and to the learning environment generally. In Mantua, as in his prior posts, Vittorino was aware of the need to avoid overcrowding in the classroom and steadfastly refused to admit more students than he and his assistants could reasonably instruct. Academic material was presented in a graduated fashion so that students did not become too easily discouraged by their tasks. Finally, subject matter was alternated to avoid boredom. The classical ideal of the *mens sana in corpore sano* (a sound mind in a sound body) also found expression in physical exercise as a part of the daily routine. As mundane as those reforms may sound now, in their day they reflected a novel attentiveness to the individual learning needs of the student.

Vittorino's concern for his students reached to all aspects of their lives. In addition to the intellectual and physical progress of his students, Vittorino took pains to assist them in their spiritual lives. Each school day began with religious services at the local cathedral. He regularly participated in the sacrament of penance and encouraged his students to do likewise. He addressed the character and moral formation of each of his students. All of this was directed to the ultimate purpose of his school: to train the individual to be of service to society.

Vittorino's Accomplishment. Over the years Vittorino educated a number of prominent Renaissance figures. The future marquis of Mantua, Ludovico Gonzaga, was among the first students. Federico da Montefeltro, the future duke of Urbino, and Taddeo de' Manfredi, the future lord of Imola, are also counted among the princes formed under the care of Vittorino. Prominent humanists such as Niccolò Perotti, Lorenzo Valla, and Giovanni Andrea Bussi, also studied there. Other humanists such as Guarino Guarini, Francesco Filelfo, and Poggio Bracciolini so respected Vittorino's work that they entrusted their son's educations to the Mantuan schoolmaster. A small number of girls from the Gonzaga family were also educated in the Casa Giocosa. These included the Marquis Ludovico Gonzaga's wife, the marchioness Barbara of Brandenburg, and his sister Cecilia Gonzaga. Cecilia was known for her command of Greek at an early age.

Unlike many other humanists, Vittorino did not write a pedagogical treatise or textbook. Very few of his letters have survived. What we know of his methods is the result largely of the recollections of his former students and their own work as teachers and theorists. It should be noted that these students of his were unanimous in their praise for this pioneer of the humanist curriculum. In his life he played an important part in the transformation of European education. He provided not only an influential new model for the future European boarding school; he also offered a new model for the schoolmaster who was to lead such a school.

BIBLIOGRAPHY

Primary Works

Vespasiano da Bisticci. *Lives of Illustrious Men of the Fifteenth Century.* Translated by William George and Emily Waters. London, 1926. Translation of *Vite di uomini illustri del secolo quindici.*

Vittorino da Feltre. "Cinque lettere di Vittorino da Feltre." Edited by Alessandro Luzio. *Archivio Veneto.* Vol. 36. 1888. Pages 329–341.

Secondary Works

Garin, Eugenio. *L'educazione in Europa, 1400–1600.* Rome, 1976.

Grendler, Paul F. *Schooling in Renaissance Italy: Literacy and Learning, 1300–1600.* Baltimore, 1989.

Woodward, William Harrison. *Vittorino da Feltre and other Humanist Educators: Essays and Versions.* Cambridge, U.K., 1897. Reprints: New York 1963; Toronto and Buffalo, N.Y., 1996.

PAUL V. MURPHY

VIVES, JUAN LUIS (1492–1540), Spanish humanist, friend and correspondent of Erasmus, More, Budé, Cranevelt, and Linacre. Born of a prominent merchant family in the Jewish community of Valencia, Vives wrote nostalgically of his native city throughout his life. Vives's parents and relatives on both sides of his family were persecuted by the Inquisition. After a long trial in 1525, his father was executed by burning, and his mother's remains were exhumed and burned in 1528. After his departure from the country, at age seventeen, Vives never returned despite the offer of a professorship of humanistic studies left open by the death of Antonio de Nebrija at the University of Alcalá in 1523.

Early Life. In 1509 Vives left Valencia for the University of Paris, where he studied until 1512 at the ascetic and reform-minded College of Montaigu, whose alumni included Desiderius Erasmus, John

Juan Luis Vives. Engraving after a sixteenth-century painting. BIBLIOTECA NACIONAL, MADRID

Calvin, Ignatius Loyola, and François Rabelais. From Paris, Vives went to Bruges, where he remained until 1517, when he moved to Louvain. He served as preceptor to William of Croy, the nineteen-year-old archbishop-elect of Toledo, from 1517 until William's premature death in 1521. He had already won the admiration of Erasmus, Guillaume Budé, and other humanists while in Bruges, and in 1519 was granted permission to deliver public lectures without holding an academic appointment at the University of Louvain, a unique exception. The 1520 publication of Vives's diatribe against the scholastic training familiar to him from his years at Paris, *In pseudodialecticos* (Against the pseudo-dialecticians), brought him to the attention of Thomas More and initiated his career as a leading northern European humanist.

England: Pedagogical Writings. At the request of his friend Erasmus, then preparing his own critical revisions of the Augustinian corpus, Vives wrote an extensive commentary on Augustine's *De civitate Dei* (The city of God) published in 1522 and dedicated to Henry VIII. Vives's annotations included controversial Erasmian opinions regarding the Immaculate Conception and predestination, sharp criticism of the gluttony and lustfulness of the clergy and papacy, and the observation that infant baptism was not practiced in the Apostolic Church. The responses of Vives's royal patron, as well as the scholarly audience, were disappointing. Nevertheless, in 1523 Cardinal Wolsey appointed Vives to a lectureship at Corpus Christi College at Oxford University, and supported his curricular reforms there. As he gained and then lost royal favor during the political and religious conflicts of the next five years, Vives divided his time between the Low Countries and England.

In 1524 he returned briefly to Bruges, where he married Margarita Valdaura, daughter of another expatriated Valencian, Bernardo Valdaura. Vives addressed his treatise on civic responsibility, *De subventione pauperum* (On aid to the poor; 1526), to the magistrates of Bruges, his adopted city. This work proposes that the war victims dispersed throughout Europe be treated like native citizens.

First for his arguments advocating European unity against the threat of Süleyman's troops, and then for his attempts to intervene on behalf of Catherine of Aragon, Vives eventually lost his position at Oxford as well as royal favor. In 1527 Catherine invited him to return as preceptor to Mary, princess of Wales, but his visits to England ended with house arrest and banishment in 1528.

Vives retired to Bruges in 1529. Although England eventually proved inhospitable to him, Vives's friendships with More and with other English humanists were mutually productive, and two of his most significant treatises on pedagogy were connected with his earliest visits to England: *De institutione feminae Christianae* (Education of the Christian woman), dedicated to Catherine of Aragon and completed in 1523, and *De ratione studii puerilis epistolae duae* (On the right method of instruction for children; 1523), a practical and theoretical guide to pedagogy written for the education of Princess Mary. The former advocated an ascetic life for women, but argued that education was compatible with female virtue, citing the example of More's daughters, whose tutor Richard Hyrde translated the work into English. Encouraged by the success of the *De institutione feminae Christianae,* he wrote a sequel on the duties of the husband, *De officio mariti* (1528), dedicated to his countryman Juan Borja, duke of Gandia. Vives's other pedagogical works were widely translated and used in schools throughout Europe; they included the *Introductio ad sapientiam* (Introduction to knowledge; 1524) and *Linguae latinae exercitatio* (Latin exercises; 1538), both

of which advocated empirical methods of education in the interest of social and moral reform.

Moral and Social Reform. Although clearly influenced by Flemish social reforms and by More's *Utopia,* Vives's enlightened and practical interpretation of Christian charity was far in advance of other proposals of the time. The works of Vives's intellectual maturity brought together his most powerful humanistic analyses of social, political, moral, and pedagogical issues during the bitter years following the deaths of Erasmus and More: *De concordia et discordia in humano genere* (Peace and conflict in human society; 1529), intended to inspire the emperor Charles V to meet the challenge of moral as well as political leadership; *De disciplinis libri xx* (Twenty books on education; 1531), not only a revolutionary program of education but also a meditation on the corruption and reform of human culture; and *De anima et vita libri tres* (Three books on the soul and on life; 1538), which has been viewed as initiating the empirical study of psychology. His unfinished apologetic *De veritae fidei Christianae* (On the true Christian faith), was published posthumously in 1543.

Assessment. Vives's contribution to humanistic studies embraces philosophy, philology, pedagogy, and social reform. His writings on education were translated into the major European languages and were influential among Catholics and Protestants alike as both practical and theoretical texts. His treatises on the intellect and the emotions contributed to the development of modern concepts of psychology based on observation and experience rather than the traditional Aristotelian categories central to Scholasticism. Vives's advocacy of the social assimilation of refugees and the education of the poor significantly influenced social programs and political and moral philosophy.

See also **Humanism,** *subentry on* **Spain.**

BIBLIOGRAPHY

Primary Works

Vives, Juan Luis. *In pseudodialecticos.* Edited by Charles Fantazzi. Leiden, Netherlands, 1979.

Vives, Juan Luis. *Joannis Ludovici Vivis Valentini opera omnia.* 1555. 8 vols. Reprint, Valencia, Spain, 1782–1790. Edited by Gregorio Mayans y Siscar. Facsimile, London, 1964.

Vives, Juan Luis. *Opera omnia.* Edited by Antonio Mestre. Valencia, Spain, 1992–.

Vives, Juan Luis. *Selected Works of Juan Luis Vives.* Edited by Constant Matheeussen et al. Leiden, Netherlands, 1987–. Six volumes have been published as of 1996.

Secondary Works

Noreña, Carlos G. *Juan Luis Vives.* The Hague, Netherlands, 1970.

Pinta Llorente, Miguel de la, and Jose M. de Palacio y de Palacio. *Procesesos inquisitoriales contra la familia judía de Juan Luis Vives.* Madrid, 1964.

EMILIE L. BERGMANN

VOIGT, GEORG. *See* Renaissance, Interpretations of the, *subentry on* Georg Voigt.

VOSSIUS, GERARDUS JOANNES (1577–1649),
Dutch humanist scholar. Gerardus Joannes Vossius was born in Heidelberg in March or April 1577. His father, Joannes, was a Dutch Calvinist minister. Young Vossius was a pupil at the Latin school in Dordrecht, and from September 1595 he studied philosophy and theology at the University of Leiden, where he was awarded the master of arts degree. In 1600 he was appointed rector of the Latin school of Dordrecht; fifteen years later he became the regent of the Leiden Estates College for prospective ministers. In spite of his neutral position in the theological and political conflict between the Dutch Arminians (Remonstrants) and their opponents (Contra-Remonstrants), he lost his post. In 1622 he obtained a professorship of eloquence and history at the University of Leiden, and in 1632 he became the first rector and professor of history and politics of the Athenaeum Illustre at Amsterdam, an academy that prepared young students for university. Vossius was married to Elisabeth van den Corput (1602–1606) and to Elisabeth Junius (1607–1649). He had two daughters and six sons, all of them gifted; all but one died before Vossius himself died in Amsterdam on 17 March 1649.

Vossius's publications on church history, such as his *Historia Pelagianismi* (The history of Pelagianism; 1618) and the *Dissertationes tres de tribus symbolis* (Three dissertations on the three early Christian creeds; 1642), paved the way for a more critical study of textual sources of religious history. Very influential were his *Institutiones oratoriae* (Lessons in rhetoric; 1606), the *Poeticarum institutionum libri tres* (Three books with lessons in poetics; 1647), and his trilogy on Latin language: the *Aristarchus, sive de arte grammatica libri septem* (Aristarchus, or seven books on grammar; 1635), *De vitiis sermonis* (On language errors; 1645), and the *Etymologicon linguae Latinae* (An etymological dictionary of Latin language; 1662). Other works were his *Ars historica* (The art of history; 1623), *De historicis Graecis libri quatuor* (Four books on Greek historians; 1623), *De historicis Latinis libri tres* (Three books on Latin historians; 1627), *Theologia gentilis* (The theolatry of the gentiles: a summary of contemporary knowledge of mythology and nature; 1641), *De artium et scientiarum natura ac constitutione libri quinque* (Five books on nature and constitution of arts and sciences; 1697), and a very successful series of textbooks for the Latin schools.

During his lifetime Vossius was one of the greatest and most influential humanist scholars. His books were used throughout the scholarly world. His work covered the entire terrain of humanistic learning, and contained everything that had been discovered and discussed in the past and in Vossius's own time. He summarized it systematically and provided it with a commentary directed to the actuality of his own days. Through his extensive correspondence with members of the Republic of Letters he helped other scholars with their work and students. Many of his students continued his work, but later generations found it too dated.

Vossius lived at the end of an era. After him, Western thought went in another direction, searching for new truths instead of demonstrating old truths. Vossius was a latecomer who closed the gate after a great period in the history of ideas, the period of the Renaissance and humanism.

BIBLIOGRAPHY

Primary Works

Vossius, Gerardus Joannes. *Gerardi Joannes Vossii et clarorum virorum ad eum epistolae* (Letters of G. J. Vossius and letters written to him by famous men). London, 1690 (Also Augsburg, 1691, and London, 1693).

Vossius, Gerardus Joannes. *Opera in sex tomos divisa* (The works in six volumes). Amsterdam, 1695–1701.

Secondary Works

Lem, Anton (G. A. C.) van der, and Cornelis S. M. Rademaker. *Inventory of the Correspondence of Gerardus Joannes Vossius (1577–1649).* Assen, Netherlands, 1993. An inventory of nearly 3,400 letters, with a list of studies on Vossius from the period 1981–1992.

Rademaker, Cornelis S. M. *Life and Work of Gerardus Joannes Vossius (1577–1649).* Assen, Netherlands, 1981. A biography with bibliographical lists of Vossius's published works, his preserved manuscripts, and publications about him up to 1981.

Wickenden, Nicholas. *G. J. Vossius and the Humanist Concept of History.* Assen, Netherlands, 1993.

CORNELIS S. M. RADEMAKER

WARBURG, ABY. *See* **Renaissance, Interpretations of the,** *subentry on* **Aby Warburg.**

WARD, MARY (1586–1645), English lay apostle and founder of the Institute of the Blessed Virgin Mary, a network of schools for girls. Born into a wealthy recusant family from Yorkshire in a time when Catholics were subject to penal reforms and regulations, Mary found her religious calling at a young age and was soon one of a wave of women who traveled to the Continent to pursue vocations in the teaching community of St. Omer, France. After an unsatisfying one-year novitiate as a Clarist sister, Mary was inspired by the example of the Jesuits to eventually establish, in 1616, an English apostolate for ladies, who would emulate the spirit of Ignatius Loyola by living uncloistered. Paul V approved the institute, and over the next fifteen years Ward established three hundred schools across the Continent "for virgins and young girls . . . that they may afterwards, according to their respective vocations, profitably embrace either the secular or the religious state."

Ward pursued her ambitions as a "Jesuitess" in the full light of public life, traveling and writing treatises on education and spirituality, though the Jesuits themselves resisted Ward and her fellow "galloping girls." In a time when the church was exerting greater pressure on female religious toward claustration, Ward eventually met with hostility and suspicion, which culminated in a 1629 church order for the suppression of her schools, and in her imprisonment on charges of insubordination for refusing enclosure. Eventually released, she returned to England where she died and was buried in her native Yorkshire. In 1701 her institute was reconstituted and her influence on the lay apostolate recognized in 1951 by Pius XII, who paid honor to "cette femme incomparable," who once predicted, in her words, that "in God it will be seen in time that women . . . will do much."

BIBLIOGRAPHY

Cover, Jeanne. *Love—the Driving Force: Mary Ward's Spirituality.* Milwaukee, Wis., 1997.
Oliver, Mary. *Mary Ward, 1585–1645.* New York, 1959.
Rowlands, Marie B. "Recusant Women." In *Women in English Society, 1500–1800.* Edited by Mary Prior. London, 1985. Pages 149–180.

SARAH COVINGTON

WARFARE. Peace, prosperity, and tranquility reigned in Italy in the 1490s, mused Francesco Guicciardini in the opening lines of his *History of Italy* (written 1537–1540), but this changed when the French invaded the peninsula in 1494: terrible events and calamities spread throughout the region and to other parts of Europe. It was the reassertion, he added with his usual pessimism, of the idea that human affairs are prey to misery like the waters of the seas to the winds. There is some truth in Guicciardini's statement. The Peace of Lodi (1454) had brought a certain amount of stability to Italy after years of continuous conflict, yet it was a peace that would not last because events on the other side of the Alps and changes in the approach to warfare guaranteed that repose would again become the exception, not the norm.

Major Wars in Europe. The majority of fifteenth-century wars were fought within the boundaries of future nation-states. They were waged either to rid the territory of an unwelcome foreign presence, or, between smaller individual states, as civil wars for control of the monarchy.

The Hundred Years' War (1337–1453) settled the Anglo-French rivalry within the territory of France by limiting the English presence to Calais, but neither the English nor the French monarchies enjoyed peace and stability from this outcome. The common path trod by England, France, and Spain since the high Middle Ages—a progressive integration of territories, which were independent or semi-independent, under the central authority of a sovereign—was often achieved by warfare. For example, murderous civil war enveloped the English countryside in the Wars of the Roses (1452–1487); the wars were not settled until the bloody battlefield of Bosworth (1485) crowned Henry VII as the final winner. He established the supremacy of the House of Tudor, which, in spite of internal and external challenges, steadily increased in strength in the next century.

French kings had to reassert their authority within the borders of their ancient land in order to reach the frontiers that later centuries would associate with the French state. This meant war against regions such as Brittany, which became part of the French monarchy only in the 1490s. The crown struggled to contain and then annex most of the territories of the duchy of Burgundy. It also had to protect itself against the menace of Spain in the west.

While wars generally benefited central monarchies in the fifteenth century, war was fatal to the smaller duchy of Burgundy. Its ruler, Charles the Bold (1433–1477), a curious, intelligent man, was eager to use new weapons and tactics on the battlefield, but his soldiers did poorly against the hardy Swiss mercenaries employed by the French. The collapse of Burgundy benefited France and eventually the Holy Roman Empire.

Warfare in the Renaissance. Battle of Eizenfeld between Imperial and Turkish armies. Detail of woodcut by Michael Ostendorfer, 1539. GRAPHISCHE SAMMLUNG ALBERTINA, WIEN (VIENNA)

For Spain, the presence of Islam on the Iberian Peninsula was unacceptable: Muslims were perceived as invaders who had come from across the sea in the distant past. They were members of a faith that Christians could not accept in an era in which religion informed every aspect of life. Moreover, once Castile and Aragon joined their destinies in 1479, Christian Spain's military strength became increasingly powerful. The Spanish monarchy reached its goal when Granada, the last Muslim stronghold in Spain, fell in 1492.

Neither the Italians nor the Germans shared the drive toward political unity under a single ruler. By the 1450s, five powers—Milan, Venice, Florence, the papacy, and Naples—had emerged as the controlling agents of the peninsula, but the ascendancy of one over the rest never happened. Germany was even more divided.

The sixteenth century opened with wars between major states of Europe, mostly fought in the territory of a third party. The small Italian states, which had been spared major fighting in the fifteenth century, were subject to the ambitions of stronger territorial monarchies. France in 1494, soon followed by the aggressive new monarchy of Spain and the ambitious if ineffective Holy Roman Emperor, Maximilian I, sent troops into Italy. Thus began the Wars of Italy, sixty-five years (1494–1559) of intermittent warfare. After the Battle of Pavia (1525), it was clear that the dominant power on the Italian peninsula was Spain, which ended up with control of Naples and Milan as well as overwhelming influence in Tuscany and sometimes over the pope. At the conclusion of the wars with the Treaty of Cateau-Cambrésis in 1559, Spain was the most powerful state in Europe.

The Italian states were direct or indirect losers of the Italian wars. Venice was potentially the strongest military power in Italy, but after its defeat at the Battle of Agnadello (1509), the city-state concentrated on keeping its borders secure on the mainland and fending off the Turks at sea.

When Charles V, the grandson of Ferdinand and Isabella of Spain, and of Maximilian I of Austria, became Holy Roman Emperor in 1519, the conflict between Spanish Habsburg and French Valois spilled beyond Italy. Great battles elsewhere, such as at Ceresole (1544), led to more battles, which did not end until the Spanish victory at Saint-Quentin in 1557 brought the wars near closure.

However, neither France nor Spain found peace. A bitter civil war between Catholics and Huguenots plagued France between 1560 and 1598. Peace remained unstable until finally achieved in the first years of the reign of Louis XIV (ruled 1643–1715). The main Spanish problem was retaining its dominions. Charles V was aware of the problem when he split his domain, leaving the central European areas to his brother, Ferdinand I, and Spain and the so-called Spanish road (the territories from Milan to Flanders) to his son Philip II (ruled 1556–1598). The inheritance brought several problems for Philip. Shortsighted policies, rapacious methods of rule, and arrogance led the Dutch provinces, part of his northern dominions, to rebel. This war in the north became larger when England emerged as the main adversary of Spain in the prologue to the eventual defeat of the Spanish Armada in 1588. Finally, Spain, Portugal, England, and France all had imperialistic ambitions in the Americas, producing more wars.

The Causes of War. On the surface, the main reason for waging war, quarrels over inherited crowns and territories, may seem identical to the reasons for war in the Middle Ages. But the concentration of power in warlike princes, especially in France and Spain, produced major changes. The limited form of medieval war, of one noble against another, or a noble against a prince, became impossible in the sixteenth century.

Princes went to war for several reasons. King Charles VIII of France invaded Italy in 1494 ostensibly because he believed that Naples belonged to his house on the basis of an ancient claim of inheritance. But a host of other reasons, especially the desire for glory, moved him more. On the eve of the Battle of Fornovo (1495), he seemed less worried about the possibility of defeat, which would have been catastrophic for his army, than the opportunity to distinguish himself on the battlefield. The European aristocracy as a whole shared his attitude. Although he did not disdain money for fighting, Charles de Bourbon-Montpensier (1490–1527) was ready to join the battlefields of Europe in the service of Francis I of France or Emperor Charles V for reasons of glory and personal honor.

Sometimes the desire to avoid a future attack moved a ruler to make a preemptive strike. The war policy of Francis I (ruled 1515–1547) is an example. Francis feared that France would be strangled from east and west when Charles V became emperor (1519). After his defeat at the Battle of Pavia (1525), when he was taken prisoner to Spain, revenge caused him to reopen hostilities. Imperialist concerns also found a place in rulers' minds. The Baltic conflicts, England's expansion into Scotland and Ireland, and especially the growing conflicts between

Warfare. *The Battle of San Romano* by Paolo Uccello (1397–1475). The battle, fought in 1423, resulted in a victory of Florence over Siena. This is one of three panels by Uccello depicting the battle; the other two are in the Louvre and the Uffizi Gallery in Florence. Distemper on wood; 1456; 182 × 323 cm (71.75 × 127.25 in.). [For the Uffizi panel, see the color plates in this volume.] NATIONAL GALLERY, LONDON/ERIC LESSING/ART RESOURCE

the European powers in the Americas all manifested the fruits of imperialism.

Religious differences were a constant characteristic of conflict in the sixteenth century. Yet, clashes based solely on religion were very few, such as the attacks on Anabaptists in the 1530s or the Schmalkaldic War (1546–1547) between Catholic Charles V and a league of German Lutheran princes. In most cases, more materialistic interests were at stake, for example, competition over trade fueled the conflicts between Christian Europe and the Turks in the Mediterranean. Religious differences made military conflicts more complex, confrontations more bitter, and negotiations more difficult, but they were not normally the immediate causes of war.

The desire to defend one's territory and to acquire what belonged to others was probably the most universal cause of wars, because it bound together all participants, from the prince to the lowest soldier. Behind most wars fought for inheritances was the desire to acquire territories. The sixteenth century accepted the notion of ownership by conquest. Yet, except for wars in the New World, conquest was tempered by the notion of legitimacy. Hence,

Charles VIII of France conquered Naples in 1495, because he thought that the kingdom belonged to him. Louis XII of France conquered Milan in 1500, because Milan was part of his inheritance. Territorial ambition was clearly important for the nobles who fought for the French king, and also for those who took up arms for Charles V. Among the rank and file, economic motivation was the stronger (and sometimes the only reason) for waging war. It is not surprising that most mercenaries came from chronically depressed areas such as Scotland, Swabia, Switzerland, Gascony, and Romagna in Italy.

For the soldiers, the above reasons do not exclude other incentives, including the quest for adventure, escape from difficulty at home, such as debts or an unwanted family, or even imprisonment. But certainly the most immediate reasons for fighting must have been poverty, unemployment, and underemployment. Sixteenth-century armies were the mirror of two groups, the aristocracy and the lower classes, those who managed war and those who fought it.

The Soldiers. Soldiers were found by conscripting one's own subjects and by hiring merce-

naries. All fit male subjects between the ages of sixteen and sixty were legally eligible to serve in the
army. (However, the average age of soldiers in the
field was between twenty and thirty-five, and a little
higher for men in garrison duties.) When soldiers
were needed, the state entrusted captains to recruit
in certain areas. This practice was common in Spain,
for example, and provided the advantage of a small
amount of governmental control over the process.
Soldiers joined voluntarily most of the time, but com-
pulsion was also employed. Recruiting the peasantry
was not enough, however, because the system did
not work properly. Perhaps one-fifth of the eligible
men avoided military service by evasion, bribery, or
legal challenge. Furthermore, the rate of attrition
from the place of recruitment to the battlefield was
high; another seventh to a third deserted before
joining the main army, and another quarter by mid-
campaign.

Hence, armies relied on mercenaries. What had
become typical of Italian warfare in the fourteenth
and fifteenth centuries, war by condottieri (contrac-
tors), spread beyond the Alps. The cantons in Switzerland and German colonels recruited and hired out
soldiers. Some states placed permanent agents in
certain regions in order to hire mercenaries. Venice,
for example, had agents who sought light cavalry in
Bosnia and pikemen in Switzerland. Mercenaries
were preferred because they were professional soldiers who performed better on the battlefield than
untrained subjects. By the sixteenth century, mercenaries became the mainstay of all armies.

At the end of a campaign, most soldiers were sent
home. Here again mercenaries were preferred, because they maintained better order than the ruler's
own dismissed soldier subjects, who, unemployed
and mostly penniless, were hated by the peasantry
through whose lands they had to pass. Some were
unwilling to return home because they were not welcome. Overnight these former soldiers could become bandits who added to the normal high level of
violence in the countryside.

Overall, the majority of the rank and file in an
army came from the poorest classes of society. A soldier's pay was often lower than that of civilian occupations, and soldiers were often cheated by their
own officers. Nevertheless, soldiering remained a favored occupation for many, because veterans could
become well-paid professional soldiers, and because
soldiers always hoped to profit from looting. Indeed,
battles could be lost when soldiers forsook the battlefield in order to loot the train of the enemy. Finally, in a society in which violence was common,

choosing an occupation that rewarded violence must
have been appealing.

Many aristocrats continued to fill the ranks of the
heavy cavalry; they took leading roles in the armies
of northern European states and in some parts of
Italy, notably Naples and Milan. But as time passed,
the nobility played a lesser role. This process began
in Italy with the development of condottieri. Those
nobles who remained in charge of mercenary bands
were often those who had to become professional
soldiers because of the poverty of their lands. The
despots of the Romagna were typical examples.

Standing Armies.   Already in 1421 the Venetian senate had proclaimed that the state needed
good soldiers both in war and in peacetime. The notion that a state must have a standing army became
an accepted belief of European states, except for England, by 1500. In addition to being more effective
in war, standing armies prevented professional soldiers from becoming vagrants or criminals during
peacetime. A professional army also limited the
power of feudal lords over their sovereign. The latter
no longer had to rely on a lord to provide subjects
for military service. The main impetus toward standing armies came from France. In the 1440s, Charles
VII (ruled 1422–1461) established the *ordonnance*
companies, essentially permanent bodies of cavalry.
Louis XI (ruled 1461–1483) created a permanent infantry about thirty years later. As the practice spread,
it produced many changes: more complex military
codes, the combined training of cavalry and infantry,
common uniforms and banners to identify units, and
a new lifestyle for the professional soldier.

A Military Revolution?   Did a military revolution, meaning the development of modern warfare, occur during the Renaissance? Although historians agree on the changes that constitute such a
revolution, they disagree on how and when these
changes occurred. The favorite dates for the military
revolution have been either the beginning or the end
of the sixteenth century. Michael Mallett and especially Bert S. Hall push the date further back. Hall
argues that the changes began in the fourteenth century and ended in the early seventeenth.

The growth in size of military forces, possibly the
main feature of the military revolution, went through
three phases. After the Black Death (1348–1350), armies grew steadily until they reached the limits of
their logistical possibilities, about thirty-five thousand. This situation persisted until 1550. Spain initiated the second phase by building chains of fortifications in order to defend its state and to suppress
internal or external attack. The third phase hap-

The Horrors of War. A battlefield scene by Urs Graf (c. 1485–1527). Drawing, 1521; 21.1 × 31.7 cm (8.25 × 12.5 in.). OEFFENTLICHE KUNSTSAMMLUNG BASEL, KUPFERSTICH-KABINETT

pened around 1600, when the rest of Europe was forced to follow Spain's example, producing costly defensive works and larger armies.

Tactics and Weapons. Developments in tactics and weaponry also characterized the military revolution, as offense and defense alternated periods of dominance during the Renaissance. Two of the greatest battles of the Middle Ages, Crécy (1346) and Agincourt (1415), demonstrated the efficiency of missile infantry (men using crossbows) against cavalry. They also showed that fortifications were impervious to any medieval artillery.

Offensive change then came from France, whose novel use of gunpowder and artillery led to the defeat of the English during the Hundred Years' War. French forces did not use heavier guns; they used smaller artillery that could be moved easily and whose impact was based on concerted shots against the walls of medieval towns, castles, and fortresses. This was very different from the earlier system of siege warfare, which depended on tremendous single shots. The new goal was to damage the walls progressively until they collapsed. The introduction of effective siege artillery changed conflict by bringing armies to the battlefield, because an army could no longer hide behind battlements but had to engage the enemy; this meant larger armies, pitched battles, and heavy casualties. The offensive force dominated.

The superiority of siege artillery lasted through the first three decades of the sixteenth century. Then the *trace italienne,* which was the Renaissance fortress built on a polygonal bastion, probably an invention of fifteenth-century Italian architects, restored the superiority of the fortress. Thus defense regained the upper hand. Sieges became too long for most armies; defenders relied on static defense and avoided pitched battles—only two major pitched battles, Nieuwpoort in 1620 and White Mountain also in 1620, were fought between the battles of Mühlberg in 1547 and Breitenfeld in 1631. The long siege, with the tedious and backbreaking work of digging trenches, sapping, and skirmishing, with the occasional attack against a breach in the enemy walls, dominated warfare.

During the period of offensive ascendancy until the 1540s, large square formations of Swiss and German pikemen dominated the center of the battlefield. The cavalry stood in the wings, while missile troops, initially men with crossbows, later harquebuses, screened the infantry. When the defense dominated, the ultimate battlefield formation was the Spanish *tercio,* a roughly square, strongly defensive formation that integrated harquebusiers and pikemen. It could attack or defend from any side.

The matchlock harquebus was the most common firearm for much of the sixteenth century. The musket, a heavier and more effective harquebus, came into use about 1560 but did not immediately replace the harquebus. The musket was much heavier (twenty pounds and six feet long) than the harquebus (twelve pounds and four feet), and more expensive. In any case, small arms were not important until later, as soldiers equipped with small arms were never numerous enough to make a difference. A more logical use of firearms was needed.

This happened with the development of linear deployment, a new type of formation, late in the century. Harquebusiers in line meant increased firepower, as pikemen in a square formation were ideal targets for the shots of the harquebus. The pikemen then had to learn to deploy in a much shallower line, which involved more sophisticated drill and much practice. Eventually the new deployments were used in northern Europe, first in Flanders under Maurice of Nassau (1567–1625) and by Gustavus II Adolphus (1594–1632) of Sweden. Changes in tactics completed the revolution of warfare.

At the beginning of the sixteenth century, large bodies of pikemen, preceded by screens of crossbowmen and flanked by heavy cavalry, had dominated the battlefield. At the end of the sixteenth century the crossbow had disappeared and the number of pikemen had been dramatically reduced, limited mainly to defensive use, while thin lines of men armed with firearms dominated. The heavy cavalry never regained its medieval role, although it remained the most fashionable branch of the army for social reasons. A new type of soldier, the light cavalryman, appeared. Finally, large standing armies became the norm.

[Paolo Uccello's *Battle of San Romano* (in the Galleria degli Uffizi in Florence), an artist's view of warfare, appears in the color plates in this volume.]

See also **Arms and Armor; Artillery; Firearms; Fortifications; Holy League; Mercenaries; Moriscos; Naval Warfare; Peasants' War; Wars of Italy; Wars of Religion.**

BIBLIOGRAPHY

General Works

Black, Jeremy. *Cambridge Illustrated Atlas, Warfare: Renaissance to Revolution, 1492–1792.* Cambridge, U.K., 1996.

Corvisier, Andre. *Armies and Societies in Europe, 1494–1789.* Translated by A. T. Siddall. Bloomington, Ind., 1979.

Hale, John R. *War and Society in Renaissance Europe 1450–1620.* London and New York, 1985.

Mallett, Michael E. "The Art of War." In *Handbook of European History 1400–1600.* Vol. 1. Edited by Thomas A. Brady Jr. et al. New York, 1994. Pages 535–562.

Oman, Charles. *A History of the Art of War in the Sixteenth Century.* London, 1937. An old-fashioned but still useful book.

Parker, Geoffrey. *The Military Revolution: Military Innovation and the Rise of the West, 1500–1800.* Cambridge, U.K., 1988.

Tallett, Frank. *War and Society in Early Modern Europe 1495–1715.* London and New York, 1992.

Works Containing Important Sections on Renaissance Warfare

Contamine, Philippe. *War in the Middle Ages.* Translated by Michael Jones. Oxford and New York, 1984.

Howard, Michael. *War in European History.* Oxford, 1976, 1983.

McNeill, William H. *The Pursuit of Power: Technology, Armed Force, and Society since A.D. 1000.* Chicago, 1982.

Special Topics

Guilmartin, John F. *Gunpowder and Galleys: Changing Technology and Mediterranean Warfare in the Sixteenth Century.* Cambridge, U.K., 1974. On sea warfare.

Hale, John R. *Artists and Warfare in the Renaissance.* New Haven, Conn., and London, 1990. On the visual representation of warfare.

Hall, Bert S. *Weapons and Warfare in Renaissance Europe.* Baltimore, and London, 1997. On artillery and fortifications.

Mallett, Michael. *Mercenaries and Their Masters: Warfare in Renaissance Italy.* London, 1974. On mercenaries.

Paret, Peter. *Imagined Battles: Reflections of War in European Art.* Chapel Hill, N.C., and London, 1997. On the visual representation of warfare.

Pepper, Simon, and Nicholas Adams. *Firearms and Fortifications: Military Architecture and Siege Warfare in Sixteenth-Century Siena.* Chicago, 1986. On artillery and fortifications.

ANTONIO SANTOSUOSSO

WARS OF ITALY (1494–1559). The Wars of Italy were the most important conflict of the Renaissance because of their location, the way they were fought, and their impact, especially on the Italian states. They can be divided into four stages. The first period began toward the end of 1494 and concluded with Spain regaining Naples in 1495. The second stage began with Louis XII's invasion of Italy on 13 July 1499. It ended temporarily with the treaty of Lyon between France and Aragon on 31 March 1504, leaving France in control of Milan, and Spain in control of Naples. A year later, Louis hired Swiss mercenaries, ending the frail peace; France and Spain met again on Italian battlefields. The most important battles were at Ravenna (11 April 1512), where the French defeated the Spaniards, and at Marignano (13–14 September 1515), where the French and Venetians defeated the Swiss. The third stage (1516–1530) saw attempts by Venice, Florence, and at times the papacy to loosen the foreign stranglehold over the peninsula. They all failed. Moreover, the great confrontation between France and Spain was resolved in favor of Spain after the Battle of Pavia (1525). The fourth stage (1531–1559) saw the firm establishment of the Spaniards over the peninsula.

Wars of Charles VIII and Louis XII. The long-held notion that the French invasion of Italy in

HOLY
ROMAN
EMPIRE

SWISS
CONFEDERATION

★ Battles of the Franco–Spanish
War for Naples, 1494–1505

☆ Campaigns of Louis XII (War
of the League of Cambrai, War
of the Holy League),
1508–1514

★ Campaigns of Francis I and
Henry II, 1515–1559

Ravenna 1512 French victory

← Invasion and retreat of the
French army under Charles
VIII, 1494–1496

Trent

DUCHY
OF MILAN

DUCHY OF SAVOY

Novara 1513 Milan

★ *Bicocca 1522*

Turin

Marignano 1515

Agnadello 1509

ASTI

Pavia 1525

MANTUA

Venice

Ravenna 1512

REPUBLIC OF VENICE

OTTOMAN
EMPIRE

MARQUISATE OF
MONTFERRAT

★ *Fornovo 1495*

MARQUISATE
OF SALUZZO

REPUBLIC OF GENOA

DUCHY
OF
MODENA

Genoa

Bologna

Ravenna 1512

REPUBLIC OF
SAN MARINO

PAPAL
STATES

ADRIATIC SEA

CORSICA
(Genoa)

REPUBLIC
OF LUCCA

Florence

Pisa

PISA

REPUBLIC
OF
FLORENCE

Urbino

DUCHY OF
PIOMBINO

Siena

REPUBLIC
OF SIENA

Marciano 1553

DUBROVNIK

Rome 1527

Pontecorvo

Benevento

Cerignola 1503

KINGDOM
OF
NAPLES

Taranto 1496

Naples

KINGDOM OF
SARDINIA

Cagliari

TYRRHENIAN SEA

Palermo

KINGDOM OF
SICILY

Reggio di Calabria 1543

AFRICA

Wars of Italy

50   100 Miles

50   100   150 Kilometers

1494 was unusual is false. King Charles VIII of France was neither an idiot, as Francesco Guicciardini portrayed him in his history of the period (written 1537–1540), nor did he place more important French goals in jeopardy. Charles based his decision on the tradition that "to control Italy was to control Europe." Since the Middle Ages Italians had been accustomed to calling in foreigners to resolve their quarrels. They saw the foreigners as "brooms" that would sweep up the mess and then be discarded. What was unusual about 1494 is that the French and other foreigners came to stay while the Italian states became their pawns.

The deaths of several Italian heads of state—Lorenzo de' Medici of Florence and Pope Innocent VIII in 1492, and Ferdinand (Ferrante) I of Naples in 1494—left Italy bereft of responsible leadership at a time of crisis. The wars began when the illegitimate ruler of Milan, Duke Ludovico Sforza (1452–1508) urged King Charles VIII of France to come to Italy. Charles VIII entered Italy in September 1494 for the purpose of seizing the Kingdom of Naples, which he claimed because he was the heir of the earlier Anjou dynasty of Naples. Sforza, in turn, expected that Charles would support his own shaky claim to Milan.

The French moved with lightning speed through Italy. The Italian states would not unite in order to stop the incursion, and they feared that their thin-walled medieval fortifications could not withstand French guns. Neapolitan counterattacks failed, and Charles conquered Naples but later was forced to withdraw. A coalition of Italian states led by Venice barred his return to France at Fornovo (in northern Italy). The Italian defeat at the Battle of Fornovo (6 July 1495)—that is, the Italians' failure to destroy the French army—rendered a French return inevitable.

Louis XII (ruled 1498–1515) of France invaded Italy again in 1499 in order to claim both Naples and Milan, the latter on the basis of another family connection. Again the Italian response was myopic. Venice used the occasion to seize territory on the peninsula, while Pope Alexander VI (1492–1503) made an alliance with France so that his son, Cesare Borgia (1475–1507), could carve out an ephemeral domain in the papal states of central and north-central Italy. However, Venice soon paid for its greed. In 1508 Pope Julius II (1503–1513) brought together in the League of Cambrai papal forces, France, Spain, England, and Maximilian I, the Holy Roman Emperor, against Venice. The French defeated the Venetians at Agnadello (1509), striking gloom and terror in Venetian hearts and causing the loss of a section of the city-state's mainland empire. Venice

survived the defeat. However, even though it was the only Italian power potentially able to challenge a foreign invader, Venice now knew its limitations. This was so even after the Peace of Noyon (1516), when Venice regained most of the territory it had lost.

Francis I versus Charles V. Initially the Wars of Italy were a contest between France and the Italian states. However, by the time of Charles VIII's hasty departure from Italy, a new, more dangerous contestant had entered the fray—the Spain of Isabella of Castile and of Ferdinand II of Aragon. France and Spain, originally allies in dividing the spoils, soon became rivals over the issue of supremacy in Italy. It was a contest that became more bitter and antagonistic when Francis I Valois (ruled 1515–1547) and Charles V (ruled 1519–1556), heir of the Spanish crown and of the lands of the Habsburgs, appeared on the scene. The prize was not just hegemony in Italy, but in the rest of western Europe. The Italians, once masters of their lands, were soon reduced to the status of bit players or spectators.

The battles of Cerignola (28 April 1503) and of the Garigliano (29 December 1503) had decided the issue of control over southern Italy in favor of the Spaniards. All future French attempts to reestablish supremacy over Naples failed. The confrontation over the French claim on northern Italy, specifically Milan, lasted much longer and was characterized by important battlefield confrontations. At Ravenna in 1512 the French won after a harsh encounter in which the power of field artillery showed its devastating impact for the first time. The contestants left twelve thousand casualties on the battlefield. French euphoria soon disappeared when, at Novara (1513), the Swiss, self-proclaimed protectors of the duchy of Milan, routed the unprotected pikemen and harquebusiers (gunmen) of the French army. At Marignano in 1515 the French took their revenge over the Swiss thanks to a combined effort of cavalry and infantry.

The French now ruled Milan, but their supremacy was illusory. The imperial forces of Charles V, who combined Spanish and Habsburg dominions, eventually won. It began with the success of the German-Spanish force over the French and their Swiss mercenaries at Bicocca in 1522. The artillery and the small arms of the imperial troops, lined up behind an obstacle, were very effective against the Swiss pikemen, causing large casualties among them. Bicocca was a preview for the most famous battle of the Italian Wars—Pavia in 1525. This battle also saw the effective use of small arms, as the Spanish forces used their harquebusiers in an offensive role, not just in a defensive manner as had become customary after their introduction at Cerignola in 1503. The imperial forces even took Francis I prisoner to Spain. Then in May 1527 the mutinous mercenaries of Charles de Bourbon-Montpensier, a combination of German *Landsknechten* (mercenary soldiers) and Spanish and Italian soldiers at the emperor's service, sacked Rome. Soon after, Florence, which had once again proclaimed its status as a republic, had to submit to the emperor and accept the return of the Medici. The crowning of Charles V by the pope at the Congress of Bologna in 1530 made formal what was already clear after Pavia. The Italian peninsula was subject to one master—Spain under Charles V.

The wars did not end in 1530, but theoretically lasted until the Treaty of Cateau-Cambrésis of 1559 with at least one major bloody encounter on Italian soil (Ceresole in 1544) and one on French terrain (Saint-Quentin in 1557). After Bologna, however, the Spaniards' main task was strengthening their hold over Italy. Italians made two more attempts to assert their independence against Spanish power. In 1552 Siena expelled the Spanish garrison left there to guard communications and called on France for help. But Spain then conquered Siena and gave the city to its ally, Florence under Cosimo I de' Medici (1519–1574). Sienese independence ended. Pope Paul IV (1555–1559) launched a war against Spain in 1556; this also failed. However, his stand may have helped preserve the semblance of independence for some Italian states. In summary, Italy had five major powers—Milan, Venice, Florence, the papacy, and Naples—in 1494. By 1559 Milan and Naples had become part of the Spanish empire. The other three kept their independence, but Venice had become a secondary power, and Florence and sometimes the papacy had fallen under Spanish influence.

Interpretations. Contemporaries and later historians remembered these wars as years of misery and humiliation for Italy. The great historian Francesco Guicciardini (1483–1540) claimed that the manipulations of Italian rulers and the papacy had caused Italy's fall. Niccolò Machiavelli (1469–1527) sometimes blamed the mercenaries, other times the papacy. In his most pessimistic mood he believed that Italians lost their freedom because they were degenerate fools. Contemporary Italian popular writers and social critics criticized the tyranny of the petty Italian princes and saw no reason to support them.

Twentieth-century scholars have suggested more general explanations based on the intellectual makeup of sixteenth-century Italians or social conditions. In a famous short note, the influential Marxist writer Antonio Gramsci (1891–1937) condemned most Italian intellectuals of the period for their subservience to two cosmopolitan ideals—the empire and especially the church. Such ideals made it easier to accept foreign supremacy and prevented them from forming a common front against the invaders.

Other historians have pointed out that many Italians were not loyal to their rulers, who exploited them or permitted the nobility to exploit them. Indeed, from the reaction of the people, Charles VIII's withdrawal in 1495 through the territory of Milan seemed more like the leave-taking of a friend than the retreat of an enemy of the state. Moreover, all the major states except for Venice were internally divided. Members of the ruling classes clashed in Florence and Naples, the ruler's illegitimacy caused divisions in Milan, and the short reigns of popes produced quick policy changes in Rome. Finally, Italian desire for stability led to acceptance of the foreigners. Although the Spaniards were hated, Italians craving peace and quiet were not motivated to political action.

The historian John R. Hale claimed that Italian culture could not be correlated to the wars. This seems to be the case, because Michelangelo (1475–1564) created *David*, his first *Pietà*, and the Sistine Chapel ceiling—great examples of balance, peace, and tranquillity—in the midst of the wars. Raphael (1483–1520) painted his supremely peaceful *stanze Vaticane* (Vatican rooms) 1510–1520, and Baldassare Castiglione (1478–1529) wrote his melancholic but serene *Il cortegiano* (*The Book of the Courtier*) at the same time. But alienation, violence, and despair can also be found in these and other artists and intellectuals, for example, the writings of Machiavelli, and the later works of Leonardo da Vinci, Raphael, and Michelangelo. The vibrant but discordant styles of the mannerist painters, especially after the Sack of Rome of 1527, are another sign of how the wars affected culture. It was a difficult and troubling time for the Italian peninsula.

See also **Pavia, Battle of; Rome, Sack of; Warfare.**

BIBLIOGRAPHY

Primary Works
Francesco Guicciardini, *History of Italy,* edited and translated by Sidney Alexander (New York, 1968), is the most important work available in English; however, this edition is an abridged version of the original Italian. Also fundamental is Paolo Giovio, *Opera*

(Rome, 1956). On Charles VIII's invasion, see Alessandro Benedetti, *Diaria de bello carolino,* translated by Dorothy M. Schullian (New York, 1967), and especially *Memoirs of Philippe de Commynes,* translated and edited by Samuel Kinser (Columbia, S.C., 1969, 1973). Most of Machiavelli's works deal in part with the Wars of Italy, especially his *Art of War* (Norwalk, Conn., 1990).

Secondary Works
The fundamental work remains Piero Pieri, *Il Rinascimento e la crisi militare italiana,* 2nd edition (Turin, Italy, 1970). Still useful is F. L. Taylor, *The Art of War in Italy 1494–1529* (1921; reprint, Westport, Conn., 1973). John R. Hale remains the authority in the field, with a series of important articles collected in *Renaissance War Studies* (London, 1983). See also Michael Mallet and John R. Hale, *The Military Organization of a Renaissance State: Venice c. 1400–1617* (Cambridge, U.K., 1984); David Abulafia, ed., *The French Descent into Renaissance Italy: Antecedents and Effects* (Aldershot, U.K., 1995); and Antonio Santosuosso, "Anatomy and Defeat in Renaissance Italy: The Battle of Fornovo in 1495," *International History Review* 16 (1994): 221–250.

ANTONIO SANTOSUOSSO

WARS OF RELIGION. Between 1562 and 1598, eight Wars of Religion reduced France to near anarchy. The religious roots of these wars lay in the clash between the French Catholic view of their religion as the one true faith and the demand by Protestant converts to worship according to their conscience. The wars' political roots lay in factional quarrels among aristocratic grandees whose competition for royal patronage mounted uncontrollably after Henry II's accidental death in July 1559 left France in the hands of immature kings and a queen mother whose single consistent objective was to maintain her sons' crown at any cost. When factional cleavages aligned with religious divisions, as they did after 1560, the danger of war loomed large.

The Guise family, a younger branch of the house of Lorraine headed by François, duc de Guise, and his brother Charles, cardinal de Lorraine, became aggressive defenders of the Catholic faith. The Bourbon, princes of the blood as descendants of a younger son of Louis IX, moved into the Protestant orbit. Antoine de Bourbon, king of Navarre, refused to commit himself despite the conversion of his wife, Jeanne d'Albret, but Antoine's younger brother, Louis, prince de Condé, accepted leadership of the French Protestant movement. The Montmorency, a third powerful clan, were divided in faith. Constable Anne de Montmorency and his four sons remained Catholic; his nephews, the Châtillon, became Protestants. Among them, Admiral Gaspard II de Coligny took second place only to Condé as a Protestant leader.

Origins. French monarchs traditionally enjoyed a close alliance with the Roman Catholic Church. Their claim to rule by divine right was firmly embedded in Catholic ritual; in return, the coronation oath bound them to protect the faith and drive out heretics. When Martin Luther's teachings were condemned as heretical in 1521, French kings were thus obliged to proceed against his followers. France had a homegrown movement of evangelical reformers who shared some but not necessarily all of Luther's theological principles. This complicated but did not stop the pursuit of heresy. The Protestant movement went underground but continued to attract supporters. By the 1550s, moreover, ministers trained in John Calvin's Geneva brought a more militant Protestantism to France. Underground conventicles formed into churches, which organized regionally and then nationally. Their first national synod met secretly in Paris in the spring of 1559.

At the same time, Henry II, having concluded peace after long wars with Spain, announced his intention of stepping up measures to eliminate heresy. Henry's unexpected death cut short his plans, but his son and heir Francis II, influenced by his wife Mary Stuart's ultra-Catholic uncles, the duke of Guise and cardinal of Lorraine, did intensify persecution. Calvinist nobles plotted in March 1560 to seize the young king at Amboise and remove him from the influence of the Guise. Word of the conspiracy leaked out, and several hundred participants were hanged as rebels. Condé was arrested for complicity and would have been executed, but Francis II's death in December 1560 cast the Guise from power. Queen Mother Catherine de Médicis declared herself regent for ten-year-old Charles IX. She freed Condé and appointed Antoine de Bourbon lieutenant general for the kingdom. Hoping that moderation would reduce factional tensions, she declared in April 1561 that no one should be injured on account of his or her religious beliefs. In September she brought together Protestant and Catholic theologians at the Colloquy of Poissy, but the discussion failed to produce conciliation or compromise. In the meantime, the Calvinists profited from the freer atmosphere to preach more openly, though public assemblies were still prohibited. The movement grew rapidly but also attracted more vehement Catholic opposition.

Catholics' anger against the Protestants, who after the conspiracy of Amboise began to be called "Huguenots," expressed itself in violent sermons and pamphlets describing the new faith as a cancer that corrupted the social body and risked provoking the wrath of God. The anger also found outlet in attacks

French Wars of Religion. Procession of the Holy League in the Place de Grève, Paris. Many participants carry guns. Anonymous painting, 1590. MUSÉE DE LA VILLE DE PARIS, MUSÉE CARNAVALET/LAUROS-GIRAUDON/ART RESOURCE, NY

on Protestant worshipers. Popular violence became common. Anger grew against the crown as well, especially when in January 1562 Catherine permitted assemblies of the new faith as long as they took place outside town walls. Two months later, Guise's troops attacked and killed Huguenots gathered for worship in Wassy. Condé called for an apology but prepared for war.

The First Wars.   The royal family was caught between the opposing factions. Catherine solicited Condé's protection, but he failed to respond and with his troops seized Orléans and other key towns. Antoine de Bourbon, having abandoned any Protestant leanings, joined a Catholic Triumvirate of Guise, Montmorency, and Marshal Saint-André (a favorite of the late Henry II). Catherine reluctantly accepted the protection they offered her but continued to attempt to negotiate peace. She succeeded in March 1563 with the Peace of Amboise, which set the pattern for later religious settlements. It allowed freedom of conscience but permitted Protestant worship only in limited social and geographical settings. Noble households could hold services for their dependents; otherwise, Protestant worship was restricted to the suburbs of one town in each judicial district. Services were forbidden in or near Paris, whose citizenry had violently opposed the peace.

Antoine de Bourbon died fighting at Rouen. François, duc de Guise, was assassinated just prior to the war's end. Factional divisions nevertheless contin-

ued to run deep. The cardinal of Lorraine, again dominating the king's council, urged more repressive measures against Huguenots and retribution against their leaders, especially Admiral Coligny, whom he blamed for his brother's death. The Huguenots responded in September 1567 by organizing another plan to seize the king and free him from Guise domination. Once again, word leaked out. The king escaped to safety in Paris, and the second War of Religion began. In November a major battle was fought at Saint-Denis. In March 1568 a compromise was negotiated on much the same terms as in 1563 (Edict of Longjumeau). Catholic opposition to the peace was strong, and neither side disarmed.

War broke out again in September. Most of the fighting occurred in southwestern France, where Condé was killed and the Huguenots notably defeated at Jarnac (March 1569). Under Coligny's leadership, in October 1569 the Huguenots were again defeated at Moncontour but rallied enough to negotiate the Peace of Saint-Germain in August 1570 on favorable terms that increased opportunities for worship and allowed them to hold certain fortified cities as a guarantee of security for a specified term. Many Catholics saw the treaty as a betrayal of trust; popular resentments remained strong and burst forth on 24 August 1572 in the wave of killings known as the Saint Bartholomew's Day massacre. The killing began when Charles IX, fearful that Huguenot leaders were again plotting to seize him, ordered these leaders—who were conveniently gathered in Paris for the marriage of Charles's sister Marguerite to the Protestant Henry of Navarre—assassinated during the night. Word got out that the king had ordered the Huguenots killed, and the circle of violence widened until approximately two thousand people lay dead in Paris. Similar waves of violence shook at least a dozen provincial towns.

Emergence of the Politique Alliance. Surviving Huguenot leaders fled to La Rochelle, one of the armed cities held by the Huguenots under the Peace of Saint-Germain. Besieged by royal armies, they surrendered in July 1573, accepting a punitive peace that denied virtually any chance to practice their faith. They began almost immediately to plan a new offensive. Huguenot propagandists publicized the horrors of Saint Bartholomew's Day and wrote treatises arguing that resistance to monarchical authority was justified when the king behaved like a tyrant. Huguenots in the South, where the Protestant population was strongest, took the more radical step of drawing up a republican constitution effectively separating them from the monarchy. In 1574 they forged an alliance with the Catholic governor of Languedoc, Henri de Montmorency, sieur de Damville.

Damville typifies the emergence among Catholics of a new advocacy of religious coexistence as a means of resolving the kingdom's quarrels. Derisively nicknamed "Politiques" by ultra-Catholics, who believed they sacrificed religious truth to political ends, men like Damville never formed a unified party. They nevertheless shared a belief that serious political and economic reforms were needed to repair the damage done by the wars and ensure lasting peace. At the same time, they saw peace as a precondition for reform and were willing to ally themselves with the Huguenots in pursuit of these goals.

Charles IX died in May 1574 and was succeeded by his brother Henry, recently elected king of Poland. Everyone tensely awaited his return. Known as an ardent Catholic, Henry disappointed the militants who hoped he would lead them to triumph over the Huguenots. The crown's debts were so enormous that he could not have raised an effective army had he wanted to. A fitful war broke out in which Henry's own brother François, duc d' Alençon, became the figurehead of the Huguenot-Politique alliance. Alençon was heir to the throne, and his rebellion threatened irreparable harm to the state. Henry III was forced to negotiate peace in May 1576. The generous terms of the Peace of Beaulieu angered ultra-Catholics, who formed a Holy League in defense of the faith under the leadership of Henri, duc de Guise (son of Duke François, assassinated in 1563). Henry III attempted to co-opt the League, hoping thereby to raise money and troops to reverse the humiliating Peace of Beaulieu. The Huguenots fought again and lost some of their gains with the Peace of Bergerac in September 1577. Another brief war in 1580 failed to change the status quo. Henry III grew increasingly unpopular. Debts mounted; popular rebellions and disorders troubled the countryside.

The Wars of the League. The death of François, duc d' Alençon (raised to duc d'Anjou after the Peace of Beaulieu), in 1584 caused a succession crisis. It seemed increasingly unlikely that Henry III would produce a son. The Protestant Henry de Bourbon, king of Navarre, was by French laws of succession heir to the throne. Ultra-Catholics revived the Holy League to oppose this prospect and in December 1584 signed an alliance with Spain to finance a new war against heresy. While the Guise recruited aristocrats, urban Leagues formed in the cities. Bowing to League power in July 1585, Henry III signed the Treaty of Nemours. Promising to eradicate heresy, he revoked the edicts of pacification, forbade practice of the Reformed faith, and ordered Protestant ministers to leave France. The Huguenots again prepared for war.

Henry of Navarre defeated the royal army at Coutras (October 1587), but when Guise's army achieved an unexpected victory against German mercenaries arriving to aid the Huguenots, Henry III began to fear his League allies more than his Huguenot enemies. He forbade Guise to come to Paris, where the League was altogether too popular. Guise came anyway. Henry III's ill-considered attempts to maintain order provoked a popular revolt, and the king fled from his capital (Day of the Barricades, May 1588). Attempts to resolve matters peacefully at the Estates General at Blois ended with Henry III's rash assassination of Henri de Guise and his brother Louis, cardinal de Guise, in December 1588. The League went into open revolt. An apocalyptic religious fervor took hold in Paris, where ultra-Catholic preachers demonized Henry III, urged penitence, and predicted divine vengeance for the kingdom's ills. Allying himself with Henry of Navarre, Henry III planned to besiege Paris but died by an assassin's hand in August 1589.

Navarre claimed the throne as Henry IV and carried on the war against the League, now commanded by Guise's younger brother, the duke of Mayenne. Paris held out against a brutal siege (1590), but in-

Saint Bartholomew's Day Massacre. The massacre of Huguenots took place on and after 24 August 1572. Anonymous print. CLICHÉ BIBLIOTHÈQUE NATIONALE DE FRANCE, PARIS

ternal divisions gradually undermined the League. In spring 1593, Henry IV took instruction in the Catholic faith; in July he formally abjured Protestantism at Saint-Denis. In March 1594 the gates of Paris quietly opened to him. He triumphantly entered the capital. The League was on the wane. Henry IV's announced policy of appeasement brought many towns over voluntarily; he took others by war. League leaders surrendered—or were bought off—one by one. Peace seemed near when Mayenne surrendered in late 1595, but Spain was preparing an army to assist the League's last holdouts.

The Huguenots, meanwhile, wanted reassurance that Henry IV, despite his conversion, would protect their rights. Uniting Catholics and Protestants to drive back the Spanish invasion, Henry IV retook Amiens in September 1597 after a three-month siege. The League's last warlord, the duke of Mercoeur, surrendered in January 1598. In April, Henry made peace with the Huguenots in the Edict of Nantes, which followed the model of earlier peace treaties in granting freedom of conscience, limiting rights to public worship, and arming towns to hold for security's sake. In May he made peace with Spain at Vervins. Catholic resistance held up registration of the Edict of Nantes, but Henry IV's policy of appeasement gave a secure enough base for the kingdom to begin at last to rebuild.

Putting an end to half a century of religious discord nevertheless proved an elusive goal. Louis XIII reopened the wars against the Huguenots in 1620, finally depriving them of military power with the Peace of Alais in June 1629. Louis XIV renewed persecution of the Protestants in order to force their conversion and ultimately outlawed the French Reformed Church entirely by revoking the Edict of Nantes in 1685. Able for more than a century to practice their faith only clandestinely, French Protestants drew strength from the memory of their struggles by recasting them as signs of divine election.

See also **Holy League; Resistance, Theory of;** *entries on the Bourbon and Valois dynasties and the Guise-Lorraine and Montmorency families; and biographies of figures mentioned in this entry.*

BIBLIOGRAPHY

Benedict, Philip. *Rouen during the Wars of Religion.* Cambridge, U.K., 1981. An excellent urban case study with broader implications.

Davis, Natalie Zemon. *Society and Culture in Early Modern France: Eight Essays.* Stanford, Calif., 1975. See "The Rites of Violence," pages 152–188, a pioneering essay on religious violence in the wars.

Diefendorf, Barbara B. *Beneath the Cross: Catholics and Huguenots in Sixteenth-Century Paris.* New York and Oxford, 1991. Focuses on popular religious passions in Paris before and during Saint Bartholomew's Day.

Greengrass, Mark. *France in the Age of Henri IV: The Struggle for Stability.* 2d ed. London, 1995. Most useful on recovery and reconstruction under Henry IV.

Holt, Mack P. *The French Wars of Religion, 1562–1629.* Cambridge, U.K., and New York, 1995. An excellent short history of the wars.

Roelker, Nancy Lyman. *One King, One Faith. The Parlement of Paris and the Religious Reformations of the Sixteenth Century.* Berkeley and Los Angeles, 1996. Examines the wars from the perspective of Politique magistrates.

Salmon, J. H. M. *Society in Crisis: France in the Sixteenth Century.* New York, 1975. The classic English-language account of the wars in their social context.

Sutherland, N. M. *The Huguenot Struggle for Recognition.* New Haven, Conn., 1980. Most useful on Huguenot demands and royal edicts.

Wolfe, Michael. *The Conversion of Henri IV: Politics, Power, and Religious Belief in Early Modern France.* Cambridge, Mass., and London, 1993. A good explanation of the complex political problems Henry's conversion posed.

BARBARA B. DIEFENDORF

WEAPONS. *See* **Arms and Armor; Firearms.**

WEBSTER, JOHN (1578/79–1634/38), Jacobean dramatist. Webster is best known for two great Italianate tragedies of blood, *The White Devil* (performed 1612) and *The Duchess of Malfi* (performed 1614), and for *The Devil's Law-Case* (written 1617–1619?), an emotionally dark, tonally discontinuous, and puzzlingly ambiguous tragicomedy. He also collaborated in several other plays and wrote some occasional verses, a city pageant, and a group of prose characters, or descriptions of personality types.

Webster was the eldest son of an affluent London coachmaker, tradesman in carts and wagons, and merchant tailor, who lived in Smithfield near the horse market. In 1605 he married Sara Peniall, a saddler's daughter, who bore him several children. His formal education remains doubtful. Although his patchwork of known sources reveals extensive reading, scholars continue to debate the extent of Webster's classical learning. In the three unassisted plays on which his reputation depends, the dramatist appears to have composed with painful slowness, incorporating unrelated quotations and sententiae from his copybook as if constructing mosaics. Webster attached himself to no single acting troupe; his most important tragedy, *The Duchess of Malfi,* was composed for the King's Men (Shakespeare's company), but his two other uncollaborated plays were acted by Queen Anne's Men, and he enjoyed earlier associations with both the Admiral's Men and Paul's Boys.

Webster's two tragic masterpieces are loosely based on scandalous murders taken from Renaissance history: *The White Devil* dramatizes the illicit love and violent deaths of Vittoria Accoramboni and Paolo Giordano Orsini, duke of Bracciano, at the hands of the Tuscan prince Francesco de' Medici; *The Duchess* stages the torture and killing of the ruler of Amalfi, Giovanna d'Aragona, together with her children and lowborn husband, by her brothers, a cardinal and a duke, neurotically fixated on preserving the aristocratic purity of their bloodline. Both plays represent an important advance in tragic depth and psychological subtlety over the cruder revenge plays of the sixteenth century; both break new ground by featuring strong-minded, independent women; and both capitalize probingly on cynical tool villains—educated but displaced commoners whom ambition and blocked advancement corrupt against the better angels of their nature. *The Devil's Law-Case,* which stages a mother's vengeful attempt to bastardize her own legitimate son, is oddly Janusfaced, commingling sardonic scorn, improbable trickery, sudden reverses, moral earnestness, and authentic feeling in ways that, despite the happy ending, have much in common with the two "nightpieces" that preceded it. Irregular, asyntactic, and vermiculate in structure, Websterian tragedy fuses elements from the traditions of heroic romance and sanguinary Machiavellian intrigue, producing characterizations of brooding penetration and complexity, situations of intense cruelty and suffering, moments of profound pathos in contexts of mockery and despair, theatrical shocks and surprises, and gloomy meditations on death. High intelligence, loneliness, depravity, terror, courage, sexual vitality, romantic commitment, commanding personal dignity, religious faith, guilt, and madness intersect richly in Webster's grotesque world, coming to life energetically through verse that can be imagistically startling, abruptly luminous or ironic, hauntingly lyrical, densely compacted, or wittily "metaphysical." The principle of *discordia concors* operates powerfully at both verbal and thematic levels. His most moving figures struggle heroically to preserve their integrity of personhood in the face of enveloping chaos and the "mist" of cosmic uncertainty. Though his major achievement consists of only three unaided plays, Webster is properly regarded (with Christopher Marlowe, Ben Jonson, and Thomas Middleton) as one of the greatest dramatists of his age after Shakespeare.

BIBLIOGRAPHY

Primary Works

Webster, John. *The Complete Works of John Webster.* Edited by F. L. Lucas. 4 vols. London, 1927. Although in most respects superseded by the Gunby et al. work (below), still valuable for its extensive apparatus.

Webster, John. *The Devil's Law-Case.* Edited by Frances A. Shirley. Lincoln, Nebr., 1972. Contains the best modernized text.

Webster, John. *The Duchess of Malfi.* Edited by John Russell Brown. London, 1964. Revised, Manchester, U.K., 1997. The best edition of the play for general readers (modernized and informatively annotated).

Webster, John. *The White Devil.* Edited by John Russell Brown. London, 1960. Revised, Manchester, U.K., 1996. The best edition of the play for general readers (modernized and informatively annotated).

Webster, John. *The Works of John Webster.* Edited by David Gunby, David Carnegie, and Antony Hamond. 2 vols. Cambridge, U.K., 1995–. The standard edition of Webster; original spelling with full apparatus.

Secondary Works

Dent, Robert William. *John Webster's Borrowing.* Berkeley and Los Angeles, 1960. Indispensable for its detailed account of Webster's appropriation of earlier and contemporary writers.

Forker, Charles R. *Skull Beneath the Skin: The Achievement of John Webster.* Carbondale, Ill., 1986. The standard comprehensive biographical-critical study of the dramatist, which addresses the minor as well as the major works in depth. The ironic intersection of love and death is seen as a unifying theme.

CHARLES R. FORKER

WECHEL FAMILY. The Wechel family, a dynasty of printers in Paris, Frankfurt am Main, and Hanau, were noted as publishers of successive varieties of Renaissance humanism between 1526 and 1627. Chrétien (Christian) Wechel (Vuechel) of Herrentals, near Antwerp, entered the Parisian book trade around 1518–1519 and bought his first printing shop in 1526. In a will dated 1550 he passed on a greatly expanded printing firm in Paris to his nephew, André (Andreas) Wechel, as well as further possessions in Cologne to another nephew, Simeon Wechel.

André prospered in Paris until forced to flee the St. Bartholomew's Day massacre of Calvinists in 1572 to Frankfurt am Main, where he reestablished himself with remarkable speed as a major force in the central European book trade. With his death in 1581, the firm passed to his two sons-in-law, Claude de Marne and Jean Aubri (Aubry), expatriate Frenchmen who had previously operated as André's agents in Vienna and Prague. About the same time, a certain Johann Wechel, presumably a relation of Simeon, arrived from Cologne and began printing in Frankfurt under a device similar to André's.

In its fourth generation, the dynasty broadened still further. In 1593 Johann Wechel's widow married a member of her late husband's staff, Joannes Palthenius, who subsequently printed under his own name. Mounting hostility to Calvinism in Frankfurt prompted Aubri to transport much of his activity to the nearby Calvinist city of Hanau in 1596. The deaths of Aubri in 1601 and Marne in 1610 saw their businesses pass to their sons—Jean and André de Marne, Daniel and David Aubri—until Claude de Marne's son-in-law, Clemens Schleich, reunited the two branches of the family firm in 1613. By the time of Daniel Aubri's death in 1627, however, the pressures of the Thirty Years' War had reduced the firm from one of the leading humanist presses of central Europe to a family of printers and engravers of purely local significance.

The later generations of the family thus shared the fortunes of what can loosely be termed "Calvinism," and the dynasty as a whole is closely linked with the changing face of northern Renaissance "humanism." Chrétien is known as a printer of the third book of Rabelais's *Pantagruel* as well as some thirty editions of Erasmus, including works banned by the faculty of theology in Paris. André distinguished himself in Paris above all as a friend and favorite printer of Pierre de la Ramée (Petrus Ramus; 1515–1572), and upon reemerging in Frankfurt after the massacre, which ended his friend's life, he waged a ferocious battle to regain his domination of Ramist publication.

But the greatest financial success and cultural significance of the dynasty derived from its exemplification of the final phase of humanism more generally in central Europe in the decades around 1600. The "humanism" embodied in Wechel imprints, to be sure, is no longer the well-defined movement promoted by the heroic early generation of humanist printers such as Aldo Manuzio in Venice or Johann Froben in Basel. Like few other central European presses in that period, the Wechels' theological publications were considerably outnumbered by their editions of neo-Latin literature and classical philology—pagan and patristic, Greek and Latin; but these in turn were eclipsed by Ramist and post-Ramist pedagogical works and by countless volumes of history and geography.

From the 1590s, moreover, the family produced an increasing proportion of books of a Neoplatonic or hermetic variety—including works by Paracelsus, Giordano Bruno, John Dee, and Giovanni Battista della Porta—and Palthenius's offshoot of the firm carried this tendency further still. Thus the term "humanism" is applied to the products of the Wechel presses not merely in the strict sense but also to designate a broad-minded, curious, outward-looking culture set apart from the increasing pressures of confessional conformity characteristic of central Europe in this era.

See also **Printing and Publishing; Ramus, Petrus.**

BIBLIOGRAPHY

Evans, R. J. W. *The Wechel Presses: Humanism and Calvinism in Central Europe, 1572–1627.* Past and Present, suppl. 2. Oxford, 1975. A rich, synthetic survey of the Wechels and their authors, with a bibliography of imprints.

Maclean, Ian. "André Wechel at Frankfurt, 1572–1581." *Gutenberg Jahrbuch* (1988): 146–176. Includes a more complete bibliography of Wechel editions, 1574–1582.

HOWARD HOTSON

WEIGHTS AND MEASURES. Weights and measures in Renaissance Europe were characterized by a profusion of national, regional, and local systems that evolved from earlier Roman, Celtic, and Germanic prototypes, with occasional influences from Greek and biblical systems. During the Roman Empire, the Roman system of weights and measures, like the Latin language and Roman law, bound the large, multicultural empire into a cohesive whole. Following the Germanic invasions of the early Middle Ages, this system of unity, precision, and standardization was shattered as native systems gained a foothold and then expanded rapidly. During the Renaissance these systems continued to proliferate at a rapid pace. Hundreds of thousands of different units of measurement evolved, due to such factors as economic development, commercial competition, demographic growth, urbanism, tax manipulations, technological progress, territorial expansion, and the impact of custom and tradition. No unified, scientific system of weights and measures would emerge during the Renaissance, and Europe would have to await the creation of the metric system in the late eighteenth and early nineteenth centuries for a solution to the metrological impasse.

Legislation and Decrees. The many metrological decrees and conciliar and legislative enactments during the Renaissance were generally poorly conceived and framed. Wording was very ambiguous, and the constant repetition of injunctions and prohibitions in the absence of proper supervisory regulation led to increased abuses. Some laws provided exceptions for aristocratic and mercantile interests, and such practices set precedents for still more exceptions. Physical standards were mentioned but rarely defined or identified properly. Some laws favored certain towns and regions to the detriment of others. Frequent repeals, and the fact that certain laws even acknowledged past failures but did not introduce new approaches or stiffer penalties, encouraged noncompliance.

Standardization efforts were further thwarted by the inordinately large numbers of officials entrusted with inspecting weights and measures and enforcing obedience to the mandates. These duties fell to a host of officials who included elite townsmen, commissioners, manorial and other rural lords and courts, church dignitaries, urban magistrates, guildsmen, port officials, justices and judges, law enforcement personnel such as sheriffs and coroners, fair and market attendees, and many others. Their duties were generally poorly defined and they seldom received training. Their jurisdictions overlapped and their remuneration often depended on the number and amount of fines levied. Hence there were ample opportunities for abuse, fraud, and corruption.

Governments were also remiss in producing enough physical prototype standards to enable effective regulation. There were too few standards for many units of measurement authorized by the central and regional governments and almost none at all for the hundreds of thousands of units employed on the local level. When physical standards were disseminated from their sources of manufacture, they frequently varied from the originals or masters. Too many centers were given permission to issue standards, and the problems were compounded when local craftsmen made copies of the masters. Variances increased at each level of manufacture, and weather conditions and constant handling further reduced the accuracy of measuring devices constructed from wood, lead, iron, and bronze.

The Variations. Of the many contributors to metrological proliferation during the Renaissance, the following were the most important. First, central governments issued a variety of standards for individual units. In France, for example, there were multiple standards for such widely used units as the *arpent* (land), *pied* (length), *perche* (length), *toise* (length), *canne* (textiles), *corde* (firewood), *mille* (distance), and *quintal* (hundredweight).

Occasionally, common local vessels without standard dimensions gained such popularity that they were accepted as standards. These included the French *baille* (coal); the English trendle (wax), prickle (fruit), costrel (wine), and coddus (grain); and the Italian *balla* (dry goods). Products also contributed to metrological proliferation, especially in those units employed for bulk-rating goods for shipment. Depending on the value, weight, and physical dimensions of a particular product, there were wild fluctuations in England for such units as the bale, bunch, dicker, fatt, hogshead, kip, pack, seron, and wey, to mention only a few.

Principal Linear, Area, Capacity, and Weight Units in England during the Renaissance.[1]

English Unit	English Equivalent	Metric Equivalent[2]	English Unit	English Equivalent	Metric Equivalent
Length			*Capacity (Wine)*		
inch		2.54 cm	cubic inch		0.01639 l
palm	3 inches	7.62 cm	pint	28.875 cubic inches	0.473 l
span	9 inches	2.286 dm	quart	2 pints	0.95 l
foot	12 inches	0.3048 m	gallon	4 quarts	3.785 l
cubit	18 inches	4.572 dm	rundlet	18 gallons	6.81 dal
yard	3 feet	0.9144 m	barrel	31.5 gallons	1.19 hl
pace	5 feet	1.52 m	tierce	42 gallons	1.59 hl
fathom	6 feet	1.829 m	hogshead	63 gallons	2.38 hl
perch	16.5 feet	5.029 m	puncheon	84 gallons	3.18 hl
furlong	660 feet	201.168 m	butt	126 gallons	4.77 hl
mile	5,280 feet	1.6093 km	tun	252 gallons	9.54 hl
Area			*Capacity (Dry)*		
square inch		6.4516 square cm	cubic inch		0.01639 l
square foot	144 square inches	0.0929 square m	pint	33. 6 cubic inches	0.551 l
rood	10,890 square feet	1,011.67 square m	quart	2 pints	1.10 l
acre	43,560 square feet	0.4047 ha	gallon	4 quarts	4.404 l
			peck	2 gallons	8.810 l
			bushel	8 gallons	35.238 l
			quarter	64 gallons	2.82 hl
			Weight (Troy)		
			troy grain		0.06 g
			pennyweight	24 grains	1.555 g
			ounce	480 grains	31.103 g
			pound	5,760 grains	373.242 g
			Weight (Avoirdupois)		
			troy grain		0.06 g
			dram	27.344 grains	1.772 g
			ounce	437.5 grains	28.350 g
			pound	7,000 grains	453.592 g
			stone	14 pounds	6.350 kg
			hundredweight	112 pounds	50.802 kg
			ton	2,240 pounds	1,016.040 kg

[1]A single description denotes widespread usage, while no description after the unit name signifies multiple divisions depending on location. Even within single descriptions, however, certain units varied widely.

[2]Metric abbreviations: km = kilometer, m = meter, dm = decimeter, cm = centimeter, mm = millimeter, hl = hectoliter, dal = dekaliter, l = liter, cl = centiliter, ha = hectare, a = acre, kg = kilogram, g = gram, dg = decigram, cg = centigram.

With the rapid urbanization of Europe during this period, weights and measures often separated into different standards depending on whether they were employed inside or outside the walls of any town. The French *danrée* for land measurement was an outstanding example of this. Similarly, some units varied depending on whether they were used on land or on sea. The French *lieue* (league) varied between two thousand and three thousand *toises,* with the greater lengths employed for sea distances. Measuring units also changed in size over time. In France the *livre* (pound) went from 5,760 grains in the late eighth century to 9,216 grains in the middle of the fourteenth century.

Some units were used for more than one measurement division. The French *aissin* was a capacity measure for grain, a volume measure for wood, and a land measure. Even when used for only one divi-

Principal Linear, Area, Capacity, and Weight Units in France during the Renaissance.[1]

French Unit	French Equivalent	Metric Equivalent[2]	French Unit	French Equivalent	Metric Equivalent
Length			*Capacity*		
aune	526 5/6 lignes	1.188 m	barrique (in veltes)		198 to 305 l
brasse	5 to 6 pieds	1.63 to 1.98 m	bichet		34 to 250 l
canne	8 pans	1.80 to 2.02 m	boisseau	655.78 cubic pouces	13.008 l
lieue	2,000 to 3,000 toises	3,900 to 5,850 m	chopine	23.475 cubic pouces	46.56 cl
ligne	12 points	2.256 mm	émine		20 to 467 l
mille	1,000 pas géométriques	1,624 m	litron	41 cubic pouces	0.8 l
			mine	6 to 16 boisseaux	78 to 208 l
palme	0.25 pied	82 mm	minot	3 to 8 boisseaux	39 to 104 l
pas	2 to 5 pieds	0.65 to 1.63 m	muid		2 to 23 hl
perche	6 aunes	7.10 m	pinte	47 cubic pouces	0.93 l
pied	12 pouces	324.84 mm	poinçon	216 pintes	201.16 l
point	1/12 ligne	0.188 mm	quartaut		67 to 103 l
pouce	12 lignes	2.707 cm	quarte		0.3 to 61 l
toise	6 pieds	1.949 m	setier		7 to 417 l
Area			*Weight*		
arpent	100 square perches	34.19 to 42.21 a	carat	4 grains	2.059 dg
jour (in square verges)		20 to 62 a	charge	300 livres	146.852 kg
			denier	24 grains	1.275 g
journal (in square verges)		20 to 62 a	drachme	60 grains	3.824 g
			estelin	28.8 grains	1.53 g
			félin	7.20 grains	0.38 g
			grain	24 primes	0.053 g
			gros	72 grains	3.824 g
			livre poids de marc	9,216 grains	489.506 g
			maille	14.4 grains	0.8 g
			marc	4,608 grains	244.753 g
			obole	14.4 grains	0.8 g
			once poids de marc	576 grains	30.594 g
			quintal	100 livres	48.951 kg
			scrupule	24 grains	1.275 g
			tonneau	2,000 livres	979.112 kg

[1]Units are listed alphabetically since France had no overall national systems until metric adoption. A single description denotes widespread usage, while no description after the unit name signifies multiple divisions depending on location.

[2]Metric abbreviations: km = kilometer, m = meter, dm = decimeter, cm = centimeter, mm = millimeter, hl = hectoliter, dal = dekaliter, l = liter, cl = centiliter, ha = hectare, a = acre, kg = kilogram, g = gram, dg = decigram, cg = centigram.

sion, however, a unit could have various methods of submultiple compilation. In England, the fother for lead of 2,100 pounds had four subdivisions: 30 fotmals of 70 pounds each, 168 stone of 12.5 pounds each, 175 stone of 12 pounds each, or 12 weys of 175 pounds each.

Certain units had more than one name. In England there were the pint/jug/stoup, butt/pipe, and rod/perch/pole/goad/verge, while in the Italian states one finds the grosso/dramma/quarro, dana-peso/denaro, and cantaio/carara/centinaio.

Many other factors contributed to the proliferation of weights and measures. Area measures were based on the amount of land required to produce an annual income, on the amount rented out for a certain fee, or the amount assessed on the tax rolls at a certain price. Measures were based on food production estimates and on human functions, physical abilities,

Principal Linear, Area, Capacity, and Weight Units in Italy during the Renaissance.[1]

Italian Unit	Italian Equivalent	Metric Equivalent[2]	Italian Unit	Italian Equivalent	Metric Equivalent
		Length			*Capacity*
atomo	12 minuti	0.00022 to 0.00058 m	ambola		1.60 to 3.25 l
			amola		0.88 to 1.38 l
braccio	5 to 6 piedi	0.35 to 1.00 m	barile		0.12 to 2.25 hl
canna		0.62 to 7.85 m	bigoncia	2 mastelli	129.6 l
cavezzo	generally 6 piedi	2.06 to 3.86 m	boccale		0.68 to 4.08 l
corda	16 canne	33.036 m	botte		0.49 to 12.25 hl
linea	12 punti	0.0017 to 0.0028 m	brenta		0.47 to 1.23 hl
miglio		1.00 to 2.52 km	caffiso (in rotoli)		5.73 to 85.96 l
palmo	generally 12 once	0.125 to 0.292 m	caldarolo		0.05 to 0.11 hl
passo		0.67 to 2.02 m	cannata		0.01 to 0.25 hl
pertica		1.57 to 6.17 m	caraffa (in barile)		0.32 to 6.34 l
piede	generally 12 once	0.223 to 0.649 m	coppello		0.08 to 3.45 l
punto	generally 12 atomi	0.00014 to 0.00585 m	emina		0.05 to 1.39 hl
			fiasco		1.99 to 2.28 l
tesa		1.414 to 2.242 m	foglietta	generally 1/4 boccale	0.28 to 1.26 l
trabucco	generally 6 piedi	2.611 to 3.243 m			
		Area	litra (in rotoli)		0.41 to 4.21 l
			mastello		0.51 to 1.14 hl
biolca		0.28 to 0.65 ha	metro (in rotoli)		0.01 to 0.35 hl
campo		0.32 to 0.61 ha	mezzaruola		0.09 to 1.60 hl
coltra	generally 4 quartieri	0.39 to 0.51 ha	mezzetta		0.50 to 27.66 l
			mezzo		0.17 to 10.29 l
giornata		0.09 to 0.45 ha	mina		0.09 to 1.31 hl
modiolo		0.15 to 0.65 ha	pinta	generally 2 boccali	0.14 to 2.26 l
opera		0.05 to 0.35 ha			
quadrato	100 tavole	34.062 a	quarta		0.09 to 82.30 l
saccato		0.51 to 0.63 ha	quartarolo		0.58 to 39.84 l
scorzo	4 quartucci	11.553 a	quartino		0.03 to 3.91 l
staro		0.04 to 0.16 hl	quartuccio		0.12 to 6.13 l
tavola		0.03 to 43.10 a	rubbio		0.08 to 3.50 hl
tomolata		0.10 to 0.84 ha	sacca		0.61 to 6.23 hl
tornatura	generally 100 tavole	0.11 to 0.42 ha	salma		0.65 to 7.74 hl
			staio (in rotoli)		0.05 to 1.50 hl
			tomolo (in square passi)		0.17 to 0.55 hl
					Weight
			acino	1/20 trapesso	4.455 cg
			cantaro	generally 100 to 250 libbre	30.12 to 93.23 kg
			carato	4 grani	1.77 to 2.14 dg
			denaro	24 grani	1.10 to 2.43 g
			dramma	72 grani	1.67 to 3.60 g
			ferlino	10 carati	1.77 to 1.88 g
			libbra	generally 12 once	0.239 to 0.980 kg
			marca	8 once	0.21 to 0.25 kg
			oncia		0.025 to 0.043 kg
			rotolo	1/100 cantaro	0.48 to 1.02 kg
			saggio	1/6 oncia	4.185 or 6.626 g
			scrupolo	generally 24 grani	0.89 to 1.20 g
			trappeso		0.82 to 0.89 g

[1]Units are listed alphabetically since Italy had no overall national systems until metric adoption. A single description denotes widespread usage, while no description after the unit name signifies multiple divisions depending on location.

[2]Metric abbreviations: km = kilometer, m = meter, dm = decimeter, cm = centimeter, mm = millimeter, hl = hectoliter, dal = dekaliter, l = liter, cl = centiliter, ha = hectare, a = acre, kg = kilogram, g = gram, dg = decigram, cg = centigram.

and time allotments, as well as the production capability or strength potential of animals. Weights and measures were frequently divided into halves, thirds, and fourths, and, where such subdivisions were impractical, into an irregular assortment of diminutives. They could vary according to the needs of specific trades or crafts. Area measures sometimes arose from linear or capacity measures. Capacity measures sometimes were determined by a vessel's calibration in the weight content of river water or whether their contents were sold in heaped, striked, or shallow containers. Finally, volume measures arose from the name or the length of some string, cord, or rope used to bind products together; from capacity measures reserved solely for wholesale shipments; and from quantity measures used for land and sea shipments transported by pack trains and ships of varying sizes and cargoes.

Tables of Equivalents. The tables accompanying this entry list some of the principal linear, area, capacity, and weight units in England, France, and Italy during the Renaissance. Coverage for the multitude of other units and variations within these systems, and for those employed in other European countries, can be found in the sources in the bibliography. The French and Italian units are listed alphabetically since they had no overall national system until metric adoption. A single description denotes widespread usage, while no description after the unit name signifies multiple divisions depending on location. Even with single descriptions, however, certain units varied widely.

BIBLIOGRAPHY

Berriman, A. E. *Historical Metrology*. London, 1953. Important for the development of English weights and measures.

Kula, Witold. *Measures and Men*. Translated by Richard Szreter. Princeton, N.J., 1986. Europeanwide in scope, with principal emphasis on social ramifications of weights and measures.

Zupko, Ronald E. *Revolution in Measurement: Western European Weights and Measures since the Age of Science*. Philadelphia, 1990. Extensive coverage of medieval and Renaissance metrologies, scientific experiments, physical standards, numerous tables of equivalents, and extensive bibliography.

Zupko, Ronald E. "Weights and Measures, Western European." In *Dictionary of the Middle Ages*. Vol. 12. New York, 1989. Pages 582–596. Dominant systems of medieval Europe plus tables of equivalents.

RONALD EDWARD ZUPKO

WEYDEN, ROGIER VAN DER (Roger de la Pasture; c. 1399–1464), Flemish painter. Van der Weyden, a cutler's son born at Tournai, is almost certainly the "Rogelet de le Pasture" who entered the workshop of the painter Robert Campin in 1427. However, he probably began his apprenticeship in his teens—as was common practice—and joined Campin in 1427 as a collaborator, not as a pupil as is generally believed. He may have trained at the workshop of the Master of Flémalle, upon whose style van der Weyden's was founded. (Campin, whose documented works are lost, is now generally believed to be the anonymous Master of Flémalle, because of his association with van der Weyden and the connections between van der Weyden's style and that of the anonymous master. However, conclusive evidence is lacking.) Van der Weyden left Campin's workshop in 1432, moved to Brussels by October 1435, and was named that city's official painter by May 1436, a position he retained for the rest of his life. He painted four large panels in the late 1430s and 1440s (now lost, with one panel reportedly dated 1439), representing the *Justice of Trajan* and the *Justice of Herkinbald* for the courtroom of the Brussels town hall.

Rogier and Italy. Bartolomeo Fazio states in his *De viris illustribus* (c. 1456) that van der Weyden visited Italy in 1450 for the Holy Year. If this is true, it is remarkable how little impact Italian art had on the content and style of his later works. (The attributions of the italianizing *Virgin and Child with Saints* [Frankfurt, Städelsches Kunstinstitut] and *Entombment* [Florence, Uffizi] to van der Weyden remain controversial.) Van der Weyden's fame obviously reached Italy early on, for Fazio devotes a "life" to him and mentions works by him in Genoa, Ferrara, and Naples. The works at Ferrara were delivered to the Marquis Leonello d'Este, and those at Naples belonged to King Alfonso V of Aragon. Van der Weyden was also admired at the Milanese court, since he was praised by the court architect Filarete (c. 1460–1464) and was thanked in 1463 by the Duchess Bianca Maria Sforza for training the young court painter Zanetto Bugatto in Brussels. (Little is otherwise known about the artists who trained and assisted in his workshop, with the possible exception of Hans Memling, who may have completed his instruction with van der Weyden.)

Authenticated Works. Van der Weyden's surviving works are neither signed nor dated and are poorly documented. However, the Miraflores Triptych (Berlin, Staatliche Museen), given in 1445 to the Charterhouse of Miraflores near Burgos by King John II of Castile, is recorded in the donation as being painted by "the great and famous Fleming Rogel." The *Descent from the Cross* (Madrid, Prado), obvi-

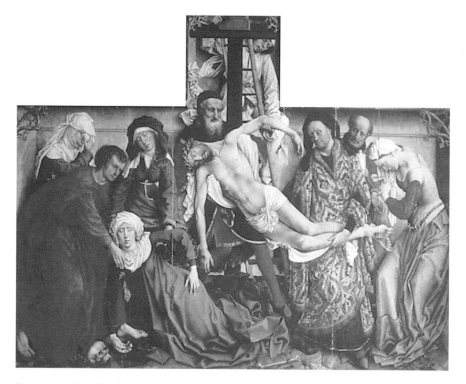

Rogier van der Weyden. *Descent from the Cross.* MUSEO DEL PRADO, MADRID/SUPER-STOCK

ously completed by the time it was copied in 1443, was reportedly acquired from the chapel of Our Lady Outside the Walls at Louvain by the regent of the Netherlands, Mary of Hungary. Mary passed the painting on to her nephew Philip II of Spain, who offered it to the Escorial in 1574. It is listed at the Escorial in the inventory of the gift, together with a *Crucifixion,* as by "Rogier." The inventory states that the *Crucifixion* came from the "Charterhouse of Brussels," almost certainly the Charterhouse of Scheut outside Brussels, to which van der Weyden made a gift of money and pictures. A number of works are attributed to van der Weyden on the basis of these three devotional paintings; they must thus form the point of departure for an assessment of his achievement.

The *Deposition* is influenced by the tradition of the *Schnitzaltar,* an altarpiece in which carved and painted figures were assembled inside boxes. Here, the actors—perhaps including the donor, second from the right—are placed on a narrow stage inside a shallow gilded box, which both underlines the theatricality of this drama, acted out so close to the viewer and above the altar, and eliminates all superfluous detail, thus allowing for focused contemplation. As the dead Christ is lowered in the center of the composition, the Virgin swoons in the im-

mediate foreground, echoing the arabesque of his pose in her *compassio.* Van der Weyden's relief-like ensemble comes alive as a result of his superb rendering of movements, emotions, and textures.

Masterly synthesis and theatrical staging are likewise characteristic of the Miraflores Triptych, which includes the *Holy Family,* the *Pietà,* and the *Final Appearance of Christ to His Mother.* These tableaux are placed just beyond painted arches, which simulate the portals of a Gothic cathedral and support carved saints and scenes from the *Life of the Virgin* on the archivolts.

In the tall, austere, and perfectly symmetrical *Crucifixion,* van der Weyden draws the viewer's attention to the pathos of the Virgin and John at the foot of the cross. The cross is raised in front of an unfolded red drapery, which serves as a precious foil for the dead Christ and both mourners seen in dramatic close-up.

Van der Weyden and Jan van Eyck. Van der Weyden's inventive skills are also evident in his transformation of van Eyck's *Virgin and Child with Chancellor Rolin* (Paris, Louvre) into *St. Luke Drawing a Portrait of the Virgin* (Boston, Museum of Fine Arts). Van Eyck's triptych of the *Virgin and Child with Saints* (Dresden, Gemäldegalerie) may be at the

Rogier van der Weyden. *Annunciation.* MUSÉE DE LOUVRE, PARIS/SUPERSTOCK

origin of the idea of reserving the large central panel of the altarpiece of the *Seven Sacraments* (Antwerp, Koninklijk Museum voor Schone Kunsten) for the representation of the central aisle of a Gothic basilica and the two side panels for the depiction of the aisles and side chapels. Mass is celebrated beyond the *Crucifixion* in the foreground of the tall central panel, while the remaining sacraments are depicted in the shorter and narrower side panels.

Van der Weyden was also an outstanding portrait painter. In his bust-length portraits *Francesco d'Este* (New York, Metropolitan Museum of Art), *Antoine, Grand Bâtard de Bourgogne* (Brussels, Musées Royaux des Beaux-Arts), and *Young Woman* (Washington, D.C., National Gallery of Art), the heads and torsos are turned in three-quarter profile toward the left before a blank ground, and one or two hands are placed at the bottom of the configuration. Van der Weyden's intensely expressive art was in great demand, and his highly original compositions, exquisite draftsmanship, and abstracting tendencies—more easily assimilated than van Eyck's daunting illusionism—influenced artists in many areas of western Europe well into the sixteenth century.

See also biographies of figures mentioned in this entry.

BIBLIOGRAPHY

Campbell, Lorne. "Rogier van der Weyden." In *The Dictionary of Art.* Edited by Jane Turner. Vol. 33. New York, 1996. Pages 117–128.

Campbell, Lorne. *Van der Weyden.* New York, 1980.

Davies, Martin. *Rogier van der Weyden: An Essay, with a Critical Catalogue of Paintings Assigned to Him and to Robert Campin.* London, 1972.

Delenda, Odile. *Rogier van der Weyden (Roger de Le Pasture).* Paris, 1987.

Dhanens, Elisabeth. *Rogier van der Weyden: Revisie van de Documenten.* Brussels, Belgium, 1995. Includes passages from all the known documents and literary accounts referring to Rogier up to the end of the eighteenth century.

MICHAËL J. AMY

WICKRAM, JORG (or Georg; c. 1505–c. 1561), Alsatian author and playwright. Because Wickram was the illegitimate son of a wealthy Colmar patrician, it can be assumed that he was excluded from many communal privileges. He probably went to a public school, learning only elementary reading, writing, and mathematics, and he never learned a foreign language. Thus excluded from much of the humanist discourse of the time, he nonetheless seems to have read extensively in vernacular texts.

Not afraid of literary challenges, in 1545 Wickram even reworked Albrecht of Halberstadt's translation of Ovid's *Metamorphoses*. He was also in charge of the city theater, and in 1531 his first Shrove Tuesday play *Die zehen Alter* (The ten ages) was published. Affiliated with the city Meistersinger, Wickram owned a manuscript of songs by Hans Sachs and also wrote songs himself. Wickram is remembered, however, not for his plays and songs, but rather for his prose texts, especially the chapbook *Rollwagen-büchlein* (Carriage booklet, 1555) which is the only text he wrote primarily to entertain, rather than to educate or to admonish. His first novel was *Der Ritter Galmy uss Schottland* (The knight Galmy from Scotland; 1539), a story about a young knight's love for a married, socially superior lady. Wickram typically relied on old sources and traditional themes, but he added his own stories and morals to the plot. His second novel, *Gabriotto und Reinhart* (1551), is based on one of Boccaccio's novellas in the *Decameron* though it differs greatly from the original. *Der jungen Knaben Spiegel* (Manual for young boys; 1555) draws its plot and its purpose from the biblical story of the prodigal son.

In an age of highly conventional vernacular literature, Wickram's work stands out for its increasing thematic and stylistic independence. Although influenced by humanist writers as well as by popular culture and literature, Wickram had few true predecessors and no successors. The importance of law and order among people living in the growing cities combined with the wish for happiness, friendship, and mutual respect expressed in Wickram's work are topics of less importance in the courtly literature that appears toward the end of the sixteenth century.

Wickram's last two prose works show the greatest independence of all. Around the time they were written, Wickram became town clerk in Burgheim on the Rhine and also changed publishers. His higher social status probably allowed him more freedom in his choice of topics and themes. *Von guten und bösen Nachbaurn* (Of good and bad neighbors; 1556) and *Der Goldtfaden* (The golden thread; 1557) use topics familiar to the reader, but they are not directly based on older texts. In *Nachbaurn* Wickram completely moves away from the courtly atmosphere found in early works; the plot focuses on merchants and craftsmen.

BIBLIOGRAPHY

Primary Work

Wickram, Georg. *Sämtliche Werke.* Vols. 1–8, 11–13. Edited by Hans-Gert Roloff. Berlin, 1967–1992.

Secondary Works

Chrisman, Miriam Usher. *Lay Culture, Learned Culture: Books and Social Change in Strasbourg 1480–1599.* New Haven, Conn., 1982. Pages 209–222.

Kleinschmidt, Erich. "Jörg Wickram." In *Deutsche Dichter der frühen Neuzeit (1450–1600): Ihr Leben und Werk.* Edited by Stephan Füssel. Berlin, 1993. Pages 494–511.

Wåghäll, Elisabeth. "Georg Wickram." In *Dictionary of Literary Biography.* Vol. 179, *German Writers of the Renaissance and Reformation: 1280–1580.* Edited by James Hardin and Max Reinhart. Detroit, Mich.; Washington, D.C.; and London; 1997. Pages 309–316.

ELISABETH WÅGHÄLL-NIVRE

WIDOWHOOD. Many factors shaped the lives of the widowed in Renaissance Europe: law, wealth, religion, age, affection, personality, and, above all, the sex of the bereaved. Widowhood affected women far more than it did men. That is, widows always outnumbered widowers: in Castile by up to twelve to one, in Tuscany by more than five to one, in England by two to one. Wives, generally younger than their husbands, usually outlived them. Widowers experienced less financial change; their occupational roles were unaltered and men normally kept all or most of the conjugal estate for life. Widowers were also at least twice as likely to remarry, and remarry quickly, driven by the sheer necessity of having a woman in the household.

Remarriage was accepted hesitantly in Renaissance cultures. Among Catholics widowhood was honored as a status next to virginity, and even Protestants and Jews expressed reservations about widows remarrying. Christian prescriptive writing on widowhood drew heavily on 1 Tim. 5:3 in the New Testament to "honor widows that are widows indeed," although the permission to young widows to remarry was reflected in reality; young widows were everywhere more likely to wed again. Popular literature generally portrayed widows as lusty and likely to harm their children's interests. The separate case of the widower was rarely considered, although some writers included widowers in their warnings against the dangers of "unequal" remarriage, a phenomenon liable to neighborly criticism in the form of charivari (a mocking serenade).

But unremarried widows also posed complex problems when patriarchal order required women to be under the control of men. Prescriptive works for widows focused on controlling the "unheaded" woman. Book three of Juan Vives's influential *De institutione feminae Christianae* (The education of Christian women; 1523) emphasized "chastity" and continued loyalty to the dead husband's expectations. Horatio Fusco and Desiderius Erasmus instead celebrated widowhood as allowing the widow to enact her independent virtue when, free of male control, she was nearest virile power.

The numbers of independent widows heading their own households in a given locality depended not only on the relative ages of conjugal partners and remarriage rates but also on inheritance law and urban or rural environments. For example, due to migration only 6 percent of households in rural Tuscany were widow-headed in 1427, in contrast to 14 percent in Florence. Law and custom particularly affected widowhood among elites. In areas were Roman law was influential, widows' rights to a share of the conjugal property and guardianship of the children were limited. The best-known case is that of elite Florentine widows who took back only their dowries if they left the households of their husbands' heirs; thus, though numerous due to great conjugal age differences, they headed only 2 percent of wealthy households.

Castile presents one of many variations on the rules of customary law that were, by and large, more favorable to widows. Widows there succeeded to substantial shares of conjugal property, including one-tenth or more of their husbands' wealth (called the *arras*) plus their own dowries and half of conjugal acquisitions, so long as they did not remarry. Consequently, high proportions of Castilian households were headed by widows (24 percent in Ávila, 14 percent in some villages). In Paris widows' customary rights were also strong, and they headed about 12 percent of households, 20 percent among wealthier taxpayers. Similar patterns prevailed in the Netherlands and in many German towns. In England, where conjugal age differences were lower, widows were fewer overall (9 percent of all women) but they still headed 13 percent of households. Common and customary law, notoriously restrictive of married women, gave widows substantial lifetime rights to conjugal and husbands' estates (rarely less than the third allowed by common-law dower plus shares of movable goods). However, actually claiming such rights was everywhere often difficult.

Legal patterns could be altered by contract or testament. Negotiated marriage settlements often extended the widow's share, and husbands' testaments could make wives executors and household heads. Fathers could convey guardianship of children and their estates in areas where it normally did not fall to widows, or take it away in areas (such as England) where by "natural law" widows were guardians.

Thus, depending on law, practice, and talent, some remarkable widows (Christine de Pizan [1363/64–c. 1430] is one extraordinary example) acquired an independent economic and social presence (and historical visibility) rarely afforded to married or never-married women. Some widows entered new masculine roles and like Maddalena Nerli of Florence or Catherine de Médicis (1519–1589) took over management of estates or even kingdoms. In many localities rights of succession in office or in craft and trade were formally recognized. But only a minority of widows carried on their husbands' businesses even until a child came of age. Only a third did so for even a brief time in Abingdon, England; even fewer in Augsburg, Germany. More appear in local listings practicing "female trades," especially supplying food and drink, perhaps perpetuating work they had previously pursued as wives, perhaps work newly adopted in widowhood.

If widowhood gave unique opportunities for independence and power to a few widows, for the vast majority bereavement entailed not only more work but also upheaval and poverty, or at best comfortable subordination in another's household. Widowhood induced mobility; in some localities half of widows moved within a year to new independent households or to share with other women, children, or kin. Poor widows were endemic, as evidenced in records of poor relief, charitable institutions, almshouses, and asylums. Any single-adult household was vulnerable, but since women's earning power was always less than men's and widows held only part of the conjugal wealth, everywhere the majority of widow-headed households were poor and everywhere widows predominated among adult recipients of charity or relief. Perhaps they were victims of a preference for nuclear families, yet widows subordinated within large households were not necessarily more economically comfortable. Perhaps the most eloquent testimony to the hardship of being a widow in a male-dominated world is the absence of hundreds of old women in listings like the Florentine *catasto* (property census) of 1427. Their invisibility brings to sharp relief the prominence of the powerful few.

See also **Marriage and Separation**.

BIBLIOGRAPHY

Primary Works

Erasmus, Desiderius. *The Christian Widow*. Translated by Jennifer T. Roberts. Vol. 66 of *Collected Works of Erasmus*. Toronto, 1988. Pages 200–257. Translation of *De vidua christiana* (1529).

Vives, Juan Luis. *A Very Frutefull and Pleasant Boke Called the Instruction of a Christen Woman.* Translated by Richard Hyrd. London, 1529, and later editions. Translation of *De Institutione feminae Christianae* (1523).

Secondary Works

Cavallo, Sandra, and Lyndan Warner, eds. *Late Medieval and Early Modern Widows.* London, 1998.

Hufton, Olwen. "Widowhood." In *The Prospect before Her: A History of Women in Western Europe.* Vol. I, *1500–1800.* London, 1995. Pages 217–250.

Klapisch-Zuber, Christiane. "The Cruel Mother." In *Women, Family, and Ritual in Renaissance Italy.* Translated by Lydia Cochrane. Chicago, 1985. Pages 117–131.

Mirrer, Louise, ed. *Upon My Husband's Death: Widows in the Literature and Histories of Medieval Europe.* Ann Arbor, Mich., 1992.

Vassberg, David E. "The Status of Widows in Sixteenth-Century Castile." In *Poor Women and Children in the European Past.* Edited by John Henderson and Richard Wall. London, 1994. Pages 180–195.

BARBARA J. TODD

WILLIAM THE SILENT

WILLIAM THE SILENT (1533–1584), count of Nassau, prince of Orange (from 1544), and stadtholder of the United Provinces of the Netherlands (from 1572). William was born and raised initially in Dillenburg in the Lutheran region of Nassau; upon his accession to the Catholic principality of Orange, the Spanish Habsburg emperor, Charles V, required that he be sent to the Flemish court of Brussels to learn Dutch and be educated as a Catholic.

William adapted well to his new role as an Orange prince. In 1549 he accompanied Prince Philip of Spain through the Netherlands, and he fought in Habsburg campaigns against the French for much of the 1550s. In 1551 he married Anne of Egmond-Buren, who gave him a considerable inheritance and, in 1554, his eldest son, Philip William. He was a widower by 1558. At the conclusion of the French wars in 1559 Philip—since 1566 Philip II, king of Spain—now returned to his homeland, bestowed on William the responsibilities of the first stadtholder (chief executive) in the Dutch provinces of Holland, Zeeland, and Utrecht.

It was not long before the powerful stadtholder found himself in opposition to his benefactor. Linked, more through his sympathies than by any illegal actions, to revolutionary movements, William was banished, his lands confiscated, his son snatched from school and transported to Spain as a hostage. A new emissary was sent by Philip II to quell rebellion and rule all the Netherlands as stadtholder. Thus was William motivated to participate in the armed revolts against Philip II in 1568. Although these uprisings were not successful, there followed

William the Silent. Portrait by Adriaen Thomasz Key (1544–1589). Oil on oakwood; 1579; 48 × 34 cm (19 × 13.4 in.). MAURITSHUIS, THE HAGUE/ERIC LESSING/ART RESOURCE

a period of intermittent, and seemingly interminable, rebellion against Spain and, for William, a life of complicated military, political, and religious maneuvering.

William had married Anna of Saxony, a German Lutheran, in 1561. In 1567 his second son, Maurice of Nassau, was born and William reverted back to the Lutheranism of his youth. By 1573, responding to both general indifference in the Netherlander populace and increasing Calvinist radicalism, he converted to the (Calvinist) Reformed Church even as he tried to steer a course of moderation between Calvinists and the Dutch Catholic minority. Forced to choose between religious tolerance and Dutch independence under Calvinist rule, William chose independence. Having divorced his Lutheran wife in 1571 on grounds of infidelity, he married Charlotte of Bourbon-Montpensier in the Reformed Church in 1575.

Plate 1. Art in Siena. *Maestà* (Virgin Mary in Majesty with Angels and Saints), 1308–1311, by Duccio de Buoninsegna (c. 1255–1318), in the Cathedral of Siena. [See the entry Siena, subentry on Art in Siena, in this volume.] MUSEO DELL'OPERA METROPOLITANA, SIENA/ALINARI/ART RESOURCE.

Plate 2. Space and Perspective. *Madonna and Child with Saints and Angels,* called the *Montefeltro Altarpiece,* by Piero della Francesca (c. 1420–1492). Federico da Montefeltro, lord of Urbino, kneels at the Madonna's feet. Painted 1472–1474; 2.5 x 1.7 m (97.25 x 66.75 in.). [See the entry on Space and Perspective in this volume and the entry on Piero in volume 5.] PINACOTECA DI BRERA, MILAN/SCALA/ART RESOURCE

Plate 6. Titian. *Venus of Urbino.* Painted 1538–1539.
[See the entry on Titian in this volume.] GALLERIA DEGLI
UFFIZI, FLORENCE/SCALA/ART RESOURCE

Plate 7. **The Ruler of Urbino.** Portrait of Federico da
Montefeltro (1422–1482), lord of Urbino, with his son
Guidobaldo, by either Pedro Berruguete or Justus of Ghent.
[See the article on Urbino in this volume, the entry on
Federico da Montefeltro in volume 2, and the entry on the
Montefeltro Family in volume 4. For a portrayal of Federico
by Piero della Francesca, see the illustration of space and
perspective in this section of color plates.] PALAZZO DUCALE,
URBINO, ITALY/SCALA/ART RESOURCE

Plate 8. The Studiolo of Urbino.
The studiolo (small study) of
Federico da Montefeltro
(1422–1482), lord of Urbino,
is paneled in illustionistic intarsia
(a mosaic made of wood).
[See the article on Urbino in this
volume.] PALAZZO DUCALE, URBINO,
ITALY/SCALA/ART RESOURCE

Plate 9. Art in Venice. *The Death of Adonis,* c. 1512, by Sebastiano del Piombo (c. 1483–1547).
[See the entry Venice, subentry on Art in Venice, in this volume; for another treatment of the story of
Venus and Adonis, see the painting by Rubens in the color plates in volume 5.] GALLERIA DEGLI UFFIZI,
FLORENCE/NIMATALLAH/ART RESOURCE

Plate 10. Art in Venice. *Woman with a Drawing of Lucretia,* c. 1530–1533, by Lorenzo Lotto (c. 1480–1556). On the table is a piece of paper with the inscription "No unchaste woman shall live through the example of Lucretia," a quotation from Livy's *History of Rome* 1.58. Oil on canvas; 95.9 x 110.5 cm (37.8 x 43.5 in.). [See the entry Venice, subentry on Art in Venice, in this volume.] NATIONAL GALLERY, LONDON

Plate 11. A Venetian Family. *The Vendramin Family,* 1543–1547, by Tiziano Vecellio, called Titian (1488 or 1490–1576). The Venetian senator Andrea Vendramin, his brother Gabriele, and Andrea's seven sons venerate a relic of the True Cross presented to a fourteenth-century ancestor, also named Andrea, who had rescued the relic when it fell into the canal. [See the entry Venice in this volume. For a depiction of the rescue of the relic, see the painting by Gentile Bellini illustrating the entry on Art in Venice in volume 6; for a depiction of the relic carried in procession, see the painting by Gentile Bellini illustrating the entry on Parades, Processions, and Pageants in the color plates in volume 4.] NATIONAL GALLERY, LONDON

Plate 12. Paolo Veronese. *Mars and Venus United by Love.* Oil on canvas; 1570s; 205.7 x 161 cm (81 x 63.4 in.). METROPOLITAN MUSEUM OF ART, JOHN STEWART KENNEDY FUND, 1910, 10.189/PHOTOGRAPH © 1988 THE METROPOLITAN MUSEUM OF ART

Plate 13. Warfare. *The Battle of San Romano,* 1456, by Paolo Uccello (1397–1475). The battle, fought in 1423, resulted in a victory of Florence over Siena. This is one of three panels by Uccello depicting the battle; the other two are in the Louvre and the National Gallery, London. [For the London panel, see the entry on Warfare in this volume.] GALLERIA DEGLI UFFIZI, FLORENCE/ERICH LESSING/ART RESOURCE

Plate 14. Rogier van der Weyden. *Portrait of a Lady.* Oil on panel; c. 1460; 34 x 25.5 cm (13.5 x 10 in.). [See the entry on Rogier van der Weyden in this volume.] NATIONAL GALLERY OF ART, WASHINGTON, D.C., ANDREW W. MELLON COLLECTION/ PHOTO BY BOB GROVE

In 1572, the provincial leaders of Holland and Zeeland were the first to declare William to be their rightful stadtholder, though they still regarded themselves as part of the Spanish empire and though Catholic portions of the population were very wary of Calvinist authorities. In 1579 the Union of Utrecht—with William's support—established a league of seventeen provinces united against Spain, but the Union of Arras consisting of Catholic Brabant and Flanders remained loyal to Spain.

In 1580 Philip II declared William an outlaw, this time offering a reward for his assassination. In the face of renewed efforts by Spain to control its unruly provinces, William encouraged the States General to declare François de Valois, the duke of Anjou, sovereign in 1581, a move resisted by his own Calvinist supporters. In 1582 William moved to the city of Delft, in the northern province of Holland, as Spanish and Catholic forces grew stronger in the south. In 1583 he married Louise de Coligny, a French Huguenot. Their son, Frederick Henry, was born the following year.

At Delft his lifelong effort to unite the provinces of the Netherlands under a federal monarchy based on the principles of a representative government was ended by his assassination. His sons, in turn, were each to become a player or a pawn in the struggle, which continued for many years.

BIBLIOGRAPHY

Swart, K. W. *William the Silent and the Revolt of the Netherlands.* London, 1978.

HUGO DE SCHEPPER

WIMPHELING, JACOB (1450–1528), German churchman and humanist. Born into the family of a Sélestat saddler, Wimpheling was educated at the local Latin school, the University of Freiburg im Breisgau (B.A., 1466), the University of Erfurt, and the University of Heidelberg (M.A., 1479; licentiate in theology, 1496). Ordained in the early 1480s, he used his income from churches in Sulz and Heidelberg to support his theological studies at the University of Heidelberg, where he also taught in the Faculty of Arts in the 1470s and early 1480s. In 1484 he accepted a position as preacher at the cathedral church in Speyer.

After rejoining the faculty of the University of Heidelberg in 1498, he was passed over for a canonicate in the Strasbourg cathedral chapter in 1501. Bitterly disappointed, Wimpheling remained in Strasbourg from 1501 to 1515, where he edited and wrote more than forty books, tutored local children, and received a small income from church offices. In 1515 he moved into the household of his sister in Sélestat, where he remained until his death in 1528.

After the outbreak of the Protestant Reformation in 1517, Wimpheling at first sympathized with Martin Luther's denunciations of indulgences and his attacks on clerical abuses and papal shortcomings. When church authorities excommunicated Luther in 1520, Wimpheling urged that the Saxon Reformer be given a fair hearing. Like many older German humanists, however, he broke with Luther after he grasped the implications of Luther's theology and the threat he posed to the unity of Catholic Christianity. Despite declining health, in the 1520s he fought to keep Lutheran preachers out of Sélestat, and in one of his last works, an edition of Hieronymous Emser's *Canonis missae: defensio* (Defense of the canon of the mass; 1524), he urged Luther and Huldrych Zwingli to preserve traditional Catholic rites and respect the office of the papacy. Such efforts disappointed many of his former students and younger colleagues who had embraced Protestantism; Wimpheling's actions also failed to placate his Catholic critics who remembered well his fiery denunciations of clerical failings before 1517.

Wimpheling was a prolific author and editor who published over one hundred works. He wrote a small body of Latin poetry and one Latin school drama, *Stylpho* (1484), which supposedly was modeled on the dramas of Terence. In his pedagogical works, most notably his *Elegantiarum medulla* (Kernel of elegancies; 1493), *Isidoneus germanicus* (German guide; 1497), and *Adolescentia* (Youth; 1500), he showed his commitment to humanism by recommending the study of classical authors to improve Latin style and by urging educators to teach morality, not just the mastery of logic and the memorization of facts. Yet he cautioned his readers about the corrupting influence of pagan poetry and warned that students should have access to only the most chaste of the ancient poets. His *Defensio theologie scholastice et neotericorum* (Defense of theology and of the moderns; 1510) was a defense of traditional scholastic theology written in response to the criticisms of the University of Ingolstadt poet Jacob Locher (1471–1528). In addition to his pedagogical treatises, Wimpheling wrote a manual for the upbringing of princes (*Agatharchia,* 1498) and several works on German history (*Germania,* 1501; and *Epithoma rerum Germanicarum* [Epitome of matters German] 1505). In his *De integritate* (On uprightness; 1505) and *Apologia pro republica christiana* (Apology for the Christian commonwealth; 1506), he earned a reputation as a fiery critic of church abuses. His two main targets were clerical immorality, especially among monks and friars, and the failure of the church to reward dedicated, well-educated priests (like himself) with suitable offices. He edited over sixty works. They include writings of humanists such as Sebastian Brant (1458–1521), Giovanni Pico della Mirandola (1463–1494), and Erasmus (1466–1536), but also works of many medieval theologians and religious writers such as Jean de Gerson (1363–1429), Henry of Langenstein, Bernard of Clairvaux, and Ludolf of Saxony.

Wimpheling's scholarship, although impressive in volume, was largely derivative and unfocused. His outlook was essentially conservative, and he firmly resisted those humanists and Reformers who called for fundamental changes in the academic or religious status quo. His views were not without influence, however. His denunciations of the clergy, papacy, and religious orders intensified the anticlericalism of many of his contemporaries, and his educational writings had wide-ranging influence. Throughout the Reformation era and beyond, countless teachers, schoolmasters, and political leaders enthusiastically embraced his belief that the purpose of education was to produce pious Christians and obedient subjects through the modest study of classical literature, strict discipline, and respect for religious and political authority.

BIBLIOGRAPHY

Primary Works

Wimpheling, Jacob. *Opera selecta*. Edited by Otto Herding. Munich, 1965–1990. Modern editions of *Adolescentia* (1965), *Das Leben des Johannes von Kaysersberg* (1970), and *Briefwechsel* (1990).

Wimpheling, Jacob. *Stylpho*. Edited by Hugo Holstein. Berlin, 1892.

Secondary Works

Knepper, Joseph. *Jakob Wimpfeling (1450–1528); Sein Leben und Seine Werke*. Freiburg im Breisgau, Germany, 1902.

Schmidt, Charles. *Histoire littéraire de l'Alsace*. Paris, 1879. See "Jacques Wimpfeling," vol. 1, pp. 1–188; vol. 2, pp. 317–340.

Spitz, Lewis. *The Religious Renaissance of the German Humanists*. Cambridge, Mass., 1963. See "Wimpfeling: Sacerdotal Humanist," pp. 41–60.

JAMES H. OVERFIELD

WITCHCRAFT. The crime of witchcraft, as it was defined in Europe during the the Renaissance, contained two main elements. The first was the alleged practice of maleficent or harmful magic, the exercise of a supernatural or mysterious power that caused death, bodily injury, illness, or some other misfortune. This type of magic, often referred to as sorcery, could harm the entire community, such as when a witch brought down a hail storm that destroyed crops. The second element was the worship of the devil. In its most elaborate form this diabolical component of witchcraft involved not only the making of a face-to-face pact with the devil but also the collective worship of him at secret nocturnal ceremonies. At these assemblies, known as sabbaths, witches allegedly engaged in cannibalistic infanticide, naked dancing, and copulation with demons. In some countries witches were believed to have flown to and from these assemblies. The word for witchcraft in most European languages could also denote the use of white or beneficent magic, although most judicial authorities considered this type of witchcraft a lesser offense and punished it more leniently.

The Learned Concept of Witchcraft. The amalgamation of the various activities included within the concept of witchcraft developed gradually over the course of three centuries. The concept was in large part the work of theologians and inquisitors. At its root lay the Christian belief, first articulated by the church fathers, that all magic derived its power from the devil. The scholastic condemnation of ritual magic in the thirteenth and fourteenth centuries linked magic to an explicit demonic pact and hence also with heresy. A longstanding monastic tradition of rhetorical invective against heretics, especially Cathars and Waldensians, identified those same individuals as members of a sect of devil worshipers who met secretly at night and engaged in promiscuous sexual activity.

In the early fifteenth century all these charges were directed against individuals who were suspected of casting spells and causing various maleficent deeds, including the killing of children. Theologians and jurists therefore began to think of witches as members of a new and particularly dangerous heretical sect, whose crimes included apostasy, conspiracy, a rejection of the moral law, and the magical destruction of life and property. The belief that witches could fly arose as the result of a learned commentary on popular beliefs regarding women who transformed themselves into nocturnal cannibalistic screech owls and other women who joined nocturnal processions with Diana, the pagan goddess. Demonologists conflated these ideas and identified the devil as the source of the witches' locomotion.

Witches. "Supposed Witches Worshiping the Devil in the Form of a Billy-Goat," c. 1460. BIBLIOTHÈQUE ROYALE ALBERT IER, BRUSSELS. MS. 11209

Witchcraft literature. The formation of the learned concept of witchcraft took place both in the courts, where suspects were interrogated, and in the minds of theologians and inquisitors who wrote treatises on the subject. More than thirty works on witchcraft, including those by the Dominican theologian and inquisitor Johann Nider, the French inquisitor Nicholas Jacquier, and the Spanish theologian Alfonso de Spina, were written during the fifteenth century. These early works laid the foundation for the publication of the most famous witchcraft treatise, *Malleus maleficarum* (The hammer of witches; 1487), by the German Dominican inquisitors Heinrich Krämer and Jacob Sprenger. This manual for inquisitors, which was widely disseminated throughout Europe, synthesized many of the prevailing learned notions of witchcraft and argued for the vigorous prosecution of the crime.

The ideas set forth in the *Malleus maleficarum* were restated and amplified in a number of late sixteenth- and early seventeenth-century treatises. The most influential of these works were written by Peter

Binsfeld, the suffragan bishop of Trier, in 1589; Nicolas Remy, the attorney general of Lorraine, in 1595; Martín del Rio, a Belgian Jesuit, in 1599; and Henri Boguet, a Burgundian judge, in 1602. Much of the material in these and other books about witchcraft was drawn from the confessions of convicted witches. The authors of witchcraft treatises, while hardly ignoring the witch's maleficent powers, were much more concerned with her apostasy and worship of the devil. The same was true of educated magistrates and clerics who identified witchcraft as a massive threat to Christian civilization. By contrast, the villagers who first suspected and accused their neighbors of practicing witchcraft were almost exclusively concerned with the harm allegedly caused by the witch's magical powers.

The learned stereotype of the witch, despite its widespread circulation, did not command universal assent. The claim that witches, as a result of demonic illusion, only imagined that they made pacts with the devil and worshiped him at the sabbath was grounded in a provision of ecclesiastical law, the canon *Episcopi*, which had been originally formulated in the tenth century. A number of sixteenth-century authors, most notably the physician Johann Weyer in 1563 and the English layman Reginald Scot in 1584, argued against the reality of the pact with the devil and on those grounds appealed for leniency in the treatment of witches. The skeptical views of Weyer and Scot did not command widespread support among educated and ruling elites until the late seventeenth century.

Witchcraft Trials. The prosecution of witches was greatly facilitated by the adoption of inquisitorial procedure in both the ecclesiastical and secular courts between the thirteenth and sixteenth centuries. Inquisitorial procedure enabled officers of the court to initiate proceedings against a person on the basis of rumor or denunciation, without first obtaining an accusation from a private complainant. It also allowed judges to determine the guilt or innocence of the accused by weighing the evidence according to established norms of judicial proof, instead of relying on the outcome of ordeals or other ancient modes of proof. The strict requirement that all capital convictions be based on the testimony of two eyewitnesses or a confession led to the use of torture in order to extract a confession when witnesses to a secret crime could not be found. The designation of witchcraft as an "excepted crime" made possible the relaxation of the strict rules that both church and state had prescribed for the application of torture. In some courts, however, especially those of the Roman Inquisition and the Parlement of Paris, judicial authorities exercised considerable restraint in the application of torture in cases of witchcraft. In England, where lay juries decided questions of guilt or innocence, torture could be administered only by a special warrant from the Privy Council and was not used in witchcraft trials.

The earliest prosecutions for witchcraft involving both *maleficium* and collective devil-worship took place in western Switzerland, Savoy, and Dauphiné during the early decades of the fifteenth century. Prosecutions became more widespread in other areas of western Europe during the later years of the fifteenth century, but after 1500 the total number of trials began to decline. A second period of prosecutions, much more intense than the first, began around 1560 and lasted until about 1630, reaching its peak in many countries during the 1590s. The total number of witchcraft trials during the fifteenth, sixteenth, and seventeenth centuries was approximately 100,000. Probably not more than half of those tried were executed.

Prosecutions and executions for witchcraft were generally most intense in those regions where the belief in collective devil worship was strong, where central political authority was weak, and where torture was applied with little restraint. The most severe prosecutions took place in German territories, especially in the small and mid-sized ecclesiastical territories in the south and west. The borderlands on the eastern boundaries of the kingdom of France, a number of Swiss cantons, and the kingdom of Scotland also witnessed large numbers of executions. Prosecutions were much less intense in England, the northern Netherlands that became the Dutch Republic, Scandinavia, Spain, Portugal, and Italy. Nevertheless almost all European countries experienced at least one large witch-hunt during the Renaissance. The judicial abuses that characterized witchcraft trials, especially in German lands, led to a demand for greater caution in proceeding against witches, the regulation or abolition of torture, and the establishment of more demanding standards of judicial proof.

The Reformation. The Protestant and Catholic Reformations played a significant role in the intensification of witchcraft prosecutions. In the most general terms the demonization of European culture that preceded and accompanied both Reformations fostered a greater awareness of satanic influence in the world. The eagerness of Protestant authorities to adhere literally to Biblical injunctions against witch-craft (especially Exodus 22:18: "Thou shalt not suffer a witch to live"), the determination of religious reformers to eliminate magic on the grounds that it was superstitious, and the efforts of secular authorities to establish a godly state by taking legal action against all moral transgressors encouraged the search for and prosecution of Satan's alleged confederates.

In Protestant countries the devaluation or elimination of sacramentals like holy water, which had been traditionally used to provide informal protection against witches, may have made victims feel more vulnerable to the effects of witchcraft and more likely therefore to have recourse to the judicial process. Witchcraft accusations did not become a tool of confessional conflict, even though Protestant clerics often identified Roman Catholicism itself with witchcraft. In the 1590s German Catholics accused Protestant demonologists, who had defined witchcraft as essentially a spiritual crime, of denying that witches were responsible for their maleficent deeds and that they actually attended the sabbath and copulated with demons.

Social and Economic Status. Approximately 80 percent of all accused witches throughout Europe were female, mainly because women engaged in the types of activities that led to the suspicion that they practiced harmful magic. Women entrusted with the supervision of childbirth and the care of infants were particularly vulnerable to accusations, which often came from members of the same sex. Some accused witches were midwives, although there is no foundation for the equation of the two groups. Others were lying-in maids, who assisted the mother after delivery and who often became the target of maternal fears regarding the well-being of the child and the domestic authority of the mother. Healers were often accused, especially when they had failed to cure their patients. The accused were frequently described as sharp tongued or quarrelsome, and they usually failed to conform to prevailing standards of appropriate female conduct. Clerical claims that women were morally weak and had insatiable sexual appetites, thus making them easy prey for a seductive devil, may have strengthened the belief of members of the ruling elite that witches were women, but the initial identification of witches came from neighbors of the accused, not the judges who interrogated and tried them.

During the early fifteenth century, when witchcraft was still associated with other forms of heresy or with the practice of ritual magic, significant numbers of men were accused. After witchcraft became more closely identified with women, men were still occasionally accused because they were related by blood or marriage to female witches. In some of the larger witch-hunts, the torture of witches in order to secure the names of their accomplices resulted in the accusation of men as well as children. In Finland, Russia, and Estonia, where practitioners of magic were traditionally men, there was no clear-cut sex-linkage with witchcraft. The same was true for certain regions of Spain and Italy.

The large majority of accused witches came from the lower levels of society. The poor, as the weakest and most vulnerable members of the community, became the natural scapegoats for the misfortunes that occurred in everyday life. The poverty of witches also provided a plausible explanation for the pacts they allegedly made with the devil. The poor, moreover, were the most likely to threaten the use of magical power as a means of retaliation against their social and economic superiors. As the most dependent members of the community, the poor, especially old, unmarried women, were likely to ask others for charity. Those who felt guilty for having refused them often relieved their guilt by accusing them of witchcraft.

Suspicions tended to build up over a period of years and then crystallize in response to particular misfortunes. The adverse economic conditions that prevailed during the period 1560–1630, especially the unprecedented rise in prices, the decline in real wages among the poor, periodic subsistence crises, and the social dislocations that resulted from widespread warfare, tended to aggravate the personal conflicts that found expression in witchcraft accusations. They also created a mood that encouraged elites as well as villagers to seek a supernatural explanation of the dislocations that were taking place.

Possession. In the late sixteenth and seventeenth centuries witchcraft became closely related to the phenomenon of demonic possession. Theologians argued that demons could enter a human body not only directly, with God's permission, but also at the command of a witch. On numerous occasions, therefore, those possessed accused individuals of having used witchcraft to cause their convulsions, bodily contortions, and other physical afflictions. Possession could also take a collective form, such as when accusations by possessed nuns in the French convents at Aix-en-Provence (1611) and Loudun (1634) led to the identification and prosecution of priests as witches. Challenges to the authenticity of specific instances of demonic possessions led to a more general skepticism regarding the guilt of the witches who were allegedly the source of the affliction. This skepticism contributed to the decline in the number of trials and executions that began in many countries in the early seventeenth century.

BIBLIOGRAPHY

Primary Works

Boguet, Henry. *An Examen of Witches.* Translated by E. Allen Ashwin. Edited by Montague Summers. London, 1929. Translation of *Discours des sorciers* (1602).

Krämer, Heinrich, and James Sprenger. *The Malleus Maleficarum of Heinrich Kramer and James Sprenger.* Translated and edited by Montague Summers. London, 1948.

Weyer, Johann. *Witches, Devils, and Doctors in the Renaissance: Johann Weyer,* De praestigiis daemonum. Edited by George Mora. Translated by John Shea. Binghamton, N.Y., 1991.

Secondary Works

Ankarloo, Bengt, and Gustav Henningsen, eds. *Early Modern European Witchcraft: Centres and Peripheries.* Oxford, 1990.

Behringer, Wolfgang. *Witchcraft Persecutions in Bavaria: Popular Magic, Religious Zealotry, and Reason of State in Early Modern Europe.* Translated by J. C. Grayson and David Lederer. Cambridge, U.K. 1997.

Briggs, Robin. *Witches and Neighbors: The Social and Cultural Context of European Witchcraft.* New York, 1996.

Clark, Stuart. *Thinking with Demons: The Idea of Witchcraft in Early Modern Europe.* Oxford, 1997.

Cohn, Norman. *Europe's Inner Demons: An Enquiry Inspired by the Great Witch-Hunt.* London, 1975.

Kieckhefer, Richard. *European Witch Trials: Their Foundations in Popular and Learned Culture, 1300–1500.* London, 1976.

Levack, Brian P. *The Witch-Hunt in Early Modern Europe.* 2d ed. London, 1995.

Midelfort, H. C. Erik. *Witch Hunting in Southwestern Germany 1562–1684: The Social and Intellectual Foundations.* Stanford, Calif., 1972.

Thomas, Keith. *Religion and the Decline of Magic.* London, 1971.

BRIAN P. LEVACK

WOLSEY, THOMAS (c. 1472–1530), English churchman and statesman. Thomas Wolsey, the son of a successful innkeeper and butcher of Ipswich (Suffolk), studied arts and theology at Magdalen College, Oxford, becoming bursar of the college and master of its dependent school. In 1501 he resigned his fellowship to serve as chaplain to a series of great men, culminating with King Henry VII, who used him as a diplomat. From 1509, as almoner to Henry VIII and a skilled administrator in the wars of 1512–1514, he rose steadily in the king's confidence. In March 1514 he was consecrated bishop of Lincoln, in September 1514 translated to the archbishopric of York, in September 1515 created a cardinal, and on 24 December 1515 became chancellor, the highest office in English government.

Political Career. Wolsey remained the king's leading minister for the next fourteen years. As a diplomat he brokered the general peace treaty of London in 1518 and the accompanying Anglo-French settlement over Tournai, captured by Henry in 1513 and now returned to France. In 1521 he held peace conferences at Calais and Bruges in the attempt to avert war between the Emperor Charles V and Francis I of France. From 1527 to 1529 he sought once again to bring these adversaries to agreement and to neutralize the old hostility between English and French. All these efforts won him the plaudits of peace-loving humanists, though he did not share their wholesale aversion to war and threw himself back into military administration with gusto in the wars of 1522–1525.

Wolsey's energy was equally evident in his judicial role. As chancellor he presided both over the court of chancery and over the king's council in star chamber. In both he encouraged a flood of litigants in search of unbiased justice and the rigorous enforcement of the king's laws. At times he stretched equitable jurisdiction too far, and repeatedly his courts were overwhelmed with business. But in general his judicial achievement was admirable. It interlocked with his wider supervision of local government through county commissions of the peace and the reestablishment of councils to oversee Wales and the north in 1525. Such interventionism was also evident in social policy. He initiated quarantine measures against plague in 1518 and grain surveys to prevent hoarding in the famine of 1528. Commissions were sent out in 1517 and 1518 to investigate the conversion of arable land to pasture and consequent depopulation, and numerous prosecutions were mounted against offending landlords.

Equally vigorous were Wolsey's efforts to increase the king's income. In 1522 and 1523 he used an innovative survey of landholding, wealth, and military preparedness, the "general proscription," to levy unprecedentedly large forced loans. In the parliament of 1523, after prolonged wrangling, he took the recently developed lay subsidy, an efficient direct tax, to its heaviest incidence yet. In 1525 he tried to levy heavier still direct taxation without parliamentary consent in the form of the Amicable Grant, but had to abandon the plan when faced with widespread noncooperation and localized revolt. Though noble councilors and courtiers cooperated with Wolsey in these ventures, there were tensions between them over his management of royal patronage, over foreign policy, and over his humiliation of great men in star chamber. Few were as disgruntled or as mala-

Cardinal Wolsey. Anonymous portrait. NATIONAL PORTRAIT GALLERY, LONDON

droit as Edward Stafford, duke of Buckingham, executed for treason in 1521, but many took the chance to criticize the cardinal when the king's confidence in him wavered. Nemesis came with his failure to obtain, whether by diplomacy at the papal court, international maneuvers, or the exercise of his own legatine authority in England, an annulment of Henry's marriage to Catherine of Aragon, which would free the king to marry Anne Boleyn in the hope of fathering a male heir. On 17 October 1529 he lost office as chancellor and on 29 November 1530, on his way south to be tried for treason following a retirement to his see of York, he died at Leicester Abbey.

Church, Patronage, and Reputation. For Protestants, Wolsey symbolized many of the faults of the contemporary church. He was a pluralist on a scale unprecedented in England, holding in addition to York successive English bishoprics—Bath and

Wells, Durham, Winchester—plus the see of Tournai and the abbey of Saint Albans. His secular duties left him insufficient time even to set foot in most of these cures. By a mistress, Jane Lark, he had a son and a daughter, and the son, Thomas Winter, was given lavish ecclesiastical promotion. He exploited his supremacy as papal legate in England, first granted in 1518, to intervene profitably in the jurisdiction of his fellow bishops and tax the clergy heavily for the crown. Yet his impact on the church was not wholly negative. He encouraged reform among secular and regular clergy alike and planned to rationalize the distribution of bishoprics. He coordinated a persuasive rather than persecutory campaign against Lutheranism and sought constructive solutions to the tensions caused by sanctuaries and benefit of clergy in the courts. Above all he aimed to improve clerical education through his grand new foundation, Cardinal College, Oxford, and its satellite schools at Ipswich and elsewhere.

Wolsey was a leading patron of the English Renaissance. At Oxford, at court, and in his household, where entertainments included plays by Plautus and Terence, he supported many of the leading humanists in England, among them John Clement, Thomas Linacre, Thomas Lupset, Richard Pace, and Juan Luis Vives. He built splendid palaces at Hampton Court, York Place, The More, and Tyttenhanger, filling them with tapestries, plate, and paintings of the highest quality. He commissioned work from the sculptors Giovanni da Maiano and Benedetto da Rovezzano, the scribe Peter Meghen, the glaziers Barnard Flower and James Nicholson, and probably the illuminator Gerard Horenbout, seeking the best in Italian and Netherlandish design. His seals and goldsmith's work and his projected tomb were particularly advanced by English standards in their use of Renaissance motifs. His chapel choir and those of his colleges were of outstanding quality and included the composers John Taverner and Richard Pygott. Thus, he certainly met contemporary expectations of the magnificence appropriate to great men. His critics, among them the historian Polydore Vergil and the poet John Skelton, felt he far exceeded them. For them his splendor was of a piece with his personal prominence in diplomacy and justice, all evidence of rampant vainglory. More sympathetic observers, among them the servant George Cavendish, who later wrote his master's biography, saw Wolsey as a case study in the propensity of fortune to raise men to greatness and then to cast them down. One of the great men of the English Renaissance was thus also one of its greatest object lessons.

See also **England**; *biography of Henry VIII.*

BIBLIOGRAPHY

Primary Work

Cavendish, George. *The Life and Death of Cardinal Wolsey.* Edited by Richard S. Sylvester. Early English Text Society 243. London, 1959.

Secondary Works

Gunn, Steven, and Phillip Lindley, eds. *Cardinal Wolsey: Church, State and Art.* Cambridge, U.K., 1991.

Gwyn, Peter. *The King's Cardinal: The Rise and Fall of Thomas Wolsey.* London, 1990.

STEVEN GUNN

WOMEN. [This entry includes six subentries:

Women in the Renaissance

Two issues arise in characterizing the condition of women in the Renaissance. The first is the nature of the lives women led in the period 1350–1650. The second is identification of what is distinctive about the Renaissance era for women: Did their social or economic condition improve? Did they gain greater access to power? Were they able to express themselves in new or different ways than in the Middle Ages? Was there—this last question frequently posed since first formulated in the mid-1970s by Joan Kelly Gadol, a pioneer of women's history—a Renaissance for women? Both issues can be addressed by looking at women's lives in three settings: the family, the churches, and high (elite) culture.

Women in the Family. Women played several roles in their families depending on their age and marital status: those of daughter (or "virgin," as contemporaries put it), wife, mother, and widow. These categories were regularly used by writers—preachers, philosophers, humanists, even ordinary letter writers—in their descriptions of women and appear to define the possibilities that the age understood to be available for those of the female gender. Male roles were, in contrast, generally defined by social position or occupation—merchant, knight, priest, peasant, barrelmaker, weaver, and so on.

In urban societies (which expanded during the Renaissance centuries and were characteristic especially of those regions of Europe most involved with the creation of Renaissance civilization), the delineation of female roles was sharper than in peasant society. Money was the crucial distinguishing element. Considerations of inheritance in a society that construed descent in the male line conditioned the way in which daughters, wives, and widows lived.

Virginity and honor. Both religious ideology and social and economic considerations demanded, above all, virginity of daughters until marriage, or for their entire lives. In Roman Catholic regions of Europe, virginity was an ideal for all people, as it had been for all of Europe prior to the Protestant Reformation. The ideal of virginity had roots in the Gospels and Epistles of the Christian New Testament, in Greek philosophy, and in patristic literature. During the eleventh century, in connection with monastic and papal reform movements, the ideal was reaffirmed. From about the twelfth century, beginning in the households of the high nobility of western Europe but radiating outward geographically and down the social hierarchy within property-owning classes, the requirement of virginity for daughters received new emphasis.

As a patriarchal model developed for the family, where identity depended primarily on descent through the male line (the agnatic lineage), and where property descended almost entirely to male heirs, the main purpose daughters served was as brides, to link two lineages. To assure the legitimacy of any heirs resulting from the marriage, it was necessary that the bride's father be able to assure the future spouse that the bride was indeed a virgin.

Increasingly in the Renaissance era, the concept of honor also depended on virginity. The violation of a daughter's virginity brought dishonor not only on the girl, but on all of her male kin. The punishment for rape, for instance, often varied with the standing of the victim's male relatives, an indicator of how serious the invasion of their honor was. Young girls who lost their virginity, whether through rape or seduction, if abandoned by their male kin, were liable to turn to prostitution—as, indeed, were impoverished wives or widows for whom prostitution offered a form of employment.

Women's skills. In addition to preserving their virginity, daughters were required to master the skills they were later expected to perform as wives and household managers. Most important were textile crafts: spinning, weaving, and embroidering, both of the ordinary furnishings and clothes worn by family members in lower-status families and of elaborate luxury products in wealthier ones. Beyond the textile crafts, generally taught by the older women of the household, young girls learned to manage the household economy, to supervise servants, and to nurse any ailing household members. Certain values were inculcated: chastity, obedience, and silence. These were thought to prepare a daughter well for her role in the second stage of her life (if she was not exempted by reason of entry to the religious life) as wife.

The dowry. When a woman of the propertied classes married, she was also expected to bring to her new husband's household that portion of her father's wealth that was to be, in most regions of Europe, her whole claim on her inheritance. That sum was the dowry. Even among the poorest ranks of the peasantry, a bride was expected to bring some tangible goods to a marriage, if only a few pots or stools to furnish the marital hut. Inherited from Greek and Roman and more ancient civilizations, the dowry had returned around the twelfth century (from its eclipse in the early Middle Ages) as a central mechanism in the establishment of a household system based on agnatic lineage. The dowry technically remained the woman's property for life, but in fact it was managed by her husband and passed on her death to her heirs (female as well as male, if the local system of law permitted a woman to make a testament and name special gifts).

In some regions of Europe, a wife might also possess property in her own name, outside the dowry assigned her (sometimes bestowed upon her by her father, who had also prescribed the dowry sum). Again, depending on locality, they might or might not be able to direct its inheritance by testamentary bequest. Other property that women were entitled to use—real estate, jewelry, clothing—often belonged to a male relative who had every right to reclaim it as needed. Whether personal items of clothing or jewelry were their own or their husbands', their display was often censured by moralists and controlled by legislation.

The function of the dowry was to permit the detachment of a woman from her father's line so that she had no further claim on the patrimony. It represented her share of her inheritance, and as such was to be as small as possible, to minimize the burden on the estate. At the same time, it had to be allotted with regard to the standard of the matrimonial marketplace, and as such was to be as large as possible, permitting the natal family to "purchase," in effect, a spouse with the highest social status (which might merely reflect glory on the bride's kin, or even win them political allies or access to power)

Court Ladies at an Outdoor Loom. Single women learned such textile crafts as weaving in order to prepare themselves to become household managers. Detail of *The Triumph of Minerva* by Francesco del Cossa in the Palazzo Schifanoia, Ferrara, Italy. ALINARI/ART RESOURCE, NY

or, more simply, wealth. If the bride's family could not afford a high-status spouse, she would need to be satisfied with a lesser one, acquired with a lesser dowry.

Marriage. Marital choice, in the framework of the dowry system, barely existed. Most marriages in the propertied classes were arranged by male kin, perhaps in consultation with mothers. Many women married men they knew scarcely or not at all. Although among the peasantry in most of Europe the age of marriage was fairly late (in the twenties) for both sexes, among the propertied classes in many regions the pattern that prevailed was that an adolescent woman married an older man (perhaps in his late twenties or thirties) already established in commerce, government, or aristocratic society; or she married a man who was even more advanced in age and who had already been married.

In these circumstances, it is hard to assume a widespread notion of marital love. A disparity in the ages of the two spouses, coupled with their lack of acquaintance prior to the marriage, and sometimes their very different daily occupations, seems to have had the effect in many cases of spiritual estrangement, especially among the wealthier classes. A quality of companionship seems more often to have characterized those marriages where both spouses were engaged in the same kind of occupation—where they were both skilled craftspersons, for instance, in textile manufacture, or where they could jointly operate a tavern or shop.

Mutuality, however rarely achieved, was the ideal recommended to couples by preachers, humanists, and other moral instructors. These authors thundered against adultery, bigamy, desertion, and abuse. Adultery was consistently viewed as a wife's crime, and a very serious one. In many locations, a husband was excused for killing a wife caught in adultery; in some, such a murder was not even designated a crime. Among the wives of European royalty, adultery was viewed as treason and generally punishable by execution. Meanwhile, men regularly engaged in sexual relations outside marriage, sometimes with concubines or mistresses resident in the same house with the patriarch's wife (who was expected to raise the offspring of these illicit relationships) and legitimate children.

Such arrangements were more typical of high-status families. Among poorer folk, marital coolness or breakdown was more often expressed through bigamy or desertion. A man who found marriage unsatisfactory might leave his parish and marry again in a more remote location. A man who believed himself deeply burdened by his wife left her, in which case her legal rights were unenforceable, and her economic condition probably pitiable.

Abuse could be found everywhere. Wife-beating was permissible (as was the corporal disciplining of children and servants), although some moralists urged moderation and others deplored the use of beatings altogether. Householders might, furthermore, imprison, starve, and debase their wives (or other family members, for that matter).

Prior to the Protestant Reformation, divorce was not available as a solution for irremediable marital breakdown. Annulment, generally on grounds of nonconsummation, the discovery of a prohibited degree of kinship, or some flaw in the marriage ritual, was often a possibility among the highest social strata. Although divorce remained impossible in Catholic regions, some Protestant reformers argued for divorce in cases of adultery or hopeless incompatibility. Their arguments were fundamental to much later legislation permitting civil divorce.

Most wives, however, remained married until they or their husbands died. Wives had serious responsibilities as workers and as managers of their household. Peasant women performed manifold duties, from tending to fowl and sheep and the vegetable garden to brewing beer and assisting with the harvest. Artisan wives performed craftwork requiring high skill alongside their husbands, or as their surrogates in their absence—sometimes attaining (less frequently as time progressed) guild membership. Wives of merchants tended shops, helped keep accounts, or managed other business records.

Among wealthier patrician and aristocratic families, women continued to perform the textile work that women everywhere were expected to do, but their labor was generally for luxury (gold-thread embroidery, for instance) rather than ordinary use. Their primary work was the running of the household: seeing to the purchase, storage, and replenishment of supplies; entertaining their husbands' visitors; supervising the servants; and nursing the ill, whether servants or family members.

Motherhood. All wives had as a paramount responsibility the conception, bearing, and rearing of children. Conception was largely unregulated, as its mechanisms were not understood. Birth control was limited to coitus interruptus (male withdrawal), of which there is evidence especially among urban patrician classes, and abortion, the latter obtained erratically and at great risk to the mother mostly by means of herbal therapies recommended by midwife-healers. When maternal lactation did not offer a period of infertility and relief from pregnancy, women often conceived anew within weeks of giving birth. Such a pattern is seen in the high birthrates in certain social groups—twenty or twenty-five children from one mother were not uncommonly reported—and indicate that births succeeded each other at nearly an annual rate.

Although among the wealthy such frequent childbirth was often viewed as desirable, even the birth of a single child could be seen as excessive to a poor or unmarried woman unable to care for the baby. That situation often led to child abandonment or even infanticide.

Whether childbirth was more or less frequent, the rate of infant mortality was high—overall, across the period and many different regions, from 20 to 50 percent of all births. Child mortality up to age twenty was also frequent. It is not unusual that a woman who had given birth to eight or ten children saw only one or two of them reach adulthood. High mortality rates must have overshadowed the experience of motherhood in ways difficult to identify. Certainly, although some women may have grown hardened to the experience of child death, many grieved powerfully at the loss of their infants.

Maternal mortality also conditioned the experience of pregnancy and childbirth. The chance of dying in any single childbirth event was about 10 percent—much higher over a lifetime in which childbirth was experienced several times. Mortality in childbirth was a leading cause of death among women, a great number of whom predeceased their husbands (who might proceed to marry one or two further wives). In the literature of moral advice, the possibility of maternal death in childbirth is one argument frequently raised for a woman to remain virginal and not marry.

Childrearing. Women's responsibility for the healthy newborn infant varied according to social class. Poor women generally nursed their own infants for about two years. Elite women, whether of mercantile, patrician, or aristocratic strata, generally did not. In these circles, arrangements were made (often by fathers) to send the child to a wet nurse, who, having perhaps recently discharged her own infant from the breast on this account, was paid for her services. Infants spent about one or two years with their wet nurses (females were perhaps weaned more abruptly than males) before returning to their mothers—who, in the meantime, might have conceived once again. The reasons for the widespread

Woman and Family. Family portrait attributed to Baldassare d'Este (1441–1504). Oil on canvas; 112 × 90.5 cm (44 × 35.6 in.). BAYERISCHE STAATGEMÄLDESAMMLUNGEN, MUNICH

pattern of wet-nursing among European elites, and the impact it had on family relationships and the psychological welfare of child or mother, are not well understood.

From its birth when it was nursed by its mother, or from its return from the wet nurse, the infant was understood to be its mother's responsibility until about age six or seven—the point at which, it was believed, rational thought became possible. In these early years, except in the cases of some wealthy women who entirely delegated the responsibility to servants, young children must have been susceptible to maternal values and instruction.

These differed, outside of instruction in devotional duties, depending on the gender of the child. Girls were kept closely confined and supervised, trained in household skills, and inculcated with those already cited values of chastity, silence, and obedience that were ceaselessly recommended to them. Boys were prepared for their further instruction by their fathers, by a school or tutor, or in apprenticeship. Peasants trained male and female children in the necessary and largely unchanging agricultural skills. In the case of the very poor, both male and female children were often sent out of the household at an extremely young age, as early as eight or nine, as servants. In the latter case, virtually the only instruction they received was the early childhood pedagogy offered by their mothers.

When a mother of young children died, her children were reared by their father and his female kin, his servants, or his new wife. When a father of young children died, responsibility for rearing those children would lie with his male kin. In his will he may have invited his widow to remain in the household to tend her children, or she might be welcomed in that role by his brothers or cousins. But children were not understood to belong to their mother. If she did not, as a widow, remain in her deceased husband's household, she would relinquish the care of her children to the lineage into which she had married, and generally would not be able to claim her offspring for her own.

Widows. Widowhood presented difficulties to women at any age when they found themselves in that condition, and for the society in which they lived as well. Difficulties involved matters of kinship (To whose household did a widow belong?) and moral issues (How could the behavior of a sexually experienced woman be controlled?).

When her husband died, depending on where she lived, a widow might remain in his household (especially if young children survived), return to her father's household (or to that of other male kin), marry again, enter a convent or other religious community, or reside alone. Competing interests surrounded her as this decision was made. Her natal family might wish her to remarry, or to return, with her dowry, to their household. Her husband's family might wish her to stay in their household, her dowry continuing to support its economy. Church and society would urge chastity upon her and express anxiety about her moral supervision: in Catholic regions, she might be urged to join a convent or religious community; elsewhere, to remarry. Her residence alone, as head of household, might signify her impoverishment and abandonment by kin. Or, if she had property, it might make her the object of suspicion. Few moralists sided with Desiderius Erasmus in allowing the possibility of a self-sufficient widow's living in chaste and productive isolation. The possibility became greater after 1600.

With regard to their roles in the family, the Renaissance era marked no special landmark for women. The patrilineal family concept of the Middle

Ages continued to reign through the eighteenth and later centuries, depending on region. The religious ideal of chastity had its origins in the early Christian centuries and, though modified under Protestantism, continued to weigh heavily until the same late era. Increased urbanization in the Renaissance did mean that large numbers of artisan, merchant, and patrician families imitated aristocratic ones in their management of household economic interests. If anything, the hold of the patriarchal family on women may have increased during the Renaissance.

Women in the Church. The hold of the patriarchal family on women also increased under Protestantism, which branched during the Renaissance from the Catholicism common to western Europe in the Middle Ages.

Protestantism. For men, Protestantism meant a new set of beliefs and standards of moral behavior. For women, it meant these things, too, and also the disappearance of the ideal of holy virginity, linked to sanctity and secluded religious community. For all women, life was to be lived out within the natal or spousal family, under the supervision of male kin. Historians differ about the consequences of this change. Did women's lives within the family become more constrained, as the patriarch, now priest in his own household, concentrated all authority within himself? Or did marriages become more companionable, as husbands and wives cooperated to create a godly society within their own household?

Some opportunities emerged for female leadership in the earliest days of Protestantism, and thereafter, within certain sects. Some female advocates of reform stated their views in writing (for instance, Argula von Grumbach), and some wives of reform leaders contributed intellectually to the first development of the movement (Katharine Zell). After the first generation, however, these voices were largely sidelined. Among the persecuted sects, notably the Anabaptists, women adherents witnessed for their faith, and many won fame as martyrs.

Catholicism. Meanwhile, many European women remained Catholics. In that church the convent remained, as in the Middle Ages, an alternative to household residence; the pursuit of sanctity remained a possible, if difficult, career.

During the Renaissance, as during the Middle Ages, women entered convents for a variety of reasons: some were adults drawn to the religious life; some were widows or refugees who sought a safe haven or were placed in safety by male kin; some were young girls placed by their kin permanently or temporarily in convents also for safekeeping, or as an alternative to marriage. Some of these women subsequently made permanent vows. Although some women lived in convents because of a sincere religious vocation, others were there to bide their time, or despite their own contrary personal choice or interest. Most women who resided in convents for any of these motives came from propertied and even aristocratic families, as convents required an entrance fee (termed a "dowry," just as in a marriage).

The variety of motivations for entering a convent colored the nature of the conventual life and explain the great variation in the way the convents or individual nuns were viewed by society at large. During the Renaissance, in some areas (for instance, in the wealthier Italian cities) the proportion of women entering convents because of their family's economic interests skyrocketed.

In addition to those women who sought to pursue a religious vocation in the convent there were others whose quest for holiness led them elsewhere. Either by preference or because their families did not provide the dowries necessary for admission to a convent, some joined communities of religious women that were not strictly cloistered, although they were supervised in some manner by members of the male clergy. A few others pursued saintly careers as single individuals, following strict routines of religious observance and ascetic practice while living in the household of a male relative, or, generally as wives or widows, engaging in charitable activities associated with a hospital or religious order.

The pattern of "holy women" seeking to pursue religious lives in unofficial communities or as individuals is a phenomenon especially characteristic of urban societies during the three hundred years before the advent of Protestantism (thirteenth through early sixteenth centuries). The Catholic Reformation greatly curtailed this kind of religious expression. Women seeking to follow religious vocations were largely limited to the single option of the convent. At the same time, conventual life was placed under much stricter regulation by male clergy, and the spiritual experiences of individual holy women were closely scrutinized for evidence of heresy, witchcraft, or feigned sanctity.

The Renaissance era saw, therefore, a continuation of the medieval mode of women's participation in the churches, as well as some striking novelties. These included the explosion of new forms of the quest for sanctity, both in unofficial communities and in individual action, the suppression of these by the Catholic reformers, and the repudiation of all traditional patterns of the female pursuit of sanctity by the Protestant Reformers.

Women in High Culture. The role of women in "high" culture—the elite world of power and ideas—also saw considerable development during the Renaissance era.

Queens and armed women. A model for female competence was posed by the numerous queens regnant and female regents who by circumstance and accident wielded power at precisely the time of the emergence of the modern nation-state during the fifteenth to seventeenth centuries. Isabella of Castile (Spain), Elizabeth I of England, and Christina of Sweden all ruled effectively in their own right. As regents for their sons, Catherine de Médicis and Anne of Austria, among others, had considerable influence on the shaping of national policy. Despite the arguments of the Scots Presbyterian leader John Knox against female governance, the capacity of these women to act decisively and intelligently was evident.

Women rulers often surrounded themselves with the imagery (in the literature they patronized, in art, and in adornment) of the Amazon or armed virago—and understandably so, as the principal verbal and artistic vocabulary to express concepts of political power was military. One powerful woman who was not a queen, the French self-appointed soldier and mystic Joan of Arc, assumed the image materially, wearing men's clothes and bearing arms.

These instances where the appurtenances of military might are associated with women may be numbered among many others that appear in the literature and art of the era, for Renaissance culture was fascinated by the image of the armed woman. Boccaccio's catalog of illustrious women featured several females who bore arms. That figure reappears in many subsequent catalogs of "women worthies" produced tediously in several languages over the next centuries. Authors of epics (Ludovico Ariosto, Torquato Tasso, Edmund Spenser) presented armed maidens as their heroines. The elevation of the image of the armed maiden may be found to relate to another contemporary phenomenon: that of female cross-dressing (which also relates to dramatic practice, where single-sex companies performed both female and male roles), especially by women who served, in cases for years, as soldiers, their gender disguised until revealed by wounding or death.

The masculinizing conceptualization of women deemed worthy of regard is also encountered as a commonplace of intellectual culture. Women who excelled in some demonstration of learning or wisdom were repeatedly said to have "exceeded their sex" or "achieved the virtue of a man." These clichés first make a regular appearance in the works of male humanists. It is as part of the humanist movement, indeed, that women make a first significant entry to the realm of intellectual discourse outside the church.

Humanists. Women appear in humanist literature almost as soon as that movement begins. By the late fifteenth century, a number of northern Italian noblewomen had managed (despite the lack of schools or tutors especially assigned to them) to acquire Latin literacy and a sound acquaintance with classical literature, most conspicuously Isotta Nogarola, Laura Cereta, and Cassandra Fedele. They produced works in all the usual genres (letters, dialogs, orations, poems), some of which dealt squarely with important issues for women: the worth of their essential nature, their access to education, their intellectual capacity. Their achievement won the attention of some leading male humanists (including Leonardo Bruni and Angelo Poliziano).

By 1500, women humanists, and the men who entered into discourse with them, had developed many of the major themes of early feminism. Humanist themes joined with those developed from female religious thought and with the pioneering insights of the French author Christine de Pizan to form the foundation of women's subsequent participation in the intellectual world. The broadening of their participation after 1500 was encouraged by the growth of printing (which permitted women authors to deal directly with publishers and bypass male-dominated institutions such as the universities); of primary schooling; and of the vernacular languages (which invited women, once again, to engage in discourse not dominated by the learned sciences, which continued to use Latin).

Writers. The sixteenth and seventeenth centuries saw an enormous increase in the number of women writers, from the handful per century of the later Middle Ages, to the dozen or so for the whole course of Italian humanism, to hundreds and perhaps thousands of mostly Italian, French, and English authors—a complete prosopographical study is necessary but is not yet at hand. Women wrote poetry, both religious and secular, and most notably love poetry; poetry by such figures as the Italian Gaspara Stampa or the French Louise Labé reached a level of unsurpassed excellence. They wrote romances, stories, novels, and plays, and they trans-

lated all of these from other vernaculars; a few, learned in Latin or Greek, also translated learned works of classical or humanist authors. They wrote diaries, family histories, and advice books.

Most important for later conceptualizations of women's roles and rights, women authors of the later Renaissance engaged in the ongoing literary debate, contending with male opponents and joined by male supporters, known as the Querelle des Femmes. In this debate, humanist arguments for women's dignity, educability, and mental capacity were extended and elaborated, notably in such works as Baldassare Castiglione's *Book of the Courtier,* Heinrich Agrippa of Nettesheim's *Declamation on the Nobility and Preeminence of the Female Sex,* Juan Luis Vives's *On the Instruction of the Christian Woman,* and various works of Erasmus.

In 1600, two of the era's foremost works in defense of women, both by women authors, were published: those of the Italians (indeed, Venetians) Moderata Fonte (the pen name of Modesta da Pozzo) and Lucrezia Marinella. In these lengthy works, the combined misogynist tradition branching from biblical and Aristotelian roots is thoroughly examined and refuted. The path then lay clear for the development of a mature feminism over the next two centuries, culminating in the work of Mary Wollstonecraft co-incident with the French Revolution.

Other women besides authors of learned or literary works helped shape the mental world of the later Renaissance centuries. Women artists (especially Artemisia Gentileschi and Sofonisba Anguissola) and musicians gained international recognition. Women patrons, the recipients of virtually every significant theoretical work on the nature of women, also supported literature, learning, and the arts beyond the confines of that theme: such patrons included Margaret of Austria, Margaret of Navarre, and Catherine of Aragon. Women artists, intellectuals, and patrons attended meetings of the academies (especially in sixteenth- and seventeenth-century Italy) where through presentations and conversation important cultural themes and styles took shape. Cultivated women of the high bourgeoisie or aristocracy, especially in France but also in England, the Netherlands, the German lands, and Italian cities, presided over salons where conversation among the learned and fashionable diffused new scientific and philosophical ideas and set standards of literary taste.

Women writers, artists, and intellectuals did not influence Renaissance culture as greatly as did their male counterparts, but the main currents of Renaissance culture won the attention of women and their supporters from the outset. Women's participation in that culture contributed to the formation of fundamental ideas about women's moral and intellectual capacities that reversed prevalent misogynist constructs and laid the foundations for modern feminism. In this sense, there was surely a Renaissance for women.

See also **Birth and Infancy; Childhood; Childrearing; Diaries and Memoirs; Education; Family and Kinship; Feminism; Honor; Household; Humanism; Jews,** *subentry on* **Jewish Women and Family Life; Life Stages; Love; Marriage; Material Culture; Midwives and Healers; Motherhood; Orphans and Foundlings; Pregnancy; Printing and Publishing; Prostitution; Queens and Queenship; Querelle des Femmes; Rape; Religious Piety; Salons; Servants; Sexuality; Sickness and Disease; Spirituality, Female; Sumptuary Laws; Virginity and Celibacy; Widowhood;** *and biographies of figures mentioned in this entry.*

BIBLIOGRAPHY

Primary Works

Erasmus, Desiderius. *Erasmus on Women.* Edited by Erika Rummel. Toronto and Buffalo, N.Y., 1996.

King, Margaret L., and Albert Rabil Jr., eds. and trans. *Her Immaculate Hand: Selected Works by and about the Women Humanists of Quattrocento Italy.* 2d ed. Binghamton, N.Y., 1992.

Wilson, Katharina M., ed. *Women Writers of the Renaissance and Reformation.* Athens, Ga., 1987.

The OVEME series (The Other Voice in Early Modern Europe, edited by Margaret L. King and Albert Rabil Jr.; Chicago, 1996–), will include twenty-six volumes of key works by and about early modern women, including those by Agrippa, Laura Cereta, Cassandra Fedele, Moderata Fonte, Lucrezia Marinella, and Isotta Nogarola. Oxford University Press is publishing the series, Women Writers in English 1350–1850, for which more than thirty works are planned.

Secondary Works

Benson, Pamela Joseph. *The Invention of Renaissance Woman: The Challenge of Female Independence in the Literature and Thought of Italy and England.* University Park, Pa., 1992.

Crawford, Patricia. *Women and Religion in England, 1500–1750.* London, 1993.

Davis, Natalie Zemon, and Arlette Farge, eds. *Renaissance and Enlightenment Paradoxes.* Vol. 3 of *A History of Women in the West.* Edited by Georges Duby and Michelle Perrot. Cambridge, Mass., 1993.

Flandrin, Jean-Louis. *Families in Former Times: Kinship, Household, and Sexuality.* Translated by Richard Southern. Cambridge, U.K., and New York, 1979.

Gottlieb, Beatrice. *The Family in the Western World: From the Black Death to the Industrial Age.* New York, 1993.

Hufton, Olwen. *The Prospect before Her: A History of Women in Western Europe.* New York, 1996.

Jordan, Constance. *Renaissance Feminism: Literary Texts and Political Models.* Ithaca, N.Y., 1990.

Kelly (Gadol), Joan. "Did Women Have a Renaissance?" In *Becoming Visible: Women in European History,* edited by Renate Bridenthal, Claudia Koonz, and Susan M. Stuart. 2d ed. Boston, 1987. Pages 175–202. Also in Joan Kelly, *Women, History, and Theory.* Chicago, 1984. Pages 12–50.

King, Margaret L. *Women of the Renaissance.* Chicago, 1991.

Klapisch-Zuber, Christiane. *Women, Family, and Ritual in Renaissance Italy.* Edited and translated by Lydia G. Cochrane. Chicago, 1985.

Kuehn, Thomas. *Law, Family, and Women: Toward a Legal Anthropology of Renaissance Italy.* Chicago, 1991.

Lerner, Gerda. *The Creation of Feminist Consciousness: From the Middle Ages to 1870.* Vol. 2 of her *Women and History.* New York, 1993.

Macfarlane, Alan. *Marriage and Love in England: Modes of Reproduction, 1300–1840.* New York, 1985.

Maclean, Ian. *The Renaissance Notion of Women: A Study in the Fortunes of Scholasticism and Medical Science in European Intellectual Life.* Cambridge, U.K., 1980.

Stone, Lawrence. *The Family, Sex, and Marriage in England, 1500–1800.* London, 1977.

Warnicke, Retha M. *Women of the English Renaissance and Reformation.* Westport, Conn., 1983.

Wiesner, Merry. *Working Women in Renaissance Germany.* New Brunswick, N.J., 1986.

MARGARET L. KING

Women and Protest

Women have participated throughout history in protests, either as direct instigators or as bystanders goading on others, but it was the particular economic and political conditions of the Renaissance and the seventeenth century that brought about a heightened character in women's outbursts of resistance. The traditional form of protest most associated with women of the lower classes centered around bread riots resulting from grain shortages, which became especially acute during the instabilities of the sixteenth and seventeenth centuries, directly threatening the domestic sphere over which women reigned. In France particularly, such disturbances were exacerbated by new burdens of taxation (especially the salt tax) imposed by an increasingly centralized state, resulting in famous female-centered riots in Lyon in 1529 and Bordeaux in 1643. Women played a small role as well in the notorious 1580 riot at Romans, as strike leaders, participants in the carnival pandemonium, or, in the case of Queen Mother Catherine de Médicis, as a tough representative of authority.

Women were also known to rise up as workers or artisans. Records from the 1300s tell of lower-paid spinners in the wool trade in England who fought merchant oligarchies, and of spinners in Cologne who demanded restrictions against unlicensed spinners. Religious riots, though not a uniquely female phenomenon, also witnessed women playing significant and visible roles, as was the case in the peasant uprisings in sixteenth-century Germany, the violence of strife-ridden France during the period of the religious wars, and the messianic instabilities during the time of the English Civil War.

The forms of female violence often involved household implements such as kitchen knives, dishes, and pewters. One Lisbon baker woman in 1580 led a group of armed female "soldiers" wielding a pan in place of a halberd. Women also helped stockpile, and often themselves threw rocks, as in the 1695 protest in Berry against process-servers who attempted to inaugurate a new tax on trades. Verbal threats were couched in the graphic language of butchery, cut throats, and cannibalism. In some cases, females even physically attacked hapless officials; this tended to provoke laughter from the crowds toward the now-humiliated victim.

Some female-centered protests did lead to a sense of female solidarity and vague assertions of equality. This was the case in the English Civil War of the 1640s and 1650s, when the women supporters of the Leveler John Lilburne protested martial law in 1649 with the words, "Have we not an equal interest with the men of this Nation in those liberties and securities contained in the Petition of Right?" In general, however, the nature of women's revolts tended to fall within generally conservative bounds, as gender was firmly subordinate to other interests and alignments. Still, while rioting women did not really come into their own until the revolutionary period in France, the Renaissance witnessed a new kind of visibility for outraged women, armed with household weapons and a moral authority, who united in a fearsome front against those unfortunate enough to face them.

BIBLIOGRAPHY

Bercé, Yves-Marie. "Les femmes dans les révoltes populaires." In *La femme à l'époque moderne: Colloque 1984, bulletin de l'association des historiens modernistes des universités*. Paris, 1985. Pages 57–64.

Davis, Natalie Zemon. *Society and Culture in Early Modern France*. Stanford, Calif., 1975.

Higgins, Patricia. "The Reactions of Women, with Special Reference to Women Petitioners." In *Politics, Religion, and the English Civil War*. Edited by Brian Manning. London, 1973. Pages 179–222.

SARAH COVINGTON

Women and Literature

The written and published word belonged primarily to men in the Renaissance, as women were hindered by a lack of educational opportunity that cut them off from universities and the elites' language of Latin. Nevertheless, Renaissance developments such as an increase in literacy, the revolutionary impact of print culture, the humanist movement, and religious reformation generated opportunities for literary women that granted them new ways in which to express themselves and contribute to a male-dominated world with voices of their own.

Context: Authorship, Patronage, Printing. The involvement of women in literature was often shaded and ambiguous, especially when it came to questions of authorship. For example, it is not clear how many women, in order to be taken seriously, published anonymously or switched gender in their noms de plume; also to be considered is a case such as the semiliterate Margery Kempe (1373–1439), whose spiritual autobiography conveys a distinctly female voice, even though it was dictated to a confessor. Patrons could also serve as hovering shadow-authors, and here women were especially influential in the Renaissance. Hundreds of dedicatory prefaces attest to the role of women who supported writers of their own gender and were behind the more female-friendly tracts written by Erasmus and Juan Luis Vives (for Catherine of Aragon), Cornelius Agrippa (for Margaret of Burgundy), and Bartolomeo Goggio (for Eleanora of Aragon).

Women also played more informal roles as supporters, correspondents, *salonnières,* translators, friends, and muses, popularizing works or providing the inspiration for virtually every important male writer or poet of the Renaissance. For elite women, the movement of humanism provided opportunities to create collections and libraries, which were not only available to male writers but were also bequeathed to daughters, granddaughters, and new generations of women readers. Finally, women played a role in shaping the new world of print, either as widows carrying on the family printing business, or as patrons like Margaret Beaufort, the mother of Henry VII, who was behind the efforts of William Caxton.

Female Genres and Literary Women. The emerging print and vernacular culture witnessed a proliferation of books directed toward and often written by women, including cookbooks, fashion books, child-care manuals, and herbals—the latter being a particularly fruitful genre for Hannah Wooley, a seventeenth-century medicine-maker and an authority on domestic crafts. Before, women who wrote had directed their efforts to a private audience, forsaking publication. Their work consisted primarily of journals, letters, spiritual diaries, religious meditations, or advice books for a limited, personal audience. The first woman writer to seriously challenge these traditions, at least on a secular and overtly public plane, was Christine de Pizan (1364–1430?), who supported herself by her craft, producing secular-minded works and polemics for a larger audience of men as well as women. Her articulations of the female experience and assertions of women's strength were carried forward by later writers such as Marie de Gournay (1566–1645). Still, while some of these "amazon" or "manly" women were upheld as models of goodness and purity by a few prominent male writers, the bulk of Renaissance literature written by men portrays women who seek more assertive identities as dangerous, monstrous, deformed, or unnatural.

Italian women writers predominated in the century after Christine, benefiting from a relatively open literary atmosphere and the sympathy of such poets as Ludovico Ariosto (1474–1533), Pietro Bembo (1470–1547), and others. Among the most acclaimed was Vittoria Colonna (1492–1547), the "literary queen" of the Italian Renaissance, whose noble Roman birth marked the beginning of a life spent at the center of the period's intellectual and political developments. Widowed from an unhappy and childless marriage at the age of thirty-three, Colonna spent the remaining twenty-two years of her life traveling, writing, and attracting a wide and important circle of acquaintances, the most famous of whom was Michelangolo Buonarroti, with whom she shared a long and fruitful correspondence. Colonna's published literary output consisted of books of verse that explore love from its lowliest, earthliest form through its most elevated, mystical, and Neoplatonic realization. Laura Terracina (1519–c. 1577), a contemporary of Colonna, lived an altogether more solitary life in her native Naples, publishing a body of work from 1548 through 1561 that included moral lamentations, poems of praise for her relatives and friends, reminiscences of her early years as a member of the Neapolitan Academy of Incogniti (The Unknowns), and, most importantly, the forty-two canto *Discorso sopra il principio di tutti i canti d'*Orlando furioso (Interpretation of the first cantos of *Orlando furioso*; 1549). Another significant writer at the time, Moderata Fonte (1555–1592), was born into high-ranking Venetian society and published religious poems, musical dramas in verse, and an important four-hundred-page didactic prose work on women before her death at the age of thirty-seven.

Marriage for Fonte and other Renaissance women proved somewhat stifling to their literary output, a situation not experienced by courtesans, who were freer to develop their intellectual and literary capabilities. Veronica Franco (1546–1591) and Gaspara Stampa (1523?–1554) offered major contributions to Renaissance poetry in lyrics that articulated knowing authority on the art of eros, with a deeper and more wrenching love occasionally entering in, spoken (in Stampa's words) by "a woman, half out of my mind." Tullia d'Aragona (c. 1510–1556), another high-class courtesan, also established herself as a literary figure in her own right by publishing works of lyric poetry, epistolary sonnets to men such as Cosimo de' Medici, and the Neoplatonic *Dialogo della infinità di amore* (Dialogue on the infinity of love; 1547).

In sixteenth-century France, love was also the theme of a few women who established themselves by the pen. Louise Labé (c. 1524–1566), the daughter of a rope twiner, dwelled in a love-soaked world, demanding her amour to "Kiss me again, again, kiss me again! / Give me one of the luscious ones you have," while on a much higher social scale stood the noblewoman Margaret of Navarre (1492–1549), sister to the king of France and one of the most important Renaissance patronesses, whose oeuvre consisted not only of poems and the great collection of stories known as the *Heptaméron* (1558), but also defenses of women and devotional works such as *Le miroir de l'âme pêcheresse* (The mirror of a sinful soul; 1531). In England the Countess of Pembroke and Lady Wroth breathed the same air as Shakespeare and Edmund Spenser, serving as patronesses, muses, and poets in their own right, but it was not until the seventeenth century that England began to witness a surge of important women writers, ranging from those who dealt in serious histories and political writings, such as Margaret Cavendish (1623–1673), to others who ventured into the altogether different terrain of bawdy worlds, cuckolded men, female lechery, and passions aflame. The most notable of the latter group was Aphra Behn (1640–1689), who earned an independent living by her plays, songs, translations, and an epistolatory novel, many of which were dedicated to female patrons.

Religious and Political Works by Women. While traditionally male genres of history, science, or philosophy remained closed to women, religious writing, which had long been a tradition among nuns and holy women, sent Renaissance women writers in new directions. The energies released by the Counter-Reformation impelled Teresa of Ávila

(1515–1582)—a woman of no Latin and little reading, though she had once enjoyed romances of chivalry—to compose spiritual works reflecting an ease with words and love of language. The Protestant Reformation, though it varied according to country, similarly focused the reading and writing habits of women, exposing them to the Bible and encouraging them to keep personal records of their spiritual lives. England in the seventeenth century especially provided an atmosphere of political and religious upheaval that women could exploit: thus, women's writings abounded in number and variety, ranging from prophecies and lamentations to works of quiet meditation and angry admonition.

Political petitions were common during the period of the English Civil War, with the amassed signatures reflecting a kind of collective female authorship, at times thousands of names strong. The Civil War also witnessed prolific publishing efforts by sectarian women, led above all by Quakers such as Dorothy White, who began one tract, "The word of the Lord came unto me, saying write, and again I say write." So compelled were religious women to write that a few such as Eleanor Davis and Anne Wentworth jeopardized or ended their marriages when those marriages interfered with an activity commanded by God. Moreover, for these writers, issues particular to women, such as motherhood, or the burdens placed on their gender often colored their publications and distinguished them from those of their male counterparts, as when the Fifth Monarchist Mary Cary wrote of a utopia where no children or dear relations would die. Such words approached a kind of self-conscious feminism that reached its height in the profound works of Mary Astell (1666–1731), who dreamed of scholarly female communities, critiqued the institution of marriage, and aspired to a world, she wrote, where women could "furnish our minds with a stock of solid and useful Knowledge, that the Souls of Women may no longer be the only unadorn'd and neglected things."

See also biographies of figures mentioned in this entry.

BIBLIOGRAPHY

Crawford, Patricia. "Women's Published Writings 1600–1700." In *Women in English Society 1500–1800*. Edited by Mary Prior. London, 1985. Pages 211–282. Includes a checklist of published writings.

Hufton, Olwen. *The Prospect before Her: A History of Women in Western Europe, 1500–1800*. New York, 1995.

Jordan, Constance. *Renaissance Feminism: Literary Texts and Political Models*. Ithaca, N.Y., 1990.

King, Margaret L. *Women of the Renaissance*. Chicago, 1991.

Russell, Rinaldina, ed. *Italian Women Writers: A Bio-Bibliographical Sketchbook*. Westport, Conn., 1994.

Wilson, Katharina, ed. *Women Writers of the Renaissance and Reformation*. Athens, Ga., and London, 1987.

SARAH COVINGTON

Women and Philosophy

The fate of the female philosopher in the Renaissance was the fate of the learned female in general, which is to say that her pursuits were constricted, often short-lived, and subject to the biases of an age in which philosophic undertakings were thought irrelevant to the identity of womanhood. Nevertheless, women did engage in philosophic activity as readers, students, patrons, and writers, despite their exclusion from universities and other institutions of learning. Humanism exposed a few elite women to texts including the works of Plato and Aristotle, the church fathers, and contemporary works of moral philosophy. Isotta Nogarola (1418–1466), a noblewoman who under male tutelage moved from the study of dialectic into philosophy, read Aristotle and the Arab philosophers, and wrote a disputation on whether Adam or Eve was the greater sinner. Elena Lucrezia Cornaro Piscopia (1646–1684) was said to have received her doctorate in philosophy in 1678 at the University of Padua after being examined on logic, natural philosophy, and Aristotle's *Posterior Analytics* and *Physics*. The careers of both women, however, were cut short by an atmosphere of hostility and resentment with Nogarola prematurely renouncing her classical studies and Cornaro dying at a young age.

The persistence in the Renaissance of the Aristotelian view of women as inferior to men intellectually and biologically surrounded the female with negative connotations, though some women used emerging ideas to challenge the dominant beliefs. Lucrezia Marinella (1571–1653) questioned Aristotle's view, suggesting that it resulted in part from a problematic relationship with his wife. Renaissance Platonism was a positive influence on the *précieuses,* a salon-centered group of learned women in late seventeenth-century France who embraced the ideas of René Descartes, Blaise Pascal, and François Fénelon. On a higher patronage level stood Queen Christina of Sweden (1632–1654) who read philosophy voraciously and brought Descartes to her country to set up a school. Women's correspondence with philosophers provided perhaps the most fertile domain of philosophic exchange; Descartes exchanged letters with Anna Maria van Schurman, known as "the learned and most noble virgin" of Utrecht, and author of a Latin treatise translated into English in 1659 as *The Learned Maid; or, Whether a Maid may also be a Scholar.* Englishwomen such as Margaret Cavendish and Lady Anne Conway—who is said to have influenced Leibniz's concept of the monad—also corresponded with men such as Henry More and the Cambridge Platonist John Norris, but it was Mary Astell (1666–1731) who took her pursuits to their furthest and most profound level.

Astell, the daughter of a well-to-do Newcastle coal merchant, was particularly interested in questions concerning the relations of the spirit and the flesh. She was the first Englishwoman to connect these concerns with a specifically feminist analysis and a call for an "academical" retreat for women, "to expel that cloud of Ignorance which Custom has involv'd us in, to furnish our minds with a stock of solid and useful Knowledge, that the Souls of Women may no longer be the only unadorn'd and neglected things." Astell's community, like that depicted in Christine de Pizan's *Book of the City of Ladies* (1405), was not realized, nor was Cornaro Piscopia's doctorate in philosophy followed by another awarded to a woman until 1732; but if women could not participate directly in Renaissance philosophy, they nevertheless were not far from the center of its production, shadowing it with their peripheral presence.

See also **Christina of Sweden; Cornaro Piscopia, Elena Lucrezìa; Marinella, Lucrezia; Nogarola, Isotta.**

BIBLIOGRAPHY

Primary Works

Astell, Mary. *The First English Feminist: Reflections on Marriage and Other Writings.* Edited by Bridget Hill. Aldershot, U.K., 1986.

Nogarola, Isotta. "On the Equal or Unequal Sin of Adam and Eve." In *Her Immaculate Hand.* Edited and translated by Margaret L. King and Albert Rabil Jr. Binghamton, N.Y., 1983. Pages 57–68.

Secondary Works

Hufton, Olwen. *The Prospect before Her: A History of Women in Western Europe.* Vol. 1: *1500–1800.* New York, 1995.

Jordan, Constance. *Renaissance Feminism: Literary Texts and Political Models.* Ithaca, N.Y., 1990.

King, Margaret L. *Women of the Renaissance.* Chicago, 1991.

SARAH COVINGTON

Portrayal in Renaissance Art

Mirroring the complexities of culture, representations of Renaissance women reflect social as well as aesthetic ideals and values. Although some images illustrate the physical reality of the era, most do not. Many portraits, such as Titian's flattering painting of the sixty-year-old Isabella d'Este as a youthful beauty (c. 1534) and Nicholas Hilliard's miniatures of Elizabeth I known as the "Mask of Youth" series (1590s),

are idealized. Similarly, mythologies and histories, like Lucas Cranach's depiction of *The Judgment of Paris* (1530), which is set in the Saxon court, and Giotto di Bondone's fresco cycle illustrating the life of the Virgin Mary painted for Enrico Scrovegni's Arena Chapel in Padua, consecrated in 1305, are imagined. But whether the woman pictured was a witch or a saint, a heroine or a temptress, a noblewoman or a member of the working class, her image was a moral admonition or an exhortation to dress and behave appropriately. Even donor portraits such as Oradea Becchetti in Carlo Crivelli's *Madonna and Child with Saints Francis and Sebastian* (1491) underscore the desired virtue of piety. Geographical boundaries had little effect on the didactic function invested in visual imagery. Although styles and mediums varied, subjects and themes recur throughout Europe.

Holy Women. Renaissance depictions of the Virgin Mary are numerous. Some, like Cimabue's *Enthroned Madonna and Child,* which was painted for the high altar of the church of Santa Trinità in Florence around 1280, are iconic. Others present the story of her life. Often, as is the case with Giotto's fresco cycle in the Arena Chapel, scenes of her life function as a foreword to the life of her son, Jesus Christ. In this particular example, the thirty-eight scenes picturing the two lives are painted on facing chapel walls. In altarpieces like Fra Angelico's Cortona *Annunciation* (c. 1434), significant moments in Mary's life are illustrated in the predella panels decorating the painting's pedestal.

Embodying the ideals of woman—chastity, piety, humility, and maternity—Mary was the paragon of feminine virtue. Images of the Madonna, whether carved of stone, printed on paper, or painted on panel, urged women to strive to live up to Mary's example. Because Mary was represented in paradoxical ways, this directive was not easily followed. The forever youthfully unblemished mother who mourns her son in Michelangelo's Vatican *Pietà* (1497–1499), for example, conveys the uniqueness of Mary as both mother *and* virgin. Similarly, Enguerrand Charonton's painting *Coronation of the Virgin* (1454), which depicts Mary flanked by saints and angels and surrounded by God the Father, God the Son, and the dove of the Holy Spirit, contrasts with countless paintings of Mary as the paradigm of humility, such as Rogier van der Weyden's *Annunciation* (c. 1435).

Although these and other images of the Madonna underscore the difficulty, indeed the impossibility, of

Women in Renaissance Art. *Return of the Virgin and Joseph from the Temple* by Giotto in the Scrovegni Chapel of Santa Maria Annunziata all'Arena, Padua. SCROVEGNI CHAPEL, PADUA, ITALY/ALINARI/ART RESOURCE

emulating her example, efforts were made to make her more accessible. In its setting and with incidental details such as a birthing stool, Albrecht Dürer's woodcut of *The Birth of the Virgin* from *The Life of the Virgin* series (c. 1503–1504), captures the sense of activity surrounding any successful birth in any German city at the beginning of the sixteenth century. Lucas Cranach's woodcut *The Holy Kinship* (c. 1509) also attempts to convey the unexceptional aspects of this very exceptional woman. He does so by showing her in the company of her parents and surrounded by an extended family of aunts, uncles, and cousins. While Dürer's and Cranach's images reflect the popularity of the cult of Saint Anne, Mary's mother, they also bring the humble Queen of Heaven down to earth. The print medium, which was relatively cheap, easily replicated, and transportable, was well suited to the theme. Presumably, these woodcuts were sold on the open market. Here

content, medium, and audience work in concert. But as Domenico Ghirlandaio's fresco cycle in the church of Santa Maria Novella, Florence (1485–1490), demonstrates, costly commissioned works could function in a related way. Lodovica Tornabuoni is in attendance in Ghirlandaio's painting of the Virgin Mary's birth, while Giovanna degli Albizzi, the wife of Lorenzo Tornabuoni, witnesses the Visitation, the moment Mary, who is pregnant with Jesus, meets Elizabeth, who is pregnant with John the Baptist.

Representations of female saints, especially those narrating events in a saint's life, functioned in similar ways. As Hans Memling's *Shrine of Saint Ursula* (1489) shows, these images, especially in combination with a holy relic, were poignant testaments to self-sacrifice. The *Shrine*, a reliquary in the form of a miniature church, illustrates six scenes of Ursula's life and martyrdom as recounted in Jacobus de Voragine's *Golden Legend.* Images of Mary Magdalen were especially popular. This purported prostitute turned saint was particularly well suited to the didactic function invested in art. Moreover, imaging the Magdalen gave artists more pictorial latitude than any other female saint. Donatello's hauntingly gaunt sculpture *Penitent Mary Magdalen* (c. 1450–1455) bears no relationship to the alluringly coy Magdalen painted by Jan van Scorel around 1530. And Scorel's Magdalen, which according to legend is a portrait of the artist's mistress Agatha van Schoonhoven, has little in common with Titian's ecstatic *Penitent Magdalen* (c. 1565).

Temptress. Images of Eve, usually in the company of Adam, are typically symbolic even when placed in what appears to be a narrative. *The Temptation* and *The Expulsion* in the Brancacci Chapel, Santa Maria del Carmine, frescoed by Masaccio and Masolino da Panicale around 1425, function in this way, as does Michelangelo's 1509–1510 rendering of these events in the central panel of the Sistine Chapel's ceiling. On rare occasions, such as Cristofano Robetta's engraving *Adam and Eve with the Infants Cain and Abel,* Eve is represented after the Fall. Frequently they suggest Eve's oppositional relationship to the Virgin Mary, and sometimes, as is the case with Jean Cousin the Elder's *Eva Prima Pandora* (c. 1538), she is conflated with another troublesome female. It is easy to see how images of witches like those by Hans Baldung Grien flourished in this environment.

The combining of Eve with Pandora reflects a sixteenth-century vogue for images of beautiful temptresses. As Donatello's bronze relief in the Siena Cathedral (c. 1425; Baptismal Font) and Fra Filippo Lippi's fresco in Prato's cathedral (1452–1466), demonstrate, depictions of the lithe Salome dancing for John the Baptist's head were nothing new. What was different was the increased number of so-called temptresses. Because their stories are about voyeurism, Susannah and Bathsheba were especially popular. Ignoring their victimization, these enticing Old Testament bathing beauties were imaged in costly paintings, like Tintoretto's *Susannah and the Elders* (c. 1555), and inexpensive prints, such as Hans Burgkmair's woodcut of *Bathsheba at her Bath* (1519). Strikingly similar to pictures of the goddess Diana, such as Titian's *Diana and Actaeon* (1559), images of this kind subtly satisfied a taste for the erotic. Many of the paintings of ideal beauty were similarly satisfying. Presented as portraits, images like Titian's *La Bella* (c. 1536) visualize the verbal

descriptions of the ideal woman found in contemporary treatises like Baldassare Castiglione's *Il cortegiano* (*The Book of the Courtier*). Marcantonio Raimondi's print series known as *The Positions* (c. 1524) represents the opposite end of the spectrum. Engraved after drawings by Giulio Romano and subsequently supplemented with graphically crude poems by Pietro Aretino, the pornographic series of images cost Raimondi several years in prison.

Depictions of the battle between the sexes also flourished. As the woodcuts by Lucas van Leyden known as *The Large Power of Women* series (c. 1512) show, humor and tragedy were uncomfortably close when sexuality was involved. The series of six includes Salome's dance for which she got John the Baptist's head and the famed poet and foolishly enamored Virgil suspended in a basket midway in its route to the bedroom of the emperor's daughter. Predictably, Eve's seduction of Adam is among the pictured incidents. In some cases it is not always clear whether a powerful woman is to be admired as a heroine or condemned as a temptress. Images of Judith are especially susceptible to this type of ambiguity. Judith can be a symbol of fortitude, as is the case with Donatello's sculpture of the heroine decapitating Holofernes (c. 1456–1459), or a naked seducer, as is the case with Jan Sanders van Hemessen's oil painting of c. 1549.

BIBLIOGRAPHY

Cropper, Elizabeth. "The Beauty of Woman: Problems in the Rhetoric of Renaissance Portraiture." In *Rewriting the Renaissance: The Discourse of Sexual Difference in Early Modern Europe.* Edited by Margaret W. Ferguson, Maureen Quilligan, and Nancy J. Vickers. Chicago, 1986. Pages 175–190.

Goffen, Rona. *Titian's Women.* New Haven, Conn., 1997.

Johnson, Geraldine A., and Sara F. Matthews Grieco, eds. *Picturing Women in Renaissance and Baroque Italy.* New York, 1997.

Lazzaro, Claudia. "The Visual Language of Gender in Sixteenth-Century Garden Sculpture." In *Refiguring Woman: Perspectives on Gender and the Italian Renaissance.* Edited by Marilyn Migiel and Juliana Schiesari. Ithaca, N.Y., 1991. Pages 71–113.

Russell, H. Diane. Eva/Ave: *Woman in Renaissance and Baroque Prints.* Washington, D.C., 1990.

Tinagli, Paola. *Women in Italian Renaissance Art: Gender, Representation, Identity.* New York, 1997.

Wood, Jeryldene M. *Women, Art, and Spirituality: The Poor Clares of Early Modern Italy.* Cambridge, U.K., 1996.

FREDRIKA H. JACOBS

Women and Science

During the Renaissance women participated marginally in the academic world of science. By the fourteenth century the medieval university had become an important center for scientific learning, most notably the study of Aristotle's writings and the pursuit of learned medicine. Scholasticism had made Latin the universal language in which discussions of knowledge took place. While there was no specific rule barring women from the universities, the theological and professional orientation of the curriculum was predicated on the assumption that university education prepared one for public activities that were overwhelmingly male, either by precedent or by custom. Lack of access to both Latinate education and learned institutions made it difficult for most women to engage in those critical discussions and revisions of ancient learning out of which a new scientific culture emerged.

The development of humanistic education outside of European universities created opportunities for a handful of women to participate in conversations about knowledge. In northern Italy especially, learned fathers occasionally educated their daughters in Latin and Greek. These crucial linguistic skills made it possible for fifteenth-century female humanists such as Isotta Nogarola (1418–1466) of Verona and Laura Cereta (1469–1499) of Brescia to study philosophy. Similarly, some women courtiers not only had access to a kind of learning equivalent to that of the university but also enjoyed the company of physicians, philosophers, mathematicians, and engineers who increasingly came to the Renaissance courts in search of patronage for their projects.

Access to knowledge is not the same as full participation, however. While there were prominent women artists, musicians, and writers by the sixteenth century, it is difficult to identify any women who were known independently for their science. More typically, wives, sisters, and daughters of prominent natural philosophers participated fully in a scientific household. For example, the Danish nobleman and astronomer Tycho Brahe's (1546–1601) sister Sophie assisted him in observing the nova of 1572, shared the secret of his elixir to ward off plague, and generally involved herself in scientific conversations at the Danish court. The Bolognese naturalist Ulisse Aldrovandi (1522–1605) married his second wife, Francesca Fontana, for her learning as well as her dowry; she participated actively in the maintenance of his burgeoning natural history collection and in the preparation of his encyclopedia of nature. The English mathematician and magus John Dee (1527–1608) at times made his wife, Jane Fromond, the object of his experimental imagination, recording her menstrual cycle and reproductive activities. In all of these instances, women facilitated the work of men as part of their domestic and familial responsibilities.

Medicine was the one arena in which Renaissance women enjoyed a greater degree of autonomy. While the increasing status and authority of physicians and surgeons in the sixteenth and seventeenth centuries restricted the number of women allowed to practice in these areas because they did not have university degrees in medicine, many communities relied on female healers for medicinal and herbal knowledge. In some instances, prominent practitioners, such as the French royal midwife Louise Bourgeois (1563–1636), used the medium of print to compete with male practitioners, demonstrating that their experience could rival academic knowledge of the human body. The greater and more vocal presence of women in Renaissance medicine suggests that it did not yet fully enjoy academic status as a science, like astronomy or mathematics, but continued to be a craft open to both sexes.

BIBLIOGRAPHY

Findlen, Paula. "Masculine Prerogatives: Gender, Space, and Knowledge in the Early Modern Museum." In *The Architecture of Science*. Edited by Emily Thompson and Peter Galison. Cambridge, Mass., 1999. Pages 29–57.

Green, Monica. "Women's Medical Practice and Health Care in Medieval Europe." *Signs* 14, no. 2 (1989): 434–473.

Harkness, Deborah E. "Managing an Experimental Household: The Dees of Mortlake and the Practice of Natural Philosophy." *Isis* 88 (June 1997): 247–262.

Schiebinger, Londa L. *The Mind Has No Sex? Women in the Origins of Modern Science*. Cambridge, Mass., 1989.

PAULA FINDLEN

WOODCUT. *See* **Printmaking.**

WORK. *See* **Agriculture; Guilds; Industry; Peasantry.**

WROTH, MARY (c. 1587–1653), English writer. Mary Wroth was born Mary Sidney in 1587, the first child of Robert Sidney (later Viscount de L'Isle and earl of Leicester) and his wife, Barbara Gamage. Wroth was niece to Sir Philip Sidney, the well-known Renaissance poet and courtier (author of *Astrophil and Stella* and *Arcadia*), and Mary Sidney, the countess of Pembroke (a poet and patron of aspiring authors). Mary Wroth wrote the first sonnet sequence in English by a woman, *Pamphilia to Amphilanthus* (1621), one of the first plays by a woman, *Love's Victory* (no date; printed for the first time in 1988), and the first published work of fiction by an Englishwoman, *The Countess of Mountgomeries Ura-*

nia (1621). Wroth is noteworthy not simply for her career as a woman writer in a period dominated by male voices, but also for the range of her authorship: whereas other English women writers at that time, such as Aemilia Lanyer or Elizabeth Cary, are known for single texts or for their work in single genres, the volume and diversity of Wroth's texts attest to her extraordinary dedication and ability as an author.

Mary Wroth spent her childhood at Penshurst, the Sidney family estate. In 1604, her parents arranged her marriage to Robert Wroth, who had been knighted the previous year by King James I. In 1614, Mary Wroth gave birth to a baby son, James, one month before the death of her husband. When her son died two years later, the estate reverted to her husband's uncle, leaving Wroth to face her husband's debts. She subsequently engaged in an affair with her cousin William Herbert (third earl of Pembroke), bearing two illegitimate children, William and Katherine, and maintaining ties with her circle of friends despite her reduced standing at court and financial difficulties. The first portion of Wroth's prose romance, *Urania,* was most likely composed during these years, and was published in 1621 with her lyric sequence, *Pamphilia to Amphilanthus.* Her play, *Love's Victory,* and the manuscript continuation of *Urania* were probably written in the early 1620s.

The publication of *Urania* in 1621 occasioned a court furor: the objections of King James's male courtiers to the book's satirical references to their private lives forced Wroth to withdraw *Urania* from sale only six months after its publication. Her primary attacker, Edward Lord Denny, specifically chose to make Wroth's gender an issue, lambasting her not only for her alleged allusions to his life, but also for her effrontery as a woman in presuming to write secular fiction and poetry, contrasting her with her aunt, the countess of Pembroke, whose translations of religious poetry were considered more acceptable writing for a woman. The resulting suppression of Wroth's text had long-range consequences: only a few copies of the 1621 published *Urania* and only one copy of her unpublished continuation of the romance survive today, while the first complete edition of her romance did not appear until 1995. Written in the face of adversity, Mary Wroth's works offer a complex representation of a remarkable range of women's voices and positions.

BIBLIOGRAPHY

Primary Works

Wroth, Mary. *The First Part of* The Countess of Montgomery's Urania *by Lady Mary Wroth.* Edited by Josephine A. Roberts. Binghamton, N.Y., 1995.

Wroth, Mary. *Lady Mary Wroth's* Love's Victory: *The Penshurst Manuscript.* Edited by Michael G. Brennan. London, 1988.

Wroth, Mary. *The Poems of Lady Mary Wroth.* Edited by Josephine A. Roberts. Baton Rouge, La., 1983.

Secondary Works

Lamb, Mary Ellen. *Gender and Authorship in the Sidney Circle.* Madison, Wis., 1990. Analysis of writings produced by the Sidney family, including Sir Philip Sidney; his sister, Mary, countess of Pembroke; his niece, Lady Mary Wroth; his daughter, Elizabeth, countess of Rutland; and an anonymous poet, most likely a woman, in his family circle.

Miller, Naomi J. *Changing the Subject: Mary Wroth and Figurations of Gender in Early Modern England.* Lexington, Ky., 1996. Full-length study of all the writings of Mary Wroth, reading Wroth in relation to a broad range of English and continental authors, both male and female, literary and non-literary.

Miller, Naomi J., and Gary Waller. *Reading Mary Wroth: Representing Alternatives in Early Modern England.* Knoxville, Tenn., 1991. Collection of critical essays on Mary Wroth, including an annotated bibliography of Wroth criticism.

Waller, Gary. *The Sidney Family Romance: Mary Wroth, William Herbert, and the Early Modern Construction of Gender.* Detroit, Mich., 1993. Cultural biography and analysis of the sexual and textual relationships of Mary Wroth and William Herbert, as writers, lovers, and first cousins in the Sidney family.

NAOMI J. MILLER

WYATT, THOMAS. *See* **Poetry,** *subentry on* **Early Tudor Poetry.**

XAVIER, FRANCIS.   *See* **Francis Xavier.**

YIDDISH LITERATURE AND LANGUAGE.

During the Renaissance, Yiddish, the Jewish vernacular originating in the German-speaking area, was the only spoken language of all Jews, regardless of age, gender, or social, cultural, or economic status, throughout the Ashkenazi Diaspora, which at that time included Germany, Bohemia and Moravia, Poland-Lithuania, northern Italy (only until the seventeenth century), the Netherlands (only from the mid-seventeenth century), and several locations within the Ottoman Empire. As a result of this wide dispersion, Slavic, Italian, Dutch, Arabic, or Turkish elements entered the spoken language in each of these locations and, together with the earlier German, Hebrew-Aramaic, and Romance common components of Yiddish, generated a great number of regional variations in the language.

Although no formal coordinating body existed, the regional elements of the spoken language were carefully kept out of Yiddish printed books with the intention of making their contents comprehensible to all potential readers, wherever they might be. A literary language was thus created, which systematically distanced itself from local usages and until the end of the eighteenth century maintained the link of all Yiddish speakers to the same body of literature. Yiddish books, written anywhere within the Ashkenazi Diaspora, were printed in various cities of Poland, Germany, and Italy as well as in Basel, Prague, and Amsterdam, and distributed throughout the Diaspora in order to reach their main addressees: men and women, young and old, who could read He-

brew but had not achieved the necessary language proficiency to understand the Hebrew literary sources.

Main Genres of Yiddish Literature.   At least until the end of the eighteenth century, Yiddish literature was largely involved in the transmission of knowledge from the Hebrew corpus. Inevitably, only the learned—mainly religious officials—could act as mediators between that corpus and the Yiddish reader. Their sense of that reader's ability to comprehend and learn combined with their conception of his intellectual, spiritual, and behavioral needs or duties to determine the selection of particular segments of the Hebrew corpus and the methods of transmission to be employed. Thus Hebrew prayers were translated literally, while the books of the Hebrew Bible were rendered in a variety of either simple or complex prose or rhyme translations, and in some cases adapted and reworked into homiletic prose and even turned into sophisticated epic poetry.

Translations and adaptations of Hebrew ethical literature appeared alongside original compositions in Yiddish inspired by Hebrew works. They had a clear didactic and moralistic purpose and contributed to the diffusion of popular religion in much the same way as did the adaptations of books of customs instructing the reader in his domestic and synagogue duties on holidays and other special occasions such as weddings, circumcisions, and funerals; the translations of special collections of the texts to be recited or sung during the festive ceremonies performed at home; and the Yiddish or bilingual Hebrew and Yid-

Yiddish Text. Title page of the Old Yiddish *Ayn Shoyn Mayse Bukh* (Book of stories) by Jacob ben Abraham of Mezhirech (Basel, 1602).

dish songs specifically composed for such occasions and marked by the fusion of Hebrew liturgical poetry and German folk song.

Fables and tales, mainly exemplary and hagiographical, were either drawn from the classical rabbinic sources or developed from homilies and oral tradition. Women in particular were provided with books on women's commandments that focused on their formal religious duties but addressed other feminine functions as well, and with voluntary supplicatory prayers covering the full range of events marking their life cycle. Translations of Hebrew travelogues and historiographies, together with some works in this genre composed originally in Yiddish, conferred knowledge about distant places and the historical past. The Yiddish "historical" song, which combined elements of the Hebrew lamentation tradition with stylistic and structural devices borrowed from the German "historical" song, supplied fresh information on current events and played a role simi-

lar to that of the newspaper (apart from one isolated and short-lived venture in Amsterdam, no Yiddish newspaper appeared until the nineteenth century).

Most Yiddish works drawing on Hebrew sources were popularizations providing additional explanation, repetition and rewording, simplification, itemization, and exemplification, assisted at times by poetical devices and graphic illustrations. The typical outcome was a paraphrastic narrative interlaced with stories, exempla, proverbs, and parables, in addition to the author's digressions and interpolations, his direct appeals to the reader, and his allusions to the realities of daily life. Some of these features pervade the few extant Yiddish autobiographical or memoiristic accounts (such as Glikl Hamel's [Glueckel of Hameln's] memoirs, written between 1691 and 1719, and Leyb Oyzer's report on the Sabbatean movement, 1711) as well as the numerous Yiddish private letters that have come down to us from this period.

Besides serving as a vehicle for personal expression by the authors and mediating Hebrew to those who could read but did not understand it, Yiddish also mediated German, a language they understood but could not read, since the association between the Roman alphabet and the Christian priesthood had created an apprehension which most Ashkenazi Jews shared at least until the late eighteenth century. Those who read the Roman script (generally officials in charge of the community's external affairs) provided faithful transcriptions into Hebrew characters of several German epic poems, in which they intervened only to the extent of eliminating, neutralizing, deprecating, or Judaizing the overtly Christian elements.

Yiddish Literature in Italy. While the eastern European branch of Ashkenazi Jewry remained attached to Yiddish both in Europe and abroad until well into the twentieth century, the Yiddish-speaking Jews who had settled in Italy after the Black Death clung to their language only until the beginning of the seventeenth century. However, during the fifteenth and sixteenth centuries the Ashkenazic communities of northern Italy (Venice, Verona, Padua, Mantua, Cremona, Brescia, Mestre) were involved in intense Yiddish literary activity and printing. This "golden age" introduced numerous innovations, gave rise to Yiddish narrative prose either in single-story booklets or in large anthologies, introduced the use of illustrations in Yiddish books, and produced fascinating Yiddish adaptations of Italian popular literature (such as the chivalric romances *Buovo d'Antona* and *Paris e Vienna*), written or inspired by Elijah Levita (1468–1549), the most outstanding personality in the history of Yiddish literature until the nineteenth century.

See also Hebrew Literature and Language; Jews, *subentry on* Print and Jewish Cultural Development; Judeo-Italian; Translation, *subentry on* Jewish Translators.

BIBLIOGRAPHY

Primary Works

Levita, Elijah. *Elye Bokher: poetishe shafungen in Yidish.* Edited by Judah A. Joffe. New York, 1949. Contains a reproduction of the 1541 first edition.

Ma'aseh Book: Book of Jewish Tales and Legends. Translated by Moses Gaster. 1934. Reprint, Philadelphia, 1981.

Paris un Wiene. Transcribed into Latin characters by Erika Timm. Tübingen, Germany, 1996.

Secondary Works

Shmeruk, Chone. *Sifrut yidish: prakim le-toldoteha.* Tel Aviv, Israel, 1978. Important historical research on Old Yiddish literature. Comprehensive bibliography on pages 294–327.

Turniansky, Chava. "La letteratura yiddish nell'Italia del Cinquecento." In *Il mondo yiddish: saggi.* Edited by Elena Mortara Di Veroli and Laura Quercioli Mincer. Rome, 1996. Pages 63–92.

CHAVA TURNIANSKY

ZABARELLA, JACOPO (1533–1589), Aristotelian philosopher, important for his studies in logic and natural philosophy. Born in Padua, he inherited the title of palatine count (which enabled him to award university degrees) from his father, Giulio Zabarella. He studied the humanities, logic, natural philosophy, and mathematics at Padua, receiving the doctorate from the university there in 1553. He then taught at the university, obtaining the first chair of logic in 1564 and, in 1568, the more remunerative second ordinary chair (or professorship) in natural philosophy, which he occupied until his death.

Among Zabarella's works the most important are his *Opera logica* (Work on logic; Venice, 1578), which included a commentary on Aristotle's *Posterior Analytics,* and his *De naturalis scientiae constitutione* (On the constitution of natural science; Venice, 1586). His commentaries on Aristotle's *Physics, On the Generation of Animals, Meteorology,* and *On the Soul,* together with a collection of thirty short works on natural philosophy entitled *De rebus naturalibus* (On natural things), were published repeatedly after his death, first in Italy (1590), then also in Germany. Apart from Padua, Zabarella's influence was most felt in Germany and in the British Isles, where the Aristotelianism he expounded remained strong until the mid-seventeenth century.

Classification of Disciplines. Zabarella was an excellent commentator on Aristotle, but he also went beyond Aristotle to address other problems of interest. Foremost among these was the hierarchy of disciplines taught in the university and particularly the relationships between the arts and the sciences. While admitting that in general usage there is considerable overlap between these two terms, Zabarella maintained that, properly speaking, sciences (*scientiae*) are concerned with the eternal world of nature and thus are contemplative disciplines, whereas arts (*artes*) are concerned with the contingent world of human beings and thus are noncontemplative, being active or productive instead.

The contemplative or speculative sciences, for Zabarella, are only three in number: divine science, also called metaphysics; mathematics; and natural philosophy. To these he opposed law, medicine, ethics and politics, and mechanics, which, for him, are all active or operative arts. His dominant interest was in natural philosophy, which he regarded as an autonomous science treating both nature and the soul, independently of metaphysics. Aristotle's *Physics* and *On the Soul* were, for him, foundational disciplines akin to Euclid's *Elements,* which perfectly filled the requirements of the *Posterior Analytics.* Both were open to fuller development through an empirical approach that stressed observation, experience, and the rudimentary "experimental methods" being developed in his time.

Medicine, for Zabarella, is not a science but an operative art that aims at maintaining the health of the human body and curing its sickness. Its end is operation, not the contemplation of nature. On this ground it cannot be a science but must be an art, though Zabarella would concede it to be the highest or noblest of the arts. To the extent that anatomy and physiology are ordered to knowledge as such, and not to operation, for him they belong to natural philosophy rather than to medicine. In this view, as in others, he was strongly opposed by Francesco Piccolomini (1523–1607), another professor of natural philosophy at Padua, and the medical faculty at the university.

Method and Order. Method, for Zabarella, also serves to differentiate the sciences from the arts. The term can be taken in two senses, either in a wide sense as a method of presenting existing knowledge, which he prefers to call an order (*ordo*) of presentation, or in a narrow sense as a method of discovering knowledge, for which he would reserve method (*methodus*) in its proper understanding. As

JACOBI

ZABARELLÆ
PATAVINI

OPERA LOGICA:

Quorum argumentum, feriem & vtilitatem often-
det tum verfa pagina, tum affixa
PRÆFATIO

JOANNIS LVDOVICI HAVVENREVTERI
Doctoris Medici, & Philofophi, in ARGENTORA-
TENSI *Academia Profefforis.*

RERVM QVOQVE ET VERBORVM
maxime memorabilium INDICES acceffe-
runt locupletiffimi.

EDITIO POSTREMA.

Cum Gratia & Priuilegio Cæfareæ Majeftatis.

FRANCÓFVRTI,
Sumptibus LAZARI ZETZNERI Bibliopolæ.

M. D. C. VIII.

Zabarella's Logic. Title page of Zabarella's *Opera logica* (Frankfurt, 1608). The work was originally published in Venice in 1578.

to presentation, he recognized only two orders, the compositive and the resolutive. The compositive order starts with first principles and then proceeds to others derived from them, and is characteristic of the contemplative sciences. The resolutive order starts with ends to be achieved and resolves these back to the means or principles for attaining them, and is characteristic of the active or operative disciplines, including medicine, ethics, and politics.

As with orders, Zabarella recognized only two methods, which he labeled demonstrative and resolutive. Demonstrative method proceeds from cause to effect and involves demonstration "of the reasoned fact" or "most powerful" demonstration,

best exemplified in the mathematical sciences. Resolutive method proceeds from effect to cause and, despite its name, also involves demonstration, but of an inferior kind, that is, demonstration "of the fact" or "from a sign." Related to this is the process of induction (*inductio*), which is helpful for discovering principles that are known naturally but are not immediately evident. Both processes are characteristic of natural philosophy and are incorporated in the demonstrative regress.

The Demonstrative Regress. Zabarella defined demonstrative regress as "a kind of reciprocal demonstration in which, after we have demonstrated the unknown cause through the known effect, we convert the major proposition and demonstrate the same effect through the same cause, so that we known why the effect exists" (*Opera logica;* Cologne, 1598, col. 481). For this conversion to occur, he points out, an intermediate "work" (*labor*) must occur. This involves induction and a "mental examination" (*examen mentale*) during which one passes from knowing the cause confusedly to grasping it distinctly. When completed, the first stage is elevated from a conjectural argument to a true demonstration, and the entire process consists of reciprocal demonstrations, one "of the fact" and the other "of the reasoned fact," yielding a conclusion that is strictly scientific.

In his commentary on the *Posterior Analytics* Zabarella identified Aristotle's proofs that the planets are near and that the moon is a sphere as instances of the demonstrative regress (*Opera logica,* pp. 836–841). Other examples of the regress he analyzed are Aristotle's proof of the existence of "first matter" (*materia prima*) from substantial change and his proof of an "eternal first mover" (*primus motor aeternus*) from local motion (*Opera logica,* pp. 484–492). Yet he made no advances through its use that would be recognized as scientific in the modern sense.

Not until late in the twentieth century was it discovered that Galileo Galilei (1564–1642) knew of Zabarella's teaching on the regress through notes he appropriated from the Jesuit Paolo della Valle (1561–1622) around 1589. It is arguable that Galileo in fact used the regress to certify his many discoveries as "necessary demonstrations" in the Aristotelian sense.

BIBLIOGRAPHY

Di Liscia, Daniel A., Eckhard Kessler, and Charlotte Methuen, eds. *Method and Order in Renaissance Philosophy of Nature: The Aristotle Commentary Tradition.* Aldershot, U.K., 1997. See essays by Nicholas Jardine, "Keeping Order in the

School of Padua: Jacopo Zabarella and Francesco Piccolomini on the Offices of Philosophy," pp. 183–209; and Heikki Mikkeli, "The Foundation of an Autonomous Natural Philosophy: Zabarella on the Classification of Arts and Sciences," pp. 211–228.

Mikkeli, Heikki. *An Aristotelian Response to Renaissance Humanism: Jacopo Zabarella on the Nature of the Arts and Sciences*. Helsinki, Finland, 1992.

Schmitt, Charles B. "Zabarella, Jacopo." In *Dictionary of Scientific Biography*. Edited by Charles Coulston Gillispie. Vol. 14. New York, 1976. Pages 580–582. Provides a basic bibliography.

Wallace, William A. *Galileo's Logic of Discovery and Proof: The Background, Content, and Use of His Appropriated Treatises on Aristotle's* Posterior Analytics. Dordrecht, Netherlands; Boston; and London, 1992.

WILLIAM A. WALLACE

ZELL, KATHARINE (1497/8–1562), German Protestant author and Reformer. The daughter of artisans, Katharine Schütz's marriage to Matthew Zell, a cathedral preacher in Strasbourg, in 1523 caused controversy as an early example of a reforming priest marrying. Her home soon won a reputation for hospitality; she harbored refugees and visited the sick, victims of plague, and those in jail. She kept in touch, by letter or in person, with many of the leading Reformers such as Huldrych Zwingli and Oecolampadius (Johannes Huszgen). Between 1524 and 1558 she published five printed works, beginning, in an unusual reversal of marital roles, with a defense of her husband titled *Christliche Verantwortung*. In a 1557 letter, or collection of letters, to Ludwig Rabus, the Lutheran preacher in Ulm, she rejected not only his savage criticism of her open doctrinality but also the confessionalist spirit he personified. Her letter appeals to the common sense of the people of Strasbourg and illustrates a charitable and inclusive outlook, which extended to radicals such as Kaspar Schwenckfeld von Ossig and Zwingli, both of whom had been her guests. Doctrinal niceties were less important to her than the integrity of one's life and witness to one's faith, which she admired in the Anabaptists, or Baptists, as she preferred to call them. This belief led her to be accused of heresy. Critical of clericalism and legalism, as a writer, speaker, and adviser she played a public role, as well as an important domestic one. She was effectively a lay pastor and Reformer and a noted advocate of religious tolerance.

BIBLIOGRAPHY

Primary Work

McKee, Elsie Anne. *The Writings of Katharina Schütz Zell: A Critical Edition*. Leiden, Netherlands, 1998.

Secondary Works

McKee, Elsie Anne. "The Defense of Schwenckfeld, Zwingli, and the Baptists, by Katharina Schütz Zell." In *Reformatorisches Erbe: Festschrift für Gottfried W. Locher*. Edited by Heiko A. Oberman. Zurich, Switzerland, 1993. Pages 245–264.

McKee, Elsie Anne. *Katharina Schütz Zell: The Life and Thought of a Sixteenth-Century Reformer*. Leiden, Netherlands, 1998.

PETER MATHESON

ZOOLOGY. Before becoming a full-fledged branch of modern biology, the scientific study of animals fell primarily under the discipline of natural philosophy. Theories drew on concepts of nature, defined by generation and corruption, and creation culminating in humanity; concrete aspects depended on relevance to daily life. In this framework the Renaissance produced an unprecedented number of writings on zoology. The authors, led by Conrad Gesner of Zurich and Ulisse Aldrovandi of Bologna, personified continuity, change, and challenge in scientific inquiry.

The Context of Tradition. The intellectual roots of zoology were in the classroom rather than in the laboratory. Aristotle's teaching, as mainspring of the university curriculum, inspired a value-based hierarchy of living beings and an emphasis on the purpose of each part and process. Albertus Magnus's remarkable commentary on the Aristotelian treatises on animals, composed around 1260, animated zoological studies for three centuries. Less philosophical information abounded in the late-classical natural histories of Pliny and the Roman rhetorician Aelian, which tended to be more narrative than descriptive, to favor the strange, and to humanize beasts. Data from these and other sources, compiled by medieval encyclopedists, were discussed in the liberal arts, medical theory, and biblical exegesis.

The ultimate practical motive for learning, the promotion of moral rectitude and devout recognition of the Creator, entailed a predilection for marvelous creatures and symbolic traits. Fable and allegory pervaded collections such as the 1559 *De miraculis occultis naturae* (Occult miracles of nature) by Levinus Lemnius, and illustrated texts ranging from heraldry to bestiaries. Animal lore, mythical and mundane, was mined for all kinds of ingredients for remedies. Most zoologists were physicians, and Aldrovandi held a chair in the history of medicinal substances. Furthermore, the understanding of physiology relied on parallels among mammals, and particularly on extrapolations from dissections of apes and pigs. Analogies highlighted the "fabric" of the human body for Andreas Vesalius, who in 1543 described

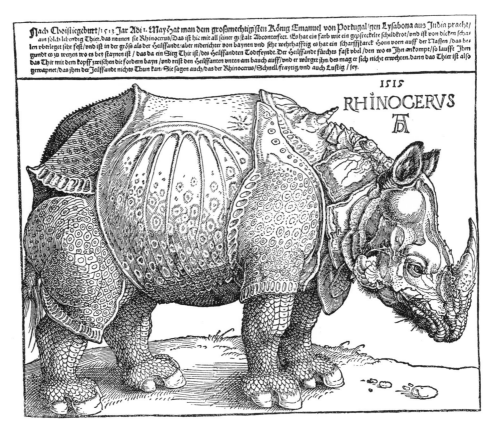

Zoological Specimen. Engraving of a rhinoceros by Albrecht Dürer, 1515. © THE BRITISH MUSEUM, LONDON

his vivisections on several animals. Comparative anatomy was introduced in Pierre Belon's natural histories of fish and birds in the 1550s, extended to a wide zoological spectrum by Volcher Coiter in 1573, and applied to horse medicine by Carlo Ruini in 1598. The role of animals in transportation and toil, nutrition and sport, remained a basic reason for their study.

New Stimuli. The climate of the Reformation intensified the search for authentic foundations undistorted by medieval transmission; paradoxically, it also reinforced supernatural interpretations of unfamiliar phenomena, particularly of abnormal births as omens. The humanist outlook encouraged study of nature in the quest for universal knowledge, an avocation rather than a scholastic career. The intense visuality documented in animal portraits, from Il Pisanello and Leonardo da Vinci to Albrecht Dürer and Jan Brueghel the Elder, enhanced perceptiveness. The cultivation of letter writing fostered scientific exchanges, exemplified by Gesner's correspondence with scores of scholars. Philological erudition gave access to several languages and precise terminology.

Original texts were restored, including Aristotle in a new Latin translation by Theodore Gaza around 1450 and Aelian in an edition by Gesner in 1556. The significance of printing is evident in the early publication of a book on animals as part of a ninth-century encyclopedia, at Strasbourg in 1467, and in the sequence of other firsts: Pliny in 1469; four Romans on husbandry in 1472; the encyclopedists Bartholomaeus Anglicus in 1471 and Vincent of Beauvais in 1478; Aristotle on animals in 1476 and, in Gaza's translation, in 1483. German, English, and French books on hunting appeared in the 1480s. A travelogue of a pilgrimage to the Holy Land was printed in 1486 with woodcuts of seven animals, including a giraffe and a great ape.

The contributions of travelers to zoology were ambivalent. Their reports, relatively free from academic baggage, stirred fresh inquiry into the natural world; narration, however, favored fantasy and hyperbole. Knowledge was enriched by accounts of Levantine fauna, most notably by Belon in the 1550s, but deepened by nearby explorations in mountain climbs by Aldrovandi and Gesner and visits to fish markets by Guillaume Rondelet. New World species such as armadillo and sloth intrigued Europeans but had less immediate impact than American plants. The first challenge was to match them with textual traditions: in 1526, the explorer-naturalist Gonzalo Fernández de Oviedo sought to apply Pliny's descriptions of the tiger to the jaguars of the Indies.

Development of Science. The principal scientific endeavor of naturalists was to gather evidence, above all from books. Gesner offered all the available literature in his *Historiae animalium* (History of animals; 1551–1587), citing 150 sources in his first section on viviparous quadrupeds. Aldrovandi, with a library of nearly four thousand volumes, named five hundred authors and titles in his *De animalibus insectis libri septem* (Seven books on insects). The preoccupation with comprehensiveness and historical perspective accounted for the inclusion of the basilisk, phoenix, unicorn, and other fabulous creatures. The weight of testimony induced Gesner and Aldrovandi, unlike Albertus Magnus, to accept that the barnacle goose could be generated from rotting wood. Such acceptances are offset by admissions of uncertainty, deference to the reader's judgment, and exposure of frauds such as the fabrication of dragons out of rayfish; the impression of credulity became exaggerated later in less circumspect posthumous editions, particularly the *Exoticorum libridecem* (Ten books of exotica) of Carolus Clasius (1605) and the anonymous *Monstrorum historia* (History of monsters; 1642).

Voracious curiosity fueled investigation and publication. Casual discoveries were often recorded without attribution: William Turner's findings supplemented an ostensible edition of ornithological excerpts from Aristotle and Pliny in 1544. Less self-effacing, Georg Bauer (Agricola) explored subterranean animals and fossils in 1549. Extraordinary items constituted the nucleus of scientific collections, none more famous than Aldrovandi's Musaeum, which by 1600 held thousands of specimens and drawings. Marvels, from monkeys to elephants, were displayed in the menageries of Pope Leo X and other potentates. The forerunners of zoos, though less linked with science than botanical gardens, benefited research at least occasionally: by dissecting lions in the Medici menagerie in 1549, Gabriele Falloppio disproved Aristotle's claim that lions have solid and marrowless bones. By more homely dissection, Gesner refuted the belief that the mouse's liver grows and shrinks with the lunar phases. Methodical examination of insects, first reported in 1552 in Edward Wotton's *De differentiis animalium* (Differences of

animals) and carried further by Aldrovandi, whetted the thirst for seeing more minute creatures. By systematically following chick development, Aldrovandi and Coiter facilitated the epochal embryological studies of the early 1600s by Girolamo Fabrici of Aquapendente, Galileo's physician and William Harvey's professor. Occasional experiments were eclipsed by the wish to capture nature as it is. The liveliest interest was in illustrations derived from original observations, communicated descriptions, and artists' sketches. Among the copious drawings in Gesner's works, many by his own hand, one is based on Albrecht Dürer's rhinoceros. Aldrovandi, with the keenest eye for bird anatomy, collected thousands of tempera paintings.

The scientific task of organizing knowledge proved more challenging in zoology than in botany. Encyclopedic purposes justified alphabetical and rhetorical arrangements within the division into quadrupeds, birds, fish, and blooded-bloodless. For imposing order on the animal world, neither the classical categories of genus and species nor Aristotle's criteria of morphology, development, and habitat seemed satisfactory. Even the largest groupings left room for confusion: Aldrovandi pictured the bat as nursing yet classified it among birds, in a transitional section toward quadrupeds; Gesner added problematic branches such as wild-tame, hornless-horned—and included the elephant among the latter. With the exception of Wotton, Renaissance authors paid less attention than Albertus Magnus to Aristotelian physiology, in other words, to the processes of reproduction, nutrition, and growth that could lead to a synthesis. If the Great Chain of Being promised a unifying construct, it compounded anthropocentrism and the disproportionate coverage of domestic companions, as well as aesthetic gradations. Indeed, the balance between handicaps and achievements leaves historians divided in the assessment of Renaissance zoology.

See also **Aristotle and Aristotelianism; Museums; Pliny the Elder.**

BIBLIOGRAPHY

Debus, Allen G. *Man and Nature in the Renaissance*. Cambridge, U.K., 1978.

Gmelig-Nijboer, Caroline Aleid. *Conrad Gessner's "Historia Animalium": An Inventory of Renaissance Zoology*. Meppel, Netherlands, 1977.

Grafton, Carol Belanger, ed. *Beasts and Animals in Decorative Woodcuts of the Renaissance: Konrad Gesner*. New York, 1983.

Hoeniger, F. David. "How Plants and Animals Were Studied in the Mid-Sixteenth Century." In J. W. Shirley and F. D. Hoeniger, eds. *Science and the Arts in the Renaissance.* London and Washington, D.C., 1985. Pages 130–148.

Lloyd, Joan Barclay. *African Animals in Renaissance Literature and Art.* Oxford, 1971.

Thomas, Keith. *Man and the Natural World: Changing Attitudes in England, 1500–1800.* New York, 1983.

LUKE DEMAITRE

ZUMÁRRAGA, JUAN DE (c. 1468–1548), Spanish ecclesiastic in Mexico. Juan de Zumárraga was born in Durango, in the Basque country of northern Spain. Zumárraga joined the Franciscan order, ultimately becoming the guardian of the convent of Abrojo, near Valladolid. He also served as a local inquisitor in efforts to suppress heresy in Castile. In 1528 he was appointed by Charles V to become bishop of the new diocese of Mexico; however, Zumárraga sailed for Mexico before he could be consecrated. In the colony he was soon pitted against the secular officials of the first royal Audiencia (court) who had been sent earlier to impose royal government in the wake of the conquest. This first Audiencia provoked widespread opposition among clerics and settlers alike.

Between 1532 and 1534 Zumárraga returned to Spain, where he was consecrated bishop. At this time he also held the title of "protector of the Indians." Working in concert with Don Antonio de Mendoza, the first viceroy, Zumárraga sought to improve the lot of the natives, especially in the implementation of the Leyes Nuevas (New Laws) that reformed abuses in the system of native labor allocations to settlers of 1542. He supervised the establishment of two schools, Santa Cruz de Tlatelolco, run by the Franciscans, to educate the sons of the native nobility, and San Juan de Letrán for mestizos. He founded one of the first hospitals in Mexico, the Hospital Amor de Dios. He also conducted several inquisitorial proceedings against native nobles for their continued embrace of pagan practices. At least one noble, Don Carlos of Texcoco, was executed for his apostasy. In 1547 Zumárraga was appointed the first archbishop of Mexico, but he died before he could be consecrated.

In 1536 Zumárraga also promoted the foundation of the first printing press in the New World, which was finally accomplished in 1539. The production of the press was notable in that it includes many works in native languages of the Indies, such as Nahuatl, the language of the Aztecs. Zumárraga in many ways established the precedent that most other archbishops in Mexico would emulate.

BIBLIOGRAPHY

Gil, Fernando. *Primeras "doctrinas" del nuevo mundo: Estudio historico, teológico de las obras de Fray Juan de Zumárraga.* Buenos Aires, Argentina, 1993.

Greenleaf, Richard E. *Zumárraga and the Mexican Inquisition, 1536–1543.* Washington, D.C., 1962.

JOHN FREDERICK SCHWALLER

ZWINGLI, HULDRYCH (1484–1531), Swiss reformer and founder of Reformed tradition. Born to a prosperous peasant family in the Alpine valley of Toggenburg, Zwingli instituted one of the first Protestant churches, beginning in 1519, with his arrival in Zürich, and articulated a distinctive understanding of the Eucharist, both of which influenced Calvin's formulations.

Zwingli's education embraced both the humanist study of classical languages, which he began under the guidance of Heinrich Wölfflin in Bern (1496–1498), and Scholasticism, which he studied with Thomas Wyttenbach at the University of Basel, where he took a B.A. in 1504 and an M.A. in 1506,

Huldrych Zwingli. Portrait by Hans Asper. KUNSTMUSEUM WINTERTHUR, ZÜRICH

and studied theology for a further six months. When he left the University of Basel to take up a pastorate in Glarus, he continued his study of Greek and the church fathers, which led him to renewed study of the text of the Bible and of the biblical languages.

Three dimensions of Zwingli's work deserve attention: his biblical scholarship, his preaching, and his understanding of the Christian community and the Eucharist. In his biblical scholarship the most enduring influence was Erasmus. As a young priest, Zwingli eagerly awaited Erasmus's Greek New Testament, which provided the basis for Zwingli's study of the Bible, done first in private and then among a circle of friends, known as the Prophecy, who in 1529 produced the first complete Swiss German Bible.

That biblical text provided the centerpiece of Zwingli's sermons, which he preached in Zürich Fridays and Sundays for twelve years. Zwingli's first sermon in Zürich, delivered on 1 January 1519, opened with the first Gospel, Matthew. His preaching style, echoing his vision of the Bible, was simple, idiomatic, and graceful. With his preaching, as his successor Heinrich Bullinger wrote, he brought the Bible alive for his congregation.

Zwingli also acknowledged his debt to Erasmus's emphasis on the ethics articulated in the Gospels: pacifism, love of one's neighbor, and a love of God realized not in ceremonies or formalized rituals, but in the conduct of one's daily life. In his articulation of the Reformed Christian community in Zürich, Zwingli insisted that worship encompassed one's behavior as well as collective acts. That understanding of the nature of the Christian community later influenced John Calvin and English Protestantism.

Zwingli's understanding of the Eucharist was anchored in his reading particularly of the Gospel of John, where spirit and flesh are radically separated, and in his humanist sensitivity to the social functioning of language. He argued that the words of the Eucharist could not be understood apart from the context of their speaking. With Jesus's body gone, the bread can only *signify* Jesus's body—it cannot be the thing itself, but can only stand, spiritually and experientially, for the body of Christ.

After Reformation was achieved in Zurich, in 1525, Zwingli worked through diplomatic and personal channels to extend his vision of reform to all of Europe. He achieved successes in Bern and Basel. His death in the battle of Cappel on 11 October 1531 cut short not only the life of one of the major reformers, but his pursuit of a vision of Christianity grounded in the Swiss commune and humanism.

BIBLIOGRAPHY

Primary Work

Zwingli, Huldrych. *Selected Writings of Huldrych Zwingli.* 2 vols. Translated and edited by E. J. Furcha and H. Wayne Pipkin. Allison Park, Pa., 1984.

Secondary Works

Gäbler, Ulrich. *Huldrych Zwingli: His Life and Work.* Translated by Ruth C. L. Gritsch. Philadelphia, 1986.

Locher, Gottfried. *Zwingli's Thought: New Perspectives.* Leiden, Netherlands, 1981.

Stephens, W. P. *The Theology of Huldrych Zwingli.* Oxford, 1986.

LEE PALMER WANDEL

Systematic Outline of Contents

The systematic outline provides a general overview of the conceptual scheme of the Encyclopedia, listing the titles of each entry and subentry.

The outline is divided into eight parts:

1. Defining the Renaissance
2. Contexts
3. Thought
4. Art
5. Literature
6. Places
7. Events
8. People

Most parts are divided into several sections. Because the section headings are not mutually exclusive, certain entries in the Encyclopedia are listed in more than one section. The main entry on a topic may appear at the beginning of a section, out of alphabetical order.

1   DEFINING THE RENAISSANCE

Renaissance
  The Renaissance in Historical
    Thought
  The English Renaissance in Literary
    Interpretation
  The Renaissance in Popular
    Imagination
  Influence of the Renaissance
  Renaissance Studies
Gothic
Middle Ages

Baroque, Concept of the
Early Modern Period

Renaissance, Interpretations
  of the
  Giorgio Vasari
  Jules Michelet
  Jakob Burckhardt
  John Ruskin
  John Addington Symonds
  Walter Pater

Bernard Berenson
Aby Warburg
Johan Huizinga
Erwin Panofsky
Hans Baron
Eugenio Garin
Remigio Sabbadini
Georg Voigt
Paul Oskar Kristeller
Economic Interpretations
Villa I Tatti

2   CONTEXTS

This part includes sections on politics, society and economic life, religion, everyday life, and culture, universities, and books, printing, and reading.

Political Contexts

Cambrai, League of
City-State
Concordats
Despotism
Diplomacy
Dynastic Rivalry
Espionage

Exploration
Faction
Finance and Taxation
Monarchy
Nation-State
Nepotism
Notaries
Oligarchies

Podestà
Popular Revolts
Prince
Queens and Queenship
Representative Institutions
Republicanism
Tyrannicide
Violence

Civility
Diffusion of Ideas
Education
Europe, Idea of
Feminism
Festivals
Glory, Idea of
Grand Tour
Greek Émigrés
Honor
Humanism
    The Definition of Humanism
    The Origins of Humanism
    Italy
    Spain
    Portugal
    Germany and the Low Countries
    The British Isles
    France
    Legal Humanism
Humor
Pasquino
Popular Culture
Querelle des Femmes
Ratio Studiorum
Rhetoric
Rhétoriqueurs
Salons
Translation
    Overview
    Elizabethan Translations
    Jewish Translators

Discovery and Recovery of the Ancient World

Classical Antiquity
    Discovery of Classical Antiquity
    Classical Antiquity in Renaissance
      Art
Classical Scholarship

Historical Themes in Renaissance
    Art
Historiography, Classical
    Classical Historians
    Greek Historians
    Roman Historians
Manuscripts
Pasquino

Aristotle and Aristotelianism
Augustine of Hippo
Cicero
Epicurus and Epicureanism
Euclid
Galen
Hippocrates of Cos
Horace
Jerome
Lucian
Ovid
Paganism
Patristics
Plato, Platonism, and Neoplatonism
Plautus, Titus Maccius
Pliny the Elder
Plotinus
Terence
Virgil

Universities

Universities
Alcalá de Henares, University of
Bologna, University of
Cambridge, University of
Coimbra, University of
Collège de France
Inns of Court
Louvain, University of
Oxford, University of
Padua, University of

Paris, University of
Pavia, University of
Saint Andrews University
Salamanca, University of

Books, Printing, and Reading

Bible
    Printed Bibles
Calligraphy
Censorship
    Censorship on the Continent
    Censorship in England
Commonplace Books
Complutensian Polyglot Bible
Dictionaries and Encyclopedias
Index of Prohibited Books
Jews
    Print and Jewish Cultural
      Development
Literacy
Manuscripts
Nürnberg Chronicle
Printing and Publishing
Typography

Aldine Press
Cromberger Press
Eguía Press
Elzevier Press
Estienne Family
Froben Press
Giolito Press
Giunti Press
Plantin, Christophe

Libraries
Brunswick-Wolfenbüttel
Vatican Library

3 THOUGHT

This part includes sections on philosophy, political thought, religious thought, and science.

Philosophy

Aristotle and Aristotelianism
Dignity of Man
Epicurus and Epicureanism
Ethnography of the New World
Fortune
Hermetism
Humanity, Concept of
Immortality
Individualism
Jewish Philosophy

Libertinism
Logic
Matter, Structure of
Metaphysics
Moral Philosophy
Natural Philosophy
Neo-Stoicism
Philosophy
Plato, Platonism, and Neoplatonism
Pliny the Elder
Plotinus
Psychology

Scholasticism
Science, Epistemology of
Skepticism
Stoicism
Virtù
Women
    Women and Philosophy

Political Thought

Absolutism
Constitutionalism
Law

Political Thought
Reason of State
Resistance, Theory of
Urbanism
Utopias

Religious Thought

Augustine of Hippo
Bible
    Texts and Textual Criticism
    Christian Interpretation of the Bible
    Jewish Interpretation of the Bible
Christian Theology
Complutensian Polyglot Bible
Conciliarism
Crusade
Devotio Moderna
Islamic Thought
Jerome
Jewish Thought and the Renaissance

Paganism
Patristics

Science and Technology

Acoustics
Alchemy
Anatomy
Astronomy
Botany
Calendars
Chemistry
Clocks
Euclid
Galen
Geography and Cartography
Geology
Hippocrates of Cos
Jewish Medicine and Science
Kabbalah
Magic and Astrology
    Magic and Astrology

    Jewish Magic and Divination
    Jewish Astrology and the Occult
Mathematics
Matter, Structure of
Mechanics
Medicine
Mining and Metallurgy
Numerology
Obstetrics and Gynecology
Optics
Physics
Ptolemy
Science
Science, Epistemology of
Scientific Instruments
Scientific Method
Technology
Women
    Women and Science
Zoology

4   ART

This part includes sections on art in general, aesthetics and aesthetic theory, surveys of artistic traditions and production in specific locations and countries, themes in Renaissance art, visual arts, architecture, performing arts, public arts, and arts of war.

Art in General

Art
    Renaissance Art
    Education and Training
    Women Artists
Classical Antiquity
    Classical Antiquity in Renaissance
        Art
Forgeries
Jews
    Jews and the Arts
Manuscripts
Museums
Patronage
    Patronage of the Arts

Aesthetics

Gothic
Grotesques
Mannerism
Paragone
Royal Iconography, English

Area Art Surveys

Austria
    Art in Austria
Britain, Art in
Croatia and Dalmatia
    Art in Croatia and Dalmatia

East Central Europe, Art in
Emilia, Art in
Ferrara
    Art in Ferrara
Florence
    Art of the Fifteenth Century
    Art of the Sixteenth Century
France
    Art in France
Genoa
    Art in Genoa
Germany, Art in
Hungary
    Art in Hungary
Milan
    Art in Milan and Lombardy
Naples
    Art in Naples
Netherlands
    Art in the Netherlands
Rome
    Art in Rome and Latium
Siena
    Art in Siena
Spain
    Art in Spain and Portugal
Umbria, Art in
Venice
    Art in Venice

Themes in Renaissance Art

Chivalry
    Chivalry in Renaissance Art
Classical Antiquity
    Classical Antiquity in Renaissance Art
Famous Men and Women
Historical Themes in Renaissance
    Art
Human Body in Renaissance Art
Jewish Themes in Renaissance Art
Religious Themes in Renaissance Art
Space and Perspective
Supernatural World in Renaissance
    Art
Women
    Portrayal in Renaissance Art

Visual Arts

Ceramics
Coins, Medals, and Plaquettes
Decorative Arts
Drawing
Emblem
Illumination
Jewelry
Painting
Printmaking
Sculpture

Architecture

Architecture
    Architecture in the Renaissance
    Architectural Treatises
Châteaux
Gardens
Palaces and Townhouses
Tombs
Villas

Performing Arts

Commedia dell'Arte
Dance
Jews
    Jews and Music
Music
    Renaissance Music

Music in Renaissance Culture
Music in Renaissance Society
Music Treatises
Transmission of Music
Performance Practice
Musical Instruments
Instrumental Music
Sacred Vocal Music
Secular Vocal Music
Intermedi
Opera
Music in England
Music in France
Music in Italy
Music in Spain and Portugal
Music in the Holy Roman Empire
Music in the Low Countries

Plautus, Titus Maccius
Theaters

Public Arts

Heraldry
Parades, Processions, and Pageants
Ritual, Civic
Tournaments

Arts of War

Arms and Armor
Artillery
Firearms
Fortifications
Mercenaries
Naval Warfare
Warfare

5 LITERATURE

This part includes sections on general and miscellaneous topics, national literatures and languages, and literary genres.

Literature in General

Aristotle and Cinquecento Poetics
Bible
    German Translations
    The English Bible
Cicero
Classical Scholarship
Dante in the Renaissance
Epic
Facezie
Horace
Literary Theory, Renaissance
Lucian
Ovid
Patronage
    Literary Patronage in England
Petrarchism
Pléiade
Poetics
    Survey
    French Poetics
Religious Literature
Translation
    Overview
    Elizabethan Translations
    Jewish Translators
Virgil
Women
    Women and Literature

Literatures and Languages

Arabic Literature and Language
Catalan Literature and Language

English Literature and Language
French Literature and Language
German Literature and Language
Hebrew Literature and Language
Italian Literature and Language
Judeo-Italian Literature and Language
Ladino Literature and Language
Neo-Latin Literature and Language
Netherlandish Literature and
    Language
Portuguese Literature and Language
Spanish Literature and Language
Yiddish Literature and Language

Literary Genres

Allegory
Bawdy, Elizabethan
Biography and Autobiography
    Europe
    England
Chivalry
    Romance of Chivalry
    English Arthurian Romance
Chronicle, Elizabethan
Diaries and Memoirs
Drama
    Religious Drama
    Tragedy
    Erudite Comedy
Drama, English
    Elizabethan Drama
    Jacobean Drama
    Jacobean Court Masque

Drama, French
Drama, Spanish
Fiction, Elizabethan
Hagiography
Historiography, Classical
    Classical Historians
    Greek Historians
    Roman Historians
Historiography, Renaissance
    Italian Historiography
    French Historiography
    British Historiography
    German Historiography
    Jewish Historiography
    Spanish Historiography
Letterbooks
Myth
Novella
Pastoral
    Pastoral on the Continent
    Elizabethan Pastoral
Picaresque Novel
Poetry
    Classical Poetry
    Religious Poetry
    The Sonnet outside England
    The English Sonnet
Poetry, English
    Neo-Latin Poetry in England
    Tudor Poetry before Spenser
    Elizabethan Poetry
    Early Stuart and Metaphysical
        Poetry

Poetry and Music
Pornography
Prose, Elizabethan
Prosody, Elizabethan

Satire
    Satire on the Continent
    Satire in England
    Satire in France

    Satire in Germany
    Satire in Italy
Satire Ménippée
Terence

6 PLACES

This part includes sections on Italy, countries and cities in Europe outside Italy, and the world beyond Europe.

Italy and Environs

Italy

Bologna
Ferrara
    Ferrara in the Renaissance
Florence
    Florence in the Renaissance
Genoa
    Genoa in the Renaissance
Livorno
Lucca
Mantua
Milan
    Milan in the Renaissance
Modena
Naples
    Naples in the Renaissance
Parma
Perugia
Piedmont-Savoy
Pisa
Rome
    The City of Rome
Sardinia
Sicily
Siena
    Siena in the Renaissance
Urbino
Venice
    Venice in the Renaissance

The Rest of Europe

Europe, Idea of

Austria
    Austria in the Renaissance
Baltic States
Bavaria
Bohemia
Brandenburg
Brittany
Brunswick-Wolfenbüttel
Burgundy
Croatia and Dalmatia
    Croatia and Dalmatia in the
        Renaissance
Dubrovnik
England
France
    The Kingdom of France
Hesse
Holy Roman Empire
Hungary
    Hungary in the Renaissance
Ireland
Mediterranean Sea
Netherlands
    The Netherlands in the Renaissance
Palatinate
Ottoman Empire
Poland
Portugal
Russia
Saxony
Scandinavian Kingdoms
Scotland
Spain
    The Spanish Kingdoms
Switzerland

Amsterdam
Antwerp
Augsburg
Basel
Bruges
Brussels
Cologne
Cracow
Groningen
Leiden
Leipzig
Lisbon
London
Lyon
Madrid
Nürnberg
Paris
Prague
Rouen
Seville
Strasbourg
Toledo
Vienna

Beyond Europe

Africa, North
Africa, Sub-Saharan
Americas
Asia, East

Columbus, Christopher
Ethnography of the New World
Exploration

7 EVENTS

This part lists entries that deal with particular events or series of events.

Armada, Spanish
Basel, Council of
Comuneros, Revolt of the
Constance, Council of
Constantinople, Fall of
Field of Cloth of Gold
Florence, Council of

Lateran V, Council of
Lepanto, Battle of
Lodi, Peace of
Pavia, Battle of
Pazzi Conspiracy
Peasants' War
Reuchlin Affair

Rome, Sack of
Thirty Years' War
Trent, Council of
Wars of Italy
Wars of Religion
    (France)

8 PEOPLE

This part includes a section listing biographies of individuals and a section listing important families, ruling houses, and dynasties.

Biographies

Abravanel, Isaac
Achillini, Alessandro
Adrian VI (pope)
Africanus, Leo
Agricola, Georgius
Agricola, Rudolf
Agrippa of Nettesheim, Heinrich
Agustín, Antonio
Alberti, Leon Battista
Albuquerque, Afonso de
Alciato, Andrea
Alemán, Mateo
Alemanno, Yohanan ben Isaac
Alexander VI (pope)
Alfonso the Magnanimous
Almeida, Francisco de
Alvárez de Toledo, Fernando
Amboise, Georges d'
Amyot, Jacques
Andreini, Isabella
Angelico, Fra
Anguissola, Sofonisba
Anjou, François de Valois, duc
    d'Alençon et d'
Anna of Saxony
Anne de Beaujeu
Anne of Brittany
Antoninus
Aragona, Tullia d'
Aretino, Pietro
Ariosto, Ludovico
Ascham, Roger
Aubigné, Théodore-Agrippa d'

Bacon, Francis
Baïf, Lazare de
Balassi, Bálint
Baldung Grien, Hans
Bandello, Matteo
Barbaro, Francesco
Barocci, Federico
Baronio, Cesare
Bartolommeo della Porta, Fra
Basile, Giambattista
Beatus Rhenanus
Beaufort, Margaret
Behn, Aphra
Bellarmine, Robert
Bellièvre, Pomponne de
Bembo, Pietro
Benedetti, Giovanni Battista

Beni, Paolo
Bernardino of Siena
Berni, Francesco
Béroalde de Verville, François
Bessarion
Bèze, Théodore de
Bidermann, Jakob
Biondo, Flavio
Boccaccio, Giovanni
Bodin, Jean
Böhme, Jakob
Boiardo, Matteo Maria
Borgia, Cesare
Borgia, Lucrezia
Boscán, Juan
Bosch, Hieronymus
Botero, Giovanni
Botticelli, Sandro
Bouts, Dirck
Bracciolini, Poggio
Brahe, Tycho
Bramante, Donato
Brant, Sebastian
Brantôme, Pierre de Bourdeille,
    seigneur de
Browne, Thomas
Brûlart de Sillery, Nicolas
Brunelleschi, Filippo
Brunfels, Otto
Bruni, Leonardo
Bruno, Giordano
Bucer, Martin
Budé, Guillaume
Buonamici, Francesco
Burchiello
Burton, Robert
Busche, Hermann von dem
Bussa de' Ponziani, Francesca
Byrd, William

Cajetan, Thomas de Vio
Calderón de la Barca, Pedro
Calvin, John
Camerarius, Joachim
Camões, Luíz Vaz de
Campanella, Tommaso
    The Life of Campanella
    Campanella the Philosopher
    Campanella the Literary Figure
Canter, Jacob
Capito, Wolfgang
Caravaggio, Michelangelo Merisi da
Cardano, Girolamo

Caro, Joseph ben Ephraim
Carpaccio, Vittore
Carvajal y Mendoza, Luisa de
Casaubon, Isaac
Castiglione, Baldassare
Catherine de Médicis
Catherine of Aragon
Catherine of Bologna
Catherine of Genoa
Catherine of Siena
Cavendish, Margaret
Caxton, William
Cecchi, Giovanni Maria
Cecil, William
Cellini, Benvenuto
    Cellini the Writer
    Cellini the Artist
Celtis, Conrad
Cereta, Laura
Cervantes Saavedra, Miguel de
Cesalpino, Andrea
Champier, Symphorien
Charles V (Holy Roman Emperor)
Charles I (England)
Charles VIII (France)
Charles IX (France)
Charles the Bold
Charron, Pierre
Christina of Sweden
Chrysoloras, Manuel
Ciruelo, Pedro
Cisneros, Francisco Jiménez de
Clavius, Christopher
Clement VII (pope)
Clement VIII (pope)
Cleve, Joos van
Cobos, Francisco de los
Colet, John
Coligny, Gaspard II de
Colonna, Francesco
Colonna, Vittoria
Columbus, Christopher
Commandino, Federico
Commynes, Philippe de
Contarini, Gasparo
Copernicus, Nicolaus
Coquille, Guy
Cornaro Piscopia, Elena Lucrezia
Corner, Caterina
Correggio
Cortés, Hernán
Corvinus, Matthias
Covarrubias y Leiva, Diego de

Families, Houses, and Dynasties

Directory of Contributors

SHEILA R. ACKERLIND
United States Military Academy
Coimbra, University of

HOWARD TZVI ADELMAN
Mofet Institute and Achva College,
Israel
Jews: Jewish Women and Family
Life
Modena, Leon
Rabbis

KENNETH B. ALBALA
University of the Pacific
Food and Drink

MERCEDES ALCALÁ-GALÁN
University of Wisconsin–Madison
Guevara, Antonio de

JONATHAN J. G. ALEXANDER
New York University
Illumination

STEPHEN ALFORD
King's College, Cambridge
Cecil, William
Saint Andrews University
Tudor Dynasty

MICHAEL J. B. ALLEN
University of California,
Los Angeles
Ficino, Marsilio
Plato, Platonism, and
Neoplatonism

RUDOLPH P. ALMASY
West Virginia University
Tyndale, William

PAUL ALPERS
University of California, Berkeley
Pastoral: Elizabethan Pastoral

IDA ALTMAN
University of New Orleans
Americas
Pizarro, Francisco

GLENN J. AMES
University of Toledo
Albuquerque, Afonso de
Almeida, Francisco de

FRANCIS AMES-LEWIS
Birkbeck College, University of
London
Mantegna, Andrea

MICHAËL AMY
Cooper Union; New York University;
City University of New York
Bartolommeo della Porta, Fra
Botticelli, Sandro
El Greco
Goes, Hugo van der
Grünewald, Matthias
Memling, Hans
Mostaert, Jan
Weyden, Rogier van der

CHRISTY ANDERSON
Yale University
Châteaux
Villas

KARL APPUHN
Columbia University
Doria, Andrea
Genoa: Genoa in the Renaissance

BRIAN G. ARMSTRONG
Georgia State University (Retired)
Goulart, Simon

GRACE ARMSTRONG
Bryn Mawr College
Villon, François

ALBERT RUSSELL ASCOLI
University of California, Berkeley
Machiavelli, Niccolò: The Literary
Figure

ALBERTO AUBERT
University of Rome
Paul IV

JERZY AXER
University of Warsaw
Poland

CLIFFORD R. BACKMAN
Boston University
Sardinia

IRENA BACKUS
University of Geneva,
Switzerland
Bible: Christian Interpretation
of the Bible
Jerome

ADRIANNA E. BAKOS
Rochester University, British Columbia,
Canada
Anne de Beaujeu
Charles the Bold
Commynes, Philippe de
Louis XI
Louis XIII

UGO BALDINI
University of Padua, Italy
Clavius, Christopher

CARL OLIVER BANGS
Saint Paul School of Theology,
Emeritus
Hooft, Pieter Corneliszoon

PAUL BAROLSKY
University of Virginia
Renaissance, Interpretations
of the: Walter Pater

FIORA A. BASSANESE
University of Massachusetts,
Boston
Colonna, Vittoria
Gonzaga, Giulia
Petrarchism

REMIGIUS BÄUMER
Albert-Ludwigs-Universität Freiburg,
Germany (d. 1999)
Conciliarism

FREDERIC J. BAUMGARTNER
Virginia Polytechnic Institute and State University
Amboise, Georges d'
Charles VIII
Diane de Poitiers
Francis II
Henry II
Louis XII
Nation-State
Renée of Ferrara
Tournon, François de
Valois Dynasty

MICHAEL G. BAYLOR
Lehigh University
Müntzer, Thomas

JAN BAŽANT
Academy of Sciences, Czech Republic
Bohemia
Prague

BRIGITTE M. BEDOS-REZAK
University of Maryland
Montmorency Family
Montmorency, Anne de

GUY BEDOUELLE
University of Fribourg, Switzerland
Bible: Texts and Textual Criticism

F. E. BEEMON
Middle Tennessee State University
Margaret of Parma

ELAINE V. BEILIN
Framingham State College
Roper, Margaret More

ISTVÁN BEJCZY
Katholieke Universiteit Nijmegen, The Netherlands
Bruges
Leiden

MARINA BELOZERSKAYA
Mary Ingraham Bunting Institute, Radcliffe Institute for Advanced Study
Bouts, Dirck
Carpaccio, Vittore
Decorative Arts
Eyck, Jan van and Hubert van
Florence: Art of the Fifteenth Century
Hilliard, Nicholas
Masaccio
Netherlands: Art in the Netherlands
Patronage: Patronage of the Arts

PHILIP BENEDICT
Brown University
Lyon
Rouen

MARGARET BENT
All Souls College, Oxford
Dunstaple, John

JERRY H. BENTLEY
University of Hawaii
Complutensian Polyglot Bible
Fernández de Córdoba, Gonzalo
Nebrija, Antonio de
Pontano, Giovanni

JILL BEPLER
Herzog August Bibliothek, Wolfenbüttel, Germany
Brunswick-Wolfenbüttel

MARCO BERETTA
Istituto e Museo di Storia della Scienza, Florence
Agricola, Georgius
Mining and Metallurgy

EMILIE L. BERGMANN
University of California, Berkeley
Vega Carpio, Lope Félix de
Vives, Juan Luis

PETER BERGQUIST
University of Oregon, Emeritus
Lasso, Orlando di

ALAN E. BERNSTEIN
University of Arizona
Middle Ages

ECKHARD BERNSTEIN
College of the Holy Cross
Bidermann, Jakob
Böhme, Jakob
Brant, Sebastian
Celtis, Conrad
Dedekind, Friedrich
Fischart, Johann
German Literature and Language
Hessus, Helius Eobanus
Hutten, Ulrich von
Murner, Thomas
Naogeorgus, Thomas
Palatinate
Sachs, Hans
Satire: Satire in Germany

DOMENICO BERTOLONI MELI
Indiana University
Monte, Guidobaldo, marchese del

DAVID BEVINGTON
University of Chicago
Shakespeare, William

PETER G. BIETENHOLZ
University of Saskatchewan
Renaissance, Interpretations of the: Jakob Burckhardt

J. W. BINNS
University of York, United Kingdom
Poetry, English: Neo-Latin Poetry in England

ROBERT BIRELEY
Loyola University, Chicago
Clement VIII
Machiavelli, Niccolò: Machiavelli's Influence
Paul V

MARIANNA D. BIRNBAUM
University of California, Los Angeles, Emerita
Corvinus, Matthias
Heltai, Gáspár
Hungary: Hungary in the Renaissance
Pannonius, Janus
Tinódi, Sebestyén

ISTVÁN BITSKEY
Kossuth Lajos University, Debrecen, Hungary
Balassi, Bálint

TINA WALDEIER BIZZARRO
Villanova University; Rosemont College
Gothic

RICHARD J. BLACKWELL
Saint Louis University
Campanella, Tommaso: Campanella the Philosopher

ANN M. BLAIR
Harvard University
Bodin, Jean

CHARMARIE J. BLAISDELL
Northeastern University
Jeanne d'Albret

W. SCOTT BLANCHARD
College Misericordia, Dallas, Pennsylvania
Satire: Satire on the Continent; Satire in England; Satire in France

KALMAN P. BLAND
Duke University
Bible: Jewish Interpretation of the Bible
Delmedigo, Elijah

SARAH RUBIN BLANSHEI
Agnes Scott College
Perugia

REINHARD BODENMANN
University of Geneva
Capito, Wolfgang

FLAVIO BOGGI
University of Glasgow
Cellini, Benvenuto: Cellini the Artist
Florence: Art of the Sixteenth
  Century
Ghiberti, Lorenzo
Leonardo da Vinci
Mannerism
Orcagna, Andrea
Pisano, Andrea
Riccio, Andrea Briosco, il
Verrocchio, Andrea del

ANDREA BOLLAND
University of Nebraska–Lincoln
Art: Education and Training

SUZANNE BOORSCH
Metropolitan Museum of Art
Printmaking

ANDRZEJ BOROWSKI
*Jagiellonian University of Cracow,
Poland*
Klonowic, Sebastian Fabian
Kochanowski, Jan
Łaski Family
Orzechowski, Stanisław
Skarga, Piotr
Szymonowic, Szymon

AGOSTINO BORROMEO
Istituto Italiano di Studi Iberici, Rome
Pius IV

BARBARA C. BOWEN
Vanderbilt University
Drama, French
Humor

GERRY BOWLER
University of Manitoba
Charles V
Monarchy

JAMES M. BOYDEN
Tulane University
Exploration
Gómez de Silva, Ruy
Pérez, Antonio

JOHN K. BRACKETT
University of Cincinnati
Crime and Punishment
Daily Life
Rape

GORDON BRADEN
University of Virginia
Renaissance: The English
  Renaissance in Literary
  Intepretation
Translation: Elizabethan
  Translations

THOMAS A. BRADY JR.
University of California, Berkeley
Bucer, Martin

WALTER BRANDMÜLLER
*Pontificio Comitato di Scienze
Storiche, Vatican*
Constance, Council of

NOEL L. BRANN
East Meadow, New York
Trithemius, Johann

M. E. BRATCHEL
*University of the Witwatersrand,
South Africa*
Lucca

DVORAH BREGMAN
*Ben Gurion University of the Negev,
Beer-Sheba, Israel*
Hebrew Literature and Language

MAUDA BREGOLI-RUSSO
University of Illinois at Chicago
Facezie
Salernitano, Masuccio

JEAN R. BRINK
Arizona State University
Poetry, English: Elizabethan
  Poetry

P. J. BROADHEAD
*Goldsmiths College, University of
London*
Augsburg

DAVID ALAN BROWN
*National Gallery of Art,
Washington, D.C.*
Renaissance, Interpretations of the:
  Bernard Berenson

DAVID BUISSERET
University of Texas at Arlington
Sully, Maximilien de Béthune, duc
  de

PETER BURKE
*Emmanuel College, University of
Cambridge*
Neo-Stoicism
Popular Culture
Reason of State

JAMES HENDERSON BURNS
University College, London
Political Thought

ROBERT I. BURNS, S.J.
University of California, Los Angeles
Alfonso the Magnanimous

COLIN BURROW
*Gonville and Caius College,
Cambridge*
Horace

GORDON WILLIAM BYNUM
University of Minnesota
Netherlands: The Netherlands in the
  Renaissance

WILLIAM CAFERRO
Vanderbilt University
Accounting
Banking and Money
Datini, Francesco
Finance and Taxation
Renaissance, Interpretations of the:
  Economic Interpretations

KEITH CAMERON
University of Exeter
Henry III

STEPHEN J. CAMPBELL
University of Michigan
Human Body in Renaissance Art

GIUSEPPE CANDELA
Arizona State University
Doni, Anton Francesco
Gelli, Giovanni Battista
Straparola, Gianfrancesco

NANCY L. CANEPA
Dartmouth College
Basile, Giambattista
Folengo, Teofilo
Tansillo, Luigi

PAULA CARABELL
Arkansas State University
Giulio Romano

CHARLES CARLTON
North Carolina State University
Charles I

ANN G. CARMICHAEL
Indiana University
Plague
Sickness and Disease

JESÚS CARRILLO
University Autónoma of Madrid
Historiography, Renaissance:
  Spanish Historiography

LINDA L. CARROLL
Newcomb College, Tulane University
Dovizi, Bernardo

GINO CASAGRANDE
University of Wisconsin–Madison
Beni, Paolo

JUAN CASANOVAS
Specola Vaticana
Calendars

REBECCA S. CATZ
University of California, Los Angeles
Asia, East

JO ANN CAVALLO
Columbia University
Boiardo, Matteo Maria

CHRISTOPHER S. CELENZA
Michigan State University
Calligraphy
Manuscripts

J. H. CHAJES
Yale University
Magic and Astrology: Jewish Magic
and Divination

CAROLYN LOUGEE CHAPPELL
Stanford University
Salons

DONALD CHENEY
University of Massachusetts
Literary Theory, Renaissance

MIRIAM USHER CHRISMAN
*University of Massachusetts, Amherst,
Emerita*
Brunfels, Otto
Sturm, Johann

GEORGIA CLARKE
Courtauld Institute of Art, London
Giocondo, Fra

PAULA C. CLARKE
McGill University
Faction
Pazzi Conspiracy

CYNDIA SUSAN CLEGG
Pepperdine University
Censorship: Censorship in England

SARAH L. CLINE
*University of California,
Santa Barbara*
Sahagún, Bernardino de

CECIL H. CLOUGH
University of Liverpool
Este, House of
Federico da Montefeltro

Ferrara: Ferrara in the Renaissance
Montefeltro Family
Umbria, Art in
Urbino

LOUISE GEORGE CLUBB
University of California, Berkeley
Commedia dell'Arte
Della Porta, Giambattista
Della Valle, Federico
Drama: Erudite Comedy

RICHARD I. COHEN
Hebrew University, Jerusalem
Jews: Court Jews

ANTHONY COLANTUONO
University of Maryland
Carracci Family
Emilia, Art in

RICHARD G. COLE
Luther College
Gutenberg, Johann

DAVID COLEMAN
Eastern Kentucky University
Juan de Ávila

PAUL COLILLI
Laurentian University
Bruno, Giordano
Poliziano, Angelo

DAVID J. COLLINS
Northwestern University
Ribadeneira, Pedro de

JAMES B. COLLINS
Georgetown University
Brittany

MARIA ANN CONELLI
*Parsons School of Design,
New York City*
Herrera, Juan de

WILLIAM J. CONNELL
Seton Hall University
Livorno
Medici, Lorenzo de': Political Leader
and Patron of the Arts

JAMES WYATT COOK
Albion College
Pulci, Antonia

BRIAN P. COPENHAVER
University of California, Los Angeles
Hermetism
Magic and Astrology: Magic and
Astrology
Pico della Mirandola, Giovanni

LESLEY B. CORMACK
University of Alberta
Geography and Cartography

FRANÇOIS CORNILLIAT
Rutgers University
Rhétoriqueurs

MARGA COTTINO-JONES
University of California, Los Angeles
Novella

ROBERT D. COTTRELL
Ohio State University
Brantôme, Pierre de Bourdeille,
seigneur de
Margaret of Navarre

SARAH COVINGTON
*Graduate School and University
Center of the City University of New
York*
Bussa de' Ponziani, Francesca
Catherine of Bologna
Catherine of Genoa
Christina of Sweden
Clothing
Glueckel of Hameln
Material Culture
Sports
Ward, Mary
Women: Women and Protest;
Women and Literature; Women
and Philosophy

ALEXANDER COWAN
*University of Northumbria at
Newcastle*
Bourgeoisie
Cities and Urban Life
Oligarchies

EUGENE CASJEN CRAMER
University of Calgary
Victoria, Tomás Luis de

JOHN R. CRAMSIE
Drury College
James I

MICHAEL HEWSON CRAWFORD
University College, London
Agustín, Antonio

BRYANT CREEL
University of Tennessee at Knoxville
Ribeiro, Bernardim

STELIO CRO
University of Louisville
Campanella, Tommaso: The Life of
Campanella; Campanella the
Literary Figure

ANNE J. CRUZ
University of Illinois at Chicago
Boscán, Juan
Carvajal y Mendoza, Luisa de
Garcilaso de la Vega
Picaresque Novel

ANTHONY M. CUMMINGS
Tulane University
Music: Transmission of Music

JOHN M. CURRIN
Instituto Tecnologico y de Estudios Superiores de Monterrey, Mexico City
Diplomacy
Field of Cloth of Gold
Henry VII

NANCY L. D'ANTUONO
Saint Mary's College, Indiana
Bandello, Matteo

HARM-JAN VAN DAM
Leiden, Netherlands
Grotius, Hugo

DAVID DANIELL
Hertford College, University of Oxford
Bible: The English Bible
Prayer Book, English

DAVID H. DARST
Florida State University
Hurtado de Mendoza, Diego

LINDA KAY DAVIDSON
University of Rhode Island
Pilgrimage

MARTIN DAVIES
Head of Incunabula, The British Library (until 1998)
Bracciolini, Poggio
Typography

ELIZABETH B. DAVIS
Ohio State University
Ercilla y Zúñiga, Alonso

J. C. DAVIS
University of East Anglia
Utopias

J. M. DE BUJANDA
Université de Sherbrooke
Index of Prohibited Books

LORENZO DEL PANTA
University of Bologna, Italy
Census
Demography

LUKE DEMAITRE
University of Virginia
Zoology

ANNA DE PACE
Università degli Studi di Milano, Italy
Mazzoni, Jacopo
Piccolomini, Alessandro
Tartaglia, Niccolò

NANCY DERSOFI
Bryn Mawr College
Andreini, Isabella
Ruzzante

HUGO DE SCHEPPER
Katholieke Universiteit Nijmegen, The Netherlands
Maurice of Nassau
William the Silent

CHRISTY DESMET
University of Georgia
Chronicle, Elizabethan

INGRID A. R. DE SMET
University of Warwick
Terence

THOMAS B. DEUTSCHER
Saint Thomas More College, University of Saskatchewan
Seminaries

JONATHAN DEWALD
State University of New York at Buffalo
Aristocracy

OTTAVIO DI CAMILLO
Graduate School and University Center of the City University of New York
Humanism: Spain

EDMUND H. DICKERMAN
University of Connecticut, Emeritus
Bellièvre, Pomponne de
Brûlart de Sillery, Nicolas
Villeroy, Nicolas de Neufville, seigneur de

BARBARA B. DIEFENDORF
Boston University
Paris
Wars of Religion

SALVATORE DI MARIA
University of Tennessee at Knoxville
Cecchi, Giovanni Maria
Drama: Tragedy
Giraldi, Giambattista Cinzio

GEOFFREY DIPPLE
Augustana College
Eberlin, Johann von Guenzburg

IAN DONALDSON
King's College, Cambridge
Jonson, Ben

JOHN PATRICK DONNELLY, S.J.
Marquette University
Bellarmine, Robert
Ratio Studiorum
Religious Orders: New Religious Orders and Congregations in Italy
Suárez, Francisco

JOHN E. DOTSON
Southern Illinois University, Carbondale
Mediterranean Sea

RICHARD M. DOUGLAS
Wellesley, Massachusetts
Sadoleto, Jacopo

MICHAEL DRISCOLL
University of Notre Dame
Liturgy

HENK DUITS
Vrije Universiteit, Amsterdam
Netherlandish Literature and Language

PETER N. DUNN
Wesleyan University, Emeritus
Alemán, Mateo

ROBERT S. DuPLESSIS
Swarthmore College
Mercantilism

FRANCIS A. DUTRA
University of California, Santa Barbara
Francis Xavier
Gama, Vasco da
Magellan, Ferdinand

EDWIN M. DUVAL
Yale University
French Literature and Language

T. F. EARLE
St. Peter's College, Oxford
Ferreira, António
Sá de Miranda, Francisco de

FRIEDRICH EDELMAYER
University of Vienna
Holy Roman Empire
Maximilian II

NOAH J. EFRON
Massachusetts Institute of Technology
  Gans, David ben Solomon
  Isserles, Moses
  Maharal of Prague

BENJAMIN A. EHLERS
University of Georgia
  Furió Ceriol, Fadrique

TRACY K. EHRLICH
Colgate University
  Gardens

CARLOS M. N. EIRE
Yale University
  Religious Piety

IVANA ELBL
Trent University
  Portugal

KARL ALFRED ENGELBERT ENENKEL
University of Leiden, The Netherlands
  Canter, Jacob

DAVID FALLOWS
University of Manchester
  Music: Instrumental Music

GIUSEPPE FALVO
University of Maryland
  Firenzuola, Agnolo
  Palmieri, Matteo

ELAINE FANTHAM
Princeton University
  Ovid

BERNARDINO FANTINI
University of Geneva
  Fabricius of Aquapendente, Girolamo
  Fracastoro, Girolamo

CLAIRE FARAGO
University of Colorado at Boulder
  Paragone

JAMES K. FARGE, C.S.B.
Pontifical Institute of Mediaeval Studies, Toronto
  Paris, University of

GIORGIO FEDALTO
University of Padua
  Christianity: Orthodox Christianity

ANTONIO FEROS
New York University
  Sandoval y Rojas, Francisco Gómez de

PAUL ALBERT FERRARA
Hofstra University
  Renaissance, Interpretations of the:
    John Ruskin

JOANNE M. FERRARO
San Diego State University
  Charivari
  Honor
  Social Status

PAULA SUTTER FICHTNER
Brooklyn College and the Graduate Center, City University of New York
  Austria: Austria in the Renaissance
  Dynastic Rivalry
  Ferdinand I
  Vienna

J. V. FIELD
Birkbeck College, University of London
  Piero della Francesca

PAULA FINDLEN
Stanford University
  Academies
  Museums
  Pornography
  Women: Women and Science

STEPHEN FISCHER-GALATI
University of Colorado at Boulder
  Mehmed II
  Ottoman Empire
  Süleyman I

SUSAN M. FITZMAURICE
Northern Arizona University
  English Literature and Language

ARNE R. FLATEN
Indiana University (Ph.D. Candidate)
  Coins, Medals, and Plaquettes
  Fiorentino, Niccolò

ANNA FOA
University of Rome
  Jews: The Jewish Community

THAYNE R. FORD
University of Wisconsin–Madison
  Ethnography of the New World

CHARLES R. FORKER
Indiana University
  Webster, John

ALISON KNOWLES FRAZIER
University of Texas at Austin
  Hagiography
  Religious Literature

CARLA FRECCERO
Santa Cruz, California
  Sexuality

LINDA FREY
University of Montana
  Maximilian I

MARSHA FREY
Kansas State University
  Maximilian I

ILSE E. FRIESEN
Wilfred Laurier University, Waterloo, Ontario
  Schongauer, Martin

CHRISTOPH L. FROMMEL
Max-Planck-Institut, Rome
  Peruzzi, Baldassare

MARY D. GARRARD
American University
  Anguissola, Sofonisba
  Gentileschi, Artemisia

LLOYD P. GERSON
University of Toronto
  Plotinus

WALTER S. GIBSON
Case Western Reserve University, Emeritus
  Bosch, Hieronymus
  Brueghel Family

MICHAEL J. GIORDANO
Wayne State University
  Du Fail, Noël

ELISABETH G. GLEASON
University of San Francisco, Emerita
  Contarini, Gasparo
  Farnese, House of
  Parma
  Paul III
  Pius V
  Spirituali

JOHN B. GLEASON
University of San Francisco, Emeritus
  Colet, John

THOMAS F. GLICK
Boston University
  Agriculture

JACQUELINE GLOMSKI
Warburg Institute, University of London
  Cracow

JEAN GOLDMAN
Glencoe, Illinois
  Drawing

GEORGE L. GORSE
Pomona College
  Genoa: Art in Genoa

EDWARD A. GOSSELIN
California State University,
Long Beach
  Lefèvre d'Étaples, Jacques

BEATRICE GOTTLIEB
New York City
  Birth and Infancy
  Childhood
  Family and Kinship
  Household
  Life Stages
  Love
  Marriage
  Motherhood
  Pregnancy
  Virginity and Celibacy

KENNETH GOUWENS
University of Connecticut
  Clement VII
  Historical Themes in Renaissance
    Art
  Leto, Pomponio
  Platina, Bartolomeo
  Rome, Sack of

JUDITH V. GRABINER
Pitzer College
  Mathematics

RICHARD L. GREAVES
Florida State University
  Puritanism

MARK GREENGRASS
University of Sheffield
  Coligny, Gaspard II de
  Epernon, Jean-Louis de Nogaret,
    duc d'
  Joyeuse, Anne de

MARGARET RICH GREER
Duke University
  Calderón de la Barca, Pedro

PAUL F. GRENDLER
University of Toronto, Emeritus
  Alciato, Andrea
  Bologna, University of
  Censorship: Censorship on the
    Continent
  Cornaro Piscopia, Elena Lucrezia
  Early Modern Period

Padua, University of
Patrizi, Francesco
Pavia, University of
Professions
Renaissance: The Renaissance in
  Historical Thought; The
  Renaissance in Popular
  Imagination
Renaissance, Interpretations of the:
  John Addington Symonds; Georg
  Voigt
Translation: Overview
Universities

CLIVE GRIFFIN
Trinity College, Oxford
  Cromberger Press

GORDON GRIFFITHS
University of Washington, Emeritus
  Constitutionalism
  Representative Institutions

MICHAEL GRILLO
University of Maine
  Religious Themes in Renaissance Art

FRANCESCO GUARDIANI
University of Toronto
  Marino, Giambattista

CAROLYN C. GUILE
Princeton University
  East Central Europe, Art in

STEVEN GUNN
Merton College, University of Oxford
  Wolsey, Thomas

HUBERTUS GÜNTHER
University of Zürich
  Bramante, Donato

ALAN HAGER
State University of New York at
Cortland
  Sidney, Philip

ROSEMARY DRAGE HALE
Concordia University, Montréal
  Catherine of Siena

MARCIA B. HALL
Tyler School of Art, Temple University
  Painting
  Raphael

BARBARA C. HALPORN
Harvard College Library
  Amerbach Family

JOHN OLIVER HAND
National Gallery of Art, Washington,
D.C.
  Cleve, Joos van

JAMES HANKINS
Harvard University
  Bruni, Leonardo

SARAH HANLEY
University of Iowa
  Du Tillet, Jean
  Marie de Médicis

MARGARET P. HANNAY
Siena College
  Sidney, Mary

RICHARD F. HARDIN
University of Kansas
  Antiquarianism

DEBORAH E. HARKNESS
University of California, Davis
  Alchemy
  Dee, John

CRAIG E. HARLINE
Brigham Young University
  Brussels

MARGARET HARP
University of Nevada, Las Vegas
  Anne of Brittany

DON HARRÁN
Hebrew University of Jerusalem
  Jews: Jews and Music

VAUGHAN HART
University of Bath
  Architecture: Architectural Treatises
  Britain, Art in
  Jones, Inigo
  Serlio, Sebastiano
  Supernatural World in Renaissance
    Art

RANDOLPH C. HEAD
University of California, Riverside
  Switzerland

JOHN M. HEADLEY
University of North Carolina,
Chapel Hill
  Cobos, Francisco de los
  Europe, Idea of
  Gattinara, Mercurino

FELICITY HEAL
Jesus College, University of Oxford
  Parker, Matthew

RICHARD HELGERSON
University of California,
Santa Barbara
  Hakluyt, Richard
  Ralegh, Walter

JOHANNES HELMRATH
Humboldt University, Berlin
Basel, Council of

DIANA E. HENDERSON
Massachusetts Institute of Technology
Poetry, English: Tudor Poetry before
Spenser

WILLI HENKEL, O.M.I.
Pontifical Urbaniana University, Rome
Missions, Christian

M. HENNINGER-VOSS
Princeton University
Euclid
Toscanelli, Paolo dal Pozzo

MAURO HERNÁNDEZ
*Universidad Nacional de Educación a
Distancia, Spain*
Madrid

JEANETTE HERRLE-FANNING
*Graduate Center, City University of
New York*
Midwives and Healers
Obstetrics and Gynecology

ANDREW C. HESS
*Fletcher School of Law and
Diplomacy, Tufts University*
Africa, North

DAVID HIGGS
University of Toronto
Inquisition: Portuguese Inquisition

BRIDGET HILL
Oxfordshire, United Kingdom
Servants

JOHN WALTER HILL
*University of Illinois at Urbana-
Champaign*
Music: Intermedi; Opera

W. SPEED HILL
*Lehman College, City University of
New York*
Hooker, Richard

RICHARD HILLMAN
University of Western Ontario
Gournay, Marie de

DALE HOAK
College of William and Mary
Edward VI

P. G. HOFTIJZER
Leiden University, The Netherlands
Elzevier Press
Froben Press

MICHAEL ANN HOLLY
*Clark Institute, Williamstown,
Massachusetts*
Renaissance, Interpretations of the:
Aby Warburg; Erwin Panofsky

MACK P. HOLT
George Mason University
Anjou, François de Valois, duc
d'Alençon et d'
Burgundy
Charles IX

LU ANN HOMZA
College of William and Mary
Alcalá de Henares, University of
Ciruelo, Pedro
Stunica, Jacobus Lopis
Vergara, Juan de

WILLIAM HOOD
Oberlin College
Angelico, Fra

ANDREW JAMES HOPKINS
British School at Rome
Scamozzi, Vincenzo

LISA HOPKINS
Sheffield Hallam University, U.K.
Drama, English: Jacobean Drama

ELLIOT HOROWITZ
Bar-Ilan University, Israel
Jews: Jewish Religious Life

LOUISE K. HOROWITZ
Rutgers University
Urfé, Honoré d'

MARYANNE CLINE HOROWITZ
University of California, Los Angeles
Diaries and Memoirs

HOWARD HOTSON
University of Aberdeen
Rudolf II
Wechel Family

EUNICE D. HOWE
University of Southern California
Rome: Art in Rome and Latium

LILLIAN HROMIKO
Kent State University
Dudley, Robert

ALAN HUNT
Carleton University, Canada
Sumptuary Laws

G. K. HUNTER
Yale University, Emeritus
Drama, English: Elizabethan Drama
Lyly, John

GARY IANZITI
*Queensland University of Technology,
Brisbane*
Despotism
Prince

MOSHE IDEL
Hebrew University of Jerusalem
Flavius Mithridates
Kabbalah

VINCENT ILARDI
*University of Massachusetts, Amherst,
Emeritus*
Lodi, Peace of

ARTHUR F. IORIO
Illinois State University
Francesco di Giorgio

JOYCE L. IRWIN
Colgate University
Schurman, Anna Maria van

RADOVAN IVANČEVIĆ
University of Zagreb, Croatia
Croatia and Dalmatia: Art in Croatia
and Dalmatia

THOMAS M. IZBICKI
Johns Hopkins University
Florence, Council of
Nicholas of Cusa

K. DAVID JACKSON
Yale University
Portuguese Literature and
Language

FREDRIKA H. JACOBS
Virginia Commonwealth University
Art: Women Artists
Women: Portrayal in Renaissance
Art

KLAUS J. JAITNER
*Director, European Historical
Archives, Florence (Retired)*
Nepotism

DE LAMAR JENSEN
*Brigham Young University,
Emeritus*
Espionage

MINNA SKAFTE JENSEN
Odense University, Denmark
Scandinavian Kingdoms

SETH JERCHOWER
*Library, Jewish Theological Seminary
of America*
Judeo-Italian

CARROLL B. JOHNSON
University of California, Los Angeles
Cervantes Saavedra, Miguel de

NORMAN L. JONES
Utah State University
Elizabeth I
Usury

CHRISTIANE L. JOOST-GAUGIER
Independent Scholar,
Washington, D.C.
Famous Men and Women

WALTER KAISER
Villa I Tatti, Florence
Villa I Tatti

CRAIG KALLENDORF
Texas A&M University
Aristotle and Cinquecento Poetics
Landino, Cristoforo
Poetics: Survey
Poetry: Classical Poetry
Virgil

HENRY KAMEN
Higher Council for Scientific Research,
Barcelona, Spain
Inquisition: Spanish Inquisition
Philip II
Philip III
Popular Revolts
Toleration

YOSEF KAPLAN
Hebrew University of Jerusalem
Conversos
Menassah ben Israel

CAROL V. KASKE
Cornell University
Allegory
Chivalry: English Arthurian
Romance

RICHARD KASSEL
Writer and Editor, New York City
Music in Italy

DONALD R. KELLEY
Rutgers University
Dumoulin, Charles
Historiography, Renaissance:
German Historiography
Hotman, François
Resistance, Theory of

IRVING A. KELTER
University of St. Thomas, Houston
Astronomy
Ptolemy

G. YVONNE KENDALL
University of Houston–Downtown
Dance

ROBERT L. KENDRICK
University of Chicago
Music: Renaissance Music; Music in
Renaissance Society

DALE V. KENT
University of California, Riverside
Medici, Cosimo de'

FRANCIS WILLIAM KENT
Monash University, Australia
Patronage: Patrons and Clients in
Renaissance Society

JOHN E. KICZA
Washington State University
Cortés, Hernán

JAN KIENEWICZ
University of Warsaw
Poland

MARIE SEONG-HAK KIM
University of Minnesota
L'Hôpital, Michel de

JOHN N. KING
Ohio State University
Royal Iconography, English

MARGARET L. KING
Brooklyn College and the Graduate
Center, City University of New York
Barbaro, Francesco
Borgia, Lucrezia
Margaret of Austria
Nogarola, Isotta
Venice: Venice in the
Renaissance
Women: Women in the
Renaissance

WILLARD F. KING
Bryn Mawr College
Ruiz de Alarcón y Mendoza, Juan

ROBERT M. KINGDON
University of Wisconsin–Madison
Calvin, John
Estienne Family

ARTHUR F. KINNEY
University of Massachusetts, Amherst;
New York University
Prose, Elizabethan

PHILIP L. KINTNER
Grinnell College
Franck, Sebastian

JAMES KITTELSON
Luther Seminary, St. Paul, Minnesota
Strasbourg

CHRISTOPHER KLEINHENZ
University of Wisconsin–Madison
Glory, Idea of
Petrarch

LOUIS A. KNAFLA
University of Calgary
Ramus, Petrus

R. J. KNECHT
University of Birmingham
Collège de France
Francis I
Louise of Savoy

JOHN R. KNOTT
University of Michigan
Foxe, John

JOSEPH LEO KOERNER
Harvard University
Baldung Grien, Hans
Cranach, Lucas

ROBERT KOLB
Concordia Seminary, Saint Louis
Oecolampadius

MICHAEL KOORTBOJIAN
University of Toronto
Classical Antiquity: Discovery of
Classical Antiquity

MARIE ELENA KOREY
Massey College, University of Toronto
Nürnberg Chronicle

JILL KRAYE
Warburg Institute, University of
London
Classical Scholarship
Moral Philosophy
Stoicism

THOMAS J. KUEHN
Clemson University
Law

MARION LEATHERS KUNTZ
Georgia State University
Postel, Guillaume

KRIS LANE
College of William and Mary
Piracy

ULLRICH LANGER
University of Wisconsin–Madison
Amyot, Jacques
Muret, Marc-Antoine

ULLRICH LANGER
(*continued*)
Ronsard, Pierre de
Turnèbe, Adrien

Y. TZVI LANGERMAN
Bar-Ilan University, Israel
Magic and Astrology: Jewish
Astrology and the Occult
Translation: Jewish
Translators

DONALD J. LARROCCA
Metropolitan Museum of Art
Arms and Armor
Artillery
Firearms

ANNE R. LARSEN
Hope College
Baïf, Lazare de
Des Roches, Catherine and
Madeleine
Du Bellay, Joachim
La Boétie, Étienne de
Malherbe, François
Marot, Clément
Pibrac, Guy du Faur, sieur de
Pléiade
Saint-Gelais, Mellin de

JOHN E. LAW
University of Wales, Swansea
City-State
Italy

ERIC LAWEE
York University, Canada
Abravanel, Isaac

LANCE G. LAZAR
*University of North Carolina,
Chapel Hill*
Varthema, Lodovico de

MOSHE LAZAR
University of Southern California
Ladino Literature and Language

EDOARDO A. LÈBANO
Indiana University
Pulci, Luigi

STANFORD E. LEHMBERG
University of Minnesota
Beaufort, Margaret
Drake, Francis
Elyot, Thomas
England
Fisher, John
Grand Tour
Henry VIII

Humanism: The British Isles
Linacre, Thomas
London

STEPHANIE LEITCH
University of Chicago
Holbein, Hans, the Elder
Holbein, Hans, the Younger

FABRIZIO LELLI
*Facoltà Teologica dell'Italia Centrale,
Florence*
Alemanno, Yohanan ben Isaac
Jewish Thought and the
Renaissance
Leone Ebreo

EMMANUEL LE ROY LADURIE
Collège de France (Retired)
Platter Family

BRIAN P. LEVACK
University of Texas at Austin
Witchcraft

F. J. LEVY
University of Washington
Vergil, Polydore

NINA S. LEWALLEN
Columbia University
Palaces and Townhouses

ELAINE LIMBRICK
*University of Victoria, British
Columbia*
Sanches, Francisco

ROBERT LINDELL
Vienna
Music in the Holy Roman
Empire

DAVID LINDLEY
University of Leeds
Drama, English: Jacobean Court
Masque
Poetry and Music

PEGGY K. LISS
West Stockbridge, Massachusetts
Isabella of Castile

HOWELL LLOYD
University of Hull
Coquille, Guy

T. H. LLOYD
University College of Swansea
Fairs

DAVID LOADES
University of Sheffield
Mary I

CHARLES H. LOHR
University of Freiburg, Germany
Metaphysics

PAMELA O. LONG
Washington, D.C.
Technology

DENNIS LOONEY
University of Pittsburgh
Ariosto, Ludovico

DEBORAH N. LOSSE
Arizona State University
Béroalde de Verville, François
Des Périers, Bonaventure
La Boderie, Guy Le Fèvre de

RONALD S. LOVE
University of Saskatchewan
La Noue, François de
Montluc, Blaise de Lasseran-
Massencôme, seigneur de

MARTIN J. C. LOWRY
University of Warwick
Aldine Press
Printing and Publishing

GREGORY P. LUBKIN
Washington, D.C.
Milan: Milan in the Renaissance
Visconti, Giangaleazzo

MARVIN LUNENFELD
*State University of New York, College
at Fredonia, Emeritus*
Ferdinand of Aragon

ANTHONY LUTTRELL
Bath, United Kingdom
Crusade

BRIDGET GELLERT LYONS
Rutgers University
Burton, Robert

GUY FITCH LYTLE
University of the South
Jewel, John

DENNIS JAMES MCAULIFFE
St. Michael's College, Toronto
Bembo, Pietro

DIANE KELSEY MCCOLLEY
*Camden College of Arts and Sciences,
Rutgers University*
Milton, John

JAMES MCCONICA
*Pontifical Institute of Mediaeval
Studies, Toronto*
Cambridge, University of
Oxford, University of

WILLIAM MCCUAIG
University of Toronto
Biondo, Flavio
Botero, Giovanni
Casaubon, Isaac
Giannotti, Donato
Guarini, Guarino
Paruta, Paolo
Pius II
Sarpi, Paolo
Scaliger, Joseph Justus
Scaliger, Julius Caesar
Sigonio, Carlo

DIARMAID MACCULLOCH
St. Cross College, Oxford University
Cranmer, Thomas

PATRICK MACEY
Eastman School of Music
Josquin des Prez

DOUGLAS MCFARLAND
Oglethorpe University
Rabelais, François

TIMOTHY J. MCGEE
University of Toronto
Music: Performance Practice;
    Musical Instruments

FREDERICK J. MCGINNESS
Smith College
Clergy: Catholic Clergy
Gregory XIII
Preaching and Sermons: Christian
    Preaching and Sermons
Sixtus V

RICHARD MACKENNEY
University of Edinburgh
Guilds
Industry

MARY B. MCKINLEY
University of Virginia
Margaret of Valois

MARY MARTIN MCLAUGHLIN
Independent Scholar, Millbrook, N.Y.
Merici, Angela
Spirituality, Female

JOHN M. MCMANAMON, S.J.
Loyola Marymount University, Los Angeles
Vergerio, Pierpaolo

ERIC MACPHAIL
Indiana University
Dolet, Étienne
Humanism: France

WILLIAM S. MALTBY
University of Missouri–St. Louis, Emeritus
Alvárez de Toledo, Fernando

DAVID MARGOLIES
Goldsmiths College, University of London
Fiction, Elizabethan

JOHN A. MARINO
University of California, San Diego
Naples: Naples in the
    Renaissance
Sicily

RICHARD MARIUS
Harvard University
Luther, Martin
More, Thomas

GUIDO MARNEF
University of Antwerp
Antwerp

ARTHUR F. MAROTTI
Wayne State University
Donne, John

DAVID MARSH
Rutgers University
Alberti, Leon Battista
Lucian

F. X. MARTIN, O.S.A.
University College, Dublin; Royal Irish Academy; Irish Manuscripts Commission
Giles of Viterbo

JOSÉ MIGUEL MARTÍNEZ TORREJÓN
Queens College and Graduate Center, City University of New York
Villalón, Cristóbal de

LINDA MARTZ
Bethesda, Maryland
Toledo

ROGER A. MASON
University of Saint Andrews
Knox, John
Scotland

JAN MATERNÉ
GIB, Brasschaat, Belgium
Plantin, Christophe

PETER MATHESON
Ormond College, Melbourne
Grumbach, Argula von
Pirckheimer, Caritas
Zell, Katharine

HERBERT S. MATSEN
Yakima, Washington
Achillini, Alessandro

THOMAS F. MAYER
Augustana College
Biography and Autobiography:
    Europe
Cromwell, Thomas
Morison, Richard
Pole, Reginald
Starkey, Thomas

JAMES V. MEHL
Missouri Western State College (d. 1998)
Busche, Hermann von dem
Cologne

CAROL BRESNAHAN MENNING
University of Toledo
Florence: Florence in the
    Renaissance
Medici, House of
Medici, Cosimo I

RAYMOND A. MENTZER
Montana State University
Bèze, Théodore de

RONIT MEROZ
Tel-Aviv University, Israel
Caro, Joseph ben Ephraim
Jewish Messianism
Luria, Isaac

CHARLOTTE METHUEN
Ruhr-Universität Bochum, Germany
Schegk, Jakob

EMILY MICHAEL
Brooklyn College of the City University of New York
Harriot, Thomas
Humanity, Concept of
Psychology

ANITA MIKULIĆ-KOVAČEVIĆ
Academy of America, Inc., Toronto
Croatia and Dalmatia: Croatia and
    Dalmatia in the Renaissance

CLEMENT A. MILLER
John Carroll University, Emeritus
Du Guillet, Pernette

DAVID LEE MILLER
University of Kentucky
Spenser, Edmund

NAOMI J. MILLER
University of Arizona
Wroth, Mary

MICHAEL MILWAY
University of Toronto
  Bible: German Translations
  Cambrai, League of

NELSON MINNICH
Catholic University of America
  Lateran V, Council of
  Leo X
  Papacy

BONNER MITCHELL
University of Missouri–Columbia
  Festivals
  Parades, Processions, and
    Pageants
  Tournaments

BRANKO MITROVIĆ
*Unitec Institute of Technology,
Auckland, New Zealand*
  Palladio, Andrea

JOHN MONFASANI
*University at Albany, State University
of New York*
  Augustine of Hippo
  Bessarion
  Chrysoloras, Manuel
  Cicero
  Constantinople, Fall of
  Gaza, Theodore
  Gemistus Pletho, George
  George of Trebizond
  Greek Émigrés
  Immortality
  Lascaris, Constantine
  Lascaris, Janus
  Renaissance, Interpretations of the:
    Remigio Sabbadini; Paul Oskar
    Kristeller
  Vatican Library

LUIGI MONGA
Vanderbilt University
  Cellini, Benvenuto: Cellini the
    Writer
  Ramusio, Giovanni Battista
  Travel and Travel Literature

MICHAEL L. MONHEIT
University of South Alabama
  Budé, Guillaume
  Humanism: Legal Humanism

CRAIG A. MONSON
Washington University, St. Louis
  Byrd, William
  Gibbons, Orlando
  Music in England

JO ANN HOEPPNER MORAN CRUZ
Georgetown University
  Education
  Literacy

JOHN S. MORRILL
*Selwyn College, University of
Cambridge*
  Stuart Dynasty

CHARLES R. MORSCHECK JR.
Drexel University
  Milan: Art in Milan and Lombardy

ANN MOSS
University of Durham
  Commonplace Books
  Dictionaries and Encyclopedias

JEAN DIETZ MOSS
Catholic University of America
  Ramus, Petrus
  Rhetoric

NICOLETTE MOUT
Leiden University, The Netherlands
  Lipsius, Justus

ANN E. MOYER
University of Pennsylvania
  Nostradamus

JANEL MUELLER
University of Chicago
  Parr, Katherine

EDWARD MUIR
Northwestern University
  Carnival
  Ritual, Civic
  Violence

ROBERT MUNMAN
University of Illinois–Chicago
  Tombs

PAUL V. MURPHY
University of San Francisco
  Gonzaga, House of
  Mantua
  Vittorino da Feltre

JAMES C. MURRAY
Georgia State University
  Vega, Inca Garcilaso de la

HELEN NADER
University of Arizona
  González de Mendoza, Pedro

JOHN M. NAJEMY
Cornell University
  Machiavelli, Niccolò: The Life of
    Machiavelli; The Political Theorist
  Republicanism

JERRY C. NASH
University of North Texas
  Montaigne, Michel de

CHARLES G. NAUERT
*University of Missouri–Columbia,
Emeritus*
  Agrippa of Nettesheim, Heinrich
  Fugger Family
  Humanism: The Definition of
    Humanism
  Pliny the Elder
  Protestant Reformation
  Reuchlin, Johann
  Reuchlin Affair

PAUL NEEDHAM
Princeton University Library
  Caxton, William

PAUL NELLES
St. Andrews University, Scotland
  Libraries

HELMUT NICKEL
Metropolitan Museum of Art, Emeritus
  Heraldry

JOSÉ C. NIETO
Juniata College
  Servetus, Michael
  Valdés, Juan de

BODO NISCHAN
East Carolina University
  Brandenburg
  Saxony

CARLOS G. NOREÑA
*University of California, Santa Clara,
Emeritus*
  Huarte de San Juan, Juan

TARA E. NUMMEDAL
Stanford University
  Anna of Saxony

LAURIE NUSSDORFER
Wesleyan University
  Rome: The City of Rome

MICHAEL O'CONNELL
*University of California,
Santa Barbara*
  Browne, Thomas

JOHN W. O'MALLEY, S.J.
Weston Jesuit School of Theology
  Catholic Reformation and Counter-
    Reformation
  Ignatius Loyola
  Religious Orders: The Jesuits
  Trent, Council of

YNEZ VIOLE O'NEILL
University of California, Los Angeles
Vesalius, Andreas

JOHN ORRELL
University of Alberta, Emeritus
Theaters

MARGARET J. OSLER
University of Calgary
Epicurus and Epicureanism
Skepticism

PATRICIA OSMOND
Iowa State University
Historiography, Classical: Classical
Historians; Roman Historians

MASSIMO OSSI
University of Rochester, N.Y.
Monteverdi, Claudio

JAMES H. OVERFIELD
University of Vermont
Bavaria
Leipzig
Wimpheling, Jacob

J. B. OWENS
Idaho State University
Comuneros, Revolt of the
Maldonado, Juan
Mariana, Juan de

MARIANNE PADE
University of Copenhagen
Historiography, Classical: Classical
Historians; Greek Historians

CLAUDE V. PALISCA
Yale University
Acoustics
Music: Music in Renaissance
Culture; Music Treatises

WILLIAM PALMER
Marshall University
Ireland

LETIZIA PANIZZA
Royal Holloway College, London
Libertinism
Marinella, Lucrezia
Tarabotti, Arcangela

JAN PAPY
*Catholic University Leuven,
Belgium*
Louvain, University of

JAMES A. PARENTE JR.
University of Minnesota
Drama: Religious Drama

CHARLES H. PARKER
Saint Louis University
Amsterdam

DEBORAH PARKER
Charlottesville, Virginia
Dante in the Renaissance

JOTHAM PARSONS
University of Delaware
Gallicanism

KEVIN PASK
Concordia University, Montréal
Biography and Autobiography:
England

ALINA A. PAYNE
University of Toronto
Architecture: Architecture in the
Renaissance
Filarete
Rossellino, Bernardo
Urbanism

LYNDA STEPHENSON PAYNE
University of Missouri–Kansas City
Galen
Harvey, William
Hippocrates of Cos

RODNEY J. PAYTON
Western Washington University
Renaissance, Interpretations of the:
Johan Huizinga

TED-LARRY PEBWORTH
University of Michigan–Dearborn
Patronage: Literary Patronage in
England

JAROSLAV PELIKAN
Yale University
Christianity: The Western Church
Christian Theology

MAUREEN PELTA
*Moore College of Art and Design,
Philadelphia*
Correggio
Donatello
Religious Themes in Renaissance
Art

SIMON PEPPER
University of Liverpool
Fortifications

MARIO PEREIRA
*University of Chicago (Ph.D.
Candidate)*
Caravaggio, Michelangelo
Merisi da

DAVID S. PETERSON
Washington and Lee University
Antoninus

WILLIAM A. PETTAS
Montgomery, Alabama
Eguía Press
Giunti Press

SUSANNA PEYRONEL RAMBALDI
University of Milan
Modena

CARLA RAHN PHILLIPS
University of Minnesota
Communication and
Transportation
Ships and Shipbuilding

WILLIAM D. PHILLIPS JR.
University of Minnesota
Columbus, Christopher
Slavery
Spain: The Spanish Kingdoms

MARTIN PICKER
Rutgers University, Emeritus
Music in France
Ockeghem, Johannes

PETER PIERSON
Santa Clara University
Armada, Spanish
John of Austria
Lepanto, Battle of

KAREN PINKUS
University of Southern California
Colonna, Francesco

EMIL J. POLAK
*Queensborough Community College of
the City University of New York*
Letterbooks

CYNTHIA L. POLECRITTI
University of California, Santa Cruz
Bernardino of Siena

JOSEPH POLZER
University of Calgary
Sculpture
Space and Perspective

JONATHAN F. S. POST
University of California, Los Angeles
Marvell, Andrew
Poetry, English: Early Stuart and
Metaphysical Poetry

WILFRID PREST
University of Adelaide
Inns of Court

DAVID PRICE
Southern Methodist University
  Bible: Printed Bibles

RUSSELL PRICE
University of Lancaster
  Virtù

BRIAN PULLAN
University of Manchester
  Orphans and Foundlings
  Poverty and Charity

CYRIAC K. PULLAPILLY
Saint Mary's College, Indiana
  Baronio, Cesare

EDDY PUT
Kessel-lo, Belgium
  Brussels

MARÍA CRISTINA QUINTERO
Bryn Mawr College
  Góngora y Argote, Luis de

ALBERT RABIL JR.
State University of New York, College at Old Westbury
  Diffusion of Ideas
  Feminism
  Humanism: Italy
  Morata, Olympia
  Querelle des Femmes
  Renaissance: Influence of the
    Renaissance; Renaissance
    Studies
  Renaissance, Interpretations
    of the: Eugenio Garin

SHEILA J. RABIN
St. Peter's College, Jersey City, N.J.
  Kepler, Johannes
  Optics
  Peurbach, Georg
  Regiomontanus

CORNELIS S. M. RADEMAKER, SS.CC.
University of Amsterdam (Retired)
  Vossius, Gerardus Joannes

CATHARINE RANDALL
Fordham University
  Desportes, Philippe
  Du Bartas, Guillaume de Salluste
  Poetics: French Poetics
  Régnier, Mathurin
  Sponde, Jean de

PIYO RATTANSI
University College, London
  Helmont, Johannes Baptista van

BENJAMIN C. I. RAVID
Brandeis University
  Ghetto
  Luzzatto, Simone

AMNON RAZ-KRAKOTZKIN
Ben Gurion University of the Negev, Beer-Sheba, Israel
  Jews: Print and Jewish Cultural
    Development

KAREN MEIER REEDS
National Coalition of Independent Scholars and Princeton Research Forum
  Botany
  Cesalpino, Andrea

PAOLO RENZI
University of Siena, Italy
  Pisa
  Siena: Siena in the
    Renaissance

STELLA P. REVARD
Southern Illinois University, Edwardsville
  Secundus, Johannes

CHRISTOPHER REYNOLDS
University of California, Davis
  Dufay, Guillaume

ELIZABETH RHODES
Boston College
  Granada, Luis de
  Montemayor, Jorge de

LAWRENCE F. RHU
University of South Carolina
  Epic

JOSEPH V. RICAPITO
Louisiana State University
  Valdés, Alfonso de

WOLFGANG RIEHLE
Karl-Franzens-Universität Graz, Austria
  Plautus, Titus Maccius

JONATHAN B. RIESS
University of Cincinnati
  Perugino
  Signorelli, Luca

DAVID RIGGS
Stanford University
  Marlowe, Christopher

FRANÇOIS RIGOLOT
Princeton University
  Labé, Louise

ELIAS L. RIVERS
State University of New York at Stony Brook
  Spanish Literature and Language

DIANA ROBIN
University of New Mexico
  Cereta, Laura
  Fedele, Cassandra
  Filelfo, Francesco

THOMAS P. ROCHE
Princeton University
  Poetry: The Sonnet outside England

ROBERT J. RODINI
University of Wisconsin–Madison
  Berni, Francesco
  Grazzini, Anton Francesco
  Italian Literature and Language

DAVID ROSAND
Columbia University
  Tintoretto
  Titian
  Veronese, Paolo

CHARLES M. ROSENBERG
University of Notre Dame
  Ferrara: Art in Ferrara

MARGARET F. ROSENTHAL
University of Southern California
  Franco, Veronica
  Stampa, Gaspara

CHARLES ROSS
Purdue University
  Chivalry: Romance of Chivalry

INGRID D. ROWLAND
University of Chicago
  Art: Renaissance Art
  Classical Antiquity: Classical
    Antiquity in Renaissance Art
  Forgeries
  Grotesques
  Naples: Art in Naples
  Pasquino
  Pinturicchio
  Spain: Art in Spain and Portugal

DAVID B. RUDERMAN
University of Pennsylvania
  Jewish Medicine and Science

ERIKA RUMMEL
Wilfred Laurier University, Waterloo, Ontario
  Erasmus, Desiderius
  Humanism: Germany and the Low
    Countries
  Peutinger, Conrad

TIMOTHY J. RUNYAN
East Carolina University
Naval Warfare

DANIEL RUSSELL
University of Pittsburgh
Emblem

RINALDINA RUSSELL
Queens College, City University of New York
Aragona, Tullia d'
Corner, Caterina
Fonte, Moderata
Gàmbara, Veronica
Tornabuoni, Lucrezia

JEFFREY S. RUTH
The Hudson School, Hoboken, N.J.
Humanism: Portugal
Lisbon

MAREN-SOFIE RØSTVIG
University of Oslo, Emerita
Numerology

SHALOM SABAR
Hebrew University of Jerusalem
Jewish Themes in Renaissance Art
Jews: Jews and the Arts

J. H. M. SALMON
Bryn Mawr College, Emeritus
Champier, Symphorien
France: The Kingdom of France
Renaissance, Interpretations of the:
Jules Michelet
Satire Ménippée

ANTONIO SANTOSUOSSO
University of Western Ontario
Della Casa, Giovanni
Gattamelata, Erasmo da Narni, il
Mercenaries
Pavia, Battle of
Warfare
Wars of Italy

MARC SAPERSTEIN
George Washington University
Preaching and Sermons: Jewish
Preaching and Sermons

JAMES M. SASLOW
Queens College and the Graduate Center, City University of New York
Homosexuality
Michelangelo Buonarroti:
Michelangelo the Poet

ALDO SCAGLIONE
New York University
Civility

HELGA SCHEIBLE
Bammental, Germany
Pirckheimer Family

JULIANA SCHIESARI
University of California, Davis
Morra, Isabella di

ZACHARY S. SCHIFFMAN
Northeastern Illinois University
Charron, Pierre
Du Vair, Guillaume
Historiography, Renaissance:
French Historiography
Le Roy, Louis
Pasquier, Étienne

WINFRIED SCHLEINER
University of California, Davis
Bawdy, Elizabethan

CECIL J. SCHNEER
University of New Hampshire, Emeritus
Geology

ROBERT A. SCHNEIDER
Catholic University of America
Duel

LUISE SCHORN-SCHÜTTE
University of Potsdam
Clergy: Protestant Clergy

ANNE JACOBSON SCHUTTE
University of Virginia
Spilimbergo, Irene di

JOHN FREDERICK SCHWALLER
University of Montana
Inquisition: Inquisition in the Americas
Zumárraga, Juan de

LÍA SCHWARTZ
Dartmouth College
Quevedo, Francisco de

CHARLES SCRIBNER III
Author and Independent Art Historian, New York City
Rubens, Peter Paul

JOLE SHACKELFORD
University of Minnesota
Brahe, Tycho
Paracelsus

SILVIA SHANNON
St. Anselm College, Manchester, N.H.
Guise-Lorraine Family

CHRISTINE SHAW
University of Warwick
Alexander VI
Julius II
Sixtus IV

DEANNA SHEMEK
University of California, Santa Cruz
Este, Isabella d'

MICHAEL SHERBERG
Washington University, St. Louis
Tasso, Bernardo

RICHARD SHERR
Smith College
Music: Sacred Vocal Music
Palestrina, Giovanni Pierluigi da

MATTHEW G. SHOAF
University of Chicago
Giotto di Bondone

DEBORA K. SHUGER
University of California, Los Angeles
Homilies, Book of
Poetry: Religious Poetry

VICTOR SKRETKOWICZ
University of Dundee
Poetry, English: Elizabethan Poetry

JANET LEVARIE SMARR
University of Illinois at Urbana-Champaign
Boccaccio, Giovanni

JOACHIM SMET
Institutum Carmelitanum, Rome
Religious Orders: Orders of Men

ALAN K. SMITH
University of Utah
Burchiello

FENELLA K. C. SMITH
Cheltenham, Gloucester, United Kingdom
Cardano, Girolamo
Pacioli, Luca

HILDA SMITH
University of Cincinnati
Behn, Aphra
Cavendish, Margaret
Makin, Bathsua
Speght, Rachel

JEFFREY CHIPPS SMITH
University of Texas at Austin
Dürer, Albrecht
Germany, Art in
Riemenschneider, Tilman

369

JOSEPH T. SNOW
Michigan State University
Rojas, Fernando de

JOHANN P. SOMMERVILLE
University of Wisconsin–Madison
Absolutism

JAMES B. SOUTH
Marquette University
Nifo, Agostino
Pomponazzi, Pietro
Vernia, Nicoletto

MICHAEL R. G. SPILLER
University of Aberdeen, Scotland
Poetry: The English Sonnet

JERZY STARNAWSKI
University of Łódź, Poland, Emeritus
Dantiscus, Johannes

C. C. STATHATOS
University of Wisconsin–Parkside
Vicente, Gil

JAMES M. STAYER
Queen's University at Kingston, Canada
Peasants' War

TIMOTHY STEELE
California State University, Los Angeles
Prosody, Elizabethan

MURRAY STEIB
Ball State University
Music in the Low Countries

SUSAN STEIGERWALD
University of Nevada, Las Vegas
Vespucci, Amerigo

LAURA IKINS STERN
University of North Texas
Notaries
Podestà

KEVIN M. STEVENS
University of Nevada, Reno
Giolito Press

JOACHIM W. STIEBER
Smith College
Eugenius IV
Nicholas V

CHARLES L. STINGER
University at Buffalo, State University of New York
Borgia, House of
Borgia, Cesare
Patristics
Traversari, Ambrogio

KENNETH STOW
University of Haifa, Israel
Anti-Semitism
Jews: The Jewish Community; Jews and the Catholic Church

MARIE MICHELLE STRAH
Miami University
Scève, Maurice

EDMOND STRAINCHAMPS
State University of New York at Buffalo
Music: Secular Vocal Music

RICHARD STRIER
University of Chicago
Herbert, George

SHARON T. STROCCHIA
Emory University
Death
Strozzi, Alessandra Macinghi

SUSAN MOSHER STUARD
Haverford College
Dubrovnik

SARA STURM-MADDOX
University of Massachusetts, Amherst
Medici, Lorenzo de': The Literary Figure

CONSTANCE A. SULLIVAN
University of Minnesota
Erauso, Catalina de

HENRY W. SULLIVAN
University of Missouri–Columbia
Molina, Tirso de

CLAUDE J. SUMMERS
University of Michigan–Dearborn
Patronage: Literary Patronage in England

RONALD E. SURTZ
Princeton University
Drama, Spanish
Torres Naharro, Bartolomé de

ROBERT BRIAN TATE
University of Nottingham
Camões, Luíz Vaz de

BRUCE TAYLOR
University of California, Los Angeles
Cisneros, Francisco Jiménez de

JOHN TEDESCHI
University of Wisconsin–Madison, Emeritus
Inquisition: Roman Inquisition

ROBERT TER HORST
University of Rochester
Encina, Juan del

NICHOLAS TERPSTRA
University of Toronto
Bologna
Confraternities
Hospitals and Asylums

ARTHUR TERRY
Colchester, United Kingdom
Catalan Literature and Language
Herrera, Fernando de

JOHN C. THEIBAULT
Independent Scholar, Vorhees, N.J.
Thirty Years' War

COLIN P. THOMPSON
St. Catherine's College, Oxford
John of the Cross
León, Luis de

JOHN A. F. THOMSON
University of Glasgow
Concordats

JOHN K. THORNTON
Rockville, Md.
Africa, Sub-Saharan
Africanus, Leo

VALENTINA K. TIKOFF
Indiana University
Seville

ACHIM TIMMERMANN
Princeton University
Austria: Art in Austria
Hungary: Art in Hungary

HAVA TIROSH-SAMUELSON
Arizona State University
Jewish Philosophy

BARBARA J. TODD
University of Toronto
Widowhood

JOHN TONKIN
University of Western Australia
Sleidanus, Johannes
Vadianus, Joachim

DAVID M. TRABOULAY
College of Staten Island, City University of New York
Las Casas, Bartolomé de
Quiroga, Vasco de

DAIN A. TRAFTON
Rockford College, Emeritus
Tasso, Torquato

CHARLES TRINKAUS
University of Michigan, Emeritus (d. 1999)
　Dignity of Man
　Fortune
　Individualism
　Paganism
　Valla, Lorenzo

TERENCE TUNBERG
University of Kentucky
　Neo-Latin Literature and Language

CHAVA TURNIANSKY
Hebrew University of Jerusalem
　Yiddish Literature and Language

RICHARD J. TUTTLE
Tulane University
　Vignola, Giacomo Barozzi da

JANE TYLUS
University of Wisconsin–Madison
　Guarini, Giovanni Battista
　Pastoral: Pastoral on the Continent
　Sannazaro, Jacopo

WILLIAM L. URBAN
Monmouth College
　Baltic States
　Russia

MARY VACCARO
University of Texas at Arlington
　Parmigianino

GINETTE VAGENHEIM
University of Rouen
　Ligorio, Pirro

ARJO VANDERJAGT
University of Groningen, The Netherlands
　Gansfort, Wessel
　Groningen

MARC VAN DER POEL
The Hague, The Netherlands
　Agricola, Rudolf

KATHERINE ELLIOT VAN LIERE
Calvin College
　Covarrubias y Leiva, Diego de
　Ginés de Sepúlveda, Juan
　Salamanca, University of
　Vitoria, Francisco de

DAVID E. VASSBERG
University of Texas Pan American
　Peasantry

JOS E. VERCRUYSSE
Pontifical Gregorian University
　Adrian VI

MATTHEW VESTER
Southern Illinois University, Carbondale
　Piedmont-Savoy

BERNARD VINCENT
École des Hautes Études en Sciences Sociales, Paris
　Moriscos

ALVIN VOS
University at Binghamton, State University of New York
　Ascham, Roger

RAYMOND B. WADDINGTON
University of California, Davis
　Aretino, Pietro
　Myth
　Satire: Satire in Italy

ELISABETH WÅGHÄLL-NIVRE
Växjö University
　Wickram, Jorg

STEPHEN WAGLEY
New York City
　Religious Orders: New Religious Congregations in France
　Renaissance: The Renaissance in Popular Imagination

G. GRAYSON WAGSTAFF
University of Alabama
　Music in Spain and Portugal

WILLIAM A. WALLACE, O.P.
University of Maryland
　Aristotle and Aristotelianism
　Benedetti, Giovanni Battista
　Buonamici, Francesco
　Cajetan, Thomas de Vio
　Chemistry
　Clocks
　Commandino, Federico
　Copernicus, Nicolaus
　Galilei, Galileo
　Gilbert, William
　Logic
　Major, John
　Matter, Structure of
　Mechanics
　Natural Philosophy
　Philosophy
　Physics
　Scholasticism
　Science
　Science, Epistemology of
　Scientific Instruments
　Scientific Method
　Soto, Domingo de

　Telesio, Bernardino
　Toletus, Franciscus
　Zabarella, Jacopo

WILLIAM E. WALLACE
Washington University
　Michelangelo Buonarroti: Michelangelo the Artist

LEE PALMER WANDEL
University of Wisconsin–Madison
　Basel
　Zwingli, Huldrych

MICHAEL T. WARD
Trinity University, San Antonio
　Salviati, Leonardo
　Varchi, Benedetto

IAN WARDROPPER
Art Institute of Chicago
　Ceramics
　Jewelry

RETHA M. WARNICKE
Arizona State University
　Catherine of Aragon
　Grey, Jane
　Mary Stuart
　Queens and Queenship

ANDREW WEAR
Wellcome Institute for the History of Medicine, London
　Anatomy
　Medicine
　Paré, Ambroise

ELISSA B. WEAVER
University of Chicago
　Castiglione, Baldassare

ALISON WEBER
University of Virginia
　Teresa of Ávila

ELEANOR F. WEDGE
Brooklyn, New York
　Brunelleschi, Filippo

SUSAN WEGNER
Bowdoin College
　Barocci, Federico
　Siena: Art in Siena

ANTON G. WEILER
Catholic University of Nijmegen, The Netherlands, Emeritus
　Devotio Moderna

JOANNA WEINBERG
Leo Baeck College, London
　Historiography, Renaissance: Jewish Historiography

DONALD WEINSTEIN
University of Arizona, Emeritus
Chivalry: Knighthood and Chivalric Orders
Savonarola, Girolamo

JAMES MICHAEL WEISS
Boston College
Beatus Rhenanus

TIMOTHY J. WENGERT
Lutheran Theological Seminary at Philadelphia
Camerarius, Joachim
Melanchthon, Philipp
Peucer, Kaspar

BARBARA J. WHITEHEAD
DePauw University
Catherine de Médicis

CHARLES WHITNEY
University of Nevada, Las Vegas
Vespucci, Amerigo

MERRY E. WIESNER
University of Wisconsin–Madison
Artisans
Prostitution

PIOTR WILCZEK
University of Illinois at Chicago
Krzycki, Andrzej

CHARITY C. WILLARD
Cornwall-on-Hudson, New York
Pizan, Christine de

JOHN ALDEN WILLIAMS
College of William and Mary
Arabic Literature and Language
Islam
Islamic Thought

CAROLYN C. WILSON
Houston, Texas
Bellini Family
Giorgione
Venice: Art in Venice

COLETTE H. WINN
Washington University, St. Louis
Aubigné, Théodore-Agrippa d'

JOHN W. WITEK, S.J.
Georgetown University
Ricci, Matteo

RONALD G. WITT
Duke University
Humanism: The Origins of Humanism
Renaissance, Interpretations of the: Hans Baron
Salutati, Coluccio

MICHAEL WOLFE
Pennsylvania State University–Altoona College
Bourbon Family and Dynasty
Estrées, Gabrielle d'
Henry IV
Tyrannicide

CAROLYN H. WOOD
Ackland Art Museum; University of North Carolina at Chapel Hill
Baroque, Concept of the

SUSANNE WOODS
Franklin and Marshall College
Lanyer, Aemilia

JOANNA WOODS-MARSDEN
University of California, Los Angeles
Chivalry: Chivalry in Renaissance Art
Pisanello, Antonio Pisano, il

D. R. WOOLF
McMaster University, Canada
Historiography, Renaissance: British Historiography

WILLIAM J. WRIGHT
University of Tennessee at Chattanooga
Hesse

ROBERT ZALLER
Drexel University
Bacon, Francis

GABRIELLA ZARRI
Università degli Studi di Firenze
Religious Orders: Orders and Congregations of Women

SERGIO ZATTI
University of Pisa
Trissino, Gian Giorgio

T. C. PRICE ZIMMERMANN
Davidson College
Court
Giovio, Paolo
Guicciardini, Francesco
Historiography, Renaissance: Italian Historiography

JONATHAN W. ZOPHY
University of Houston–Clear Lake
Habsburg Dynasty
Nürnberg

REBECCA E. ZORACH
University of Chicago
France: Art in France

RONALD EDWARD ZUPKO
Marquette University
Weights and Measures

Index

Page numbers in boldface refer to the main entry on the subject. Page numbers in italics refer to illustrations, figures, and tables. Page numbers followed by gen refer to the genealogical tables. Page numbers preceded by Pl. refer to the color inserts.